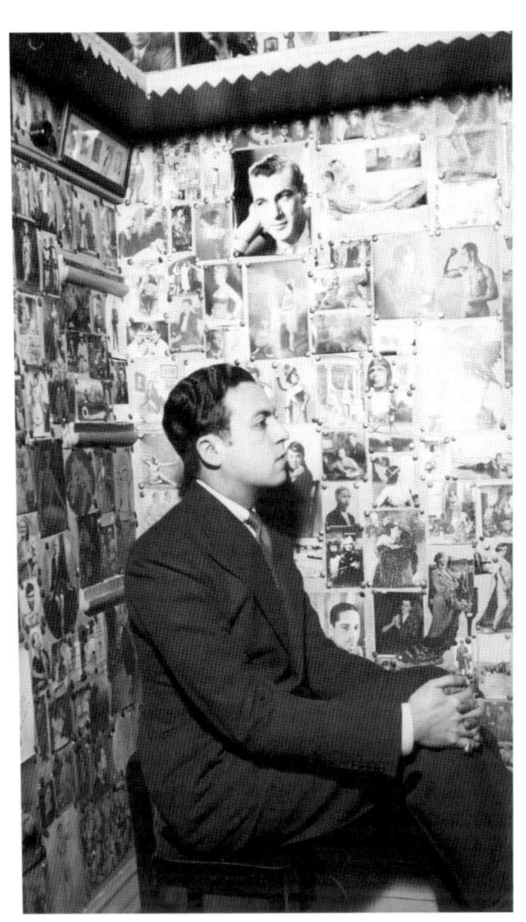

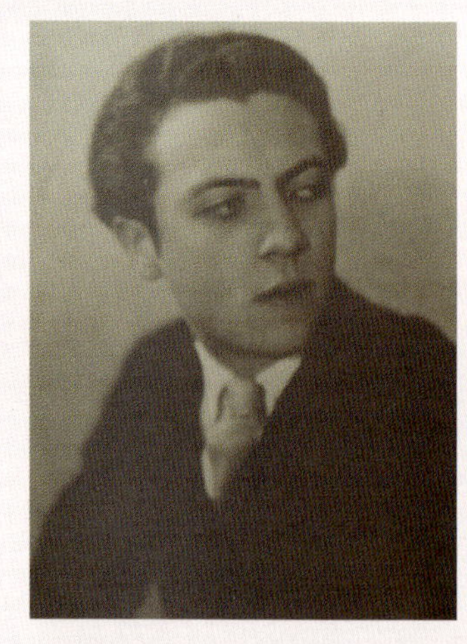
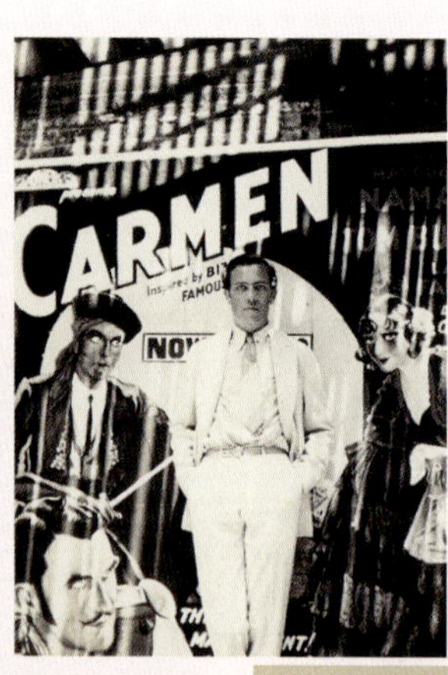
CARMEN
NOW
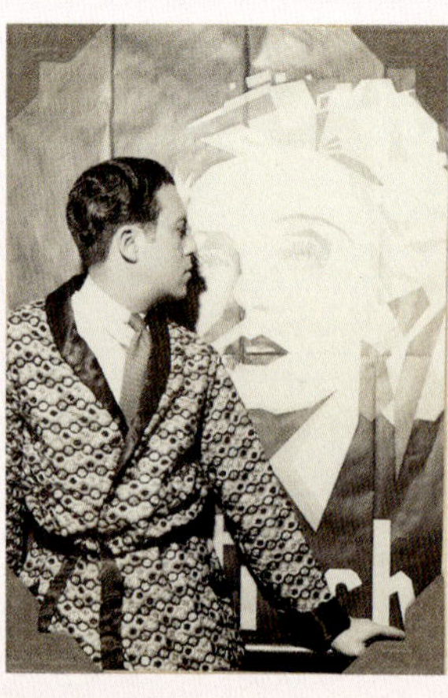
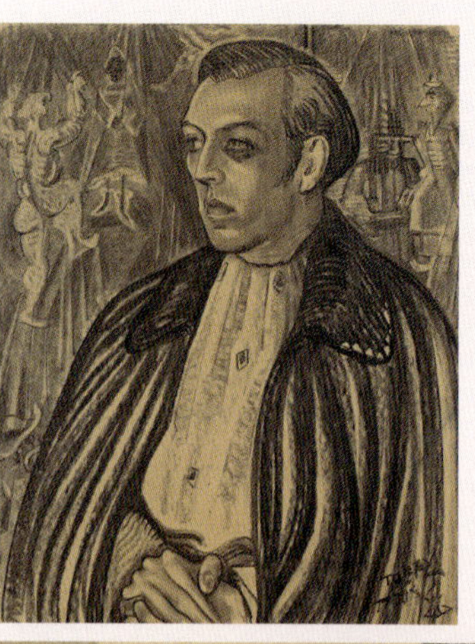
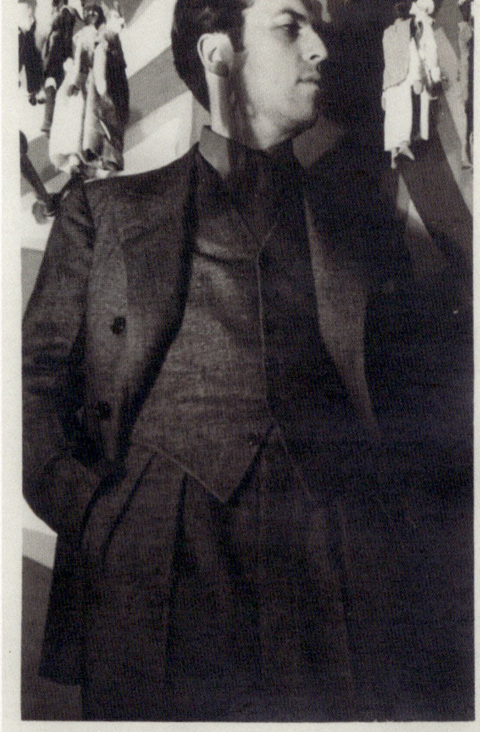
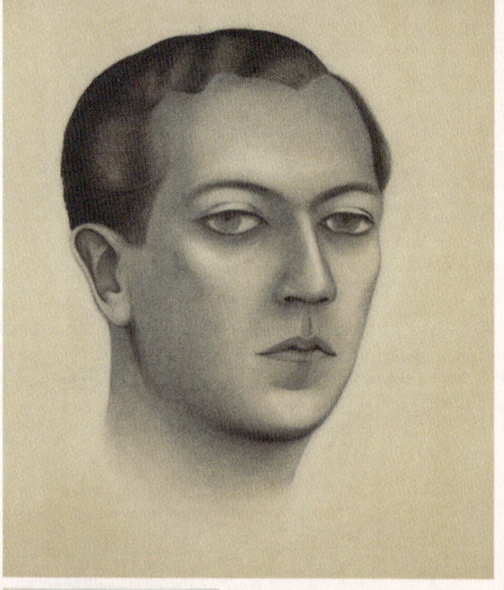
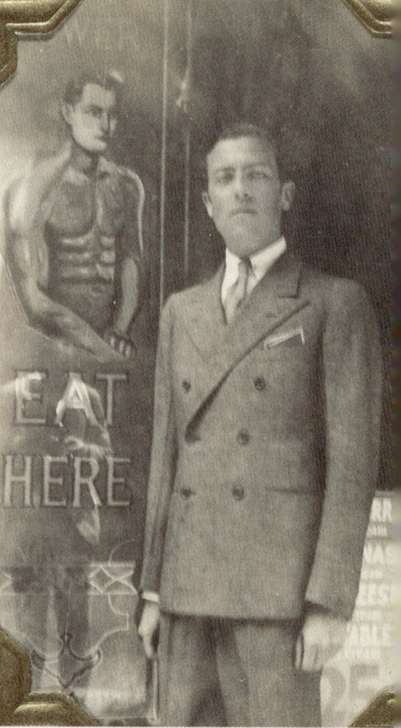
EAT
HERE
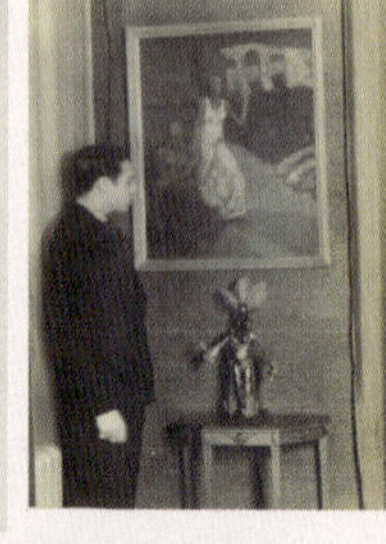
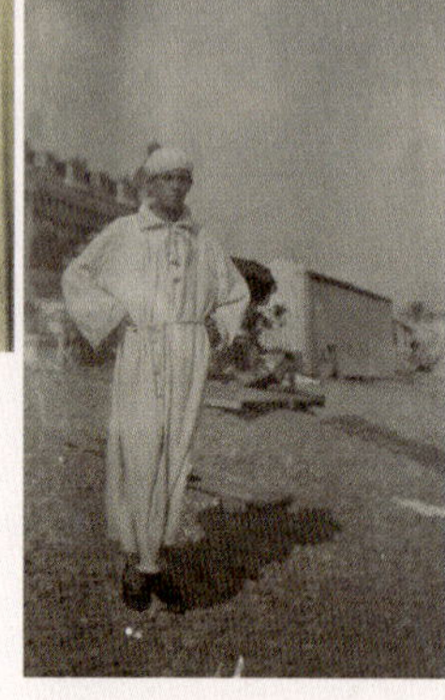
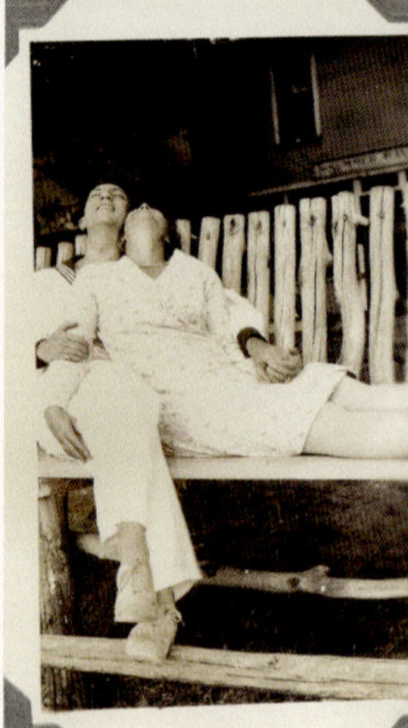
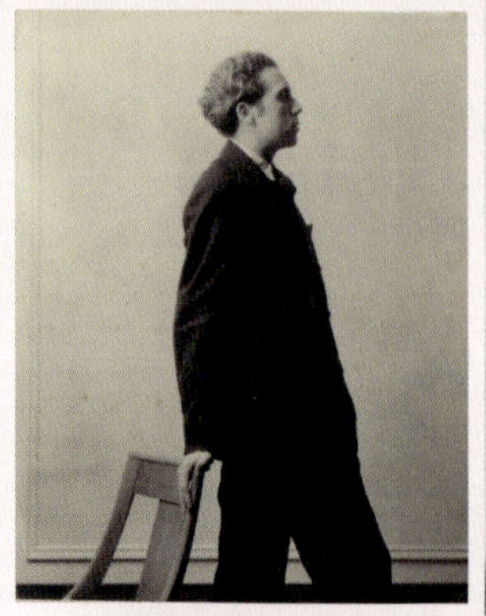
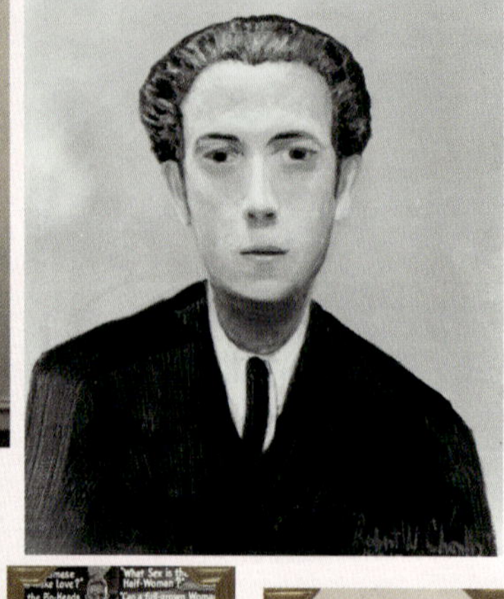
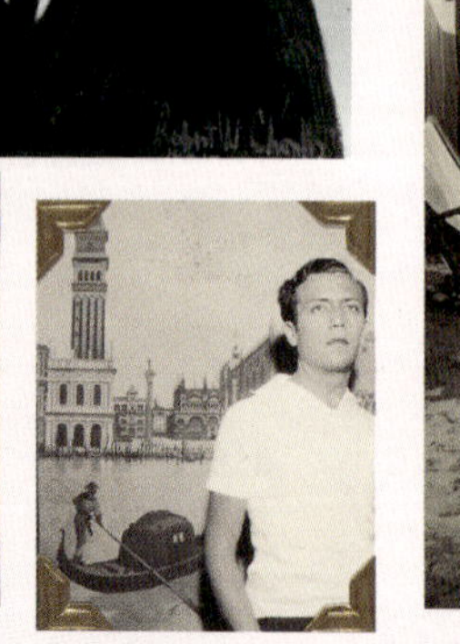
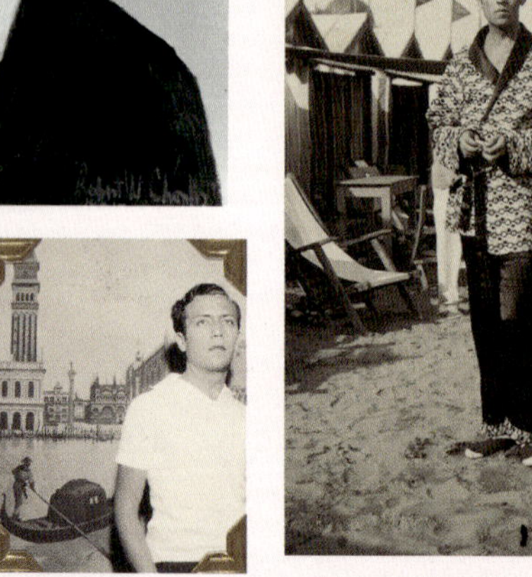
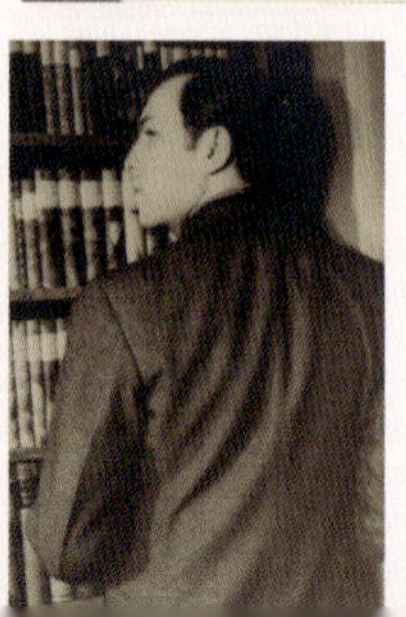

Queer Moderns

Max Ewing's Jazz Age New York

Alice T. Friedman

PRINCETON UNIVERSITY PRESS

PRINCETON AND OXFORD

Princeton University Press is committed to the protection of copyright and the intellectual property our authors entrust to us. Copyright promotes the progress and integrity of knowledge. Thank you for supporting free speech and the global exchange of ideas by purchasing an authorized edition of this book. If you wish to reproduce or distribute any part of it in any form, please obtain permission. Requests for permission to reproduce material from this work should be sent to permissions@press.princeton.edu

Published by Princeton University Press, 41 William Street, Princeton, New Jersey 08540
In the United Kingdom: Princeton University Press, 99 Banbury Road, Oxford OX2 6JX
press.princeton.edu

Cover images: (top) George Platt Lynes, *Max Ewing Reading Cocteau's Les Enfants Terribles*; (bottom) *Max Ewing and Zena Naylor*, December 1929. Max Ewing Collection. Yale Collection of American Literature, Beinecke Rare Book and Manuscript Library. Used with permission of The George Platt Lynes Estate.
Pages i, ii, ix, x, 242, 243: Portraits from Max Ewing's *Carnival of Venice* (small prints from a series of four albums entitled *Les Amants de Venise*).
Pages 248–49: Carl Van Vechten, "Love at First Night" and "Gay Honeymoon," double page collage with Max Ewing's photographs of the Ritter brothers and found text, from Carl Van Vechten's scrapbook.
Page 270: Anon., "One side of Max Ewing's Gallery of Extraordinary Portraits in his clothes closet," 1928. Max Ewing Papers.

Library of Congress Cataloging-in-Publication Data
Names: Friedman, Alice T., author.
Title: Queer moderns: Max Ewing's Jazz Age New York / Alice T. Friedman.
Description: Princeton: Princeton University Press, [2025] | Includes bibliographical references and index.
Identifiers: LCCN 2024036055 (print) | LCCN 2024036056 (ebook) | ISBN 9780691267340 (hardback)
| ISBN 9780691267357 (ebook)
Subjects: LCSH: Modernism (Art)—New York (State)—New York. | Homosexuality and the arts--New York (State)
—New York—History--20th century. | Gay artists—New York (State)—New York—History—20th century.
| Ewing, Max—Friends and associates. | BISAC: ART / LGBTQ+ Artists | HISTORY / LGBTQ+
Classification: LCC NX456.5.M64 F75 2025 (print) | LCC NX456.5.M64 (ebook) | DDC 700/.4110866097471—
dc23/eng/20241016
LC record available at https://lccn.loc.gov/2024036055
LC ebook record available at https://lccn.loc.gov/2024036056

British Library Cataloging-in-Publication Data is available

Editorial: Michelle Komie and Annie Miller
Production Editorial: Terri O'Prey
Text Design: Jack Design
Jacket Design: Jack Design
Production: Steven Sears
Publicity: Jodi Price
Copyeditor: Lachlan Brooks

276 color + 40 b/w illustrations
This book has been composed in
GT Alpina, National, and Miller

Printed in Italy
10 9 8 7 6 5 4 3 2 1

For Cameran

Contents

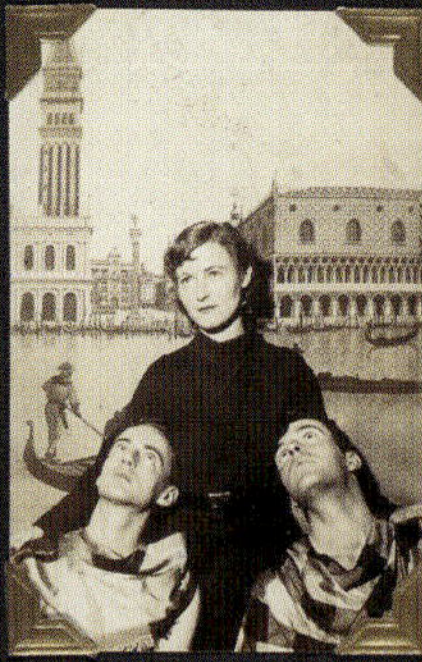
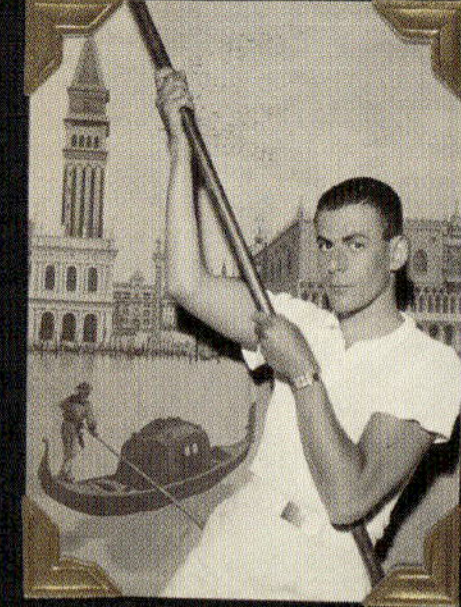
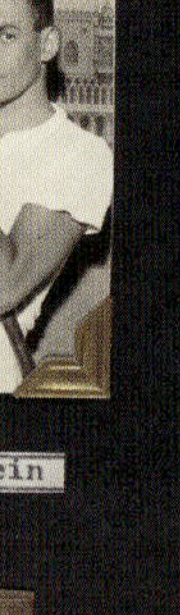
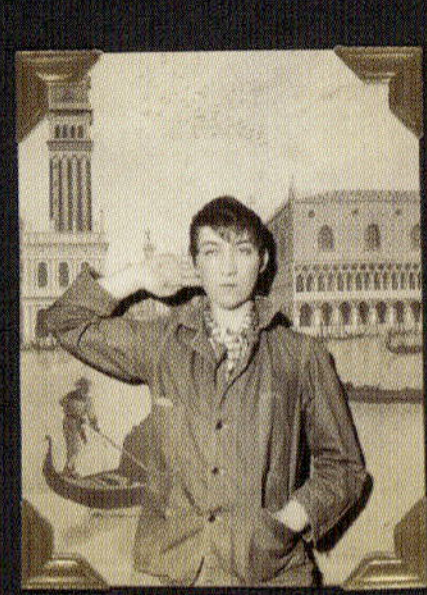
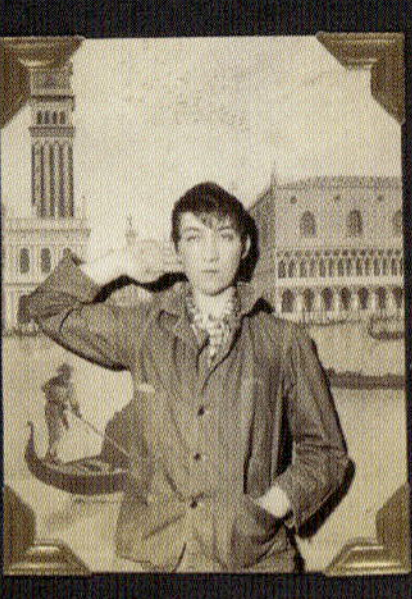

Lois Moran
Georg Lynes

Lincoln Kirstein

Julian Levy —

Miguel Covarrubias

Berenice Abbott

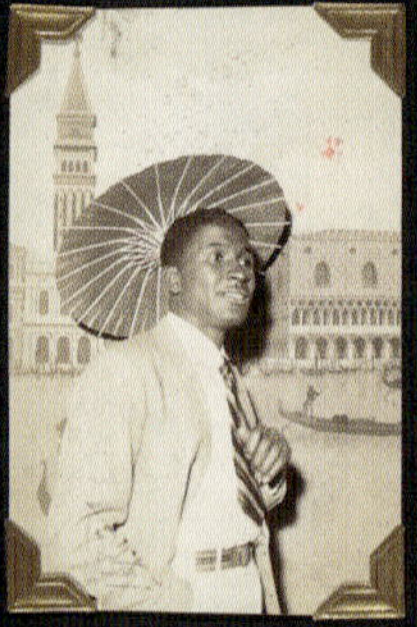
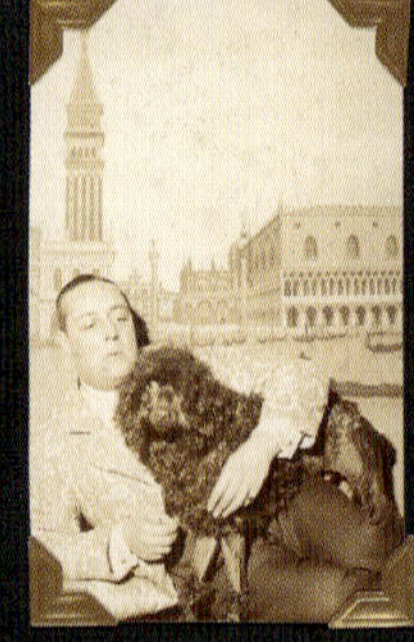

Leonard Franklin

Edward Wassermann

George Platt Lynes

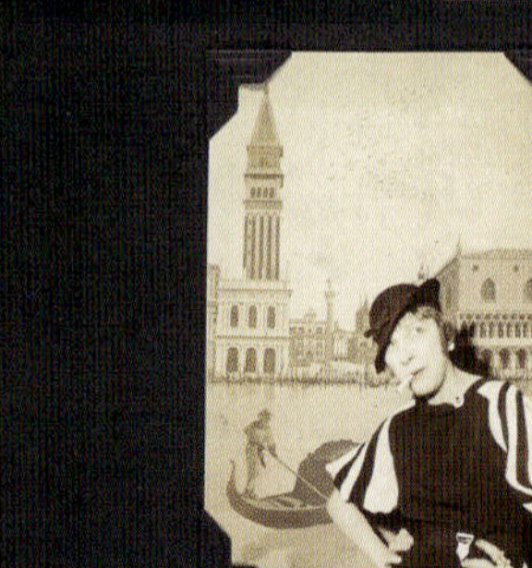
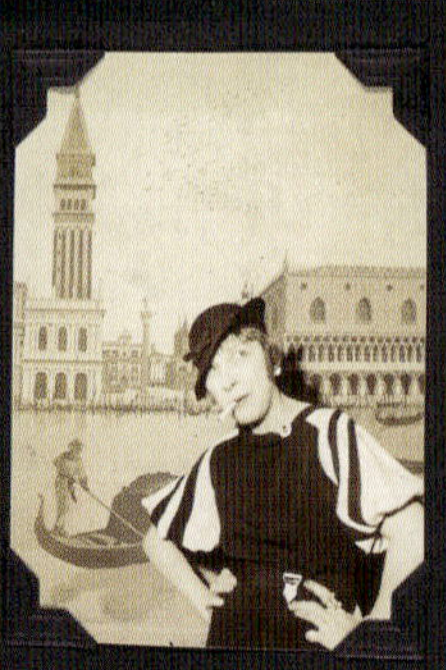

Jack Pollock

Louise Hellstrom.

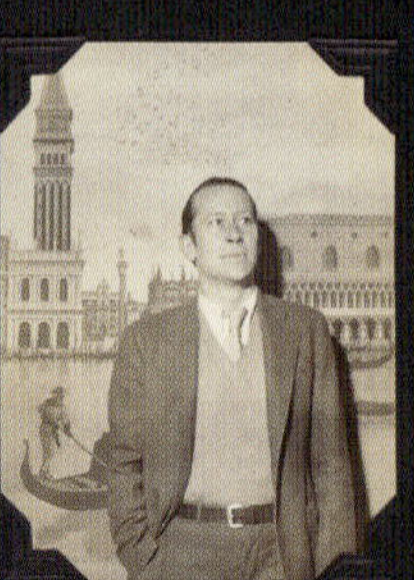
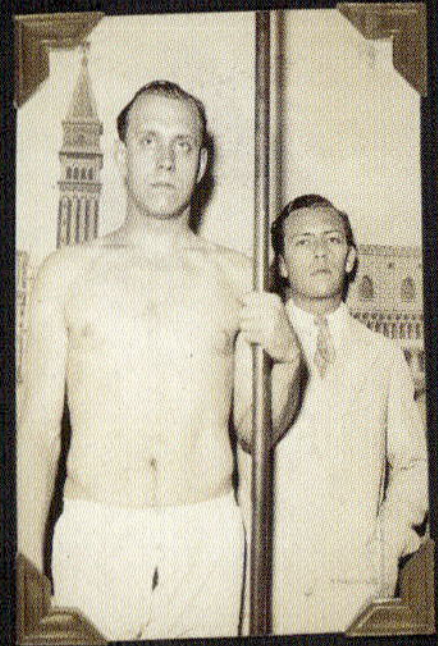
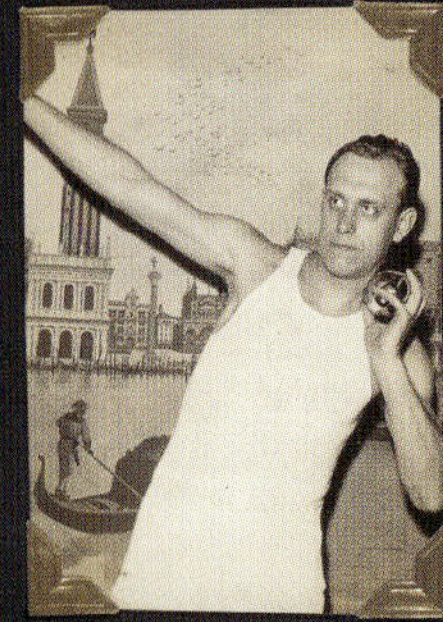

E E Cummings

Herbert Buch
Max Ewing

Herbert Buch

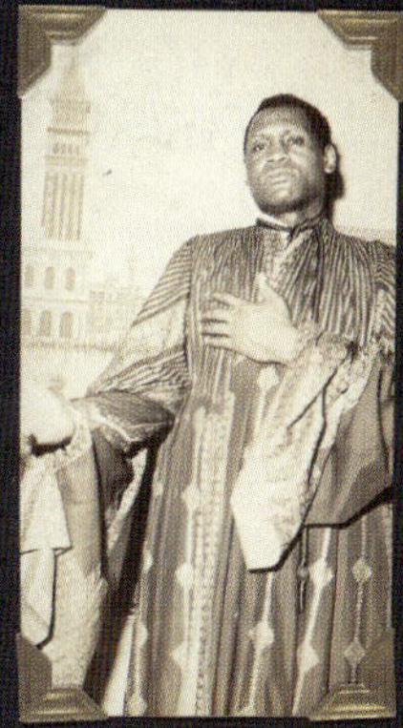

Paul Robeson

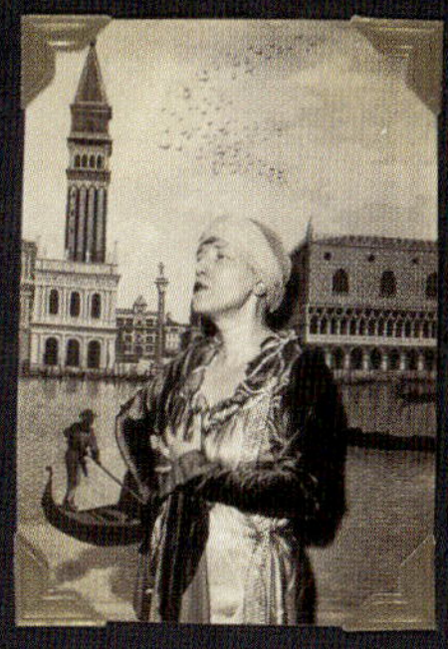

Muriel Draper

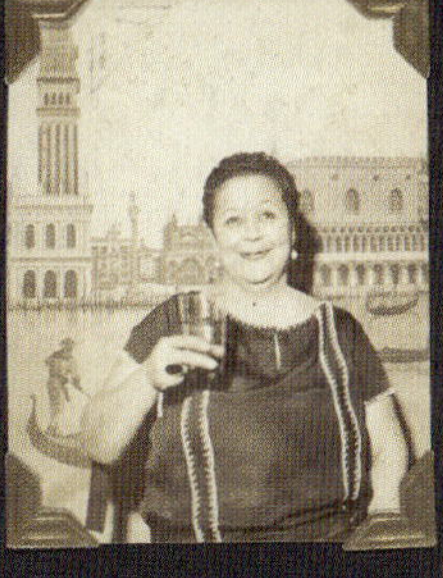

Mamie White

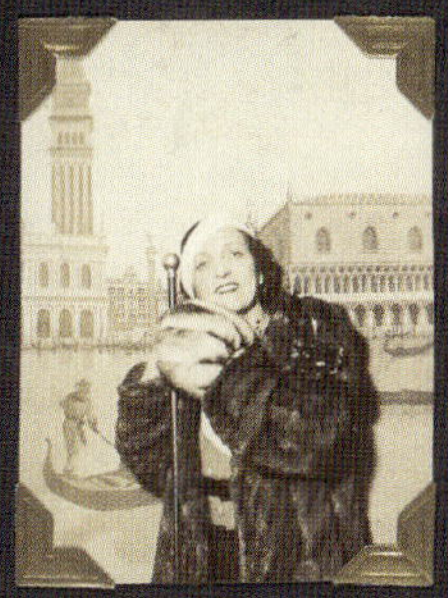

Paul Meeres

Marguerite Namara

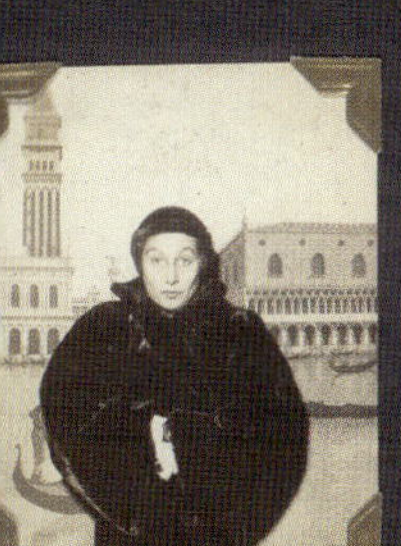

Aline MacMahon

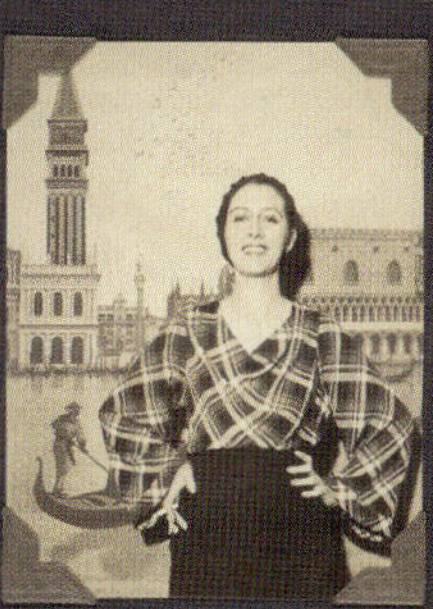

Marion Morehouse

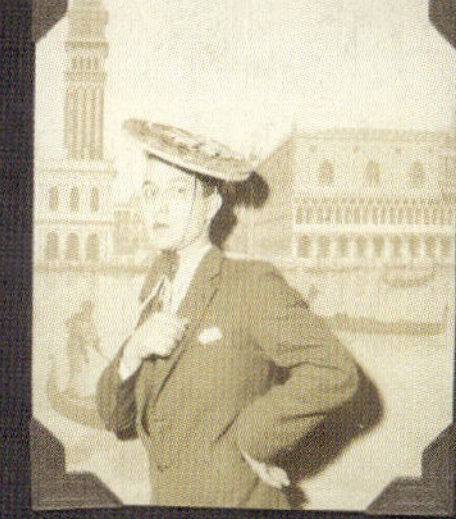

Isamu Noguchi

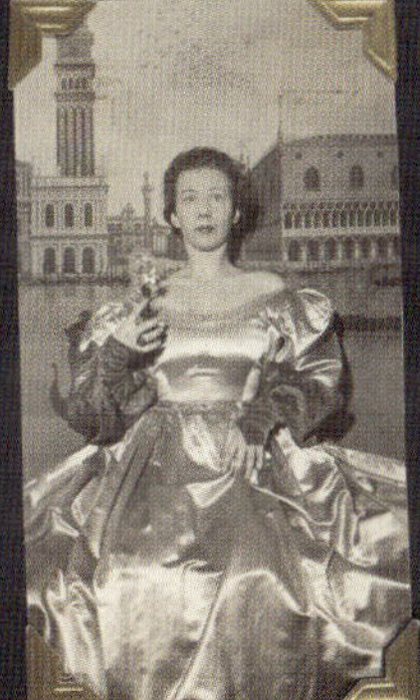

Agnes de Mille

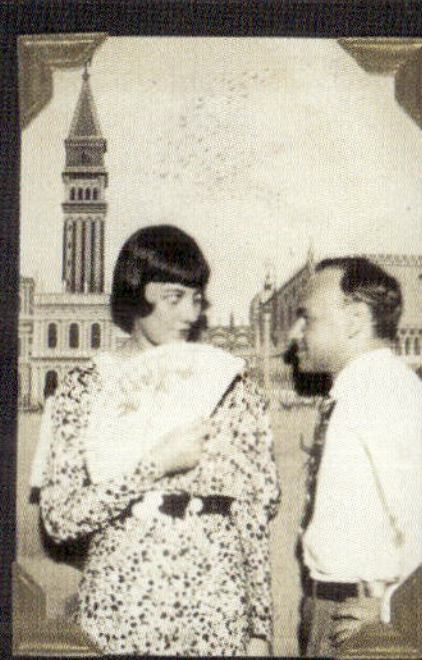

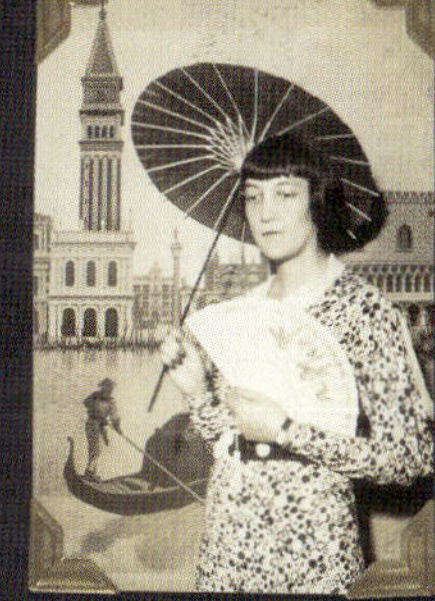

Amanda
and Gilbert Seldes

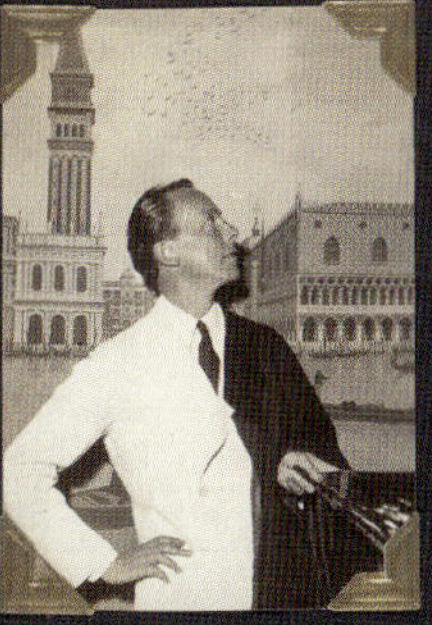

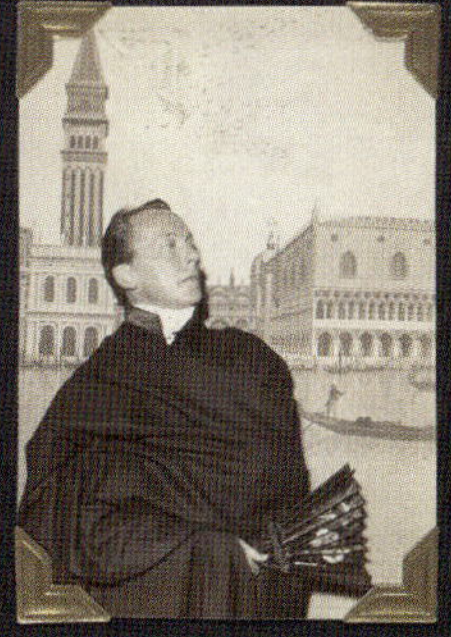

Robert Locher

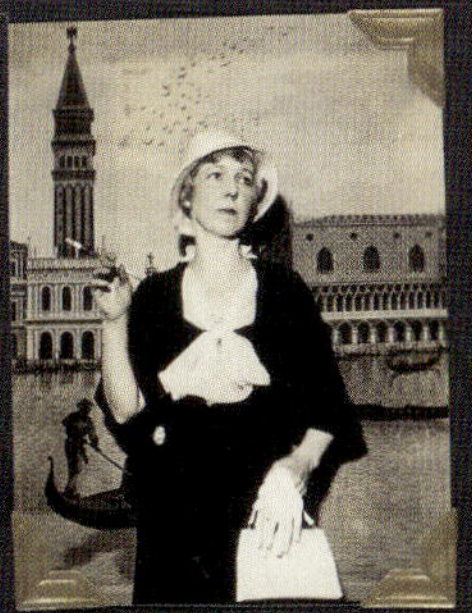

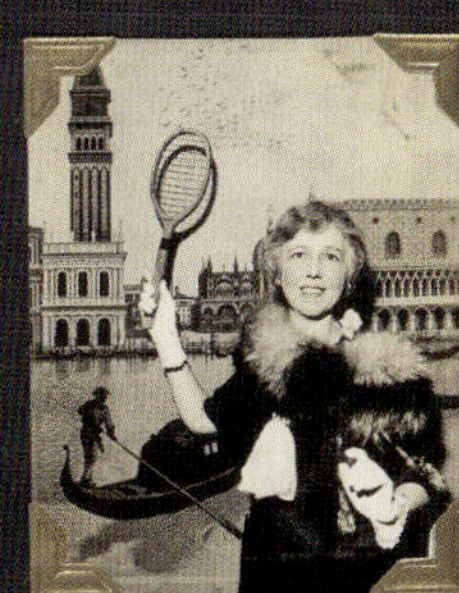

A Menace At Tennis In Venice
Dorothy Sheldon

REDISCOVERING QUEER NEW YORK

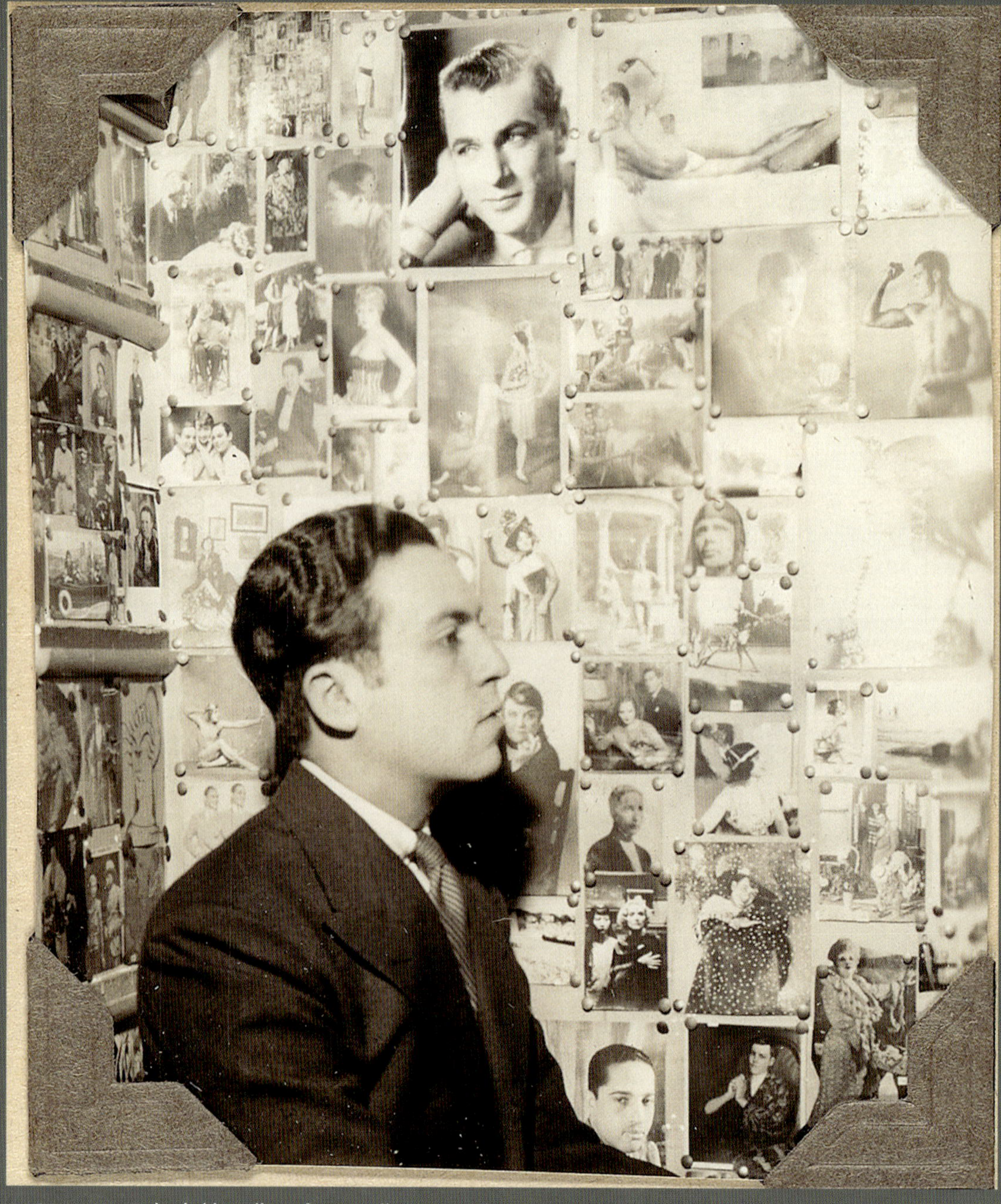

0.1 Anon., Max Ewing in his *Gallery of Extraordinary Portraits*, 1932. Max Ewing Papers, Beinecke Rare Book & Manuscript Library, Yale University, New Haven, Connecticut (henceforth Max Ewing Papers).

In the winter of 1934, the bodybuilder and artists' model Bill Ritter wrote to his friend Max Ewing (1903–34) (fig. 0.1), a queer musician, author, and photographer, who had recently left New York to try his hand as a scriptwriter in Hollywood.[1] Ritter's letter, one of a series exchanged by the two men between the spring of 1933 and the late winter of 1934, is full of details about the New York social scene that Ewing was missing out on. "Fred [Bill Ritter's brother] and I [are] spending most of my time in dear old Harlem," he wrote, noting that it was "very gay there this season":

> Clinton Moore's cocktail hours have been pretty good lately a new crowd of English boys are taking the place by storm. Met George Lynes the other night at some awful dizzy party, you can imagine how these partys [*sic*] effect me, out all night and then work the next day, some fun. You remember the pictures George took of us he claims they were in a French magizine [*sic*] he wants us to come up and then at the same time take more pictures. We recently went to some of the bigger partys in town, started the season with a drag, as usual then came the Bowery Ball, the Mad Hatters etc. Fred and I crashed the gayest of society's balls this year, the Peacock and the Packard Motor Ball they were really gala affairs and we met plenty of different people. Despite everything I still manage to keep in fair condition, intend taking some new pictures soon if any come out OK will send you copies.[2]

Bill Ritter's distinctive voice — colloquial, upbeat, and decidedly queer — and his recollections of his experiences in New York City are just two of the many extraordinary revelations of the Max Ewing Papers, a substantial collection of letters, photographs, and printed ephemera primarily related to music, theater, and opera between the mid-1910s and June 16, 1934, the date of Max Ewing's death. This archive was assembled and donated to Yale in 1943 by his friend and mentor Carl Van Vechten (1880–1964), a writer, collector, and portrait photographer.[3]

The most outstanding discovery in all among these materials is, of course, the queer persona and panache of Max Ewing himself. It is through his papers, and especially the hundreds of detailed letters that he wrote — often three or four times a week, at great length — for the amusement of his family and friends in his hometown of Pioneer, Ohio, that the people and places in New York's queer bohemia of the 1920s and '30s come alive with a vitality, nuance, and pathos that are rare in the field of queer studies, or indeed in cultural studies as a whole. As many scholars have noted, homophobic prejudices and laws have frequently caused the erasure, mutilation, and outright destruction of archives like Ewing's.[4] His remarkably candid observations of people and places allow us to see the world through his eyes, creating a unique picture of the city and its archipelago of queer spaces, joyfully animated and inhabited by Ewing and his contemporaries. His photographic projects, including his *Gallery of Extraordinary Portraits*, an installation in the walk-in closet of his New York apartment (1928–33), and his *Carnival of Venice* portrait series (1932–33), were efforts to immortalize the celebrities, acquaintances, and friends he loved and admired and to place himself squarely within the protected space of the "queer family" album that he created.[5] This book is thus both a celebration of the unlikely survival of Max Ewing's papers and photographs, and of the man himself.

The significance of Ewing's distinctive voice and his lively descriptions of his life in New York becomes readily apparent if we revisit George Chauncey's foundational contribution to queer history, *Gay New York: Gender, Urban Culture, and the Making of the Gay Male World, 1890–1940*, published in 1994. Chauncey's book drew back the curtain on a little-known world of queer experience in the first half of the twentieth century, shattering the myth that this world was too dispersed and shrouded in shame and secrecy to ever be known, and calling out the emergence of institutionalized homophobia in subsequent decades as the principal cause for its disappearance from the historical record.[6] Chauncey's richly documented discussion of the complexities of queer, urban culture in New York — from the drag balls of Greenwich Village and Harlem where straight tourists "came to gawk at the drag queens on display," to the secret underworld of queer codes "of dress, speech, and style that enabled [gay men] to recognize one another on the street, at work, and at parties and bars" — convinced historians that gay male subculture not only existed in the decades before Stonewall, but that it was alive, well, and *resilient* in the face of homophobia.[7]

While first-person narratives and private reflections from diaries and letters do indeed contribute to the richness and ground-breaking discoveries of *Gay New York*, most of its many revelations come from close readings of newspapers, legal documents, institutional records, novels, and other printed sources. Max Ewing's private letters confirm many of Chauncey's conclusions, but they also radically extend the scope of our knowledge by taking us behind the scenes into private homes and inviting us to private parties that we would otherwise never visit. An inveterate name-dropper intent on educating and impressing his parents, Ewing tells us about the famous people he met — Igor Stravinsky, Gertrude Stein (1874–1946), Pablo Picasso, Serge Diaghilev, Natalie Barney (1876–1972), Romaine Brooks (1874–1970), Virgil Thomson (1896–1989), and Cole Porter, to name just a few from his European travels — describing their conversations, clothes, and social interactions. He also makes it clear that, while much of queer life was indeed often lived in the public eye — in bars, restaurants, and theaters, for example — the greater part of day-to-day living was experienced in private, just as it was for everyone else.[8]

Better still, Ewing's letters tell us about decor, fashion, and gossip with extraordinary, often jaw-dropping, vividness. The experience of reading his letters is thus as powerful and game-changing for historians of today as the discovery of the letters exchanged by the "Merchant of Prato," Francesco Datini, and his wife Margherita in the fourteenth and fifteenth centuries was for the feminist turn toward the history of private life and "material culture" in Renaissance Studies. Published by historian Iris Origo in 1957, these letters reveal details of daily life and the private realities of relationships that were previously thought to be unknowable.[9] Here as well, in words and images, we meet people from Ewing's queer world — the Ritter brothers, Clinton Moore, George Platt Lynes (1907–55) and many others — and we come to know them in entirely new ways.

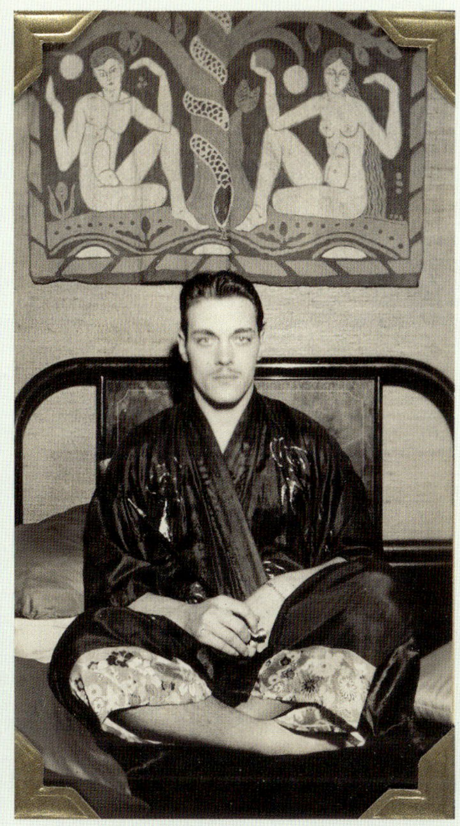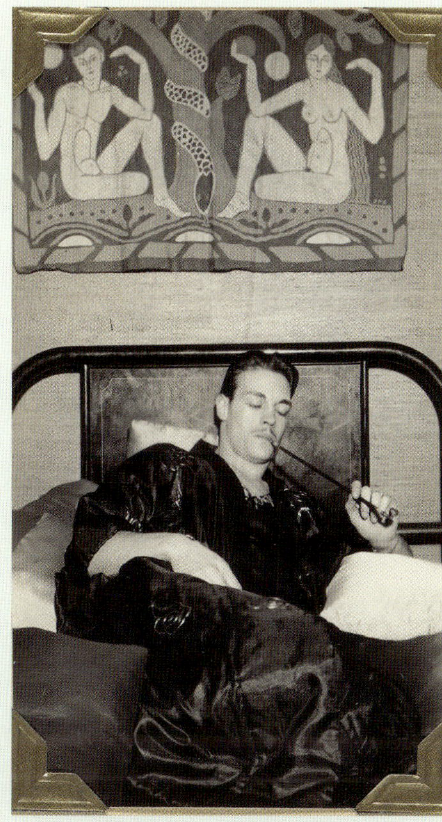

0.2 Max Ewing, *Two Portraits of Fred Ritter*, April 1932 (detail of fig. 5.2). Max Ewing Papers.

The Ritter brothers first encountered Max Ewing and the aspiring photographer George Platt Lynes sometime around 1930, either at Coney Island, where Ewing and Lynes would go to take pictures of bodybuilders at outdoor gyms and swimming pools, or at one of the many Harlem parties and drag balls they attended. These gala fashion shows were primarily performed by glamorous African American cross-dressers and judged by celebrities, including (on more than one occasion) Ewing's white friends Carl Van Vechten and Muriel Draper (1886–1952). Bill Ritter, Fred Ritter, George Lynes, and Max Ewing soon became part of an interracial group of young people who went out to clubs and "rent parties" in Harlem practically every night, and attended the frequent queer-themed events that Ritter alludes to in his letter.[10] The brothers proved to be not only amusing and energetic companions on all-night rambles, but were also talented models who were more than willing to pose, nude and clothed, in photographers' home studios. From 1930 on, Ewing regularly photographed Fred Ritter at his apartment on West 31st Street, either wearing one of the elegant, silk dressing gowns that Ewing had acquired in France in 1926 (fig. 0.2), or nothing at all.

Unlike George Platt Lynes, who built up a professional practice in fashion photography, Ewing was an amateur who used his Kodak camera to take casual snapshots, self-portraits, and staged portraits, including a series of over a hundred images produced between April 1932 and January 1933 that he titled *The Carnival of Venice*. The *Carnival* included portraits of celebrities and friends posed in front of a pull-down window shade printed with a view of the Piazza San Marco from the water, complete with gondolas and a flock of birds in the sky

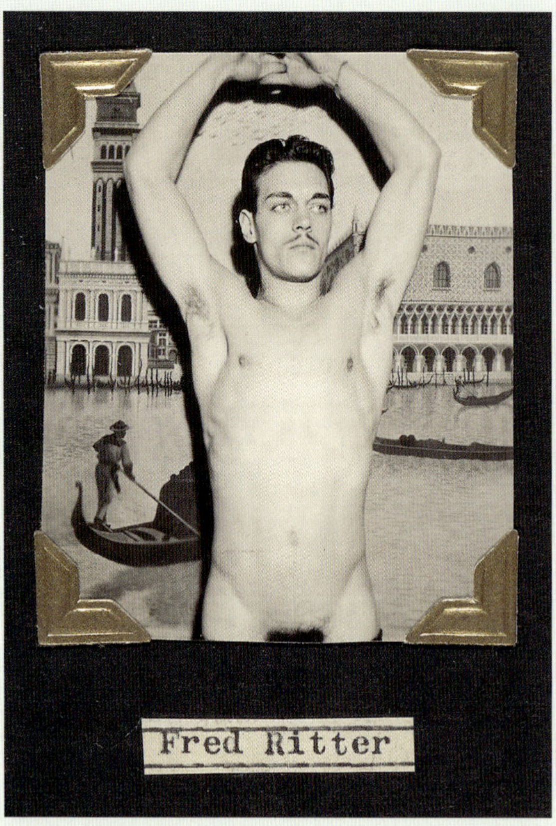

0.3   Max Ewing, *Fred Ritter* from *The Carnival of Venice* (small print from a series of four albums entitled *Les Amants de Venise*), 1932. Max Ewing Papers.

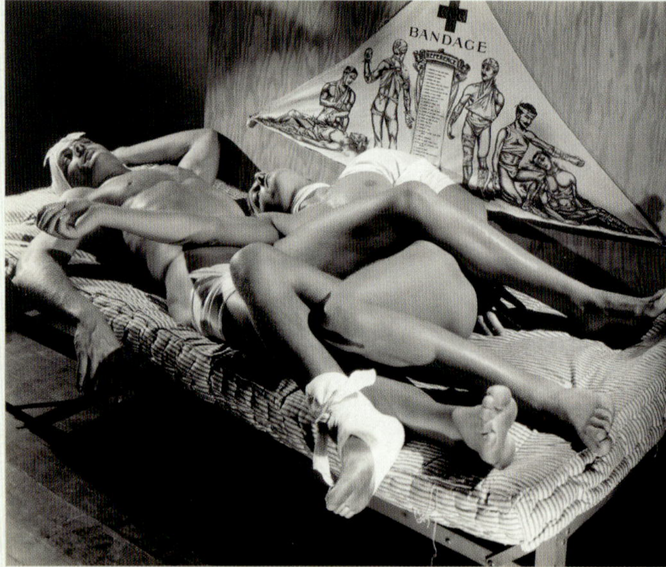

0.4   George Platt Lynes, *Untitled (the Ritter Brothers)*, c. 1934, gelatin silver print, 7 × ½ × 9½ in. (19 × 24.1 cm). The Museum of Modern Art, New York.

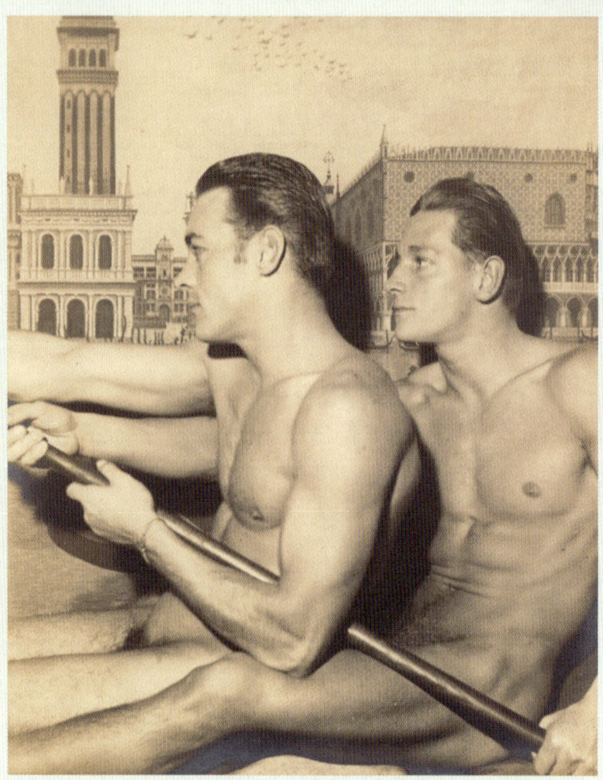

0.5   Max Ewing, *The Ritter Brothers*, from *The Carnival of Venice* (detail of fig. 5.55).

(fig. 0.3). This collection was exhibited in a one-day show at the Julien Levy Gallery in New York on January 26, 1933, culminating in a party at the gallery where the sitters were asked to bring the props and wear the costumes they had chosen for their portraits — or to wear nothing at all, if that's how they had appeared in Ewing's *Carnival* — much to the amusement of guests and critics alike.[11]

Both brothers allude to the Venice series in their letters to Ewing: in July 1933, for example, Fred wrote that he missed the little West 31st Street studio that Ewing had left behind when he moved to Hollywood, commenting, "I shall always remember it as [I] have numerous pictures which you took of me in about every corner of it, including Venice which you made so famous." On February 12, 1934, he wrote again, sharing the latest gossip and reporting that "Geo Lynes … is planning on getting a fifteen room apartment near the east river and using it for something, he is also going to photograph brother and I in bed, quite a contrast from the canals of Venice, also Geo had a picture of brother and I he took placed in the Photographie, some French publication."[12]

Lynes's well-known photograph of the two men (fig. 0.4) is one of the images that established the artist's successful career, and it is most likely the photo of "brother and I in bed" that Ritter was referring to in his letter. It is among the best-known examples of a newly emerging genre of queer art photography that that was largely invented by Lynes in the 1930s as an outgrowth of his innovative approach to commercial fashion photography.[13] His increasingly sophisticated work was closely watched by both Ewing and Ewing's mentor Carl Van Vechten, a writer, critic, collector (notably of queer erotica), and photographer who began making portraits in his home studio at about this time.

Ewing's goals were different from those of either of his friends. His snapshot of the Ritter brothers posing nude (fig. 0.5), for example, one of a number of images of the two men in the *Carnival of Venice* series, is a decidedly amateur effort in which the brothers crowd together awkwardly on a narrow bench with their legs and arms intertwined. The photograph is only known to us from a copy preserved by Van Vechten in his scrapbooks of queer images and ephemera now at Yale University's Beinecke Library; the image, collaged together with texts clipped by Van Vechten from magazines and newspapers, is a world away from Lynes's glamorous studio photographs or Van Vechten's own carefully lit portraits, as Ewing himself recognized. For him, the process of taking pictures was a way of getting to know people and documenting his wide circle of friends and acquaintances: for the *Carnival of Venice* series, he invited nearly everyone he knew to his home and asked them to pose with whatever props or costumes they preferred, chatting and working with them to create portraits that they liked.

Ewing's process was in that way quite similar to that of his friend Berenice Abbott, another emerging professional photographer, who drew out her sitters as she worked with them in the studio.[14] Yet Ewing went even further: when photographing his most beautiful male subjects, including the Ritter brothers, he encouraged his sitters to take off their clothes, both for his own pleasure and for theirs, and unlike Abbott, he viewed the project as a camp performance by photographer and subject rather than a serious, artistic venture. Here as elsewhere, Ewing included self-portraits in the series, ensuring that he would be recognized as both the creator of the performance and an embedded member of the group.

Ultimately, through these experiments, Ewing sought to create a complex self-portrait in which the people captured by his camera represented different aspects of his own New York life, from uptown to downtown. The denizens of the city's "queer bohemia" that he memorialized — Black and white, young and old, gay and straight — were a disparate group, including not only established *salonistes* like Muriel Draper and famous actors like Paul Robeson (1898–1976), but also little-known writers, critics, and artists at the beginning of their careers. Ewing's sitters included Lincoln Kirstein, Agnes de Mille, Miguel Covarrubias, Isamu Noguchi, E. E. Cummings, Taylor Gordon, George Platt Lynes, and Berenice Abbott. Many members of this interracial group, who regularly came together for the raucous, alcohol-fueled parties of the sort referenced by Ritter in his letter, were creating new forms of art as part of a self-styled, American avant-garde. They were also connected to one another and to the spirit of their time by their openness to fluid gender norms and sexualities, key elements in Ewing's own emerging identity and values. Thus, as a group, Ewing's portraits form a multifaceted picture of a distinctive time and place in US history, one that soon faded away amid the cataclysmic economic and cultural changes of the 1930s.

These friends lived outside the norms of mainstream America. They forged intimate and sometimes sexualized friendships, open heterosexual marriages, and unlikely partnerships of various kinds, like Ewing's or Lincoln Kirstein's bond with the much-older Muriel Draper (both men were gay, and she was heterosexual) or the long-lasting queer "throuple" created by George Platt Lynes with Glenway Wescott (1901–87) and Monroe Wheeler (1899–1988), a marriage of a sort that lasted from the late 1920s to the 1940s.[15] Many of Ewing's queer friends, including Van Vechten, Lincoln Kirstein (1907–96), Robert Locher (1888–1956), and Esther Murphy (1897–1962) were married or linked to partners of the opposite sex, and a similar arrangement was made by the African American actress Edna Thomas with her husband Lloyd Thomas and her white lover Olivia Windham.[16] Here, as in all other areas of their lives, the members of this circle crossed the boundaries of commonly accepted behavior, pushing the limits of social and cultural values. They embraced new definitions of intimacy, believing that sexual and emotional engagement were merely two points on a wide spectrum of ways that people could be close, and that intimate friendships defied categorical (and, of course, medical) definitions of homosexual and heterosexual love.[17]

This was certainly also the case with Ewing's lengthy love affair with Muriel Draper and his unlikely, loving friendship with the boxer Jack Pollock, a relationship that was flirtatious and undoubtedly erotic, but probably never consummated. Members of Ewing's circle were obviously not simply "tolerant" of queerness, but actively embraced the nonconformity and the free expression of individual personality that were central to their ideas of what it meant to live as a modern person. One might even go so far as to suggest that "queer bohemia's" active engagement with various forms of intimacy and embrace of indeterminacy were among the most significant elements dividing the avant-garde of the 1920s into two different and distinct "modern" worlds in New York, Paris, and along the jagged coastline of the Riviera, from Antibes to Roquebrune and Menton. The well-known, dominant group of modern artists, centered around writers and artists like Hemingway, Picasso, Le Corbusier, Zelda and F. Scott Fitzgerald (1896–1940), and Gerald and Sarah Murphy, often seemed to take for granted not only conventional, binary gender roles and notions of sexuality, but also, in the case of Hemingway and Le Corbusier, the necessary performance of a defining, heroic, and often homophobic hypermasculinity.[18] The other "moderns" — the "queer bohemians" who are the subject of this book — included Esther Murphy, her sister-in-law Noël Murphy (1896–1982), and her lover Janet Flanner, as well as Natalie Barney and Romaine Brooks, Cecil Beaton (1904–80), Carl Van Vechten, Florine Stettheimer (1871–1944), Muriel Draper, and of course, Max Ewing himself: this latter coterie seems to have devoted a great deal of their energy to blurring the normative categories embraced, albeit tacitly, by the former.

Moreover, these two groups inhabited different versions of the same cities. Of course, there was overlap, and there were friendships and family relationships that crossed between the two. As we know, both groups shared key locations and institutions — from the Ballets Russes, to the Shakespeare and Company bookshop and Gertrude Stein's home and studio in Paris, to the Julien Levy Gallery, the Askews' salon and the Stettheimers' apartment in New York. Nevertheless, there were clear yet invisible boundaries that separated the heteronormative spaces — both physical and psychic — from the "queer archipelago" of places, both public and private, that existed alongside them. As we shall see, Ewing's Paris, his New York City, and his Riviera were not the same as the places of the same name inhabited by the married Murphys or the Picassos, the MacLeishes, or John and Katy Dos Passos.[19] As close as he was to Esther Murphy in the mid-1920s, for example, and as much time as he spent in Paris, Juan-les-Pins, and Venice in 1926–27, Ewing never even met her brother Gerald, who preferred not to be reminded of what he called "his defects" in matters of sexuality and masculinity.[20] The epitome of expat American glamour and gracious living in the 1920s, Gerald and Sara Murphy may well have dedicated their lives to "Making It New," as Gerald famously put it, but their own internalized homophobia did not number among the old-fashioned values they set out to confront — not to mention the homophobia of their friends.[21] In practice, "queer bohemia" was a world unto itself.

For Max Ewing's mentor Carl Van Vechten, preserving a record of this fragile and ephemeral world through photographs, letters, clippings, and random bits of advertising became a life's work.[22] Indeed, it is thanks to him that we know Max Ewing, the Ritter brothers, and many others in their circle at all. In the spring of 1934, Ewing's meteoric rise through the ranks of the avant-garde came to a crashing halt, ending with his suicide in Binghamton, New York on June 18, as he desperately tried to return to New York City from his childhood home in the tiny town of Pioneer, Ohio. The deaths of both of his parents in the span of two years, the deepening economic Depression, his frustrated ambitions in Hollywood, and his forced return to Pioneer — the place he had escaped from just ten years earlier — to care for his ailing mother and ultimately settle her estate, sent him into a spiral of depression from which he never recovered. Though Van Vechten was shocked and saddened, like everyone else, when he learned of Ewing's suicide, he immediately began gathering up Ewing's letters, photographs, playbills, programs, sheet music, and other ephemera with the intention of creating an archive, both for the benefit of future researchers, as he explained to

Ewing's family, and "as a slight memorial to his charming soul."[23] In 1943, he donated the Max Ewing Papers to the Beinecke Rare Book & Manuscript Library at Yale University.

Most of Ewing's letters describe his daily activities and experiences during the ten years (1923–33) that he lived in New York City and in Europe, recording the names of the many people he met and socialized with. He was a graceful and insightful correspondent with a keen eye for fashion and an ear for language, and also surprisingly candid when he wrote about his love interests and his aspirations for artistic and social success. He spared no effort in explaining these things to his father and mother, and although he never went into detail about his sexual activities (not surprising in letters from a young man to his parents, then as now), it is obvious that they accepted him for the decidedly queer — and talented and gregarious — young man that he was, and encouraged him to pursue his social ambitions and artistic passions, especially his dream of a career as a concert pianist. This extraordinary collection of Ewing's letters from the 1920s and early 1930s is complemented by another, much smaller group, written during his mother's final illness and after her death in April 1934: these documents, which include letters from Ewing's friends, among them the boxer Jack Pollock, present a lyrical and heart-wrenching portrait of a man in a state of despair, exiled from the glamorous life of the city and unable to sustain the sophisticated, queer identity he had created for himself in New York. These papers fill out our picture of a life that was brilliantly and fully lived, yet tragically cut short.

Carl Van Vechten also donated his own substantial archive of letters, manuscripts, books, and photographs — an invaluable resource for much of our knowledge about avant-garde New York in this period and the Harlem Renaissance in particular — to Yale University in 1941, creating the James Weldon Johnson Memorial Collection for the study of African American history and culture.[24] Another large group of documents and images from his collection relates to Van Vechten's interest in queer history and includes a collection of eighteen scrapbooks of ephemera and erotica embellished with Van Vechten's collaged captions: these include many of Ewing's photographs of male nudes. Some of these were gifted to Van Vechten by Ewing during his lifetime, and others were found among Ewing's papers after his death and quietly added to Van Vechten's own collection. Additional items, such as a program from the Egyptian Theatre in Hollywood for a revue entitled *Duck Soup to Nutty Nuts*, which shows "The 4 Marx Sisters" in drag — inscribed "Dear Carl, For one or another of your collections of Amatory Curiosa, Max" (fig. 0.6) — were shared with Van Vechten by Ewing and other collectors.[25] Van Vechten closed these scrapbooks to researchers (and even the Beinecke's own librarians) for a period of twenty-five years after his death. Now fully accessible, they not only fill out our picture of queer visual and social culture in this period, but also open up an extraordinary window onto the private lives of New York's avant-garde circle in the 1920s and '30s.

Guided by Max Ewing and Carl Van Vechten, we get to know this coterie of artists, writers, and socialites and the queer spaces they inhabited in ways that were not possible before. Moreover, thanks to Van Vechten's extraordinary efforts to preserve even the smallest and seemingly most inconsequential bits of ephemera, these archives create new opportunities to write inclusive historical

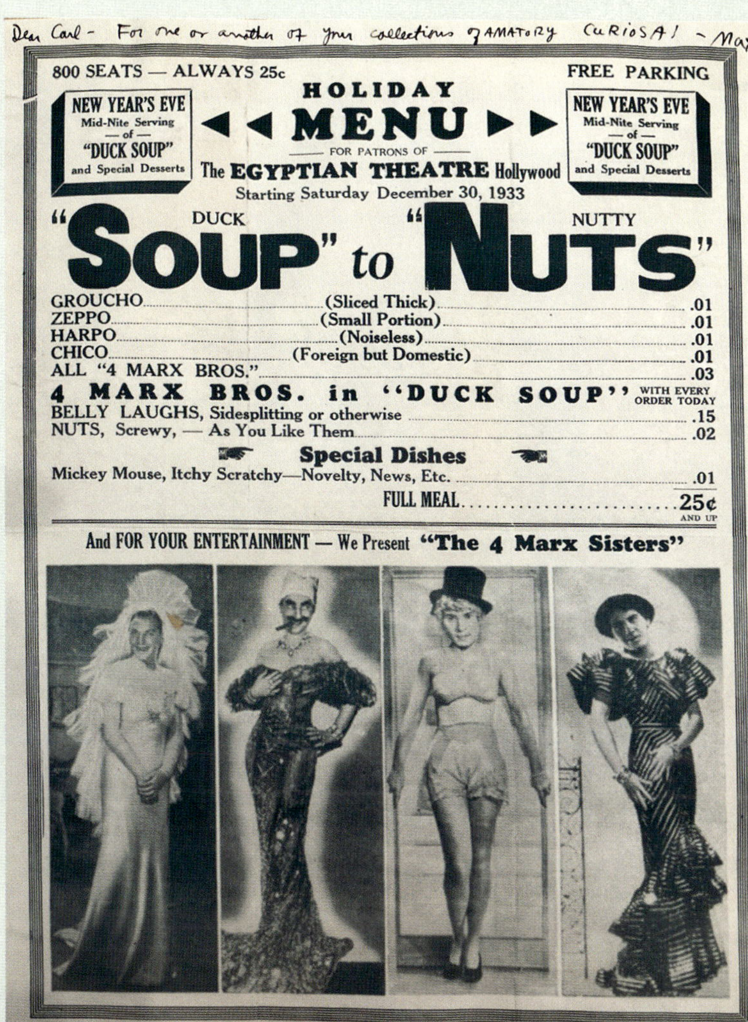

0.6 "Duck Soup to Nutty Nuts," menu from the Egyptian Theatre, Hollywood, California, December 30, 1933. Carl Van Vechten Papers, Beinecke Rare Book & Manuscript Library, Yale University, New Haven, Connecticut (henceforth Carl Van Vechten Papers).

narratives at a moment when research on Black and queer history is changing the way we view the art and culture of the twentieth century. This book tells Max Ewing's story, but — just as Van Vechten had hoped — his life, his words, and the images he left behind enable us to explore a world that has remained secret and largely forgotten for decades.

Chapter 1

ALL THAT GLAMOUR
AND LONELINESS
NEW YORK IN THE 1920S

It was typical of our precarious
position in New York that when
our child was to be born
we played safe and went home
to St Paul — it seemed inappropriate
to bring a baby into all that
glamour and loneliness …

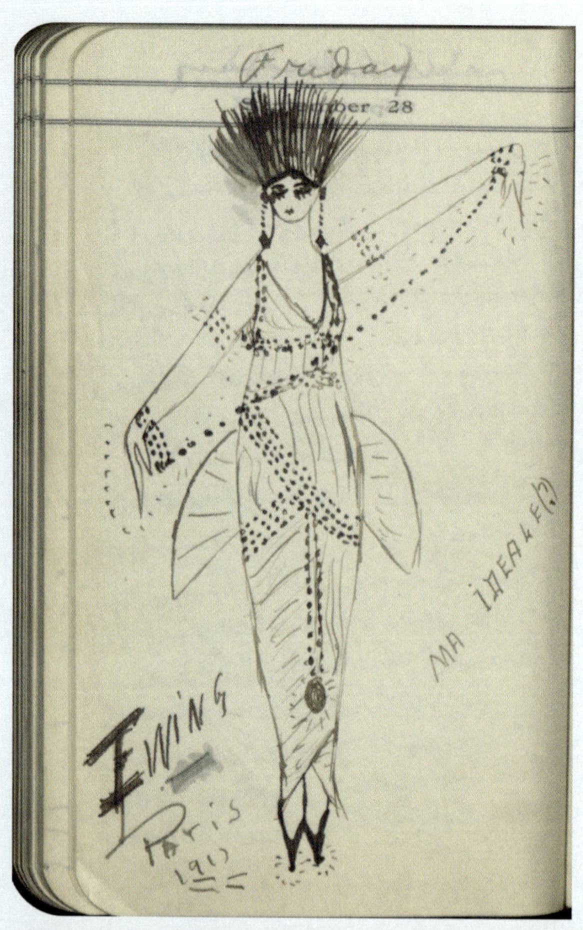

1.1 Max Ewing, "MA IDEALE (?)," Max Ewing's diary, September 28, 1917. Max Ewing Papers.

1.2 Max Ewing, "Scene from Extravaganza," Max Ewing's diary, July 10–11, 1917. Max Ewing Papers.

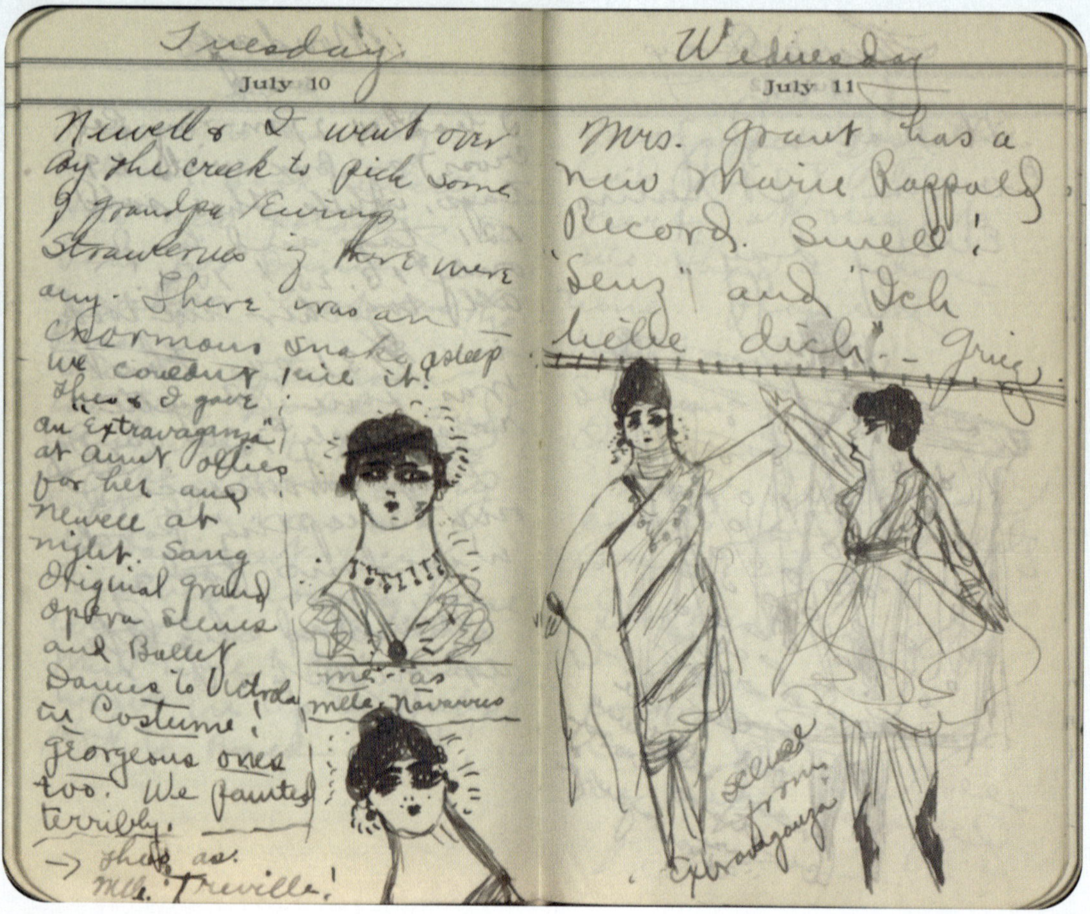

Max Ewing (1903–34) was a starstruck, small-town boy who moved to New York City from the tiny farming town of Pioneer, Ohio in the fall of 1923, a few weeks before the beginning of his senior year at the University of Michigan.[1] Impatient to get on with his training as a concert pianist and ready to begin a new life in the glamorous world of New York City that he knew — or thought he knew — as an avid fan of opera and movies, Ewing was like a character in a story by F. Scott Fitzgerald, anxious to experience firsthand the sparkling evenings at the theater, brilliant art exhibitions, and alcohol-fueled parties of his imagination. Queer, handsome, melodramatic, and most definitely a nonconformist in the eyes of his Midwestern neighbors, Ewing dreamed of life in the city, complete with the tinkling sound of ice in cocktail glasses and the animated voices of bohemian New Yorkers, and he imagined himself fully immersed in that world long before he actually arrived.

BEGINNINGS: PIONEER, OHIO, AND ANN ARBOR, MICHIGAN

From an early age, Ewing shaped his life around fantasy and playacting, creating a series of stage sets and costumes for use in at-home performances, which were inflected with a camp sensibility that knowingly referenced international glamour and the elite culture of New York, Paris, and Venice. As his diary from 1917 makes clear, by the age of fourteen, Ewing was already building up the knowledge of French fashion and high culture that would provide him with an entrée into that world, designing evening gowns inspired by Poiret (fig. 1.1) and using a storage room above his parents' dry goods store to produce lip-synched reenactments of film and opera roles played by his favorite stars — sometimes even performing in French, which he studied in school (fig. 1.2).

This was the first of the many queer interiors that Ewing would create, a safe zone of fantasy and experimentation nestled inside the store in Pioneer where his parents protected their young son from the homophobic prejudices of school friends and neighbors. Though his letters often refer to their many efforts at encouraging him to take part in the "normal" life of the town — ball games and dances, for example — Ewing remained firm, reading his highbrow books and inventing dresses and outfits. He was stubborn and snobbish, and he could be a brat: in one letter from 1928, he asks his parents "how you ever put up with me when I refused to go into a movie and insisted in [*sic*] sitting in a car to read Walter Pater."[2] He stuffed his scrapbooks full of celebrity photos and clippings, collected records to play on his Victrola, attended the opera in Toledo and Detroit with his father, and went to the latest movies as often as possible, using his diary to record the titles of the films he saw.[3]

Ewing's prosperous parents, John and Clara (figs. 1.3 and 1.4), cherished their unusual son and nurtured his musical talents, paying for concert tickets, piano lessons, and theater excursions, and subscribing to magazines from which he learned about the latest fashions and opinions of big-city critics. The Ewings clearly set their sights on moving up in the world, and from the beginning set themselves apart: both parents began their careers as clerks in one of the two dry goods stores in Pioneer, but soon after their marriage in 1901, they purchased the rival store and went into business for themselves, making a success of the newly renamed "Ewing Store."[4] As Ewing's uncle noted in a reminiscence on his brother and family written after his nephew's death, "they were successful from the start and within three or four years they had the store paid for. They built a new residence from their store profits and began to accumulate," investing their "accumulations in stocks and bonds, bought and sold at profits [*sic*], and by 1932 the face value of their securities was $125,000" — a substantial sum amounting to about $2,500,000 today.[5] While A. E. Ewing noted that the depression of 1928 "played havoc" with their securities and "reduced the value by one half," it is clear that the family became very well off in these years. Max Ewing often wrote to his parents about dividend checks and investments, and, fortified by their small-town status and their financial security, the tight-knit family trio — joined by Max's doting grandmother, who lived nearby — prospered in Pioneer.

Ambitious and hardworking, the Ewings invested in their son's success by providing him with a generous allowance for his piano lessons, paying for his comfortable living quarters at college and in New York, and supporting his taste for fashionable clothes. They also clearly accepted his queer passions and peculiarities with a loving shrug and with their eyes firmly focused on his future success — and they expected their family and neighbors to fall into line. Indeed, Ewing's letters and other communications make it clear that he was candid with both of his parents about almost everything: his snobbish opinions, especially when it came to the citizenry of Pioneer, Ohio; his desire to educate himself in all aspects of high culture, understanding that he would ultimately reinvent himself as an urban sophisticate; and his superfan adoration of glamorous divas, handsome leading men, and famous writers. He was even quite open about his sexuality, though he stayed within the boundaries that the family had established: he could write or talk about his crushes and even hint at his desires, but he could not venture beyond the jokey, camp humor that veiled his true nature, hiding the details of his feelings and keeping his private experiences from his parents and everyone else. The family loved and supported him, and they believed that he had the talent to make it. Fortified by that love, by his parents' acumen as financial investors, and by the camaraderie that came from sharing his obsessive interest in fashion, movies, and celebrity gossip with his mother, Max Ewing turned his outsider experience in small-town America into a fully formed and empowered queer identity: as long as he had his parents, and his mother in particular, he was alright, secure and protected in the cocoon of his family. Their bond was sustained by regular visits and the frequent exchange of letters, rich in detail and filled with gossip.

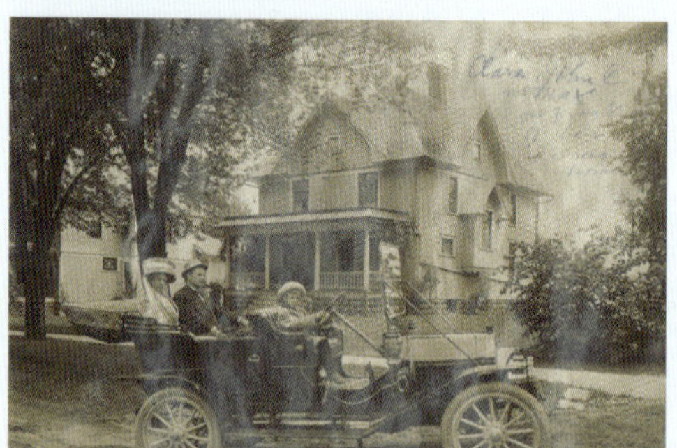

1.3 Anon., John and Clara Ewing with Max at the wheel in front of their new home in Pioneer, Ohio, c. 1908. Max Ewing Papers.

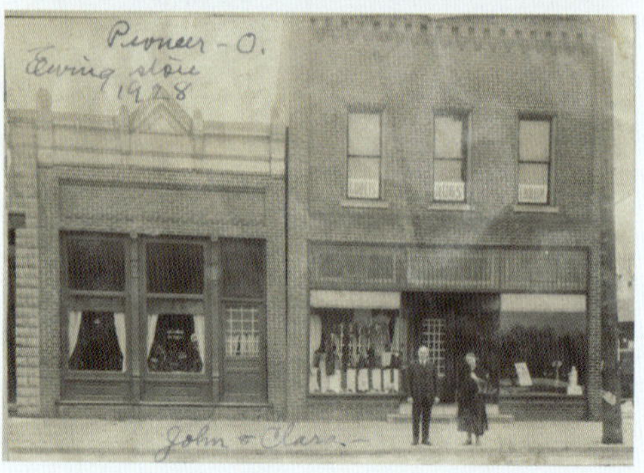

1.4 Anon., John and Clara Ewing in front of the Ewing Store, Pioneer, Ohio, 1928. Max Ewing Papers.

In 1920, Ewing enrolled at the University of Michigan in Ann Arbor, where he studied music, psychology, and literature. He enjoyed the company of "a big circle of completely congenial friends" who shared his devotion to the arts and literature, and wrote to his parents that he was "living outside myself more than I ever did before."[6] His friends put on plays and performed the latest music, and Ewing described one such event after the final recital of his junior year on June 16, 1923, touching on all the topics — from his clothes, to the guest list, to his own artistic aspirations — that would become the staples of his correspondence with his family:

> I wore a tuxedo with soft broadcloth shirt and a flowing Windsor tie. Esther wore an evening gown of green spangles and a brilliant headdress. She sang the "Hymn to the Sun". ... I can't enumerate all the guests ... Andrew Haigh, the pianist from New York came, and is coming up to see me tomorrow. I'm so awfully glad to have found him. He is in <u>everything</u> in N.Y. that I hope to be in. ... It's been such awfully fine fun — the sort of thing I've always been crazy to do, and never quite did. My French parties upstairs in the store, etc. were feeble attempts in this direction. This was the <u>real thing</u>. A really good concert, the right kind of music, right kind of décor and surroundings, and above all the <u>right kind of people</u>. I'm awfully happy over it. It's my farewell to Ann Arbor and a rather brilliant one.[7]

Over the course of the previous year, Ewing had become increasingly restless in college and infatuated with the work of the critic and author Carl Van Vechten. He studied the role of the young man of the world Peter Whiffle, the title character in Van Vechten's recently published, eponymous novel (1922), and immersed himself in Van Vechten's criticism of the arts and literature, writing a breathless appreciation of his work for the Michigan student newspaper in December 1922. That article, which was widely viewed as a declaration of independence from the traditional teaching of the rather conservative arts faculty at the university, was soon republished in the *Detroit Free Press*, and thus became accessible to a broad audience.[8]

Ewing characterized Van Vechten as a "wit-laden but fair-minded critic, refreshing essayist, and most captivating of raconteurs, indefatigable diver into the sea of all-but-unknown books and bringer to the surface of strange and precious things, thorough-going epicure and cosmopolite," establishing his own bona fides by dropping the name of the opera superstar Mary Garden, with whom he had spoken briefly in her backstage dressing room the month before. He also wrote directly to Van Vechten to introduce himself:

> I want to say to you this much about myself. I am nineteen, grew up in a world of my own in and about Toledo, exactly Peter-fashion, with piano-playing my greatest interest. Since coming to the university (three years ago) my interest in musical "criticism" — hateful term — has almost outbalanced my interest in piano playing alone. I am coming to NY next year to study piano.[9]

His young admirer's very public display of devotion pleased Van Vechten so much that he wrote back, encouraging him to drop out of college and inviting him to visit his home in New York for a more extended conversation.[10] By that point, Ewing had already resolved to move on, and he scolded his parents for remaining in Pioneer, Ohio, where he saw no future for himself or for them:

> Life in a small town is endurable if one is surrounded by the right kind of people and friends. Life in a city can be wonderful even if one has no friends, because of the goings-on. Life in a great city *with* plenty of congenial friends is then the ideal life. And the very worst life, it seems to me, is that in the village where there are neither people nor events. And that is what Pioneer is becoming as fast as it can … I will be there with you off and on throughout the summer, when I am not working with Tom [Dewey, a college friend and future Republican politician]. But you must know that after next fall I can never spend any time there. After I am twenty-one [on April 7, 1924], I cannot go on spending my summers lying around in Pioneer. And you would not want me to. Once I have decided for sure what I am going to do, and I expect to decide that next year, I am going to walk a straight path, and that, you will agree, is the only thing to do. So, if you want to furnish the house, and live on in Pioneer, without me or anyone else or anything to amuse yourselves with, I maintain that it is a strange taste! And I hope you won't do it. But we get this far every time we bring the subject up. It is most discouraging … [11]

New York City, 1923–26

Max Ewing arrived in New York in late September 1923. Thanks to a generous allowance of around $3,000 per year (nearly $54,000 in today's dollars), plus occasional gifts from his parents for special requests, he soon managed to find a room to rent at 152 East 22nd Street where the landladies were flexible about his need to practice the piano during the day; he then set about the business of getting to know the city and his mentor.[12] Ewing's regular visits to Van Vechten's apartment — which began almost immediately in early October 1923 — and their nightly adventures together mark the beginning of a long and intimate friendship between the two men, one founded on a queer sensibility that they shared: a love of the city in all its dimensions, devotion to the theater, books, and music, a zeal for collecting objects and images, and a hunger for immersion in the glamorous social whirl of downtown parties, literary salons, and all-night barhopping in Harlem.[13]

Van Vechten and Ewing were both products of middle-class, Midwestern families. Van Vechten was born in Cedar Rapids, Iowa in 1880, making him a generation older than Ewing, but both were viewed by friends and family as eccentric outsiders whose flair for the dramatic, from music and fashion to restaurants, nightclubs, and travel, determined their public and private activities. Indeed, the two men shared not only an ironic sense of humor, but also a critical eye for detail in writing and visual culture that enabled them to cast an aura of knowing, camp performance over everything they said and did.

Van Vechten — "Carlo" to his friends — welcomed Ewing into his home and turned on the charm, mesmerizing the handsome twenty-year-old with his witty stories and famous connections. As Ewing described it in a letter dated October 9, 1923:

> Last evening I spent with Carl Van Vechten, alone, in his rooms on
> E. 19th st. … He wants me to come often. He goes out little. He has
> heard all the music, seen all the plays, known all the artists, read all
> the books, seen all the pictures, visited all the capitals, & now he's
> tired of it all. He would rather spend a night talking with me than go
> out, he says. His cat was lovely. We talked music, books, & pictures.
> He likes me. He can introduce me to anyone I want to know.[14]

The following day he wrote another letter about the experience, noting that "the young man who spent last Monday evening with Carl Van Vechten in a red & yellow silk-lined room in 'Fairfax Arms' was a creature I can't recognize today at all. My body was there, yes. But where on earth was I? … You must take me as I am, and overlook my craziness-es [*sic*] … Van Vechten says I'm fascinating."[15]

Max Ewing had also scored an enormous coup in being accepted as a piano student by the distinguished Russian musician Alexander Siloti, who had settled in the United States in 1921 and taught at Juilliard from 1925 to 1942.[16] On Monday, October 15, Ewing let his parents know that his piano had been delivered and that he had started to practice in earnest. By the beginning of December, he could report that he was full of "*pianoistic* enthusiasm," having "learned more in the last six weeks about piano playing" from Siloti, than he "had in the past six years in Pioneer and Ann Arbor."[17] Nevertheless, the bulk of his October letter was taken up by news of another visit to Van Vechten's apartment the previous weekend, and a description of his first meeting with Van Vechten's wife, the actress Fania Marinoff (fig. 1.5), when she returned home from the theater. He was breathless with excitement and clearly smitten by every detail of the evening, not least the intimacy that was signaled by the exchange of books and music, the casual dropping of famous names, and the sharing of unfamiliar foods from a New York delicatessen.

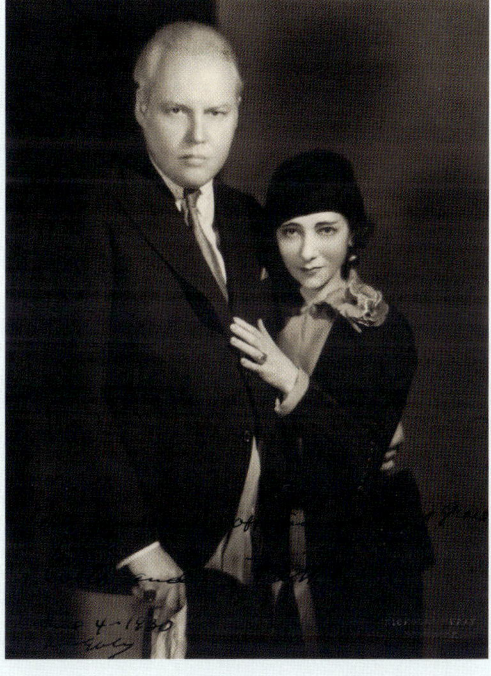

1.5 Nickolas Muray, *Carl Van Vechten and Fania Marinoff*, 1930. Carl Van Vechten Papers.

This was exactly the sort of heady urban experience he had dreamed about for his entire life:

> Van Vechten sent for me to spend Saturday [October 13] evening with
> him, and I had the most wonderful time. I like him so much better
> than the first time. I never had so much to talk about with anyone!
> He likes me and is going to have me be invited *"everywhere."* If it were
> not my nature to accept everything more or less as a matter of course
> I would be quite bowled over by my good fortune. … Van Vechten gave
> me a copy of the new Knopf edition of Rimsky-Korsikoff's [*sic*]
> "My Musical Life," which he (V. V.) has edited, a beautiful book which

sells for $8.oo. He wrote in it a whole page inscription beginning: "To Max Ewing who may write or play or ... qui sait?" (Qui sait in French, pronounced "key say" and means "who knows") I stayed until Marinoff (the wife) came in from the theater. She is delightful, small and dark, intense and vivacious. She apologized for having her wig off and her make-up still on, and showed me a stiff new bathrobe she just brought home! She went out to the Third Avenue delicatessen and brought chicken sandwiches and cheese and ripe olives, and the three of us, with the cat, had supper. ... Two hundred people were turned away from Marinoff's play Saturday night, and naturally she was happy. I want to see it before long, but I have already acquired the New Yorker's habit of putting plays off. I know I'm here for the season, and that the play will have a long run, and my attitude becomes "I'll see it next month"!![18]

"I'm so fortunate," he gushed, "I almost believe in a Destiny!"

> Obstacles that get into most people's way seem to shun me. What I want to do most of all is play the piano very wonderfully, and I am in the way of doing it. I have the talent ... and the will to work ... I go to one of the five or six greatest teachers in the world, and he accepts me on the spot, and for no very convincing reason offers to take me at practically half price. I go to Van Vechten and Marinoff, two of the most prominent people in the American world of music, books, and the theater, and they both like me, and offer to open all the doors in NY to me ... I have youth, health, a certain type of beauty, what a real authority maintains is talent, the opportunity to develop it, enough funds to live, not luxuriously, but comfortably in the most stimulating atmosphere in the world.[19]

Ever the pampered darling of his parents, Ewing couldn't resist the urge to add a bit of "I told you so" in closing:

> And, because I did not waste my high school and college days at ball games, dances, and movies, as you constantly begged me to do, but spent my time reading and "cultivating something" inside, I have, now, entry, thru V. V. and others, to the most brilliant artistic circles in the most brilliant city in the world. I should be perfectly happy. I am. I hope you can feel this with me.

Ewing fell in love with the city, describing his late-night walks through Madison Square ("It is not like anything else on earth. The lights in the Metropolitan Life Tower and the buildings around it seem like Fairyland") and Central Park, where he explored the depths of the "Wilderness" (a well-known cruising spot, a detail that he did *not* share with his parents) in the darkness, marveling that "the lighted skyscrapers against the strange black sky seem unbelievable and not real buildings!" Like his friend Berenice Abbott, who photographed the glamorous New York skyline at night a few years later (fig. 1.6), Ewing could see himself in the glittering city: he delighted in its secrets and

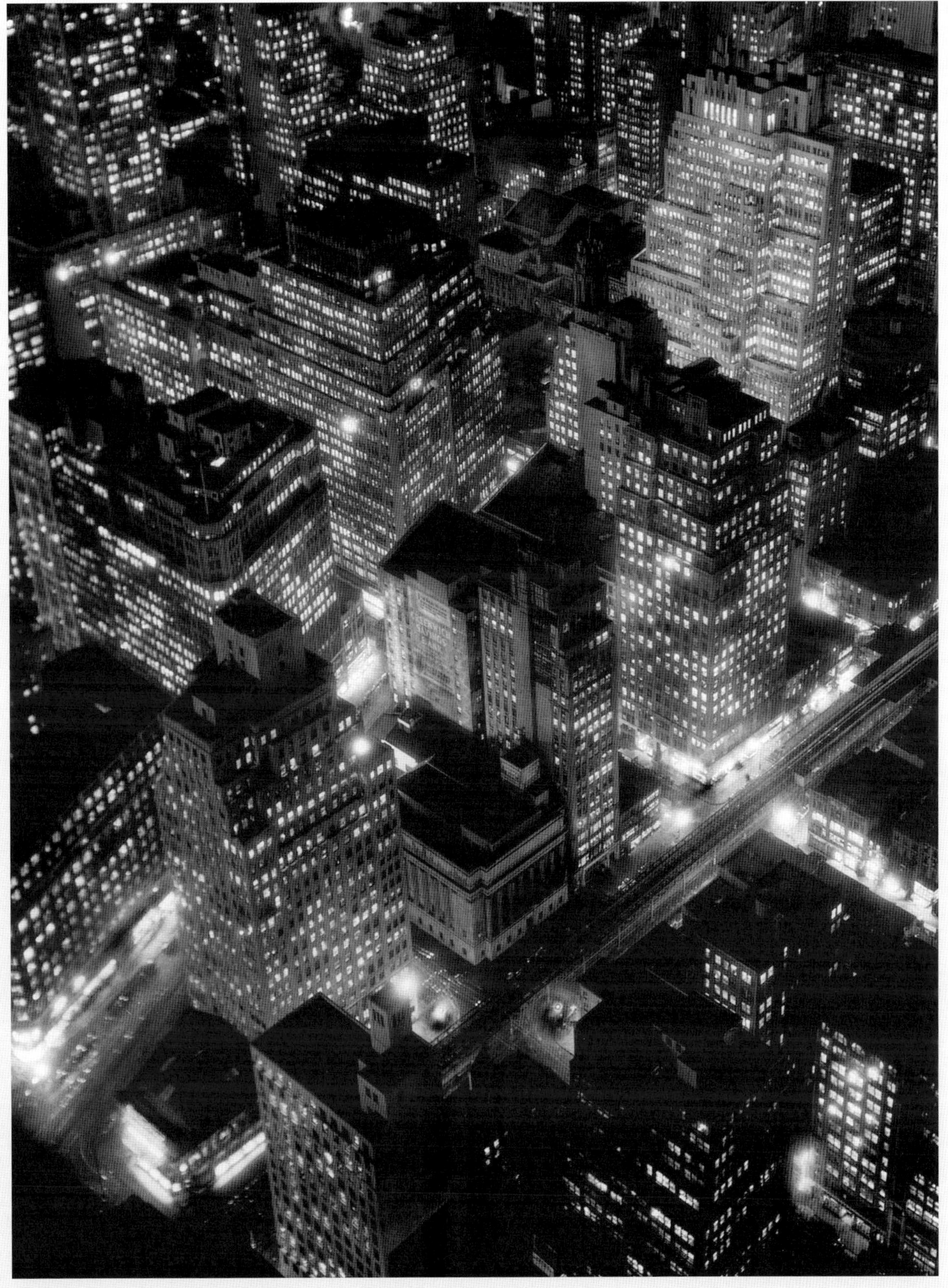

1.6 Berenice Abbott, *New York at Night*, c. 1932, gelatin silver print, 13⅜ × 10⅝ in. (34 × 27 cm). Philadelphia Museum of Art.

readily recognized it as a place where he could, at last, be himself. He soon discovered his favorite small shops and restaurants, including "a lovely place where I always go to luncheon — in a basement on Irving Place," and the Automat, which he described as "the white tile joint on 23rd Street" where he could "save on the waitress's tip." With his college friend Tom Dewey (later Governor of New York), he tried a "different place every Sunday," including a "coffee house down on Stuyvesant Square" where they had a "lovely 4 course chicken dinner for one dollar."[20] Before long, he started receiving regular invitations to parties where food and drink were on offer: as he gleefully reported to his parents just a month after his arrival in the city, "By day I practice. I go to Siloti for a lesson on Tuesday morning. By night — I meet everyone, hear everyone, see everyone!"[21]

In November, he decided to try to earn a bit of extra money by teaching piano students for $5 an hour, but nothing much seems to have come of that project; he rarely mentioned his pupils and it is clear that his parents supported him not only in those first few months in New York, but throughout his life. The plan that all three Ewings had agreed on was that he was to study piano seriously (he practiced at least three hours a day), meet lots of celebrities and powerful friends, and become famous.

New York City was filled with many opportunities and many distractions. Ewing made friends with a young dancer named Stuart Mackall from the Denishawn School who came to see his collection of Geraldine Farrar memorabilia — "he has a big one too," he boasted, "but I'm sure it can't equal mine" — and he asked his parents to send him their Kodak camera so that the two could take some snapshots at Long Beach or Brighton; unfortunately, those images are missing. He also continued to practice and write songs: with a group of Michigan friends who called themselves the "Revue du Groupe des Sept" — a play on "Les Six," the much-admired group of contemporary composers, including Darius Milhaud, Georges Auric, and Francis Poulenc, among others — he staged a revue of music and dance on May 8, 1924 for an audience of fifty that included Van Vechten and Marinoff.[22] The program included *Chocolate Thunder,* Ewing's oratorio for tenor and piano with texts by Gertrude Stein.[23]

Such activities soon gained him the attention of a wider circle of artists and writers and enabled him to expand on the literary and cultural connections that he had made through Van Vechten the previous year. As he wrote to his parents, after his recital he had been invited to the home of Samuel Hoffenstein (1890–1947), a writer and producer who was interested in using Ewing's lyrics in a new production; through Hoffenstein (who would go on to have a successful career as a screenwriter in Hollywood) and his wife, Ewing encountered a group of older, well-established artists and theater people, including the costume designer and socialite Louise Hellstrom (b. 1891), whose glamorous outfits, theatricality, and European sophistication were deeply appealing to the young man intent on moving up in the world of culture. He reported on all of these adventures in his letters: "Mrs. Hallstrom [*sic*] wants copies of my songs with Gertrude Stein texts to take to Gertrude in Paris this summer," he boasted, adding breezily, "She says Gertrude is a 'sweet old sport' and would like me."[24]

Within a year of his arrival in New York, Ewing was regularly attending Louise Hellstrom's Sunday gatherings and Van Vechten's parties, making contact with such luminary figures as the artist Joseph Stella (1877–1946), the composer Edgard Varèse (1883–1965), Jane Heap (1883–1964) (editor of the *Little Review*), and, notably, Hellstrom's lover, the artist and bon vivant Robert Winthrop Chanler (1872–1930), whose raucous parties in his home on 19th Street were a mainstay of the bohemian social scene. Writing to his parents throughout the fall of 1924, he regularly described Hellstrom's parties, listed her guests, and provided the details of her striking outfits (see fig. 5.42). In one letter, for example, he added a little sketch, noting that Hellstrom's dress was "the most smart new thing from Poiret … with transparent red lace panels up the sides and flaming neck scarf. Velvet bodice and velvet shoes," boasting that "Nothing escapes me."[25]

This was indeed the case: Ewing took in the details of everyone's clothing and remembered every conversation, working hard to know and exploit the many new acquaintances he collected. A letter from November 10, 1924 is typical:

> Yesterday was Mrs Hellstrom's weekly Sunday Afternoon. I made a most notable connection — this time with Carol Robinson one of the most talented young American pianists, a life-long pupil of Fannie Bloomfield-Zeisler … just back from Paris … a soloist with the NY philharmonic. … Well, we're both crazy about the same kind of modern music, and we're going to work together on some 4 hand arrangements of Stravinsky's music and play sometime this winter at Jane Heap's new salon when she opens it. It's going to be a combination book-shop and gallery for new sculpture and paintings … Jane Heap is the most brilliant original woman mind in America, and anything she starts, *ends*![26]

Once again, the extraordinary qualities and enormous historical value of Max Ewing's letters are on full display here: rich in detail about projects and people at the very heart of the new avant-garde, Ewing's letters delineate a detailed picture of the loosely connected circle of artists, writers, and supporters of the arts and music that thrived in New York in the 1920s and '30s. Ewing wanted nothing more than to be part of that world, and with his good looks, his charm, and his talents as a musician, it was easy for him to make friends; people like Louise Hellstrom and Jane Heap — and, of course, Carl Van Vechten — were always on the lookout for new talent and happy to support him.

By the spring of 1924, Hellstrom had emerged as the latest in a long line of strong women — Geraldine Farrar, Mary Garden, and Marguerite d'Alvarez among them — whose charisma, connections, and theatricality Ewing found irresistible. Soon this group would include the *saloniste* Muriel Draper, whom Ewing met the following spring: from that moment in 1925 — a point in time that Ewing remembered as magical and life-changing — Draper would become his beloved companion, confidante, and mentor, displacing Louise Hellstrom and everyone else in his orbit.[27] For now, however, it was Hellstrom, together with Bob Chanler, who occupied center stage in Ewing's life.

Balancing out his relationships with older friends and mentors, Ewing also acquired an intimate circle of men and women his own age through his involvement with the *Grand Street Follies*, an annual parody of the most successful Broadway shows, featuring singers, dancers, and comedians drawn from the world of vaudeville and off-Broadway theater.[28] The *Follies* was performed at the Neighborhood Playhouse, a well-established community theater with ties to the Henry Street Settlement; as Ewing informed his parents,

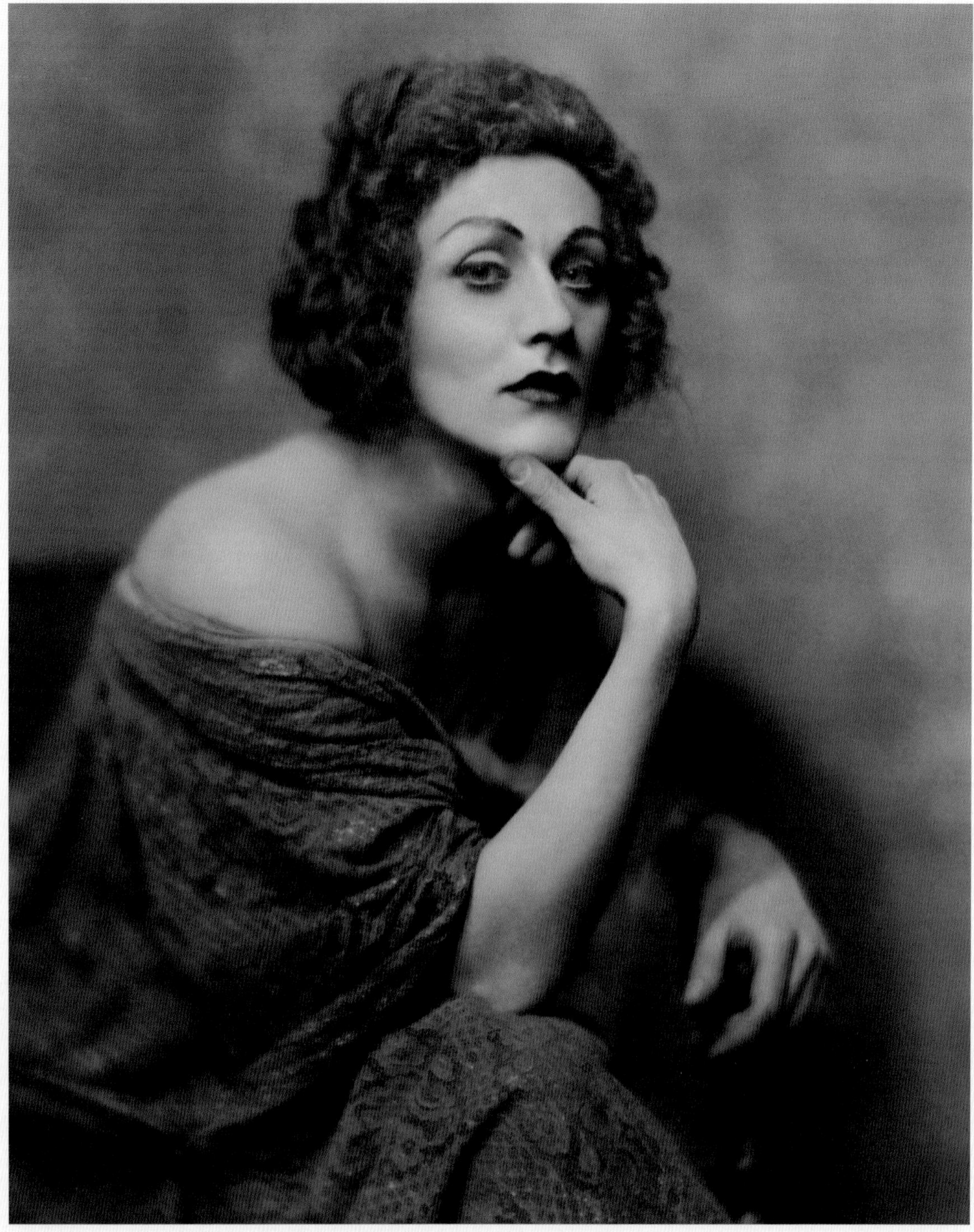

1.7 Nickolas Muray, *Actor Albert Carroll in the Character of Emily Stevens, Vanity Fair*, November 1, 1924. Condé Nast. Gift of Theodore T. Newbold in memory of Lee Witkin 1984.

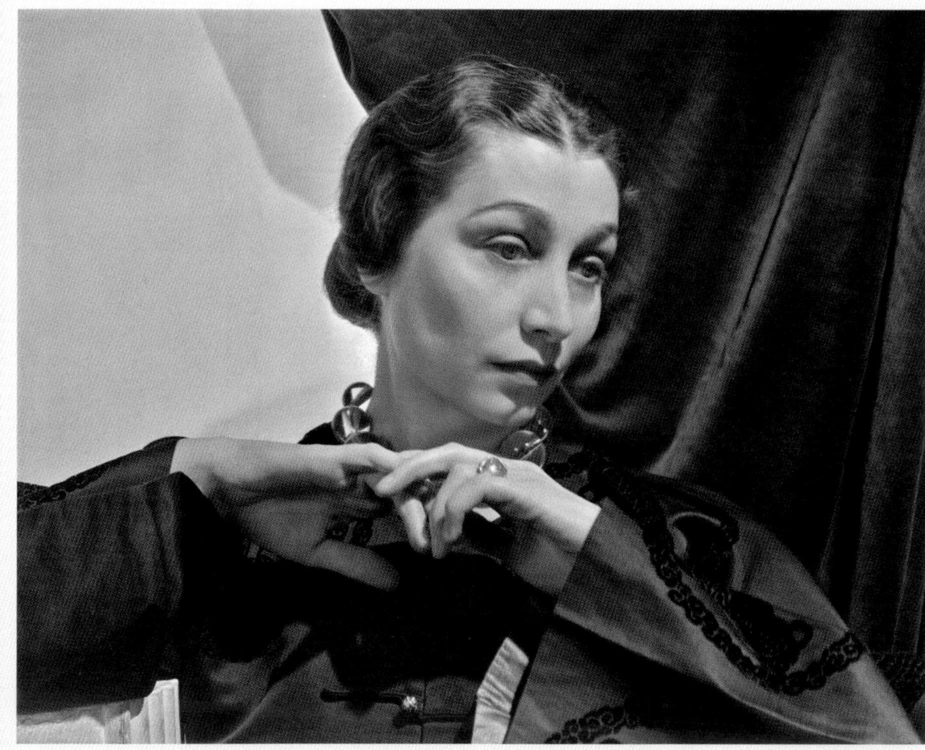

1.8 Cecil Beaton, *Aline MacMahon*, 1932. Cecil Beaton Archive, Condé Nast.

the theater was "miles downtown in the very heart of the Lower East Side — and it gets only very discriminating people who are willing to take the trouble to get there. It gets none of the Times Square transients who merely want to 'see a show.'"[29] Working as a piano player and composer for the 1924 production, Ewing — who had always been a fan of popular music and vaudeville — met the drag actor Albert Carroll (1895–1956) (fig. 1.7) and acquired a lively circle of other new friends from the theater: like many young people in the 1920s, this group shared a commitment to gender and sexual nonconformity that made Ewing feel at home in the city.[30] This was his first exposure to an "out" drag artist like Carroll, who was famous for his gender-bending impersonation of the actress Emily Stevens and made no effort to conceal his identity, on stage or in private.

Ewing chronicled these experiences in his letters to his parents, writing on June 5, 1924, to tell them about his night out with his new friends: "Albert Carroll gave a dinner party at Bruno's [in Washington Square], then a theater party at the Casino, and after that a supper party for me and Marion Morehouse who is about the most beautiful fashion model in New York."[31] Like Carroll, Marion Morehouse (1906–69) — an up-and-coming model who was often photographed by Edward Steichen for *Vogue* in the 1920s (Ewing boasted that "she poses for the big costume designers here, and sits for the Fifth Avenue photographers") — would prove to be a loyal companion for more than a decade. Both she and the poet E. E. Cummings (1894–1962), her life partner from the 1930s on, appeared in Ewing's *Carnival of Venice* series in 1932, as did the actress Aline MacMahon (1899–1991) (fig. 1.8), another lifelong friend from the *Follies* with whom Ewing became close in these years. At the heart of the group was the lesbian power couple Helen Arthur (a former lover of Henry Street founder Lillian Wald) and Agnes Morgan, principal writer and producer of the *Follies*, with whom Ewing would eventually fall out as he competed for a larger role in the annual production.[32]

The brilliant MacMahon (who had recently graduated from Barnard College) consistently promoted Ewing's efforts as a songwriter and used her employment by the Shubert Organization to help him establish his career in show business, albeit with limited success; she too remained a lifelong supporter, keeping in touch even after she had moved on to Hollywood and become famous as a character actress in such films as *Gold Diggers of 1933*.[33] Carroll, Morehouse, MacMahon, and the others welcomed Ewing into their quirky, woman-centered circle and he relished every performance and after-party. His scrapbooks and his *Gallery of Extraordinary Portraits* included numerous photos and clippings documenting his friendships with members of this group.

Not surprisingly, Ewing's parents were increasingly worried that all of this heady theater business and nightly excursions around town was taking precious time and energy away from their son's piano studies, gently suggesting that he was perhaps becoming "too predominately social"; he reassured them, rather disingenuously, that he was actually going out far less than he had the previous year.[34] The truth is that he had discovered a whole new universe of kindred spirits and an irresistible, ongoing performance of personality among these new friends. He adored the daily round of makeup, costumes, and performances in live theater, and he was thrilled by the drama and intrigue of a hothouse environment filled with young people. Although he reassured his parents that he was "in a perfectly normal way again" with his mind firmly focused on "Bach and octaves" following the successful opening of the *Follies* in May 1924, they were clearly right to be concerned.[35] Throughout his early life in Pioneer, Ewing had yearned for this glamorous, queer world: now that it was right in front of him, now that he had experienced it himself and was part of a group, he fell head over heels in love and never looked back.[36]

SHAPING THE INTERRACIAL AVANT-GARDE:
ROBERT CHANLER AND CARL VAN VECHTEN

Like Van Vechten's diaries and F. Scott Fitzgerald's novels, Max Ewing's letters from the 1920s make it clear that, despite Prohibition (or perhaps because of it), the members of his extended social network in New York City — friends and acquaintances from uptown and downtown, the East Side and West Side, young and old, Black and white — often partied hard, gathering nightly to drink, talk, dance, and socialize late into the night. Although these groups often ended up at bars or restaurants in Harlem or Greenwich Village in the early hours of the morning, they usually gathered first at "teas" and "cocktail parties" in private homes, including the Park Avenue townhouses of wealthy friends or the apartments and studios where women like Morehouse and MacMahon lived, or indeed, the ramshackle loft above a garage on the far East Side of New York where Muriel Draper lived and hosted her salon. Such impromptu parties, fueled by bootleg liquor and the creative and sexual energies of people who lived for new ideas and experiences, would prove to be the unlikely melting pot that forged a queer, interracial avant-garde art movement out of the random friendships and activities of a disparate group of individuals. Here again, Ewing's powers of observation and his passion for sharing his experiences with his family make his letters an invaluable source of information about the workings of this coterie in the 1920s and early '30s.

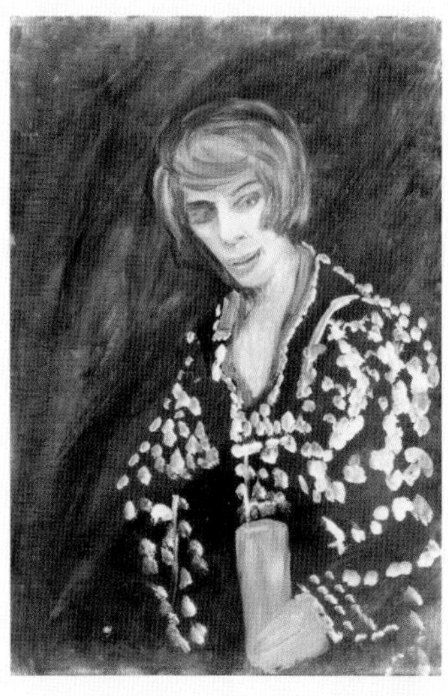

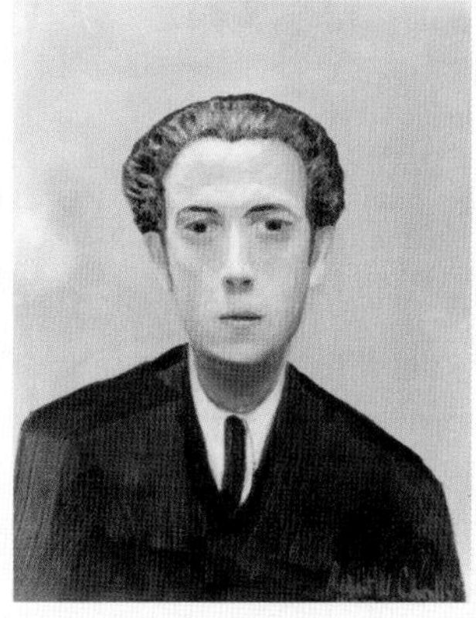

1.9 Robert Winthrop Chanler, *Louise Hellstrom*, 1924. Private Collection, Woodstock, New York; Peter A. Juley Photograph Collection, Smithsonian American Art Museum, Washington, DC.

1.10 Robert Winthrop Chanler, *Max Ewing*, 1925. Peter A. Juley Photograph Collection, Smithsonian American Art Museum, Washington, DC.

Among the best-known party venues in New York during this period was Robert Chanler's double townhouse, nicknamed "The House of Fantasy," at 147–149 East 19th Street.[37] Here the tall, burly artist — the pivot point of a love triangle that included Louise Hellstrom and the beautiful Broadway actress Clemence Randolph — presided over raucous gatherings, famous both for the generous pitchers of "cocktails" on offer and for the enormous crowds of drunken revelers (some of whom had actually been invited) who attended the nightly festivities. Chanler, who collected animals for use as models in his paintings and housed them in the basement of his home, was an outsize figure given to loud enthusiasms and angry outbursts: Ewing described his eccentric habits for the benefit of his parents, noting in passing that Chanler loved his piano playing, whether he played jazz or "little things" or, on one occasion, the music of the eighteenth-century composer Gluck.[38] His wild parties often erupted in dramatic scenes, including drunken fistfights and heated arguments among the attendees, including — more often than not — Louise Hellstrom, who frequently took issue with her lover's behavior or the comments of one or another of his guests. Chanler painted her portrait in 1924, and Ewing included a photo of the picture (fig. 1.9) in his *Gallery of Extraordinary Portraits*, the exhibition of his collection installed in the walk-in closet of his West 31st Street apartment in 1928.

Chanler also painted Max Ewing's portrait in 1925 (fig. 1.10), and Ewing sent a photograph of the painting to his parents on March 12, noting that "friends of Chanler's think it is the best portrait he ever made."[39] Although the original and the photograph of it are both now missing, we are fortunate that a signed and dated image was recorded by the photographer Peter Juley, together with the sitter's name written directly along the edge of the negative. The photo is part of the vast collection of Juley's studio archive held by the Smithsonian American Art Museum.[40] His images read like a who's who of the downtown scene between 1925 and 1930.

In 1928, Chanler again attempted to capture Ewing's handsome features; this time he was wearing the elaborate eighteenth-century costume he had rented (and later purchased) when he accompanied Romaine Brooks to a party in Marchesa Luisa Casati's garden in Paris in 1926.[41] This painting, also now missing, can be identified among the works in an exhibition of some thirty-five Chanler

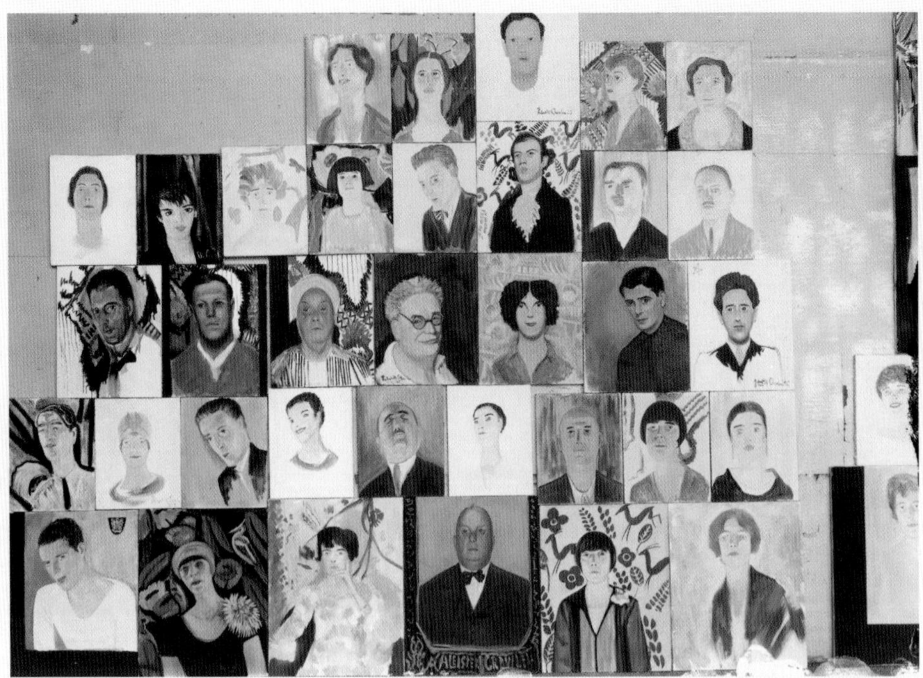

1.11 Anon., Exhibition of portraits by Robert Winthrop Chanler, 1927 or 1928. Peter A. Juley Photograph Collection, Smithsonian American Art Museum, Washington, DC.

portraits photographed by Peter Juley, which shows the extent of his effort to record the members of his social circle (fig. 1.11). Here the sitters range from recognizable figures like Jean Cocteau and the occultist Aleister Crowley (his portrait is captioned in large block letters) to anonymous men and women who can no longer be identified. We know from another surviving Juley photo that Chanler also painted Ewing's friend Albert Carroll, the star of the *Grand Street Follies*, wearing a coat and tie (fig. 1.12); were it not for the fact that here again the sitter's name is scrawled along the edge of the film negative, he, like many others, would remain anonymous.

As Carl Van Vechten later recalled, Chanler's paintings were created in an upstairs studio where a butler produced "bowls of succulent rice and curry and huge pitchers of Bronx cocktails" while the roiling crowd of drunken revelers partied on the floors below.[42] He worked in a uniform,

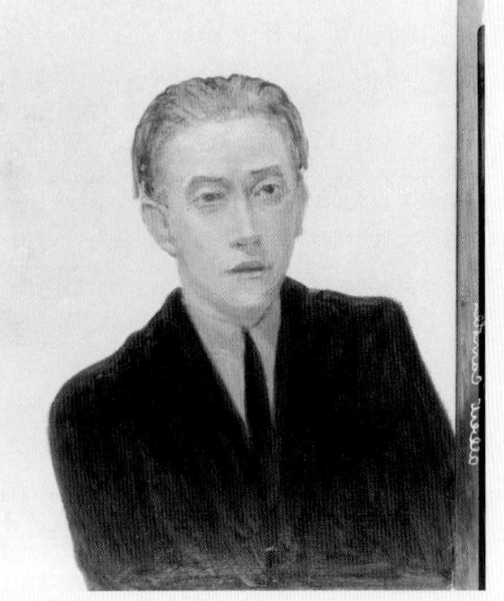

1.12 Robert Winthrop Chanler, *Albert Carroll*, c. 1928. Peter A. Juley Photograph Collection, Smithsonian American Art Museum, Washington, DC.

rectangular format, using a close-up view, with his sitters sometimes posed in front of boldly patterned backdrops; these portraits, painted in a simple, whimsical style, often have the character of photographs, an approach that clearly influenced both the encyclopedic scope and the distinctive style favored by Carl Van Vechten in his decades-long portrait series, begun in 1932, recording his own vast circle of friends and acquaintances. Chanler's project may also have served as a model for both Ewing's *Gallery of Extraordinary Portraits* and his *Carnival of Venice* series from 1932 as both reflect a similar impulse to document his circle and memorialize his own place in it. Van Vechten and Chanler admired and contributed to Ewing's efforts in this as in other projects: all three were

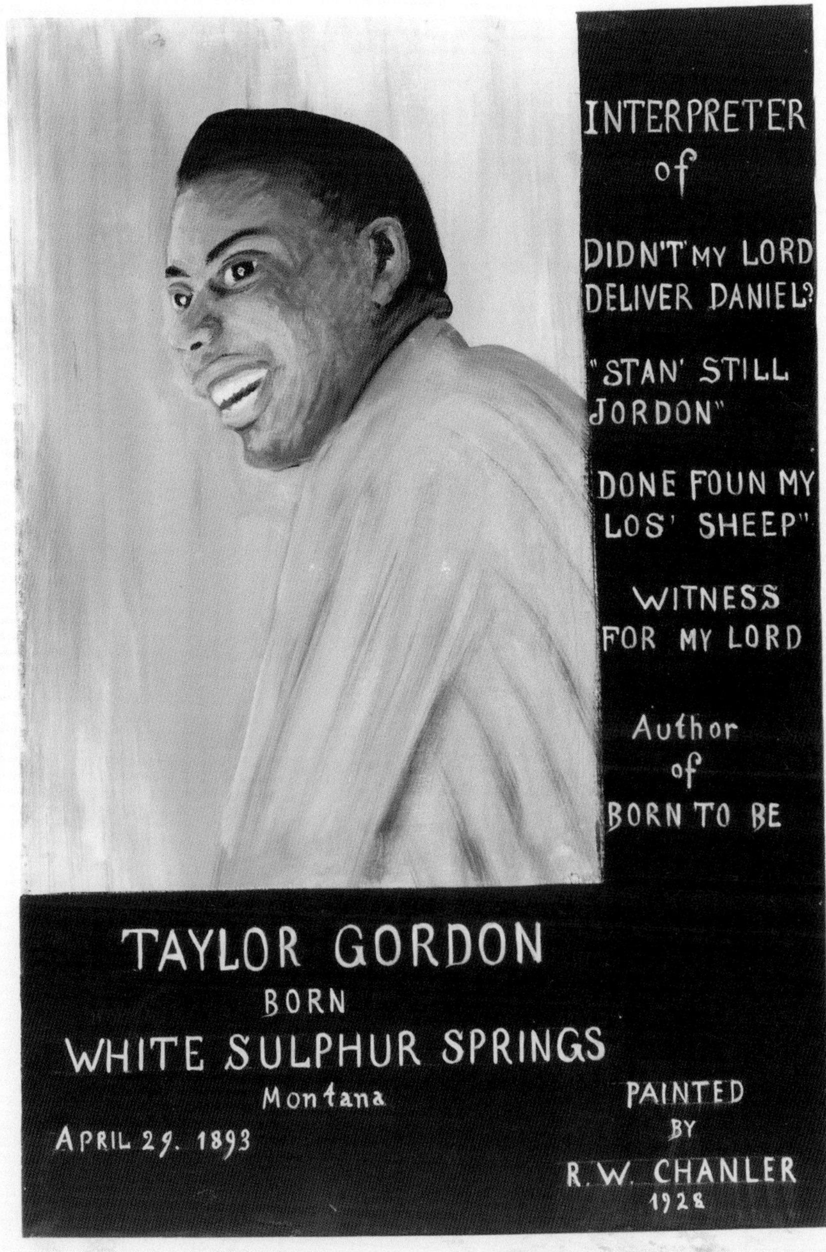

1.13 Robert Winthrop Chanler, *Taylor Gordon*, 1928. Peter A. Juley Photograph Collection, Smithsonian American Art Museum, Washington, DC.

motivated (like Andy Warhol in the *Polaroid* snapshots he produced from the late 1950s on) by a desire to capture the electric atmosphere of the times by recording the faces of their diverse circle as they might appear on any given day or night. The uniform format and style of the images enhanced the pseudoscientific character of these collections, but despite the invaluable record each created, in the end all such efforts were like trying to capture lightning in a bottle. As members of a largely forgotten coterie, many of the people, Ewing included, in Chanler's portraits remain oddly still and remote to us today.

There are, however, a few significant exceptions. In 1928, Chanler painted another denizen of his gatherings at the "House of Fantasy," the African American singer Taylor Gordon (1893–1971): in this case, the portrait was captioned not only with the sitter's name, but also with his unlikely birthplace in White Sulphur Springs, Montana, and the titles of some of the best-known spirituals for which he became famous (fig. 1.13).[43] Gordon was a rising star in Harlem and — like Albert

Carroll — became well-known among a certain sector of New York music lovers; he was a close collaborator with the musician J. Rosamond Johnson (brother of the writer and activist James Weldon Johnson [1871–1938]), and a favorite of both Carl Van Vechten and Muriel Draper. For a brief period in the 1920s, he was also a close friend and companion of Max Ewing, since both young men were part of the of the extended, interracial group that attended raucous parties like Chanler's and all-night excursions to Harlem nightspots. These friends also met at serious gatherings in the homes of cultural leaders like Van Vechten, Draper, and A'lelia Walker (1885–1931) (the African American heiress and arts patron) where readings of literature and performances of new musical and literary works took place.[44]

From his first months in New York, Max Ewing was an active participant in this world, a cultured reader and musician who revealed his talent for staying the course on the nightly rounds that Van Vechten organized, just as he did at Robert Chanler's parties or in the gatherings hosted by his young friends from the Neighborhood Playhouse. As described in Ewing's letters to his parents and detailed in Van Vechten's daybooks throughout the 1920s, these extended walkabouts often involved all-night drinking, dancing, and impromptu performances of music, as well as spirited debates about relationships, the arts, politics, and interracial culture.[45]

TROUBLE IN BOHEMIA: RACISM

Ewing's early letters often include comments about his friendship with Taylor Gordon and the limitations that racism imposed on it: by offering first-person recollections of social gatherings, drag shows, and cultural events where white and Black people came together, his comments take us beyond the well-documented accomplishments of the principal figures of the Harlem Renaissance and shed new light on both the complex friendships that cemented the movement and the range of places — private homes, restaurants, concert halls, and Harlem bars and cabarets — in which they came to fruition. It is thus worth looking carefully at Ewing's reminiscences in hope of better understanding the unique, interracial contributions of his circle, as well as the areas in which he — and other white friends — fell well short of their progressive ambitions.

As historians Steven Watson, Chad Heap, and Kevin Mumford have shown, throughout the 1920s, many Harlem clubs like Pod and Jerry's, Small's Paradise, the Nest, and the Clam House became increasingly popular by catering to the interests — social, sexual, and cultural — of new customers, including residents of Harlem, white tourists, and members of the New York avant-garde.[46] Upscale white patrons flocked to the theatrical floorshows of nightclubs like The Plantation and the Cotton Club, where a whites-only policy excluded Black customer. Music-lovers and especially queer patrons like Van Vechten, Ewing, and their friends preferred Small's Paradise on 7th Avenue and the nearby Hot-Cha Club, a mixed-race venue where they could drink, dance the Charleston, eat "Chinese" food, and listen to the musical performances of Jimmie Daniels (1907–84), a handsome singer and dancer whom they would come to know as a friend and member of their intimate, queer circle. Tiny basement bars like The Sugar Cane, or "buffet flats" and impromptu "rent-parties" in private homes occupied the other end of the scale, offering sex shows, sex-for-hire, and bootleg liquor at bargain prices.[47] Throughout this period, and ending only after the

Depression had taken its toll on New York and its inhabitants, members of Van Vechten's circle could be found in these small, domestic venues as well as in the larger clubs.

As historian Henry Louis Gates, Jr. put it in a frequently quoted comment, in the years of its greatest popularity "Harlem was surely as gay as it was Black."[48] Van Vechten, Ewing, and their friends were attracted by both, dedicating themselves to the pursuit of new experiences with the obsessive energy and focus that characterized all of their activities. As collectors, they had larger ambitions as well: over the course of his long life, Van Vechten acquired thousands of books and attended just as many concerts and performances, hoping to deepen his knowledge of American and European culture; he also acquired works of art, playbills and other ephemera, knickknacks, jewelry, and colorful clothing from which he created the outlandish outfits for which he became known. From the 1920s on, his greatest passions were African American artists, musicians, and writers, and he saw himself as both their most ardent promoter and dealmaker, introducing Black friends like Langston Hughes (1901–67) and Nella Larsen (1891–1964) to prominent white publishers like Alfred Knopf (1892–1984), and guiding white friends through the Harlem neighborhoods that he visited on his nightly pilgrimages.

Van Vechten's energy as an explorer was prodigious, and his appetite for alcohol, food, conversation, dancing, and new experiences often exceeded his ability to fully acknowledge the men and women around him, much less admit to his own physical limitations. He often stayed up all night, listening to records, talking with friends, and trolling through bars and nightclubs across the city. He danced with men in drag, ate unfamiliar foods, and talked to just about everyone. His diaries record his frequent hangovers and stomach aches.[49] In 1932, he took up photography, motivated by the desire to document the people he met and talked to, learning to develop his own negatives and spending long hours in the darkroom making portraits, focusing in particular (though not exclusively) on Black friends and acquaintances. In this, as in most everything else, Max Ewing was his devoted student and follower.

While primarily focused on pleasure and entertainment, the activities of their interracial group might also be understood as an extended cultural and artistic experiment shared by a coterie of dedicated artists and intellectuals, many of whom were queer and nonconforming, and by others linked by their commitment to creating a more diverse and vital American culture. At the center of this group were Carl Van Vechten and his wife Fania Marinoff, the writers Langston Hughes and Nella Larsen (along with her husband, the prominent African American physicist Elmer Imes), the actor and activist Paul Robeson, the wealthy, gay financier Edward Wasserman (1890–c. 1955), the singers Taylor Gordon, Rosamond Johnson, and Nora Holt (1890–1974), and, of course, Muriel Draper, whose salon on the far East Side of Manhattan attracted a sophisticated, interracial crowd.[50] In private spaces like Van Vechten's apartment in Midtown Manhattan and the homes of a handful of Black writers and musicians in Harlem, members of the circle could come together, shielded from the judgments of segregated and homophobic US society. Harlem nightspots and theaters, with their relatively permissive attitudes toward sexuality and racial "mixing," were, for similar reasons, treated like second homes by Van Vechten, Draper, and their circle. Although no one could escape the pervasive, structural racism of the time, many members of the avant-garde genuinely cared about creating something new. No one was more passionate about the project of interracial community than Van Vechten, and yet no one made bigger mistakes.

As the author of a 1926 novel entitled *Ni***r Heaven*, Van Vechten remains a controversial and maligned figure. Like F. Scott Fitzgerald, but without the flair for creating the sort of complex characters that give novels like *The Great Gatsby* (1925) or *Tender is the Night* (1934) their enduring appeal, his novels focused on questions of American social, cultural, and geographical mobility by means of satire and knowing irony, recounting tales of drunken wife-swapping and idle gossip among white, upper-class New Yorkers. Drawn from his own experiences, Van Vechten's fiction betrayed his penchant for name-dropping, social-climbing, and sexual innuendo. He brought the same glib tone and knowing voyeurism to *Ni***r Heaven* as he did to his other work, despite being a white outsider in the world he described. In a later novel, entitled *Parties*, for example — a book published in 1930 that greatly influenced Ewing's own frothy novel *Going Somewhere* (1932) — he bragged about the excesses of the 1920s, noting more social events "were held in one day in Manhattan than in a month elsewhere" ensuring that "a man with an extensive acquaintance … could drink steadily in New York from the beginning of cocktail time until eleven in the evening without any more expense than that entailed by car- or cab-fare."[51] The entries from his daybooks in this period confirm his enthusiastic participation in this social whirl, frequently listing parties where he was the last to leave, and often noting that he crawled into bed by three or four in the morning or went out for breakfast at dawn, still wearing his evening clothes from the night before.

With his many Black friends and his ardent pursuit of African American culture, Van Vechten felt he was the exception who had risen above the racism of ordinary Americans, yet as the literary historian Emily Bernard points out, he "sealed his fate when he set himself up as a white observer who told stories about Black people whose lives he could never fully know, capping off his efforts by using an epithet that 'no white man should use.'"[52] Among the scholars who have grappled with Van Vechten's complex legacy, Bernard is the most clear-eyed and sympathetic: as she points out, Van Vechten's "novel would have disappeared like most 1920s potboilers were it not for the off-color scenes and its title," noting that his "representations of Black sexuality offended those" — including friends like Walter White (1893–1955) (later head of the NAACP), James Weldon Johnson, and W.E.B. Du Bois — "who believed that Black uplift should be achieved through the politics of respectability." Bernard explains, "With his title he had violated the unwritten law that forbade a white man's using the word ni***r"; worse still, he obviously "knew the law," yet "believed" — as friend and fan of Black culture — "that he was entitled to use the term."[53]

As difficult as it is to imagine from today's perspective, Van Vechten clearly felt he could move around the city and speak freely, not as a white man but as someone "in the know" who loved Black culture and Black bodies. He wanted so badly to be hip that he even added a footnote to the text of his novel when the word ni***r first appeared in the text, cautioning his readers that "while this informal epithet is freely used by Negroes among themselves, not only as a term of opprobrium, but also actually as a term of endearment, its employment by a white person is always fiercely resented," adding that "the word Negress is forbidden under all circumstances."[54] Sadly, he failed to recognize that many of his comments sounded false and disingenuous: "A combination of naiveté and arrogance led him to believe he was unique," Bernard writes, "a white man who had transcended his whiteness" and an "honorary Negro," the title conferred by Zora Neale Hurston, his loyal friend and supporter.

As Van Vechten discovered, individual relationships could not alter the fundamental calculus of power in racist America. "Friends and foes alike wasted no time in vehemently — and loudly — rejecting Van Vechten's new book," Bernard explains: "The distinguished sociologist and activist W.E.B. Du Bois suggested that readers should 'drop the book gently in the grate,' and the Black writer Countee Cullen accused him of 'coining money' out of the work of Black artists."[55] According to his biographer Edward White, some readers even felt that they saw "a ghostly shadow of the blackface tradition" in his "mania for blackness"; for many historians and critics, this shadow continues to hang over his reputation to this day.[56]

These criticisms barely dented Van Vechten's confidence or his commitment to his project. On November 27, 1925, he noted in his daybook, without comment, that "Countee Cullen comes in and we talk about my title *Ni***r Heaven*. He turns white with hurt & I talk to him." The remainder of that entry suggests the prodigious energy that he brought to the cause: he spent the rest of the day and evening immersed in African American literature and music, reading Charles W. Chestnutt's *The Marrow of Tradition*, writing an article on Bessie Smith, and attending a concert by the famed Black tenor Roland Hayes at Carnegie Hall where he ran into the Black physician Rudolph Fisher and encountered Muriel Draper with Max Ewing: "Then we went to Rosamond Johnson's," he added, "where we met Harry Block [an editor at Alfred A. Knopf]. All of us went to the midnight performance of *Plantation Review* at Lafayette. Ethel Waters, Eddie Rector [African American tap dancer]. Afterward saw Bill Robinson, Taylor Gordon, Muriel, & Max, etc., & met Ethel Waters. Home at 3:30."[57] The frantic pace and the long list of places and friends is typical of Van Vechten's life in this period.

Van Vechten was convinced that the benefits of bringing everyone together — and lubricating social events with plenty of liquor — far outweighed the emotional or reputational costs. Along the bumpy road he and his friends traveled, he took the pitfalls and the pratfalls of his circle in stride. At one of Van Vechten's sprawling parties on West 55th Street, the assembled company famously witnessed an increasingly inebriated Bessie Smith wreak havoc, turning down the "lovely, lovely dry martini" that her host had offered, and loudly demanding a whiskey instead; after downing that drink and a number of others in rapid succession, she sidled up to the famed white contralto Marguerite d'Alvarez as she performed an aria for the guests, slapping her on the back and exclaiming, "Honey, don't let *nobody* tell you you can't sing." Bessie then sang a number of her own songs, to the delight of the crowd, but as her friend Ruby Walker and other guests recalled, when she finally turned to leave, she "flew off the handle," throwing her hostess, the tiny actress Fania Marinoff, to the floor. Marinoff had reached up and demanded a hug and kiss goodbye, but Bessie reacted angrily, screaming, "Get the fuck away from me! … I ain't never *heard* of such shit!"[58]

Van Vechten and his guests tried to shrug it off, but the drama betrayed the deep-seated racial politics that bedeviled their experiment, as well as the pervasive homophobia that so often reared its ugly head.

Max Ewing may or may not have been present at that legendary party, but his letters reveal that he too was a longtime fan of Bessie's music: he had heard her perform in Harlem a number of times in 1925 and 1926, and in 1929 she autographed a photo for him (fig. 1.14), which he preserved in his collection.[59] More important, he would have understood very well the multiple subtexts that were at work in that awkward social encounter at Van Vechten's home, recognizing the undercurrents of racist and homophobic prejudice as well as the white privilege on view for all to see. After all, Van Vechten was a mentor to him in innumerable ways, not just as a champion of avant-garde and African American arts, but in matters of queer culture and survival as well. Well before he even arrived in New York, Ewing studied the queer subculture of which he and Van Vechten were a part: indeed, Van Vechten's campy new novel *The Blind Bow-Boy*, published in 1923, was very much on people's minds during his first few months in the city, and he and Van Vechten attended a party together to celebrate its publication.[60]

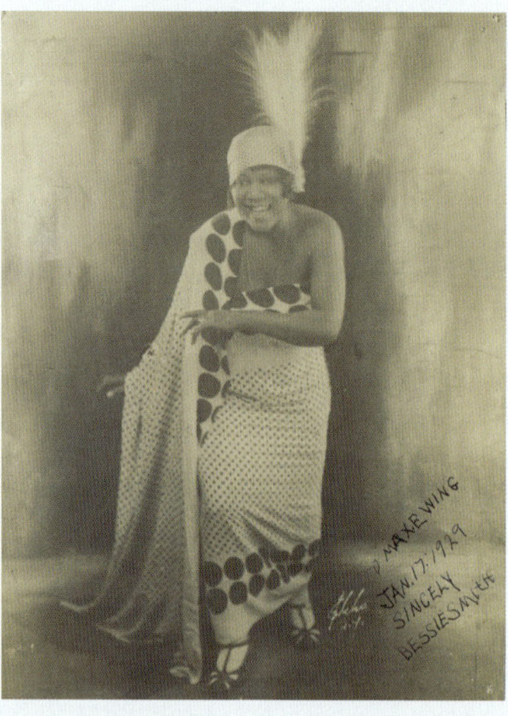

1.14 Anon., *Bessie Smith*, from Max Ewing's scrapbook (inscribed "Jan. 17, 1929"). Max Ewing Papers.

As with Van Vechten's other novels of the 1920s, the *Blind Bow-Boy* sheds light on the attitudes of the author and his circle. In the view of the literary critic Kirsten MacLeod, the novel can be appreciated as a work of what she calls "arched brow" modernism, which "approaches serious subject matter in a blithely sophisticated manner typified by characteristics associated with the body language of the arched brow — knowing, wry, cynical, and sardonic."[61] MacLeod highlights the serious messages in the work, which she claims are concealed "beneath an easy manner and arched brow"; in support of her arguments, she refers to a letter from Van Vechten to his friend Emily Clark, in which he confessed that his "formula consists in treating extremely serious themes as frivolously as possible." MacLeod's efforts to reframe the book — which at first glance seems simply to be another of Van Vechten's superficial satires — as a serious work of modernist fiction by unearthing its queer content helps us understand its attractions for Ewing and others. As she notes, the main character "Campaspe" speaks of hiding seriousness behind "a light and gay surface" in much the way that we now understand camp as a performative style that plays with notions of normativity and transgression: "If the novel is gay in the sense of 'brilliant,' 'showy,' and 'carefree' at its surface," MacLeod writes, "it is gay, in the sense of 'homosexual,' underneath," noting that — as the historian George Chauncey also pointed out — "the use of gay as

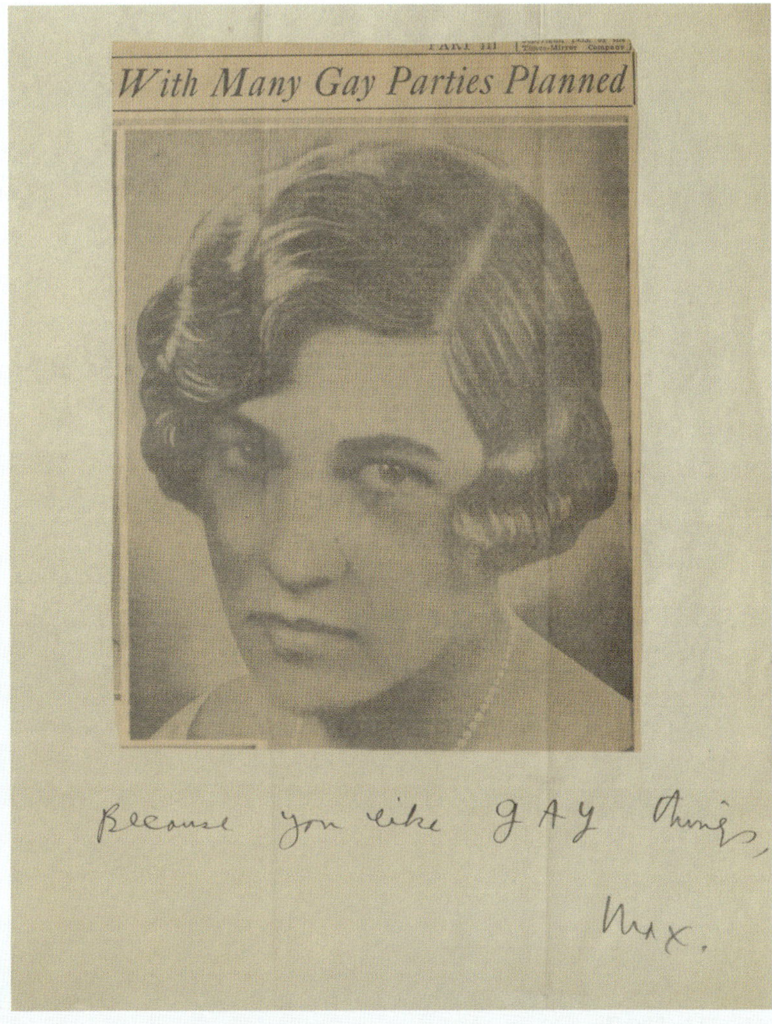

1.15 "Because you like GAY things," newspaper clipping sent by Max Ewing to Muriel Draper, 1926. Muriel Draper Papers, Beinecke Rare Book & Manuscript Library, Yale University, New Haven, Connecticut.

a code word was emerging in this period in the homosexual and bohemian circles Van Vechten circulated in."[62] If there is any doubt that Ewing was fully aware of this slang usage, it is immediately put to rest by a clipping that he sent to Muriel Draper in the mid-1920s showing a portrait of a young woman with the caption "With Many Gay Parties Planned"; to this Ewing has added the inscription "Because you like GAY things"[63] (fig. 1.15).

"Surely as gay as it was Black": for Ewing, Van Vechten, and their friends, explorations in Harlem included both sorts of entertainment. As denizens of Small's Paradise and the Hot-Cha, as well as friends of headliner Jimmie Daniels, they were privy to a great many carefully guarded secrets. According to Chris Albertson, Bessie Smith's biographer, Daniels recalled that Van Vechten maintained a secret pied-à-terre in Harlem that was painted entirely black with silver stars on the ceiling "that glowed pink from strategically located red lights": "It was a seductive place," Daniels recalled, "there were no chairs or tables, just red velvet cushions, and some of them were more like beds — well, I guess they were beds. It was a decorator's nightmare, and Carlo acted quite differently when he was there. I don't think Fania even knew about the place."[64]

With such seductions on offer, it is hardly surprising that Ewing didn't focus much on his piano lessons. Though he often blamed this on damage to his finger — writing to a Michigan friend on November 7, 1925 that he had "Gashed his finger," and didn't have to practice, later claiming that the injury occurred because of his participation in the New York performance of his friend George Antheil's *Ballet Mécanique* in 1927 — his priorities emerged very early: "I have gone out constantly," Ewing wrote to a friend in 1925:

> Exhibitions and luncheons by day. Dinners, theaters, and suppers at night. "The Man With a load of Mischief" Monday; "The Green Hat" (at last thank god) Wednesday night; Harlem with Carl Van Vechten Thursday night, the Palace yesterday afternoon to see Estelle Winwood and Adele Rowland … "White Gold" (Australian for "wool") at the Lennox Hill tonight; Mischa-Leon's song recital tomorrow afternoon, "The Grand Street Follies" … tomorrow night; "Young Woodley" with Arleen Hunger Monday night. …
>
> And Harlem Thursday night! We went first to Rosamond Johnson's. Do you know his book of spirituals? He and TAYLOR GORDON are giving a recital of them at the Garrick next Sunday night, and if it isn't a riotous occasion nothing will ever be. This boy, TAYLOR GORDON, has been singing in some Negro act in vaudeville during the past few years, and never sang a spiritual in his life until a month ago when Johnson got hold of him and began to coach him. He now sings 30 of them like no one on earth.[65]

Like many others in New York in the 1920s, Ewing was hooked on the energy and excitement that swirled around him, and the very real sense that change was in the air.

ENTER MURIEL DRAPER

A few months before he wrote the above words on June 3, 1925, Ewing recorded another event that would change his life forever: he had a date to meet "the magnificent Muriel Draper." As he explained to his grandmother, "After Jane Heap, she is the biggest woman-mind in New York. And she wears the most amazingly stunning clothes in America, rich costumes of black and white veils, with white velvet turbans over her closely clipped hair. She runs a smart interior decoration salon to make money."[66] Ageless, eccentric, and charismatic, Draper (fig. 1.16) was a force to be reckoned with, whose in-home salon was legendary, and she was equally famous for her charismatic hold on women and men alike.[67] In his autobiography of 1929, for example, Taylor Gordon singled out Muriel Draper for praise, combining the breathless admiration of a suitor with the hyperbole of a superfan:

> What a place this world would be if everyone was free of their inhibitions like Princess Muriel Draper is. Having the greatest wisdom of any and being a marvelous writer, is not enough for her. She knows how to drape her shapely figure in all materials — window curtains, silk bedspreads, satins, Spanish shawls — so no matter where or how big the party may be, people always ask, *Who is that woman?*

Who indeed? By the time that she met Taylor Gordon and Max Ewing, Muriel Draper had been cultivating the arts of seduction — intellectual,

emotional, and physical — for
over two decades, hosting a long-
running salon in London before
World War I and reestablishing
herself in New York after her
separation from her husband Paul
Draper in 1915.[68] As she recounted
in her autobiography, *Music at
Midnight* (1929), she had a long
and distinguished career as a
writer, activist, and promoter of
the arts in both places, and her
parties attracted a distinguished
group of artists and writers whose
careers and networks she
fostered.[69]

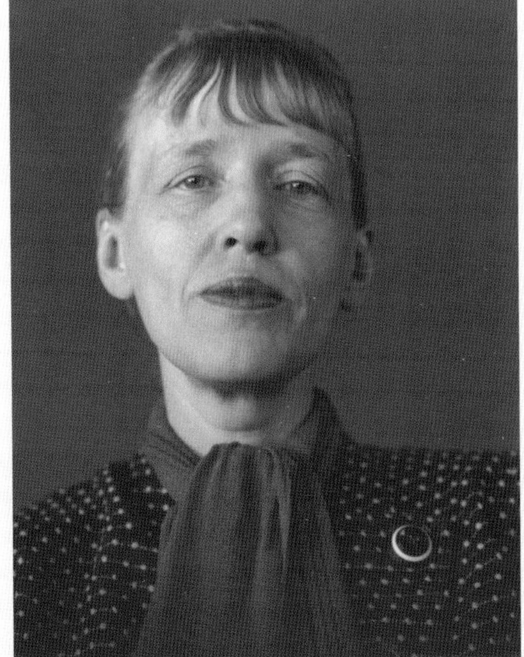

1.16 Edward Weston, *Muriel Draper*, 1933. Center for Creative Photography, Arizona Board of Regents.

According to the historians
who have studied her impact,
many people found her
combination of laser-sharp intellect, insatiable curiosity, and eccentric glamour
irresistible, and, perhaps more important, inspirational. In London, she hosted
Arthur Rubinstein and Henry James, among many others, taking the former as
her lover and charming the latter beyond all expectations. Her sexual appetite
and availability, undimmed by the passage of years, was still very much a factor in
the web of relationships she created with young men in New York, including
Ewing, Lincoln Kirstein, Walker Evans (1903–75), the wealthy brothers Leonard
and James Amster (who ran the antiques department at Bergdorf Goodman), the
composer George Antheil (1900–59) (who believed her to be the only person in
America who understood modern music), and the artist Mark Tobey (who
delighted in drawing her sensuous body and unusual features). The letters of her
many suitors fill the folders of the archive she donated to the Beinecke Library.[70]

Such was Draper's power that, many years after her death, the actress
Marian Seldes, whose parents Gilbert (1893–1970) and Amanda Seldes had been
Draper's close friends, reported in an interview with Steven Watson in 2003
that even as a child she experienced Draper's irresistible appeal and grew
to love her: "Anyone who knew her will remember her forever," Seldes observed,
describing the years in which she was close to Draper as "the golden times
because people like Muriel Draper existed." As Seldes put it, Draper "was
perhaps the most dramatic person I had ever met or knew, like someone from the
stage, a character, a theater person, grand, adorable, funny, daring."[71]

Max Ewing fell even harder than most. For a period of nine years, he was
first and foremost among her admirers, serving as her escort, her confidant, and
constant companion. His letters to her are passionate and possessive, often
suggesting physical intimacies — "I kiss your eyes," he wrote from Europe in fall
1926. In a much later letter, from the 1930s, he ended by saying, "Don't kiss etc.
etc. etc. anyone else." Yet, unlike many of her other acolytes, including Tobey and
Kirstein, he seems to have steered clear of the easygoing sexual intimacy that
was, for many, the most compelling aspect of Draper's mystique.[72] What Ewing
saw and heard at her all-night gatherings isn't recorded in his letters to his

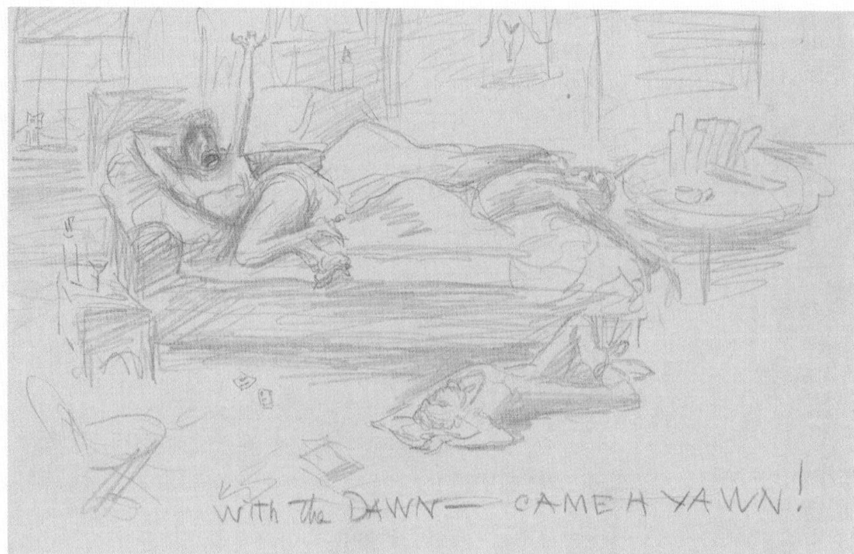

1.17 Mark Tobey, *With the Dawn—Came a Yawn!*, n.d. Muriel Draper Papers, Beinecke Rare Book & Manuscript Library, Yale University, New Haven, Connecticut.

parents, but Tobey's sketches (fig. 1.17) and Kirstein's diaries give us a good sense of what went on, celebrating her distinctive features, her ample curves, her loose-limbed sexiness, and the ever-present miasma of sexual drama that surrounded her.[73]

Writing to Draper from Paris the following year, Ewing described his first meeting with her as a life-changing event that had "a hot halo around it."[74] She was, as he told his parents, "the most stunning woman in America," and "the most tremendous personality I have ever encountered." "To talk with her is to experience explosion," he wrote: "She has a mind that flys [*sic*] faster than lightning. What it takes most people ten years to know about you, she knows after an hours [*sic*] conversation. She has the kind of mind that could attend a 60-ring circus, and not miss a move of any muscle of any performer in all the 60 rings. Nothing escapes her. Nothing will ever escape her." Comparing her to the diva Mary Garden, he summed her up with enormous insight: "I think they are the two most magnificent women in the world. Mary of course is magnificent because of what she has done. Muriel is magnificent because of what she drives other people to do."[75] This last observation would prove to be remarkably prescient.

Ewing and Draper shared a love of classical music, opera, dance, and literature. A close friend of Gertrude Stein, Mabel Dodge (1879–1962), and Carl Van Vechten since before World War I, Draper supported herself by writing (*Music at Midnight* was a bestseller), by giving lectures on current events and women's issues, and by picking up occasional jobs as an interior decorator.[76] Often penniless, she ran her salon on the fumes of conversation about art and creative genius and through the power of her own tireless, seductive energy. For all but a few naysayers (including Kirstein's parents, who considered Draper a "menace," and his sister Mina Kirstein Curtiss, who found her manipulative and deceitful), the atmosphere around her was intoxicating.[77]

To Max Ewing's delight, Draper's salon focused on words, images, and the ambitions of young men, reflecting the tastes and proclivities of its hostess. Ewing was a regular there, as were Gordon, Kirstein, Walker Evans, and George Platt Lynes, along with a large and constantly changing cast of characters. She exposed her young friends to an even broader range of New York society than Van Vechten did, introducing them to a who's who of the upper echelons of wealth and power. She herself was devoted to high culture: with Ewing and others, including her good friend Esther Murphy (sister of the expatriate artist and host Gerald Murphy), she regularly attended the theater, opera, and concerts, and she was careful to point out the celebrities in attendance for the benefit of her companions — information that Ewing gleefully passed on to his parents. Draper could also be a lot of fun, and she loved to perform, qualities that endeared her to the twenty-two-year-old Ewing from the very start of their relationship: on October 6, 1925, for example, he wrote to his college friend Edgar Ailes that "I go to tea daily at the almighty Muriel's and today she is coming to tea here. We are occupied with a song recital she and I are going to stage to amuse Mary Garden (and 39 others) when Mary goes thru town to Chicago. Muriel is going to sing all the song hits of the years 1908–1912, commencing with Honey Boy and continuing thru the worst period."[78]

Like Ewing, she could be snobbish and disdainful of everything and everyone she considered ordinary: Ewing was extremely pleased to be on the guest list for Muriel's "big party" on New Year's Eve in 1925, a group that included "the Otto Kahns, Vanderbilts, Mortimer Schiff and Sara King to represent the SOCIAL element. Then the Van Vechtens, Noël Coward, Laurette Taylor, Eva Le Gallienne, Mary Garden … Florence Mills, Michael Arlen, Glenn Hunter, Stokowski, Nazimova, E. E. Cummings, George Gershwin" — as Ewing summed it up, "in short, everyone in New York of any importance actual or potential."[79] As he never tired of reminding his family, thanks in large part to Draper's mentoring, he had truly "arrived" in New York by the end of his second year in the city, and his proximity to important people was the proof.

Draper curated both her networks and the decor of the spaces that she presided over with a discerning eye. Despite her lack of funds, her reception rooms were artfully staged with glistening silk drapes, silver candlesticks, and gilded baroque-revival furniture discovered in thrift shops or donated by friends. These rooms were documented by Walker Evans in a series of images showing Draper's home on May 29, 1934, the day after a bachelor party held for Draper's son "Smudge" (fig. 1.18). Walker's photos suggest that Draper also had a talent for theater and masquerade, and fashioned her home as an elaborate stage set that highlighted her performances and those of her friends.[80] Moreover, in addition to her salon gatherings, Draper was a devoted follower of the popular spiritualist

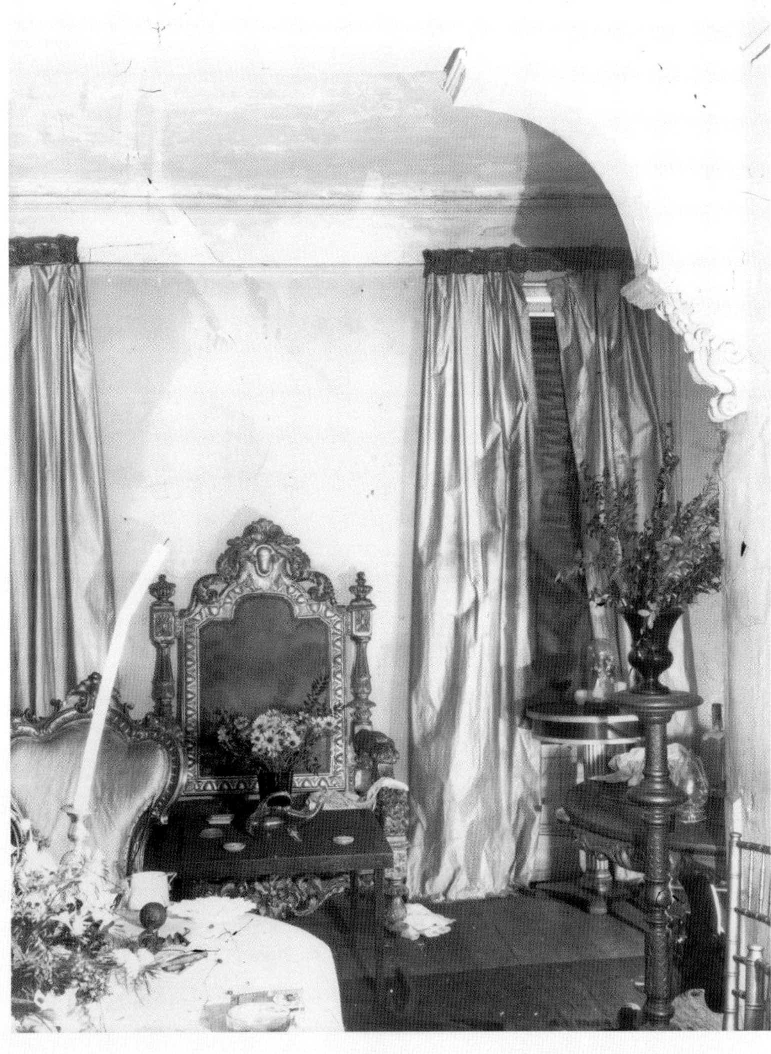

1.18 Walker Evans, *Table Setting and Throne Chair in Muriel Draper's Apartment, New York City*, 1934, film negative, 6½ × 8½ in. (16.51 × 21.59 cm). Walker Evans Archive, Metropolitan Museum of Art, New York.

George Gurdjieff, and often held meetings in her home, hosting international guests and fellow travelers that included Jane Heap and Margaret Anderson (1886–1973), women who became particularly close friends of Ewing's as well, despite his complete lack of interest in spiritualism. Draper's home had the character of a private club where strangers came and went, met new friends in the reception rooms, and got to know one another over cocktails and conversations that sometimes continued in the bedrooms upstairs.

These unusual qualities made Muriel Draper famous as a leader of New York's "High Bohemia." She was full of life, and full of opinions, and she had an uncanny ability to make people fall in love with her by giving them the impression that she could see deep inside them and truly understand them: "She gave you her interest," Seldes recalled, and "she looked right at you."[81] That intensity — which for many of her friends and acquaintances felt like love — was a sort of drug for Ewing and other young people. His letters to her, mostly written from Europe in 1926–27 and after he had returned to Pioneer in 1934, often ended with him telling her how he yearned for her company. He too was clearly more than a little bit in love with her, and he believed — rather foolishly, as it turned out — that their bond represented a marriage of sorts. Indeed, as the years went by, Ewing became more and more obsessed: he photographed her regularly and he even created a series of small sculptures showing her in various guises, including one piece fittingly entitled *Muriel Destroying Young Men* (discussed in chapter 4). He made her the star of the *Carnival of Venice* series (fig. 1.19), placing her double portrait, in the costume of a Renaissance queen, opposite that of Paul Robeson dressed as Othello. He continued to shape his world around Draper's until the very end of his life, striving to become an elegant, knowledgeable man-about-town worthy of her attention.

Ewing recorded the successful completion of his self-fashioning by having his portrait taken by the studio photographer Edwin Townsend in May 1924 and again in 1925 (fig. 1.20), adopting the long hair, baggy clothes, and mannered slouch of a bohemian artist. Late in 1925, he moved from his rented rooms on 22nd Street to the Hotel Warrington on Madison Avenue at 32nd street, an apartment hotel where he felt he could finally express himself by furnishing his own quarters and where he could receive the sort of guests he now counted among his friends. In November 1925, he again reassured his parents that the time, energy, and money he was spending on dinners out, furniture, and new clothes was worth it because they gave him the look and lifestyle he needed in order to make his mark: "This is a great life, if you don't weaken," he boasted. "And I certainly don't weaken. I flourish. I made a marvelous new statue this week, and I am painting more of my furniture red and black. Only wait until you see my quarters [when you visit] in February," he boasted, adding, with characteristic bluntness, "I want some soft, white silk shirts. Stiff collars don't fit with my type of looks."[82] No aspect of his self-invention was overlooked or omitted in his letters to his family.

The following month, Ewing announced that he was going to Paris, writing that he hoped to debut there "and return to America with a serious musical reputation behind me. God knows that debuts in Aeolian Hall don't mean anything anymore. … look at Andrew Haigh. Who will ever hear of him again? He is a music-teacher in a Michigan small town, and that's what he'll go on being."[83] Thanks to his association with people like Van Vechten and Draper, Ewing's

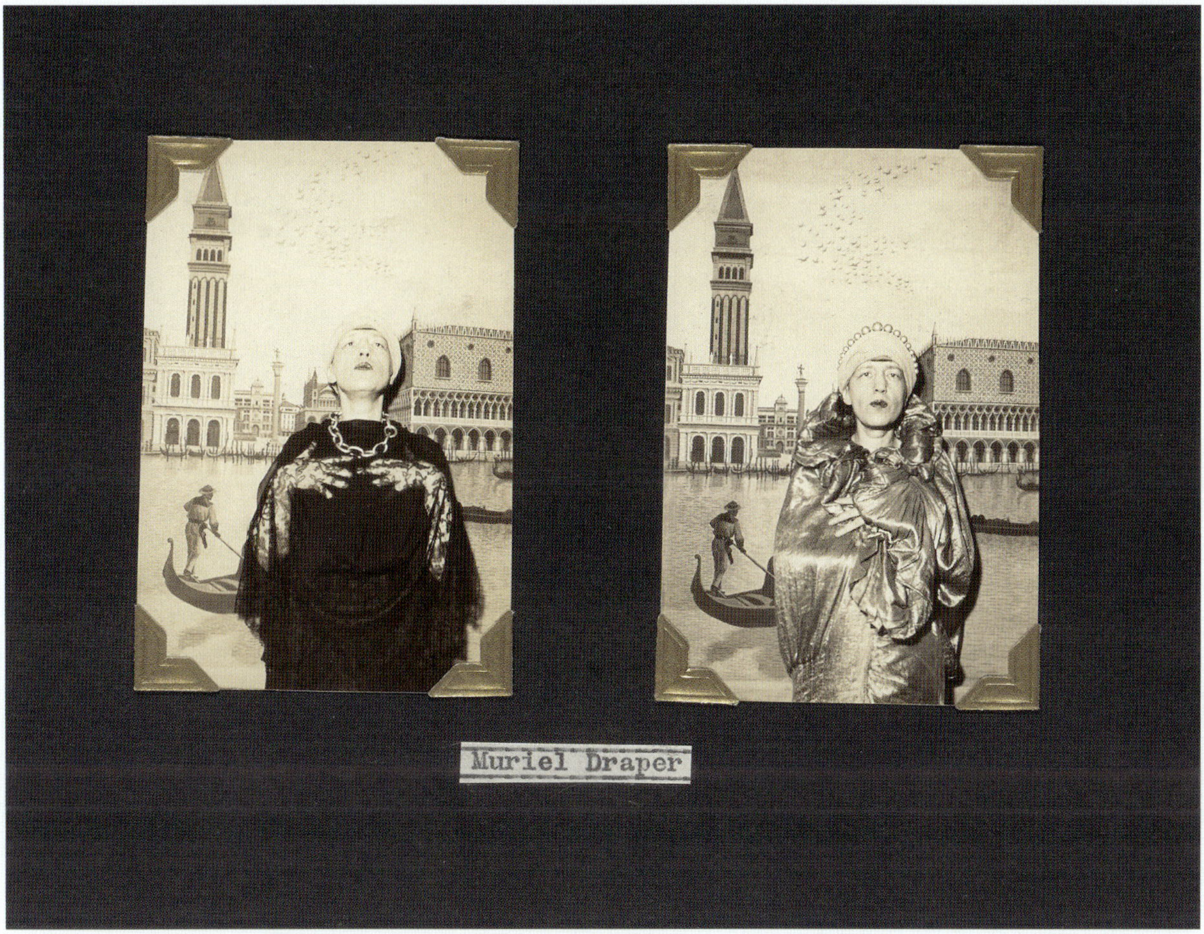

1.19 Max Ewing, *Muriel Draper*, from *Les Amants de Venise*, 1932. Max Ewing Papers.

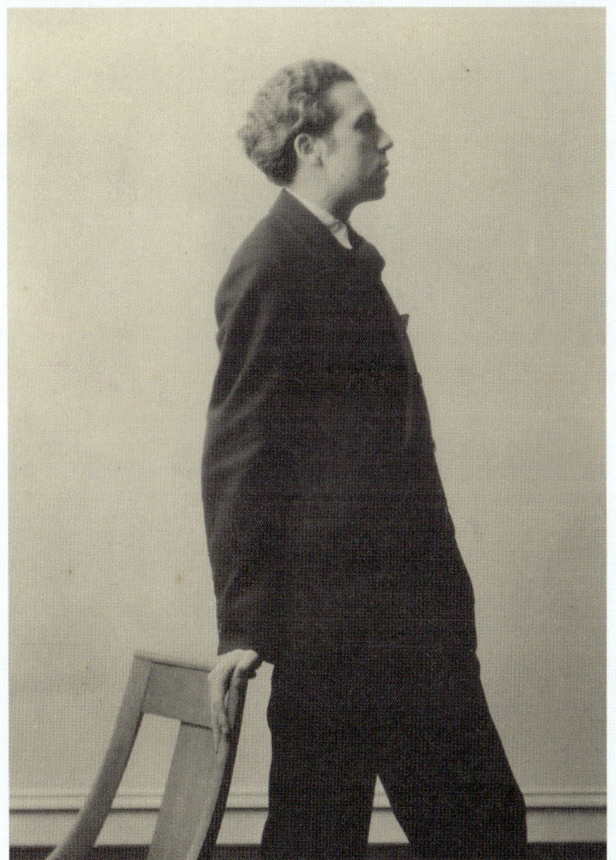

1.20 Edwin F. Townsend, *Max Ewing*, 1925. Max Ewing Papers.

aspirations had clearly been upgraded over the short span of years that he had lived in the city: this was, after all, the same Andrew Haigh of whom he had said, "He is in *everything* in N.Y. that I hope to be in," when he first moved to New York in 1923.[84]

He may have felt ready to spread his wings, but his parents were concerned that he was flying too high. He replied to their worried letters with a combination of boastful self-confidence and childish defensiveness, writing on February 1, 1926, "Yes, I am a difficult young man: … I wanted everything in New York, and everybody in New York, and now I am getting them, and I want everybody in Paris." He also reassured them about his plans for his European trip, joking that he had heard from a friend of Muriel Draper's "in Milano," and that it looked as though "it's going to be a girl or a boy in every port."[85] What the Ewings made of this camp humor is not recorded. Their son's comments about his sexuality are often tantalizingly vague, but, overall, a clearer picture begins to emerge. His relationships with men, at least as he described them for his parents, were often fraught with tension; he was always extremely guarded about his feelings — though his confessions of love to Muriel Draper were an obvious exception — and he frequently pulled away when things got too complicated. His greatest love was reserved for his mother, his confidante, booster, and fellow fan of film and fashion.

Clearly nothing and no one would ever come between him and his ambitions: his description of his parting with Albert Carroll, the *Grand Street Follies* actor, in early February 1926 is a case in point. He wrote to his parents with remarkable candor about his "fading" feelings for Carroll, telling them that there had been an embarrassing scene about his upcoming trip to Europe: "It is very strange to have had a very deep and very poignant and very personal and very great feeling about someone," he explained,

> and then to find after a period of time that absolutely every trace of that feeling has vanished and that no feeling of any kind remains for that person, and that he might as well be anyone at all. A year and a half ago it was very important, almost necessary to me to see and listen to and be with Albert Carroll, and that last night he was just a young man who happened to be in the room, and that it made not the least difference to me whether he stayed or went. I made that clear to him and he said he was going to weep, and I suggested that he go before that. He went on his knees and begged me not to go to Europe, and I made it clear that nothing he could do would keep me from sailing. And it was all very trying.[86]

Whatever else he was, Ewing was single-minded and strategic in his pursuit of his own goals, and he could be as cold and resolute at times as he was warm and generous at others. Two days later, he chided his mother once again for worrying about him: "In the past five years," he crowed,

> I have gotten myself from the nonentity of Pioneer Ohio into the Robbins box at Carnegie Hall and into the program of the Manhattan Opera House and into the consciousness of everyone in town … And all without any slightest help from you, except financial. Without the

financial help everything would have been twice as difficult, of course.
But the money has nothing to do with my direction of myself really. …
The values I attach to things, these are not yours at all. Hearing
Mary Garden sing Melisandre in Baltimore — one night — is vastly
more important to me that a month of golfing and the rest of it in
Coral Gables.[87]

The first phase of his transformation was complete. To Muriel Draper and Carl Van Vechten, he owed his greatest debts, in large part because they had served as his role models, showing him not just *how* to fashion himself into a new person — and a queer person at that — with evident good taste and social know-how, but also demonstrating that *self-invention could be an end in itself*, that life could be a process of continual change and adaptation to surrounding conditions, emotions, and fashions. For those lessons, he "loved them good and true," as he wrote to Van Vechten in his Christmas card for 1923, naively oblivious to the dangers inherent in placing his trust in people for whom change was a constant and a way of life. Reinvention may well have been a skill that Ewing would perfect during his time in New York and, briefly, as a member of the "smart set" in Paris, on the Riviera, and in Venice, but he doesn't seem to have learned the lessons about the dangers of glamour and loneliness that his friend Scott Fitzgerald described so vividly in his stories and novels. With his knowing camp humor and critical eye, Ewing strove to come across as worldly and cynical, but in his heart of hearts he remained wide-eyed and vulnerable, unprotected in the fast-paced world to which he so fervently aspired.

On the eve of his first trip to Europe in April 1926, however, Ewing was still buoyed along on a wave of optimism and excitement. He said goodbye to his friends in New York, and went to "an elaborate tea" at Van Vechten's where he met the famous conductor Eugene Goossens and his wife, promising to see them again in Europe. He worked hard to cement his friendships with the people, both young and old, he had met through Draper and Van Vechten, meeting with Aaron Copland to hear his new piano pieces, having his portrait sketched by Miguel Covarrubias (1904–57), and going to parties where celebrities like Marguerite d'Alvarez performed and Broadway stars like Julia Hoyt and Aline MacMahon made appearances.[88] Everyone he knew or met in New York — including Jane Heap and d'Alvarez and, of course, Draper and Van Vechten — helped him plan for his trip, providing letters of introduction, addresses, hotel and restaurant suggestions, and tips about bars and nightclubs.

He bought a trunk and packed up his "most treasured things," including "the Geraldine [Farrar] albums, the best-bound books, the best photographs, music, papers, etc." He put everything into storage, including his Chanler portrait and some clay sculptures of Muriel Draper that he was working on.[89] He thanked his parents for the many wonderful things they had done for him — "You have been marvelously sweet about this going of mine," he wrote, "and I can't tell you how much I appreciate it" — and left on the SS *De Grasse* in mid-April, eager to begin his next big adventure in Europe.[90]

Chapter 2

PARIS, THE RIVIERA, AND VENICE, 1926–27

Max Ewing's extraordinary letters from Europe, written to his parents every few days during his two extended trips in 1926 and 1927, are so filled with famous names and places that they make us wonder whether they were created as part of an elaborate hoax to deceive unsuspecting researchers. The range of people he mentions and describes — from Gertrude Stein and Alice B. Toklas (1877–1967), to Josephine Baker, George Antheil, Serge Diaghilev, Natalie Barney, Romaine Brooks, and Cole Porter — sometimes seems entirely too good to be true. Indeed, his earliest letters often read like fictional treatments for the script of *Midnight in Paris*, the 2011 romantic comedy in which a present-day American writer is magically transported to a party at the home of Gertrude Stein, where he meets Fitzgerald, Hemingway, Picasso, and the fabled artists of the 1920s. Like "Gil," the hero of that film, Ewing experienced many things during his visit to Europe that sound like the stuff of fantasy.

Max Ewing dreamed of Paris for many years before he actually got there, taking to heart the experiences of the well-traveled title character of Carl Van Vechten's *Peter Whiffle* (1922). As he wrote in an appreciation of Van Vechten's work, published while he was still a student at the University of Michigan, "No one could read the opening chapters [of *Peter Whiffle*] devoted to the soft, exquisite beauty of Paris in the May twilight, 'the gray buildings swathed in a bland blue light and the air redolent with a strange fragrance' without resolving to embark at the earliest possible opportunity."[1] Within a week of arriving in the city, Ewing reported to his family that he had seen the sights and explored the streets around the Paris Opéra and along the Seine, and — thanks to letters of introduction from Muriel Draper and Carl Van Vechten — visited Gertrude Stein's home twice, sharing tea and Russian Easter cake with her "lovey" Alice B. Toklas, and meeting a number of their friends, including the painter Pavel Tchelitchew (1898–1957), the pianist Allen Tanner (Tchelitchew's lover), and the French writer René Crevel (1900–35), all queer young men handpicked by Stein for the amusement of her new friend. In his letters, Ewing readily adopted the tone of a Paris insider, writing to his mother when he left Stein's home after one such gathering: "She is a divine creature who looks like her pictures but like nothing else on earth! Very dynamic and very sweet and the best American brain in Paris … when I left she told me to come in <u>any evening</u> without bothering to telephone even."[2]

For Ewing, like many other young people of his generation, Paris was the place to be: the epicenter of glamour and the arts, and a dreamworld of elegant boulevards, glistening shop windows, and hidden arcades filled with treasures that delighted the mind and the senses. Since the mid-nineteenth century, Paris had come to stand for the idea of modern life itself, a legendary city in which not only to observe (and perhaps emulate) the passing parade of fashionable people, but also to experience exciting physical and psychological freedoms — from late nights and late meals to sexual awakenings and avant-garde social gatherings — that were delightfully *foreign* to Americans, especially those who, like Max Ewing, had grown up in the small towns and rural hinterlands of the United States. After his whirlwind apprenticeship in the arts and culture of New York's bohemia, Paris was the logical next step in Ewing's process of self-invention.

Visiting Stein's salon during his first weeks in the city, Ewing carefully observed the people, sights, and sounds that surrounded him: as usual, he focused his attention on the details that would enable him to project a convincing

image of the modern intellectual and well-dressed man-about-town that he
hoped to become. Writing to Muriel Draper on May 1, for example, he reported
that while he "liked Gertrude Stein" and enjoyed her conversation, he resented
her stubborn insistence that New York had been outstripped by Paris in terms of
creativity and artistic production: "after eight days here" he noted, he still felt
that "New York is the center of the universe." "In Paris," he added, "only the old
seems to belong." He was still mulling over his disagreement with Stein the next
day, and wrote to Draper again to explain: "To show you how far Gertrude is from
N.Y. talk," he insisted, "she read Langston Hughes's *The Weary Blues*, and in
speaking of it sometime later she recalled the title as *The Weary Blacks*!"[3]

Stein was fifty-two when Ewing met her, and her salon was a well-
established destination for young artists and writers who, like Ewing, visited Paris
in hopes of adopting its sophisticated ways. Her affection and sponsorship were
coveted prizes that Ewing was, of course, very pleased to have received, telling
his mother that "we went on talking-talking after Miss Toklas had gone to bed";
"Gertrude Stein likes me," he boasted, "and that is all anyone could ask."[4] He was
"delirious" with Paris, he said, and delighted by the many parties, new friends ("It
took more than two years to get at the grandest people in New York," he crowed,
but "it has taken less than 2 weeks to do it in Paris"), and beautiful sights, but he
remained stalwart in his defense of his adopted city, with its own distinctively
American culture and conversation. Indeed, wherever he went, Ewing couldn't
help but compare the things he encountered to the glamorous salon he planned
to create in his own apartment in New York when he returned: "Of course for $70 a
month for an apartment in Paris I could live like the Prince of Wales," he insisted
to his mother. "But I think I shall buy a lot of furnishings here instead and then
transplant them to New York, which is after all the city of my epoch."[5]

For students of the art and culture of the 1920s and early '30s — and
indeed, for any fan of the "Lost Generation" who has even dreamed, like the
writer in *Midnight in Paris*, of being whisked off to this glittering world of creativity
and camaraderie — any of the firsthand recollections contained in Max Ewing's
letters would be jewels in and of themselves; as a group, and as a record of the
wonderful things that happened to one young man in these years, they are
astonishing. Even Ewing himself had to take a breath and marvel at his good
fortune, as he wrote to his parents on June 25, 1926: "Dear Family, it is sometimes
difficult for even me to believe what is happening for me. And it must sound even
stranger to you, that such things should come to me at once, without my going
after them. This trip is simply Cinderella's dream, my life begins to seem like an
experience of high fantasy and not reality at all."[6]

Establishing his Parisian bona fides was an important part of the journey,
just as it was for the thousands of others who flocked to Paris in the 1920s, filling
the terraces and cafés and small hotels in search of culture and a good time at
bargain prices. The strength of the dollar meant that Americans of modest or little
means — people like Hemingway, or Janet Flanner and her partner Solita Solano,
or indeed like Ewing himself — could live very comfortably in Paris, staying in
decent but inexpensive lodgings or apartments and eating (and, of course,
drinking) very well for months or even years on end: "Nothing costs anything,"
Ewing wrote to Muriel Draper, "A taxi would go to Nice for a dollar."[7]

For Ewing and his friends, and for well-to-do expatriates like the Steins,
or the American socialite Lorna Lindsley, or Esther Murphy and her brother

Gerald — a painter and set-designer whose glamorous parties at his Villa America in Cap d'Antibes and close friendship with Picasso, Hemingway, and the Fitzgeralds were made famous by Calvin Tomkins's *Living Well Is the Best Revenge* (1971) — Europe was an enormous playground filled with beautiful things to be enjoyed and acquired at bargain-basement prices. Historic houses, spacious apartments, and studios like the Steins' home at 27 rue de Fleurus could be rented or even purchased relatively easily: among the most glamorous residences was that of Noël Murphy (fig. 2.1), who owned a fantastic top-floor apartment on the Île-Saint-Louis overlooking the Seine and Notre Dame. Like her brother-in-law Gerald (she was the widow of his older brother Frederic, who had died in 1924), she spared no expense on parties and tickets to the theater and opera, and although she was a consummate snob, she shared her enthusiasms with her chosen friends.

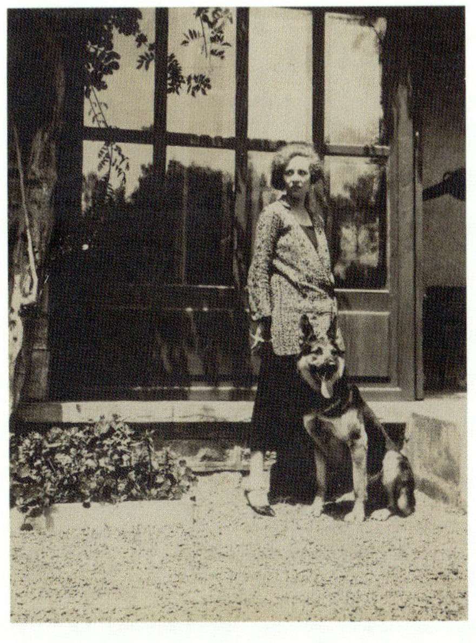

2.1 Anon., *Noël Murphy*, 1923. Sara and Gerald Murphy Papers, Beinecke Rare Book & Manuscript Library, Yale University, New Haven, Connecticut.

Ewing met Noël Murphy early in his stay in Paris, and she invited him to practice on her Steinway grand piano two or three times a week: she was a trained singer who shared his love of music and interest in avant-garde trends, and he happily accompanied her to concerts and gatherings where she introduced him to her friends. While many expatriate artists and writers lived very frugally, the opportunities for luxury and pleasure were ample, and the freedom from the strictures of American life was exhilarating for everyone. In one early letter from Ewing's first Paris trip, for example, he described how Noël Murphy and Lorna Lindsley — who were close friends at the time — purchased a manor house in Orgeval, outside of Paris, in 1926, on an afternoon's junket. Ewing marveled at the bargain price the women paid: "Lorna and Noel drove out of town the other day and bought a country estate in half a day the way you bought Clear Lake [the Ewings' summer cottage in Indiana.] They got a lovely 7-room house, acres of ground, with a stream running through, and 200 fruit trees, 40 minutes from Paris, grand roads — and they paid $2400.00. $1200 a piece! Did you ever hear of such ridiculous figures?"[8]

In an unlikely twist of fate, the sprawling house and garden that Noël and Lorna purchased became a gathering place for the expat lesbian community after Noël met and fell in love with Janet Flanner — the *New Yorker*'s Paris correspondent, who wrote under the pen name "Genêt" — in 1930, and it would remain so until Noël's death in 1982.[9] Noël was classy enough to be accepted by Stein and Toklas, who sometimes went to Orgeval for Sunday lunch, and she grudgingly accepted Flanner's younger friends, including her ex-lover Solita Solano (who remained a lifelong member of Flanner's extended "family"), Margaret Anderson, Esther Murphy, and a host of other women. Although it soon became clear that joint ownership created more problems than it solved, particularly given Noël's deepening relationship with Flanner and her lesbian friends, the purchase of the Orgeval property clearly demonstrates both the extraordinary privilege and the unusual complexities that the tight-knit American community experienced.

Such opportunities represent just a few of the many factors that kept young people coming to Paris in the 1920s. The city was rife with experimentation, and not least in terms of artistic and sexual conventions. Writers, musicians, dancers, and artists could take chances there and, for queer men and women especially, the *fluidity* and lack of concern for conventional morality and American proprieties were enticing. In Paris, married and formerly married young Americans like Janet Flanner, Solita Solano, and Gerald and Sarah Murphy came to test the limits of those bonds or throw them off altogether; for those who were curious about matters of love and sexuality, like Esther Murphy or Max Ewing, the city not only offered a crash course in modernity but also in the various shapes of intimacy — dyads, triangles, and all manner of polygons — that linked individuals and groups together.[10]

Ewing made a splash in this world, particularly among the American women, but he kept his eyes open and focused on his goals. As he did when he first arrived in New York, he worked hard to quickly acquire an insider's knowledge of the city, studying the map of Paris by walking the length of the principal streets, starting with avenue de l'Opéra, the rue de Rivoli, and the rue de la Paix, browsing in booksellers' stalls along the river, then moving on to the neighborhood around the Luxembourg Gardens where his chic Hotel Foyot, and the homes of Stein, Barney, and other friends were located. During his first days in Paris, he took the bus to Montmartre and browsed in the shops, perhaps checking out the gay bars and clubs while he was there, not that he shared such experiences with his mother. Writing home on May 3, 1926, he chided her for worrying that he was alone and far from home: "Stop thinking that I'm 'in a different world,'" he scolded, "I already feel as much at home in Paris as anyplace. Of course I have been here so long *in my imagination* that it naturally seems like an old stomping ground. But as a matter of fact apart from imagination I do know my Paris better than some taxi drivers!"[11]

In the same letter, he carefully explained the objectives of his visit and the roles he was playing as a visitor to his newly adopted city: "I am trying to lead three different lives in Paris and they keep me going. I am here in three capacities: 1) a sight-seer of things old, and investigator of things new, artistic and otherwise; 2) as a piano student with a certain amount of work to keep going; 3) as a visiting social celebrity in demand every day for lunches, teas, dinners, suppers, theaters, and so forth!"

For each of those roles, he had to dress the part, and for that, as his parents knew very well as store owners and followers of fashion, he needed an entirely new wardrobe. Ewing's father was a careful and fastidious dresser, his mother (herself a former salesclerk and buyer for a large and varied clientele) had an eye for the details of fabric and fashion, and their son learned to follow their high sartorial standards from an early age, producing elaborate getups — one thinks of the costumes that Ewing and his friends concocted for their teenage opera performances — and always looking his best.[12] While he was in Paris, the epicenter of sophisticated men's fashion, Ewing quickly emerged as the living embodiment of the elegant, modern man described by John Potvin in *Deco Dandy*, his study of queer masculinity in the 1920s: he cultivated an elegant yet effortless appearance, adopting the affable conversation and

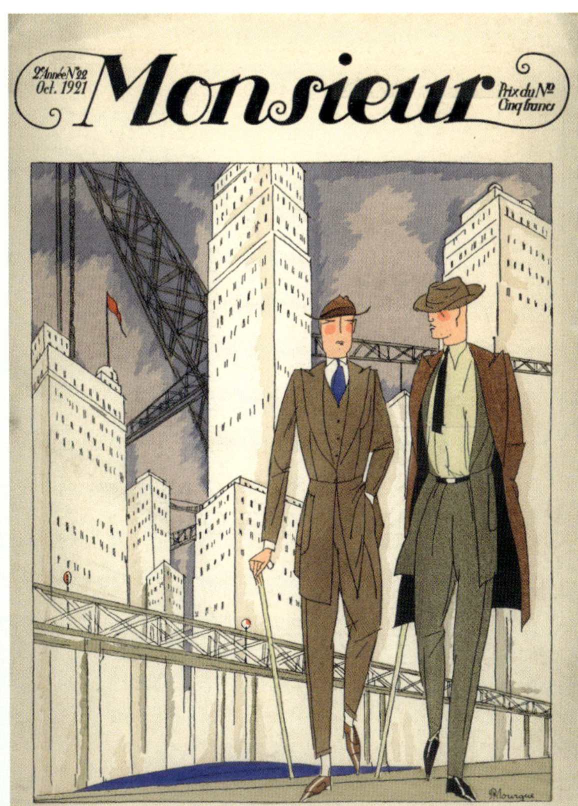

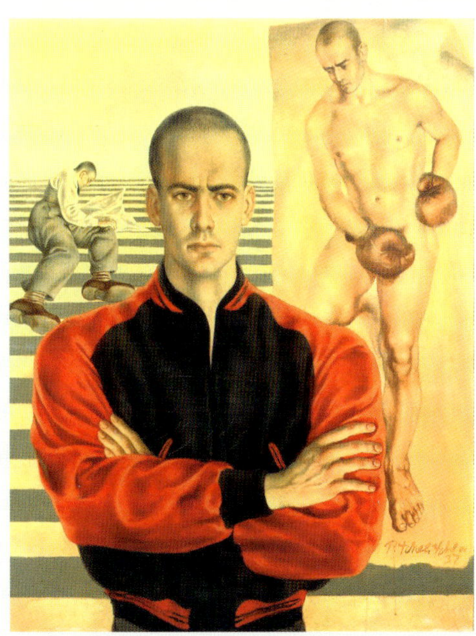
2.2 Cover of *Monsieur*, October 1921. Collection of John Potvin, Montreal.

2.3 Pavel Tchelitchew, *Portrait of Lincoln Kirstein*, 1937, oil on canvas, 46 × 36 in. (116.8 × 91.4 cm). Collection of the School of American Ballet, New York.

gracious manner of a fashionable bachelor.[13] Indeed, throughout his life, Ewing and his circle in Paris and New York embraced the fashions, sophisticated attitudes, and wide-ranging activities — from shopping and reading to daily exercise and physical culture — that magazines like *Monsieur, Le Goût du Jour,* and *Fantasio* recommended.

In the service of that dandified, elegant image, Ewing became a dedicated consumer, shopping not only for men's clothing, but for all of the equipment, accessories, and elements of interior decor that were necessary for the modern urban dweller, a role that depended not just on achieving a "look" but on adopting a modern "lifestyle." On May 20, for example, he wrote to inform his mother about the purchase of yet another suit, a bargain he knew she would appreciate: "Bought myself a gorgeous house suit — a lounging suit — black satin trousers and a jacket of black and silver brocaded silk with elaborate satin belt. Such suits cost around $50[.]oo in New York and I paid $8[.]75. It seems a pity not to buy everything in sight when prices are like this."[14]

Through the flattering cut of a jacket (fig. 2.2), or the pattern and fabric of a dressing gown, or the adoption of carefully planned exercise regimens, Ewing, like many in his circle in Paris (and ultimately in New York where the fashion continued into the 1930s), signaled his sophisticated tastes, fashionable habits, and fluid sexuality.[15] Though it may at first seem difficult to decode, a portrait like Pavel Tchelitchew's 1937 portrait of the young aesthete Lincoln Kirstein — Ewing's contemporary and rival for Muriel Draper's attention — clearly celebrates his adoption of this mode by representing each part of his multisided persona (fig. 2.3). Thus, he is depicted as both an athlete and an aesthete, a classical nude in boxing gloves, and modern-day prince in the mold of Bronzino's elegant Medici portraits.

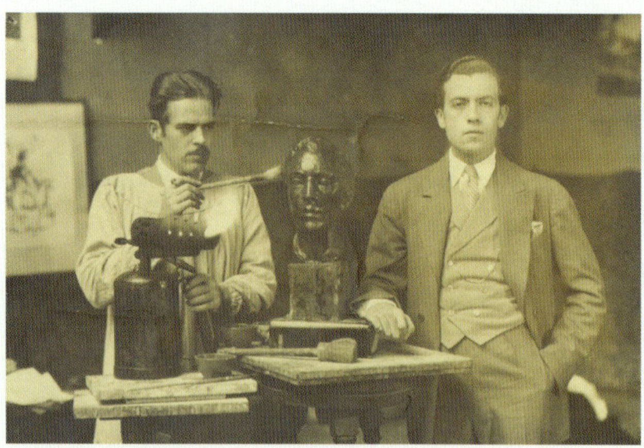

2.4 Anon., Roy Sheldon sculpting a bust of Max Ewing in Paris, from *The Gallery of Extraordinary Portraits*, 1926.

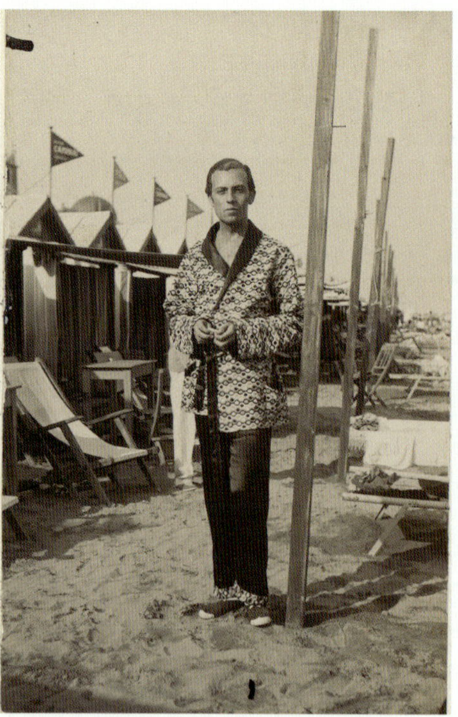

2.5 Anon., Max Ewing at the beach in Venice, 1926. Max Ewing Papers.

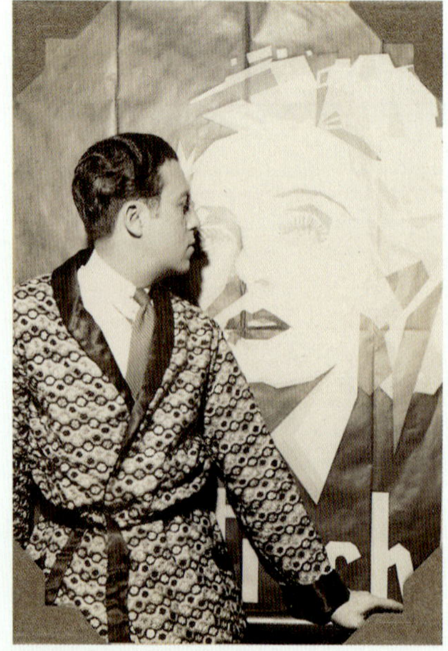

2.6 Anon., Max Ewing with poster for Marlene Dietrich's *Shanghai Express*, 1932. Max Ewing Papers.

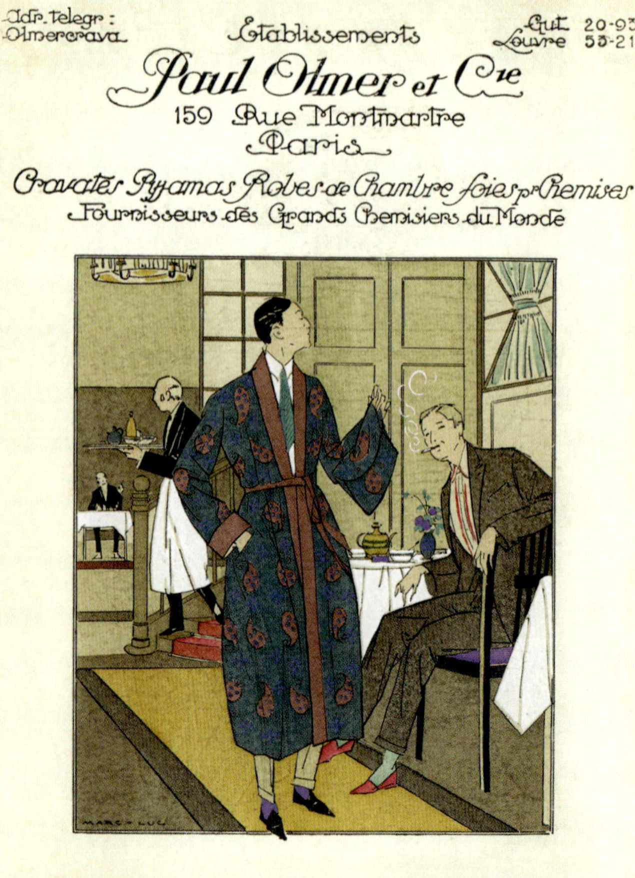

2.7 Marc Luc, Pierre Olmer et Cie advertisement, *Monsieur*, February 1921. Collection of John Potvin, Montreal.

Ewing may not have had anything like Kirstein's aristocratic self-confidence or financial resources, but he aspired to a similar role. Whether through his obsession with fashion and tailoring or his newly acquired interest in boxing, Ewing was intent on becoming a modern dandy. While he made it very clear to his parents that he didn't look very carefully at women his own age (though he clearly studied the chic costumes of his beloved Louise Hellstrom and Muriel Draper), he could wax poetic about the cut and fabric of a man's suit, as he did on May 16, describing the one he had just purchased for himself: it was made of a "dark material" he wrote, with

> slightly padded shoulders which gives it a military shape at the top — then tight hips which make it very swank. Very long loose trousers gathered slightly at the top. Double breasted coat with wide lapels — single breasted vest also with lapels. With black oxfords and straw-colored light-weights spats. A gay black and white handkerchief and a white gardenia in my button hole I am a sight that I would enjoy looking at if I had the chance! Seriously, a very handsome suit and only $40[.]oo.[16]

Ewing had himself photographed wearing that very suit in the Paris studio of his friend, the artist Roy Sheldon, who was sculpting a bust of him, and he included that image, which wonderfully captures his successful transformation from wide-eyed American tourist to confident Paris dandy, with poster for Marlene Dietrich's *Shanghai Express*, (fig. 2.4). We are also fortunate that Ewing made sure to save a snapshot of himself wearing the same short robe that he bought in Paris and sported on the beach at the Lido in Venice a few months later (fig. 2.5). The highly patterned jacket, memorialized in a snapshot taken in his New York apartment in 1932 (fig. 2.6), was — like the dressing gown he purchased in 1927 — so perfectly à la mode that it could have been lifted directly from the pages of *Monsieur*, the gentleman's fashion magazine (fig. 2.7).

For Max Ewing and his parents, such purchases clearly represented money well spent if they gained him an entrée into the elite cultural and social circles of New York and Paris. They knew that his quest for recognition as a concert pianist also depended on making the right connections and on keeping up his handsome, well-groomed, and fashionable appearance. He clearly had his parents' blessing as he acquired more clothes and accessories in shops around the city, yet he couldn't resist the temptation to push his luck (and their indulgence) just a little bit further, using a well-worn strategy familiar to shoppers everywhere, wondering aloud about where to draw the line between the necessary and the merely desired: "I want to have some photographs taken by Man Ray who does the finest possible," he wrote:

> I want an evening cape, want a better looking lightweight top coat. I want an absolutely swell dress suit. I want books and hangings for my apartment. None of these things are necessary at all. I don't and won't actually <u>need</u> any money for food and shelter until August. ... And when one is 23 — and it is spring — and Paris — and one is 'sitting on

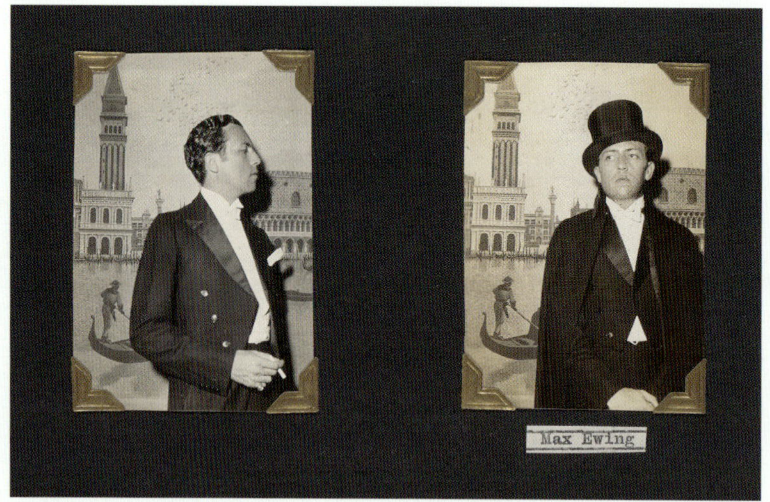

2.8 Max Ewing, *Self Portrait in Evening Wear*, from *Les Amants de Venise*, 1932.

top of the world' — one wants to get more — do more — have more than just the necessary![17]

In June he ordered the long-desired evening cape, and informed his parents that "it is going to be so beautiful I can hardly stand it," adding that he would "no longer need to feel overshadowed at concerts and plays by the glory of Muriel's clothes."[18] He would later enshrine his triumphant new look (fig. 2.8) in a photograph, a double self-portrait in evening clothes that was part of his *Carnival of Venice* series.

MODERN MUSIC AND DANCE

Thus attired and armed with knowledge about art and culture, Ewing threw himself into the social and cultural whirlwind of Paris, and his social calendar quickly filled up with parties, concerts, lunches, and dinners. Thanks to letters of introduction from Draper, Jane Heap, and Carl Van Vechten, and to his own good looks and charm, he made friends easily: in May, he was taken to supper at Maxim's ("the famous Maxim's you have heard of all your life," as he told his mother) by Lorna Lindsley; in June, he went to a dinner party given by Lady Rothermere, the financial backer of Diaghilev (her husband owned the *Daily Mail*), at her apartment on the Quai Voltaire, where he met the artist Romaine Brooks (fig. 2.9) — "the best of American portrait painters," as he explained. Later that night, he was driven in a Rolls-Royce to a performance of the Ballets Russes where he was

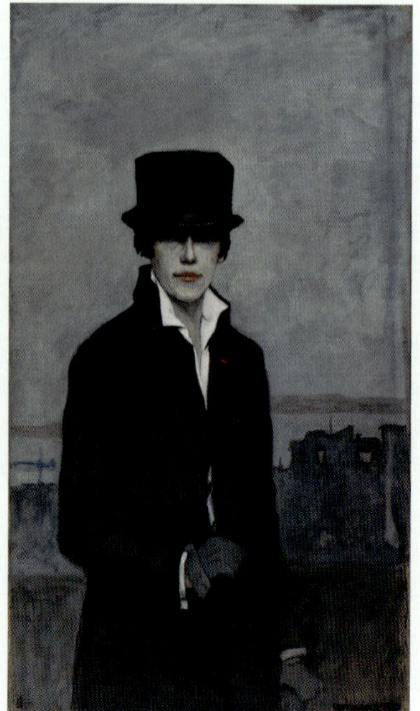

2.9 Romaine Brooks, *Self-Portrait*, 1923, oil on canvas, 46¼ × 26⅞ in. (117.5 × 68.3 cm). Smithsonian American Art Museum, Washington, DC. Gift of the artist, 1966.49.1.

"squeezed into a box with Diaghilev … and Picasso the greatest of painters, the Count and Countess de Beaumont, Marcelle Meyer pianist and Poulenc composer, and several others!!" Romaine's chauffeur had driven him back to his hotel at the end of the evening, he said. She is a "grand person," he added, noting — with characteristic snobbery of the sort that would have delighted his new friend — that, unlike Pioneer, "Paris has been marvelous for I have not once had to see or listen to any stupid people."[19]

Ewing's energy and dedication to the project of self-invention knew no bounds, and the list of famous names and unlikely encounters piled up quickly. On May 6, he was taken by Noël Murphy to a party at the home of a wealthy American couple named Mills — patrons of modern music — where he met the young American composer George Antheil (fig. 2.10) and other members of the avant-garde circle.[20] The event turned out to be a particularly memorable occasion for Ewing, as it marked the beginning of his close friendship with Antheil: in a letter to Muriel Draper, he described him as "marvelous," and an "amiable, sweet and modest person," noting that Antheil had played excerpts from his new *Ballet Mécanique*, which were "terrific and all I always thought they ought to be."[21] Ewing met and heard other aspiring musicians at

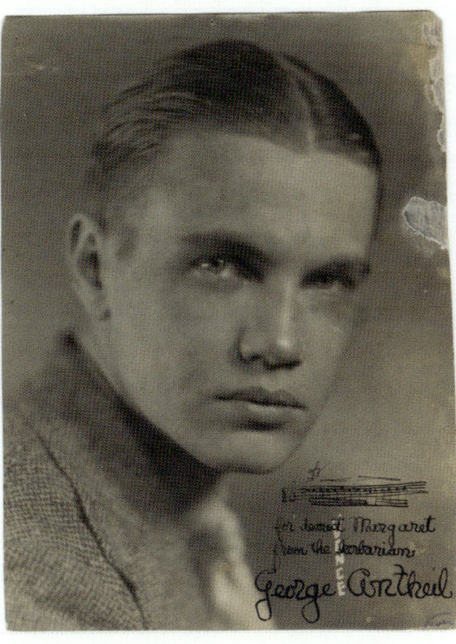

2.10 Anon., *George Anthiel*, c. 1925. Elizabeth Jenks Clark Collection of Margaret Anderson, Yale Collection of American Literature, Beinecke Rare Book & Manuscript Library, Yale University, New Haven, Connecticut.

the same event, and reported on all of this to Draper with characteristic candor: the guests had included George Copeland, "who played superbly," he said, and Virgil Thomson, "who played nauseatingly" (although he doesn't give any indication of why), and Rolf de Maré, director of the Ballets Suédois — which Ewing had seen in New York in 1923 — who "sat beneath a huge Picabia and only that."[22]

Ewing and the New Jersey–born Antheil — fellow Americans and young outsiders in an expat world dominated by Harvard graduates (like Thomson) and no small degree of class snobbery — soon became frequent companions. Ewing spared no effort in describing his enthusiasm for Antheil and his music: on May 13, for example, he wrote to say that he had spent the afternoon at Antheil's apartment, declaring, "He is without any doubt the most vital of all young American musical genius, and far and away the most advanced composer," explaining that "he left several years ago because there was no recognition in America for anyone so far beyond it as he was," adding — optimistically — that "things are changing … and New York at least is ready for almost anything."[23]

For both Ewing and Antheil, the composer's new work, and especially his *Ballet Mécanique*, represented that change: it was a raucous celebration of the clanging noise and unstoppable energy of modern America, written for multiple pianolas (only one was played in the Paris performance; in New York these would be entirely replaced by pianos), airplane propellers, bells, and whistles that had caused a riot when it was first performed in Paris the previous year.[24] As early as 1921, before he moved to Europe, Antheil had written to Muriel Draper to plead for her support (and letters of introduction), describing what he called "his dream of steel and the future," and explaining that his music took on "the color of machinery:" "New steel is blue — white — a strange radiance. New machinery … buildings — porcelains — colors … the aesthetic of the future."[25] Ewing was enchanted by his young friend's poetic way of speaking and his bold ideas; his full-throated enthusiasm for Antheil's work sealed the deal on their friendship, even if Muriel Draper remained unimpressed.

The week after the Millses' party, Ewing was invited to the home of Sylvia Beach (1887–1962), the publisher of James Joyce and proprietor of the legendary bookstore Shakespeare and Company, where he again heard Antheil play his own work; by the end of the month, the two men — together with Antheil's wife and other new friends — had achieved an easy familiarity: "I see the Antheils all the time," he explained to his parents, "George is a sweet little Barbarian, of Polish descent, but born in New Jersey and grew up there. He has lived in Europe the last four or 5 years. He has a very chic German wife. She speaks practically no English, he practically no French, I practically no German, so we talk 2 at a time, since each two of us have a language in common."[26] They often ate dinner together and went on weekend outings, including a boat trip on the Seine with Ed Cushing, the music critic of the *Brooklyn Eagle*. Even after Ewing left Paris for the summer, returning again a few months later in September 1926, they picked up right where they had left off: as he wrote to his parents on September 19, he had gone "with the Antheils to the country to lunch with a boy named Bravig [Imbs, a writer and friend of Stein's] … to a restaurant called 'Little Venice'"; then they all went punting in "ridiculous little boats."[27]

Ewing's support for his friend never wavered: as Antheil moved closer to securing a date for a spring 1927 premiere of the *Ballet Mécanique* at Carnegie Hall in New York, Ewing began making plans for the occasion, sending printed announcements to his parents and to as many friends as he could think of. He even agreed to play the difficult piano part in the concert himself (the original idea of using twelve mechanical pianolas had to be scrapped) with eleven other pianists including Antheil himself, Aaron Copland, Colin McPhee, and two of Ewing's friends; that decision would prove to be life-changing because it was there, pounding on the keys repeatedly to achieve the clamorous effect that Antheil sought, that he would permanently damage his finger and thus be forced to give up his hopes for a career as a concert pianist.[28] In his letters home, however, he described the "Antheil thing" as "great fun and of great importance to me." Even after the much-hoped-for debut turned out to be a technical and critical disaster — and even after Antheil abruptly left New York, canceling a planned second performance and fleeing back to Paris — Ewing remained a loyal friend and a champion of the project.[30]

Indeed, Ewing was an avid fan of modern music in all its forms: from his earliest days in New York City, he sought out musicians of all types, fully embracing the variety and the wealth of choices on offer throughout the city, regardless of the factionalism of the New York music scene of the 1920s. He attended concerts and recitals by fellow piano students and famous performers alike, and he made a habit of hearing the work of new composers whenever possible, saving programs and handbills to record the performances he heard and the people he met. Thus, on November 17, 1924, he sent his parents the program from a lecture and recital sponsored by the modernist "League of Composers": it featured, among other offerings, his friend Carol Robinson playing Antheil's "Jazz Sonata," as well as new work by Aaron Copland ("Passacaglia" and "The Cat and the Mouse"). Copland became a good friend, visiting Ewing's apartment to play his latest compositions on Ewing's Steinway before he left for Europe; the two also met up in Paris in a few months later.[31] Ewing also made a point of hearing the modernist composer Henry Cowell perform at Aeolian Hall in January 1926, and he heard him play again in Paris a few months later.[32] Unlike Antheil and Copland, however, neither Cowell nor Virgil Thomson would become more than acquaintances, even after Thomson returned to the United States and collaborated with many of Ewing's New York friends on his new opera *Four Saints in Three Acts*.

Like many young musicians of his generation — with the exception of Antheil, who challenged his (and everyone else's) authority — Ewing reserved his greatest admiration for Stravinsky, whose work he played and studied: in New York and Paris, Stravinsky was the gold standard by which Ewing and other aspiring musicians measured their sophistication and technique. Thus, it was especially thrilling for him to be able to write home on May 28, 1926, to report that he had met the great man himself at the Pleyel Piano Company's rehearsal space in Paris: as he told his parents, he had been practicing Stravinsky's "Serenade" on the piano in his studio there when someone knocked on the door and stuck his head inside to see who was playing — it turned out to be Stravinsky himself.[33]

SAPPHIC PARIS: MARGARET ANDERSON AND GEORGETTE LEBLANC

Music and musicians were not, of course, Ewing's only interest on the cultural scene: on the contrary, his social life soon began to focus around the remarkably diverse and sprawling world of expat lesbians, starting, of course, with Stein and Toklas. That world included not only the so-called "Women of the Left Bank," who clustered around the long-running weekly salon of the American Natalie Barney on the rue Jacob and the nearby bookshops of Sylvia Beach and her lover Adrienne Monnier (1892–1955), but also the snobbish, closed circle of titled aristocrats and monied patrons of the arts in the elite neighborhoods of the Right Bank.[34] Remarkably, members of both cohorts welcomed the handsome young American into their midst.

Soon after his arrival, Ewing developed a close friendship with Margaret Anderson (fig. 2.11) and her lover Georgette Leblanc (1869–1941), glamorous women well-known for the pivotal roles they played in the art worlds of Chicago, New York, and Paris since before World War I.[35] Through Louise Hellstrom, Ewing had gotten to know Anderson's friend and former partner (in life and literature) Jane Heap, and she provided him with letters of introduction to many of her friends in Paris: these included Anderson, who, with Heap, had been founder and editor of the *Little Review*, and Leblanc, who had been the companion and muse of the Nobel-prize-winning playwright Maurice Maeterlinck decades earlier. The resourceful Georgette, then close to fifty, was still in demand as a performer, and

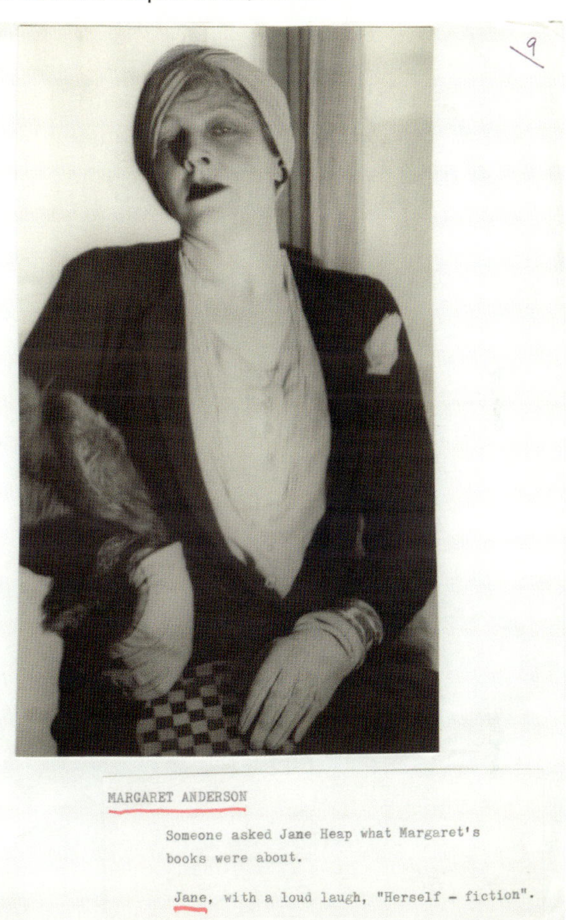

2.11 Berenice Abbott, *Portrait of Margaret Anderson*, from her scrapbook, c. 1928. Elizabeth Jenks Clark Collection of Margaret Anderson, Yale Collection of American Literature, Beinecke Rare Book & Manuscript Library, Yale University, New Haven, Connecticut.

in 1924, she had starred in *L'Inhumaine*, the modernist film by Marcel L'Herbier. Moreover, both Anderson and Georgette Leblanc had at one time been close to George Antheil, who shared a house with Anderson and Heap in New Jersey in 1921. Georgette had also worked with him and Fernand Léger on the 1924 film version of the *Ballet Mécanique*.[36] While there had been a "rupture" in their relationship with the volatile composer, by the time Ewing came along, their mutual interest in modern music, and Anderson's own training as a concert pianist, quickly cemented their bond. Moreover, Anderson was a follower of Gurdjieff and a friend of Muriel Draper's, and this too added to her appeal.

Margaret was exactly the sort of theatrical, opinionated person that Ewing adored: like Muriel, she was worldly, older than he was, and had strong opinions about everything; she loved music, and people either loved her or hated her. As Janet Flanner described her in a profile in the *New Yorker* after her death in October 1973, Anderson was "the born enemy of convention and discipline, a feministic, romantic rebel with an appetite for Chopin and indiscriminate reading. But conversation was her real passion."[37] She was argumentative and impulsive; Gertrude Stein hated her because she always thought she was right. Of course, Max Ewing adored her.

As Ewing wrote to his parents, "Margaret is a grand person and we got on marvelously … Something *clicked* when we met, as it does not very often on first meeting with a person," adding a caveat, as would become his lifelong habit: "Of course the greatest *click* in my life was when I met Muriel last year and we both clicked so hard we nearly died of it." The rest of his letter, written on May 9, 1926, is a treasure-trove of gossip and elaborate descriptions of glamorous decor and fashion that he knew his mother would enjoy:

> Margaret Anderson lived for years with Jane in N.Y. and now she lives here with Mme. Maeterlinck in a beautiful apartment in the Rue de l'Université. The lights are all in great blue and green cylinders on the floor and the walls are painted gray, with bright black oil-cloth curtains. Margaret was dressed in handsome black satin trousers and a green velvet smock, and she is doing nothing but play the piano these days. She says she will take me to meet everyone in Paris I want to know, or take me to any house where I want to go.[38]

Margaret Anderson made good on her promise, shepherding her new companion around to meet her friends and see the sights of the city: one day, for example, they were "driving through the Place Vendome to get two chocolate malted milks at Sherry's" — the American ice cream parlor that had recently opened a branch in Paris — when they saw Mary Garden walking on the street; they asked for their taxi to turn around so that they could speak to her, but they were too slow and she disappeared. Next they stopped at the Pleyel studios to take in the latest sounds, "eavesdropping while [George] Auric and [Francis] Poulenc and two others rehearsed 'Les Noces' on the pianos."[39] Herself an accomplished pianist, Margaret often visited Max at Pleyel and listened to him practice, and the two attended concerts and cultural events together, including a literary festival dedicated to the work of Jean Cocteau. One noteworthy Saturday in May, she and Georgette took him to tea at the studio of Constantin Brâncuși (1876–1957) where, as he reported in a letter to Muriel, the artist "made us coffee

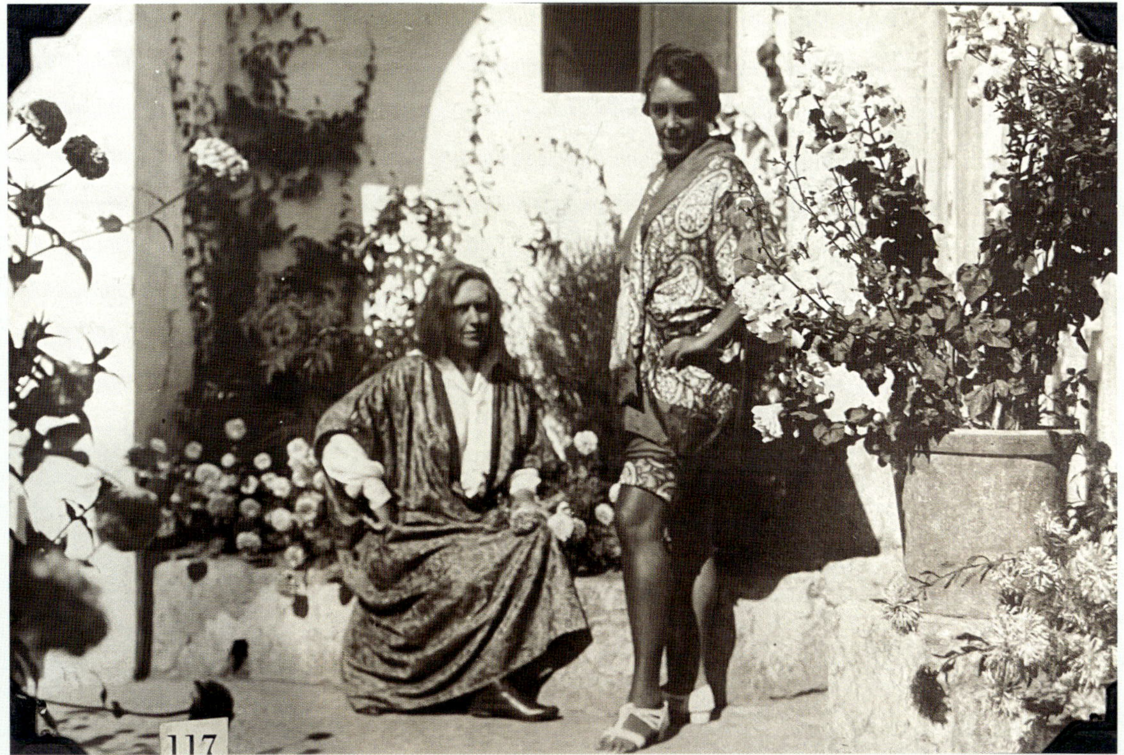

and did a Charleston or two, and I gave him your love."[40] From there, they went on to Le Select, the café "where too many people sit," according to Ewing, and talked about Muriel. No wonder they "got on famously."[41]

2.12 Anon., *"Natalie Barney and Romaine Brooks Amid Floral Decorations (Capri),"* from *The Gallery of Extraordinary Portraits*, n.d.

NATALIE BARNEY AND ROMAINE BROOKS

Throughout his time in Paris, Ewing worked hard to see and learn as much as he could. On May 21, for example, he wrote to Muriel Draper to tell her about a performance by the African American singer and dancer Josephine Baker, whom he referred to as "*the grande étoile noire,*" at the Folies Bergère: "She wears two ostrich feathers; and is let down through the roof in a rose-cage to do a Charleston on a brown mirror, which seems a procedure almost worthy of the Barney house," implying an insider's knowledge of the goings-on at Natalie Barney's infamous lesbian gatherings.[42] It isn't at all clear from his letter which of the two women Ewing was more excited to finally see in person: he and Draper had both heard a great deal about Barney that spring from their talkative friend Esther Murphy, whose obsessive yet unrequited crush on the beautiful and openly queer *saloniste* was a never-ending topic of conversation. As we know from Ewing's letters, and from Lisa Cohen's portrait of Murphy in *All We Know: Three Lives*, the brilliant, voluble Esther (who, according to Cohen, had become "a visible presence in sapphic New York and Paris" in the mid-1920s) shared her enthusiasm about Barney with anyone and everyone who would listen, as was indeed her way with most things that interested her.[43] Ewing was thrilled to be able to report back his own firsthand observations of Barney and the goings-on at her rue Jacob gatherings: he and Esther were even recognized by name in the hand-drawn diagram of the "Salon de l'Amazone" and its denizens that was included in Barney's autobiographical *Aventures de l'Esprit* in 1929.[44]

The glamorous Natalie Barney (1876–1972) (fig. 2.12) was famous for many things, not least of all her Paris home and garden — set back from the street by a leafy courtyard and a high, stone wall — which had become a de rigueur pilgrimage destination for visiting young people, queer men and women, and curious tourists of every description.[45] For nearly seven decades, from the end of World War I until her death at the age of 95, her large reception rooms and the curious little "Temple de l'Amitié" that sat at the foot of her garden offered an ideal setting for the sprawling weekly gatherings and avant-garde performances she hosted — and also for the trysts and flirtations of queer couples, including Barney herself and her many lovers. As described by Janet Flanner, the Barney salon was part mixer for the lesbian smart set — a place where, as she put it, "a new rendezvous among ladies who had taken a fancy to each other or wished to see each other again" might be planned — and part cultural center and clearinghouse.[46] Although her life partner Romaine Brooks tended to steer clear of the gossip and sexual intrigues that Natalie Barney thrived on, preferring to socialize with a more exclusive, upper-class coterie in and around her own Right Bank studio (a group that included such figures as Brooks's former lover Winnaretta Singer, the Princesse de Polignac), both women remained at the center of lesbian social life and in many ways defined the "queer space" for which Paris in the 1920s became so well-known.[47]

Barney's independence, dramatic flair, and queer coterie were the stuff of legend for people like Max Ewing and generations of other young people who made the pilgrimage to rue Jacob to see and be seen. On June 26, 1926, Ewing described the evening he spent at Barney's salon in a letter to Muriel Draper: "I went to the Barney Friday … There was tea about a table and two or three new books came up for momentary mention … but most of the talk was concerning the ball of the night before, a Proustian conversation devoted to why Duchess de so and so was not invited, and why Princesse de so and so was." "The Barney is all right," he added, "She laughs easily and when she should, and is a diplomat."[48]

Indeed, he was soon spending a good deal of time with both Barney and Brooks, visiting their homes on rue Jacob (Barney) and rue Jules Chaplain (Brooks); at the latter, he reported, he was ushered into the studio to view Brooks's "portraits of Casati and the Capriands," referring to the circle of friends from the artist's time at Capri, where she had a home.[49] Over the course of the spring and summer of 1926, he got to know the two women fairly well, and he described Romaine — who is often characterized as an antisocial recluse — in a letter to his parents as "frightfully rich … and a delightful sport to be with."[50] No doubt she too was drawn to his good looks and charm, and also perhaps to the unapologetic dandyism that he embraced, a style that was not unlike her own (fig. 2.13).

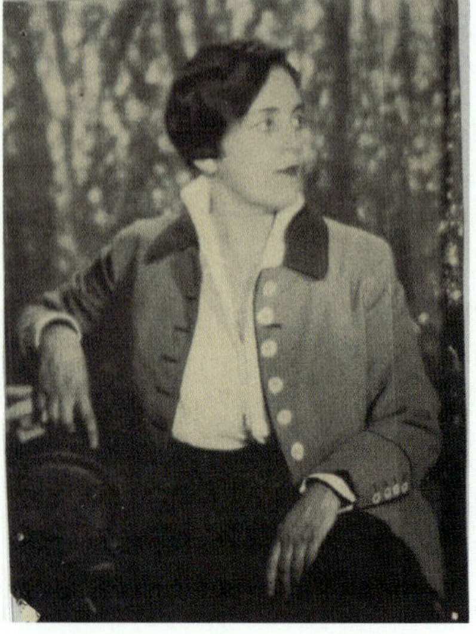

2.13 Man Ray, *Romaine Brooks*, from *The Gallery of Extraordinary Portraits*, c. 1926. Man Ray Trust.

Romaine clearly picked her friends very carefully, unlike Barney, who lived for the ready supply of new people, and new conquests, she encountered at her gatherings. The wealthy Brooks had no time for anyone whom she viewed as ordinary, American women in particular, or merely curious, and she certainly didn't socialize with women who weren't of her class. Ewing, on the other hand, was a handsome young man who, like her, was queer, well educated, and amusing in a camp sort of way. Over the course of the following two years, they became close friends.

Ewing's descriptions of his adventures with Barney and Brooks in Paris in 1926 and 1927 are full of fascinating and previously unknown details, despite the reams of paper that have been devoted to the pair, who are second only to Gertrude Stein and Alice B. Toklas in the pantheon of lesbian history. In a letter from June 1926, for example, he described a lavish costume ball that the three (and others "in their party") attended at the home of Elisabeth "Lily" de Gramont, Duchesse de Clermont-Tonnerre, a figure of enormous appeal and social standing, as well as a key player in the lesbian social scene, who would later be included in his closet *Gallery of Extraordinary Portraits* (fig. 2.14). Indeed, Lily was the third member of a lifelong "throuple" with Natalie and Romaine: having first met in the spring of 1909 (an anniversary they celebrated every year until Lily's death in 1954), Natalie and Lily had signed a "marriage contract" on June 20, 1919 that bound them together as "eternal mates," in a union that was then, and would ever be, challenged by infidelities and jealousies, as the document explicitly acknowledged. Nevertheless, Romaine was a partner and fixture in Natalie's life for more than fifty years.[51]

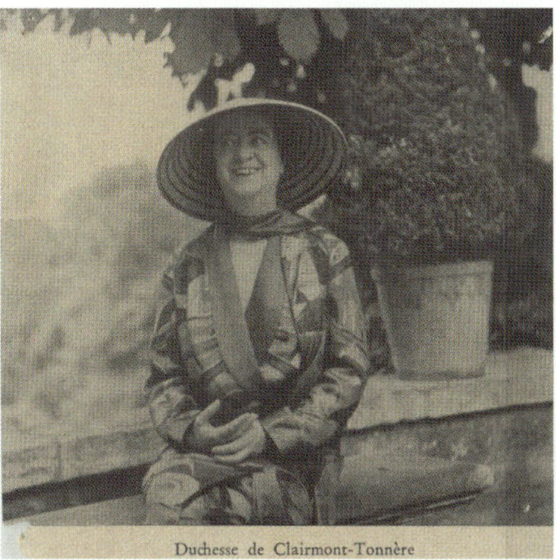

2.14 Anon., *Lily de Gramont, Duchesse de Clermont-Tonnerre*, from *The Gallery of Extraordinary Portraits*.

While it is unlikely that Brooks would have shared any of this backstory with a new friend like Max Ewing, it is also clear that both Barney and Brooks were, for a period of time, remarkably close to the young man. He described a magical evening of dancing and people-watching, a garden filled with lights, and an enormous house where an American jazz band played on one floor while an orchestra played sixteenth-century French music on another. At the party, he had glimpsed the Marchesa Casati "who used to be the greatest hostess in Venice." "She was the only woman I have ever seen," he reported to his parents, "who could compare" with Muriel Draper and Mary Garden in "extravagant allure."[52] At Brooks's suggestion, he had rented a costume "of 1830s Paris" while she herself went as a "Spanish Grande Dame." In a letter to Muriel Draper, he provided a bit more detail: Romaine "went as something Spanish, matador or citizen, I'm not sure which," he wrote, while Natalie Barney "went *Chinese*," in a costume "lighted by electric bulbs which she shot on and off by a hand battery." "At one time," Ewing added, "they both danced to the tune of 'Yes Sir She's My Baby.'"[53]

Stories like this caused his stock to rise considerably with Esther Murphy, and in March 1927, when he was briefly back in New York, he reported that he was "seeing quite a lot of Esther": "I go to all of Esther's dinners. I am one of the few people she knows who know Miss Barney in Paris, so we get on excellently well. Every time I see her I can talk to her about Miss Barney, and altho I have said all I know a hundred times it is always fresh to her!"[54] "Last year she never paid so much attention to me," he reported, "but this year she is all attention, and it all because in the summer I MET THAT WOMAN — NATALIE BARNEY, I'm sure."

A few days later, he wrote that he had talked with Esther about Miss Barney "for five solid hours" at dinner: for Esther, who tended to be obsessive about anything that interested her, the topic of the beautiful and unapologetically lesbian Barney never got boring. Ewing was game to share everything he knew, and he often had to repeat his stories for her more than once: "The conversation becomes mad but always fascinating," he added generously. By early May 1927, Esther felt ready to try her luck again with Miss Barney in person: "Esther sails on the 21st and has been buying a wardrobe all week. She is now all set to captivate Miss Barney. Miss Barney. Miss Barney. Miss Barney."[55]

Romaine Brooks was of minimal interest to Esther, but it was she, rather than Natalie Barney, who became Ewing's close friend over the course of two summer visits to Italy and the south of France in 1926 and 1927. In July, Romaine asked him to accompany her to Venice, mentioning that he could meet the Marchesa Casati, "under less formal circumstances than those attending a ball at the Duchess de Clement's [sic]."[56] A few weeks later, Ewing informed his parents that he was going to "ride along with Mme Romaine Brooks from Paris to Venice in her huge car with chauffeur," traveling to Monte Carlo for ten days on his own (so he could visit the writer Glenway Wescott in Villefranche), then rejoining Brooks in Aix-les-Bains and continuing "the rest of the way [to Venice] with her across lower France and northern Italy, Turin, Verona, and those towns." "Romaine wants to paint me too," he boasted, "and this is a great thing, for everyone on earth has sat to her. Ida Rubenstein, and Cocteau and Casati and d'Annunzio himself."[57] In anticipation of their stay in Venice, Ewing worked on his tan, suffering through "the burning process" to achieve the desired result. "My brown eyelids make my eyes look bluer," he told his parents, but by October, when he had returned to Paris, he had already begun to lose "his Italian complexion," because of the "gray French climate"; fortunately, he reported, he could "fake it by putting on a careful and elaborate French man's makeup — and Houlingant's brown powder achieves about the same results as the Italian sun."[58]

Ewing and Brooks visited Venice together in August 1926: Ewing had reserved a room at the Hotel Beau Rivage overlooking the Grand Canal, and Romaine went by motorboat, "with all her luggage" to an apartment she had rented for the summer. For a few weeks, the two were inseparable and intimate friends, so much so that the normally reserved Brooks confided a great deal of her life story to him. He reported on those developments to Muriel Draper in amazement:

> The trip with Romaine is an absolute hallucination. She can be terribly amusing. But all day! And for five days! Every story. Every event in her life she told me. From Jane Heap dropping the matches through her door, to Casati posing for her portrait. Casati removed everything but her stockings. That she would not do. So Romaine started to paint hoofs instead of feet, thinking Casati would be furious, but no, she was delighted and the portrait remains, nude with hoofs. And every amour of her life she told me![59]

His letters from that summer and the following one offer a rare insider's glimpse of the social life and attitudes of the elite club of European aristocrats and their American friends who flocked to Venice for the season. Early in their first visit, for example, Romaine took him to the Lido where he wore his beautiful new lounge suit on the beach, reporting to his mother that the Lido was "the last word in modernity," where "you hear only American jazz and the Charlestons never stop."[60] "Nobody ever dresses until night," he added, and "the beach pajamas are very gay, but their wearers are too fat: too many vulgar American, German, and English tourists are here." With his own well-cultivated snobbery now reinforced by that of his elegant lady friends, he declared that he couldn't "stand the sight of them."

He also picked up on the political opinions of aristocratic friends: "There is an excitement that is marvelous," he told his parents, "and it is due of course to Mussolini."[61] Indeed, Ewing's letters from Venice offer significant new information about this circle, revealing the details of Romaine Brooks's love affair with Daisy, Countess di Robilant, a wealthy Italian feminist and fascist, whose advocacy on behalf of women and children — and support for strict abortion laws — earned her a top position in Mussolini's government.[62] Questions about Brooks's politics have always lingered over her historical reputation, given her close relationship with Gabriele d'Annunzio and her extended residence in Italy during World War II; Ewing's letters confirm Brooks's longstanding association with Mussolini's supporters, and — at least in Ewing's telling of the story — her apparent acceptance of his policies in the 1920s.[63]

Throughout the summer of 1926, Ewing and Brooks attended all-night parties in Venetian palaces belonging to (or rented by) Italian marchesas, English duchesses, French princesses — including the American heiress Winnaretta Singer, the Princesse de Polignac, who had purchased the Palazzo Contarini as a present for her husband twenty-five years earlier — where everyone did the Charleston and Ewing sometimes played the piano with the African American entertainers who had been hired for the occasion. At one "grand soirée" in honor of Baroness Erlanger at the palace of Madame Lina Cavalieri, Ewing reported that he had danced with "four German film actresses" who were "very pretty in pearls and yards of chiffon, if you like them pretty in yards of chiffon. I do not. I danced with some of them. But girls are such bores."[64] He played the piano for "Count Cellani to do a Charleston, which he did almost as well as a Harlem negro," and he boasted that the Marquis Guido Sommi (an avant-garde musician famously painted by Tamara de Lempika) was "trying to arrange with Toscanini for me to give a concert in Milano": "Get used to his name for it will probably come up often in my life," he wrote, but needless to say, it never did.

In August 1926, he boasted that "life in Venice this month is almost rivalling the eighteenth century for magnificence," continuing:

> The newest thing is the <u>Dance-Boat</u> which Cole Porter and Elsa Maxwell <u>have launched</u>. It is huge floating night-club with tables around the side and dancing in the center and negro musicians at one end, and blue and gold lights everywhere. At midnight it sails out from Venice to the Lido and back. The Venetians whose homes it passed objected. They are not particularly rich people and could not stand the sight of other people going by behaving so expensively. So now the Dance Boat has put up curtains, and is completely enclosed by red spangled drapes. Nobody can see in, and everyone is satisfied. Isn't it all divine and ridiculous?[65]

Cole Porter's party at the Ca' Rezzonico a few days later, one of many he hosted that summer, was "epochal," Ewing reported:

> for it was the first party ever given in Venice by Americans which the Venetian royalty deigned to go to. The Countess Rubiliant [*sic*] went, and the famous Countess Morosini who was the lover of the Kaiser, and they stayed until morning. … Romaine Brooks has made a sensational entry into Italian society, and the French American Princess Polignac is furious and jealous with rage, and the intrigues on all sides are fantastic. It is almost the most inaccessible aristocracy left in Europe, and after only a month here both Romaine and I find ourselves mixed up in the middle of it. These people never knew any Americans like us, and they seem both amazed and delighted.[66]

Although Ewing didn't offer more details, we know from other sources that the party was indeed "epochal," like most of Porter's gatherings: all of the beautiful people were there, drugs were plentiful (perhaps it was in Venice that Ewing developed his fondness for cocaine, which he would later claim was a remedy for his many sinus infections), alcohol flowed, and the music and dancing continued through the night and into the following morning. Porter surrounded himself with exactly the sort of people that Ewing felt most comfortable with, a combination of titled aristocrats, musicians of all kinds, queer bohemians, and beautiful young men like Boris Kochno, the Diaghilev dancer with whom Porter had fallen madly in love in 1925.[67]

In early September, Baroness Erlanger — a wealthy socialite and arts patron whose portrait Brooks had painted in 1924 (fig. 2.15) — invited Ewing to the Villa Malcontenta, the Palladian country house on the Brenta Canal outside Venice that she and her husband Bertie Landsberg had recently purchased and planned to restore. For entertainment, Ewing reported, "all the guests were given little chisels with which to pry away the whitewash" in the *salone*; "It is the most fascinating business. You keep prying away and come upon a portion of a body … And you don't know if it is the front or the back."[68] He signed the guestbook, and excitedly described the progress he was making with his career prospects:

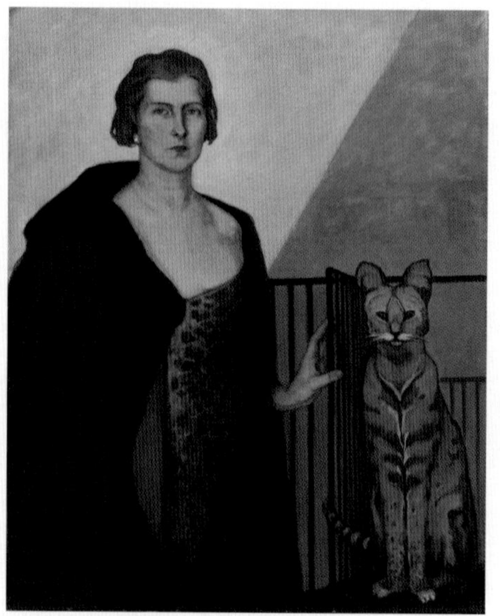

2.15 Romaine Brooks, *La Baronne Emile D'Erlanger*, c. 1924, oil on canvas, 41⅞ × 34⅛ in. (106.4 × 86.7 cm). Smithsonian American Art Museum, Washington, DC. Gift of the artist, 1968.18.5.

> Baroness Erlanger said she would like to take me to play for the Princess de Polignac. The princess is the most influential person in Paris musically, and it is she who forced Stravinsky on the world. But she is also the greatest snob both socially and artistically in Europe, and she has to be handled with great care. I decided that after ten weeks without a piano I did not want to play for her here. She might

be particularly mean about it, as she is not a friend of Romaine's and
she would know I was. Years ago the Princess was in love with
Madame [Olga] de Meyer and as Mme de Meyer did not respond to
her affection the princess declared she would spend the rest of her life
destroying Mme de Meyer's position and she has. Almost no one will
receive Madame de Meyer because the Princess de Polignac will not
recognize her. That's the kind of Princess she is! So the Baroness said
she would try to arrange for me simply to meet the Princess
informally at her palace here and then play for her at her home in
Paris in October — all this being a great help toward a possible
concert in Paris next season.[69]

Ewing assured his parents that, whatever heady experiences he was having, he
always kept his eyes on the prize: "An English baroness bent on presenting me to
the oldest French Princess. One has to steer an extremely difficult course between
these powers, but it is certainly a magnificent game!"

Even in this exciting company, and with all the glamorous adventures he
had had in Europe, he could not resist comparing the wonderful people around
him to Muriel Draper — and, of course, he found them wanting: "All of these
people are very brilliant and spectacular in their way. But after Muriel they all
seem like nothing. Draper is really the only woman of our time who combines all
the qualities of extravagant brilliance of mind and of appearance, and who is at
the same time of the greatest simplicity and the most rarely sympathetic nature
in the world. She is incomparable, and alone in our epoch, and to have her as
my nearest friend is the greatest thing I can have."[70]

With his confidence in Draper and her New York world unshaken — and
excited to spend the fall and winter season with his friends — Ewing began to
make plans to return to New York. He filled his last months in Paris with all of the
pleasures that the city could offer: he took piano lessons with Marcelle Meyer, a
new-music virtuoso, who declared him to be — as he told his parents — "a big
talent" in need of an "immense lot of grinding technical training"; he met up
with an American friend, Robert Gorham, "about the handsomest spectacle the
world contains," and went with him to the opera and to a "Montmartre men's
nightclub" where they "made a most magnificent entrance."[71] He was introduced
to the artist Eugene McCown and saw his new paintings, which "Jane [Heap]
is going to exhibit in New York this winter." He hoped to buy one for himself, he
said, but he settled for a "grand evening suit" and a "very swell brown street
suit" instead.[72]

It was time to go home: his Italian tan was fading in the French climate and
Romaine was still in the south, unable to "break away from" the Countess
Robilant.[73] He said goodbye to Margaret Anderson and called at Lorna Lindsley's
for tea; on October 21, Sylvia Beach and Adrienne Monnier gave a dinner party for
their American friends — "the Antheils and Galantières and me" — who were all
leaving town. He wrote that he "almost shed tears at the idea of going even briefly
from these adorable people," but he was excited by the prospect of America and
longed for the sight of the "Woolworth Building in the sky."[74] With the Galantières
for traveling companions, Ewing set sail for New York on the SS *Berengaria* on
October 23.

Muriel Draper and Esther Murphy were at the dock to meet him on October 31.[75] He took up residence at the Hotel Warrington on Madison and 32nd Street after weeks of apartment hunting; by November, he was fully back in the swing of things, going to parties, and teas, and concerts, and buying black and gold drapes for his large room at the hotel, decorating it in shades of black, white, silver, and gold. He bought an "amusing Venetian window blind from Muriel," he reported, painted with a view of the Piazza San Marco; by the time his parents came to visit, he wrote, the room "will be terribly nice."[76] He went out with Carl Van Vechten and Donald Angus (1899–1990); Muriel gave a tea for him, and he went to a concert given by his friend Taylor Gordon … and these were just the highlights.

On December 5, he reported on the frenzied pace of activities in the holiday season: a party at Small's in Harlem, a "grand dinner party" at Esther Murphy's, a tea at Eddie Wasserman's, a theater party with his Paris friends the Galantières, and a dress rehearsal with Aline MacMahon in the star role. He also reported that Muriel was planning a party for Osbert Sitwell who was newly arrived from London, and mentioned that he hoped to get his only piano student, Teddy Bernstein, started again with lessons.[77] Most exciting of all, he noted, Muriel was planning a party for her friend Glenway Wescott (1901–87) (fig. 2.16), the handsome young writer on whom Ewing had long had a superfan's crush, following his work and his movements with avid attention: Wescott, who was then living in France with his lover Monroe Wheeler (1899–1988), was planning to be in town for January and February before returning to Europe again, and Ewing wrote that the prospect of meeting him was "vastly dramatic and exciting."[78] The couple's visit to the city would indeed prove momentous, but not for the reasons that Ewing had hoped: it wasn't Max Ewing but another young friend of Muriel's, George Platt Lynes, who would become part of Glenway's and Monroe's lives, meeting the two men in February 1927 and immediately forming a passionate bond with Monroe — and of necessity with Glenway as well — that would last for more than a decade.[79] Ewing observed the drama from the sidelines, as was his habit, drawing closer to Lynes and worshipping Wescott from afar.

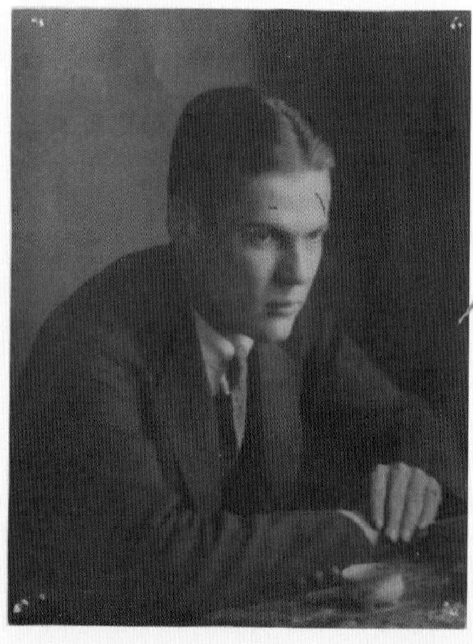

2.16 Doris Ulmann, *Glenway Wescott*, from *The Gallery of Extraordinary Portraits*, c. 1925. (Note the pinholes in the corners of the image.)

In March, George Antheil arrived in New York for his debut concert, and Ewing was there to meet him and his wife when they docked. "Antheil is certainly the craziest, sweetest angel," he wrote, "I don't know how New York will act about his mad music."[80] At his concert the previous month in Budapest, there had been a riot and 250 people were arrested, he reported, but "any city where he is becomes immediately exciting." Antheil was especially keen to see Muriel Draper, and had told Ewing that "anything he writes or does in his life will be due to her stimulus."[81] Their devotion to Draper and certainty about her prescience were clearly two other things the two men had in common.

By the end of the month, rehearsals for the *Ballet Mécanique* had started in earnest. The score was impossible, Ewing told his parents, and a few of the pianists had already quit:

The whole thing was of course written for mechanical pianos,
pianolas with rolls, and with no regard for what actual hands can play.
It became impossible to get the rolls cut for twelve pianolas, so actual
pianists are being used. Since part of it is simply impossible for
anyone to play, then anyone can play it as well as anyone else, so I am
not alarmed. Everything is going ahead about it. Pathé News are
going to take news-reel films of the performance which promises to
be as riotous as anything in America.[82]

Ewing had high hopes both for the event and for his future friendship with Antheil;
even when the much-anticipated performance on April 10 turned out to be a
disaster and not the *succès de scandale* that he and Antheil had hoped for, he put
on a brave face, writing that while "some of the papers were violently angry about
it, they gave it endless space and attention."[83] As the historian Carol Oja has
written, problems with the wind machine, the siren, and the performers produced
a chaotic scene in Carnegie Hall: the promoter and producer Donald Friede
recalled, "The first few moments of the *Ballet* went off smoothly, and the audience
listened carefully … and then … all hell … broke loose."[84] Ewing was
understandably bowled over when he received a letter from the event promoters
Boni and Liveright informing him simply that "due to Mr. Antheil's indisposition"
the second performance of the *Ballet Mécanique* on April 20 was canceled, and
thanking him for his "cooperation and willingness to play at the concert."[85] For his
part, Antheil went silent and sailed back to Europe.

Whatever his private feelings about the concert and Antheil's sudden
disappearance, Ewing quickly pivoted, rejoining his friends at the *Grand Street
Follies* and planning his return to Europe. His pursuit of Glenway Wescott was an
ongoing preoccupation, and he began to lay the groundwork for an encounter in
France the following summer. Planning his moves carefully, he embarked on a new
friendship with the writer and Columbia professor Lloyd Morris (1893–1954) — "it
was because he was Glenway's best friend in America that I sought to know him,"
he confessed — which progressed well beyond his original expectations: "I made
every effort to interest him in me," he noted gleefully, "and now he is so interested
that it is almost difficult!"[86] But Morris's offer of a cozy vacation in Nice, and an
ongoing connection to Glenway Wescott, who lived nearby, were irresistible.

His continued friendships with Van Vechten, Hellstrom, Chanler, Eddie
Wasserman, and, of course, Muriel Draper, filled out his social calendar. At a
party in his apartment at the beginning of May, Taylor Gordon read aloud from
Gertrude Stein's "Miss Furr and Miss Skene" "and their regularly being gay" to the
delight of his friends, who "went into violent hysterics laughing."[87] A few days
later, he went with a group to a party at the private apartment of A'lelia Walker on
Edgecombe Avenue. Paris may have had its nightclubs and bars, but New York
was blessed with the delights of Harlem and its wealthy heiress: "She lives in this
absurd apartment far uptown, amid much silken splendor," he wrote:

with divan-like beds hung from ceiling to floor with red, green
and yellow taffetas, with elaborate canopies, and hundreds of satin
cushions. Her own bed is very white and frilly with a white lace
umbrella over it that conceals a reading lamp. Japanese prints and
Indian embroideries hang around, and all sorts of odd trappings.

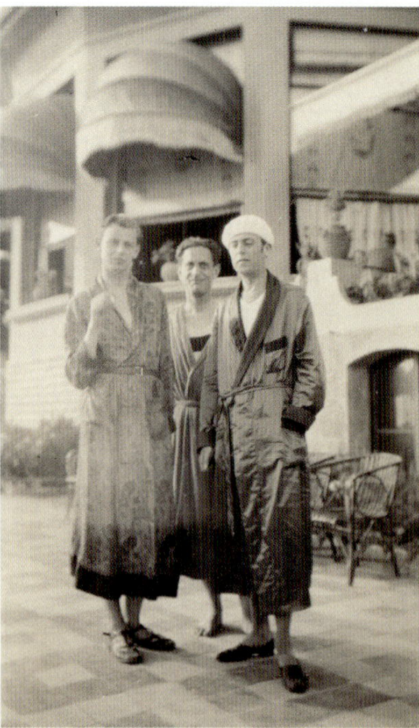

2.17 Anon., Max Ewing with Derek Patmore and Lloyd Morris, Juan-les-Pins, July 1927. Max Ewing Papers.

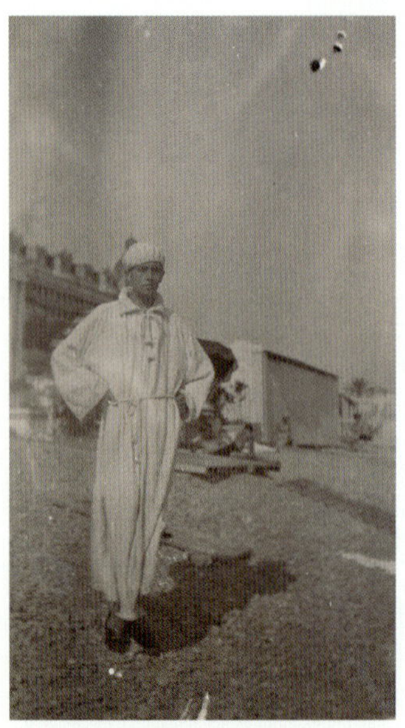

2.18 Anon., Max Ewing at Juan-les-Pins, 1927. Max Ewing Papers,.

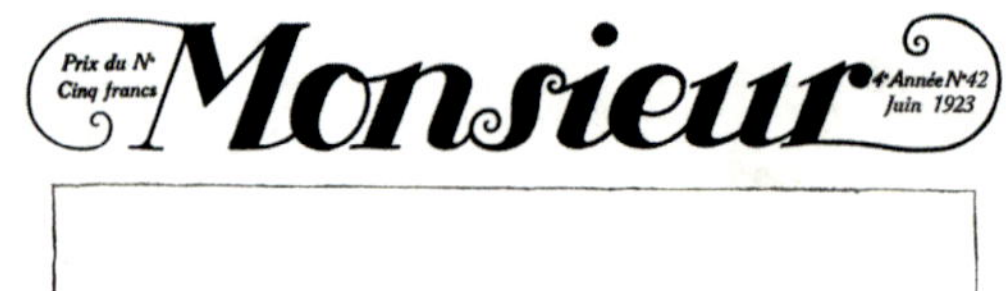

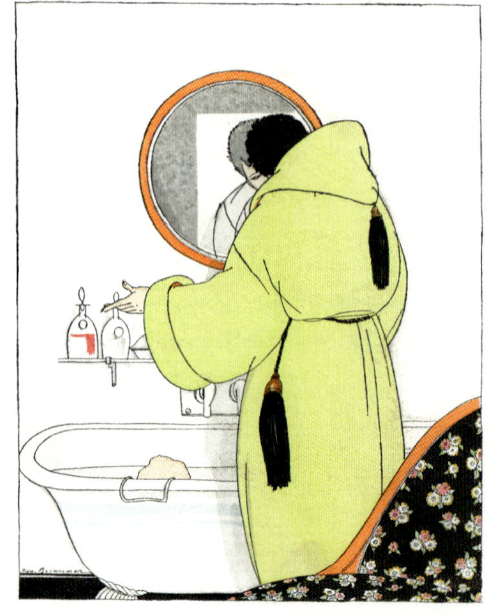

2.19 Zyg Brunner, cover of *Monsieur*, June 1923. Collection of John Potvin, Montreal.

This apartment is just a small place she uses when she is not in her big town house or at her country estate on the Hudson! After her party she took the best of it to the opening of a new night club in Harlem called Vo-De-O which was sumptuous and noisy and crowded with very well-spangled well-jewelled people. A'lelia became bored and finally went away home, leaving her guests behind her, like Queen Victoria in a temper.[88]

Another night, he took Muriel and Esther, George Lynes, and Marion Morehouse to the Neighborhood Playhouse to see the *Grand Street Follies* (for which he had written the musical score), noting that he was "terribly pleased with, and proud of, my connection to the whole thing," and hoped his parents would share that with him. When the show moved uptown to a theater on 44th Street, he saw his name in lights "visible half a block away." His mother came to visit at the end of the month and he showed her around the town and introduced her to his friends: by June, many of them were sailing back to Europe, and he too began to pack up his things and put his piano in storage.[89]

Ewing had always intended to return to Europe for another summer, and he booked passage on another Cunard ship, the *Mauretania*, to depart on June 19. Once back in Paris, he called on Margaret Anderson and other old friends, but his focus was on a planned trip to the south of France with Lloyd Morris, which, he hoped, would allow him another meeting with Glenway Wescott. He was soon caught up in the revelry of the young, well-to-do lesbian set — newly arrived from New York — including Esther Murphy, Alice DeLamar, and Eva Le Gallienne (1899–1991), the beautiful Broadway actress with whom DeLamar was then in love. These women had money to spend, and Ewing was in awe of the luxuries — fancy cars, chauffeurs, expensive hotels, beautiful clothes — that they enjoyed.[90]

He also planned to spend more time with Natalie Barney and Romaine Brooks, who once again invited him to join them on their travels in the south of France and Italy. The couple seemed to genuinely care for him, and he proved to be an excellent companion and, for Brooks in particular, a trusted confidant. In July he headed off to explore the queer entertainments at the beach resort at Juan-les-Pins, near Antibes, meeting up with Lloyd Morris and another friend named Derek Patmore (1908–72), an "English boy," who aspired to be a writer but would go on to publish a number of successful books on interior design.[91] Though he was not invited to visit the Murphys' nearby Villa America at Cap d'Antibes, Ewing did cut a fashionable figure on the beach, recording his friends in a series of snapshots that showed them posing in their robes and beach shoes (fig. 2.17). In describing the image to his parents, he noted that his new dressing gown (purchased especially for the trip) was made of gold-colored satin that "doesn't photograph well."[92] In another photo from the summer of 1927 (fig. 2.18), taken either in the south of France or at the Lido in Venice, Ewing wears a loose-fitting wrap made of thick toweling with decorative tassels, once again looking like he had walked straight out of the pages of *Monsieur* (fig. 2.19). His elegant beach attire no doubt endeared him to his queer young friends, and to the snobbish Barney and Brooks as well.

As it turned out, Lloyd Morris and Glenway Wescott had a falling out that summer and vowed never to see each other again, leaving Ewing with few opportunities to come into contact with his idol.[93] Thus, at the beginning of August, he moved on to the Italian Riviera, staying in Rapallo, where Natalie Barney and Esther Murphy met up with him on August 5. Romaine motored over from Venice so that the four friends could drive to Gardone together to visit d'Annunzio at the "palace" near Lago di Garda that "the king and Mussolini had given him … and everything else he wants in order to keep him out of their politics."[94] They would then go on to spend a few days touring together: he was excited, he wrote, and "Esther is much excited too, and neither of us can quite believe that we are actually travelling with NATALIE BARNEY who was for two years a constantly discussed phantom."[95] Snapshots of the group, taken when they stopped at Mendola and Verona, show them all in characteristic poses:

Ewing (photographed by Barney) gazes calmly at the camera in his dapper white suit, while the tall and gangly Esther — who was still madly in love with Barney — looks down shyly as she stands beside her idol, who poses as a Roman sculpture on a marble pedestal (figs. 2.20 and 2.21) in order to minimize — or, knowing the mischievous Barney, to highlight — the great difference in their heights. These photos show Barney in a way that the familiar, well-published portraits do not: young, playful, and fashionably dressed, like Esther, in a striped skirt. As Ewing wrote to his parents, after recording such a momentous event, his camera promptly gave up the ghost and had to be repaired for three days since "it was more than his Kodak could stand!"[96]

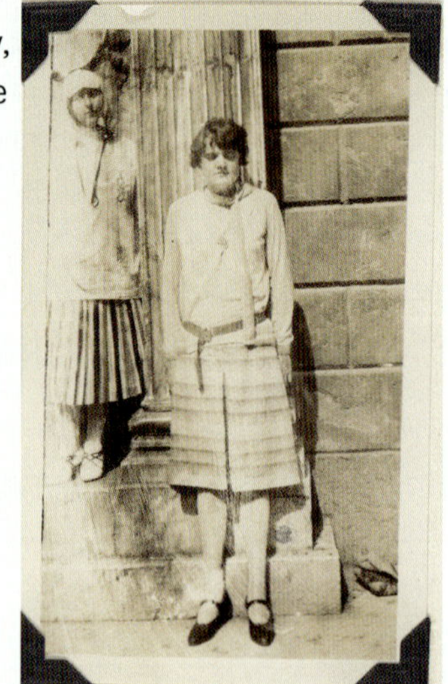

2.20 Max Ewing, *Esther Murphy and Natalie Barney* [standing on a plinth] *in Verona*, 1927. Max Ewing Papers.

The successful trip he took with these women — all three so important to Ewing and his sense of accomplishment — was the culmination of his European experience. After traveling back to Venice and lunching once more time with Romaine on August 17, 1927, he sped back to his hotel on her boat *The Romaine*. He could not resist sharing the gossip that "her boatman left the Princess Polignac to run this boat, so now Romaine and the princess are greater enemies than ever!" and then embarked on the last leg of his journey by himself.[97] Brooks planned to stay on in Venice and had rented a floor of the Lucheschi Palace, close to the Ca' Rezzonico on the Grand Canal: "She has given up her house in Capri and her place in London, and sent the furnishings here," he reported to his parents (who may not have taken an interest in that granular level of detail), "it is quite severe, with lots of gorgeous African things, a great contrast to the florid gold and marble of most of the palaces here." He also admitted it was unlikely that he would be back in Venice anytime soon, since "Mussolini is succeeding in making Italy extremely prosperous and the exchange is no longer profitable for Americans, as it still is in France."[98]

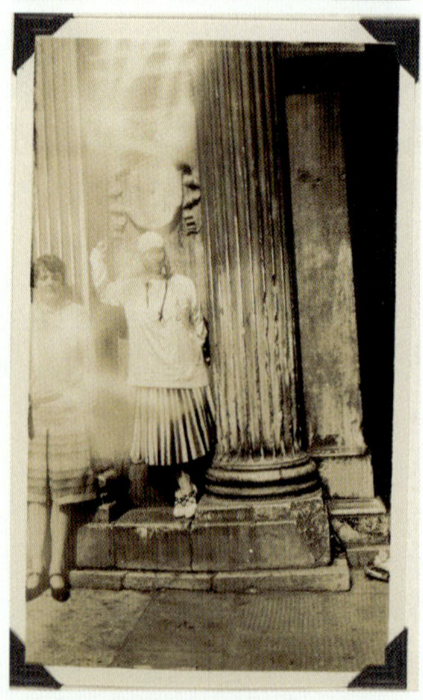

2.21 Max Ewing, *Esther Murphy and Natalie Barney in Verona*, 1927. Max Ewing Papers.

A few days later, Ewing traveled to Vienna, continuing on to Munich — which he loved — and Berlin, which he deemed "the only city over here that makes any very remarkable connection of its own with the year 1927."[99] His letters recount the details of the concerts and plays he attended, but don't include even a hint about the notorious queer nightlife of Berlin (one of Van Vechten's favorite haunts) or any other city. He appears to have spent most of his time alone, which was not a condition he was comfortable with, although once again he kept his tone light and chatty, leaving the question of his day-to-day activities unanswered. By the end of September 1927, he was in Paris again. His friends Alice DeLamar and Esther Murphy had both sailed home at the end of the summer, and "Miss Barney" was back in Santa Margarita with her new love, Dorothy Wilde, Oscar Wilde's niece. Things were quieting down. On November 16, 1927, he once again set sail for New York on the RMS *Majestic*.

MAX EWING IN LOVE

Thanks to his elegant manners and good looks, Ewing found it easy to make friends wherever he was, and he enjoyed writing about his adventures in Paris with the easy reportage of a local. As always, however, he took great care to shield his family from the private details of his queer life, editing his letters and thus leaving us with many questions as well. As we know, he spared no effort in reporting on the parties, concerts, and dinners he attended. His vanity was flattered by the attention he received, and he was particularly excited by the invitations he got from artists, which enabled him to pose and preen as the object of another's gaze: he was delighted to share in the pleasure that his good looks gave them. In a long letter to his parents, written on May 17, 1926, he described one such his experience:

> Two days ago I was lunching at Duval's on the Rue de Rivoli
> when Walter Lowenfels [a well-to-do young poet and aspiring
> publisher he had met through Muriel Draper in New York] came
> along with a quite beautiful bearded man who proved to be Mark
> Tobey. ... in the middle of the meal Mark Tobey decided he had
> to make a portrait of me. He asked me if I would sit for him every day
> next week and I hope to be able to though I am going to London
> the 27th and we are both pretty busy. ... Yesterday AM I was invited
> to Mme Romaine Brooks' to see her portraits of d'Annunzio and
> many other people. She said she too would like to paint me
> and asked me back next Wednesday PM.[100]

Although neither Mark Tobey nor Romaine Brooks were in those years the famous artists they would later become, Ewing was proud of their attention and enjoyed the long hours he spent with them. If Brooks ever completed a portrait of Max Ewing, it has yet to come to light, but we are fortunate to have the drawing that Tobey completed in 1926 (fig. 2.22). While he jokingly complained to his parents that Tobey's efforts made him look a "little bit more Oscar Wilde than necessary," he confessed that he liked the picture a lot: "I'm wearing a cape and scarf and topaz," he reported, "and he has drawn in a most amusing background," noting that the work would be exhibited in New York the following winter.[101]

Ewing had traveled to Europe in 1926 and 1927 for many reasons, not least of which was his fervent desire to leave the banality and the straitlaced conventions of the American Midwest behind. He wanted to meet new people, to hear great music and see art, to experience great cities like Paris, London, Vienna, and Berlin firsthand, and to hobnob with wealthy socialites in their theater boxes and palaces on the Grand Canal. From his earliest days in Paris, he had sought out the queer, bohemian world that he had heard so much about, observing the many varieties of love and friendship that were possible if one got far enough away from places like Pioneer, Ohio. He also discovered that there were many different ways to be committed to another person, or to a group of people, one loved: as we have seen, first and foremost among his teachers were the American women he befriended — Gertrude and Alice, Natalie and Romaine and Lily, Margaret, Jane and Georgette — but queer men like Glenway and Monroe and Ewing's new friend George Lynes also opened up new worlds of

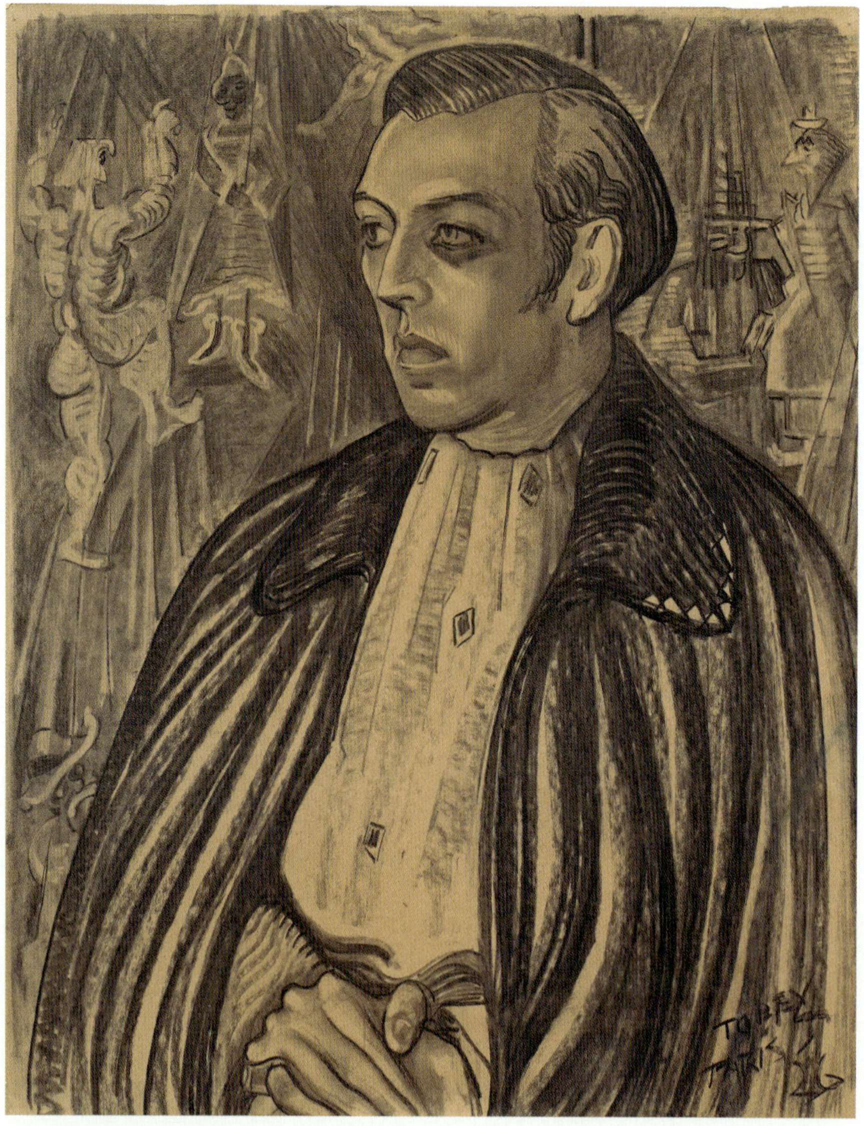

2.22 Mark Tobey, *Portrait of Max Ewing*, 1926, charcoal on paper, 25½ × 20¼ in. (64.8 × 51.4 cm). Birmingham Museum of Art. Gift of Mr. Charles W. Ireland in honor of his mother, Mrs. Pauline Ireland Van Sant, 1979.277. Image © 2018 Mark Tobey / Seattle Art Museum, Artists Rights Society (ARS), New York.

unconventional emotional and sexual experience to him, even if those were often held at a remove.[102] Of course, that was also one of the great lessons he had learned from Van Vechten and Marinoff in New York: they may have fought and struggled, walked out and come back together again on a regular basis, but (like Robert Chanler and Louise Hellstrom and Clem Randolph) they stayed committed to one another no matter who else they slept with, queer or otherwise.

For his part, Ewing seemed happier watching others fall in love than losing his own head, or his heart — at least as far as we can tell from his letters to his parents — but there was one great exception to this rule: his beloved Muriel Draper was never far from his thoughts. Moreover, although the "beautiful" Mark Tobey was thirteen years his senior, their meeting in Paris confirmed that they had quite a bit in common: both men were gay, and both were in love with Muriel Draper. For years Tobey drew her incessantly, sending her caricatures that lovingly described her unconventional looks, her commentaries on people and things, and the peculiar way in which she lived.[103]

Of course, we don't know what they talked about during the long sessions in the studio when Tobey drew Max Ewing's portrait, but we do know that Ewing went to some lengths to analyze the nature of his attachment to Draper, placing his friendship with Mark Tobey in that context. "There is not any limit to the breadth of beauty which I want to give my life," he wrote:

> More and more I realize that I am not a person who was cut out to do just one thing and I cannot help it that my interest continues to embrace more things than piano-playing. … But it is more and more apparent to me that people are important, or great, or whatever you want to call it, on account of what they <u>are</u> more than what they <u>do</u>. It is Muriel of course who has demonstrated this most clearly. She is regarded on 2 continents as the greatest woman in the world, and she actually <u>does</u> nothing. She just <u>is</u>. Mark Tobey is returning to America in the fall because he says that an hour's conversation with her is a greater inspirational stimulus to him than all of Europe and everyone in it. My sensitivity and receptivity and reaction to things and people in general is such that I know I shall someday <u>write</u> about it all, as well as play. It is a long way to a complete finding of myself, but I shall get there, and I know my <u>direction</u>.[104]

Like all of the young men who contended for Draper's attention and sexual favors in the late 1920s, Ewing's relationship with her was complicated: they shared a close physical and emotional intimacy for many years, but he knew well that he could never fully possess her. Indeed, he may have come first in her affections — or thought he did — for a time, but he was well aware that he was not her only suitor. She wouldn't have it any other way.

Perhaps that was the reason that Tobey sought him out and seemed to genuinely care for him as a friend.[105] When the two men returned to New York in the winter of 1927, Tobey presented him with a painting entitled *Draper's Training School*, now lost but preserved in a photo showing Ewing surrounded by the books and art in his home (fig. 2.23). The entry for the painting in Ewing's catalogue of the *Max Ewing Collection of Incredible Portraits*, a supplement to Ewing's 1928 catalogue of the *Max Ewing Collection of Extraordinary Portraits*, described the painting as follows: "Muriel Draper Painted Red, Lying on Elevated Track, With Entourage of Acrobats, Tents, Negroes and Trains."[106] Ewing had the picture framed, and, as the snapshot clearly shows, he displayed it prominently in his apartment.

Ewing tried to keep Draper close in every way possible: even when he was surrounded by the wonders of Europe, and by the many brilliant and beautiful men and women he encountered there, he yearned for her company and approval. The tone of his letters is unfailingly ardent and tender: in late May 1926,

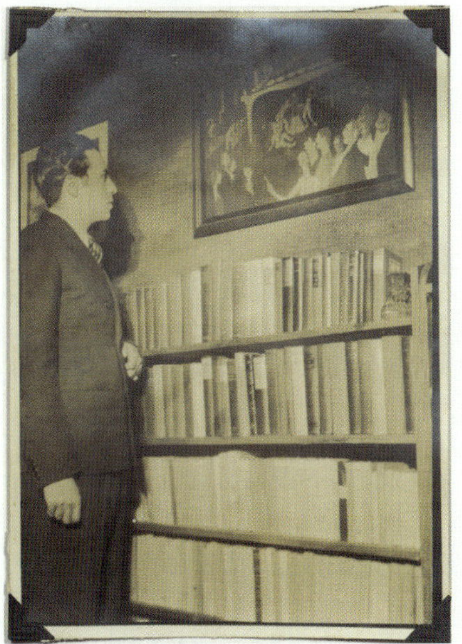

2.23 Anon., Max Ewing in his apartment with Mark Tobey's *Draper's Training School*, 1930. Max Ewing Papers.

for example, he wrote a note to her confessing that he "needed to hear" from her that morning, adding that it was "the first time in years that I have needed … to hear anything from anyone."[107] He often pleaded with her to "come over straightaway" and join him in his travels; a number of letters end with the words "I want you," and in one he simply signed off, "I kiss your eyes." In June 1926, he described his recollection of their first meeting at the Ritz a year earlier: "That night has around it, more and more, all the time, a hot halo, and always since it everyone but you has steadily shrunk, collapsed, or vanished from me. They … seem like pieces of people, or like things Augustus John didn't finish! For me only you is entire, and I knew that as well when I went to Ohio last summer as I did when I came here this spring."[108] Whatever the exact nature of their intimacy, it was passionate, physical, and life-changing.

GLENWAY WESCOTT, MONROE WHEELER, AND GEORGE PLATT LYNES
Muriel Draper may have been the love of Max Ewing's life, but she was by no means his only passion. As a young teenager, he became an ardent fan of movie stars, opera singers, and real-life heroes; as an adult, the habit of loving glamour from afar never left him. He embraced celebrity in all its forms, filling his scrapbooks and the walls of his *Gallery* with images that kept his beloveds close to him.[109] Worshipping idols from afar was a comfortable and familiar role, even as he came to understand himself — in college or before — as decidedly queer. He became an ardent fan of Carl Van Vechten's, and he began to form an enduring crush on the beautiful, openly gay novelist Glenway Wescott, whose work had begun to appear in literary magazines. Ewing added his portrait — in multiple versions — to his scrapbooks as well.

As noted earlier, since 1925, Wescott had lived with his lover Monroe Wheeler in the south of France, and before he sailed to Europe in the spring of 1926, Ewing sent Wescott a fan letter at his hotel in Villefranche-sur-Mer.[110] When Wescott eventually responded, he was beside himself with joy:

> Put it down, Parents, in your book of my life, that on this first day of April 1926, I received a good-six typewritten letter from one Glenway Wescott in Villefranche France, a letter filled with greatest appreciation, thanks, and good wishes, a letter of the highest cordiality which leaves me to feeling like Parsifal after he has found the Holy Grail, or Perry after he has reached a Pole, or something. … Glenway Wescott was my last sea, the one human being on earth who refused to even recognize my existence, and now here he comes with a letter of thanks.[111]

While traveling in the south of France with Romaine Brooks in July 1926, Ewing took a step closer: he motored over to Villefranche from his hotel in Monte Carlo in hopes of seeing Wescott and "his man," as he referred to him, and while it isn't clear if he actually achieved his goal or simply made the pilgrimage to observe the scene, he soaked up the storied atmosphere of the town where another of his idols, the writer Jean Cocteau, lived in the Hotel Welcome. As he reported to his parents on July 23, "Glenway Wescott and his man live there in the winter. Cocteau goes there and Mary Butts goes there. They all live at the Hotel Welcome, and it became the most cosmopolitan little community, in the midst of the most primitive surroundings."[112] On July 29, however, he wrote from Italy in a state of great excitement, reporting that he had actually met his hero: "The day we left was one of the most wonderful of my life," he gushed:

> We sat for hours at breakfast on a terrace with Glenway Wescott. He does not yet know who I am. … Glenway is the most charming personality, the most handsome boy, the most brilliant talker (except Muriel) and most informed and distinguished mind I have ever encountered. … Things turn out as I want always. I go for years after something or someone and I never fail getting it. He has always wanted to meet Romaine.[113]

While he had to admit that Wescott had no idea who he was, Ewing was in awe — and kept his distance.

Ewing's romanticized, diffident response to Wescott is revealing: as the reaction of a closeted young man to the sight of his beloved, it is categorically different from the bold, almost predatory, sexual move that his new friend George Platt Lynes would make when he first encountered Wescott and Wheeler in New York in the winter of 1927.[114] As the story would be told for years after, at that first meeting in the couple's hotel room, the importunate Lynes caught sight of a photograph of Wheeler — who was not even present at the time — and promptly fell head over heels in love. He "took it for granted" — as Wheeler later recalled — that Monroe "was to be his," despite the fact that Wescott and Wheeler, still in their mid-twenties, had already been in a committed, though nonmonogamous, relationship for some eight years.[115] From that day until February 1943, when Lynes informed the two men by letter that he was leaving them, the triad remained unbroken, weathering the many challenges that such a complex constellation of relationships presented.[116]

It is important to note that Lynes's fateful meeting with Wescott and Wheeler took place a number of months after Ewing had first encountered Wescott in France, but their long-standing friendship brought Ewing a great deal closer to the couple than he had been before: throughout the spring and summer of 1927, he could observe the ups and downs of Lynes's lovesick passion for Wheeler, and he knew well the complicated, shell-shocked reactions of all three men. Unlike Ewing's highly mediated relationships with Draper and Wescott, or the fantasy world of queer friends and lovers he created in his *Gallery of Extraordinary Portraits*, this unlikely triad and its sexual intimacies was real and challenging. Lynes was smitten and persistent and — perhaps because he saw himself so clearly as Monroe's lover, even when that meant literally inserting himself and cutting Glenway out of the picture (fig. 2.24) — his ardor was unstoppable.[117]

2.24 George Platt Lynes, *Self-Portrait with Monroe Wheeler*, collage of gelatin silver prints, image: 7½ × 4¾ in. (19.1 × 12.1 cm); sheet: 7⅞ × 5 in. (20 × 12.7 cm). Philadelphia Art Museum. Purchased with the Lola Downin Peck Fund, 2015.

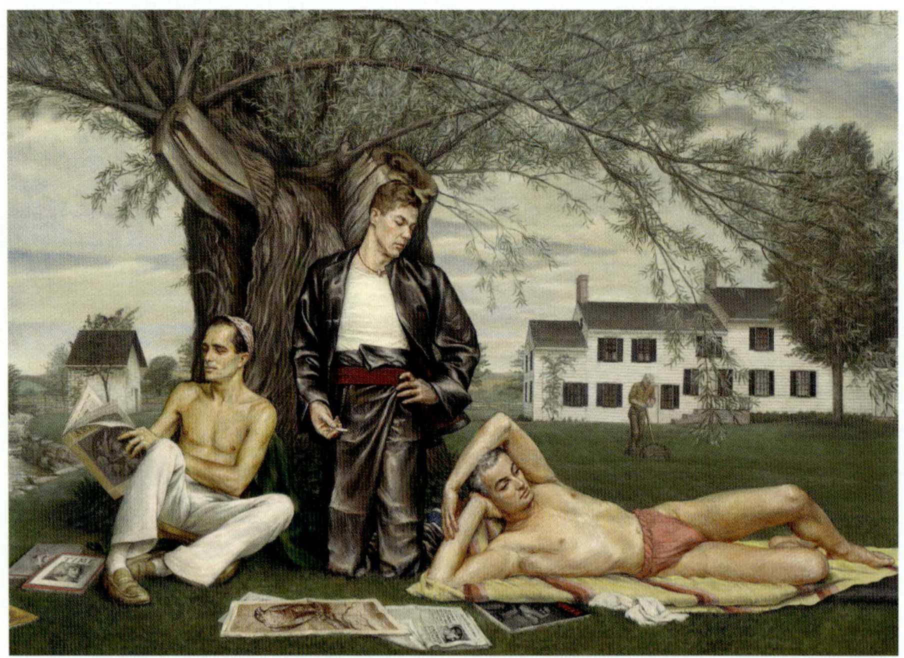

2.25 Paul Cadmus, *Stone Blossom: A Conversation Piece*, 1939–40. Museum of Fine Arts, Boston. Juliana Cheney Edwards Collection and Seth K. Sweetser Fund, 2010.753.

The complex family that Lynes, Wheeler, and Wescott created would later be brilliantly depicted in Paul Cadmus's *Stone Blossom: A Conversation Piece* (1940) (fig. 2.25), a portrait of the three men resting in the landscape around their country home. There Wescott, dressed in a silk suit (perhaps a gift from Monroe, who had traveled to Japan a few years earlier) kneels awkwardly between the two men and gazes to his left at the reclining, seminude Lynes, who like Wheeler — depicted on the opposite side — seems lost in his own thoughts, isolated yet content. Lynes's beauty and self-awareness are unmistakable, as are the supreme self-possession of Wheeler, and Glenway's awkward position between them. Although Glenway would confess his insecurities to his private diary in these years (noting in particular that George acted like a falconer who could send him off like a falcon to pursue his own love interests, secure in the knowledge that he would return), the painting suggests a certain stasis and intimacy; it is also a rare image of queer domesticity, offering us an unlikely view of a private moment of psychological complexity as seen through the eyes of their friend.[118]

Though Ewing and Lynes would remain close friends for many years, there is no record of whether they ever talked about George's ongoing affair or broached the possibility of Ewing's feelings of jealousy in the face of George's intimacy with his beloved Glenway Wescott.[119] While the incomplete nature of the archival evidence leaves us guessing, the tone of Ewing's surviving letters certainly confirms our overall sense that he preferred the distanced adoration of a fan and admirer to the messy intimacy and emotional volatility of the sort that Lynes and his two lovers endured. Indeed, Ewing would later joke with his friend Esther Murphy that his passion for Glenway Wescott was as hopeless as hers for Natalie Barney.[120]

Both men figured prominently in Ewing's *Gallery of Extraordinary Portraits*, and for reasons that we can only guess at, Ewing kept a picture of Lynes, shown posing by the harbor at Villefranche in 1928, in his own album of travel

photographs (fig. 2.26). The photo shows him in the way
that Ewing no doubt wished for himself: relaxed, tanned,
and sexy, wearing the fashionable attire of a *matelot*
(sailor), with a striped jersey and bell-bottom trousers,
showing off his trim body to greatest effect. This outfit
would become the enduring uniform of the younger,
cosmopolitan generation in New York, London, Paris,
and the south of France for many years to come: Ewing
owned a similar striped jersey that he wore in a number
of snapshots, most of them taken not in Villefranche
but by the lake at his parents' summer cottage in Clear
Lake, Indiana.

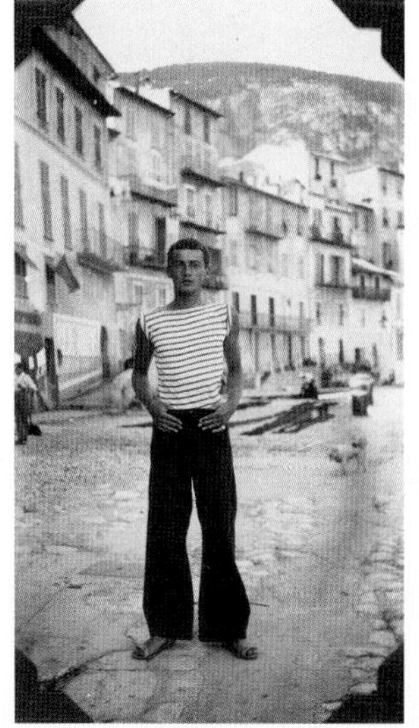

2.26 Anon, George Platt
Lynes at Villefranche,
1928. Max Ewing Papers.

Given all of the emotional energy that Ewing
expended on distant idols like Draper and Wescott, it
was perhaps inevitable that he would be unlucky in love
when he turned his romantic attention to the real-life, flesh-and-blood young
men he encountered in Europe. Far from the constraints of Pioneer, or the
gossipy, tight-knit circle in New York, he was free to experiment, but his letters
merely offer only a glimpse of the many unhappy love affairs, always short-lived
and tragic, that he pursued while he was there. While he is never explicit —
the bulk of the surviving letters in the archive were written to his parents, after
all — it is possible to read between the lines: he often described his romantic
feelings and his crushes on the "boys" whose beauty or charm he admired.
It isn't at all surprising that he didn't go into detail: even queer people themselves
often preferred to use the catchall label of "friend" in most circumstances,
and one would hardly expect him to spell things out for his parents in any case.
Moreover, as with love letters generally, forthright and explicit discussions of sex
were generally confined to letters exchanged by lovers themselves — letters
of precisely the kind that we don't have in this case. We are left in the dark about
the details, which is no doubt the way that Ewing, and many others before and
since, preferred it.

CONSTANT LAMBERT

Ewing's two-week affair with the composer Constant Lambert (1905–51)
(fig. 2.27) — aged twenty-one to Ewing's twenty-three, and, like Glenway Wescott,
exactly the type of fair-haired, androgynous young man that he was most
attracted to — began at the end of May 1926 with an invitation from Lorna Lindsley
to meet "a divine English boy who wrote the score of one of the new Russian
Ballets."[121] He was immediately smitten, describing him to Draper on June 1 as
"twenty-one and magnificent."[122] He had attended the premiere of the Diaghilev
production of *Romeo and Juliet* — with music by Lambert and sets by Max Ernst
and Joan Miró — on May 18, where he was seated in Diaghilev's box along
with Lambert, Lady Rothermere, Romaine Brooks, Picasso, and others. For
Draper's benefit, he described in detail the famous *Protestation* mounted by Louis
Aragon, André Breton, and other surrealists, complete with whistles and printed
handbills (he saved one and sent it along with his letter) that rained down on
theatergoers from the balcony above. By June 8, Ewing told his parents that he
"had seen no one but Lambert" over the previous weekend, going to lunch with

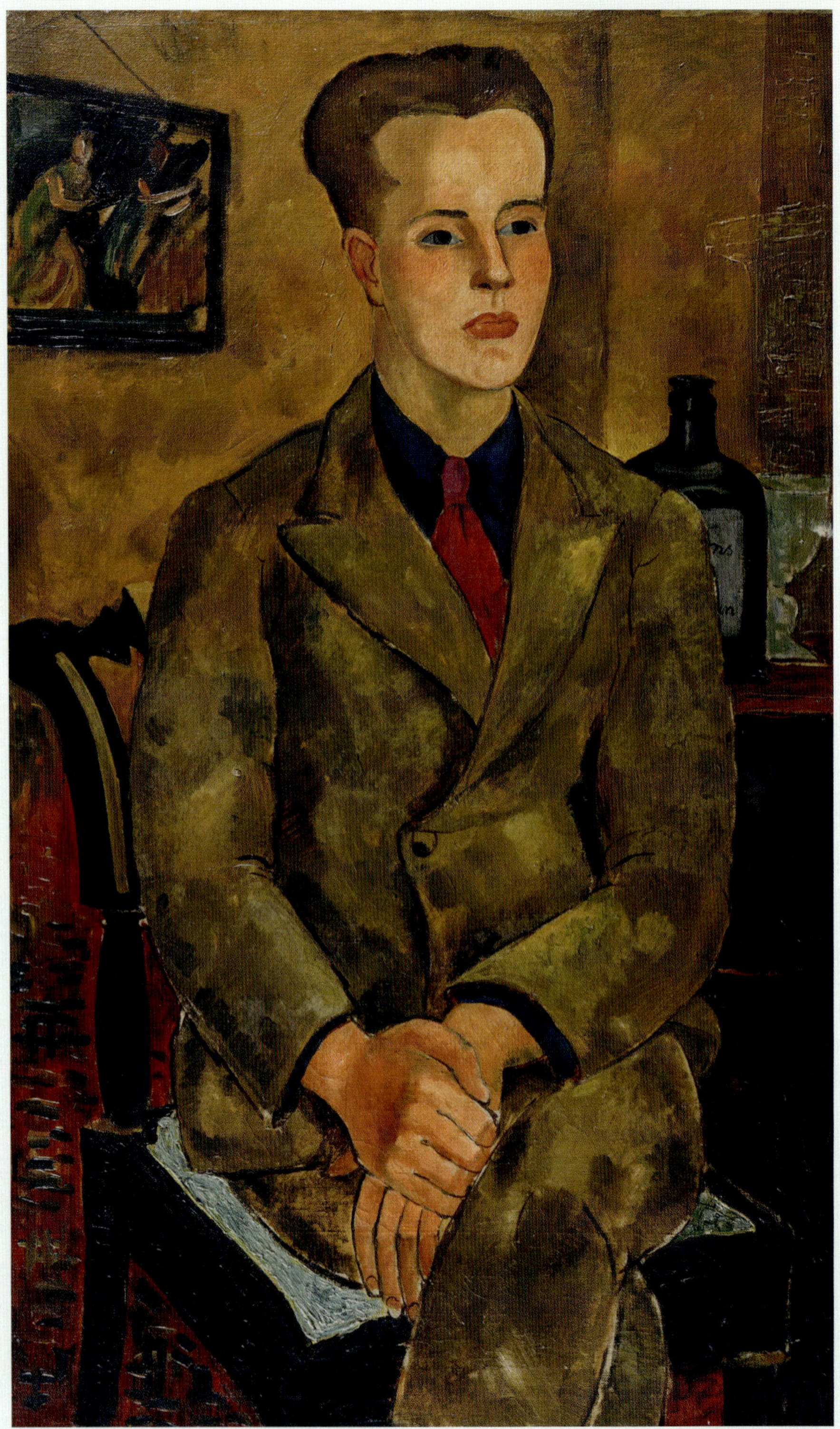

2.27 Christopher Wood, *Constant Lambert*, 1926. National Portrait Gallery, London.

him in the country, walking with him along the banks of the Seine to St. Cloud, and then attending an opera performance by his beloved Mary Garden.[123]

On June 11, 1926, Ewing noted that Lambert and his patron Lady Rothermere would shortly be heading to London with the production, and he informed his parents that he planned to follow them.[124] On more than one occasion, he confided to Draper that he found Lambert "distracting," but provided few details, noting only that after the Garden performance they had "sat up the entire rest of the night on a Montparnasse sidewalk," and seen the sun come up on the Place du Panthéon "on a frigid sad pink morning."[125] By the time he wrote to his parents about his adventures with Constance Lambert, however, the relationship was already upended by emotional turmoil: "I became terribly tangled up, emotionally, with Constant Lambert," he admitted, "and I think I'll not see him for a few weeks now."[126] He confessed that he had hoped to take Lambert to Venice for a week in August, explaining that Lambert was "by far the most delightful person I have found in Europe." Clearly this plan would never come to fruition: the intensity of the connection had set off warning bells for one or both of them, and suddenly the relationship was over. In an extraordinary note to Lambert, dated only "Tuesday" (probably June 15), Ewing backpedaled furiously, begging Lambert to see him again: "Constant Lambert: Let me see you one time before you leave Paris — Wednesday at lunch, or Thursday at tea, or whenever you say. But I do not want that unpleasantly fantastic scene this morning to be a final one. And I shall not see you in London. Max Ewing."[127] In the end, the two men parted without further contact, though Ewing was in the audience for Lambert's recitation of Edith Sitwell's poems in *Façade*, an experimental collaboration with music by William Walton at the New Chenil Galleries in London on June 29. He sent the program for the concert to Draper, along with one for a private performance in Paris of Ezra Pound's musical setting of the poetry of François Villon on which he wrote, "I had to miss this for that."[128]

What Lambert — who married twice and conducted a long-standing love affair with the dancer Margot Fonteyn in the 1930s — made of all this is not recorded. Despite the evidence of his intimacy with Ewing, and the exclusively homosocial world in which he lived, his biographer Andrew Motion notes that "despite spending a great deal of his life surrounded by homosexuals," he was "undeviatingly heterosexual."[129] In a world that tolerated any sort of intimacy but demanded complete discretion, the "unpleasantly fantastic scene," had been precisely the sort of thing that Ewing — and no doubt Lambert as well — sought to avoid at all costs. Both men adored the theatrics of stage and screen, but controlled their public images with great care. Ewing's yearning for distant stars like his beloved opera divas and, of course, Glenway Wescott, or even Muriel Draper, was a significant part of the persona that he constructed over the years, a mask that deflected scrutiny with elegance and a touch of camp humor. Early in their friendship, Muriel Draper had told him — in her insightful but rather tactless way — that she saw in him a "vicious, cerebral histrionism," and that some in their circle resented the unflappable composure that enabled him to keep his true feelings to himself.[130] With characteristic aplomb, and more than a touch of practiced self-preservation, he summed up his feelings after seeing the London performance of Edith Sitwell's *Façade* in April 1926: "It is odd the way geography affects feelings — in Paris C. Lambert interested me immensely, in London not at all."[131]

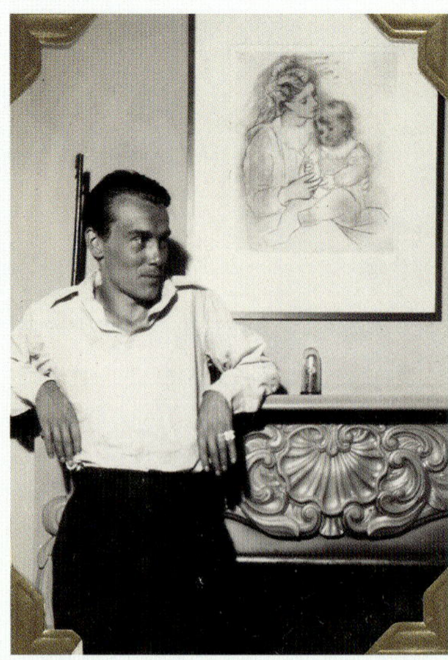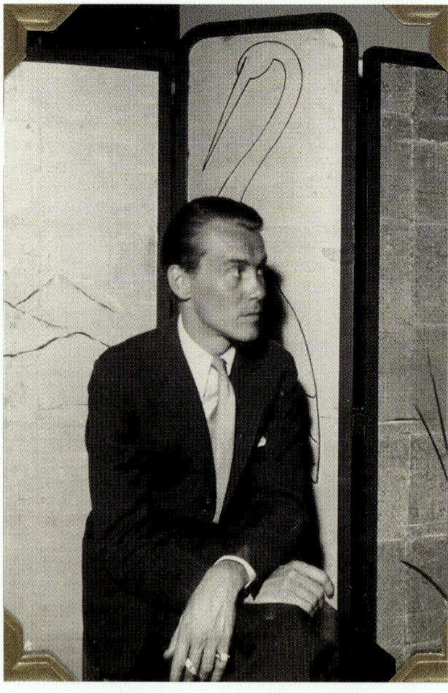

2.28 Max Ewing, *George Dangerfield*, 1932. Max Ewing Papers.

In any case, by the time Ewing and Lambert encountered one another again in London the following year, in November 1927, both had moved on, although Ewing clearly still valued the connection with his successful friend enough to remind his parents that "Constant has written a new ballet which Nijinska has just produced in Buenos Aires," adding, "When Constant left Paris a year ago last summer we agreed to never see each other again, and we did not see each other in London when I was here before. But that is all over now and everything is all right."

GEORGE DANGERFIELD

In any case, Ewing had already embarked on another affair, this time with a young Oxford graduate whom he had met in Paris (fig. 2.28). George Dangerfield was a year younger than Max, and a writer who would become, in the 1930s, the literary editor of *Vanity Fair* and, much later, a prize-winning historian and professor at the University of California, Santa Barbara.[132] The uneven pattern of their relationship is a familiar one to us now, though in this instance the shame and heartbreak seem to have been shared by both men: on October 22, 1927, Max wrote from Paris to say that his piano lessons with Marcelle Meyer were going well, that he was studying hard and seeing "George Dangerfield every day," adding that "he could be quite content to see no one else for a period of time." Six days later, Ewing wrote again with bad news, describing his broken heart and confusion in the aftermath of their breakup: he had hoped that Dangerfield "might be coming to America with me to stay," and "for a week or so it seemed so. Now he has lost his courage about leaving a girl he is engaged to — and we both cry ourselves sick every day. It's all over now save the aching which will go on in both of us for a long time. But the hardest aches end, and I'm ready to sail with Derek" — his friend Derek Patmore, whom he had met a few months earlier at Juan-les-Pins — "when he is ready."[133]

The end of this love affair was hard, but Ewing had clearly grown up a lot since the scene with Constant Lambert in 1926. Thus, he ended this letter to his parents by summoning up the unruffled countenance of the worldly American that he hoped (and wanted them to think) he had become: "I work — work — work," he wrote; "The weather remains glorious … The Luxembourg Gardens are a blaze of flowers, and just the beauty of them draws tears. Paris is not 'Gay Paree' — it is a city of pasts and tears. New York is the place to be. No one has time there for tears." By October 31, 1927, the case was closed: "The George Dangerfield thing is over," he wrote to his parents:

> I went with him to hear Mary Garden at the *Opera Comique* yesterday, and I shall never see him again. It is very hard on him. He could not bring himself to go away with me. But now that he has known me he cannot bear to go back to his former life in England. He talks of committing suicide, and if he does I don't know how I'll stand it. He is in such a state of hysteria he might do it.[134]

Characteristically, Ewing didn't stick around long enough to find out. By mid-November, he was on his way home again to New York.[135]

THE GALLERY IN THE CLOSET

As soon as Ewing was back in the city and settled into his new apartment on the top floor of the Life Building at 19 West 31st Street, he embarked on creating a 3D scrapbook of photographs and clippings, the *Gallery of Extraordinary Portraits*, which he installed on the walls of his walk-in closet. His plan was to transform his new place into a salon and theater of memory, where words, images, the sounds of conversation, music, and laughter — sometimes enhanced by theatrical lighting — served to transport him and his friends to a glamorous world of fantasy. In this way, the men and women that he had come to know in Europe — Romaine and Natalie, Constant Lambert, Stravinsky, and the dancers of the Ballets Russes — could be made real again for the benefit of his friends in New York. He added a number of self-portraits to the display, thereby including himself in the illustrious group as both a participant and physically present narrator.[136]

For their part, these friends left barely any record at all of Max Ewing. Gertrude Stein immediately wrote to Van Vechten in July 1934 after she was informed of Ewing's suicide, praising his youthful poetry, recalling, "Poor Max Ewing, with his little mouth and pretty ways."[137] Only the designer Derek Patmore, his queer, young friend from Nice and, later, Paris and New York, remembered him in his memoirs, writing many decades later that Ewing had been "a habitué of the [Draper] household" and "a gifted young pianist" who had studied with Marcelle Meyer but "become infected by the mad 'exoticism' of the twenties." "When I first knew Max in Paris," he recalled:

> he had fallen a victim to the sailor craze initiated by Jean Cocteau and Francis Carco, and exploited by Diaghilev in his ballet *Les Matelots*. The French sailor had become a literary symbol — he represented the desire for escape and adventure, and the same time he symbolized a wayward innocence. Max Ewing was so infatuated with these ideas that he used to dress up as a French *matelot* and wander about the Paris streets in this costume. Even in New York he was always being tempted by some new eccentricity, and Muriel Draper encouraged him in his exploits.

Patmore went on to note that Ewing had been "an outstanding pianist" who "might have had a great career had not one of his fingers suddenly become paralysed," adding that he later wrote "one witty novel, *Going Somewhere*" in the style of Evelyn Waugh. As he looked back on that period of his life, Patmore summed Ewing up with the detached kindness of someone who had survived when his friend had not: "With his pale white face, side-whiskers, and whimsical smile, Max was a personality of unusual charm. But he could never come to terms with life. A few years later, he committed suicide by walking into a lake [*sic*] in the Middle West carrying two loaded-down suitcases."[138]

Even with many friends and admirers, it would seem that Max Ewing faded into obscurity soon after his death. Nevertheless, two extraordinary portraits created by Romaine Brooks during her time in New York City in 1935–38 — one of Carl Van Vechten (fig. 2.29) from early 1936, and one of Muriel Draper from 1938 (fig. 2.30) — suggest that Ewing was perhaps not alone in memorializing his friendships through images. Brooks's portraits have long puzzled historians, yet viewed through the lens of the new evidence detailing her intimacy with Ewing over the course of two long summers in 1926 and 1927, it seems possible that they represent her private effort to remember her friend in the way she knew best.[139]

The circumstances surrounding these commissions remains obscure. The art historian Betsy Fahlman suggests that Van Vechten may have paid for Draper's portrait because her own finances would never have allowed for such an expense (he later acquired the work for his own collection in any case), but in the absence of any evidence to the contrary, it is worth speculating that Brooks — who always used her paintings to memorialize personal connections, and who didn't need the fees — independently embarked on both projects as a way of getting to know the two people who had meant more to Ewing than anyone else in the world.[140]

It is easy to imagine that over the course of their brief but intense friendship, Ewing had spoken with Romaine Brooks about his adoration for both Van Vechten and Draper, and it requires little imagination to reconstruct the language he would have used, since we know it so well from his letters. Could Brooks — who came to New York City expressly to reapply for US citizenship and not to paint — have filled up her time in the city by looking into the faces and drawing out the stories of Max Ewing's beloved mentors? Ultimately, the ghostly images of the young African American men who peer out from behind Van Vechten's chair in his portrait, as with the malevolent, basilisk-like figure that emerges in Draper's unfinished likeness, seem to suggest something of what Brooks knew or had heard from Stein or others about her subjects' distinctive passions and their hold on her young friend. Derek Patmore remembered Draper as "a vivid potent personality," who "enjoyed having power over people"; was it possible, he wondered, that "she was not too dominating a force for some of the young American writers and poets who felt drawn to her house"?[141] Her fixed stare in Brooks's portrait and the "razor-sharp profile," described by Brooks-specialist Cassandra Langer suggest little of her much-vaunted charm but say a great deal about the authority she wielded over her young acolytes, Ewing in particular.[142]

These questions cannot be answered at present. Perhaps new evidence will come to light to guide research into Brooks's motivations for making these

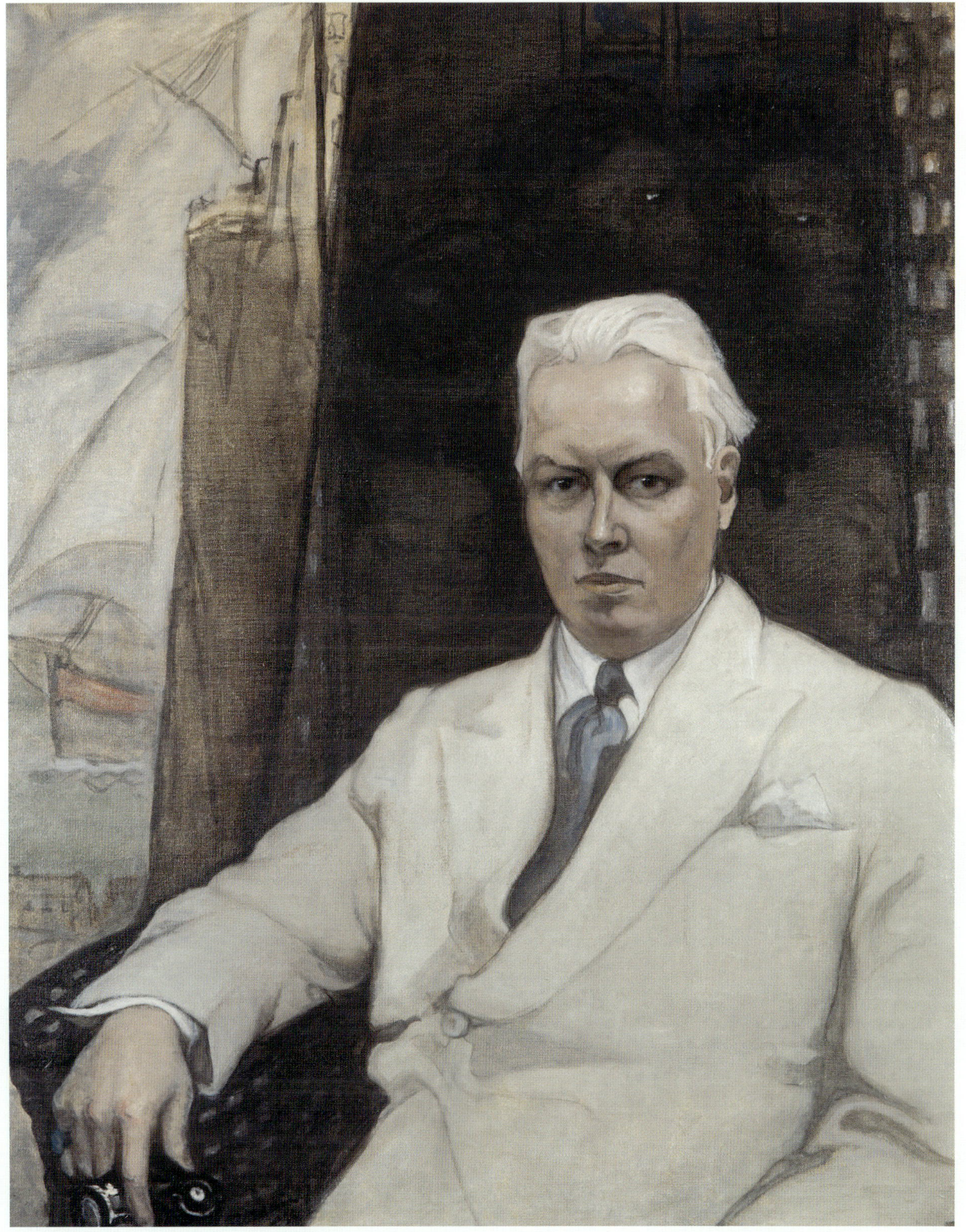

2.29 Romaine Brooks, *Carl Van Vechten*, 1936, oil on canvas, 46 × 38 in. (116.8 × 96.5 cm). Carl Van Vechten Papers.

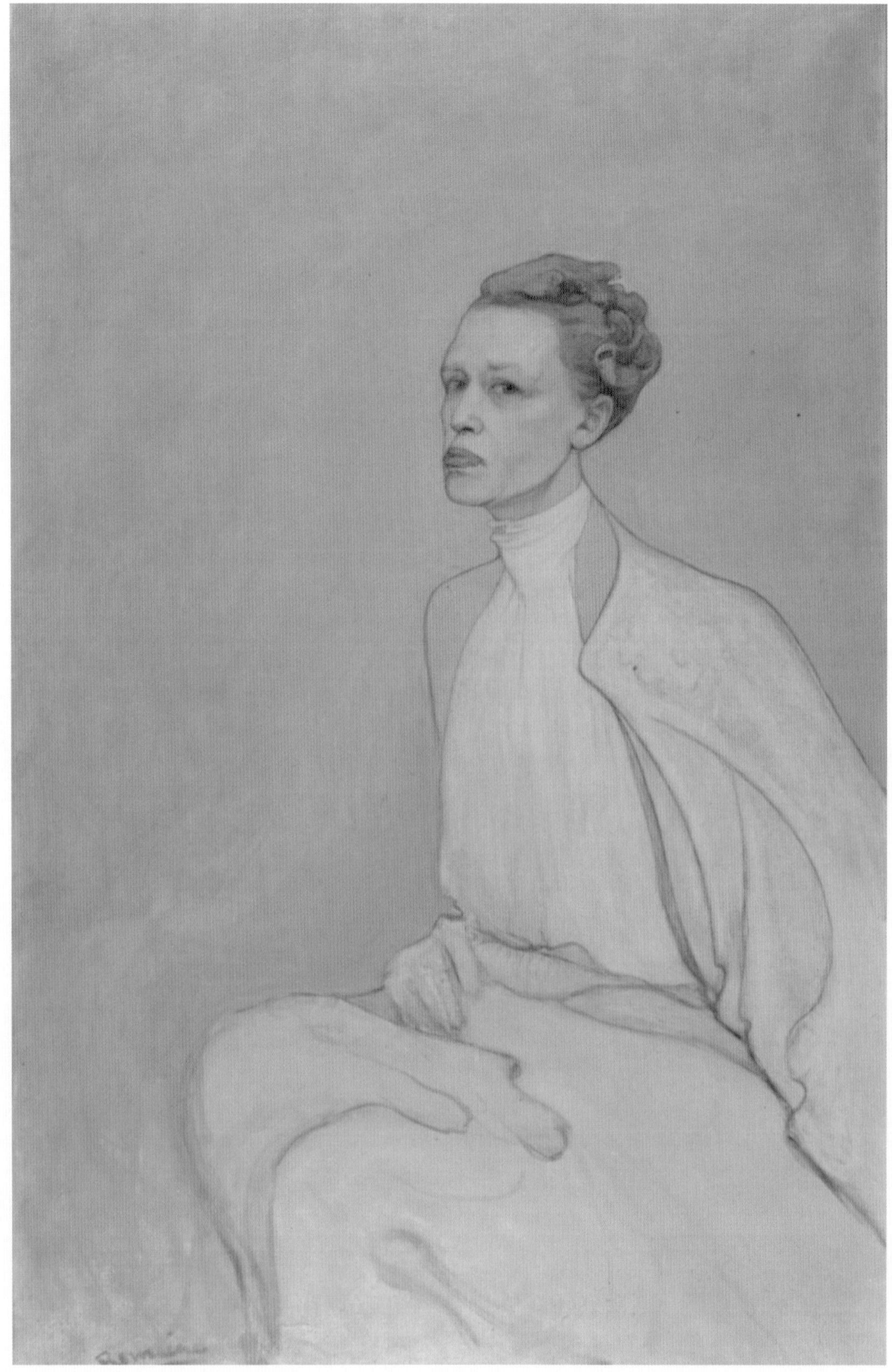

2.30 Romaine Brooks, *Muriel Draper*, 1938, oil on canvas, 46 × 30 in. (117 × 76.5 cm). Carl Van Vechten Papers.

works, her only two portraits from her stay in the United States.[143] In the meantime, the portraits, donated to Yale together as part of Van Vechten's archive, can serve as a memorial to the improbable intimacy that Ewing and Brooks shared in Europe — a triumph that buoyed Ewing up and, indeed, shaped both his social standing in New York and his view of himself when he returned to the city in November 1927.

Chapter 3

THE GALLERY OF EXTRAORDINARY PORTRAITS, 1928–33

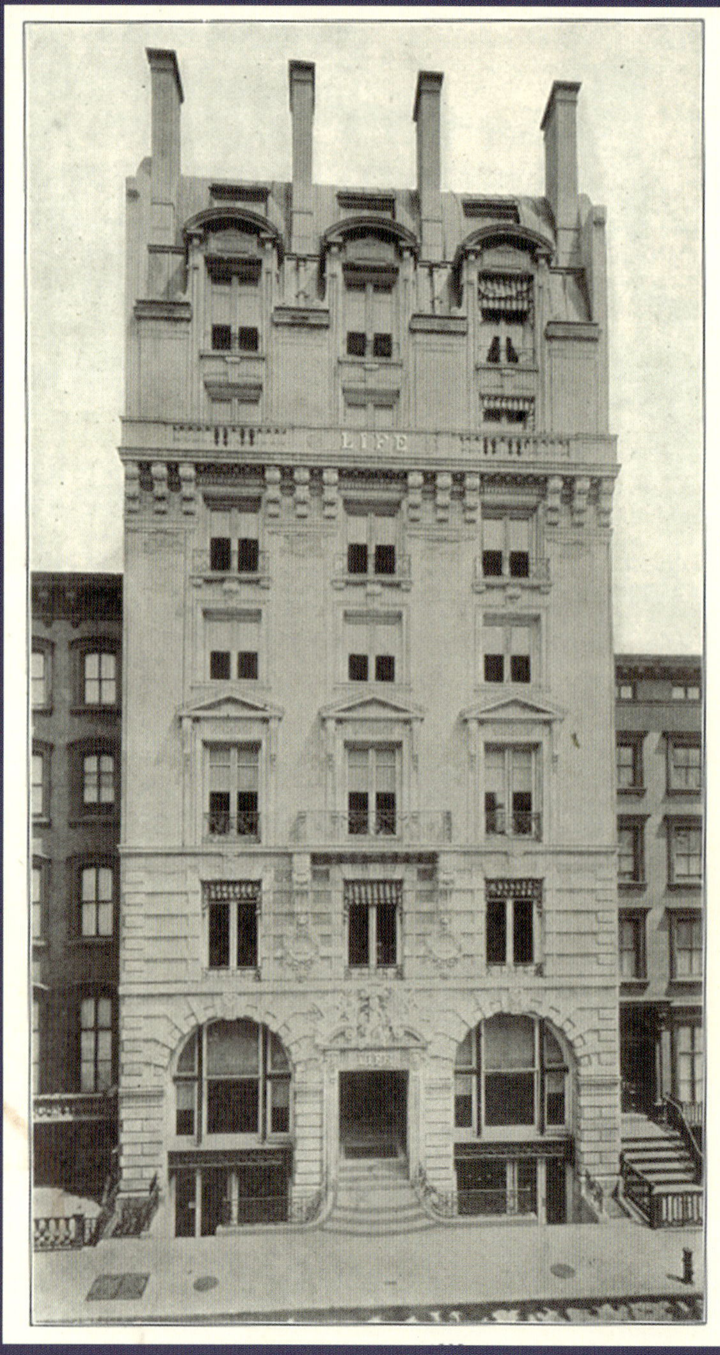

3.1a Carrère and Hastings, "The Life Building, 19 West 31st Street, New York City," *Architectural Record* 27, no. 1 (January 1910): 32.

Unless otherwise noted, all images in this chapter are from Max Ewing's *Gallery of Extraordinary Portraits*.

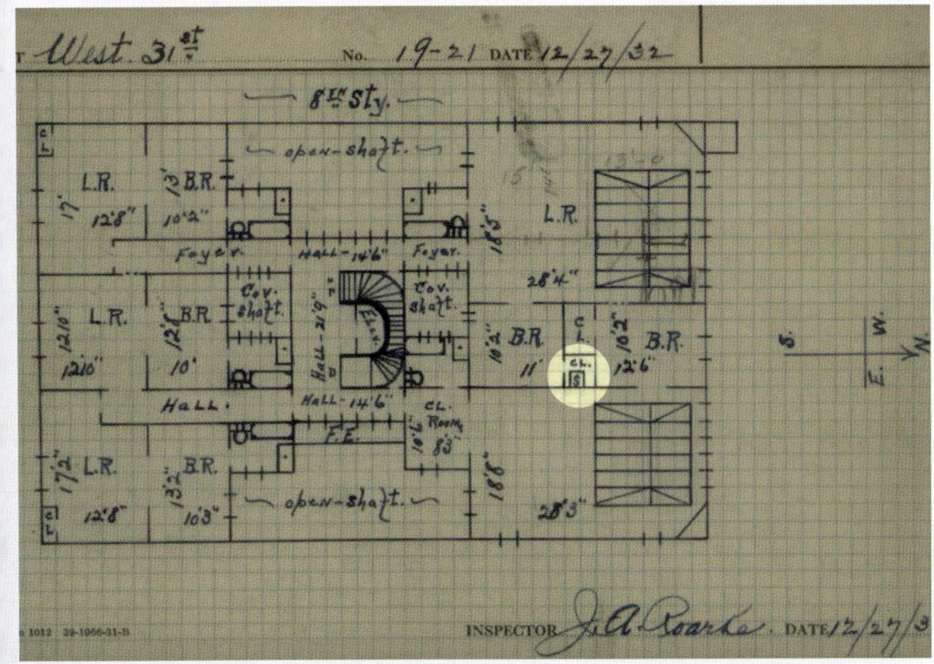

3.1b Plan of 19 West 31st Street, 8th floor. The closet was c. 4 × 4 ft and had a sink ("S") in it, shown on the plan. New York City Department of Housing Preservation and Development.

Seeing Europe firsthand had changed Max Ewing, and his heady experiences of glamour, culture, and sexual freedom convinced him that his strategy was the correct one: he would continue to meet people and throw himself into the social whirl of New York's "High Bohemia," hoping for a big break in his career as a musician. Thus, when he returned to the city in the fall of 1927, he picked up where he left off, attending concerts and plays, drinking and dancing in Harlem, and going to lots of parties where he encountered not only the usual crowd — Muriel Draper's salon circle and her Gurdjieff friends, the Askews and their crowd of Harvard intellectuals, and the Van Vechtens and their ever-expanding coterie of literati and entertainers from Broadway and Harlem — but also a host of new friends and acquaintances, including the hard-partying heiress A'lelia Walker, the handsome African American librarian and man of letters Harold Jackman (1900–60), young writers like E. E. Cummings, and the singer and actor Paul Robeson, who, like other talented members of Ewing's cohort, would frequently entertain at his parties.[1] Ewing's letters suggest a new confidence about his career, his social status, and his sexuality, as well as a deepening knowledge of the city and of the wide variety of places and spaces it offered.

Toward the end of November 1927, Ewing moved into a spacious, top-floor studio in the Life Building at 19 West 31st Street (figs. 3.1a and 3.1b) that suited him perfectly. The handsome brick and limestone structure, designed in 1893 by the firm of Carrère and Hastings, architects of the New York Public Library, had been built to provide offices, studios, and living spaces for the staff and artists of *Life Magazine*, including its most famous illustrator, Charles Dana Gibson, whose former studio Ewing occupied. Though the magazine had vacated the premises some years before, the building — populated almost exclusively by "bachelors," a catchall label for a new urban cohort of unmarried young men (many of them gay), who, like Ewing, had gravitated to the city in search of work and a degree of independence — offered a range of hotel services and retained some of its clubby, artistic cachet.[2] As he wrote to his college friend Edgar Ailes: "I am sick of living in hotels and in trunks which I have done for more than two years.

My apartment was formerly the studio of Charles Dana Gibson, and is very spacious and pleasant, a most unusual place to find in the middle of New York."[3]

On November 27, 1927, Ewing informed his parents that he had "found the place in New York that I've always had on my mind and wanted and now I've taken it and move in tomorrow," adding that

> it has a perfectly enormous room with fireplace — three windows facing north, 1 facing south, and two facing west. There is a small alcove bedroom, a good-sized closet and a bath. The closet has a sink in it and I can make coffee there if I want to. … It is furnished and provides full hotel service, maid, towels, etc. … It is an extraordinary place to find in New York — and piano playing is allowed at all hours, for I am on the top floor — the 8th floor.[4]

He knew that the place was expensive ($1,500 a year, or over $2,000 a month in today's dollars) but, as he explained, he had a friend who paid that much for a lesser place in the Ansonia, a fashionable apartment building on the West Side; besides, he argued, he expected to inherit $2,250 from his aunt's estate. In fact, he had gone ahead and signed a one-year lease (he ended up staying for over five) and assured his parents that "Muriel [had come] to see it before I took it and she thought I ought to take an option for a ten year lease because it was such an amazing place."[5]

Ewing's intention from the first was to make his New York home a showplace where he could entertain his new friends. He had written to his parents from Europe the previous summer to let them know that he was acquiring items for his home and "looking forward to furnishing that place in New York," adding, "God knows I have wanted to furnish a room all my life … [and] make it a place where I can receive all the people I mean to receive."[6] This news hardly came as a surprise to anyone who knew him, least of all his family: clothes from the dress-up box, theatrical costumes, and all manner of fashionable attire such as the suits and accessories he acquired in Europe were integral to the various

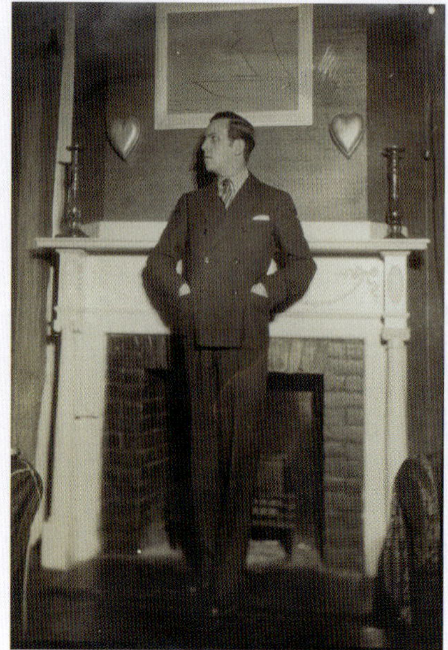

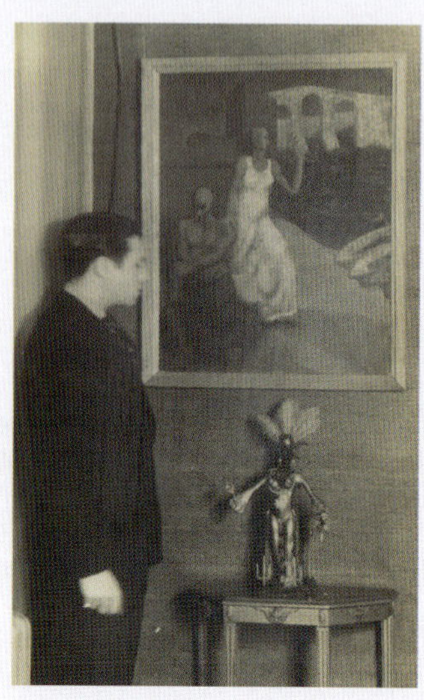

3.2 Anon., Max Ewing at West 31st Street, 1929. The painting above the fireplace is by De Hirsh Margules. Max Ewing Papers.

3.3 Anon., Max Ewing with painting by Eugene McCown, c. 1930. Note Ewing's *Muriel More So* on the table. Max Ewing Papers.

roles he intended to play in the city, and his plan to make his mark in interior design was simply the next step in the process of creating his own distinctive world of sophisticated glamour.

Ewing clearly modeled his decor and weekly social gatherings on those of his prominent friends, albeit on a smaller scale.[7] He decorated his apartment with a combination of furniture donated by Muriel Draper and some newly acquired pieces, covering the walls with works of art, including paintings given to him by the Greenwich Village artist De Hirsh Margules (fig. 3.2), and by the Paris-based artist Eugene McCown (fig. 3.3), whose career was championed by Ewing's friend Jane Heap.[8] His collection would come to include *Draper's Training School*, a large canvas given to him in 1927 by Mark Tobey (see fig. 2.23) that he made part of his *Gallery of Extraordinary Portraits*, as well as a series of his own sculptures showing Draper in a variety of roles, including *Muriel Enlightening the World* (complete with electric light bulbs) and *Muriel Destroying Young Men*.

In his letters to his family back in Pioneer, Ohio, he proudly elaborated the details of his guest lists and his menus, as well as the names of the entertainers he hired to perform for his friends. His parents continued to pay his expenses and delighted in his adventures in New York and his growing collection of A-list associates. Ewing's pace was frenetic, but everyone agreed that his strategy seemed to be working: the young man with big dreams and a campy, queer manner that didn't fit the mold in small-town America was finding his place in the world.

THE GALLERY IN THE CLOSET

Although it isn't clear when Ewing first conceived the idea of displaying his portrait collection in his walk-in closet (fig. 3.4), the gallery project progressed rapidly once he had settled in to his new apartment. He had collected photos and memorabilia of his favorite stars since childhood, amassing large holdings of ephemera related to the careers of the great opera divas Mary Garden and Geraldine Farrar, which he preserved in albums and document boxes, later diligently safe-guarded by his mother in the family home. He was always a dedicated scrapbooker, scouring newspapers and magazines for clippings and photos: the many reviews, advertisements, playbills, and autographs he amassed served as souvenirs of the performances he attended and the stars he encountered as a boy in Detroit and Toledo, and later in New York, Paris, London, and Vienna. He loved all forms of glamour and celebrity, yearning to share in the drama of the world stage, so different from the ordinary, day-to-day experience of Pioneer, Ohio.[9]

Ewing's *Gallery* was intended to serve a similar purpose but on a larger scale, enshrining his devotion to his celebrity heroes, past and present, and authenticating his ties to his famous friends through their portraits, many of which were inscribed with personal messages.[10] The gallery was also a queer space, like the storeroom above the Ewings' store in Pioneer where Max and his friends dressed up in costumes and put on plays. It was an immersive environment where Ewing could celebrate his identity and enthusiasms: tucked within the confines of his own apartment, the *Gallery* functioned as both a private, 3D scrapbook and as Ewing's self-invented realm of queer, interracial confraternity, a family that became real because he had so diligently assembled his collection of portraits and shown it to his friends.

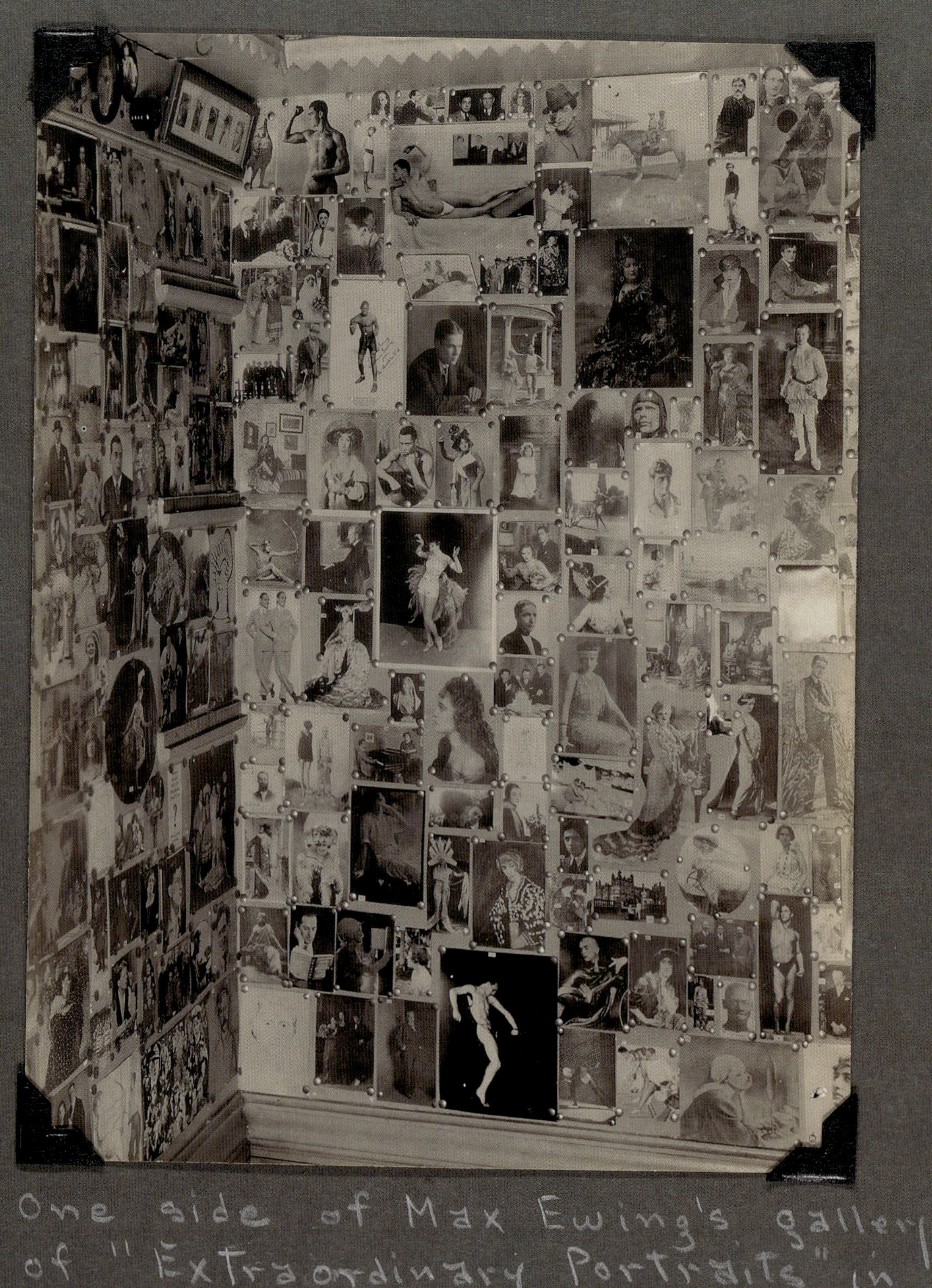

3.4 Anon., "One side of Max Ewing's Gallery of Extraordinary Portraits in his clothes closet," 1928. Max Ewing Papers.

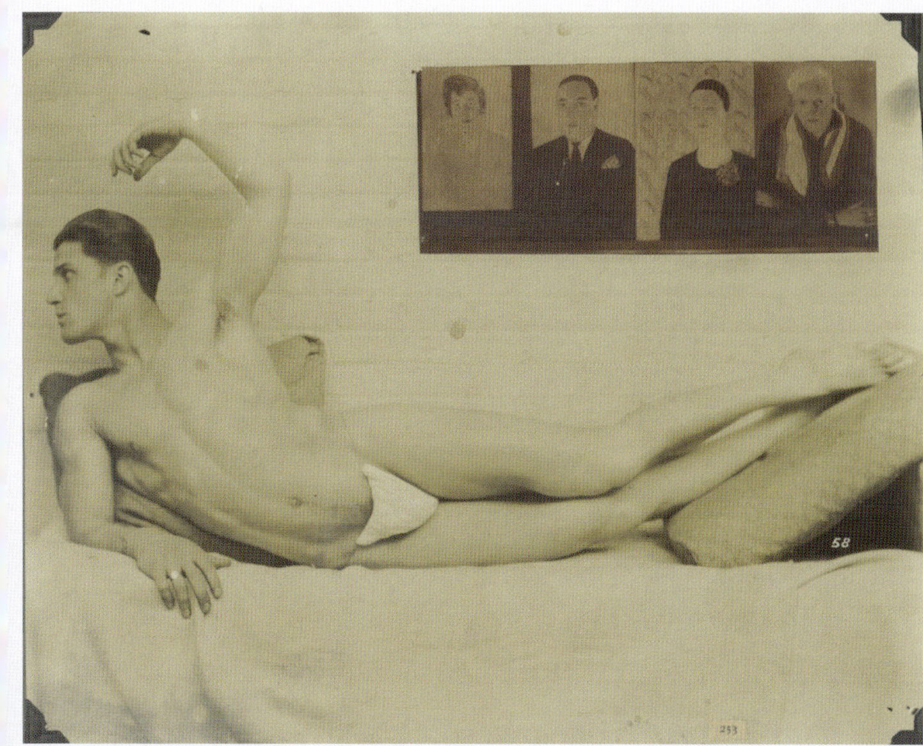

3.5 Anon, *Tony Sansone Reclining.* Note the Robert Chanler portraits of Emily Vanderbilt, Edward Wasserman, Boonie Goossens, and Carl Van Vechten in the background.

The images of nude and seminude male dancers and athletes — from the boxers Kid Chocolate and Max Schmeling to the bodybuilder Anthony Sansone (1905–87) (fig. 3.5) — were among the largest images in the display, and they created a celebration of a different kind, one that set an edgy, queer tone that delighted Ewing and his guests. The *Gallery* was thus part autobiography, part paean to the glamour of movies, books, and popular entertainments, and part monument to the queer cultural heroes of Ewing's own generation and of the recent past, including Marcel Proust, Oscar Wilde, Gertrude Stein, Havelock Ellis, and Serge Diaghilev, who appeared on the walls among many lesser-known figures. Soon after he began to install his treasures on the wall, he decided to produce a privately printed catalogue with numbered entries so that his guests could identify his heroes.

We might therefore think of Ewing's closet *Gallery* as a "queer family romance," a concept adapted from a 1910 essay by Sigmund Freud by the art historian Whitney Davis to shed new light on queer collecting as a "*conscious* remaking of one's lineage, a conscious imagining of a natal culture more satisfying than one's own."[11] Viewed in this light, Ewing's collection was not only a form of self-invention, but also a literally all-encompassing 3D story about celebrity glamour, male beauty, and queer history into which Ewing inscribed himself. That this newly created "family" effectively removed Ewing from his American roots goes without saying: while he remained close to his parents (and especially to his mother, whom he later described as "both the audience and the backer of [his] show"), he knew from an early age that his rightful place would never be back at home with them.[12]

In addition to the experiences of looking and talking that took place in its small closet space, Ewing's *Gallery*, which was constantly changing and growing from 1928 until Ewing left New York for Hollywood in early summer 1933, became both a tiny stage set for the recitation of his amusing stories and a magical cabinet of curiosities, filled with a diverse array of rare finds. The fact that Ewing's performances took place within the confines of a small, windowless room — a room into which his guests had to be invited — made it all the more vivid as a site of secret revelations. In some ways, the *Gallery* seems tantalizingly reminiscent of the "closets" from which men and women "came out" during the gay liberation movement of the 1960s, but without the crucial elements of pride and new-found freedom that marked those disclosures of queer sexuality.[13] Here irony and camp theatrics — the fundamental qualities of queer *artifice* — served to mask the nagging feelings of shame and doubt that Ewing and his queer friends undoubtedly experienced in these homophobic times: his tragic death six years later, and the suppression (and in some cases, outright destruction) of many items in his collection are vivid reminders of the dangers of self-disclosure in public or within the family.[14] These factors make the survival of so many of the portraits and stories related to Ewing's *Gallery* all the more remarkable.

In this endeavor, as with most things in Ewing's short life, Carl Van Vechten proved to be an inspiration, a mentor, and a fellow traveler, not only in the world of photo collecting but also in the arts of performance and queer self-invention. As noted earlier, Van Vechten had spent decades of his life before he met Max Ewing amassing a huge collection of books, manuscripts, paintings, knickknacks, clothing, and keepsakes; in the mid-1920s, the two men bonded over their mutual dedication to the search for new acquisitions, particularly those related to queer, curious, and risqué subjects.[15] In many respects, it can also be argued that Van Vechten "collected" the young man himself both before and after his death in 1934, first by encouraging his devotion and friendship and keeping him close, next by making his own photographic portraits of Ewing (along with hundreds of self-portraits and thousands of portraits of others), and ultimately by diligently acquiring, cataloguing, and establishing the Max Ewing Archive as a memorial and as a historical artifact that he donated to Yale. Van Vechten had a long-standing commitment to documenting queer history — his many scrapbooks in the Beinecke Library offer ample evidence of that — and he clearly recognized that Ewing was a comrade-in-arms whose activities should be encouraged and, ultimately, preserved for posterity.

———

Ewing's and Van Vechten's shared interest clearly went beyond friendly banter about divas, bodybuilders, and the curiosities they found in sex shops, extending at times to serious conversations about the writings of sexologists and psychologists and their own status as queer outsiders: in December 1930, for example, Ewing told his parents that he and Van Vechten had attended a lecture by the noted German physician and gay rights activist Magnus Hirschfeld, who was then on tour in New York: "Today CVV and I spent in the German quarter of East 86th Street," he wrote, "where we went to hear Dr. Magnus Hirschfeld lecture in German, so we didn't understand all he said by any means, either of us, but we listened to him for three hours! Then we dined in a German restaurant …"[16] There is no record of the Ewing parents' response to this revelation about their son's interests, or any evidence to suggest whether they had any idea what he was talking about, but they were, of course, familiar with his efforts to keep up with everything new and significant in the city, and with both his long-standing passion for collecting and his devotion to his mentor.

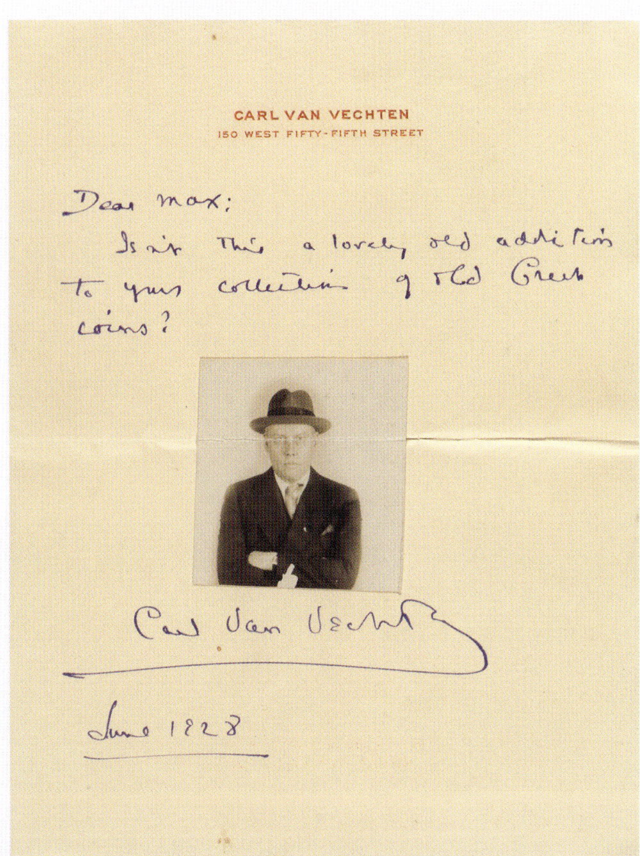

3.6 Letter from Carl Van Vechten to Max Ewing, June 1928. Max Ewing Papers.

Thanks to Van Vechten's encouragement and influence, the *Gallery* served as both a superfan's record of the stars in his queer firmament and as a living monument to the part he himself played in an extraordinarily diverse network of friends and acquaintances. The fact that the artist Robert Chanler, a close friend of both Ewing and Van Vechten, was also in the process of creating an encyclopedic record of his circle through his own quickly painted portraits — including, as we saw earlier, images of Ewing, Hellstrom, Taylor Gordon, and others — may also have inspired both men to think about expanding their collecting efforts in this direction. In any case, Van Vechten's pivotal role in the making of the *Gallery* is confirmed by Ewing's note to his parents in March 1927, reporting that "Carl Van Vechten, who left here the other night with so many pictures of me, outdid himself this morning by sending me pictures of himself."[17] These images included a large reproduction of Chanler's recent portrait of Van Vechten wearing "A Red Shirt and Navajo Bracelet," inscribed to "Dear Max," and presumably intended for inclusion in the *Gallery*, where it was ultimately displayed.

In June 1928, Van Vechten sent along another image of himself, a small portrait that appears to be a passport photo (fig. 3.6) pasted onto a piece of personal stationary, to which he added the handwritten inscription: "Isn't this a lovely old addition to your collection of old Greek coins?"[18] His camp, joking manner is entirely characteristic of an author who adopted the supercilious tone and conversational patter of an insider in novels like *The Tattooed Countess* (1924) and *Parties* (1930) — to say nothing of his offensive, failed efforts to portray himself as an expert on African American culture in the 1926 book for which he remains best known. As we know, it was a manner that Ewing often adopted in his communications with his parents and friends, but the younger man's wide-eyed enthusiasm for the things that he saw and experienced in New York and Europe, and his sincere expressions of love, belie such efforts at sophisticated cynicism. Both modes are present in his *Gallery*, which included another significant gift from Van Vechten: an X-ray of his own skull presented to Ewing in July 1928 (fig. 3.7) as an example of the sort of curiosity that both men loved.[19]

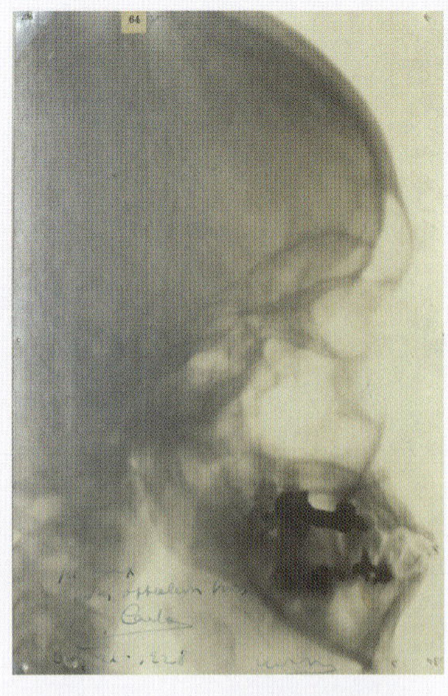

3.7 *X-ray of Carl Van Vechten's Skull*, inscribed "to Max with affection from Carlo July 21, 1928."

In light of the significant role that Van Vechten played in Ewing's life, it is not surprising to also find many other portraits of Van Vechten among the images on display, including a reproduction of his friend Florine Stettheimer's portrait (fig. 3.8) from 1922. Stettheimer's salon gatherings, hosted by the artist, her sisters, and their mother at their Alwyn Court apartment on West 58th Street, were the most intellectually ambitious and decorous of the many such venues that Van Vechten, a friend since at least the mid-1910s, and Ewing (who met the Stettheimers through Van Vechten in early 1929) attended in New York.[20] There, art-world luminaries, including Marcel Duchamp (1887–1968), Gaston Lachaise, Alfred Stieglitz (1864–1946), and Leo Stein, gathered with members of the Stettheimers' inner circle, a group that included many queer and bisexual friends.[21] The salon was also well-known for the performative quality of the sisters' dress and etiquette and for the highly ornamented decor that characterized both the family apartment and Florine's Bryant Park studio, both of which were frequently commented upon in Ewing's letters of the late 1920s and '30s. Surviving photographs show the hanging lace and tassels, the carved white and gold furniture, and the "billowing cellophane curtains hanging between rooms" that historian Cécile Whiting has characterized as "interior décor taken to its fantastical, whimsical, and feminine extreme."[22]

As will be discussed in the following chapter, like Van Vechten, Stettheimer and her sisters recognized something special in the young man who became their consort and confidant, visiting them regularly from 1929 until the time of his departure from New York City in late spring 1933. Indeed, as the 1922 portrait of Van Vechten clearly shows, Florine had an uncanny ability to see and paint the unusual and often well-hidden aspects of her sitters' lives and personalities. In her representation of Van Vechten, for example, the writer sits on a red stool at the center of a circular rug decorated with red roses; he holds a cigarette in one hand and crosses his arms and legs in a theatrical pose; he is wearing purple socks and a purple tie, and his pointy shoes barely touch the floor. All of these elements could be taken as signs of Van Vechten's queer identity. He is surrounded by the things he loved and, indeed, frequently shared with Max Ewing: cats, books, toys, a typewriter, a piano, food, and flowers. Behind him, a mask of his actress wife, Fania Marinoff, hangs on the wall: she was an indispensable and much-loved — albeit frequently embattled and vexed — part of Van Vechten's life, and her image not only symbolized the tools of her stagecraft, but also suggested something of the disguise she provided for

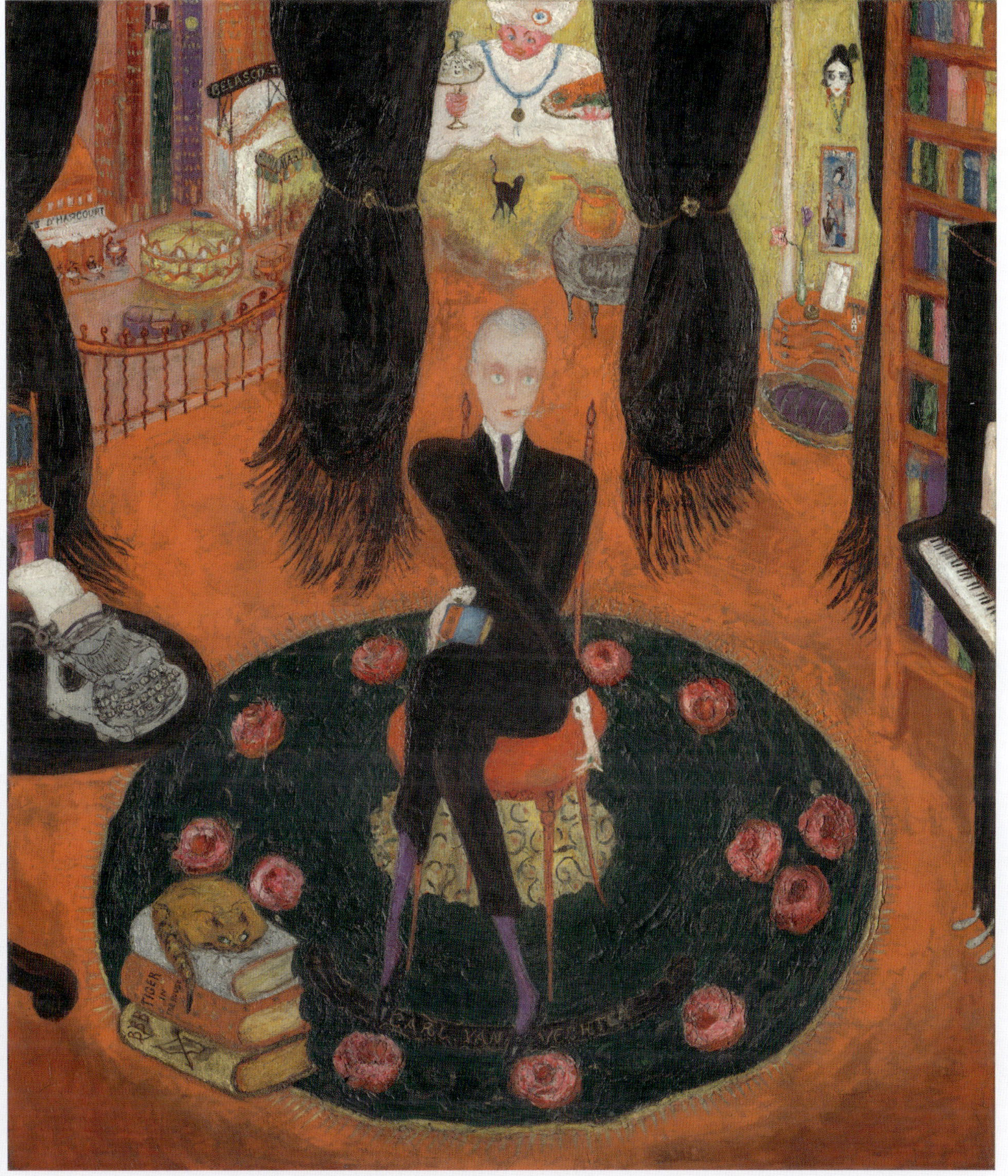

3.8 Florine Stettheimer, *Carl Van Vechten*, 1922, oil on canvas, 30½ × 26 in. (77.5 × 66 cm). Yale University Art Gallery, 1973.95.13.

her husband, whose queer bisexuality and late-night exploits were legendary. Ewing knew the portrait very well, as it hung in a prominent position in the middle of Van Vechten's private library.[23]

As the *Gallery* evolved in 1928, it came to include portraits of other friends from this period as well: each was special to Ewing and each contributed to the telling of his story. Thus, we find a photograph given to him by his friend Taylor Gordon, the African American singer whom he had met in 1925, one of two portraits he kept of the singer: clearly visible in the photo that depicted one side of the installation, the portrait showed Gordon on horseback with a white child of the same age; it was, according to Ewing's catalogue, inscribed: "To Max Ewing that he might know my start."[24] As a Black man in the overwhelmingly white social and cultural milieu created by Ewing and his friends, Gordon was engaged in an ongoing process of self-invention that culminated in his autobiography of 1929, entitled *Born to Be*, which included an introduction by Muriel Draper.[25] The book, with characteristically cartoonish illustrations by their friend Miguel Covarrubias, describes Gordon's childhood in White Sulphur Springs, Montana, his early years as a child servant in a bordello, and his road to success as a singer of spirituals, detailing the complexities of his career, his adventures on the stages of New York, London, and Paris, and his unlikely experiences in the drawing rooms of Harlem and Park Avenue. Here, again, we find the familiar ironic, knowing style that was characteristic of Ewing's "set": Gordon singles out Draper (the object of his adoration — another thing he shared with Ewing) for her charisma and her fashionable yet eccentric dress, and he praises Carl Van Vechten for his skill as a mixer of cocktails. Gordon's half-serious "glossary" of Harlem slang, included for the benefit of his white readers — similar to the one Van Vechten published in his novel of 1926 — nods to his own ambivalent role between uptown and downtown. Indeed, Gordon's Cinderella-like transformation from provincial striver to New York insider was an accomplishment that he wrote about with genuine pride. Like so many in this corner of New York's bohemia — including Draper herself, whose memoir *Music at Midnight* was published in 1929, the same year as Gordon's — he felt the need to narrate his journey and explain himself to those around him, knowing very well that there was a substantial readership for both the celebrity gossip and the rags-to-riches story that he told.

Ewing's photo of Gordon as a child was prominently displayed in the first installation of the *Gallery* (see fig. 3.4). In a later image of the *Gallery* dating from 1932 (see fig. 0.1), Gordon appears in a tiny newspaper clipping as the dapper, urban sophisticate that he ultimately became: in a small but widely circulated press clipping (fig. 3.9), barely visible on the side wall immediately to the left of Ewing's shoulder, Gordon is shown in Harlem with Nancy Cunard, the wealthy activist and promoter of African American culture whose *Negro Anthology* was published in 1934, accompanied by the white photographer John Banting. The image, in which Banting is cropped out, bears the caption "Ain't Misbehavin'," an obvious

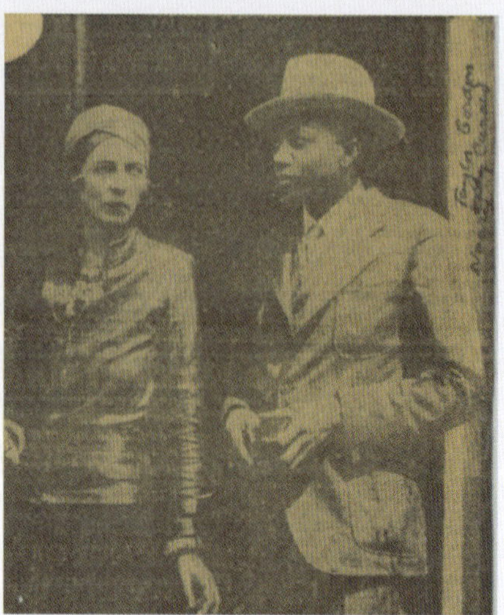

3.9 Newspaper clipping of Taylor Gordon and Nancy Cunard in Harlem (with John Banting cropped out), 1932.

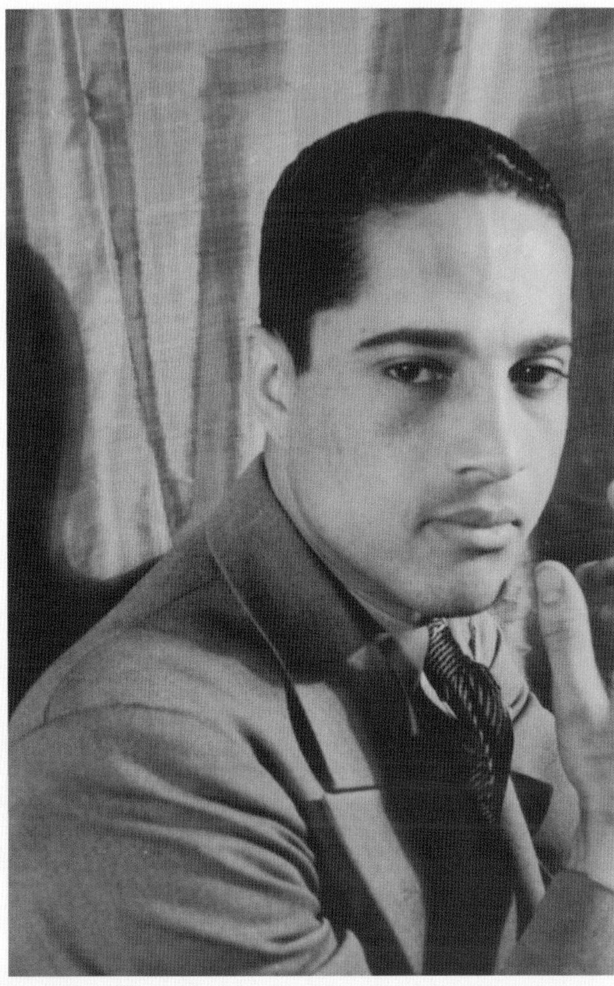

3.10 Carl Van Vechten, *Paul Meeres*, 1932. Carl Van Vechten Papers.

reference to Cunard's "scandalous" relationships with Black men, including Henry Crowder, the jazz musician with whom she was living at the time.[26] Gordon's friendship and public persona — and their mutual embrace of interracial friendship — were important to Ewing, as the many portraits of Gordon in his collection make clear. Moreover, although his image in the newspaper was used to taunt Cunard about her interracial love life and to appeal to the endless appetite of readers for salacious gossip, Gordon also achieved a certain degree of celebrity from the photograph, a fact that was always of interest to Ewing.

In the 1932 view of the closet (fig. 0.1) we can also recognize other changes in the installation that signal Ewing's evolving sense of himself. Notably, there is now a large portrait of Paul Meeres (1902–62), the much-admired and sought-after Harlem entertainer, by Carl Van Vechten (fig. 3.10), clearly visible in the middle of the display. The beautiful Meeres was a Bahamian dancer whose career Ewing and Van Vechten followed closely as ardent fans: the portrait was one of the first that Van Vechten, newly obsessed with making photographs in his home studio, created in the spring of 1932. Indeed, for a number of years, beginning in 1928, Van Vechten, Ewing, and their friend George Platt Lynes — and no doubt countless other gay men in New York as well — became active followers of "the brown Valentino," as he was known, frequently making the journey to Harlem in the spring and fall of 1928 to see him perform at Small's Paradise, the cabaret where he danced.[27] Ewing included his portrait in the *Gallery* from the first, listing

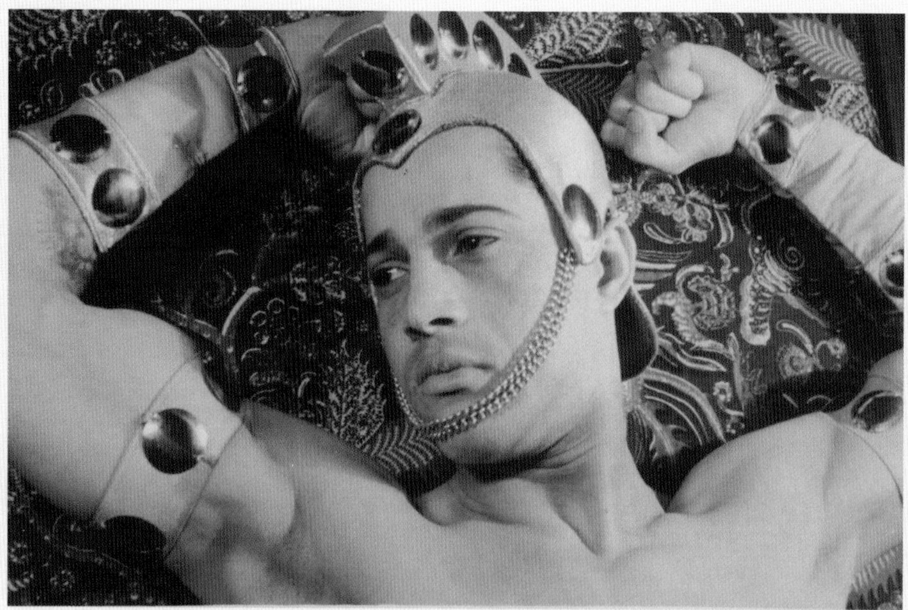

3.11 Carl Van Vechten, *Paul Meeres as a Roman Soldier*, April 1, 1932. Carl Van Vechten Papers Relating to African American Arts and Letters.

two images — alas, now lost — of Meeres "As Valentino" (catalogue no. 124) and "Holding a Cigarette in Harlem in 1928, Gift of Mr. Meeres, Signed at Some Length" (catalogue no. 227).

George Platt Lynes was apparently the first in the group to photograph Meeres, both clothed and nude, in his studio, writing to his lover Monroe Wheeler on December 6, 1929 about the photographs he had just taken, adding that Meeres was "slighter than Sansone, but finer, subtler and more plastic," adding that he was "the most beautiful man I have ever seen."[28] In 1932, Ewing and Van Vechten, both longtime admirers, also turned their lenses on Meeres, capturing his handsome face and extraordinary physique in every conceivable pose, including studio shots by Van Vechten of Meeres dressed in an Indian costume and in the guise of a "Roman Soldier" from his show at Connie's Inn (fig. 3.11).[29] Ewing's own efforts included snapshots of Meeres in a dapper suit, and a series of full-length, frontal nudes, taken as part of his *Carnival of Venice* series in April 1932, discussed in chapter 5.[30]

The 1932 view of the *Gallery* also reveals a glossy pinup of the Hollywood star Gary Cooper (see fig. 0.1), which shares pride of place in the top row next to Ewing's idol, the bodybuilder and model Anthony Sansone. Ewing must have relished the juxtaposition of the glamorous film star and the nude athlete, who reclines on a divan (see fig. 3.4 and 3.5). The collection also includes a large nude portrait of the boxer Max Schmeling flexing his right arm (fig. 3.12), a photo that would no doubt have captured the attention of viewers — both men and women — unaccustomed to seeing such explicit images. As a group, these photos reflect Ewing's interests in the early 1930s: he became a huge fan of Gary Cooper, and even started a club — complete with printed membership cards and lavish events — that he called "The GaryFlappers." Unsurprisingly, he also sought out Cooper when he went to Hollywood in 1933, and wrote to his friends about the rare sightings that he was able to experience during his visits to the studios. He was also increasingly interested in looking at the bodies of naked men, and far less shy about seeking them out in whatever context he could find them: the boxing ring, the bodybuilder's studio, or indeed through the lens of his own camera.

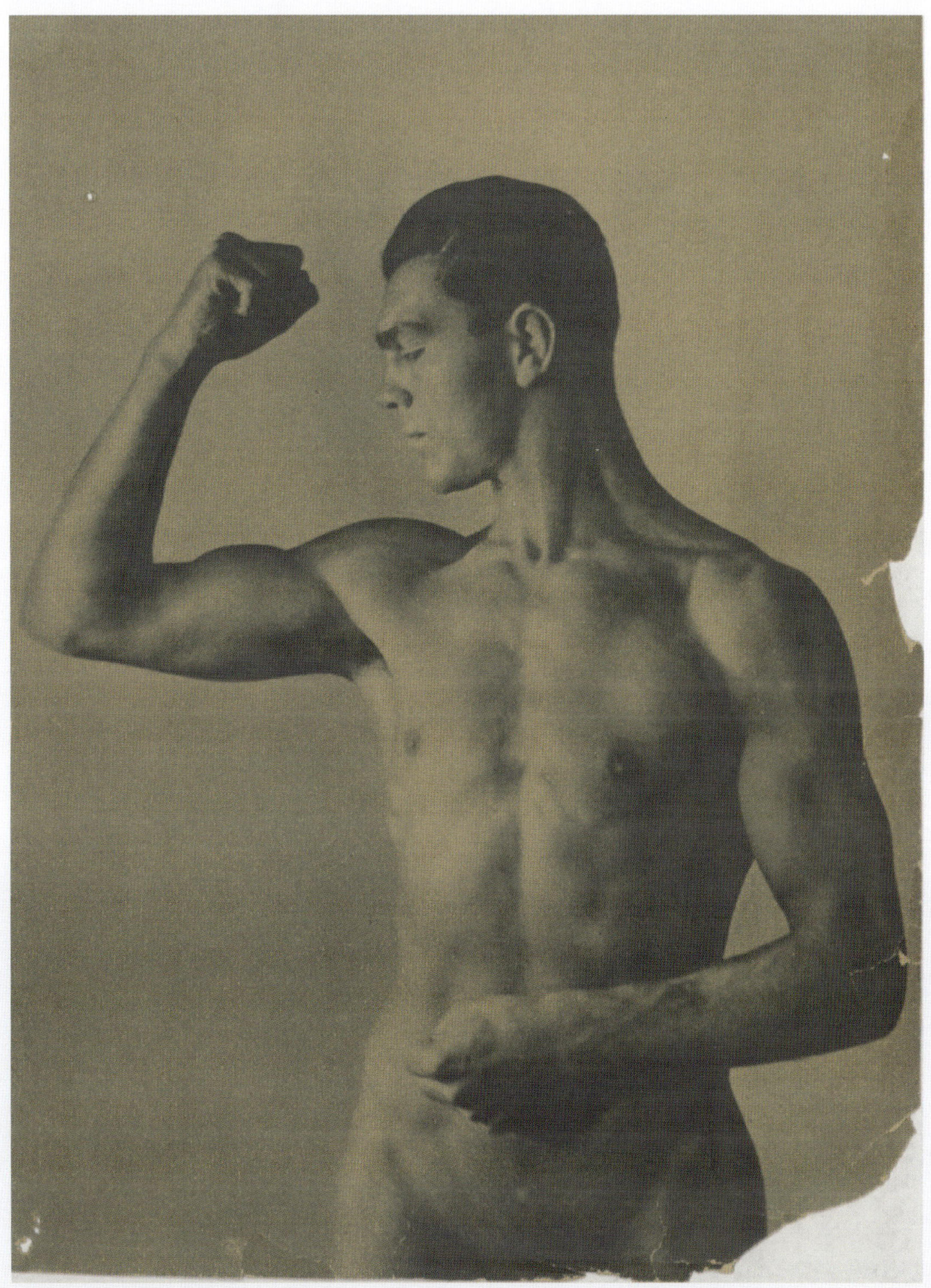

3.12 Anon., *Max Schmeling*.

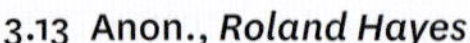

3.13 Anon., *Roland Hayes*.

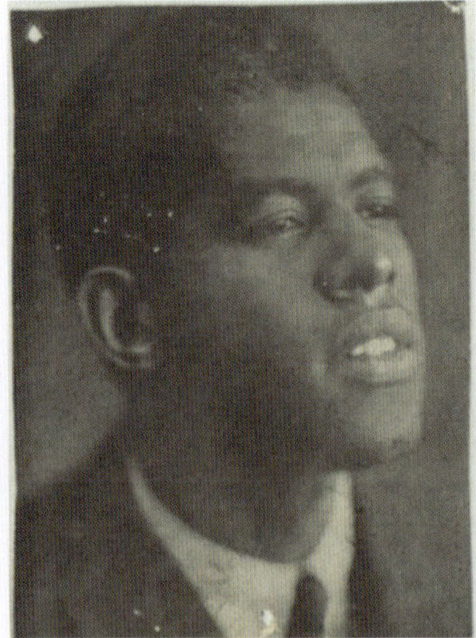

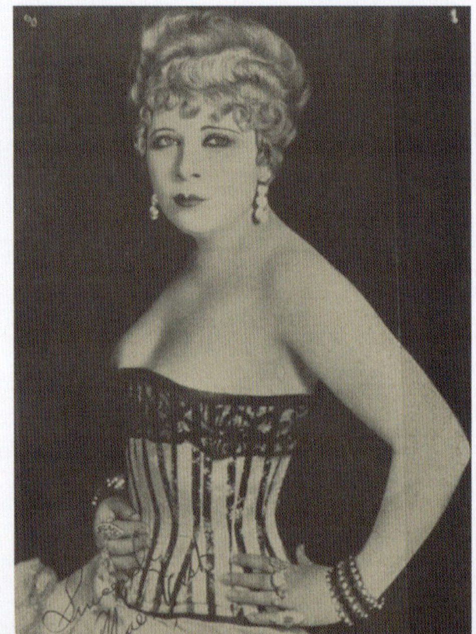

3.14 Anon., *Mae West*.

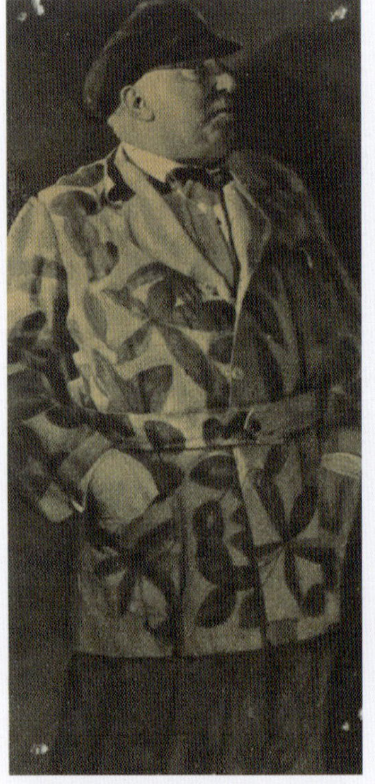

3.15 Anon., *Paul Poiret*.

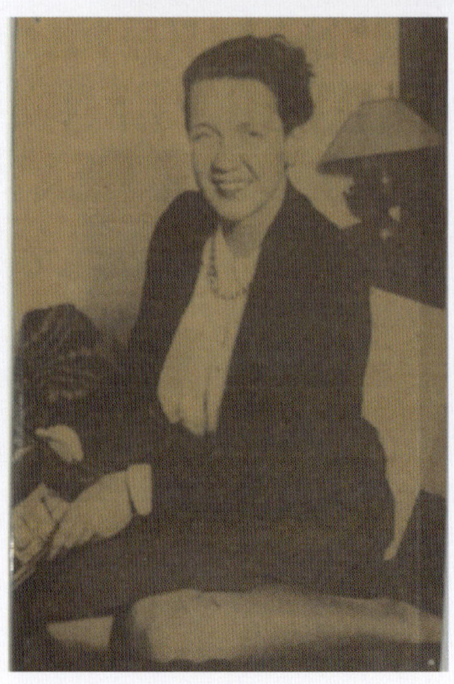

3.16 Anon., *Natalie Hammond*.

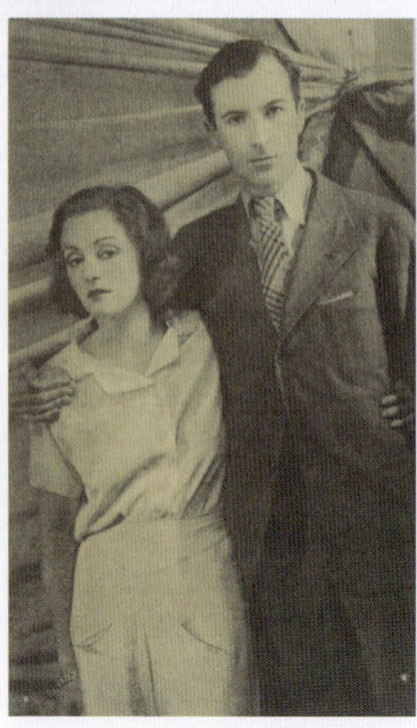

3.17 Anon., *Tallulah Bankhead and Cecil Beaton*.

Other images in the display suggest Ewing's deepening interracial friendships, his expanded social circle of wealthy lesbians and popular entertainers, and his increasingly sophisticated camp humor. Among the most visible are the small portrait of the African American singer Roland Hayes (fig. 3.13), a clipping of a young Mae West, whose 1927 comedy *The Drag* made her a queer icon, wearing a bustier in a photo taken from a German periodical (fig. 3.14), and a glossy pinup of the French cabaret performer Mistinguett flanked by the Rocky Twins, two androgynous young men who visited Ewing's apartment and met a group of his friends in November 1930. The appearance of these stars in Ewing's own home was clearly a *coup* that thrilled the starstruck Ewing: as he wrote to his mother, "The Rocky Twins are coming here at tea time today, and I am having some people in to meet them. They are enchanting boys — the Peggy Hopkins Joyces [an actress famous for her many marriages, divorces, and lavish lifestyle] of their sex — not that they get married but they manage to be given jewels on the same scale that Peggy does. They even wear diamonds in their garters!"[31]

These portraits were grouped at the center of the main wall, next to a clipping of the French fashion designer Paul Poiret (fig. 3.15) that had been repositioned to create a new dialogue between them. Adding to the camp cacophony is a small photo of Ewing's close friend Natalie Hammond (1904–85) (fig. 3.16), the wealthy theater producer and prominent member of New York's lesbian elite, who frequently hosted Ewing and other friends for elegant dinners and parties at her penthouse apartment on Park Avenue, adjoining a matching one belonging to her lover, the artist and stage-designer Alice Laughlin. Through Hammond, Ewing met many other glamorous lesbians, including Hollywood idol Tallulah Bankhead (1902–68), who poses with the fashion photographer Cecil Beaton in the photograph that Ewing displayed in his *Gallery* (fig. 3.17), Mercedes de Acosta (1892–1968), Eva Le Gallienne, and Peggy Fears (1903–94), the actress and producer. Ewing was particularly proud of these high-flying connections: as a group, these women (and their portraits) extended his circle of queer celebrities and transformed his *Gallery* quite definitively from fantasy collection to real-life photo album.

THE CATALOGUE AND THE COLLECTION

For the five years that it remained on the walls of Ewing's walk-in closet, the *Gallery* served as the focus of his social life, drawing diverse crowds to his apartment for parties and performances that often coincided with his weekly "Mondays," modeled on Draper's weekly "Thursdays."[32] From the beginning, it became clear that some sort of handlist or catalogue was needed: most people came to the apartment to see themselves on the walls, but many were curious about the other portraits as well. On October 31, 1928, Ewing wrote to Van Vechten about the success of his endeavor: "The picture gallery in my closet is by this time a close rival of the Uffizi and I am thinking of issuing a catalogue (almost a necessity for the convenience of visitors, inasmuch as most of the subjects are shown in almost unrecognizable guises), charging admission and having a *vernissage*."[33] Ewing mentioned the catalogue again the following month when he wrote to his parents to tell them that the *Gallery* was "the rage": "Everyone is coming to see it and bringing along friends … Namara and Mindret, Robert Gorham and Anthony Sansone whose body is the most perfect in existence," noting, "All got out their catalogues and studied the gallery conscientiously for

two hours. And they all want to come back to do it still more thoroughly."[34]
As he explained:

> It has become a really amazing room, containing some of the most
> rare and remarkable photographs of prominent people in the world.
> It is really important as a collector's collection but I like it simply
> because it amuses me so much. A printed list of its contents will make
> everyone in New York want to come and see it; will flatter everyone
> who is included, and most of New York is; and will serve as Christmas
> cards to mail out instead of stupid stereotyped ones; and it will
> please me more than any printed document since the Sonnets
> [his self-published 1924 collection *Sonnets from the Paronomasian*].
> Of course, the expense will be nothing compared to that.[35]

Ewing was delighted that the *Gallery* was proving to be a draw for the very
people he hoped to attract: the well-known lyric soprano Marguerite Namara,
who was a friend of Van Vechten's and a star of the Broadway stage, the screen
writer Mindret Lord, the handsome dancer Robert Gorham (an old friend from
Paris about whom he had once written to his parents, "Robert is just about the
handsomest spectacle the world contains") and, of course, his idol, Anthony
Sansone.[36] These people all came from very different social and cultural realms,
to say the least. A printed and numbered catalogue clearly seemed to be the best
way to deal with that.

In early December 1928, Ewing's parents sent him the money to have the
catalogue of the *Max Ewing Collection of Extraordinary Portraits* professionally
printed, and he wrote to them on December 14 to tell them, with characteristic
hyperbole, how delighted he was with the result: "My gallery catalogues are off
the press, and I am as pleased with them as with
a new doll at the age of four. Will mail you one in
a day or so. Thank you very much. I would have
enjoyed nothing else as much for Christmas. I
am sure too that all the people I send them to
will be just as much amused as I am, so you can
see it is a Christmas gift for the whole world!"[37]
Taken together, the *Catalogue* (fig. 3.18) and
later *Supplement* contain some three hundred
entries, many corresponding to images that are
visible in the 1928 photograph of the gallery, and
others that survive — complete with pinholes
in the corners and their original numbers
attached — in folders and scrapbooks at Yale.
Some photos by well-known photographers,
notably a number of images taken by Ewing's
friends Berenice Abbott, George Platt Lynes,
and Cecil Beaton, have disappeared over the
years. Still others entered Ewing's collection after the catalogue and supplement
were printed, as the 1932 view of the closet and the many surviving images not
listed in the printed version clearly show.

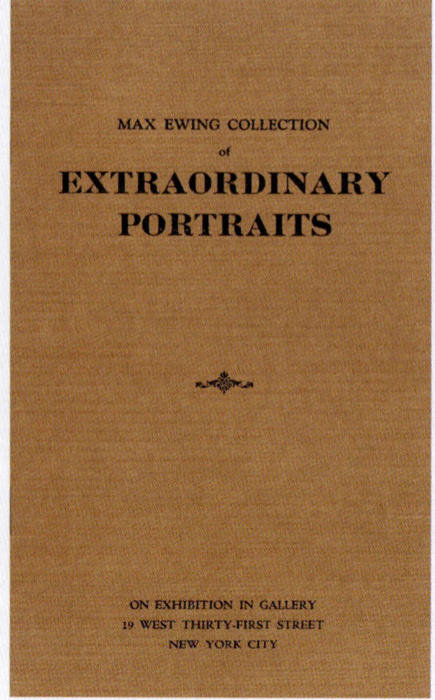

3.18 Catalogue of *The Max Ewing Collection of Extraordinary Portraits*, December 1928. Max Ewing Papers.

Given the fragility of so many of the items, it is remarkable that the *Gallery* remained intact and that so much of it survives, but Ewing clearly intended for his collection to be preserved: when he left New York City for California in 1933, he organized the photos and placed them in folders and albums to await his return. Because he never came back to collect them, and because Van Vechten was able to convince Ewing's family to preserve his papers and photos so soon after his death, most of these items are still exactly as he left them, complete with the identifying numbers he pasted on them. Moreover, although we know that retaining the nudes and homoerotic photographs in the archive was particularly uncomfortable for some family members, who asked Van Vechten to discard them before giving the collection to Yale, many of those also survive, albeit some with the addition of hand-painted "*cache-sexes*" for modesty. Others were transferred to Van Vechten's own scrapbooks. As with every archive, loose images have been rearranged by researchers, librarians, and archivists over the years. Remarkably, the bulk of the collection is intact.

As a group, the images in Ewing's *Gallery* can be organized into six, loosely overlapping categories: 1) images clipped from newspapers and magazines showing opera singers, musicians, and stage actors, many of them famous stars; 2) celebrities and popular heroes, like the dashing young aviator Charles Lindbergh, whose solo flight between New York and Paris made news in 1927, or the dapper Prince of Wales, who appears in numerous images and collages; 3) writers and philosophers — past and present, Black and white — associated with queer and avant-garde culture, and with the so-called "Harlem Renaissance" of the 1920s and early '30s; 4) professional and amateur photos of bodybuilders, dancers, and athletes, including Anthony Sansone, Max Schmeling, Robert Gorham, Serge Lifar, and Gene Tunney, many posing nude or partially clothed; 5) images by the aspiring young photographers among Ewing's friends, including Berenice Abbott, George Platt Lynes, Cecil Beaton, and Carl Van Vechten, some of which were gifts from the artists themselves; and 6) snapshots from Ewing's travels in Europe in 1926 and 1927, including photos he took in Northern Italy when he traveled with Natalie Barney, Romaine Brooks, and Esther Murphy. Remarkably, a portrait of Ewing by Barney also survives.

Ewing's father owned a Kodak folding camera that he borrowed soon after his arrival in New York, writing in March 1924 to ask his parents to send it to him in New York so that he could take some "snaps" during an outing to "Long Beach or Brighton" with Stuart Mackall, a dancer he "liked" from the Denishawn School.[38] He brought that camera with him to Europe in 1926 and 1927, and he added some snapshots from that trip to his closet. Over time, he also added some of his own photos of nude and partially clad men to his *Gallery* or pasted them into his scrapbooks. He supplemented these with images from the *Carnival of Venice* series, begun in the spring of 1932 and exhibited at the Julien Levy Gallery in January 1933.

No doubt most visitors would have been particularly impressed to discover their own portraits among the hundreds of others that their friend had managed to squeeze into his closet. For opera buffs and fans of serious music like Muriel Draper, and for collectors of ephemera like Van Vechten — and perhaps also for Henry McBride, the art critic from the *New York Sun* (whom Ewing had met through Romaine Brooks in Paris) who toured the *Gallery* in March 1929 — it was the breadth of the celebrity memorabilia, much of it signed and inscribed, and the number of rare items, that were particularly startling. Among the most heavily featured celebrities was Geraldine Farrar, an internationally famous diva whom Ewing had loved since his early teens: his *Gallery* featured at least a half a dozen pictures of her, one of which was personally inscribed to Ewing in 1924 as a souvenir of her performance in *Carmen*. Another photo showed Farrar in a "candid" shot, boarding a train with the actor Lou Tellegen (catalogue no. 134). Perhaps his most treasured item of Farrar memorabilia was a 1915 photo presented to her by Sarah Bernhardt, inscribed and signed by the actress, which Farrar had gifted to Ewing herself (fig. 3.19).

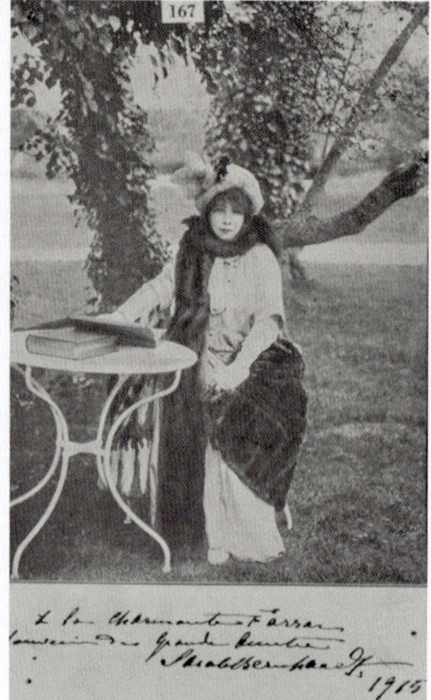

3.19 Anon., *Real photo postcard of Sarah Bernhardt inscribed to Geraldine Farrar.*

The display also featured ten images of the beloved diva Mary Garden (fig. 3.20), a star whom Ewing had heard in concert many times throughout his life, including a performance in Paris that he attended with another one of Mary Garden's superfans, Ewing's friend Margaret Anderson. One rare item (catalogue no. 185) was a still image from a home movie by the publisher Alfred Knopf showing Carl Van Vechten with Garden "on board the SS Mauretania" in 1928. The display of this sort of personal and intimate photography was perfect for establishing Ewing's bona fides as a fan and insider.

Ewing documented his devotion to other popular figures as well: there were three portraits of Marguerite Namara (one of which was signed), including a clipping showing Namara "on a boat with Charlie Chaplin," and another of the singer with Mindret Lord in Antibes (catalogue no. 67). Photos of the popular contralto Marguerite D'Alvarez, who was then appearing on Broadway, were also featured, as were a clipping of Maria Jeritza as *Carmen*, a portrait of the concert pianist Myra Hess, and a photo that depicted a small statuette of Ewing's French piano teacher Marcelle Meyer, who was famous for her interpretations of the works of Darius Milhaud and Igor Stravinsky.[39]

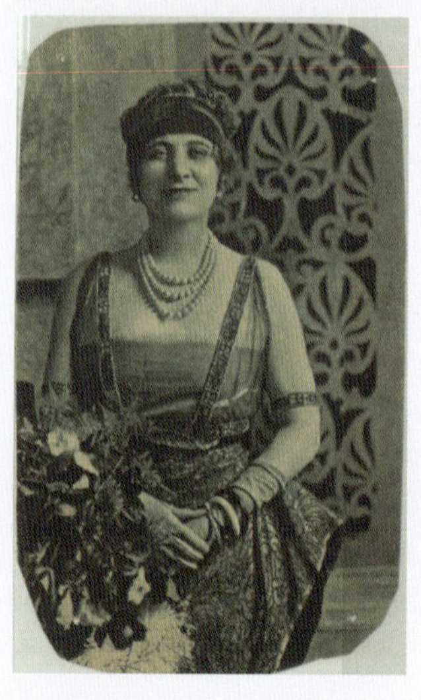

3.20 Anon., *Mary Garden.*

Both of those well-known composers and other avant-garde musicians, including Ewing's sometime heartthrob, the contemporary composer Constant Lambert, were represented in the *Gallery*; Lambert appears both in a portrait painted by Christopher Wood (see fig. 2.27) and in two snapshots showing him mugging for the camera, later preserved in Ewing's scrapbooks. Ewing had briefly met Stravinsky (fig. 3.21) by chance while practicing the piano at the Pleyel studios in Paris, and he was particularly proud that his sojourn in Europe brought him into contact with important members of the European avant-garde. Indeed, the photo of Darius Milhaud showed him with another of Ewing's personal idols, Jean Cocteau, in 1920 (fig. 3.22): in the catalogue, the fashion-conscious Ewing added a comment, "*Dernier Chic*," to the photo of the two dapper young men standing

arm-in-arm, dressed in suits and carrying hats;
the handsome, young Cocteau carries a cane.

We know that Ewing met Jean Cocteau
during his first trip to Europe, having traveled to
Villefranche in 1926 in hope of meeting Glenway
Wescott: like Wescott, Cocteau is a featured star of
the *Gallery* and is portrayed in a number of
portraits, though hardly in the same scope (ten
photos) or variety that is lavished on Wescott,
Ewing's idol. The handsome Wescott was not only
captured in these images — among them photos
that show off his left and right profiles, as indicated
in Ewing's catalogue notes — but also in a small,
framed miniature (catalogue no. 300, now lost),
described in the *Supplement* in the sort of
excessive detail that one might lavish on the golden
reliquary for a saint: "Glenway Wescott (Gold
miniature mounted and framed with baroque
extravagance). Enclosed in effulgent *cadre d'or*
with minute carved *embellissements* in black, and
inlaid with *joyaux* and *bijou* of worth unknown)."[40]

By 1928, two years after Ewing had written
him a gushing fan letter, Ewing's relationship with Wescott had changed
profoundly, largely because of his close friendship with George Platt Lynes, whom
Ewing had met at the beginning of 1927. Lynes had just begun a passionate love
affair with Wescott's longtime lover Monroe Wheeler, quickly entering into the
three-way relationship with the two men that would last for nearly two decades.
Through his friend, Ewing drew closer to their orbit and could now see them all in
a completely different way, though his letters to his parents never describe their
parties or daily lives in detail. We learn from other sources that, in those years,
Lynes and Ewing shared an appreciation for the sort of explicitly queer
photography that both men produced and collected.

GEORGE PLATT LYNES: ANOTHER WORLD
Everything about George Lynes was different, not
only from Ewing himself but from the other queer
people he knew. He was a risk-taker whose dramatic
and often outrageous words and bold actions where
Wescott and Wheeler were concerned — so unlike
Ewing's with Constant Lambert or George
Dangerfield — seemed to signal a willing embrace of
his sexuality, his passionate nature, and the unlikely
triangular shape of his love affair. But the two young
men had much else in common: Lynes had traveled
to Europe in search of queer, modernist idols like
Cocteau and Gertrude Stein in 1925, the year before
Ewing made the journey to Paris, and the two friends
(fig. 3.23) quickly discovered that they shared not
only those passions and experiences, but also a love

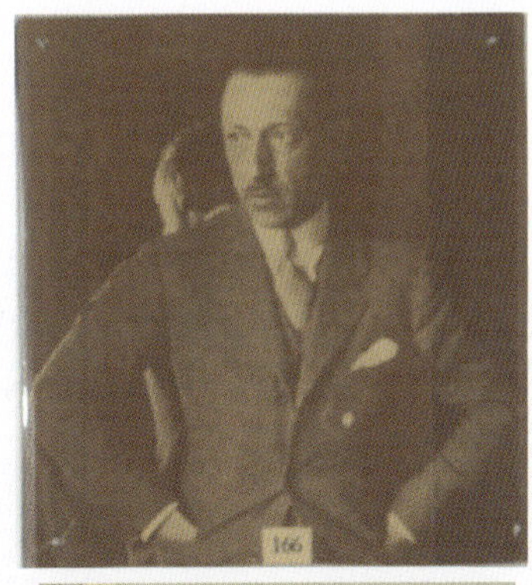

3.21 Anon., *Igor Stravinsky*.

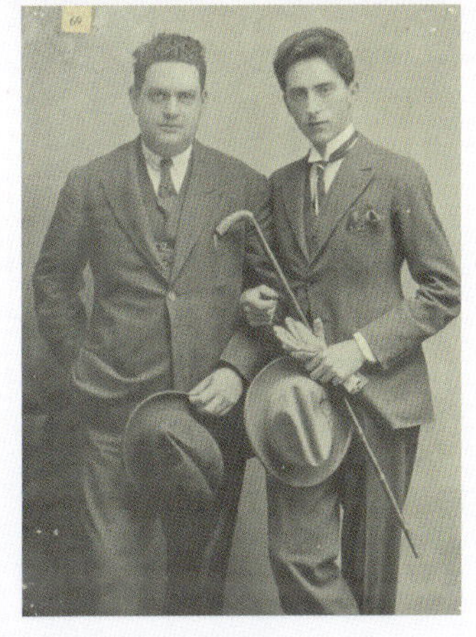

3.22 Anon., *Darius Milhaud
and Jean Cocteau*.

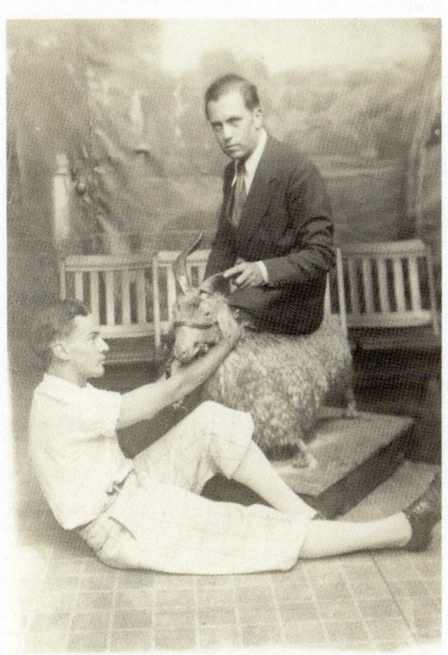

3.23 George Platt Lynes
and Max Ewing at
Palisades Park, 1929.
Max Ewing Papers.

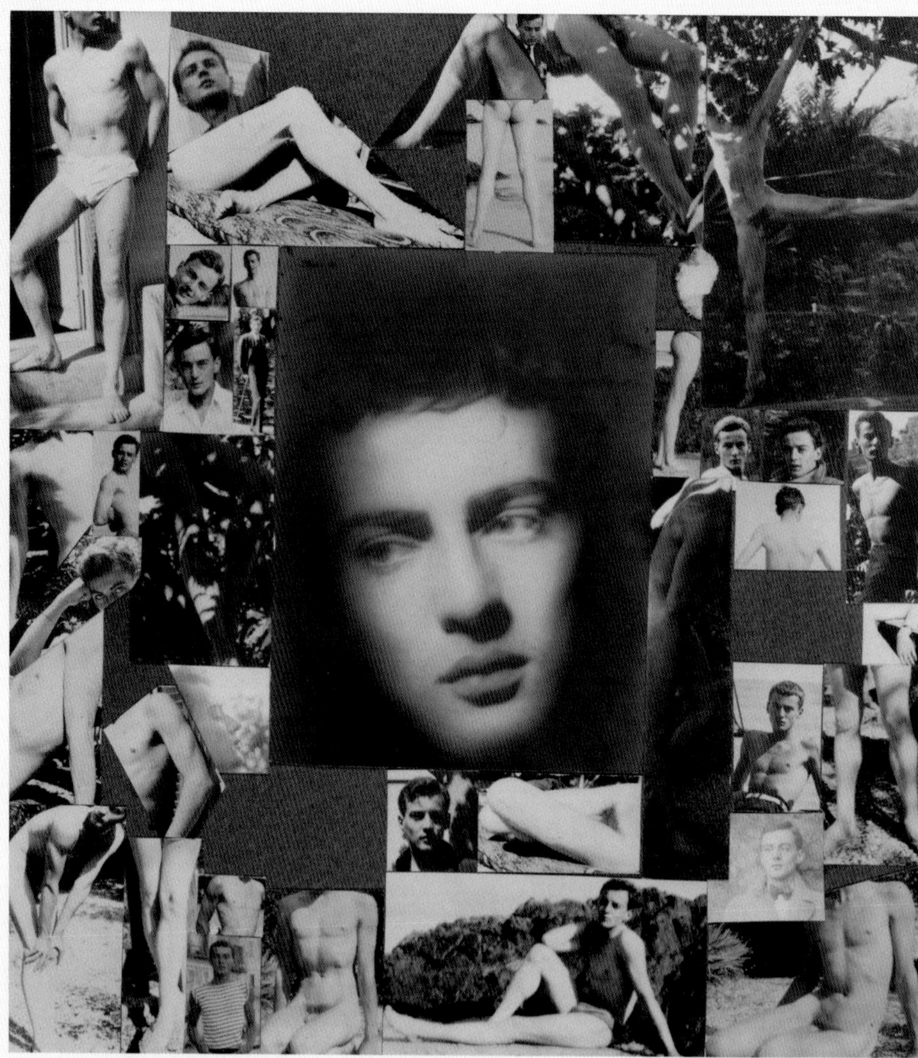

of literature, photography, and fashion. While Ewing collected images for his *Gallery* and took snapshots with his Kodak, by 1928, Lynes was already beginning to embark on a serious effort to cast himself as a professional photographer. This would, in turn, inspire Ewing to try his hand at art photography as well, resulting in the *Carnival of Venice* portrait series, which he began in 1932. More important, the two men shared a passion for looking at beautiful, preferably nude, male bodies, and they traded images from their collections of photos showing bodybuilders, athletes, and male models. For Lynes, whose collaged self-portrait, made from images that date from the late 1920s, speaks volumes about his supreme confidence in the beauty of his body (fig. 3.24), looking through the lens of a camera and making photographs soon became a way to capture and enhance that experience of visual pleasure: one always feels his presence in the images, whether as subject or observer. Ewing, though always the shy and distanced observer, soon began to experiment with portraits (including nudes) and self-portraits as well. For both men, photography was relational and interactive: circulating their photographs among friends was a way of participating in and creating queer community, as noted by Nick Mauss and Angela Miller in their recent book on Lynes's work and his collaboration (from the 1930s until the 1950s) with Paul Cadmus, Jared French, and Margaret French, who worked under the name of PaJaMa.[41]

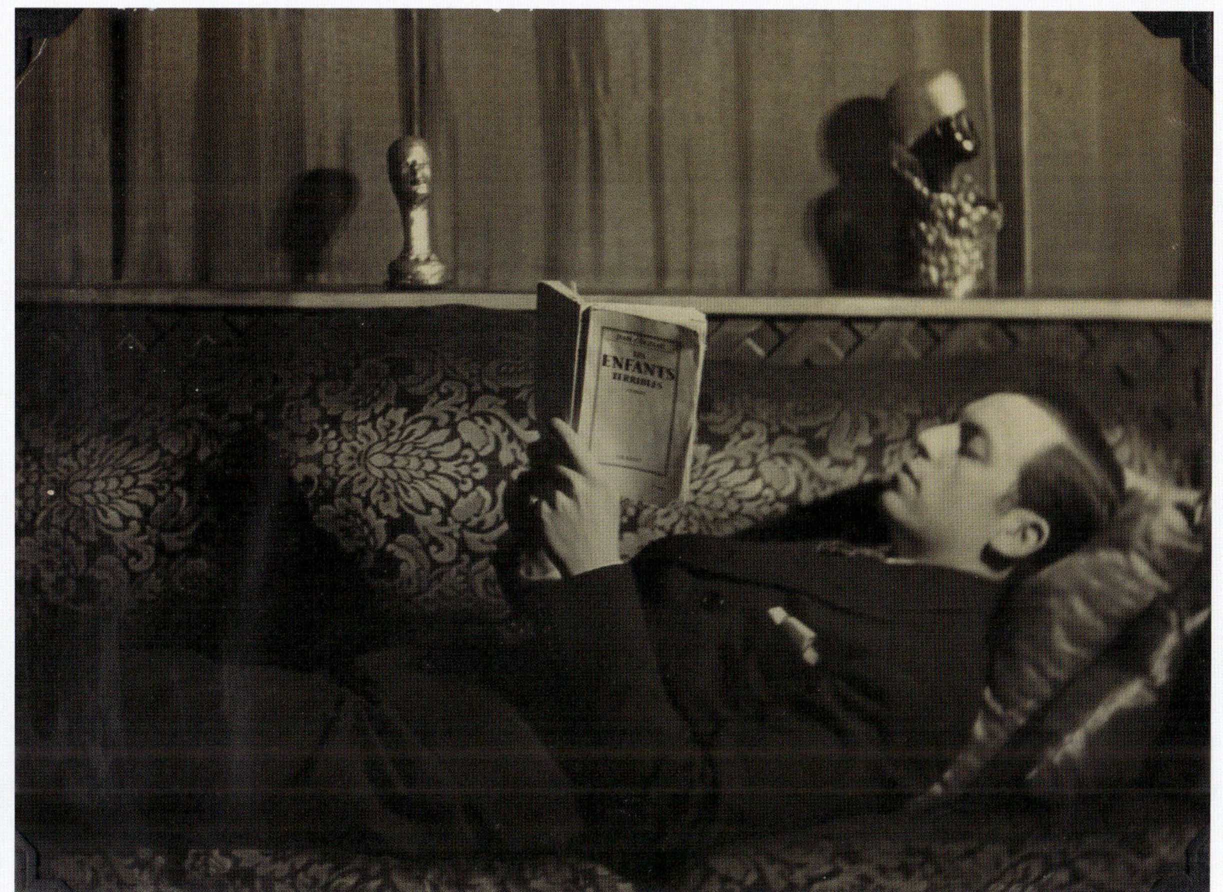

3.25 George Platt Lynes, *Max Ewing Reading Cocteau's Les Enfants Terribles*, December 1929. Max Ewing Papers.

Clearly Lynes was an enthusiastic supporter of and contributor to Ewing's collection and *Gallery*. He appears in the catalogue a number of times, both as the subject of portraits (catalogue no. 164: George Platt Lynes, "photograph widely known under title: 'The Archangel'"; no. 237: "George Lynes [gift of Adlai Harbeck]"), and as the creator and donor of others. On April 7, 1929, Ewing's twenty-sixth birthday, he wrote to his parents to say that Lynes intended to tour the *Gallery* when he returned to New York after May 1, and that he hoped that "Glenway and Monroe" would come along.[42] Perhaps it was on that occasion that Lynes gave Ewing copies of his most treasured portraits from his time in France, three snapshots of Gertrude Stein from March 1929 and another of Jean Cocteau, "holding a spyglass as soldier holding gun," according to the *Catalogue*, all of which remain in the archive. According to Lynes's biographer Allen Ellenzweig, the latter was taken with Monroe Wheeler's Kodak the previous year.[43] That image was prominently displayed near the top of the closet wall, close to the well-known portrait of Cocteau firing a gun by Berenice Abbott from 1926, the same year that Ewing traveled to Villefranche.

It is significant that one of Lynes's earliest efforts as a professional photographer, for which he made use of the new photography equipment given to him by a friend of Wescott and Wheeler, shows Ewing, dressed in a coat and tie, reading a copy of *Les Enfants Terribles* while lying on the couch in his apartment in December 1929 (fig. 3.25); two clay heads that Ewing had recently sculpted can be seen on the shelf behind him.[44] Later in 1932, Ewing wrote to Lynes about the photo, requesting a "shiny print of that picture you took of me on the couch here

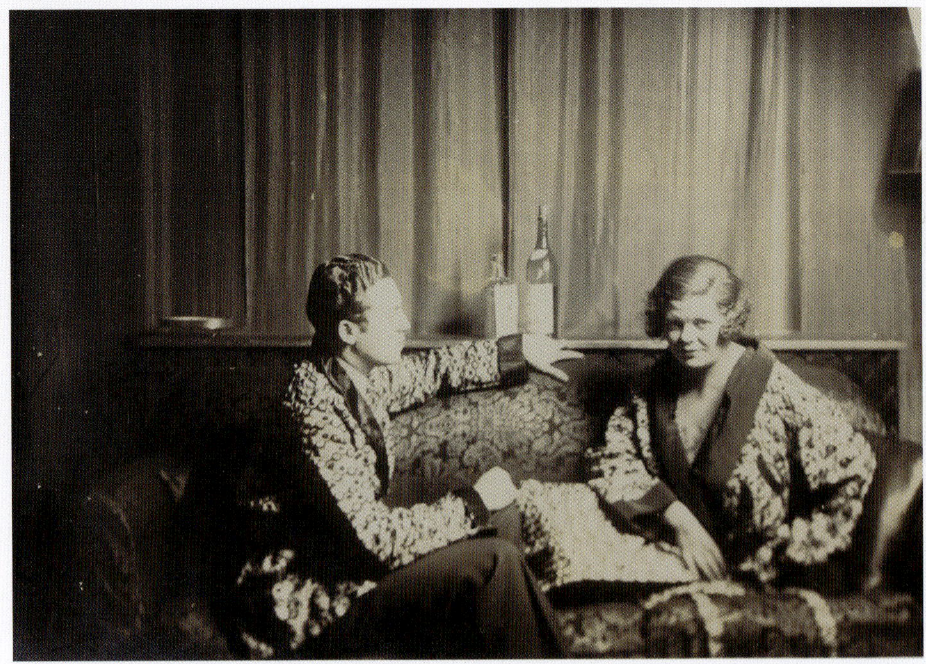

reading *Les Enfants Terribles*," but "in case you are too busy to attend to even this," he joked, "then I will just have to struggle along on some new ones of Berenice Abbott's."[45]

The same month, Lynes produced another portrait of Ewing in which he posed with the British writer and socialite Zena Naylor (fig. 3.26); both are wearing the elaborately patterned dressing gowns he acquired in Paris. In an undated letter from December 1929, he wrote to his parents to tell them: "The photos that George Lynes took of me and Zena Naylor are quite good. I will have them for you to see at Christmas."[46] He also wrote to his parents on February 3, 1930, to let them know that Lynes had come in and photographed him.[47] These rather stiff portraits of Ewing (see fig. 4.1) also survive in the archive.

BODYBUILDERS AND BOXERS

The two friends shared a fascination with the popular Harlem entertainer Paul Meeres (who had been a dance partner of Josephine Baker early in his career), and both men photographed him on a number of occasions. Here the racial and sexual politics were more controversial than in the case of Sansone: for queer, white men like Lynes, Ewing, Van Vechten, and others, outings to Harlem clubs such as Small's Paradise, the Hot-Cha, and the Sugar Cane not only provided opportunities to dance and flirt with other men, both Black and white, but also to see talented and beautiful Black singers and dancers perform on stage, often in revealing costumes. First among these were Paul Meeres and Jimmie Daniels, both of whom were frequently photographed by these men in the 1920s.

In another example of their shared enthusiasms, Ewing and Lynes both got to know the bodybuilder Fred Ritter around this time; Ewing met him late in 1930, and Lynes soon thereafter. In a letter of December 11, 1930, Ewing mentions to his parents that he has "a free pass to Texas Guinan's Club Argonaut," and that he is "Using it tonight with Marion Morehouse, the fashion model, and a boy named Fred Ritter." That same night, as he informed his parents, he gave "a recital of his songs at his house" and his "friends Ettie and Florine [Stettheimer] came" — once again creating the sort of mind-boggling juxtaposition of disparate worlds and

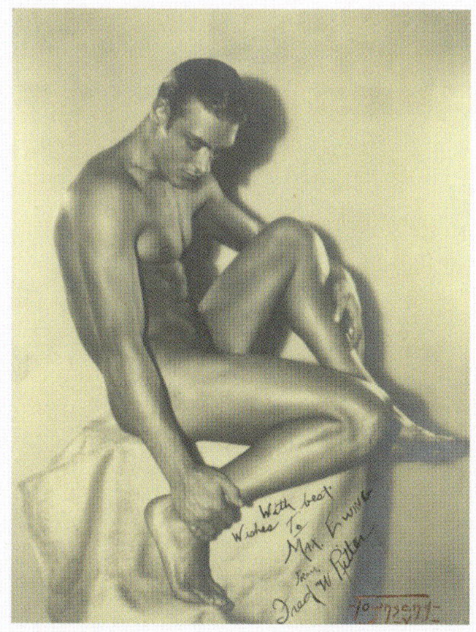

3.27 Edwin Townsend, *Fred Ritter*, inscribed to Max Ewing, c. 1931.

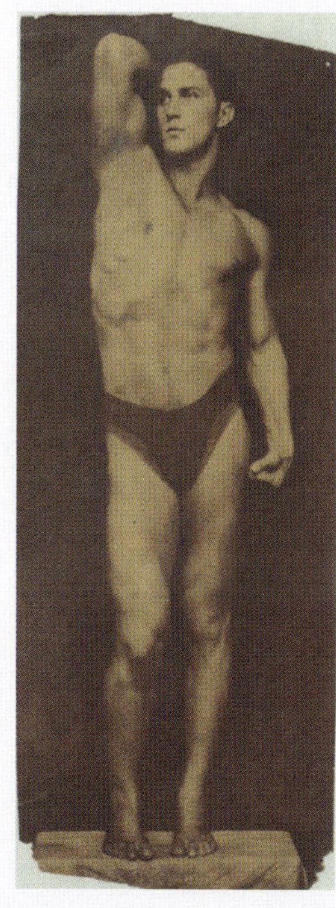

3.28 Anon., *Anthony Sansone*, with "cache-sexe" added later.

experiences that we have by this point come to expect from him.[48] Photographed in 1931 by Edwin Townsend in a series of commercial publicity shots that would be useful in his budding career as a model (fig. 3.27), Ritter inscribed one of the images to Ewing, who kept it in his scrapbooks; Ritter's height and weight are recorded on the back in the same hand.

Encouraged by George Lynes, Carl Van Vechten, and other friends, Ewing arranged his *Gallery* in a way that prominently featured the nude and semi-clad images of bodybuilders, dancers, and male models; some of these men — including Ritter, Anthony Sansone, Robert Gorham, and Paul Meeres — visited the apartment and toured the collection on multiple occasions. Indeed, as noted earlier, Sansone and Gorham were among the first to see the closet *Gallery* in November 1928. Ewing's collection of Anthony Sansone's portraits housed a number of nudes, including "Sansone in cache sexe flexing right Arm" (fig. 3.28); "Anthony Sansone nude and flexing partout (reluctant gift of Mr. Sansone)"; and Sansone "in the (practically altogether reclining along a white brick wall with feet poised on a pillow peculiarly placed (very unusual item showing tendency toward sur-realisme). Gift of Mr. Sansone" (see fig. 3.5), an image that is clearly visible in views of the *Gallery* (see fig. 3.4). No doubt the photo of "Sansone wearing nothing at all signed to me 'best wishes 1929,'" was among the treasures of the *Gallery*. Sansone was an entrepreneur whose "look book," entitled *Modern Classics* (1930), featured an "artistic" cover photo by Edwin Townsend; he became a particular favorite of Ewing's and Lynes's, and both men acquired photographs directly from him. As the historian Allen Ellenzweig noted in his biography of Lynes, the photographer reported in a July 12, 1929 letter to Monroe Wheeler that he had recently run into Sansone and Max Ewing eating together and was invited to join them; "the outcome of their meal," as Ellenzweig notes, was that "George was richer by several photographs."[49]

In August 1929, Lynes showed his growing collection of images of male nudes, including the images of Sansone that he had recently acquired, to Glenway Wescott and Monroe Wheeler when they met at Lynes's home in New Jersey.

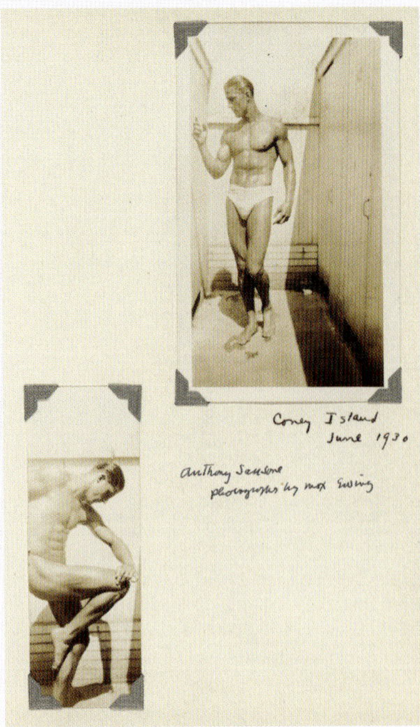

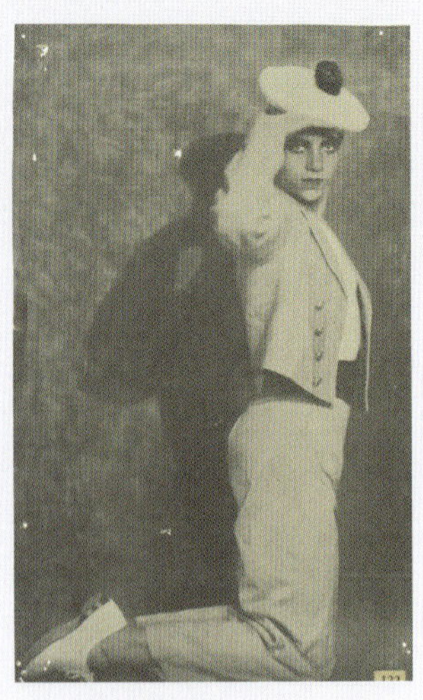

3.29 Max Ewing, snapshots of Anthony Sansone at Coney Island, June 1930. Max Ewing Papers.

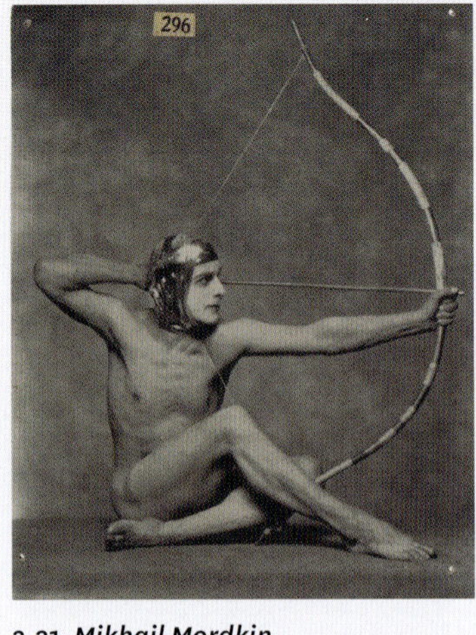

3.31 *Mikhail Mordkin.*

3.30 *Serge Lifar in Les Matelots.*

The two men encouraged him to pursue his own work in that arena, and Lynes photographed Sansone at the end of 1929, around the same time that he made his portraits of Ewing and Zena Naylor.[50] Ewing also took a number of snapshots of Sansone, using his Kodak camera on an excursion to the bodybuilder's training camp at Coney Island in June 1930 (fig. 3.29): these photos are preserved in his scrapbooks at Yale. These and many other images of scantily clad men were prominently displayed and listed in the *Catalogue* in a way that was intended to amuse, surprise, and even shock Ewing's friends, particularly people he knew from the highbrow worlds of opera, music, and literature in which he customarily moved.[51] He delighted in creating such unexpected revelations, since everything in his *Gallery* revealed a different part of who he was. The exhibition thus featured a nude photo of Charles Laskey, the bodybuilder and dancer who had performed at his first big party in April 1928, inscribed "To my sincere friend Max Ewing, with best regards, Charles L. Laskey," as well as two signed, nude photos of Robert Gorham that survive in Van Vechten's scrapbooks: in one, Gorham is shown "As Adam, wielding opportunely leafing branch." In addition to these, a photo of the much-admired Diaghilev dancer Serge Lifar, lying bare-chested "in the surf" at Juan-les-Pins, is clearly visible in the 1928 view of the closet: the image is one of a handful of portraits of the dancer on view in the *Gallery*, most of which showed him performing in various stage roles, including the queer fan-favorite *Les Matelots* (fig. 3.30). A relatively tame portrait of another Diaghilev dancer, described in the *Catalogue* as a "nude" image of "Mikhail Mordkin wearing nothing but a silver turban" (fig. 3.31), was also prominently displayed.

Like dance, sporting events offered ample opportunities to see male beauty on full display and in motion. As early as 1928, Ewing, Van Vechten, and Lynes started attending boxing matches and getting to know a number of boxers themselves, entertaining these men in their homes, just as they did with jazz singers, dancers, and male models. This focus on athleticism and exercise was not simply an eccentricity of the avant-garde in New York; as historian John

Potvin and others have shown, physical fitness and
training became fashionable elements in the education
and daily routine of the "modern" man, from the
European bachelor "dandy" to the boxing and basketball-
playing artist celebrated by the Bauhaus and in
Le Corbusier's magazine *Esprit Nouveau*.[52] Ewing was
excited to report to his parents that he had gone to one
of Gene Tunney's bouts at the end of July 1928, and he
included a number of images of the prizefighter in his
Gallery (fig. 3.32), including a jokey photo that purported to show the
resemblance of Tunney to Beethoven. This sort of thing no doubt perplexed the
people who knew Ewing not only as a snob but also as a "queer boy" who had
always preferred the company, and interests, of his girlfriends. For Ewing and his
queer circle, however, these photos not only provided myriad opportunities
for sustained looking at male bodies but had the added value of shocking their
well-mannered and proper acquaintances.

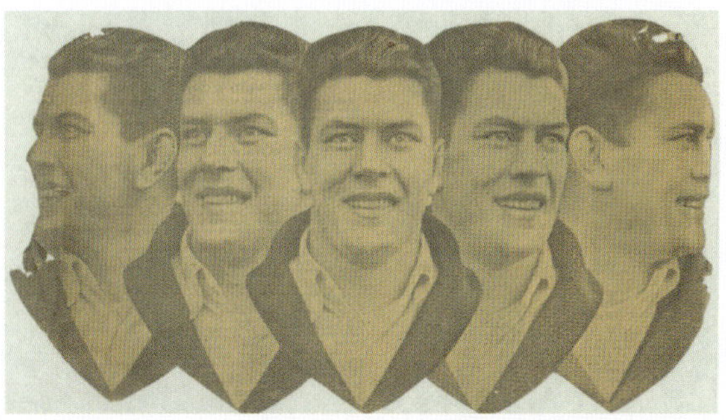

3.32 *Gene Tunney.*

It obviously took a bit of explaining on Ewing's part for Ewing's parents to
adjust to his newfound interest in these pursuits. Ewing responded to his parents'
questions in a letter from August 1928 that explained his point of view with the
sort of swagger that they had grown accustomed to:

> My going to the fight is nothing to be surprised about. I am all right
> about all those things now. And not at all as intolerant as I once
> was, or as exclusive in my enthusiasms. More and more it becomes
> apparent that it doesn't matter particularly what you do if you
> do it well enough and I am willing to grant you that a swell fighter is
> about as valuable as a swell singer, and a lot more so than a bum
> singer, so there you are … What I mean is that almost everything
> interests me now, whereas only a few things did once. Of course I do
> think that Mary Garden and Glenway Wescott are more ultimately
> important personages than Gene Tunney. But Tunney is a spectacular
> beauty who behaves in a charming and often amusing manner, and
> is therefore treasurable.[53]

Tunney was not the only athlete featured in Ewing's closet exhibition:
images of the famous fighter known as Kid Chocolate, including one personally
inscribed to Ewing, a photo of Jack Dempsey ("as Rodin's
thinker"), and a number of Max Schmeling (see fig. 3.12)
were also displayed. A portrait of a beautiful Paul Robeson
(fig. 3.33), stripped to the waist also occupied a prominent
position, high up on the wall, flanked by images of two
actresses in picture hats. Robeson had been a star football
player at Rutgers and in the NFL before receiving a law
degree at Columbia and embarking on a career as an actor
and singer.[54]

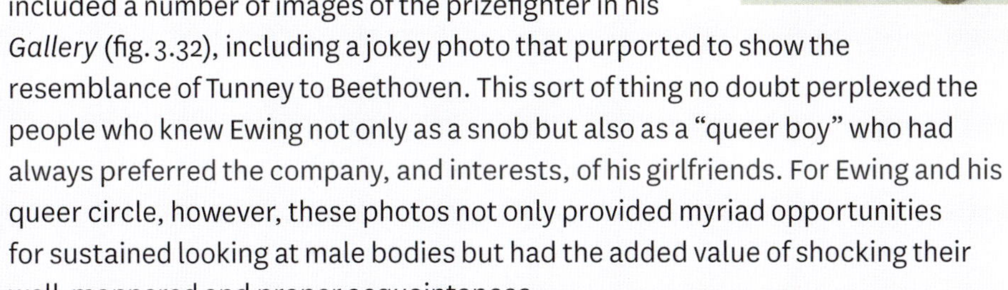

3.33 *Paul Robeson.*

Ewing clearly delighted in such visual juxtapositions
and also in jokey word games, particularly when it came to
images of queer heroes and literary giants: unlikely surprises in the fantasy
universe he created evolved from the sort of time travel that occurred when he

placed a portrait of "Oscar Wilde and Alfred Douglas on a Marble Bench" to the right of a photo of Charles Lindbergh in his aviator's cap.[55] He also hung a well-known photograph of Marcel Proust directly above a rare early portrait of his new friend, the up-and-coming photographer Cecil Beaton — one of the "Bright Young Things" whom Ewing had met (with Constant Lambert and the Sitwells) in Paris and London in 1926–27, standing by the sea (fig. 3.34).[56]

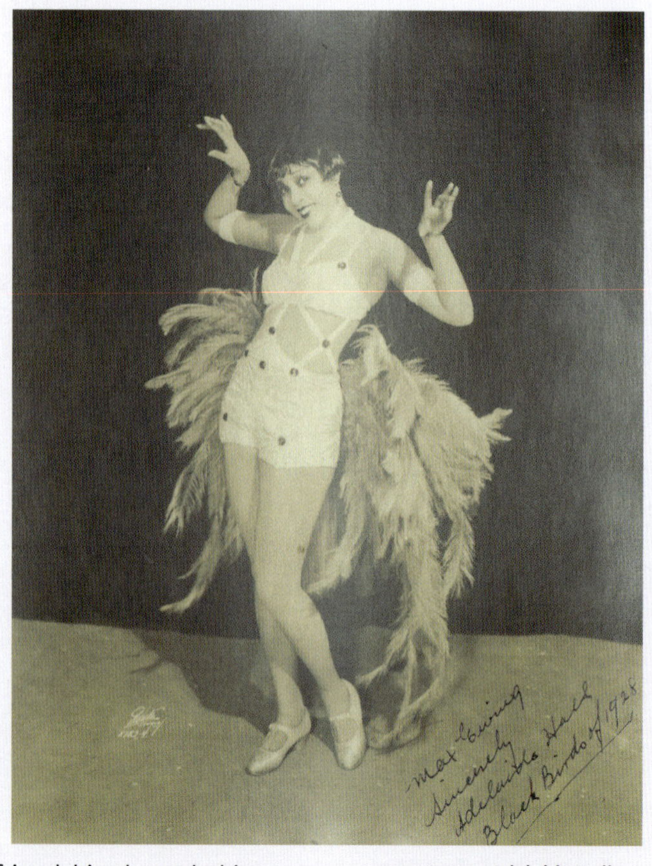

3.34 Cecil Beaton, *Self-Portrait by the Shore*, c. 1926. Cecil Beaton Archive, Condé Nast.

In the middle of the same wall is Radclyffe Hall, the cross-dressing author of the banned lesbian novel *The Well of Loneliness* (1928), who is visually paired with the African American cabaret performer Adelaide Hall (fig. 3.35), the star of the Harlem revue *Blackbirds of 1928*, seen posing in her skimpy cabaret costume, complete with tail feathers (see fig. 3.4). Another camp joke resulted from the pairing of a portrait of the popular comedian Beatrice Lillie — known for the double entendres in such songs as "There are Fairies at the Bottom of Our Garden" — who married Sir Robert Peel in 1920 and was thus awarded the title "Lady Peel" — with a historical 1827 portrait of *Lady Peel* painted by the British artist Thomas Lawrence, held in the Frick Collection.[57] This sort of unlikely mashup and camp irony — which Ewing and his friends clearly loved — featured prominently in the *Catalogue* as well, where unlikely lists of people with the same first or last name produced some remarkable gatherings of wildly different sorts of people, including George Lynes, George Sand, George Eliot, George Antheil, and the New York fireman George Lorz, who had posed for a statue of *Civic Virtue*.

BERENICE ABBOTT IN
PARIS AND NEW YORK: 1926–32

As a group, Ewing's portraits formed an imaginary band of friends and supporters who cheered him on in his effort to combine the many parts of himself. Indeed, many portraits harkened back to his time in Europe, and Paris especially, where his friendships brought him into contact with a glamorous world of queer culture that was far more widely accepted than it was in the United States — even in the avant-garde (and tentatively multiracial) community he knew in New York. Many of these photos were given to Ewing by the photographer Berenice Abbott, a close friend for a number of years.

3.35 Anon., *Adelaide Hall*, inscribed to Max Ewing. Max Ewing Papers.

While clearly very different from the raucous and risqué bond he shared with George Lynes, Ewing's friendship with Berenice Abbott spoke to an equally significant part of who he was. Ewing had perhaps met Abbott in Paris in 1926, where, having apprenticed with Man Ray, she created memorable portraits of avant-garde artists and writers like Jean Cocteau and James Joyce, as well as a series of well-known images of her fashionable lesbian friends. These included the *New Yorker* correspondent Janet Flanner and her partner, the writer Solita Solano; Margaret Anderson and Jane Heap (fig. 3.36), editors of the *Little Review*; and Djuna Barnes, the writer who had created *The Ladies Almanac*, fancifully describing the amorous adventures of the world around Natalie Barney and her Paris salon.[58] Ewing owned a number of these and displayed them in his *Gallery*.

Although it is startling to discover these now-famous photographs among the newspaper clippings and other ephemera in Ewing's *Gallery*, his friendship with Abbott makes sense: they shared not only their youthful Paris experiences, their nonconforming sexual orientation, and their membership in the queer, cultural community in New York, but also, first and foremost, their love for photography, and — in those years, at least — for portraits in particular. Indeed, when Ewing needed an "author portrait" for the jacket of his comic novel *Going Somewhere* (a highly mannered work of light fiction written in the style of Carl Van Vechten, published by Alfred A. Knopf in 1933), he passed over Lynes in favor of Abbott, boasting to his parents in 1932 that he had been "photographed by Berenice Abbott who is conceded [*sic*] to be the best portrait photographer in New York and Paris. She is impossibly expensive if you pay her. But now being a public and professional figure, I do not pay her, and she does it for the glory!"[59] (fig. 3.37).

During his visit to Paris, Ewing became particularly close with Margaret Anderson (who, oddly enough, does not appear in the *Gallery*), Jane Heap, and Georgette Leblanc. Heap, a close friend of Muriel Draper's and a member of the Gurdjieff circle in New York and London, had adopted the habit of cross-dressing in a suit and tie. As Abbott's portrait shows, she cut a dapper and somewhat startling figure. Ewing took note of this in a letter to his parents dated October 3, 1926, informing them that he would be sailing home with Heap on the *Berengaria* at the end of the month: "You can't imagine what an extraordinary looking couple we make," he wrote, for "after Muriel Draper, who is first in everything, Jane Heap

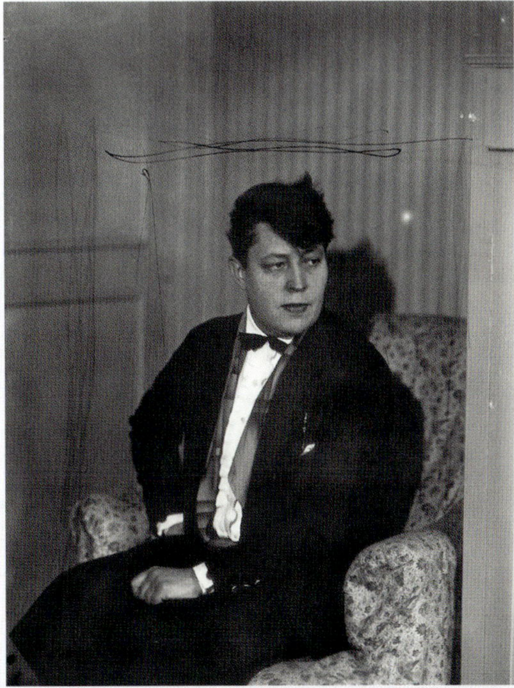

3.36 Berenice Abbott, *Portrait of Jane Heap*, c. 1928, gelatin silver print, 4¼ × 3 in. (10.8 × 7.8 cm). Estate of Berenice Abbott. Getty Images.

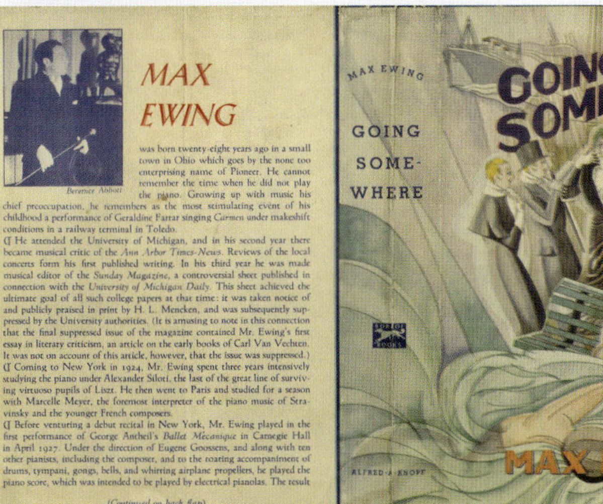

3.37 Max Ewing, *Going Somewhere*, 1933. Cover illustration by Robert Locher; Author photo by Berenice Abbott. Max Ewing Papers.

is the most striking looking woman I've ever seen. Not beautiful in the Marion Morehouse way, but beautiful as a man is beautiful. I adore her."[60]

On the *Gallery* wall, Abbott's portrait of Heap could be found among many other denizens of lesbian Paris, including *saloniste* Natalie's Barney and both of her life partners, the Duchesse de Clermont-Tonnerre and Ewing's dearest friend, the artist Romaine Brooks (see chapter 2). Brooks and Barney appeared together on the *Gallery* walls in a number of other snapshots, including one described as "Natalie Barney and Romaine Brooks Amid Floral Decorations (Capri)" (see fig. 2.12).[61] Barney's photograph of Ewing, and Ewing's startling photographs of Barney with Esther Murphy in Verona, were all displayed as well and survive in Ewing's archive.

Other luminaries of the international avant-garde included F. Scott Fitzgerald "looking at a book" (*Catalogue* no. 215) and Josephine Baker "(Nude. With Necklace and Bracelets)," an image from a performance that Ewing had written about in his letters from Paris.[62] A portrait of Cole Porter, whom he had met when he visited Venice with Romaine Brooks, and another of Noël Coward (fig. 3.38) were also on display. The collection also included a rare image of Stein's and Flanner's friend Ernest Hemingway hunting in Florida (fig. 3.39). Ewing had not actually met the famous writer in Paris, but he certainly knew a great deal about him and his work. Two photographs of Gabriele D'Annunzio, whom Ewing had met during his travels, made the cast of characters complete.

3.38 *Noël Coward.*

Ewing placed himself squarely in the middle of this unlikely group, using a photo in which he is being sculpted by his friend Roy Sheldon in Paris in 1927 (see fig. 2.4) as a pivot point high on the wall in the *Gallery*. The image created a vivid souvenir of the glamorous Parisian world that Ewing so fondly recalled, and it gave him a chance to show himself at his most handsome and fashionable, wearing the beautiful suit and waistcoat he had purchased on his trip.[63] Through his clothes and manners, grooming and exercise regime, Ewing had completed his transformation from a small-town Midwestern boy to a sophisticated, international dandy, firmly situated in a star-studded firmament of his own creation. With the realization of his *Gallery*, his self-fashioning was complete and his position in the queer, new world of New York's extended bohemia was secure: like a Renaissance prince, or an Elizabethan nobleman, Ewing's guests could come to know his network of friends, supporters, and distant acquaintances through the portraits with which he surrounded himself.[64]

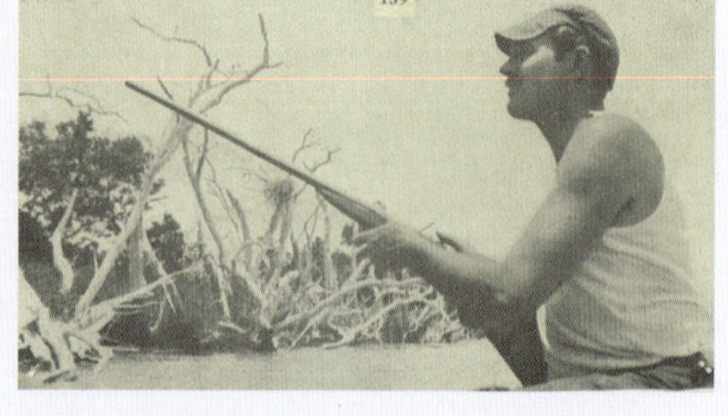

3.39 *Ernest Hemingway.*

VISITORS TO THE CLOSET: PRINCESS EUGÉNIE MURAT

One of Berenice Abbott's best-known and least understood photographs, her portrait of the Princess Eugénie Murat (fig. 3.40), stands out in the 1932 view of the *Gallery*: this image opens up a window onto another aspect of the world that Ewing and the photographer shared. In 1929, Murat visited New York from Paris, taking the bohemian crowd by storm: she cut a broad swath through Ewing's circle and the nightspots of Harlem, and Abbott soon fell head over heels in love with her.[65] The entirely unreliable princess was an opium-smoker and a terrible flirt, and her affair with Abbott, such as it was, ended badly after Murat returned

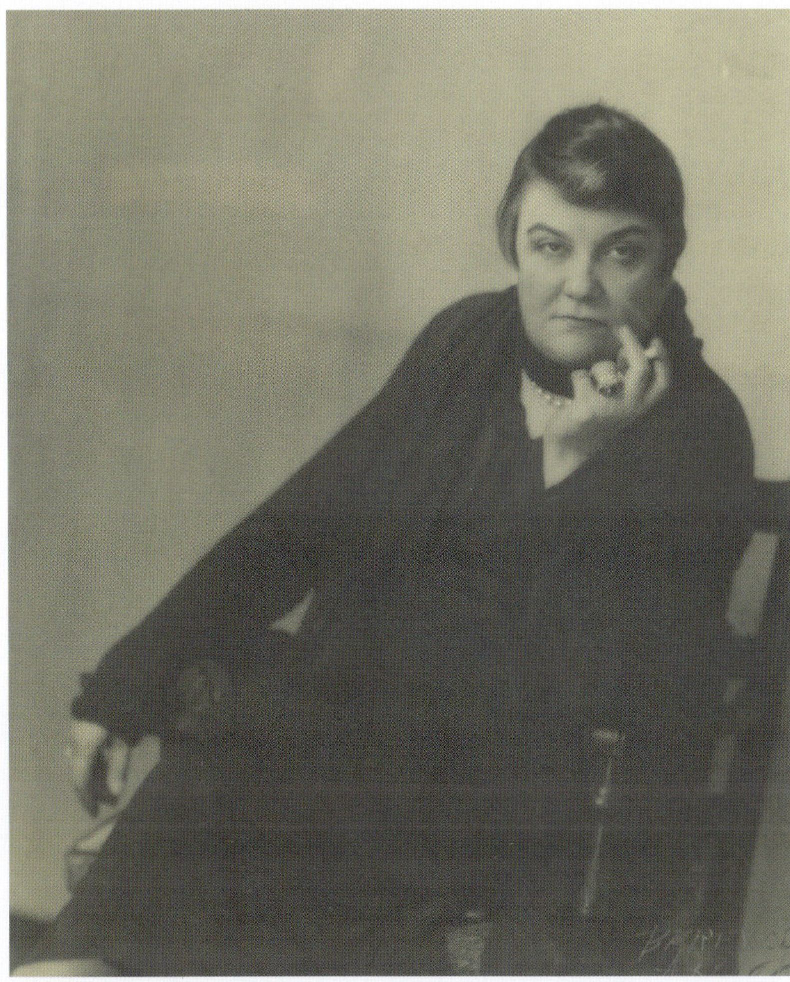

3.40 Berenice Abbott, *Princess Eugénie Murat*, 1929, gelatin silver print. Estate of Berenice Abbott. Getty Images.

to France and — having moved on both literally and figuratively — rescinded her offer to host Abbott at her home and provide financial support for her career in photography.

For a short, intense period in 1929, Abbott and Ewing shared their fascination with Murat, following her progress, documenting her activities, and even collaborating on a "Speak-a-Phone" recording of a dialogue entitled "Êtes-vous Polygame?," written by Ewing, in which Abbott took the part of the princess and Ewing played the interviewer.[66] The recording survives in the Yale collection, bizarrely yet vividly suggesting the lengths to which both young people would go in their efforts to capture the essence of the strange creature who had appeared in their midst, seemingly out of nowhere. Ewing described her arrival on the scene in February 1929:

> Douglas Parmentier the head of Harpers came here … the man
> Emily Vanderbilt wanted to marry. He planned to bring the Princess
> Murat here today but she was out all night last night, and when
> he stopped for her today at teatime she was still unable to be roused!
> She is a strange, grand creature … She arrived here unannounced
> and everyone wonders what she is up to in America. I met her once at
> Gertrude Stein's in Paris, and she remembered the occasion when
> I saw her at Muriel's the other night. Friend of Barney and Duchess
> de Clermont-Tonnerre.[67]

Not long after, on March 7, 1929, he wrote to his parents to let them know that Murat had come to his apartment to view the *Gallery*:

> Yesterday PM the Princess Murat came here to make her postponed visit to the Gallery ... the princess is about fifty years old, large, and awfully strange looking, and frightfully amusing. She was married to the Prince Achille Murat, though she has had many famous love affairs since then ... She is like a child of five, in her general confusion, and excitement, and bewilderment, and vagueness. She carries a little notebook around in which she puts down her engagements and addresses, but she usually gets them down wrong.[68]

The fact that Murat looked like no princess that anyone in New York had ever seen or imagined didn't deter her admirers: Ewing loved the story about how some photographers from Pond's, the cold cream company, arrived at her hotel to take her picture for an advertising campaign and refused to believe that she was indeed a princess until she decked herself out in her jewels. These antics only made her more fascinating to Ewing and Abbott, who captured her queer image in a brilliantly memorable portrait taken in New York around this time.

On June 9, 1929, Ewing described two parties that he organized for the Princess Murat and her friends in his home, bragging that "Georges Carpentier the famous handsome French boxer arrived here last week too, and the Princess was trying all last evening to reach him to ask him to dinner with us one night soon. I hope she arranges it, for I should love to meet him."[69] He also reported that Bessie Smith and Dudley Murphy (the theater director) had come to a different event at his house, and that Bessie Smith had performed for his friends, including the Princess Murat and the fashion model Marion Morehouse: "In no other city in the world," he gushed, "would the best Irish film director bring the greatest coloured blues singer in the world to see you, with the world's most famous fashion model there at the same time — and the most amusing of French princesses ask you to dine with the most celebrated of European boxers — all within two days!"

VISITORS TO THE CLOSET: MERCEDES DE ACOSTA AND CECIL BEATON

This was a very heady period of parties, Harlem nightclubs, and in-home entertaining for Ewing. On February 6, 1929, he welcomed a glamorous group of visitors to his apartment, once again highlighting his connections to the most famous and sought-after people in New York, as well as his contacts among the tight-knit circle of lesbian theater women, including Mercedes de Acosta, and the actresses Eva Le Gallienne and Blyth Daly. The star-studded (and mostly queer) list of visitors that he drew up to report to his parents is something that we have come to expect from Ewing: "The tea hour resembled Grand Central Station at the time of the Christmas Rush," he wrote:

> Mercedes de Acosta brought Cecil Beaton the English photographer and artist whose drawings now fill the pages of *Vogue*. Gladys Calthorp came, and seemed to be wearing any number of ear rings ... she is the most renowned English woman stage designer ... Noel [*sic*] Coward's

boyfriend Allen Vincent [was here, as well as] Robert Gorham and
Anthony Sansone, Albert Carroll, Dorothy and Roy Sheldon.[70]

In an undated letter written at about this time, he described a dinner at Natalie
Hammond's penthouse, adding that it was "the most amusing I have ever gone to
in New York"; the guests included "Texas Guinan, Lou Tellegen, Mercedes de
Acosta, Count Vasselyi and myself."[71]

A number of photographs in the collection commemorate these
friendships and events, including an image of de Acosta and her lover Greta
Garbo wearing trousers (fig. 3.41), a 1931 photo showing Garbo as the sphinx
(fig. 3.42), and one of Marlene Dietrich in a top hat and tails. Ewing also owned
a handful of portraits of Tallulah Bankhead (including the image in which she
appears with her friend Cecil Beaton (see fig. 3.17) and photos of Eva Le
Gallienne — all famous and, of course, closeted, lesbian actresses. Such was the
range of Ewing's activities and the diversity of the circles he moved in, from
nightclub owners, to intellectuals and heiresses, actresses and titled aristocrats:
indeed, the week after Hammond's party, he noted that his friend Virgil Thomson
"had performed a selection of songs from his new Gertrude Stein opera at Carl
Van Vechten's party and that Draper's friend Mabel Dodge was also there."[72]

More surprising is the number and variety of portraits that Cecil Beaton,
newly arrived in New York City on assignment for *Vogue*, presented to Ewing as
gifts for his *Gallery*.[73] These include an image from a privately printed Christmas
card, perhaps from 1926, showing Beaton in drag (fig. 3.43), as well as an early
self-portrait standing by the sea (see fig. 3.34). Other rare images from the start of
Beaton's career — his first public exhibition was in November 1927 at the Cooling

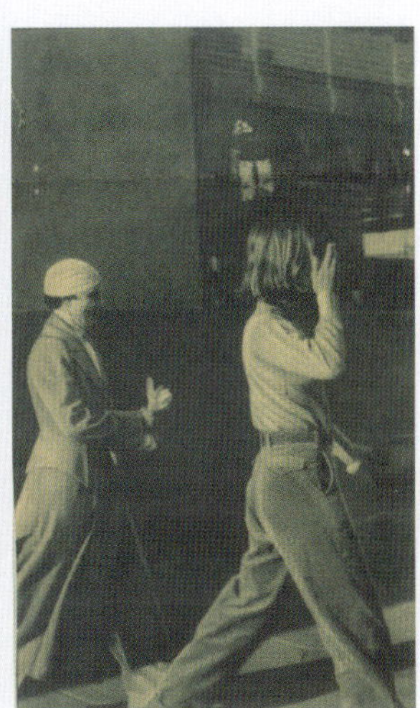

3.41 *Mercedes de Acosta and
Greta Garbo.*

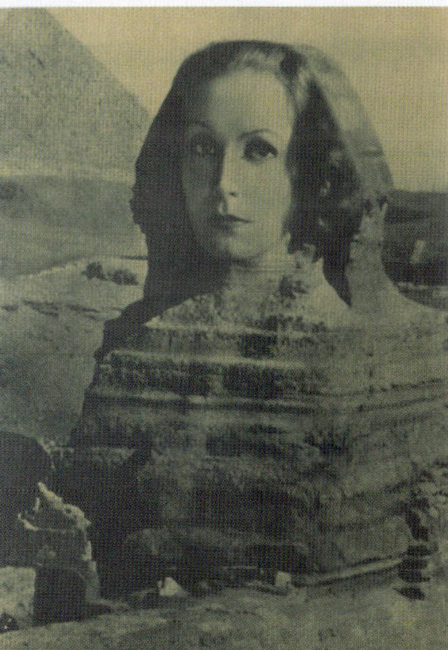

3.42 Clarence Sinclair Bull, *Greta
Garbo as the Sphinx*, 1931.

3.43 *Cecil Beaton in Drag*, Christmas card,
c. 1925.

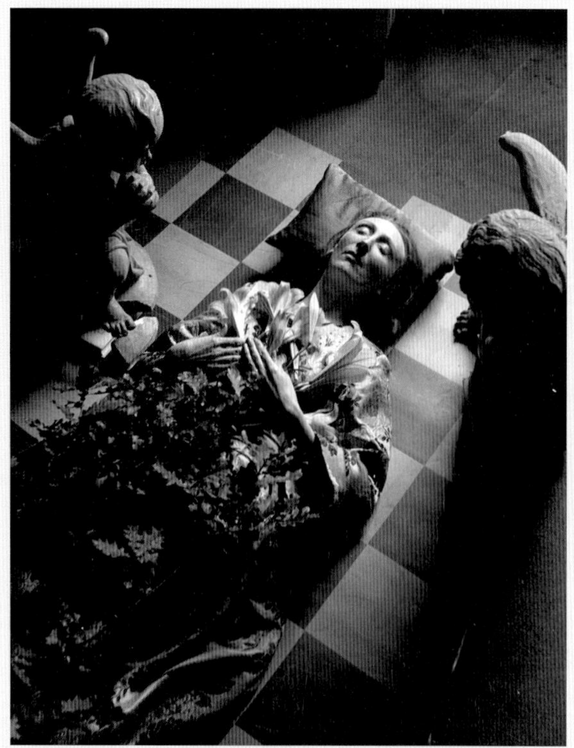

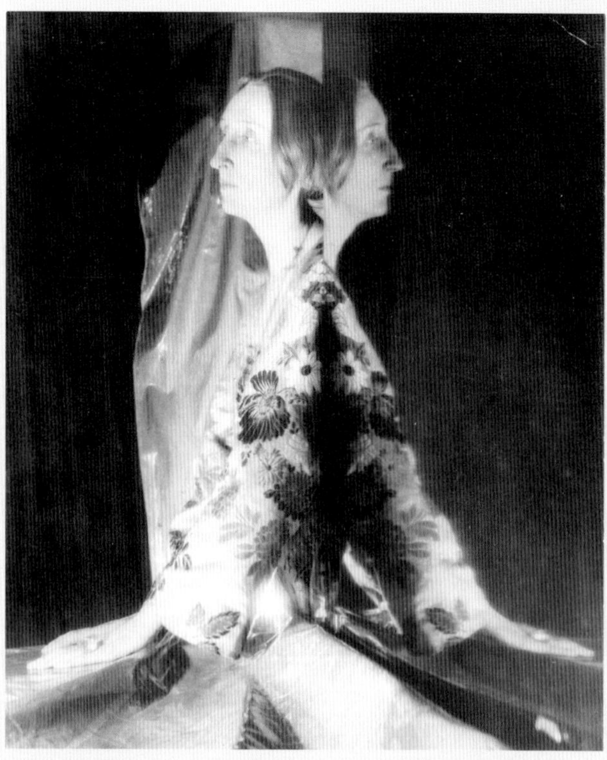

3.44 Cecil Beaton, *Edith Sitwell*, 1927, bromide print, 8 × 5⅝ in. (20.3 × 14.4 cm). National Portrait Gallery, London. Accepted in lieu of tax by H. M. Government and allocated to the Gallery, 1991, NPG x40362. Cecil Beaton Archive, Condé Nast.

3.45 Cecil Beaton, *Edith Sitwell as a Janus*, 1927, bromide print on white card mount, 9½ × 7⅝ in. (24.2 × 19.3 cm). National Portrait Gallery, London. Accepted in lieu of tax by H.M. Government and allocated to the Gallery, 1991, NPG x40361. Cecil Beaton Archive, Condé Nast.

Galleries in London — can also be found in Ewing's collection, including two portraits of Edith Sitwell in dramatic poses, one showing her lying on the floor in the guise of a Gothic effigy ("Edith Sitwell Lying Gothic Fashion," cat. no. 136) (fig. 3.44), and the other showing her as a two-faced Janus (fig. 3.45), listed in the *Catalogue* (no. 218) as included "by kindness of Cecil Beaton of the London Salon of Photography."[74] Ewing had met the Sitwells through Muriel Draper and attended a performance of *Façade: An Entertainment*, an experimental rendition of Edith's spoken poetry with music by William Walton, in London in 1926. They traveled in the same circles during this time: Beaton attended Muriel Draper's New Year's Eve party in New York City in December 1928, as did Ewing.[75]

Like George Lynes, the young Cecil Beaton was a queer, boyish photographer with whom Ewing shared a number of interests and affinities. A middle-class boy with huge social aspirations, he was determined to record and commemorate his connections to famous friends, not only through his own photographs but in his home as well. At Ashcombe, the country house where he lived and endlessly redecorated from 1930 to 1945, he curated a collection of signed handprints, left by his many friends and celebrity guests, in a small bathroom: like Ewing's closet *Gallery*, this was both a curiosity and a memorial.[76] From an early age, he had performed on the amateur stage and frequently appeared in drag along with friends from his circle of "Bright Young Things," the band of beautiful, aristocratic, young socialites that he assembled in a raucous group around him.[77] They were often photographed in costume and in full makeup at parties and gala events, and Beaton's home was fashioned to match their changing moods and the fantasy images of his elaborate stories.

Beaton and Ewing also shared a refined, camp sensibility and the studied performative social manner of queer men who used artifice, snobbery, and humor to defend themselves from prejudice and even homophobic violence. Beaton was unusually candid about his experiences growing up queer in early twentieth-century England: in his private *Diaries*, he described having been taunted and dumped in the river by a group of drunken men at a party when he was young, and like Janet Flanner — who also wrote about her ambivalence toward being a queer, young outsider in a homophobic society — he was very clear about how hard he tried to conform before he embraced his queer identity. He was also a success, and to a large extent overcame his self-hatred.[78] Thus, by his very presence in Ewing's *Gallery*, surrounded by other queer contemporaries, Beaton's example was affirming and, no doubt, also "amusing," as Ewing and his friends were fond of saying; there was strength in numbers.

VISITORS TO THE CLOSET: A'LELIA WALKER AND THE DENIZENS OF THE DARK TOWER

Another visitor to the closet, also photographed by Berenice Abbott in 1929, was A'lelia Walker, the heiress and daughter of millionaire entrepreneur Madam C. J. Walker, whom Ewing knew as a major patron of the arts and as a tireless and generous party-giver and hostess in her own right.[79] Oddly, Walker is not represented by an image in Ewing's *Gallery* or a listing in his *Catalogue*, though Van Vechten had a glamorous, inscribed photo of her (fig. 3.46), and Ewing owned a handful of images of her that he pasted into his scrapbooks. A'lelia Walker is described in a number of key letters from Ewing to his family, and their friendship is documented by letters from her to Ewing that survive in the archive. Like Van Vechten and so many others in their circle, A'lelia was a complex figure, a woman of enormous style with a huge personality, a supporter of both "high culture" and every conceivable form of entertainment on offer in Harlem, and as active in the world of business as she was in the pursuit of pleasure. Her Harlem salon, one of the key sites of the Harlem Renaissance, included all of the prominent Black writers and artists of the day — from Langston Hughes (fig. 3.47), shown in a portrait in the *Gallery* by the expat New York painter Winold Reiss, to Countee Cullen and Paul Robeson, both of whom were also represented in Ewing's collection, along with many other African American friends and associates.

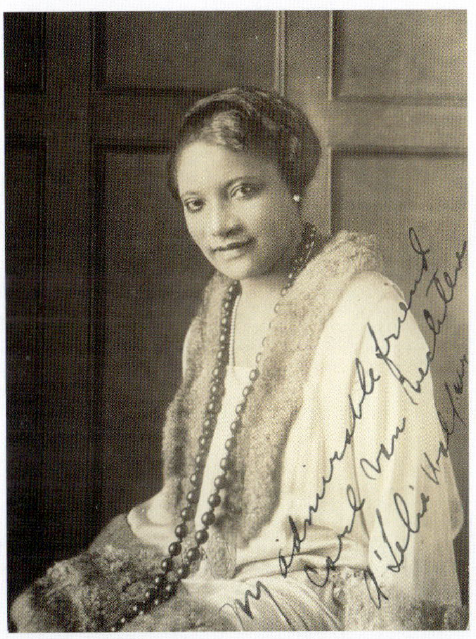

3.46 Anon., *A'lelia Walker*, inscribed to Carl Van Vechten. James Weldon Johnson Collection. Beinecke Rare Book & Manuscript Library, Yale University, New Haven, Connecticut.

Ewing had known A'lelia Walker for a number of years, dating back to 1927, when he first attended a party at her home on 136th Street. At that time, he described her to his parents — who, like Ewing himself, had never encountered anyone, white or Black, with such wealth and charisma — in glowing terms, but also with the casual racism of his circle:

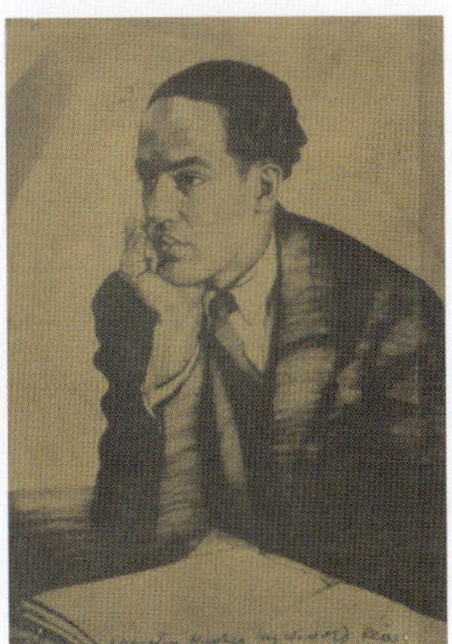

3.47 Black and white copy of Winold Reiss's, *Langston Hughes*, c. 1925.

> A'lelia inherited millions from the Anti-kink preparations of her mother, and she lives in New York in superb pomp, with silver turbans on her head, and diamond clusters

on her shoulders and velvet poppies on her hips, and very brown.
She told me two weeks ago at Muriel's that she was not going to
Europe this summer because she had just invested another million
and half dollars in some project and was going to stay in town this
summer to watch it grow. She is a superb creature and she adores me.
She is having this party Friday night for Carl Van Vechten, whom
I haven't seen for several weeks.[80]

On April 18, 1928, Walker again invited him to a party at her home, writing,
"I am to be hostess at the Dark Tower Sunday April 21 and I thought probably you
and your friends would like to be present at that time."[81] This was an invitation of
some consequence: not only were Walker's crowded parties well-known for the
enormous number and variety of the guests who attended, but also for her
permissive attitudes toward the behavior of her friends, both queer and
heterosexual. In fact, Walker had two different residences in Harlem. One was a
spacious apartment at 80 Edgecombe Avenue, where raucous parties featuring
casual sex, abundant alcohol, and drugs were on offer: this was described by
Van Vechten as a "pied-a-terre" on the label of his color photograph of A'lelia's
apartment building, indicating that it was something of a private annex to
her well-known business office and residence nearby.[82] The latter, a stately
building that served as the headquarters of the Madam C. J. Walker
Manufacturing Company, founded by A'lelia's mother, was a double-fronted
mansion at 108–110 West 136th Street, designed by the prominent African
American architect Vertner Tandy. It was both the New York home of the Walker
Company and the elegant residence of Madam C. J. Walker and her daughter.

Madam Walker, a self-made entrepreneur in the haircare and cosmetics industry
who knew more than a thing or two about branding and image-making, had also
commissioned the well-respected Tandy to build an expansive, neoclassical
country house for her on the banks of the Hudson River in Irvington, New York,
which she named Villa Lewaro. There, she entertained her friends, her business
associates, and an army of direct-sale "agents" who sold the company's products
in customers' homes. The most successful of the women "agents" had been
invited to the villa to celebrate their contributions to the company.[83] Mother and
daughter were thus very well-known not only for their broad cultural interests,
but also for their skill at literally building up their architectural brand as well as
their institutional and commercial empires. It was at 136th Street that A'lelia
established the "Dark Tower" as a "tearoom," a speakeasy, and a cultural center
featuring readings by poets and performances by Black musicians in a *moderne*
interior created by the émigré designer Paul Frankl.[84]

 Though Ewing had only a small closet in his midtown apartment to work
with, a place that in no way rivaled A'lelia's Harlem empire, he understood the
urge to create a new identity by shaping spaces, hosting events, and stage-
managing performances. He therefore cultivated the glamorous A'lelia Walker to
the fullest extent of his abilities. On April 29, 1929, he wrote home to report that
A'lelia had visited his apartment and toured his collection: "A'Lelia Walker came
with a retinue of four young men," he wrote, "dripping jewels. Her entrance even
startled the Princess Murat, who was here too, and we went from here to a dress

rehearsal of the Follies." He went on to describe a party at the "Dark Tower" that he had attended a week earlier, recalling that "one woman from Philadelphia had 36 silver bracelets on her arm," and reporting that A'lelia's apartment was hung with rose and green taffeta: Jules Bledsoe, the star of "Showboat," performed for the guests, and he recalled that, as the "evening wore on, he taught the Princess Murat to do the dance called the Bim-Bam, which was an odd sight too."[85]

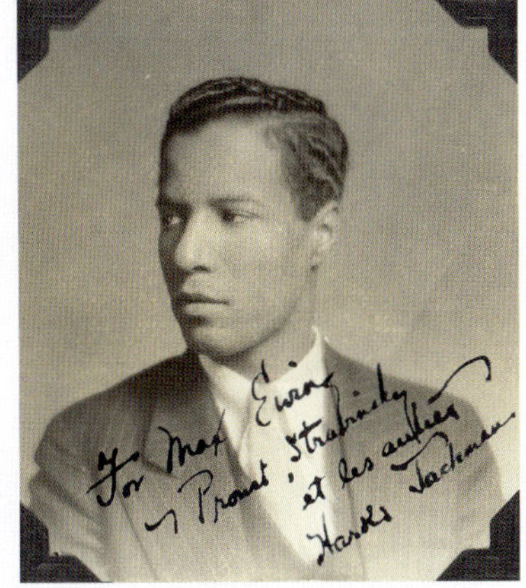

3.48 Anon., *Harold Jackman*, inscribed to Max Ewing, c. 1929. Max Ewing Papers.

Though the "Dark Tower" was ultimately closed down as a formal performance venue, private events continued at Walker's residence until her death in 1931: writers like Langston Hughes gave readings of their work, figures like Paul Robeson and Harold Jackman — who was known to some as the "most beautiful man in Harlem" (fig. 3.48) — offered performances and lectures, and there were, of course, innumerable parties. Ewing was very much a part of this crowd, writing in April 1929 that he and Jackman had walked "all the way downtown to the Battery" together, and shopped for "white duck sailor pants" at the Army Navy Store. Like Ewing, Jackman shaped his image as a sophisticated dandy who loved Paris and all things French, as the inscription — "Proust, Stravinsky, *et les autres*" — that he penned on his portrait (one of a number in the collection) suggests.[86]

In May 1929, Ewing and Muriel Draper attended a reception at the "Dark Tower" for the writers Nella Larsen and Walter White, the head of the NAACP, "both of them Negro novelists who have written outstanding books this year," adding for his parents' benefit — in the patronizing tone that was customary in their circle — that "Muriel and I went to this conscientiously, for they are very proud of achievements like this, and enjoy proper recognition."[87] Like Van Vechten, his dedication to African American culture was sincere and wide-ranging: he had portraits of many of the most prominent Black writers in his *Gallery*, but also like his friend, and Draper as well, he never relinquished his power as a white person or gave up on the mindset that established a world of difference between the two groups: the "we," as in "Muriel and I," as opposed to the "they" of the "Negro writers" who had written "outstanding books." On the contrary, that difference was baked into American culture.

He was on more familiar ground as a dedicated fan of entertainers like Florence Mills (fig. 3.49), the star of the Harlem extravaganza *Shuffle Along*, or Paul Meeres, Gladys Bentley (who performed at the Clam House in a top hat and tails), Adelaide Hall, and Jimmie Daniels.[88] In this he was not alone among either white or Black arts patrons in Harlem: as Langston Hughes explained in his autobiography *The Big Sea* (1940), as a young man he had wanted to see Florence Mills on stage so badly that he managed to persuade his father to allow him to attend Columbia University in New York rather than send him to Paris or Berlin. Her show, according to Hughes, "gave just the proper push — a pre-Charleston kick — to that Negro vogue of

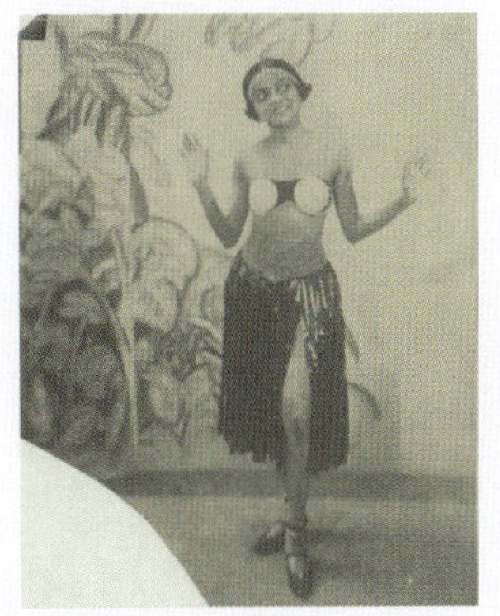

3.49 Anon., *Florence Mills.*

the 1920s, that spread to books, African sculpture, music, and dancing."[89]
"At almost every Harlem upper-crust dance or party," Hughes recalled:

> one would be introduced to various distinguished white celebrities
> there as guests. It was a period when almost any Harlem Negro of any
> social importance at all would be likely to say casually: "As I was
> remarking the other day to Heywood — ," meaning Heywood Broun.
> Or: "As I said to George — ," referring to George Gershwin. It was
> a period when local and visiting royalty were not at all uncommon in
> Harlem. And when the parties of A'Lelia Walker, the Negro heiress,
> were filled with guests whose names would turn any Nordic social
> climber green with envy. It was a period when Harold Jackman,
> a handsome young Harlem school teacher of modest means, calmly
> announced one day that he was sailing for the Riviera for a fortnight,
> to attend Princess Murat's yachting party.[90]

In Max Ewing's letters, we get a sense of the how this unlikely combination
of people — well-known to him as they were to Hughes — briefly reshaped the
cultural and social landscape of New York City in the 1920s. Yet there was also
a great deal that he didn't tell his parents or even his friends: Ewing knew
Hughes — who called A'lelia Walker "the joy-goddess of Harlem's 1920s" —
not only as an aspiring writer and friend of A'lelia's, but also as a
member of the queer circle that gathered around Van Vechten
and shared his Harlem adventures in out-of-the-way clubs and
nightspots.[91] These men also attended the crowded, all-night
parties held at A'lelia's home, together and separately, and
although we only get a glimpse of the goings-on at these events
from their writings, one extraordinary recording in the Lesbian
Herstory Archives offers a more detailed view. In an oral history
created in the 1980s, the African American dancer Mabel
Hampton describes how, as a young, queer woman in the 1920s,
she was escorted to a party at A'lelia's home by her white
girlfriend and treated to a series of revelations that she never
forgot: when they arrived, they were asked to hand over their
clothes by a liveried butler, and after making their way through a
warren of rooms and closed doors, spent the next twenty-four
hours lounging on floor pillows in heavily curtained rooms,
surrounded by other guests — "men and women, women and
women, and men and men" as Hampton put it — who were
listening to music, talking, smoking "dope," and casually "making love."
"Everybody did whatever they wanted to do," she recalled some six decades
later, "some of them did one thing, the others did the other," while "girls
with no clothes on," served them with food and drinks: in Hampton's opinion,
the experience was "marvelous."[92] She also remembered that although
A'lelia didn't take part in these activities herself, she would come into the room
from time to time just say to say hello. We can only wonder about whether Ewing
or Van Vechten or other friends had similar experiences.

Other illustrious African American figures represented in the *Gallery*
include McCleary Stinnett, "the bootlegger" (fig. 3.50), whom Ewing had met

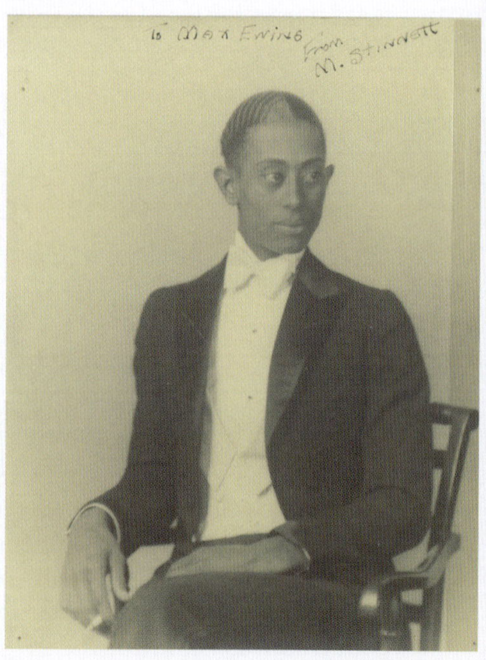

3.50 Anon., *McCleary Stinnett*, inscribed to Max Ewing.

at one of Van Vechten's parties (Van Vechten also photographed him, in 1933), acquiring his dapper, inscribed portrait for his collection. Stinnett visited Ewing's apartment on the same day that Florine Stettheimer and Charles Demuth (1883–1935), "two of the most important living painters," came: "Florine had never been here though her sister Ettie had," Ewing noted.[93] Ewing also kept a photo of the dancer Earl "Snake Hips" Tucker (fig. 3.51), along with numerous clippings of showgirls and singers. Despite his giddy admiration for well-known Black entertainers, Ewing — like Van Vechten — saw himself as very different from the stereotypical white tourists and celebrity-hounds who jammed the streets of Harlem on weekend nights. As Hughes had written (and no doubt made clear to his friends), this sort of visitor was dismissed out of hand by Black Harlemites and by right-thinking whites who deplored their voyeurism:

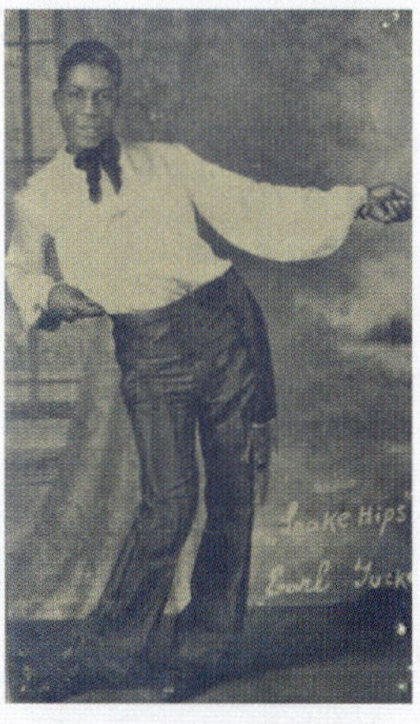

3.51 Anon., *Earl "Snake Hips" Tucker*.

> The Negroes said: "We can't go downtown and sit and stare at you in your clubs. You won't even let us in your clubs." But they didn't say it out loud — for Negroes are practically never rude to white people. So thousands of whites came to Harlem night after night, thinking the Negroes loved to have them there, and firmly believing that all Harlemites left their houses at sundown to sing and dance in cabarets, because most of the whites saw nothing but the cabarets, not the houses.[94]

Most such people were too arrogant and racist to even notice the icy coldness in the polite reception they received; Ewing and his friends made earnest efforts to be different.

From Van Vechten and others, Ewing had learned to think and act in a new way, and while both far too often fell short of their own ideals, the change they represented was significant. When A'lelia Walker died in 1931, Ewing mourned both her passing and the generosity of spirit that had fostered the new world that she and her interracial coterie had briefly created. Langston Hughes reported that he had himself attended Walker's enormous funeral, along with Muriel Draper, Dorothy Sheldon, and Rita Romilly (a Gurdjieff follower); we know that Ewing was also there.[95] As Hughes would later write, with her passing, the bold era of interracial culture had well and truly come to an end: "That was really the end of the gay times of the New Negro era in Harlem," Hughes recalled, "the period that had begun to reach its end when the crash came in 1929 and the white people had much less money to spend on themselves, and practically none to spend on Negroes, for the depression brought everybody down a peg or two. And the Negroes had but few pegs to fall."[96]

Ewing believed that the loss of people like A'lelia Walker and Robert Chanler (who had died the previous year) had robbed the world not only of the extraordinary parties where he had first encountered the raucous racial and sexual diversity of the avant-garde, but also of the sort of big, unconventional personalities who demonstrated by their own actions that small-town conventionality, racism, and homophobia could be overcome. As he wrote to his parents on October 2, 1931, paraphrasing Gertrude Stein, "My generation is no good. I don't know any one my own age with any spark of vitality, originality, or of any particular interest to anybody. It is a lost generation, growing up in the backwash of after-the war. A dead generation foundering through a dead era. Whenever someone like A'lelia dies it seems worse than when a young person dies to me."[97] Though he still revered Carl Van Vechten and Muriel Draper as his lodestars, he was gradually coming to realize that he would ultimately have to find his own way.

Ewing's letters and his *Gallery* offer a record of his journey. While some visitors might enjoy his closet display as an edgy, extended performance piece centered on celebrity fandom and gossip, Ewing's collection of portraits clearly also opened up fraught — and potentially dangerous — questions about desire and visual pleasure, foregrounding a distinctly queer and interracial sensibility, and placing Ewing's passion for beautiful male bodies, both Black and white, on full display. After all, Ewing's collection wasn't simply the usual sort of paean to white America's most admired Black celebrities: these photos showed Ewing's Black friends, men like Taylor Gordon, Harold Jackman, and Langston Hughes with whom Ewing had become close. Moreover, while much has been written about the complexities of Van Vechten's relationships, it is clear from the *Gallery* that Ewing's experiences of race and sexuality avoided the extremes of overidentification and adulation embraced by his older friend. Although he had learned a great deal about these matters from Van Vechten, he charted his own course.

The depiction of his complex, humorous, and often startling evolution into adulthood through found and original images — one in which highbrow writers and philosophers are juxtaposed with bodybuilders, divas, and cabaret entertainers with an apparent lack of hierarchy or concern for social propriety — was Ewing's goal from the start. Indeed, the collection was intended to raise questions about who he "really was" by revealing disparate parts of himself to his visitors, crossing boundaries of culture, race, and sexual identity with a camp sense of humor and a mannered elegance that enabled him to keep his distance. In so doing, it foregrounded a topic that his friends knew well, underscoring the pleasures and dangers of self-invention and the consequences of "passing" as something that one was not, as Fitzgerald had shown so compellingly in *The Great Gatsby* in 1925. This was a familiar anxiety that another member of their extended circle, Nella Larsen, had brought to life in *Passing*, her novel of 1929; like Ewing, Gordon, and others in their circle, Larsen experienced these complexities firsthand.

Where matters of race and sexuality were concerned, no one was entirely safe — or entirely free of prejudice. As Ewing reported to his parents in April 1928, he had recently given a party in honor of the socialite Emily Vanderbilt, whom he had met through Esther Murphy, but he had had to exclude Taylor Gordon and other Black friends from the guest list so as not to create a stir: "At the party we were all sorry not to have Taylor Gordon and other Negro friends," he commented breezily:

> but their absence was due to Emily, who is in the throes of her divorce suit, and as Bill Vanderbilt is very conventional, he could never understand the toleration of Negroes as guests, and could only see some scandalous aspect of their being there, and Emily is afraid he

would cut down her alimony on the grounds of her being too wild
a woman, who entertains black men and so forth. Thus life is
very complicated in the high places, and the party remained white.[98]

Carl Van Vechten's diaries are filled with similar comments about restaurants and
bars being unwilling to seat the "mixed" groups he socialized with, and he
frequently sidestepped these barriers by simply moving on to other venues that
were more accepting. While both he and Ewing disdained their contemporaries'
racism, they frequently gave in to the limits imposed on them rather than making
a fuss. The same was true of homophobia and the dreaded label "homosexual,"
and as we know from historian George Chauncey's study of *Gay New York*, it
was getting worse rather than better as new laws were written and long-ignored
restrictions already on the books were suddenly enforced.[99]

    For Ewing, the photo collection and the closet *Gallery* — his "amazing
room, containing some of the most rare and remarkable photographs of
prominent people in the world" — offered a creative outlet in which to hold up
a mirror for his friends to see their diverse and unusual world for themselves.
It also highlighted the contradictions that haunted their relationships and the
progressive aspirations by which they defined themselves. Indeed, when Ewing
came to create his own works of sculpture and his own photographic portraits
in the years between 1930 and 1933, these complexities — framed by a very queer
mixture of celebration, defiance, ambivalence, shame, and pride — would once
again be on full display.

THE MAKING OF AN ARTIST

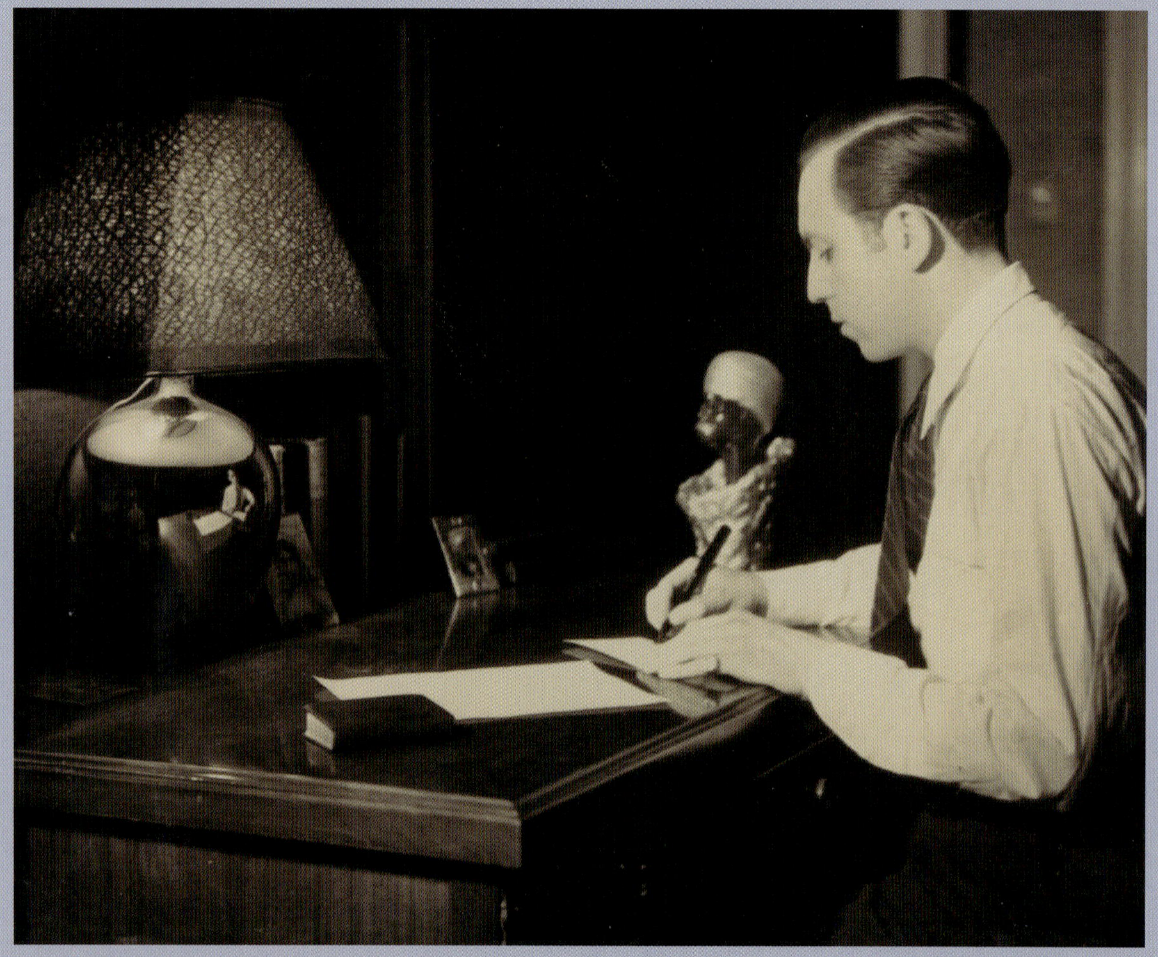

4.1 George Platt Lynes, *Portrait of Max Ewing at His Desk*, 1930. Max Ewing Papers.

Despite a successful run in 1929, Ewing's work with the *Grand Street Follies* was winding down, and references to his former friends in that world or to his piano students became fewer and farther between in his letters to his family.[1] Frustrated in his efforts to place his songs in Broadway shows or with publishers, and sidetracked as a performer because of an injury to his finger sustained during rehearsals for Antheil's *Ballet Mécanique*, Ewing began to reimagine himself as a sculptor and photographer, embarking on a series of portraits of Draper in 1930 that would, somewhat surprisingly, earn him a place in the *Surréalisme* exhibition at the new and influential Julien Levy Gallery in 1932.[2]

Ewing practiced less and partied more, going out nightly to Harlem nightclubs and elegant dinner parties with a crowd of young friends, including the models Fred Ritter and Marion Morehead, and hobnobbing with members of a circle of wealthy lesbian socialites and theater professionals — close friends of Esther Murphy and Alice DeLamar — that included Natalie Hammond and Alice Laughlin, an artist couple dedicated to the Theater Guild, as well as the Broadway star Eva Le Gallienne, who founded the Civic Repertory Theater with the backing of Alice DeLamar, and Tallulah Bankhead, the actress who would go on to enjoy great and often lurid fame and fortune in Hollywood. The writer Mercedes de Acosta was also part of this set, and she is mentioned frequently in Ewing's letters of this period, and especially in letters dating from Ewing's short stay in Hollywood in 1933, where he took note of de Acosta's turbulent love affair with Greta Garbo.[3]

Glamorous new companions and entertainments expanded Ewing's familiar round of concerts, lectures, afternoon teas, and cocktail parties with longtime friends like Taylor Gordon, George Platt Lynes, Edward Wasserman, and Carl Van Vechten. He enjoyed Muriel Draper's near-daily companionship, and the leading role he played in the circle of devoted followers that she hosted at her home on the far East Side of Manhattan; these people and places remained a constant in Ewing's life. Oddly, the stock market crash of October 29, 1929 seems to have been more of an incentive than a deterrent to this frantic social whirl, though Ewing and his working friends, unlike those with trust funds like Wasserman and Van Vechten (who had inherited a fortune from his brother in 1928), felt the pinch as jobs dried up and the Depression wore on.[4]

As the new decade began, Ewing was poised to leap into new creative ventures, including writing a book — which eventually appeared as *Going Somewhere* — and creating a group of sculptures, mostly made of found objects, showing Muriel Draper in a variety of roles. In 1932, he also took up photography, producing a number of portraits, including a group of male nudes, for his *Carnival of Venice* series. Like the Draper sculptures, the *Carnival* photographs were exhibited at the Julien Levy Gallery — with the nude images modestly cropped — in a one-day show with an opening party on January 25, 1933, to which all of the people that Ewing had photographed were invited and asked to appear, clothed or nude, as they had looked in their portraits.

Ewing's *Carnival of Venice* series, described at length in the following chapter, represents his most lasting contribution to the art of his time. As a musician, collector, writer, artist, and socialite throughout the 1920s, he often seems little more than a charming dilettante, which was, in fact, the way that Julien Levy (1906–81) remembered him in his memoir — but he was clearly more than that.[5] He began his New York life as a serious musician and continued to practice daily until the early 1930s before abandoning that dream due to his injury. He then turned to sculpture and photography, producing portraits that are playful, appealing, and often insightful: these works enable us to add names and faces to the avant-garde circle in New York in the 1920s and '30s. Compared with the many hard-working, professional photographers among his friends, Ewing was simply a talented amateur with a "queer eye" that shaped the character and content of his work. Nevertheless, he had high aspirations and, in the years between 1930 and 1932 in particular, he saw himself as an artist and worked in a variety of media.

As we turn our attention to Ewing's career in the visual arts, it is particularly significant that the winter of 1929–30 marked the beginning of Ewing's friendship with Ettie (1875–1955), Carrie (1869–1944), and Florine Stettheimer, the three sisters whose salon on the Upper West Side was such an important site for the evolution of the American avant-garde.[6] As he wrote to his parents in February 1929, "I had tea yesterday at the Stettheimers. That is a long story … they are among Carl Van Vechten's closest and oldest friends. I met Ettie at the Gertrude Stein opera performance at Carl's … They are a marvelous and incredible family, and don't forget about them: Carrie and Florine and Ettie STETTHEIMER."[7] This important friendship, which lasted until Ewing's death in 1934, extended his reach into the world of art in three significant ways. First, it helped cement his relationship with the circle of serious artists and musicians who joined forces to produce *Four Saints in Three Acts*, the modern opera by Gertrude Stein and Virgil Thomson. Florine Stettheimer was an integral part of that coterie, not only as a hostess and promoter, but also as set and costume designer, bringing her love of glittering surfaces and diaphanous fabrics (well-known to her friends from the decor of both the Stettheimer apartment at Alwyn Court on West 58th Street and her studio at Bryant Park) to the startlingly original look of the new production. Ewing had first encountered Virgil Thomson in Paris in May 1926, at a party that he attended with Noël Murphy, and in February 1929 he heard private performances of Thomson's opera at Carl Van Vechten's apartment. A more complete performance and lecture by Thomson took place in December 1932 at Muriel Draper's salon, for which occasion she had a Steinway piano delivered to her home.[8] As a musician and composer himself, and as a longtime admirer of Stein's poetry, Ewing felt close to the project. He was thus truly bereft when he missed the opening in Hartford, Connecticut because his mother's illness kept him tied to Pioneer, Ohio in the winter of 1934.

Second, Ewing's friendship with the Stettheimers offered him an entrée into an exclusive social milieu, and provided him with regular invitations to private gatherings that had a more serious and conventionally respectable art-world character than either Van Vechten's parties or Draper's East Side salon. A regular feature of bohemian New York since World War I, the parties hosted by Ettie (a novelist and philosopher), Carrie (a dedicated hostess and creator of the Stettheimer "Dollhouse" at the Museum of the City of New York), and especially Florine (a painter and poet), forged a distinctive new American modernism that spoke to the deepest parts of Ewing's artistic identity. At the Stettheimers' home, he encountered many internationally known artists, writers, and musicians, including those he listed for his parents on October 1929: the critic and translator Lewis Galantière, Henry McBride, "the art critic of the New York *Sun*" (who had come "to see the clothes closet" the previous March, no doubt at the Stettheimers' suggestion), Jean Lescaze, "a French architect," Philip Moeller, director of the Theater Guild, Maurice Sterne, "sculptor," and his wife Hilda Hellman.[9] The sisters' close friendships with these and other leaders of the New York avant-garde — Marcel Duchamp, Charles Demuth, Alfred Stieglitz, and Georgia O'Keeffe (1887–1986), among others — made their salon unique.[10]

Third, as has often been noted by historians of American modernism, the Stettheimers' salon included a mix of queer and straight members who were welcomed to their home on an equal footing: for the three sisters, themselves unmarried and of a certain age, art, talent, style, and intellect trumped any and all conventional notions of status and value. At Alwyn Court, Ewing came into contact with people who took themselves seriously. While their conversation, fashion sense, decor, and Florine's own remarkable paintings were often tinged with elements of "arched brow" irony (to use the phrase coined by Kirsten MacLeod), this had little of the self-parody that Ewing was familiar with from his experience of queer humor and camp performance.[11] The Stettheimers were never abject, and among their friends Ewing gained a new confidence.

Moreover, as upper-class Jewish women, the Stettheimers viewed the world through a lens of critical sophistication and with a vivid awareness of their own outsider status. The choices they made were intended to create a distinctive identity and an elegant presence in the city. Ewing especially enjoyed writing to his mother about the details of the lavish meals they served (all organized by Carrie) and the eye-popping originality of their clothing: he described one dinner party in January 1930, for example, where the sisters "looked dressed for a ball … Florine had on white satin trousers underneath a trailing affair of spangled net … Ettie had on a black lace creation and was wearing a red wig … the third sister Carrie wore a golden crown, and a golden throat band, a gold dress and over it a cape of black lace."[12] He had strong affinities with both their snobbery and their sense of style: in their company, he began to think of himself — like their other friends and like the sisters themselves — as a person with a voice and a privileged view of the world — in short, as an artist.

THE MURIEL DRAPER STATUES AND JULIEN LEVY'S *SURRÉALISME* SHOW
Despite these heady experiences among a diverse and dazzling crowd of women, Max Ewing's first sustained project as a visual artist (rather than as a collector or curator) was, perhaps not surprisingly, an expression of his love for Muriel Draper.[13] For Ewing, she would always hold pride of place in his personal Parnassus, and, indeed, he had been making small clay figurines — perhaps more accurately described as totems or votives — of both her and Glenway Wescott since the mid-1920s. In a letter written just before he left for Europe in April 1926, he mentioned that he had taken a painted portrait by Robert Chanler and some of his "statues" to Muriel Draper's house for safekeeping.[14] One of these figurines (figs. 4.1 and 4.2) was listed in the 1929 supplement to the catalogue of the *Max Ewing Collection of Extraordinary Portraits* as "No. 299: Muriel Draper with head held high (very odd item clay statuette by Max Ewing shows Mrs Draper's head attached to a

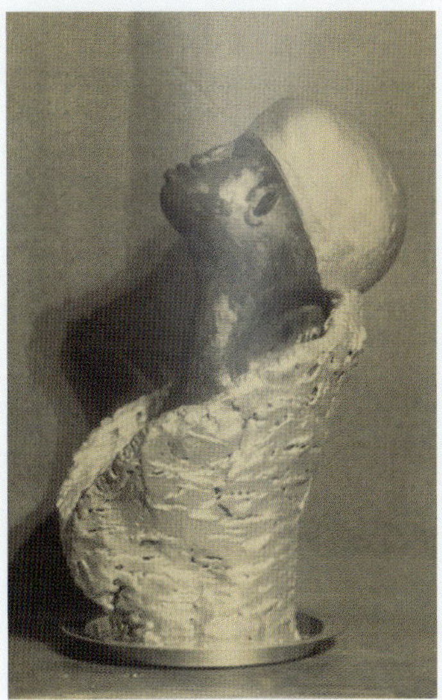

4.2 Anon. (Ralph Steiner?), photograph of Max Ewing's *Portrait of Muriel Draper*, clay figurine, 1929. Max Ewing Papers.

body not her own. Sculpture photographed by Ralph Steiner. Photograph framed with classic severity in black and white)." It is worth noting here that Ewing also took the trouble of having this work photographed by Ralph Steiner, an artist friend who by this point had a gallery show in New York.[15]

As we know, Ewing had for some years been infatuated with Draper, her animated conversation, her chic fashion sense, and her uncanny ability to make young people like him feel that they had been seen and heard for the first time. She was clearly also one of the most significant cultural leaders of her generation. In 1963, Carl Van Vechten explained her prodigious ability to create new connections in the worlds of art, literature, and music: "Muriel's house soon became the meeting place for literally hundreds of ill-assorted people who were attracted to her by her wit, her charm, her somewhat offbeat beauty, her conversation, and her entertainment," he wrote, "Muriel MADE many other people's parties … She seemed to attend all theaters and concerts. … She seemed to read all books."[16] For the young man from Pioneer, Draper represented everything he hoped to become in New York. More than anyone else, Draper gave him the confidence to see himself as a player on the social scene — her scene — and as a critic, writer, and artist in his own right. His portraits were his attempt to communicate that love in a form that captured more than his words could express, and his talismanic images kept her close.

Variants of Ewing's clay portraits of Draper appear in the background of photographs taken by George Platt Lynes In December 1929 and February 1930. A small bust showing Muriel with black skin and a golden turban (see fig. 4.1) sat on Ewing's writing desk, and a similar figure, joined by an abstract head of a man (probably Glenway Wescott), is clearly visible in an earlier image showing Ewing lying on the sofa in his living room (see fig. 3.25). Ewing noted the day of Lynes's visit to his home with characteristic glee: "George Lynes came Friday with all his outfit and photographed me again sitting at the piano, sitting at the desk, sitting at the telephone, recording all my habits of daily life for posterity."[17]

A further indication of Ewing's growing sense of confidence is his request that Lynes come back to his apartment at the end of the month to photograph the clay figures individually and provide him with copies of the photos for distribution. Unfortunately, on this occasion the dueling egos of the two aspiring young photographers came into conflict when Ewing objected to the price (three dollars) that Lynes was asking for "additional prints." Calling that price "absurd," Ewing complained to his parents that it was "as much as well-established and experienced photographers on Fifth Avenue get for prints and I won't pay George such prices."[18] Ewing wrote that he intended instead to get an "ordinary commercial photographer to come in" and get "cheap prints by the dozen." That plan doesn't seem to have come about, however, and the Steiner photos of two clay figures are the only images that survive.

The significance of these sculptures for Ewing's emerging identity as an artist is signaled by the many invitations he made to his friends to come to his apartment to see them. On January 29, he wrote to his parents to say that he "Ran into friend and invited him to come see the statues of Muriel. I have made two more much bigger ones, and painted them gold and silver. They are really amazingly good too."[19] On February 1, Van Vechten recorded his visit to West 31st Street in his daybook, and on February 3, Mark Tobey came to tea "to see the statues," as did Roy and Dorothy Sheldon, George Davis, and Lloyd Wescott

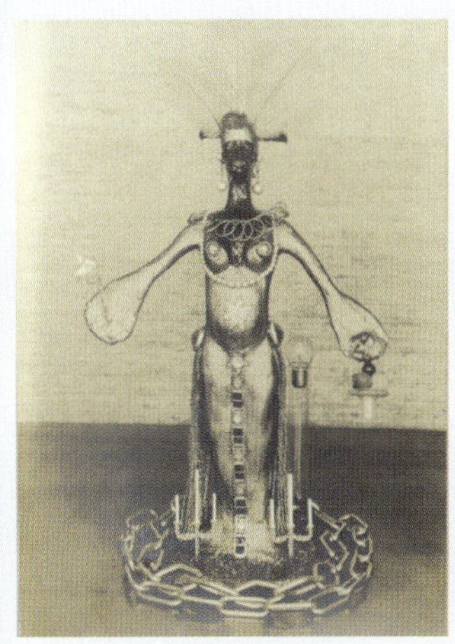

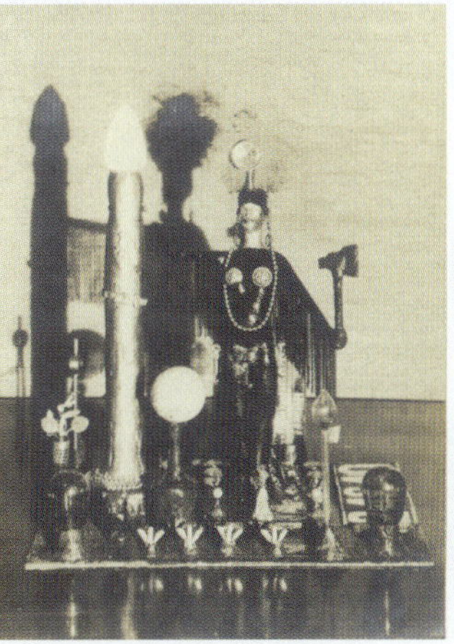

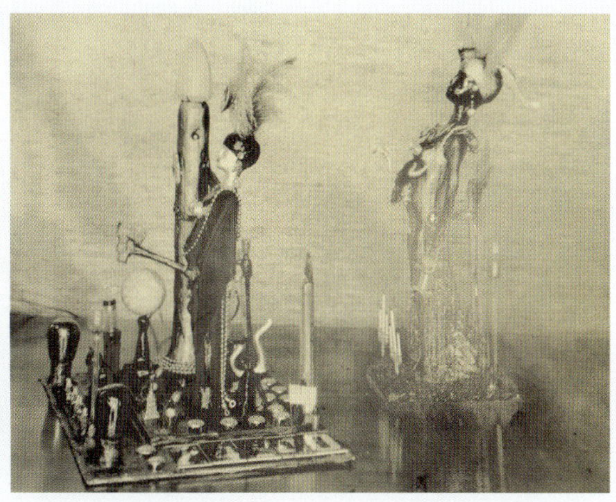

4.3 Anon. (Ralph Steiner?), photograph of Max Ewing's *Muriel More So*, 1930. Max Ewing Papers.

4.4 Anon. (Ralph Steiner?), photograph of Max Ewing's *Muriel Enlightening the World*, 1930. Max Ewing Papers.

4.5 Anon. (Ralph Steiner?), photograph of two of Max Ewing's Muriel statues from the side, 1930. Max Ewing Papers.

(Glenway's brother).[20] These were just a few of the many friends who visited Ewing's apartment to view his work.

Encouraged by his friends' approval, Ewing also began to expand his output, embarking on a series of elaborate full-length figures of Draper in mixed media, using clay, costume jewelry, artificial flowers, lightbulbs, metal disks, and other found objects.[21] These figures, measuring about 15–18 inches high, were captured in multiple, high-contrast images (figs. 4.3–4.5) by an unknown photographer and eventually published in a University of Michigan student literary publication called the *Inlander* in June 1930.[22] Entitled *Muriel More So* and *Muriel Enlightening the World*, the sculptures show Draper bejeweled and bedecked in extravagant evening gowns and turbans with feather crests, her breasts and hips accentuated by glittering ornaments; in one she is represented as a white woman, while in the other her face and neck are Black and her paddle-like arms are gilded. Lightbulbs and candelabras complete the assemblage. Ewing was particularly proud that for his second effort, *Muriel Enlightening the World*, he worked out a way to have the sculpture actually light up, as he boasted to his parents in on February 21:

> Dear Folks — Here is another note being written with great discomfort on the bench, because the desk is full of another statue, the fifth so far and the best. It is a lamp, this new one … I started with the Statue of Liberty Enlightening the World as my model, but I departed quite a bit from the original! This statue developed out of a criticism of my last one which was entitled *Muriel More So*. You may recall in her book there is a chapter devoted to her visit to Mabel Dodge's in Florence, when Carl V. V. and Robert Edmond Jones were there, and Jones, who was painting her said, "Muriel, everything about you should be <u>more so</u> — your aigrettes in your turban should be higher, your earrings should be longer, EVERYTHING about you should be MORE SO.["] So I made this statue just about as more so as it could be. One startling feature of it was that it had electric flash light bulbs for breasts. Everyone looked at these in amazement,

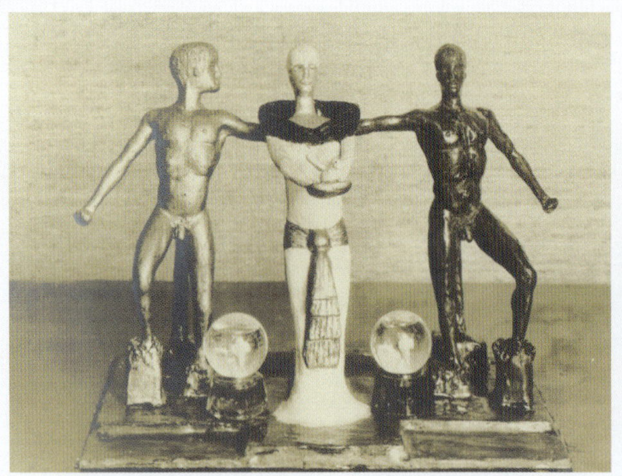

4.6 Anon. (Ralph Steiner?), photograph of Max Ewing, *Muriel Reconciling the Races*, 1930. Max Ewing Papers.

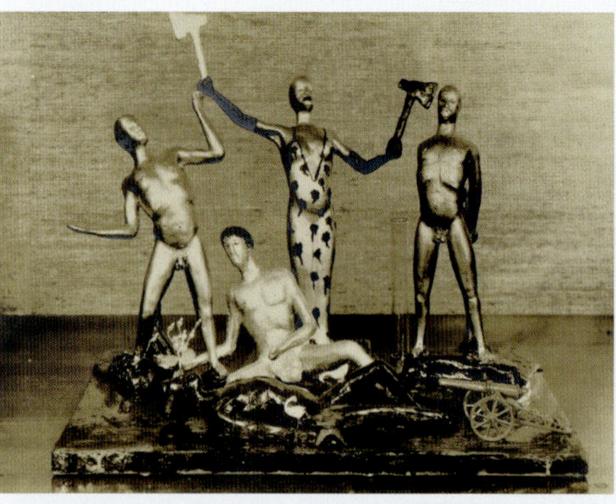

4.7 Anon. (Ralph Steiner?), photograph of Max Ewing, *Muriel Destroying Young Men*, 1930. Max Ewing Papers.

and then said "Do they light?" … they did not light and I felt that was asking too much. But I decided to show them I could make something that would light. So I bought the framework for a desk lamp, left nothing but the standard and the bulb … and the effect is magnificent! It does not look like a lamp covered in clay but like a statue with wire inside! The figure of Muriel painted black and red stands beside the column which is gold, and when it is lighted up it lights the whole room. For two years I have been going to buy a desk lamp, but now I have made one far better than anyone could buy! She is holding a red battle axe in her right hand and the light in her left, and a miniature speaker and two red plumes are coming out of her head. Mrs. Seldes and Namara and Mindret came yesterday and nearly died of pleasure. Julia Hoyt is coming tomorrow. Muriel says these statues will be the greatest record of and comment on her life when she is dead.[23]

He promised to send his parents copies of the latest photos, concluding that he had "never done anything in New York that gave so many people so much pleasure."

To accommodate the steady stream of visitors who came to see both the *Gallery* and the statues, Ewing began hosting a series of weekly gatherings at his apartment, noting that "the statues continue to cause havoc."[24] On May 20, 1930, he unveiled a newly completed figure of Glenway Wescott — "his masterpiece," as he called it.[25] He was encouraged by the praise of other artists, including the sculptor Roy Sheldon, who had made a portrait bust of Ewing in Paris, shown in a photograph in the *Gallery*: Sheldon "professes to be immensely impressed by my statues, considering I know nothing of anatomy and have never studied modeling," he wrote to his parents; "He comes to see all my 'works,' as soon as they are finished, and finds each better than the last."[26]

Two other sculptures from 1930, also portraits of Muriel Draper, survive in photographs. Unfortunately, Ewing doesn't appear to have written to his family about them or left any sort of documentary evidence that would help us make sense of them. Entitled *Muriel Reconciling the Races* (fig. 4.6) and *Muriel Destroying Young Men* (fig. 4.7), both sculptures featured images of Draper clad in an evening gown and turban and surrounded by male nudes, both Black and white, in dramatic poses. For both works, the title and date "1930" is added to the paper mounts, with Ewing's home address included as well.

Here again Ewing included found objects, artificial flowers, and even a toy cannon, placing Draper at the center of mixed media assemblages. *Muriel Reconciling the Races* is a relatively modest, though accomplished, figural composition that adopts the formal character of a monumental public sculpture celebrating Draper's well-known commitment to interracial understanding and the advancement of "the Negro," as she and her contemporaries referred to Black Americans. *Muriel Destroying Young Men*, on the other hand, is more complex and challenging, for a host of reasons: here the figure of Draper wields an axe — as she did in the earlier images — and carries a torch or a saber in her other hand; her head is tilted back as she attacks the young men on either side of her. The two standing figures — abstract, bald, and apparently gilded — appear to be heroic personifications, whereas the two figures that lie at her feet seem more like portraits of people Ewing and Draper actually knew: could these represent Lincoln Kirstein and Taylor Gordon, Draper's two most ardent suitors, shown here in postures of sexual vulnerability, or, indeed, could the white-skinned figure be Ewing himself? With its dark hair and slim figure, the white man reclines awkwardly on the ground with his legs parted; a strategically placed flower (perhaps in light purple, like the pansy prominently displayed in Stettheimer's portrait of Virgil Thomson of the same year) serves as a modest covering, while the other figures in the group are entirely nude. At the front of the group, a Black man lies fully face down on the ground, his ankles submerged in the shiny black surface of the "water"; a small toy bird, perhaps a crane, stands beside him.

As he prepared to create both of these sculptural groups, Ewing gave serious attention to improving his technique as a sculptor of male anatomy, working with a nude model hired for the purpose. This appears to have been his earliest contact with Fred Ritter, mentioned earlier, a young model whom he would befriend and photograph frequently until the time he left New York in the fall of 1933. In October of 1930, Ewing referred to Fred Ritter as "a new boy I like," and described an evening with him and the model Marion Morehouse as guests at Texas Guinan's elegant new nightclub; the following March, he reported that his "friend the model and athlete Fred Ritter" had gone to Florida to open a "sun bathing establishment" that had failed because "in the whole two months there were only six sunny days at Miami, so no one did any sun bathing."[27] Further, Ewing's collection of programs and clippings includes a page from *Klein's Bell*, a bodybuilding magazine, dated July 1931, which describes Ritter's fitness program and his "Measurement Record," and reproduces one of the nude publicity photos taken earlier that year by E. F. Townsend in New York.[28] As noted earlier, Ewing also had a personally inscribed copy of an image from the same series in his collection.

Like these publicity photos, nearly all of the surviving snapshots and study photos of Ritter in Ewing's archive have been modestly posed and strategically cropped. A number of images in Ewing's scrapbooks, however, show him in the West 31st Street apartment wearing the treasured silk dressing gown that Ewing had acquired in Paris years before, and others show him modeling nude (fig. 4.8). Understandably, these photo sessions were not something Ewing would choose

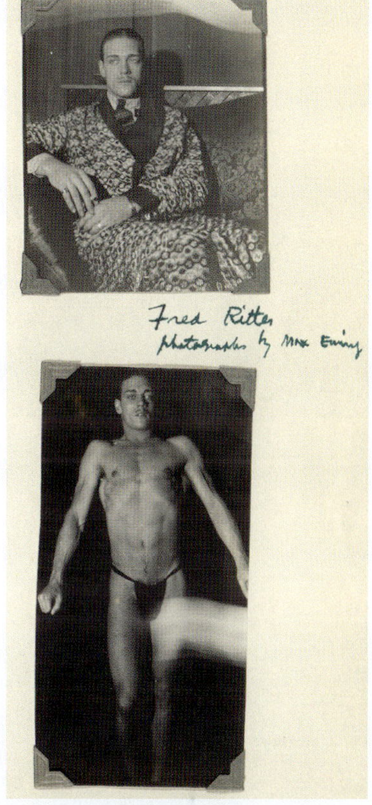

4.8 Max Ewing, *Fred Ritter clothed and nude* (cache-sexe added later). Max Ewing Papers.

to share with his parents or with others beyond his close circle of friends.
After his death, such images were a source of embarrassment for his family, who
floated the idea that they could be removed from the archive entirely.[29] Van
Vechten clearly had other plans: although the family's preference was that the
nude photographs, like those from the *Carnival of Venice* discussed in chapter 5,
be destroyed, he tucked them away in his own scrapbooks and made sure that
his collection at Yale would be available — albeit not until twenty-five years after
his death — to researchers.[30]

In one of the surviving Ritter images, a black cache-sexe has been inked
in by Ewing or Van Vechten at a later date. Like a number of photographs of
Anthony Sansone in the *Gallery*, illustrated in chapter 3, this nude image was
clearly retouched; nevertheless the peculiar pose, with clenched fists and arms
outstretched, suggests that it was a study for the nude figure on the right in
Muriel Reconciling the Races. As such, it is not only an image of particular
importance in Ewing's evolving education as an artist, but also evidence of his
increasing desire to look closely at male nudes through the lens of his camera,
just as his friends George Lynes and Carl Van Vechten would do.

An undated letter from Ewing to Lynes written at about this time sheds
new light on this matter. In it, Ewing asks Lynes to print a group of nude photos for
him because "the drug store returned the negatives with the legend, 'Sorry but
these are unprintable,'" explaining that they were snapshots of the models who

> posed for one of the young men about to be destroyed in my projected
> masterpiece 'Muriel Destroying Young Men.' Knowing that whatever
> statute makes them unprintable has been broken often by you,
> I am sending you the negatives trusting that you will print me two
> of each, and send printing bill for same, and do the job promptly,
> and mail prints to me as soon as made, for I am already at work on
> the statues.[31]

Ewing also explained that the poses were the model's "ideas of poses signifying
impending destruction," noting that he was an "experienced poser" who claimed
to be "an ex-fencer, an ex-sailor on a Portuguese cruiser, an ex-trapeze artist in
a South American circus, a deserter from a warship in Mexico, an enthusiast from
the cabarets of Lisbon, and an adagio dancer on Eighth Avenue," who "adores
being photographed," adding that "these pictures were his idea."[32] The model he
refers to may not be Ritter or Paul Meeres, who were familiar to both men by
name, but Meeres is mentioned specifically in a different letter about engaging
models for photo shoots, in which Ewing tells Lynes that Zena Naylor will bring
Meeres along to the "photographing orgy next Monday," adding, "She thought he
would be happy to pose for anyone who would like to photograph him, and
he would probably even *trapeze* if given anything to do it on."[33] From Lynes's
correspondence with Monroe Wheeler, we know that he had taken nude photos of
Meeres a few months before, in early December 1929, but the specific identity
of Ewing's model for this particular project remains a mystery.[34]

These missing photos and the single surviving retouched example from
1930 raise a number of questions about the evidence in the archive as we now
know it. Ewing clearly wasn't shy about sharing many of the details of his life in
New York with his family. He often wrote to his parents about his close friendships

with other men and about "boys" he "liked"; he also shared stories about the dramatic goings-on occasioned by the complex relationships between the "boyfriends" and "girlfriends" of his friends and associates, almost all of whom were in open heterosexual marriages that allowed them to present a respectable face to the world. Nevertheless, there were clearly limits about what and how much was revealed. In 1926, Ewing seems to have had a conversation with his mother that went into greater detail about these matters: he chides her for her negative reaction to "the sexual question" they discussed the previous summer, calling her attitude a "defense mechanism" about things "that you do not happen to have paid attention to and to have known."[35] While we, of course, can't be certain about what he was referring to here, we can infer that Ewing had filled her in on the latest gossip about his circle in New York, and perhaps even told her about his own experiences. Talking with his mother in person, he may have chosen to confide more details, going beyond his usual veiled references and the camp hints he often dropped in his letters.[36]

Anything more explicitly "queer" than that — and obviously the male nudity shown in the *Muriel* sculptures or the snapshots that preceded them fit into this category — would have been a bridge too far, not only for Ewing's parents but for American society in general. This was certainly true for the members of Ewing's extended family who survived him and his parents, and for those who made decisions about his papers and photos after his death.[37] Thus, it is significant that a letter about the creation of the Yale archive from Max's cousin Doris Ewing to Carl Van Vechten advises him that any decisions about the fate of Ewing's nude photographs — which she calls his "naked sex assortments," with obvious discomfort — would ultimately be up to Van Vechten and to Ewing's "models."[38] Van Vechten had apparently found a way to guide her to a point of ambivalent acceptance about the collection, stubbornly insisting to her that the historical importance of her cousin's papers and photos really did trump private, family concerns. The result is that some of the nude photos, like the Ritter images, though few and far between, do indeed survive in the Ewing collection, and like a trail of bread crumbs, lead us back to the complexities of Ewing's queer life in New York. He undoubtedly moved between radically different geographic, social, and psychic spaces around the city — from the niceties of the Stettheimers' drawing room to the restaurants and bars of Harlem, Times Square, and Midtown that served as centers of queer and homosocial culture — and he was adept at shape-shifting when necessary.[39] Like Charles Demuth or Lincoln Kirstein, who noted his nightly activities in his diaries, he may also have frequented gay bathhouses and cruising spots throughout the city, but he knew how to suppress those details about his life when necessary.[40]

What the archive does make abundantly clear is that by summer of 1930, Ewing was actively using his camera not only as a way to supplement the images in his *Gallery*, but as a device to look more closely at male bodies, clothed and unclothed. In July 1930, for example, Ewing photographed Anthony Sansone posing nude and "artistically" at his training camp in Coney Island (fig. 4.9), adding to the already numerous clippings, postcards, and photos of the bodybuilder displayed in the *Gallery*. Ewing may also have

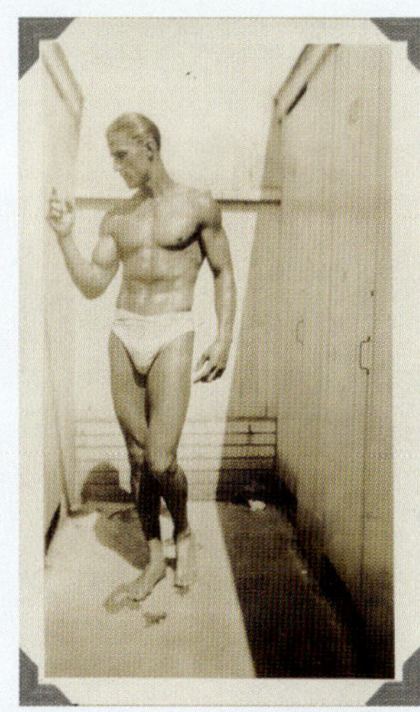

4.9 Max Ewing, snapshot of Anthony Sansone posing at Coney Island, July 1930. Detail of fig. 3.29.

photographed Paul Meeres at this time, but those images, along with many portraits of him listed in the catalogue of the *Gallery*, can no longer be located. We know that George Platt Lynes took a series of photos of Meeres in late 1929, but by that point, Lynes, Ewing, and Van Vechten had been avid fans of the entertainer for at least a year and had often seen him dance in Harlem. As early as October 1928, Ewing boasted that Meeres had visited his home and seen his photo collection firsthand; he was thrilled that he was the only one of his friends, including Van Vechten, who had managed to lure the beautiful dancer back to his own home, bragging that "everyone who came to Smalls [*sic*] gave him their telephone number and begged him to come and see them."[41] A photo of Meeres taken at Ewing's apartment three and a half years later, in April 1932, still exists (fig. 4.10), but by that point Ewing had already embarked on the *Carnival of Venice* project in which Meeres played such an important role as a model.

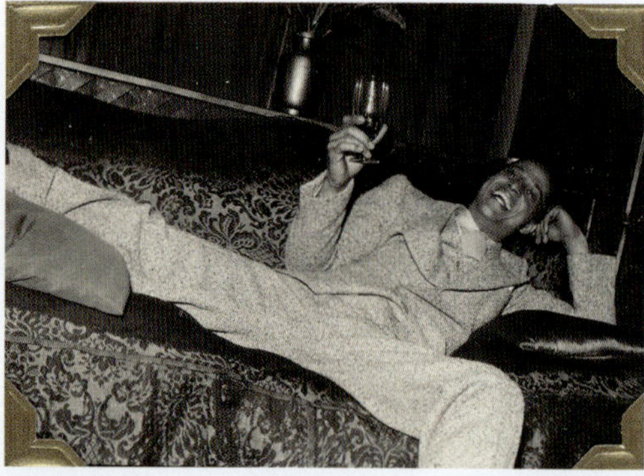

4.10 Max Ewing, snapshot of Paul Meeres in Ewing's apartment, July 15, 1932. Max Ewing Papers.

In 1930, Ewing also took his first photographs of Muriel Draper, who, like Sansone and Meeres, was someone he wanted to capture with his camera and study at leisure. The three surviving images (figs. 4.11 and 4.12) from Ewing's photo album show Draper artfully posed in the bright sunlight of her garden at 312 East 53rd Street. Though none of these is in sharp focus or even competently exposed, the two close-up portraits — one showing Draper wearing wide trousers and leaning over the back of a chair with her eyes closed, the other with her head down and legs spread wide — are clearly attempts to create expressive portraits of the sitter. Indeed, though George Platt Lynes's portrait of Draper, shot in a studio with expert lighting and equipment (fig. 4.13) is by far the more professional effort, there is clearly something more tender and intimate about Ewing's snapshots. Nevertheless, Ewing was particularly impressed with Lynes's efforts, which in Lynes's own view revealed how much progress he was making on both a technical and artistic level. Indeed, as he reported to his lover Monroe Wheeler, when the portrait was shown at a party hosted by their friend John McAndrew (1904–78), everyone including Muriel was very excited to see it, not least of all Max Ewing who was so thrilled that he "forgot" for a moment "to be the suave young man-about-town," as Lynes put it.[42]

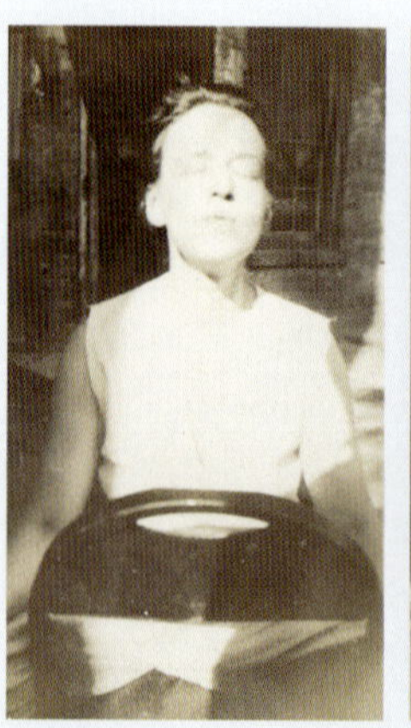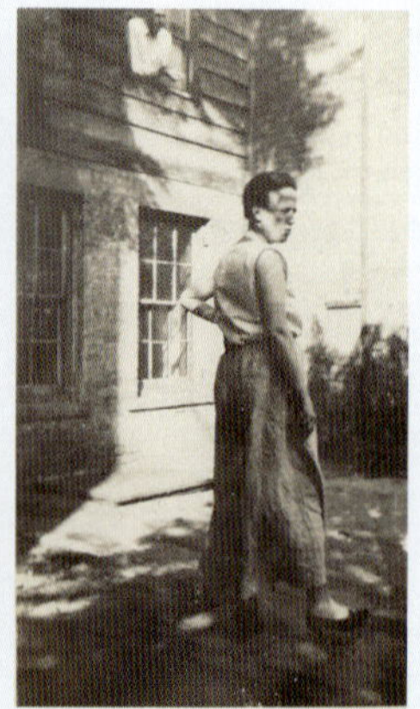

4.11 Max Ewing, *Muriel Draper in Her Garden*, July 1930. Max Ewing Papers.

Although Ewing reported to his parents in February 1930 that Muriel was very pleased with his sculptures, it would appear that his own pride and inflated sense of his artistic ability had deafened him to the nuances in her reaction.[43] A letter from Draper to Carl Van Vechten from 1930 suggests a very different story to the one Ewing told: in it, she pushes back on Ewing's efforts to capture her and literally put her on a pedestal. "He finds me easier to live with on his own terms either in words or sculpture," she complained to Van Vechten with characteristic insight, "and in a few years will not know MY me at all. I on the other hand, find HIS me an embarrassing stranger."[44] Her assessment hit the mark. The profusion of sculpted images scattered about Ewing's apartment *did* create a sort of "shrine to Muriel," as the British writer Harold Acton described

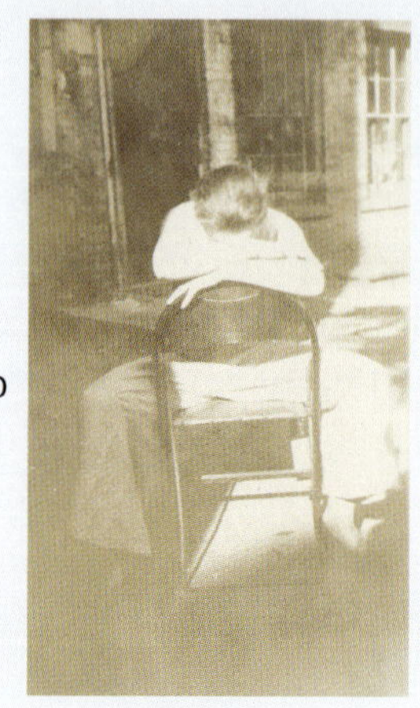

4.12 Max Ewing, *Muriel Draper with Head Down*, July 1930. Max Ewing Papers.

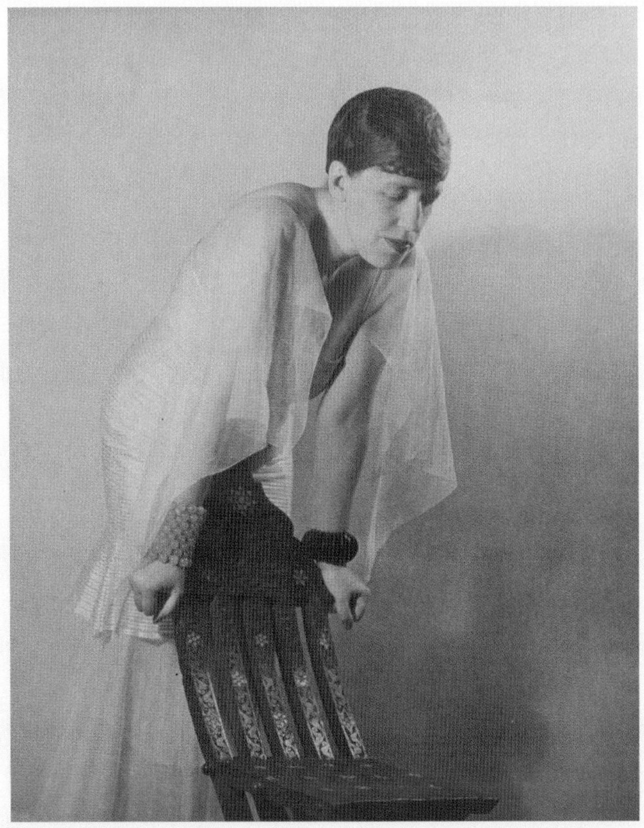

4.13 George Platt Lynes, *Muriel Draper*, 1931, gelatin silver print, 9½ × 7⅝ in. (24.1 × 19.3 cm). The Art Institute of Chicago. Gift of Patricia and Frank Kolodny in memory of Julien Levy.

it, noting, "On every piece of furniture there was a head or figure of her, in some places surrounded by candles."[45] Many years later, as he was preparing to donate the archive to Yale, Van Vechten wrote to Draper about Max's infatuation: "When he wrote to you, he wrote to YOU. In a strange way he was obviously in LOVE with you. All he wanted from you, however, was All your time, and All your attention. I guess he would have given you as much in return, but never his inside, nor even the extremes of his outside."[46]

No doubt it was this quality of the bizarre and totemic in Ewing's portraits of Draper that motivated Julien Levy to include the two standing figures in his *Surréalisme* show in January 1932, exhibiting them together with works by Pablo Picasso, Salvador Dalí, Max Ernst, Man Ray, Marcel Duchamp, and George Platt Lynes, who objected to having his name included as a member of that movement.[47] Ewing, on the other hand, was thrilled: "It may interest you to know that two of my fantastic statues of Muriel are on public exhibition for two weeks at the Julien Levy Gallery in Madison Avenue," he boasted to his mother, "They are having there an exhibition of French Sur-Realiste [*sic*] art and asked to show my statues even though not French. I guess that part of the public which has not see[n] them already will see them now!"[48] Ewing felt that this exhibition proved that he had become a real artist, and he relished the chance to put his work in front of his public.

FLORINE STETTHEIMER'S *CATHEDRALS OF FIFTH AVENUE* (1931–32)
Looking back on the world that Ewing inhabited, it sometimes seems like everyone — young or old, Black or white — knew everyone else: thanks to their frequent attendance at parties, concerts, operas, lectures, and art openings, many of the members of the bohemian social and cultural set in New

York — particularly those who, like Max Ewing, were friends of Muriel Draper and Carl Van Vechten — could recognize each other by sight or even by name. Clearly there were circles within circles, some younger and some older, some more focused on drinking or drugs, some with affinities for art, politics, or literature, and even some made up entirely of people in search of spiritual enlightenment, as was the case with those who gathered at the homes of Draper or Jane Heap to study the writings and teachings of George Gurdjieff. As a sprawling, loosely defined group, however, the avant-garde of the 1920s and early '30s in New York was surprisingly — but only briefly, as it turned out — cohesive.[49]

An undated invitation list for a large party at Muriel Draper's home in the late 1920s is a case in point: it includes over a hundred names, and in some cases the addresses, of the extended circle that Draper counted among her friends and acquaintances, many of whom are familiar to us from Ewing's letters or his *Carnival of Venice* portrait series of 1932. Among the people listed there, we find not only the socially prominent Askews, the gallery-owning Dudensings, Carl Van Vechten, the writer Gilbert Seldes (1893–1970) and his wife Amanda (c. 1903), Harold Ross (editor of the *New Yorker*), Edmund Wilson, "Stieglitz and Georgie O'Keeffe," Mr. and Mrs. Barr (of MoMA), and the "Misses" Stettheimer, but also many younger people as well, including Mercedes de Acosta, the actress Lilyan Tashman, Walker Evans, E. E. Cummings, George Antheil "and wife," Lloyd and Edna Thomas, "Stinnette" (the supplier of bootleg liquor), "Covarrubias and Rosa," Taylor Gordon, and Cecil Beaton.[50] This multiracial group ranged widely by income, age, and interests, but everyone seemed to have something distinctive and original to offer. Though Draper was well-known for her open-house parties, particularly on New Year's Eve, and for her catholic tastes (especially in young men), she was also recognized as an intellectual snob whose salon was sophisticated and exclusive. Her circle of friends reflected her high standards and her interest in modern art and ideas.

Even with his high-culture bona fides, it seems at first highly unlikely that Max Ewing would be welcomed into the inner circle of the Stettheimer sisters — Ewing who collected pinups of scantily clad athletes, stayed out late at Harlem clubs and drag shows, sculpted totemic figures of his beloved surrounded by nude men, and entertained a motley crew of raucous drinkers at his weekly Monday parties. Yet this was, in fact, the case, just as it was for Carl Van Vechten and other queer friends. What each group knew of the details of the others' lives is unclear, yet they were drawn together by their shared love for the vibrant city in which they lived. Florine's paintings and poetry reveal a visceral, fully embodied pleasure in the rhythms and textures of New York and a sense of wonder that Ewing shared. Stettheimer translated those emotions into her work, forging a new, modern manner that upended her Beaux-Arts training and replaced it with the colorful, shimmering images that we recognize as distinctively her own. Florine frequently described her feelings in her poems, making her purpose clear: "For a long time," she wrote:

> I gave myself
> To the arrested moment
> To the unfulfilled moment

To the moment of quiet expectation
I painted the trance moment
The promised moment
The moment in the balance
In mellow golden tones …
Then I saw
Time
Noise
Color
Outside me
Around me
Knocking me
Jarring me
Hurting me
Smiling
Singing
Forcing me in joy to paint them.[51]

For people who loved art, music, fashion, and good conversation in the
way that Ewing and his friends did, such dramatic words and the passionate,
sensual response that they expressed were the glue that held otherwise unlikely
friendships together. Indeed, from November 1929 on, Ewing and the Stettheimer
sisters (who were all well into their 50s) began to see each other regularly, visiting
each other's homes, sharing gossip and ideas, and gradually becoming closer.
On November 18, 1929, for example, Ewing wrote to his parents with news of his
latest visit to Florine's studio:

> Florine Stettheimer had an afternoon party at her studio — Muriel
> had never seen her paintings and it was a great event when she
> saw them. Florine refuses to exhibit them publicly, and she asks two
> hundred and fifty thousand for each picture, which is more than
> anyone can get who is still alive. The result is that these magnificent
> masterpieces can only be seen by people who Florine chooses to invite
> to see them. The Van Vechtens were there and all sorts of people, and
> I went with them to Madame Alvarez's party where there were dozens
> more, including the Princess Ghika, Dick Hammond, etc.[52]

Though Ewing exaggerated the exclusivity of access to Florine's paintings —
she did, in fact, show her work regularly in public exhibitions — and inflated the
exorbitant prices that she charged for her work (guaranteeing that the paintings
would remain at home with her), there is no doubt that the invitation to the
Stettheimers' home indicated that he had gained access to the inner circle,
together with Draper and, of course, the family's close friend Carl Van Vechten.[53]
Florine's studio, hung with Nottingham lace and resplendent in white and gold
with "billowy cellophane curtains" was, as her friend Henry McBride described it,
"one of the curiosities of the town; and very closely related, in appearance,
to the work that was done in it."[54]
Here Ewing encountered a distinctively modern sensibility much like
his own, a fusion of art, decoration, fashion, and camp irony that historian

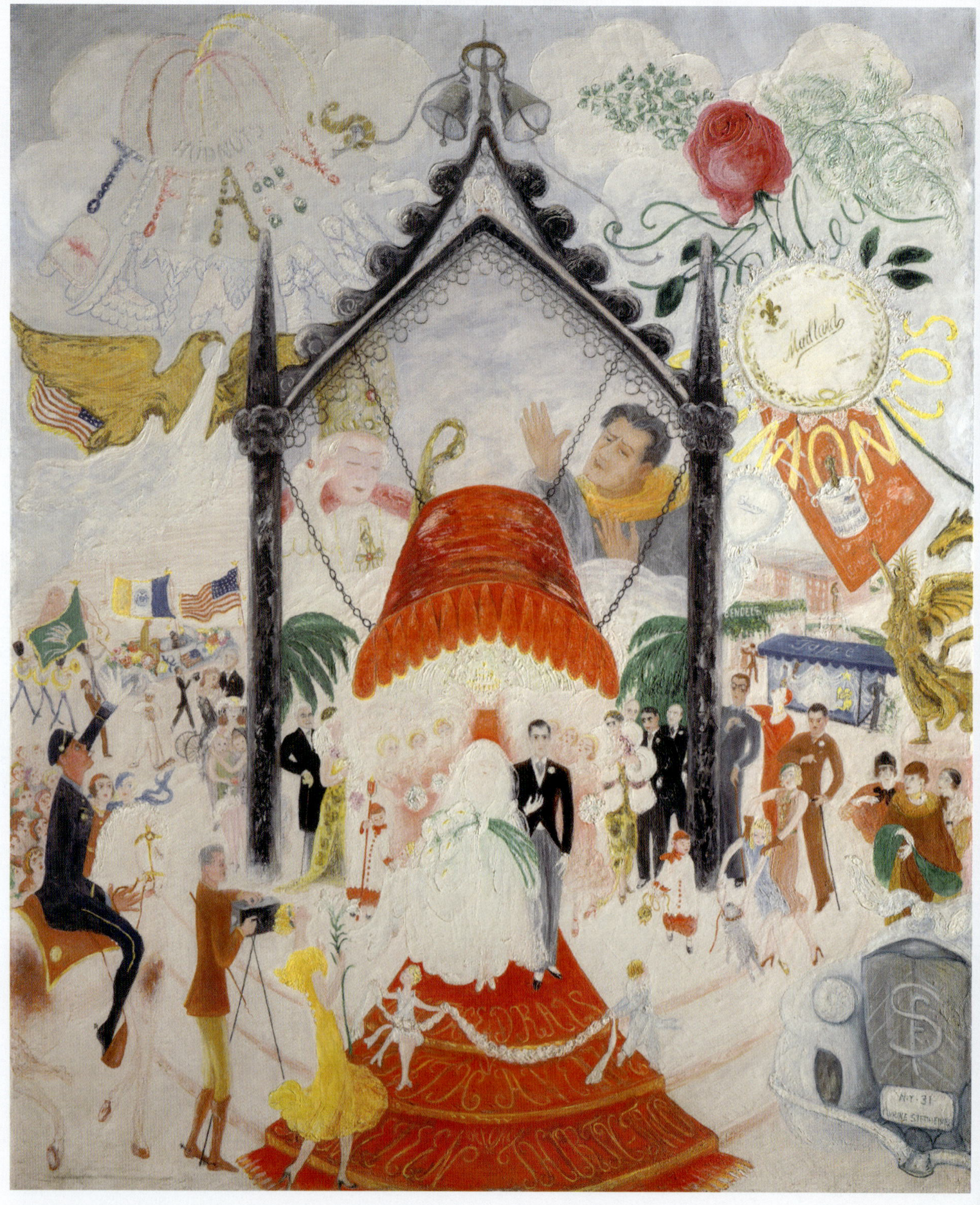

4.14 Florine Stettheimer, *The Cathedrals of Fifth Avenue*, 1931, oil on canvas, 60 × 50 in. (152.4 × 127 cm). The Metropolitan Museum of Art, New York. Gift of Ettie Stettheimer, 1953, 53.24.4.

Christopher Reed has called "The Amusing Style," in reference to the Bloomsbury artists and critics of the time. This very queer, urban, jazz-inflected, version of modernism was about as far as an artist could go from "the machismo of Hemingway's novels, Mies Van der Rohe's buildings, or other manifestations of what became canonic modernism," as Reed explained.[55] In Florine and her sisters, Max Ewing recognized a family of kindred spirits, while they, in turn, enjoyed his intelligent conversation and queer, quirky view of the world.

When the social season restarted after the summer in 1930, Ewing was invited to dinner at Alwyn Court, where he met the photographers Arnold Genthe and Montgomery Evans on November 7. A month later, he gave a recital of his songs at his apartment and Ettie and Florine came; in the same letter that recorded their visit to his home, Ewing also mentions Fred Ritter and brags that he now had a free pass to Texas Guinan's racy Club Argonaut, a new nightclub where the Stettheimer sisters would never have set foot.[56] He clearly lived in many worlds at once, and he seemed to enjoy the constantly changing landscape as he moved about the city.

Thanks to the Stettheimers, he also began to spend more and more time around artists, and his view of himself began to change. On February 5, 1931, he attended a party given by his friends Beatrice and Robert Locher at which he saw Florine Stettheimer in the company of an assortment of designers and theater people, including Eyre de Lanux (a furniture designer and friend of Muriel's, best known for her work with Eileen Gray and her connection to lesbian Paris), Edla Frankau (an actress in the *Grand Street Follies*), the set-designer Aline Bernstein, and John Mosher (the film critic for the *New Yorker*).[57] In April, he attended "high tea" at the Stettheimers' with Georgia O'Keeffe and Philip Moeller, the founder of the Theater Guild, noting that "Florine asked me to come to her studio tomorrow to see her portrait of Gertrude Stein which she has been painting for a year without ever having seen Gertrude."[58] A month later, he met the French sculptor Gaston Lachaise at the Stettheimers' apartment and visited his studio to see the "bronze bust he made of Carl." Ewing had clearly earned the sisters' trust and friendship: during that summer and the following one, he was a weekend guest at their home in Tarrytown, attending their Fourth of July celebration and various informal house parties throughout July and August.[59]

It was in the context of the Stettheimers' exclusive world — a world of art and companionship depicted in a number of Florine's paintings of the previous decade, including the well-known *Studio Party* of 1917–19 and *Sunday Afternoon in the Country* of 1917 — that Ewing was inspired to consider how he might use his camera to make his own contributions to the world of art. Clearly, the notion that he could also become an artist himself was nurtured by the example of Florine Stettheimer. As she put it in one of her best-known poems, "Our parties, / Our picnics, / Our banquets, / Our friends, / Have at last a raison d'être, / Seen in color and design: / It amuses me / To recreate them, / To paint them."[60] Ewing was enchanted by the idea: his own *Gallery of Extraordinary Portraits* was a similar effort to record his friends and enthusiasms, and he decided to supplement it with his own photographs.

Whether or not Ewing knew Florine's *Cathedrals of Broadway* (1928), the first in the series of large canvases celebrating the people and culture of New York in the 1920s, he soon became familiar with her second painting in the series, entitled *The Cathedrals of Fifth Avenue* (fig. 4.14), which she was working on in

1931 and 1932. As he explained to his mother on June 4, 1932, Florine had unveiled the work at an exclusive gathering in her studio, and invited him to be among the small number of people who would be able to see it:

> This afternoon I went to Florine Stettheimer's studio in the
> Beaux-Arts building to see her new painting called CATHEDRALS
> OF FIFTH AVENUE. It is a big canvas satirically depicting
> a Fifth Avenue wedding scene outside St. Patrick's Cathedral.
> Many people are recognizable in the picture, including Muriel
> Draper, Otto Kahn and Max Ewing. Only four people were invited
> to its first showing today — myself, Muriel, Carl, and Henry
> McBride, the art critic of the Sun. So that was today.[61]

Ewing was thrilled by the painting: Stettheimer placed him side by side with Muriel Draper in front of St. Patrick's Cathedral, watching with a group of art-world luminaries and prominent New Yorkers as a bride and groom and their wedding party emerge from the church.[62] Many of the figures in the painting were identified by Henry McBride in the catalogue of the exhibition of Stettheimer's work at MoMA in 1946. On the right side of the painting, next to a Rolls-Royce that bears the date 1931 and the initials "FS," we see the artist and her sisters, fashionably attired as always, standing close together; to the left of that group, the artist Charles Demuth (carrying a cane) stands behind the gallerist "Mrs. Valentine Dudensing and her daughter," with Muriel Draper "leaning on Max Ewing's shoulder" close by.[63] In the left foreground, the society photographer Arnold Genthe records the ceremony, as Lucie Bigelow Rosen, the patron of contemporary music, rushes past in a yellow dress to offer the couple a white lily. Another vignette in the background on the left shows "Charles A. Lindbergh parading in an auto" at the ticker-tape parade held in his honor on May 7, 1929. As Ewing pointed out, the white-haired figure wearing a black top coat to the left in the crowd is the financier Otto Kahn, easily identifiable from contemporary photographs. We can clearly identify the dark-haired artist Miguel Covarrubias and his wife Rosa, who wears an elegant yellow evening gown, on the right-hand side of the composition, and directly behind them, the shadowy but easily recognizable face of Virgil Thomson — with whom Stettheimer would collaborate on *Four Saints* — which appears beneath a green palm frond. As we know, Ewing met Thomson in Paris in 1926 and heard his new work played in private performances at friends' homes in the winter of 1929. Like Ewing and others, Thomson became a member of the Stettheimer circle around this time.[64]

The art historian Barbara Bloemink, the leading expert on the art of Florine Stettheimer, describes the painting as a feminist critique of marriage, focusing on "the commercialism and acquisitiveness commonly associated with the event by New York society women."[65] Whether meant as satire or celebration, the work is pitched in a key of camp irony that we know well from Max Ewing and his queer friends, even as it shows that Stettheimer knew her 5th Avenue shops, restaurants, and luxury goods with a connoisseur's familiarity and attention to detail.[66] She lovingly depicts the display windows and distinctive logo of Tappé, the house of French couture on 57th Street, spells out the names of Tiffany's and Altman's department store in the puffy clouds above the scene, and renders the lettering on top of a box of Maillard's chocolates in meticulous detail, then frames it with the gilded name of Delmonico's restaurant, creating a sort of radiant sun that floats in the sky opposite a golden eagle carrying an American flag in its talons.

All of the establishments that Stettheimer highlights were famous 5th Avenue landmarks, just as the Dudensings' Valentine Gallery, located at 57th Street, Otto Kahn's mansion at 1 East 91st Street, and the home of Lucie and Walter Rosen at 37 West 54th were among the leading venues for art along the same avenue. All were also associated with the extraordinary and well-documented efforts of Jewish collectors and philanthropists to contribute to the culture of New York. As established gallerists, Valentine Dudensing and his beautiful wife, Bibi, who was photographed by Van Vechten in 1937, played a leading role in bringing modern European art to the city, and they appeared on the list of guests for Muriel Draper's party described above. They were also friends of the larger-than-life painter and party-giver Robert Chanler, who painted a glamorous portrait of Bibi Dudensing in 1927.[67] Lucie Bigelow Rosen was a devoted supporter of the inventor Leon Theremin, who held concerts in her home and became a skilled performer on the electronic instrument he invented.[68] While the Walter Rosens, who built Caramoor in Katonoh, New York, as a vast summer estate, or the Otto Kahns, who recreated a French-style chateau on Long Island, were clearly on an entirely different plane and enjoyed wealth and status well beyond that of the comfortable West Side Stettheimers, all were members of a group of German Jewish Americans who would have recognized each other and the outsider status that mainstream America conferred upon them. The presence of these people in *Cathedrals of Fifth Avenue* suggests that Stettheimer's depiction of New York in 1931–32 was perhaps more complex and layered than has previously been suggested, albeit in her characteristically ebullient style.

In *Cathedrals of Fifth Avenue*, for example, Ewing is paired with his beloved Muriel Draper, whom Florine recognized as his companion and soulmate. In addition, Ewing and Draper are placed next to the painter Charles Demuth, a close friend of the Stettheimer family, who was known to be gay. Demuth was in a longstanding, intimate partnership with the married graphic artist Robert Locher, a member of Draper's intimate circle and a particular friend of Florine's.[69] Long after Demuth's death in 1935, she included a portrait of Locher in her *Cathedrals of Art* (1942–44), casting him as the "compère" or interlocutor, a role she had become familiar with from *Four Saints*: the handsome, doll-like figure in that painting looks so strikingly similar to the groom in *Cathedrals of Fifth Avenue* that it raises the question of whether Stettheimer was, in fact, using Locher's image as a way to highlight the performative nature of the society wedding, especially given that Demuth stands among the onlookers.[70] Like much else about Demuth, Locher, and indeed Florine herself, the answer remains a mystery.

Ewing was often in Tarrytown with the Stettheimers the following summer, though he also visited the top of the Empire State Building with Florine in July because she was "so bored and lonely" in the "pastoral splendor" of the country that she decided to return to town for a week by herself.[71] Sometimes he went up to the country with Van Vechten or Draper, where they might run into the Knopfs or other friends, while at other times there were very few guests besides themselves. Little changed in the Stettheimers' comfortable world during the dark days of the Depression, as Ewing reported to his mother:

It was beautiful on the hills above the Hudson. We had cocktails and
hors d'oeuvres on the lawn — eggs in jelly, lobster, salad, salami,
liverwurst, celery, wafers etc. We all ate heartily as if it were the whole
meal. Then Carrie announced that we were going in to supper.
We were quite appalled by going into SUPPER after eating so much
in the garden. When we went in it was an enormous dinner, with
roast duck and everything that goes with Thanksgiving! So we did the
best we could and felt quite stuffed for hours.[72]

For the young man from the frugal heartland of the United States, this was indeed
a brave, new world of extraordinary people, lavish meals, and unusual gatherings,
one in which he was determined not just to fit in but also to leave his mark.

CARL VAN VECHTEN TAKES UP PHOTOGRAPHY, 1932

Carl Van Vechten was a lodestar that Max Ewing followed throughout his life, and
thus it was perhaps inevitable that Van Vechten's turn toward portrait
photography in 1932 would play a significant role in Ewing's decision to take up his
camera as well. Ewing and Van Vechten had shared clippings, portraits, and
ephemera for years, and Van Vechten was, as we know, a particularly active

contributor to the *Max Ewing Collection of
Extraordinary Portraits* installed in Ewing's walk-in
closet. The two men saw each other regularly, and
Ewing was a member of the queer circle of handsome
young men — Van Vechten's "jeunes gens assortis," as
his friend Mabel Luhan had once called them — whom
he frequently brought together at restaurants and bars,
and in his own home for relaxed evenings of drinking,
listening to records, and sharing photos and gossip.[73]
The core group included the artist Prentiss Taylor
(1907–91) (a close friend of Langston Hughes), the
financier Edward Wasserman, Van Vechten's lover
Donald Angus, and an ever-changing assortment of

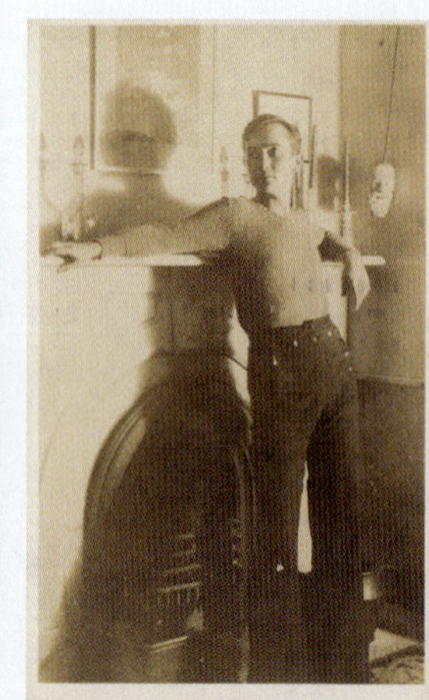

4.15 Real photo postcards of
Max Ewing and Prentiss Taylor
from the series *Famous
Beauties of the XXth Century*.
Max Ewing Papers.

young male writers and entertainers. In late 1931 or early 1932, Van Vechten and
Ewing put together a collection of five real-photo postcard portraits that Van
Vechten titled the *Famous Beauties of the XXth Century*, including recent photos
of Max Ewing, Prentiss Taylor (fig. 4.15), and Donald Angus; the two older men
appeared as young beauties in portraits taken decades earlier.[74] Although Van
Vechten had many projects underway at the time, and had recently become
obsessed with learning to fly an airplane, the project of documenting his extended
circle of friends and acquaintances was clearly not far from his mind in winter
1931–32. A surviving list with notations in Ewing's hand is evidence that Ewing
helped his friend catalogue the images for his collection as early as February 1932.[75]

We know that Van Vechten also began staging and producing his own
photographic portraits in January 1932, writing to his brother-in-law to say that
he had purchased a Leica and become obsessed with photography.[76] As he wrote
to Ewing on an undated photo-postcard with the caption "Early home of Carl Van
Vechten Cedar Rapids Iowa," "I am getting a camera and am going to become an
Artist Photographer — with subjects that the others have missed."[77] He soon
began taking portraits of his wife, his friends, and even random people he met on

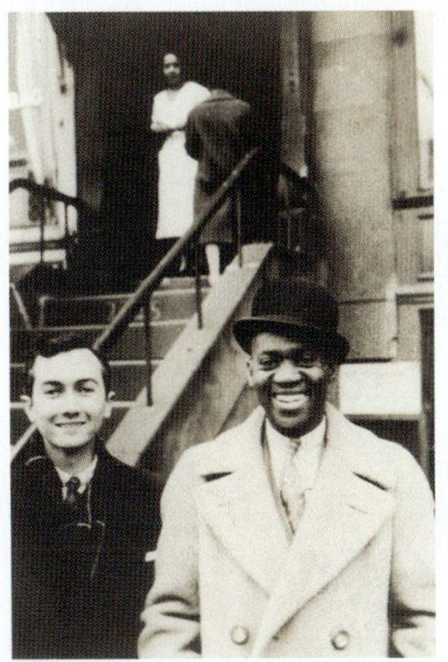

4.16 Carl Van Vechten, *Prentiss Taylor and Bill Robinson*, February 6, 1932. Carl Van Vechten Papers.

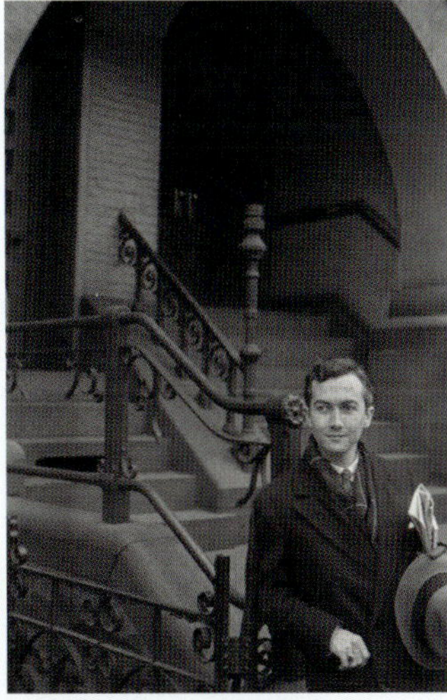

4.17 Carl Van Vechten, *Prentiss Taylor*, February 6, 1932. Carl Van Vechten Papers.

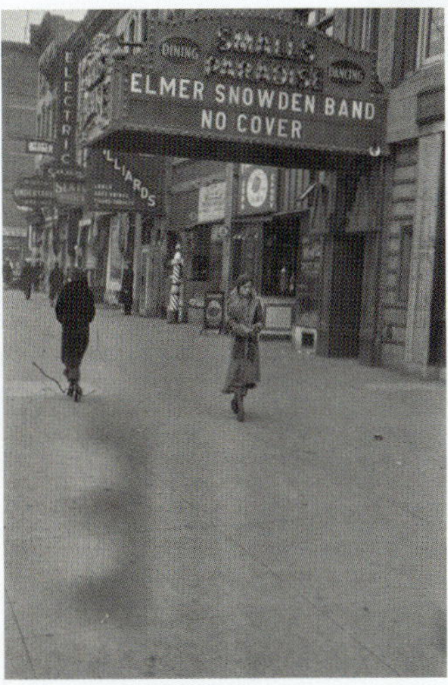

4.18 Carl Van Vechten, *Smalls Paradise*, February 6, 1932. Carl Van Vechten Papers.

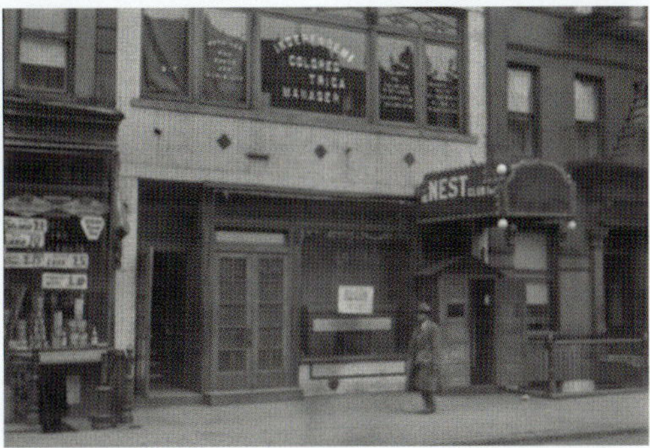

4.19 Carl Van Vechten, *The Nest*, February 6, 1932. Carl Van Vechten Papers.

the street with the same sort of frenzied energy that he brought to everything he did. On February 7, 1932, he wrote to Max Ewing about his newfound passion, boasting that he couldn't decide whether to make his "first show Harlem or celebrated sitters," adding that "O'Keeffe is posing for me in a quilt [*sic*] with skis and cat-tails. The title is: What Stieglitz Missed."[78]

Over the preceding days, Van Vechten had been out on the streets of Harlem, taking snapshots of Prentiss Taylor, a frequent collaborator and companion in his earliest efforts, some of which show Taylor posing with the dancer Bill Robinson in a variety of outdoor settings (figs. 4.16 and 4.17).[79] He also photographed a handful of streetscapes, recording the marquees of Small's Paradise (fig. 4.18), Connie's Inn, and the Nest (fig. 4.19) — his favorite Harlem nightclubs — with people walking past. Van Vechten soon turned his camera on other Harlem spots and entertainers: on February 27, 1932, he photographed Prentiss Taylor posing with both Gladys Bentley, the famous, cross-dressing Harlem entertainer, and the celebrated singer and composer Nora Holt, a long-standing friend of Van Vechten's and a leader of the Harlem Renaissance (fig. 4.20).[80] In Van Vechten's photo, Bentley appears in conventional women's clothing, including a fashionable cloche and a coat with a white fur

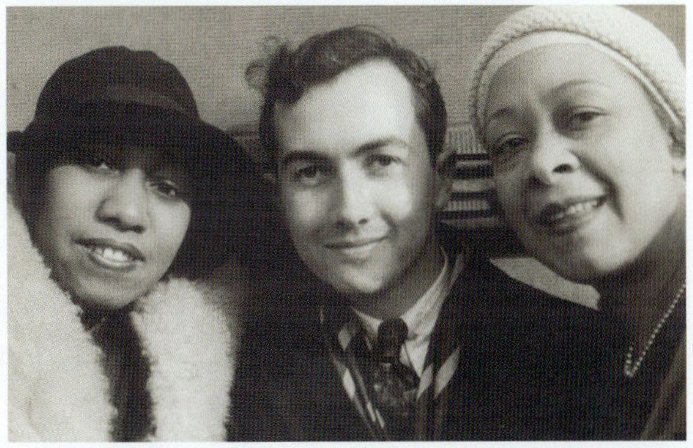

4.20 Carl Van Vechten, *Gladys Bentley, Prentiss Taylor, and Nora Holt*, February 27, 1932.

collar, clearly a very different look from the costume she wore when she performed at the Clam Shack in a white tails and a top hat (fig. 4.21).

While portraits were Van Vechten's passion, interesting cityscapes and details did not escape his notice, including the view from the window of his apartment (fig. 4.22), captured on March 5. The photo shows the sun glistening on the Empire State Building with the surrounding buildings in silhouette, an image that he liked so much that he used it as a postcard for his own correspondence.

Realizing that he lacked the skills to shoot indoors, Van Vechten asked George Lynes to teach him about lighting, writing to Ewing that they had blown all of the fuses in his apartment when they began to experiment with different setups. He added that he had made a portrait of Lynes at the time and that Lynes had made one of him; both are, alas, now lost.[81] It is notable that Lynes's own career as a portrait photographer was also taking off at this time, culminating in his first solo show at the Leggett Gallery in the Waldorf Astoria, which ran from March 1 to 19, 1932. Ewing was well aware of that event and kept the invitation, designed and printed by Lynes's lover Monroe Wheeler, in his collection of programs, announcements, and treasured ephemera.

Van Vechten went on to produce thousands of portraits over the following four decades, not only creating a remarkable record of his own extended network, but also creating an invaluable archive of portraits of Black writers, entertainers, activists, and other men and women — from Nella Larsen to Mary McLeod Bethune — who left their mark on American arts, politics, and culture.[82] Less well-known are the private portraits and domestic scenes that he made early in his career, many of which only survive in contact sheets, yet these too offer invaluable evidence, albeit of another kind: they document, sometimes haphazardly, the details of his disparate and often complex interests by showing us the things he saw around him and the things he wanted to look at. Among the most revealing are the self-portraits, many taken with the aid of Prentiss Taylor or Donald Angus, which show him posed at his desk or against a background of carefully arranged books, posters, works of art, and knickknacks behind him (fig. 4.23).

One particularly fascinating series shows Van Vechten at the end of March, posing in his pajamas in front of his closet; in one he is with his wife Fania Marinoff, who is fashionably dressed in a coat trimmed with white fur collar and cuffs (figs. 4.24 and 4.25). Another series shows Marinoff being served tea by the Black housekeeper Edith Ramsey, who wears her uniform and white apron as she poses for the camera (figs. 4.26 and 4.27).[83] While hardly surprising, given the profound racial contradictions that ran deep among Van Vechten's circle of "reformers" and advocates for Black culture, these images are nonetheless startling.

On March 2, 1932, Van Vechten made a series of portraits of Max Ewing and Donald Angus (figs. 4.28–4.30) showing his friends in both formal poses and informal conversations in his study. Like Van Vechten himself, Ewing was a man of many faces, both literally and figuratively, vain and self-absorbed, but also full

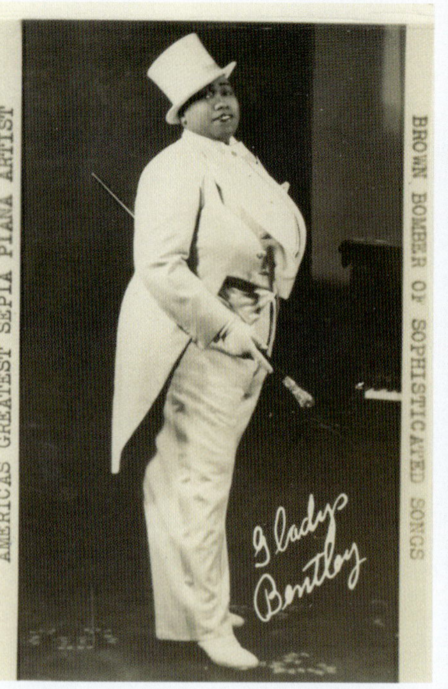

4.21 *Gladys Bentley: America's Greatest Sepia Player—The Brown Bomber of Sophisticated Songs*, c. 1946–49, silver and photographic gelatin on photographic paper, with ink on cardboard, 5¼ × 3⅜ in. (13.3 × 8.6 cm). Collection of the Smithsonian National Museum of African American History and Culture, Washington, DC., 2011.57.25.1.

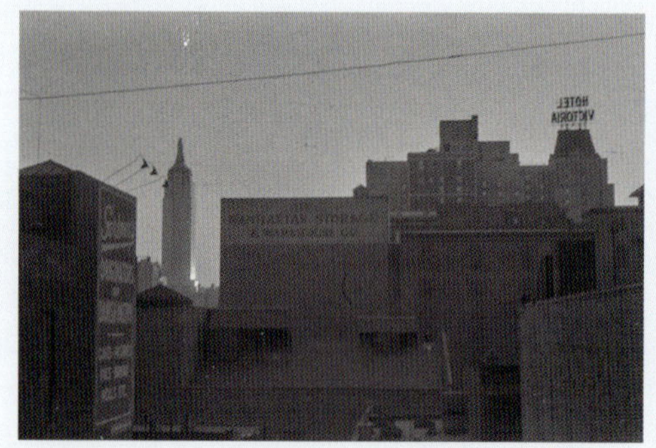

4.22 Carl Van Vechten, *View from My Apartment Window*, March 5, 1932. Carl Van Vechten Papers.

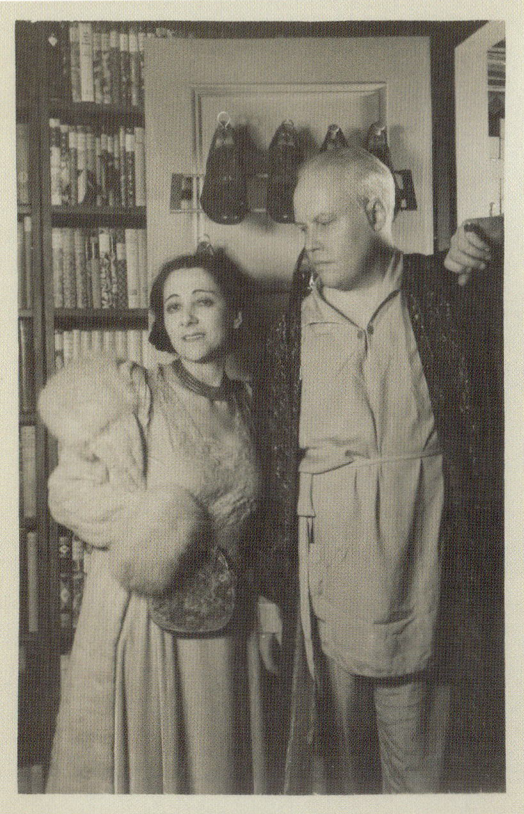

4.24 Carl Van Vechten "assisted by Prentiss Taylor," *Self Portrait in Pajamas with Fania Marinoff*, March 30, 1932. Carl Van Vechten Papers.

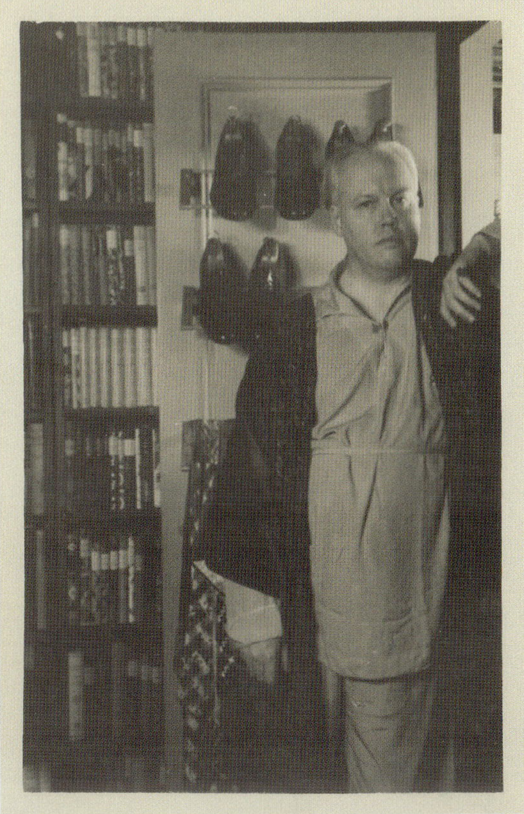

4.25 Carl Van Vechten "assisted by Prentiss Taylor," *Self Portrait in Pajamas*, March 30, 1932. Carl Van Vechten Papers.

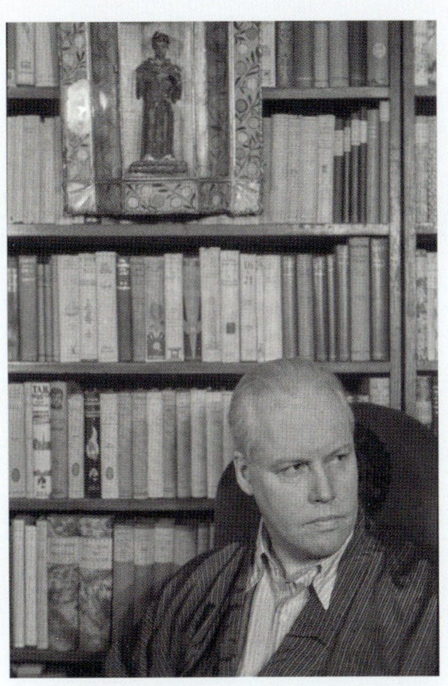

4.23 Carl Van Vechten, *Self Portrait*, February 20, 1932. Carl Van Vechten Papers.

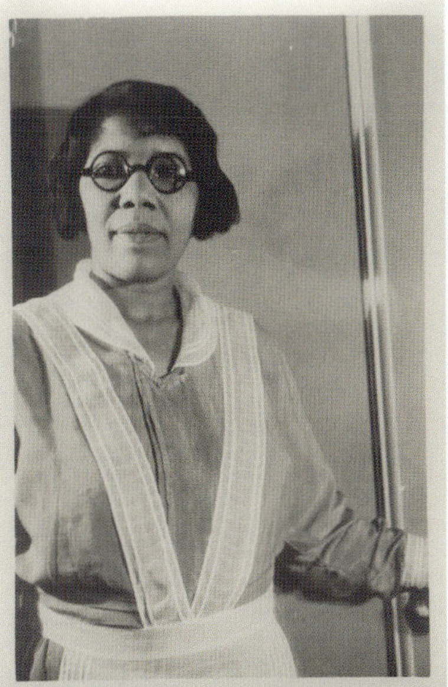

4.26 Carl Van Vechten, *Edith Ramsey*, March 9, 1932. Carl Van Vechten Papers Relating to African American Arts and Letters.

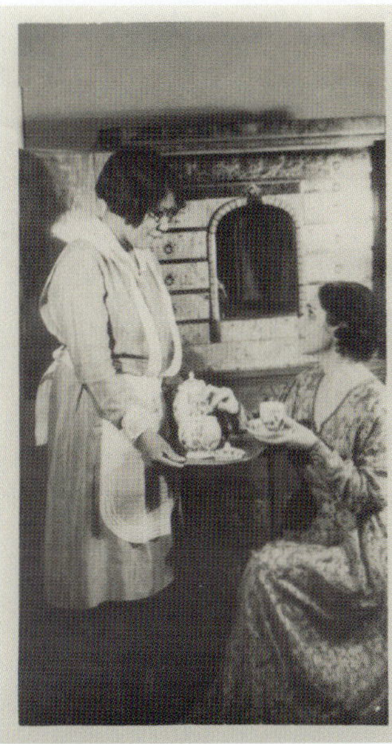

4.27 Carl Van Vechten, *Edith Ramsey and Fania Marinoff*, March 9, 1932. Carl Van Vechten Papers Relating to African American Arts and Letters.

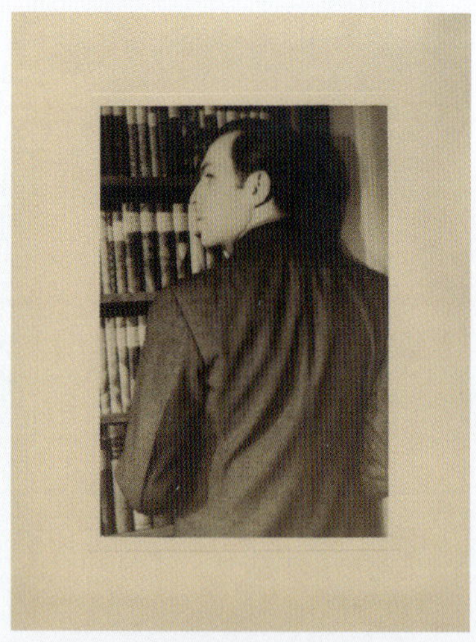

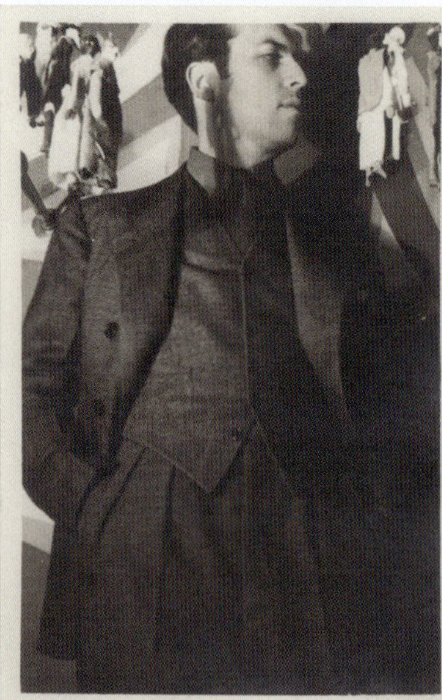

4.29 Carl Van Vechten, *Max Ewing*, March 2, 1932. Carl Van Vechten Papers.

4.28 Carl Van Vechten, *Max Ewing (Facing Away)*, March 2, 1932. Carl Van Vechten Papers.

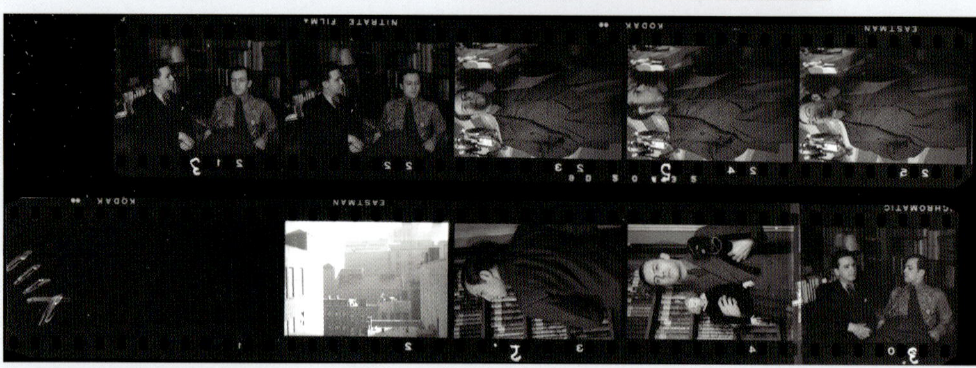

4.30 Carl Van Vechten, *Max Ewing and Donald Angus*, from a contact sheet, March 2, 1932. Carl Van Vechten Papers.

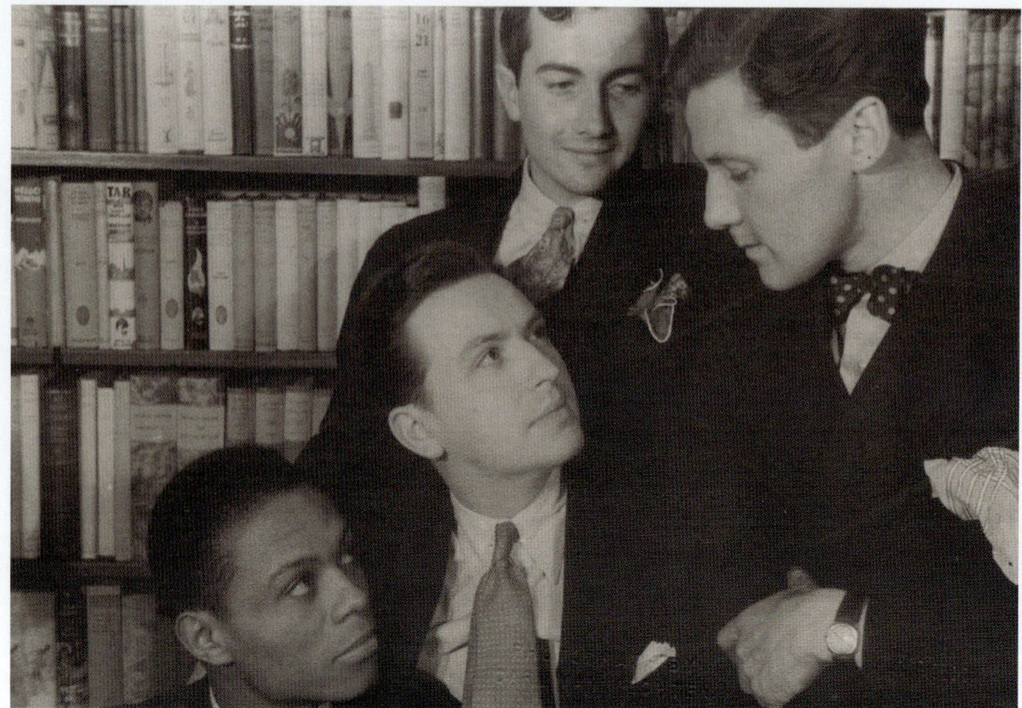

4.31 Carl Van Vechten, *Jimmie Daniels, Donald Angus, Prentiss Taylor, and Tonio Selwart*, March 5, 1932. Carl Van Vechten Papers.

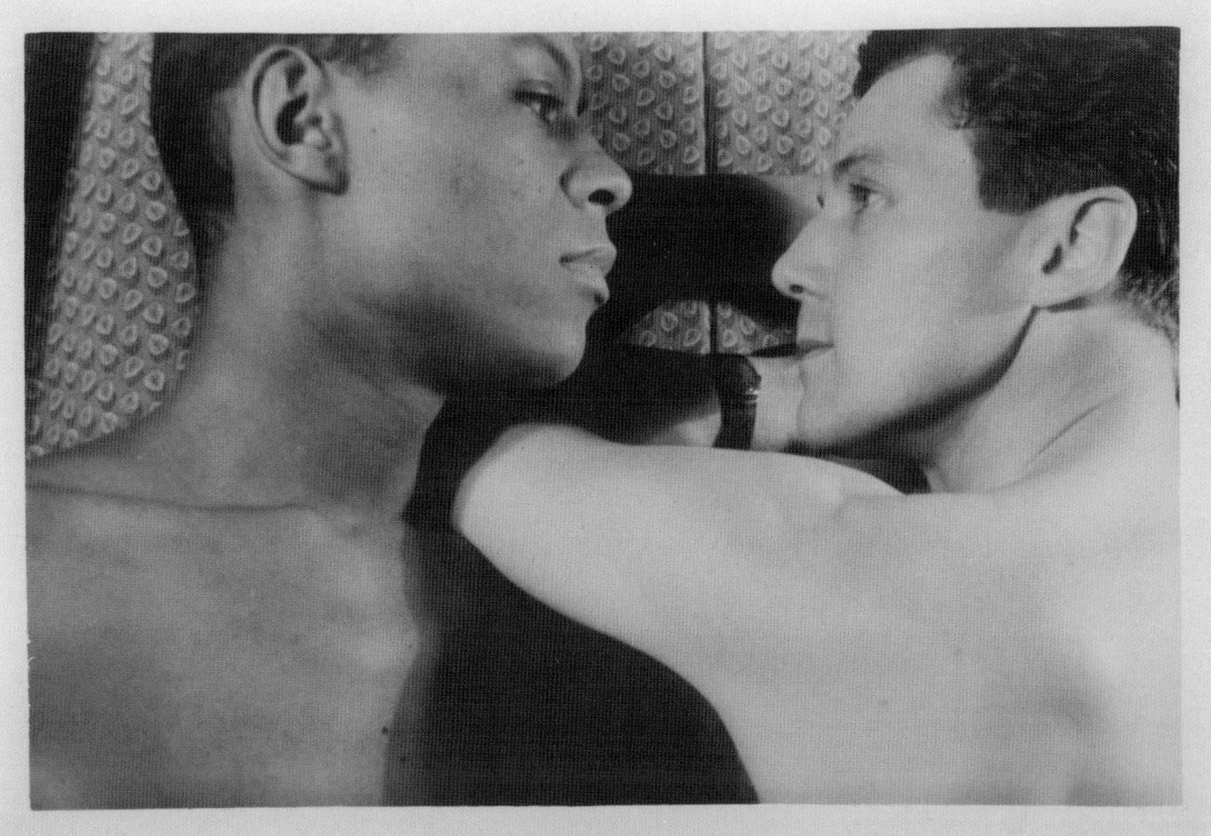

of camp humor and theater. In Van Vechten's portraits, the atmospheric lighting, and the dapper suit and patterned suspenders were all intended to show off Ewing's good looks to full advantage. In one image, he poses against the background of a Mark Tobey painting. In another, he holds two large dolls (including a black cat) and stares at the camera with a blank expression. In photos of Ewing and Donald Angus sitting together in Van Vechten's study, Ewing has his jacket off and looks away from the camera; the series depicts the sort of comfortable queer companionship that Van Vechten fostered in his home.[84]

Another series of images taken a few days later, on March 5, is even more remarkable. These include a group portrait (fig. 4.31) of Donald Angus and Prentiss Taylor posing with Tonio Selwart (1896–2002), an actor, and Jimmie Daniels, the entertainer who was the star at Hot-Cha Club in Harlem. In these images, the four men — looking dapper in their suits and ties — stand close together against a backdrop of books: they clasp hands and exchange loving looks in a tableau of queer beauty and desire. The extreme rarity of such an image hardly needs to be remarked upon: not only is it intimate and informal, it also offers striking visual evidence of the relationships that existed between Black and white men in Van Vechten's circle. We know about these connections from written documentary evidence; to see them represented so lovingly and vividly in a photograph is another thing altogether.

Other images shot the same day go even further in their depiction of queer and interracial intimacy: in one photo (fig. 4.32), Daniels and Selwart appear to be lying naked in each other's arms as they gaze intently at one another. Selwart's arm rests on Daniels's shoulder, and the two men's faces are so close together they could kiss. Neither man appears shy about taking part in this scene; in fact,

4.32 Carl Van Vechten, *Jimmie Daniels and Tonio Selwart*, March 5, 1932. Carl Van Vechten Papers Relating to African American Arts and Letters.

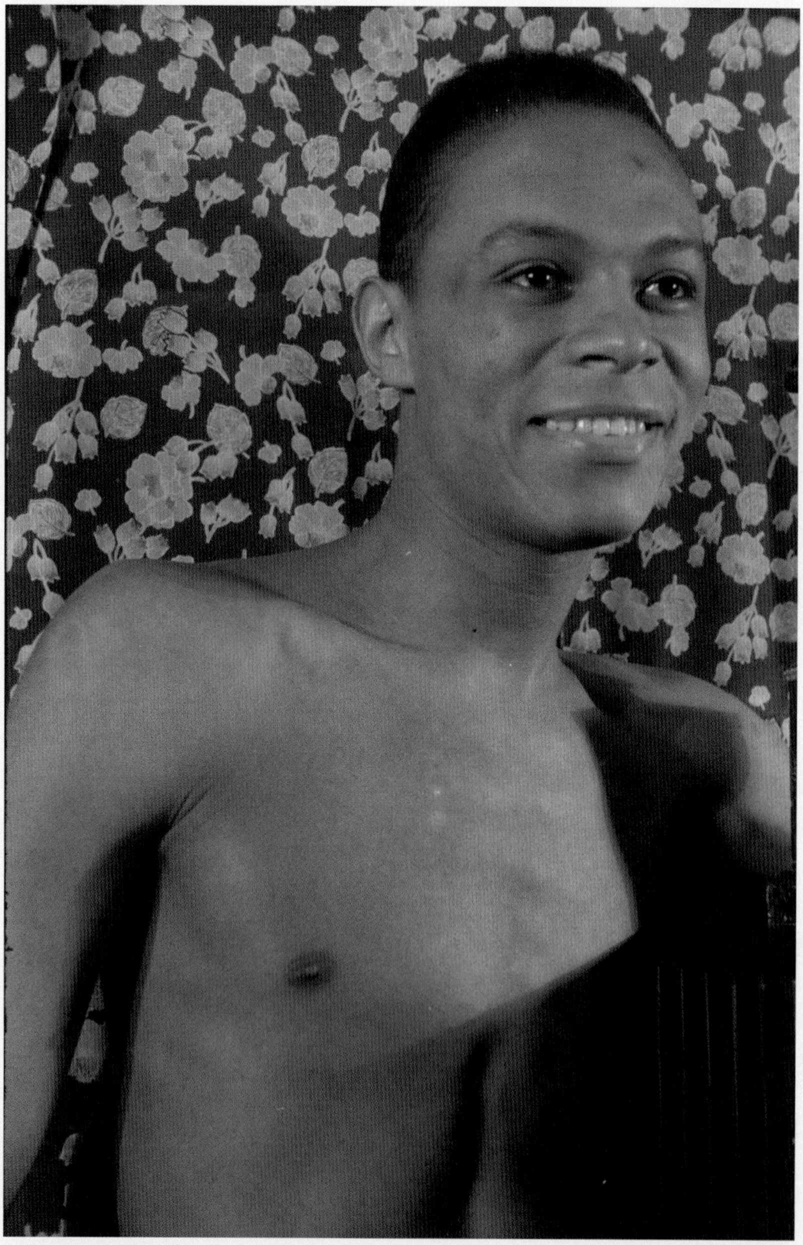

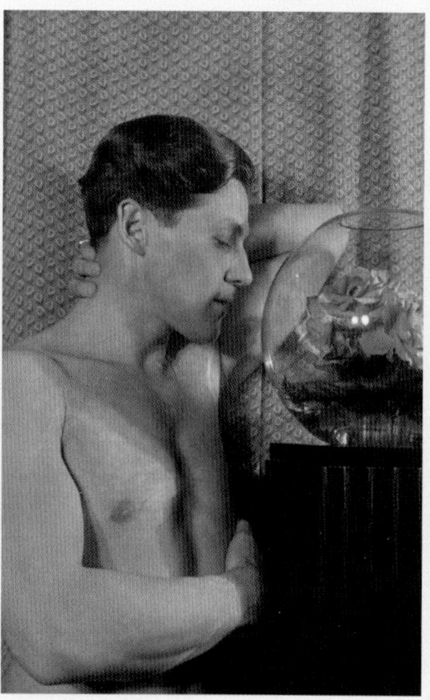

4.34 Carl Van Vechten, *Tonio Selwart with a Rose Bowl*, from contact sheet, March 5, 1932. Carl Van Vechten Papers.

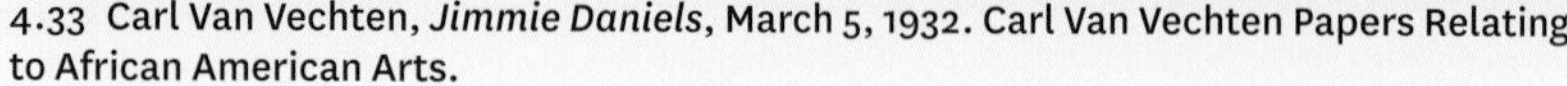

4.33 Carl Van Vechten, *Jimmie Daniels*, March 5, 1932. Carl Van Vechten Papers Relating to African American Arts.

Selwart had posed nude for George
Lynes the previous year, and both men
were used to being looked at and
admired. These photos thus tell us a
great deal more about queer intimacy
in Van Vechten's world than words
can document.

Two more portraits stand out
from the March 5 session in Van
Vechten's home. In one, Jimmie
Daniels is again bare-chested, posed
against a boldly patterned backdrop,
a broad smile of unguarded pleasure
spreading across his face (fig. 4.33).
Not only was Daniels among the most
popular entertainers in Harlem, he
was also well-known both for his voice
and his suave good looks. In another, a
bare-chested Tonio Selwart peers dreamily at a glass rose bowl or terrarium,
posing in profile with one muscular arm around his torso and the other looped
around his neck to show his body to greatest advantage, suggesting the rather
camp complexities of Van Vechten's gaze (fig. 4.34). Making these images was
clearly a coup for Van Vechten, who was still an amateur photographer but
already well established as an avid fan of Harlem nightlife whose home was a
protected, private space where his friends could gather.

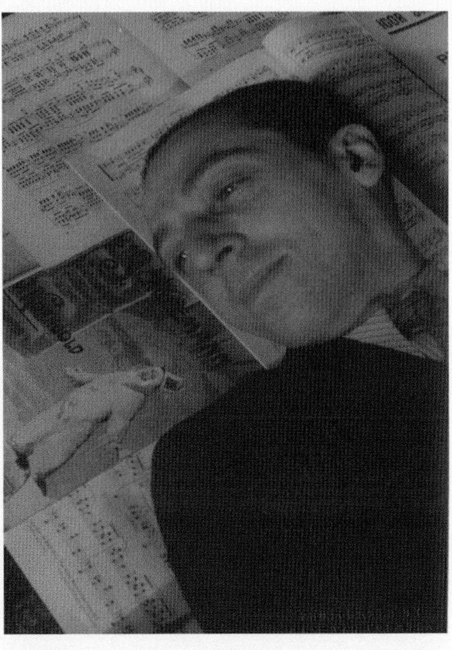

4.35 Carl Van Vechten, *Aaron
Copland*, March 11, 1932. Carl
Van Vechten Papers.

These photos also speak volumes about the early hit-or-miss nature of his
work, just as the range and variety of his many other images, including the
cityscapes and street scenes, tell us about the many experiments with subject
matter and lighting that he made in the early years of his career. Over the course
of only a few months in the winter and spring of 1932, he devoted himself to
learning his new trade, producing hundreds of images every day, and recording
the faces and characteristic appearances of the many people he knew. These
include Aaron Copland lying against a backdrop of sheet music on March 11
(fig. 4.35), Nora Holt on March 18, Frida Kahlo and Diego Rivera on March 19,
James Weldon Johnson on March 20, Luther E. Allen, Nella Larsen, Dorothy
Randolph Peterson, Jerome Sidney Peterson, and Prentiss Taylor on March 26,
and Langston Hughes (fig. 4.36) the following day — to name only a few of the
people who appear in the surviving prints and contact sheets. On March 31,
he photographed Muriel Draper and her two sons (fig. 4.37), the first of many
portraits he took of his dear friend. By April, his photographs began to assume
the style and character that we have become familiar with: sitters posed against
boldly printed backdrops, often carrying props or wearing fashionable clothing.

As a group, these portraits reveal Van Vechten's emerging style and the
body of work that Ewing measured himself against. Both men were collectors and
possessed the competitive spirit that led them to boast about their acquisitions,
even as they shared their "finds" and worked hard to impress one another.
Thus, while Draper and the Stettheimers encouraged Ewing to think of himself as
a creative artist, it was Carl Van Vechten who ultimately set the bar that Ewing felt
he had to jump over. By the spring of 1932, he would turn his attention to portrait

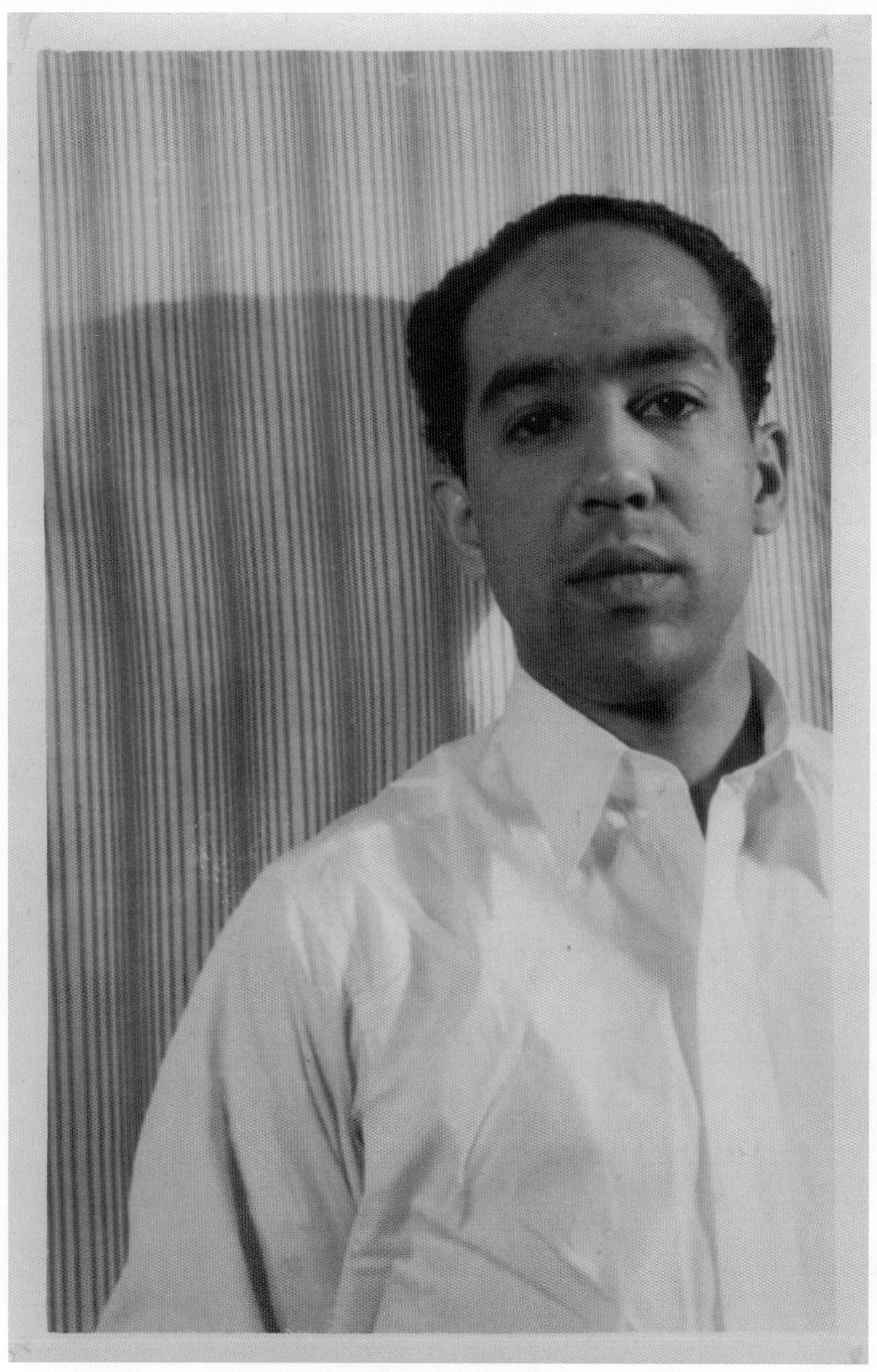

4.36 Carl Van Vechten, *Langston Hughes*, March 27, 1932. Carl Van Vechten Papers.

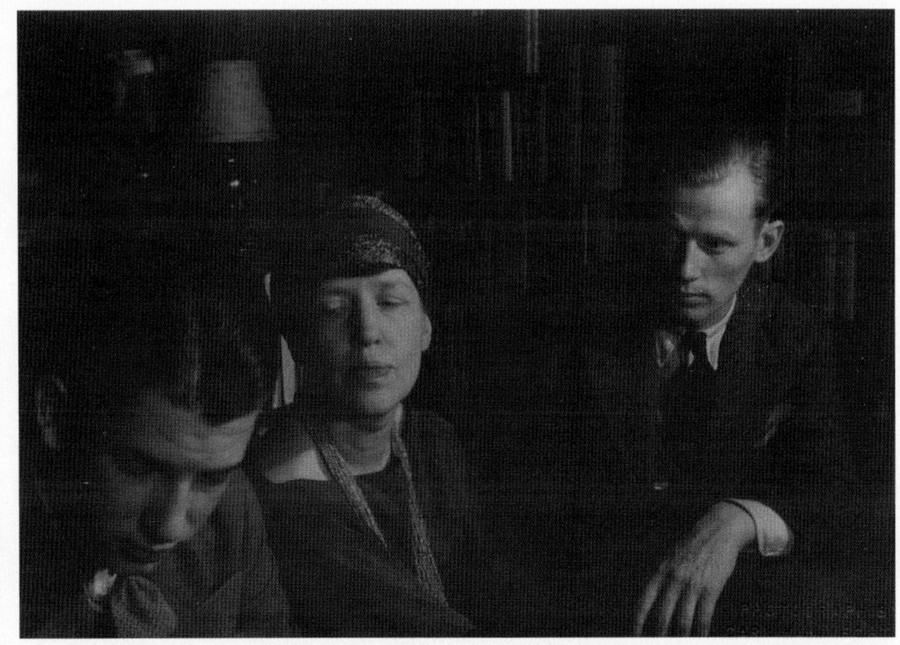

4.37 Carl Van Vechten, *Muriel Draper with Paul Draper, Jr., and Raimond Sanders "Smudge" Draper,* March 30, 1932. Carl Van Vechten Papers.

photography, hosting gatherings in his apartment and using camp irony and male nudity to capture the attention of his friends, just as he had with his sculpture projects and the gallery he created for his *Collection of Extraordinary Portraits*.

A letter from Ewing to his mother, written December 3, 1932, suggests something of the mixed emotions he experienced: "I have not gone to Carl's lately because he has been so engaged in photography he has given no parties," he wrote, "He takes pictures day and night and is as excited as a child over them. Some of them are really good. Some are not. The Stettheimers showed me the pictures he took of them and said I was the only person alive whom they would show them to, they were so bad." Ewing was confident that his own work was better: "I took a picture of Martha Winslow as a nun in Venice and took it out to her last night. She was so pleased she ordered a dozen to give away for Christmas, so that makes me a few dollars profit from her."[85] He knew that the part about the money would impress his mother, but, as always, social status and notoriety were his primary goals. Thus, following Van Vechten's lead, in April, 1932, he picked up his "little snapshot Kodak," and began working on his *Carnival* project, asking everyone he knew to pose in front of the Venetian window shade in his bedroom and giving them the choice of putting on costumes from his dress-up box or wearing nothing at all.

Chapter 5

THE CARNIVAL OF VENICE, 1932

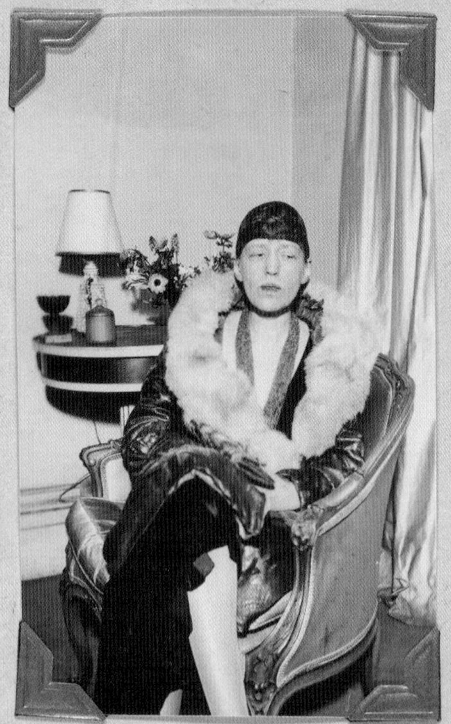

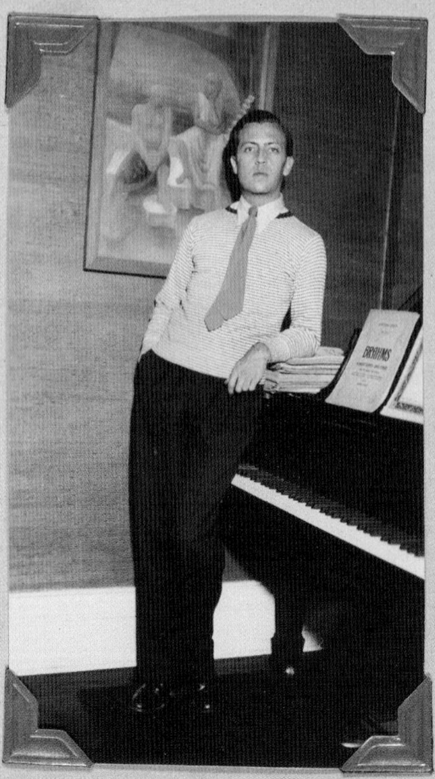

5.1 Snapshots of Muriel Draper and Max Ewing, April 18, 1932, from Max Ewing's *Snapshots 1932*. Max Ewing Papers.

The month after he posed for a series of portraits in Carl Van Vechten's home studio, Ewing wrote to his mother about his own photography project, describing a recent snapshot session in which he teamed up with Muriel Draper to take pictures of himself standing by his piano at West 31st Street. Later the same evening, they made a series of portraits of her in her own home, fashionably attired in her characteristic turban and fur-trimmed coat.[1] Ewing enclosed some examples of that work with his letter and preserved a set of prints in his scrapbooks with the date April 18, 1932 inscribed on the page (fig. 5.1). He also sent along a few images (though he didn't specify which) from his recently begun *Carnival of Venice* project, boasting that "My little snapshot Kodak is taking amazingly good pictures now both indoors and out," and explaining — in his usual fashion — that "The Venetian scene is not really Venice, but only my bedroom in front of my painted window blind. It is very convincingly like Venice however!"[2]

Not surprisingly, Ewing failed to mention another group of photos taken the previous week in that same bedroom (fig. 5.2): two of these showed the model Fred Ritter sitting on Ewing's bed and wearing his black Chinese silk dressing gown and Japanese pajamas, pretending to smoke opium from a long-handled pipe; another showed Ritter wearing a white terrycloth bathrobe that falls open to reveal his chest as he stares seductively at the camera; a fourth image showed him perched on the ledge above the radiator, wearing nothing at all except for a pair of open-toed velvet slippers.

By the spring of 1932, Ewing had been photographing Ritter, both in costume and nude, for two years. As we know from both Ritter's letters to Ewing and Ewing's letters to his parents, the two men had developed an easygoing friendship that included nights out at Texas Guinan's swanky new nightclub and a shared appreciation, thanks in part to Ewing's patronage, for Ritter's increasing success as a bodybuilder and model. No doubt this unusual friendship, like the photographs that Ewing and Ritter staged in Ewing's bedroom, was envied by other members of the queer circle: in George Lynes's case, this was soon remedied by his own use of the Ritter brothers as nude models, while other less daring friends, like Van Vechten and Edward Wasserman, were happy to admire the young men when they saw them at parties and clubs, but always kept them at arm's length. In any case, like so much else in Ewing's life, it was hard to take his relationship with Fred and Bill Ritter very seriously, much less his efforts as a portrait photographer, especially given the chasm in style and technique that was opening up between Ewing's amateur work and that of his professional friends.

Nevertheless, it is notable that Ewing's snapshot series does indeed subvert the expected form and content of the genre in significant ways, making queer use of the popular Kodak camera to produce images that the company, which had emphasized heterosexual family harmony, children's activities, and American holidays since its earliest beginnings, could hardly have predicted, much less accepted.[3] Ewing's repurposing of both the technology of the Kodak camera and the normative content of the snapshot elevated his project to the status of art, just as his inclusion of self-portraits among the highly staged images of his friends shifted the reading and time frame of the series into the future. Ewing's hope was that later viewers would look at the images after his own lifetime and understand that he was both part of a glamorous community of artists, actors, and writers and in control of the fashioning of their portraits. Like Andy Warhol, who used the new technology of the Polaroid camera to

capture the faces of his friends and the random
people he encountered, embracing both the
unpredictability and immediacy that his snapshots
conferred on his subjects, Ewing imbued his project
with camp irony and ambiguity, giving himself and
his friends an enduring presence and even a sort
of immortality.[4] In short, he had high hopes for his
work and his status as an artist.

Perhaps this is why Ewing encountered such
a negative reaction when he tried, in his usual breezy
yet expectant way, to win his friends' approval for
what he himself viewed as a serious artistic
endeavor, if not exactly the start of a burgeoning new
career. On April 22, he sent Van Vechten a handful of
his Ritter snapshots, which he knew would pique his
curiosity, hoping to set the record straight about his
work: "I am enclosing some snapshots," he wrote:

> recent handiwork of mine which I hope will
> not infuriate you as they infuriated Eddie
> Wasserman. He maintains that it is
> absolutely inexcusable for me to take any
> pictures because he says I only do it because
> you do. This seems fanciful in view of my
> widely publicized preoccupation with
> photographs … But anyway here they are. …
> The pictures of myself and of Fred Ritter were taken not in Venice,
> but in my bedroom. You see it has surprising pictorial advantages.[5]

Fred Ritter
april 12 – 1932

5.2 Max Ewing, *Four
Portraits of Fred Ritter*,
April 12, 1932, from Max
Ewing's *Snapshots 1932*.

Ewing wanted Van Vechten to approve of his latest efforts, but he couldn't
resist a bit of petulant competitiveness as he strayed deeper into Van Vechten's
territory: "Monday I am taking to Knopf's the Berenice Abbott prints," he boasted,
"and some other pictures I have got together in case they ever need them. If you
think they would reproduce at all I wish you would send me extra copies of the
ones you took of me from the back, and also those with the dolls. I don't want to
relinquish the only copies I have."[6] Van Vechten responded with good humor,
writing back to say that he would "only be infuriated if you take more or better
pictures than I do."[7]

On June 23, Ewing tried again, joking and flirting in his usual way, in hopes
that Van Vechten would acknowledge his efforts and perhaps accept his invitation
to pose for the *Carnival of Venice*. A few weeks earlier, he had taken some
portraits of their friend Edward Wasserman, and the results were obviously
disappointing. "I'm afraid Eddie has belittled my photography to you!" he wrote:

> I admit the scenes in the Casa Wasserman were unsatisfactory.
> But I lay this to the confusion of the mirrors and the dog and the
> zebras and the grass and the glass and all that. I am enclosing a
> picture for you which will prove to you that when I function in my
> own bedroom I am not far from perfect,— as a photographer,

I mean, of course. I trust that sometime you will consent to join the innumerable caravan of Venetians who are filing through the Grand Canal in the Maison. Any time you say.[8]

The photographs in question (fig. 5.3), taken on June 7 in Wasserman's living room (which clearly show a large folding screen by Robert Winthrop Chanler, decorated with a scene of fighting zebras), were even worse than Ewing's earlier efforts.[9] In one snapshot, Wasserman reclines awkwardly on an Art Deco chaise, while in another he sits on a white sofa with En Cas, his black poodle, who disappears into the dark shadows of Wasserman's lap. In response, Van Vechten held fast to his refusal to participate in the *Carnival of Venice*, repeating the excuse that he was much too busy in his own darkroom to sit for a portrait. He sent Ewing a postcard declining his invitation to come to West 31st Street, explaining that "I practically live in the <u>dark</u> now." He also tried to again reassure his friend that the problem wasn't with his work *per se* but with the type of work he was doing: "It isn't that your photographs are not good enough — they appear to be superb," he remarked, "it's that I am living in such an atmosphere of subjective photographs that I don't seem to be able to snap into the objective kind. Some time no doubt … Anyway I am sending you some pictures to console you!"[10] As we saw in the previous chapter, by the middle of 1932, Van Vechten was already deep into the frenzy of portrait-taking that would become his life's work, and while he was never actually unkind to the young man who had been his companion and admirer for the past nine years, he wanted no part of Ewing's efforts.[11] Eventually, Ewing got the message and stopped asking, writing to say that "I do want you and Marinoff in the series, but [I] don't want to be a nuisance and plead."[12]

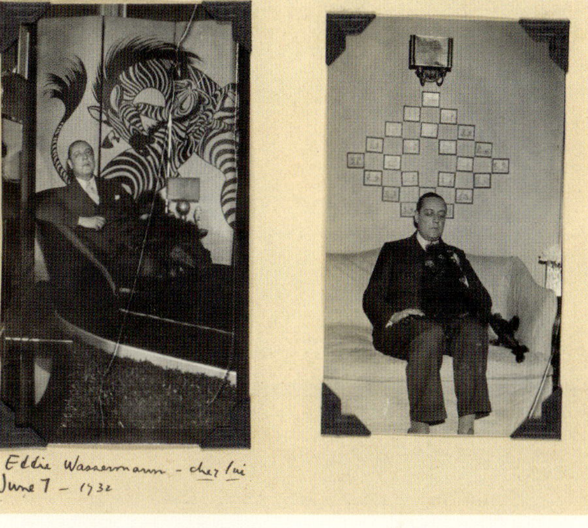

5.3 Max Ewing, *Two Portraits of Eddie Wasserman*, from Max Ewing's *Snapshots 1932*.

CREATING *THE CARNIVAL OF VENICE* AND *LES AMANTS DE VENISE*

Despite the unenthusiastic response of his friends, Ewing redoubled his efforts on the *Carnival of Venice* over the summer, photographing as many people as he could persuade to pose for him in front of the painted window shade in his apartment. Fortunately, over time his technique began to improve and the series started to take shape. Edward Wasserman sat for him again with En Cas, this time wearing a fancy, brocade jacket and looping an arm around his restless dog (fig. 5.4).[13] A number of much more famous people also accepted Ewing's invitation, including Paul Robeson, whom Ewing had met through Muriel Draper and Carl Van Vechten, who came to the apartment on July 19. Robeson, by then already well-known and used to having his photograph taken, struck a variety of dramatic poses in front of a Russian travel poster bearing the slogan "See USSR" (fig. 5.5),

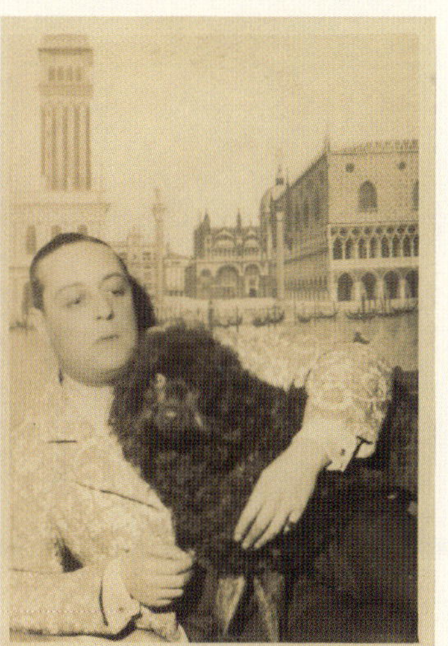

5.4 Max Ewing, *Eddie Wasserman and "En-Cas,"* from *The Carnival of Venice*.

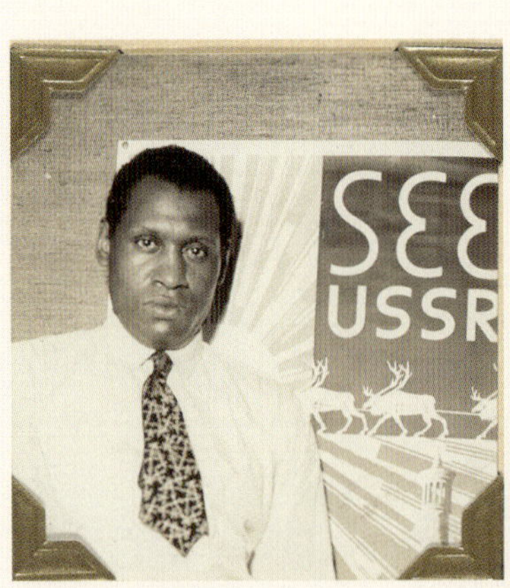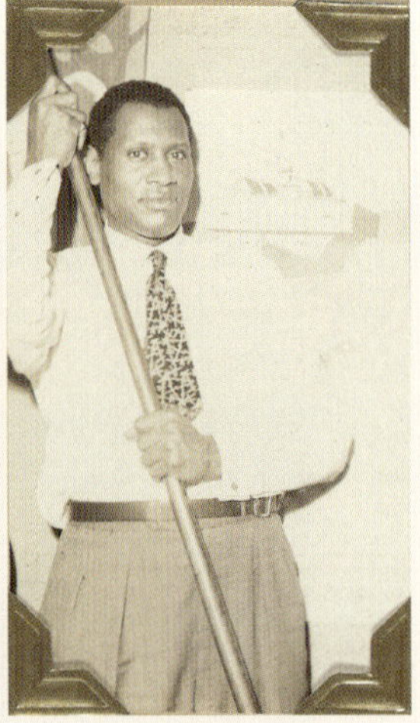

5.5 Max Ewing, *Two Portraits of Paul Robeson*, from Max Ewing's *Snapshots* 1932.

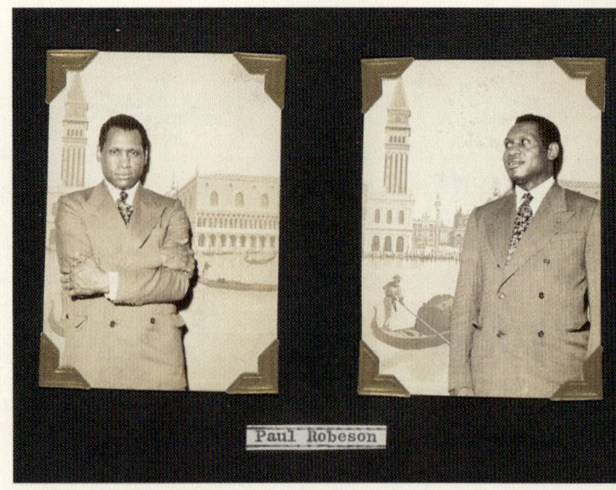

5.6 Max Ewing, *Portraits of Paul Robeson*, from *Les Amants de Venise*, 1932.

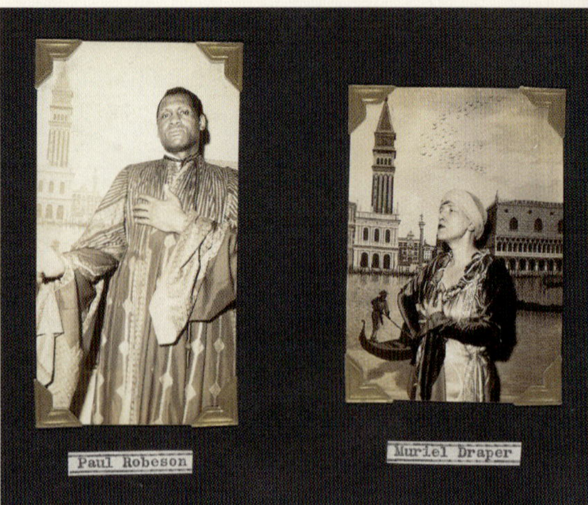

5.8 Max Ewing, *Paul Robeson and Muriel Draper*, from *Les Amants de Venise*, 1932.

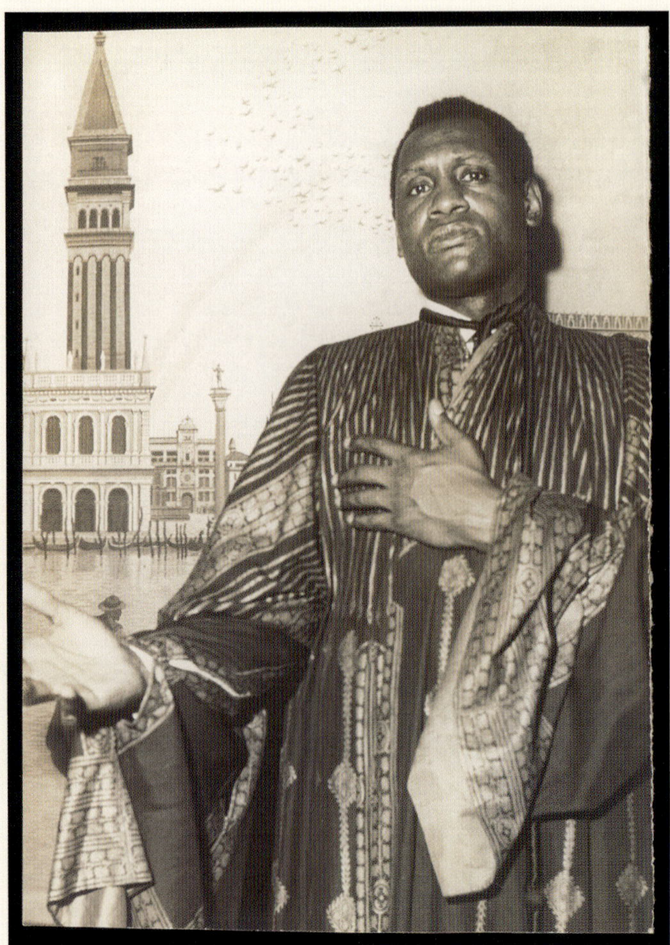

5.7 Max Ewing, *Paul Robeson as Othello*, from *The Carnival of Venice*.

perhaps a preview of his first visit to Russia in December 1934. Robeson also posed in a dapper suit and tie as a visitor to "Venice" (fig. 5.6). Ewing's favorite photo was one in which Robeson appeared as Othello (fig. 5.7), a role he had famously performed in London.[14] Experimenting with his sitter's gestures, expressions, and distance from the camera, Ewing evidently achieved good results, capturing Robeson's characteristic expression and stance as he reprised his theatrical role for the portrait.

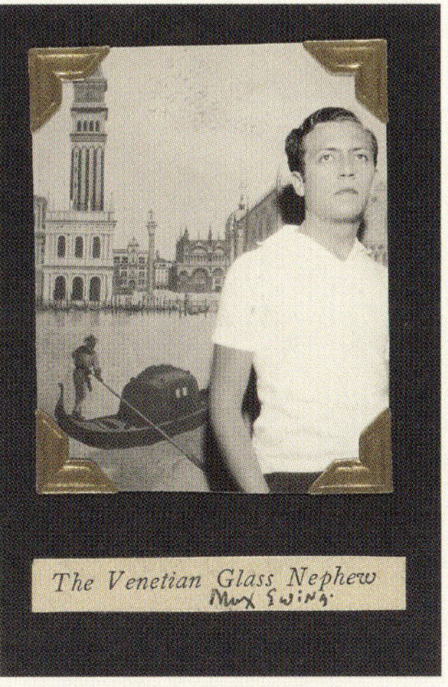

5.9 Max Ewing, *Self Portrait ("The Venetian Glass Nephew")*, from *Les Amants de Venise*.

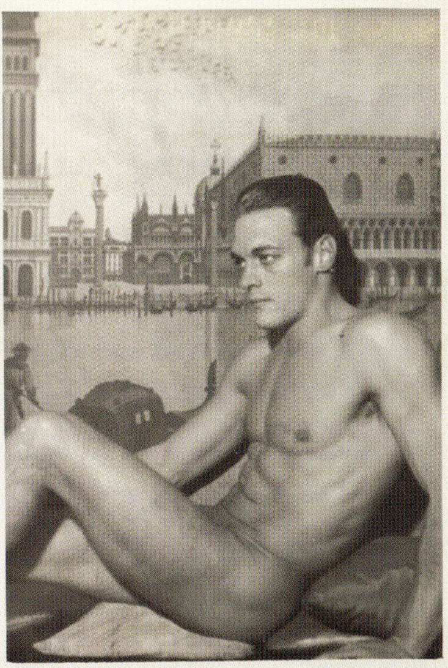

5.10 Max Ewing, *Fred Ritter Nude*, from *The Carnival of Venice*.

Ewing had photographed Muriel Draper "in Venice" earlier that month, wearing what he described to his mother as "her elaborate old trappings, which still look well in photographs, but are a bit too worn to actually wear places."[15] When he created a series of four small albums of his *Carnival* snapshots (collectively titled *Les Amants de Venise*), he paired the Robeson Othello with a portrait of Muriel from early July (fig. 5.8), placing the Robeson-Draper images at the beginning of a series. Ewing led off another of the small albums with a self-portrait captioned "The Venetian Glass Nephew" (fig. 5.9), using the nickname Van Vechten had bestowed on him in July when he acknowledged receipt of another batch of photos.[16] Although we don't know exactly which images Ewing sent, these gifts to Van Vechten could well have included more nude photographs of Fred Ritter (fig. 5.10; and see fig. 0.2), or portraits of his handsome actor friend Dick Clemmer, wearing Ewing's jaunty sailor shirt (fig. 5.11),

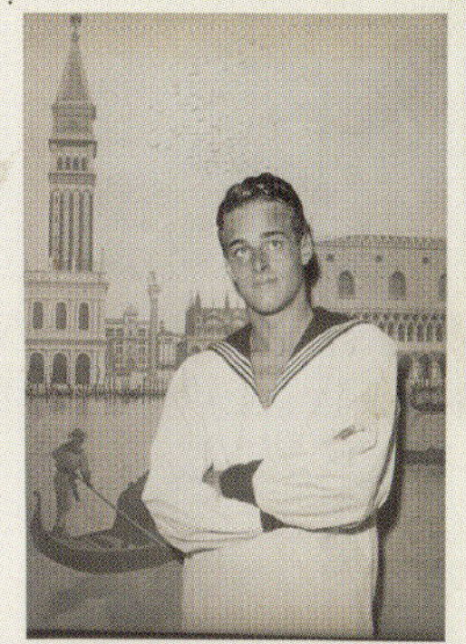

5.11 Max Ewing, *Richard Clemmer*, from *The Carnival of Venice*.

or a bare-chested Lloyd Wescott (George Lynes's roommate at the time), who donned a pair of shiny athletic shorts and pretended to play basketball on the Grand Canal (fig. 5.12). Ewing knew that any of these photos would have delighted and (he hoped) impressed his friend. So, too, would a series of new photos of Paul Meeres, who (to Ewing's giddy surprise) accepted his invitation to visit on July 15, striking a number of poses, both clothed and unclothed; the nudes were cropped for inclusion in the surviving *Carnival* series (fig. 5.13), but the original, full-length portraits were shared with Van Vechten,

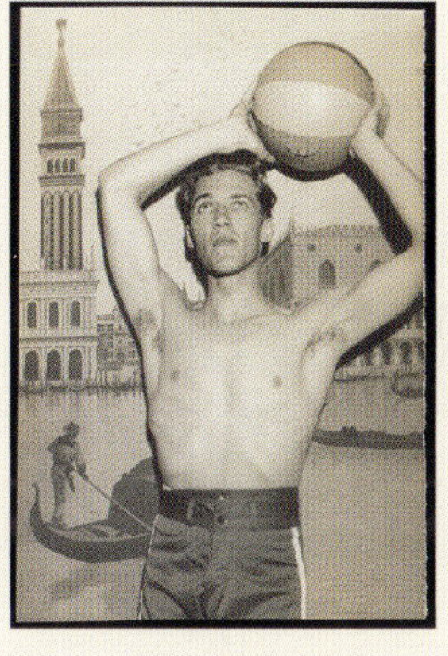

5.12 Max Ewing, *Lloyd Wescott Playing Basketball on the Grand Canal*, from *The Carnival of Venice*.

who was one of Meeres's biggest fans, and no doubt with others as well. In any case, Ewing's uncropped photos of Ritter and Meeres reappear in Van Vechten's own scrapbooks.

Ewing's efforts were viewed with a critical eye by George Lynes and Carl Van Vechten, both of whom had photographed Meeres a number of times over the years, but Ewing simply plowed ahead. "I am sending you … some selections from my *Carnival of Venice*," Ewing wrote to Lynes on July 25:

with which I am preoccupied just at present. You may or may not remember the Venetian window blind in my bedroom. Anyway, there it is, serving as a background for a lengthy caravan of Venetians who

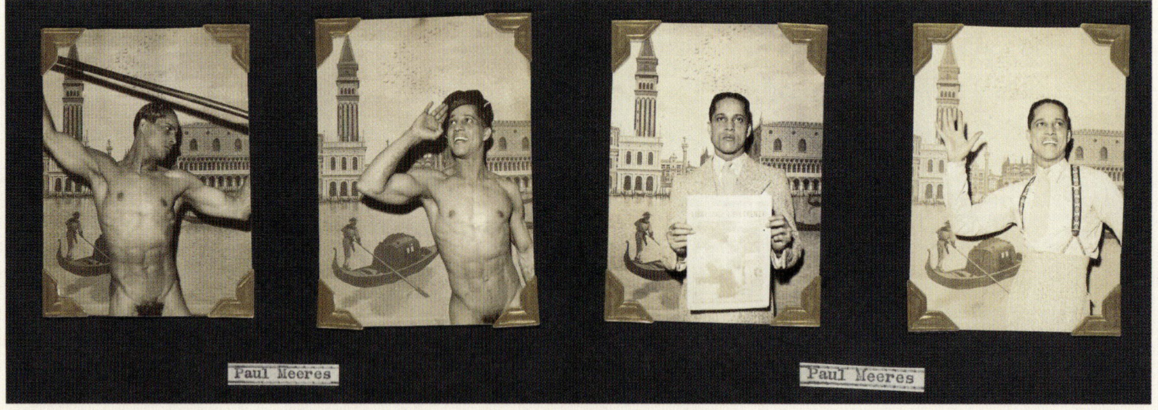

5.13 Max Ewing, *Paul Meeres, Nude and Wearing a Suit*, from *Les Amants de Venise*.

are passing in and out long enough to be photographed, all on the same location on the Grand Canal. ... You must join the list when you return, and you had better be deciding in advance what to be wearing and doing. I am trying to vary the list as much as possible and the other night I photographed freaks! Paul Robeson dressed as Othello for one of the Venetian scenes, and Paul Meeres did all sorts of things. It is quite a delightful Carnival of Venice. And all the scenes enlarge beautifully. Lloyd is not entirely recognizable playing basketball in the Canal, but I am an erratic photographer and do not pretend to have mastered all the mysteries. The picture of me is called A Frog He Would A-Wooing Go. ("So off he went in his opera hat.") What have you to say?[17]

Ewing wore his top hat and tails in his self-portrait (see fig. 2.8), looking away from the camera and — in one image — holding a cigarette like a debonair man of the world.

He did indeed manage to vary his list of sitters "as much as possible," as he told George Lynes. He convinced the twenty-five-year-old Lincoln Kirstein (fig. 5.14) to pose for him "in Venice" that summer: tan and fit from his workouts in the gym, Kirstein looks warily at the camera and holds a long pole that Ewing had given him to look like a gondolier's oar. Kirstein was part of the queer Harvard elite and already a rising star in the New York art world. He was also Ewing's principal competition for Muriel Draper's attention and affection, and unlike Ewing, had an ongoing sexual relationship with her.[18] Here he appears in his own street clothes and stares directly at the camera, confident in his talent and status, while also perhaps somewhat quizzical about his role in Ewing's project.

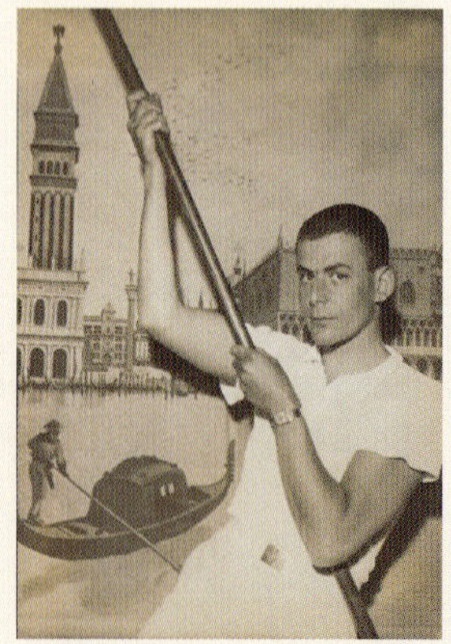

5.14 Max Ewing, *Lincoln Kirstein*, from *The Carnival of Venice*.

At the other end of the spectrum covered by Ewing's series were the "freaks" that he referred to in his letter to Lynes. In a group of images that he proudly presented to Van Vechten, he included the diminutive Joe Gould, an alcoholic writer who had become a fixture on the streets of Greenwich Village, juxtaposed with the figure of Herbert Buch, a muscular athlete who was evidently at least a foot taller (fig. 5.15). Often homeless and hungry, Gould had a talent for insinuating himself into parties, receptions, and gallery openings where free food and drink were served. He could be a nuisance, especially when he harassed the women guests, but he was widely regarded as a local curiosity. Here, he appears as a harmless pixie, sporting a necktie over his bare chest and smoking

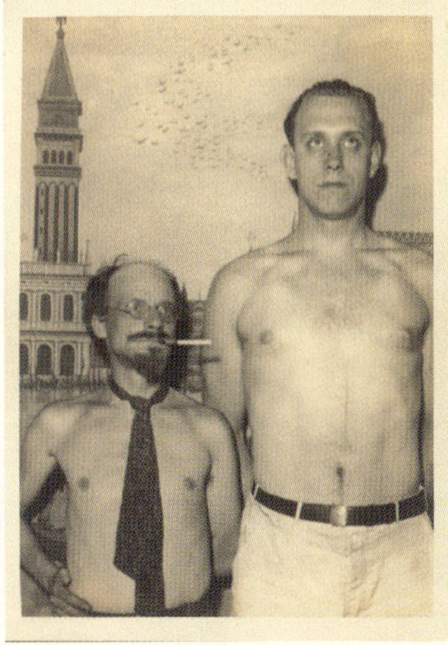

5.15 Max Ewing, *Herbert Buch and Joe Gould*, from *Les Amants de Venise*.

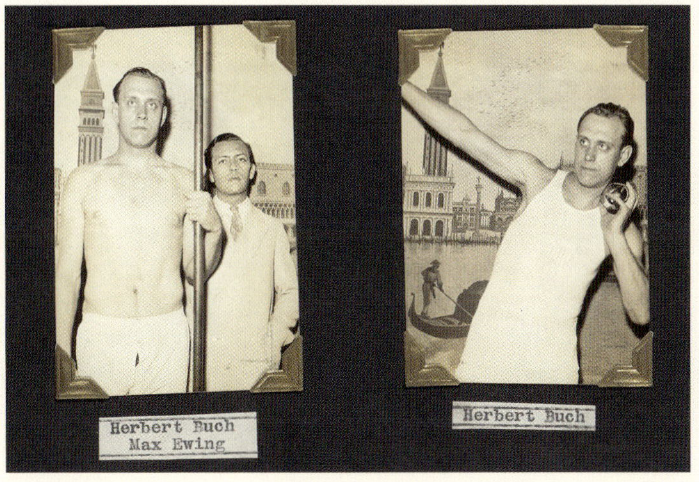

5.16 Max Ewing, *Self Portrait with Herbert Buch*, and *Herbert Buch*, from *Les Amants de Venise*.

a cigarette in the long black holder he used with the butts he scrounged. In another image, Buch — though neither a bodybuilder nor an entertainer of the type that Ewing preferred, nor even a friend — was persuaded to pose shirtless. Still another image portrays Ewing himself, sporting a white, summer suit and a blank expression, posed with the strapping Buch, who wears only partially unbuttoned boxers. A companion photo shows Buch in a sleeveless undershirt pretending to throw a shotput (fig. 5.16).

These portraits of Gould and Buch appear lighthearted, risqué, and campy, qualities that we know to be entirely characteristic of the social and artistic persona that Ewing sought to establish among his friends. As always, he chose to focus on amusing appearances and avoid any sort of deep psychological investigation into the inner lives of his sitters. Ewing's photos of Joe Gould are a case in point. He tells us nothing of the character of the sitter that is so evident in the portrait painted by Alice Neel the following year (1933), where Gould appears as a diabolical, priapic figure, perched on a pedestal with his legs spread apart to reveal three oversized penises (fig. 5.17).[19] According to Neel, Gould loved the image, which was too graphic and shocking to be exhibited publicly, but Ewing was only interested in his clownish appearance and diminutive size. More important, he knew well that his eccentric photos would appeal to Van Vechten's playful sense of humor and collector's zeal for curiosities. He sent the Gould / Buch photos along to Van Vechten on July 22 with a note of explanation: "I enclose two noteworthy additions to my Carnival of Venice," he quipped, "note the influence of Freaks" — referring to the recently released film of that name (1932), which satirized the lives of sideshow performers.[20] Ewing owned a lobby poster for the film, which he sometimes displayed in his apartment, and he knew that Van Vechten would enjoy the reference.

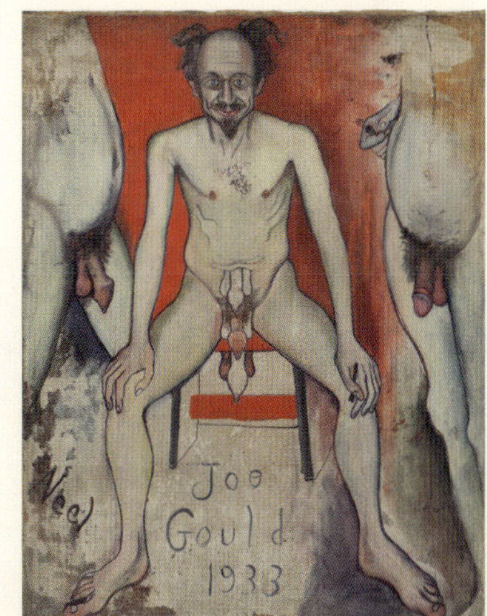

5.17 Alice Neel, *Joe Gould*, 1933, oil on canvas, 39 × 31⅛ in. (91.1 × 79.1 cm). The Estate of Alice Neel.

"A LENGTHY CARAVAN OF VENETIANS"

Ewing clearly didn't intend or imagine a coherent series, but rather a haphazard collection of portraits that evolved according to his whims and the availability of sitters. The collection of images that emerged is a lively gathering of distinctive

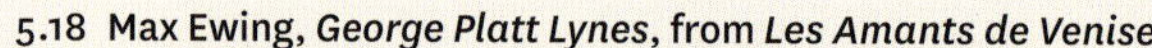

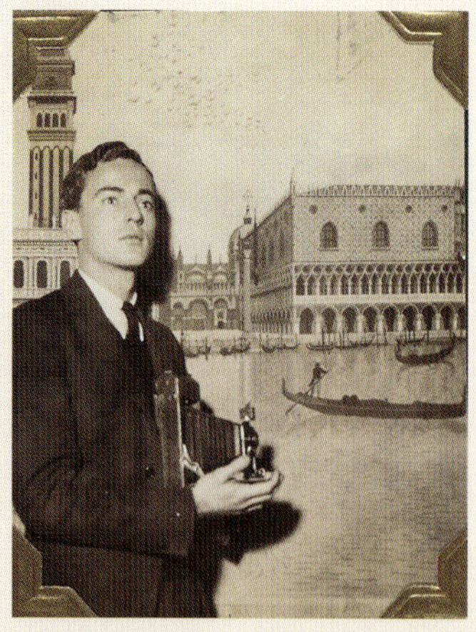

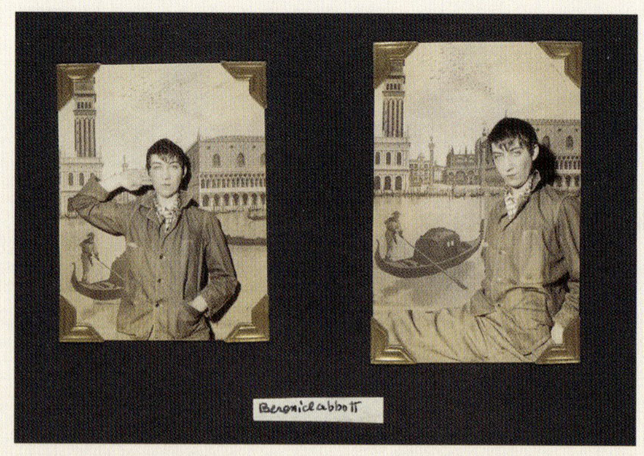

5.19 Max Ewing, *Two Portraits of Berenice Abbott*, from *Les Amants de Venise*.

faces and personalities: for Ewing, it was one thing to record the names of people who attended his parties or visited the same Harlem nightclubs as he did, but it was quite another to meet these people face-to-face and capture their expressions, costumes, and characteristic poses. He was especially proud of knowing the younger members of the bohemian circle, many of whom went on to become the prime movers in twentieth-century arts and culture, bringing modern art, dance, and literature to enthusiastic US audiences. In Ewing's photographs, which retain the immediacy of the Kodak snapshots they are, these people come alive through their body language and the small details of their portraits: Lincoln Kirstein's Cartier watch and buzz-cut hair, George Platt Lynes's uplifted chin and the graceful hand that cradles his camera (fig. 5.18), and Berenice Abbott's chic, gamine haircut — a look adopted during her Paris years — and confidence as she jauntily salutes the photographer (fig. 5.19).[21]

Some of the people Ewing photographed were long-standing friends from his earliest days in New York, like his beloved Esther Murphy (fig. 5.20), the now-famous singer Taylor Gordon (fig. 5.21), the successful *Vogue* model Marion Morehouse (paired with Isamu Noguchi, who wears a flat, little women's hat and strikes a camp pose with his hand on his hip) (fig. 5.22), and Aline MacMahon (fig. 5.23), looking somewhat less imposing here than she did in Cecil Beaton's glamorous portrait (see fig. 1.8). He also photographed Alice DeLamar, the lesbian heiress and bon vivant who had recently taken him and a group of friends to Palm Beach and the Bahamas (fig. 5.24). His friend and confidante Dorothy Sheldon appeared in at least two portraits, including one "playing tennis on the Grand Canal" (fig. 5.25): Dorothy was a dancer formerly married to Lewis Galantière and now the wife of sculptor Roy Sheldon, with whom Ewing had spent many happy months in Paris. As he wrote to his mother, "I suggest that you start a gallery of your own which will include most of my friends, and if you forget what they look like you can look them up in Venice for identification. The serious picture of Dorothy is quite good — the tennis scene a scream!"[22]

Other sitters included Mamie White (fig. 5.26), former companion of the glamorous A'lelia Walker whose Harlem homes Ewing had visited on a number of occasions. Langston Hughes, Natalie Hammond, the Stettheimer sisters, and, of course, Carl Van Vechten all managed to avoid Ewing's camera. He had better luck with the glamorous opera diva Marguerite Namara (fig. 5.27) — a long-standing presence in Ewing's

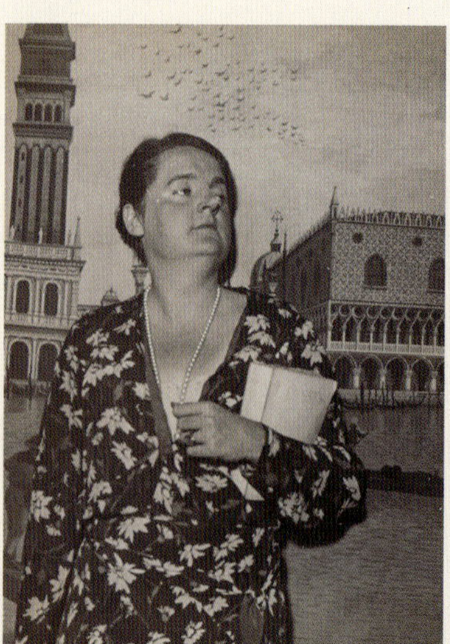

5.20 Max Ewing, *Esther Murphy*, from *The Carnival of Venice*.

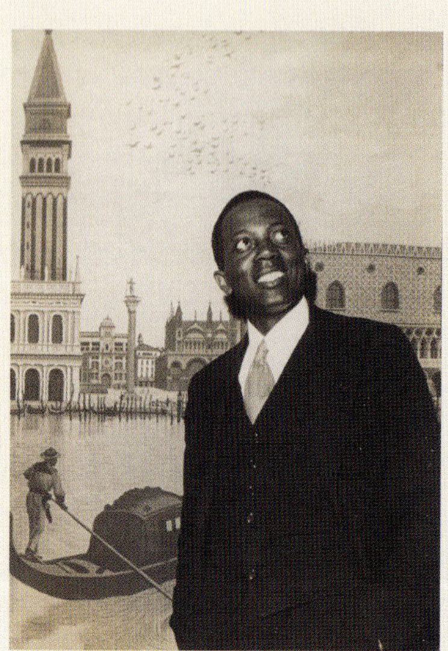

5.21 Max Ewing, *Taylor Gordon*, from *The Carnival of Venice*.

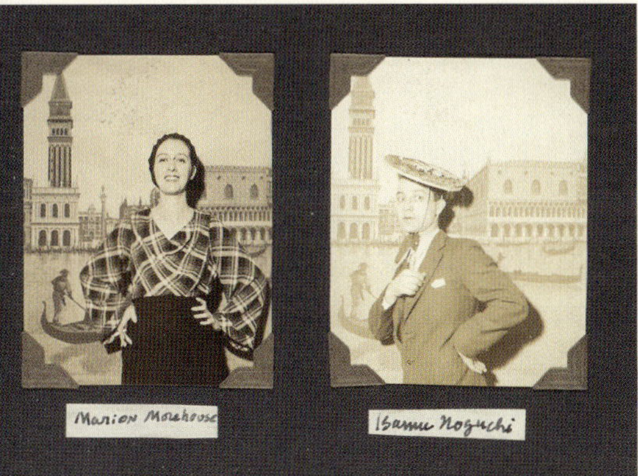

5.22 Max Ewing, *Marion Morehouse and Isamu Noguchi*, from *Les Amants de Venise*.

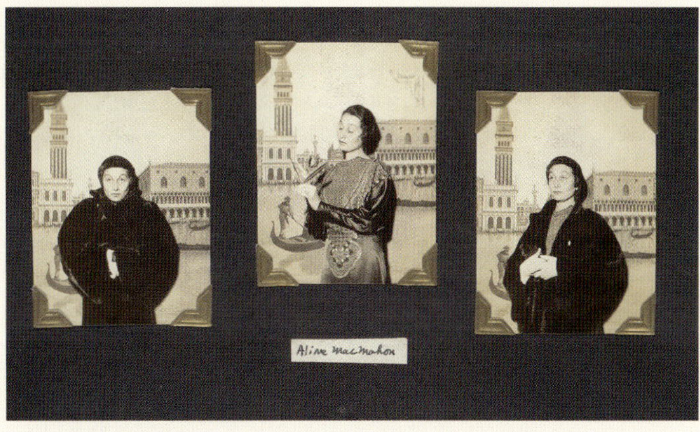

5.23 Max Ewing, *Three Portraits of Aline MacMahon*, from *Les Amants de Venise*.

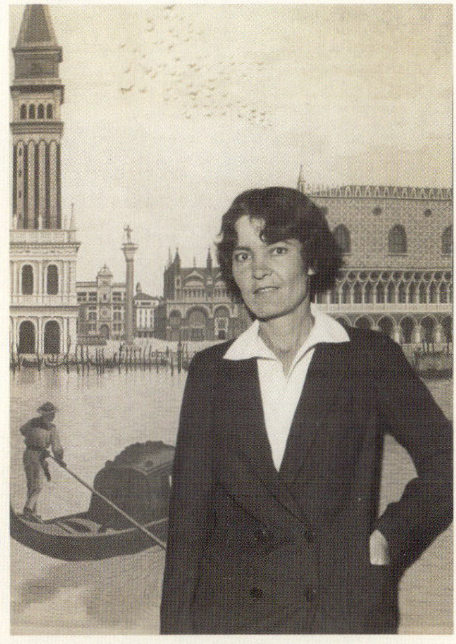

5.24 Max Ewing, *Alice DeLamar*, from *The Carnival of Venice*.

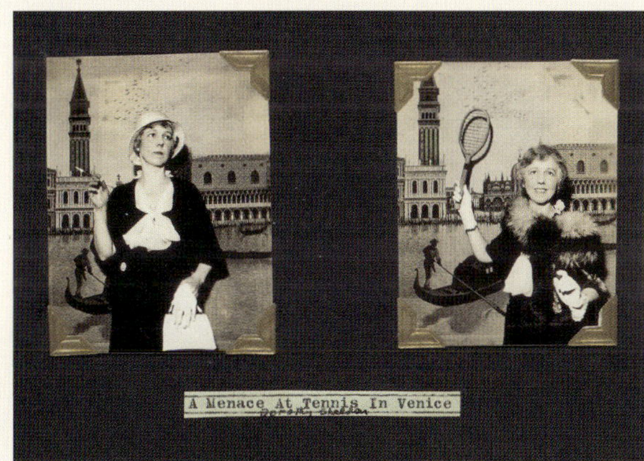

5.25 Max Ewing, *Two Portraits of Dorothy Sheldon*, from *Les Amants de Venise*.

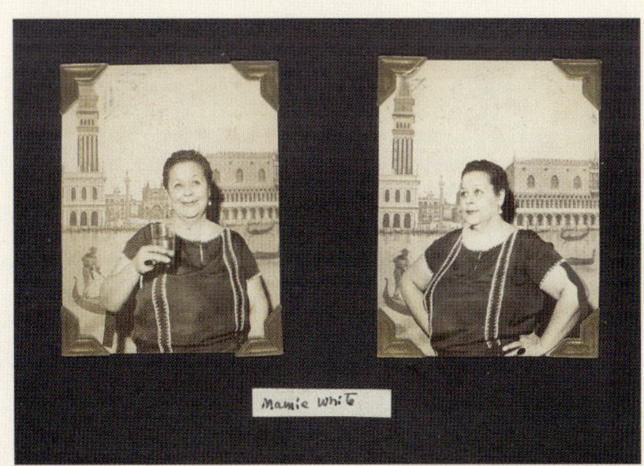

5.26 Max Ewing, *Two Portraits of Mamie White*, from *Les Amants de Venise*.

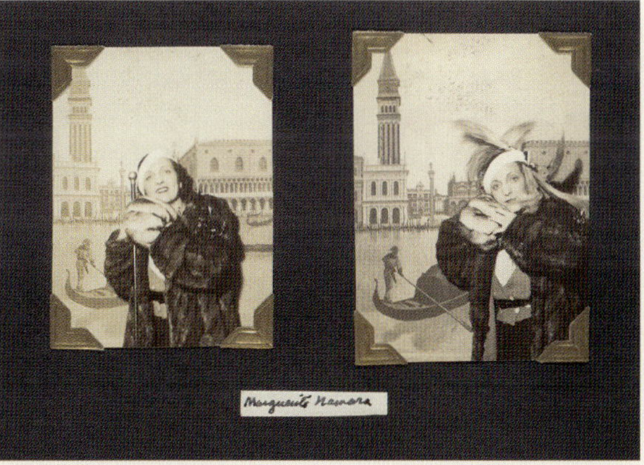

5.27 Max Ewing, *Two Portraits of Marguerite Namara*, from *Les Amants de Venise*.

scrapbooks and later in his *Gallery,* who obviously knew how to strike a pose —
as well as the young movie star Eva Casanova and her husband Lou Tellegen
(the former husband of Geraldine Farrar, now on his fourth marriage), who
appeared in elegant evening dress.[23] For Ewing, an ardent fan, these portraits of
famous actors and opera royalty were special treasures that never ceased to
give him pleasure, like the photos that covered the walls of his *Gallery.* He wrote
to his mother excitedly about almost every one of them.

The sheer number and variety of images suggests that by the end of 1932
Ewing had hit upon a winning combination of consistency and serendipity when
photographing his subjects, placing his Kodak camera in front of a scene that
didn't vary at all except for the changing identities of his sitters and the props
they chose. Lighting, focus, and camera angle hardly changed from one image to
the next, making it easier for Ewing to improve the quality
of his portraits while putting very little effort into
developing his skills. While he learned to enlarge his own
images and experimented with lighting equipment, he
remained unwilling to upgrade his equipment or setup. As
with his sculptures, he ultimately gave up on the *Carnival*
project, and photography, altogether. While he was thrilled
by the attention he gained through the exhibition and party
at the Julien Levy Gallery and proud of the enthusiastic
responses of some of his friends (he even managed to
publish four of his photos in *Town and Country* in February
1933), he lacked the discipline to take his work to the next
level. As he wrote to his cousin Doris in August 1932:

> I'm doing a large series called The Carnival of
> Venice. They enlarge beautifully and look very
> professional. You must come over for a sitting in
> the Grand Canal. It takes no time at all for
> me to snap you. I have been so successful with
> my pictures that I now have some tempting offers
> to do them professionally. The trouble is that
> with me when a thing ceases to be a caprice I lose
> interest in it and am not so good at it.[24]

Despite Ewing's lack of professional commitment,
the result of his effort is an extraordinary collection of
nearly a hundred portraits created over period of ten
months between April 1932 and January 1933. The
photographs were printed in various sizes and preserved in
Ewing's photo albums, all now at Yale: these include a large
presentation volume of forty-eight portraits entitled *The
Carnival of Venice,* as well as the four small albums of mounted snapshots titled
Les Amants de Venise and *The International Festival of Venice.* These small
albums contain approximately thirty portraits, mounted two per page. A fourth
small album contains only ten images, including "portraits" of puppets
representing Gary Cooper and Marlene Dietrich.[25] As noted earlier, a handful of
full-length nudes from the same series survives in Carl Van Vechten's archive at

THE CARNIVAL OF VENICE

PHOTOGRAPHS By MAX EWING

Long after I had learned about Max Ewing's talents and had become familiar with, but not at all tired of his talents, I discovered something totally unexpected and very disarming about him: he always tells the truth. The more highly-colored, the more removed from the ordinary his accounts of things may be, the more certain they are to be literally true, to the smallest detail. He chooses that smallest detail rather well.

In his novel, *Going Somewhere,* he follows another method, which is probably the contemporary version of the baroque. Against such a rich background as this, you say, surely nothing quite so unfancy as the conversations of these New Yorkers could take place. I advise you to take up the argument with yourself before you take it up with the author.

The photographs in his Carnival of Venice also appear before a high background. They were all taken in his New York studio-apartment. Into this apartment entered, as you will see from the catalog, some representatives of the Faubourg Saint-Germain, of Piccadilly, of Wall Street, of Broadway, of Park Avenue, of Harlem, of Hollywood, and of Coney Island. The photographer was not serious about his business. The subjects came because he invited them and told them they could be whatever they liked in Venice. I doubt whether Mr. Ewing was trying to penetrate to the subconscious desires of his subjects. I think that he wanted to make a series of entertaining and admirable photographs. In that endeavor, as in all his others, he has succeeded.

GILBERT SELDES

1. Berenice Abbott	39. Joella Levy
2. Duke de Arcos	40. George Platt Lynes
3. Joseph Brewer	41. Robert Locher
4. Madeleine Boyd	42. Aline MacMahon
5. Frank Bishop	43. Marion Morehouse
6. Claire Bishop-Huchet	44. Paul Meeres
7. Hugh Brooke	45. Tom Mabry (Death in Venice)
8. Ruth Baldwin	46. John McAndrew (as Tarzan)
9. John Becker (as Proust)	47. Lois Moran
10. Herbert Buch and Joe Gould	48. Marguerite Namara
11. Dorothy Crawford	49. Isamu Noguchi
12. Miguel Covarrubias	50. Mae Noble
13. E. E. Cummings	51. Paul Osborn
14. Princess Nina Chavchavadze	52. Florence Osborn
15. Richard Clemmer	53. Jack Pollock
16. Marion Carstairs	54. Joe Paulin
17. Eve Casanova	55. Allen Porter
18. Lucia Davidova	56. Rita Romilly
19. Irma Duncan	57. Alice Robinson
20. Muriel Draper	58. Paul Robeson (as Othello)
21. Alice De La Mar	59. Fred Ritter
22. Mrs. George Dangerfield	60. William Ritter
23. Agnes de Mille	61. Boonie Goossens Reagan
24. George Emanuel	62. Gilbert Seldes
25. Paul Flato and Spivy	63. Amanda Seldes (as Madame Butterfly)
26. Lewis Galantiere	64. Dorothy Sheldon
27. Taylor Gordon	65. Tonio Selwart
28. Barrington Hall	66. Marion Tiffany Saportas
29. Janet Harbeck (as Dietrich)	67. Spivy
30. Louise Hellstrom	68. Esther Strachey
31. Samuel Hoffenstein	69. Mrs. Frederic Stettenheim
32. Edith Hoffenstein	70. Lou Tellegen
33. Mabs Jenkins	71. Comtesse de Villeneuve
34. Lincoln Kirstein	72. James Whitall
35. Kate Drain Lawson	73. Edward Wassermann and En Cas
36. R. Ellsworth Larsson	74. Lloyd Wescott
37. Peggy Le Boutillier	75. Mamie White
38. Julien Levy	76. Sister Martha Winslow

JULIEN LEVY GALLERY
602 MADISON AVENUE, NEW YORK
One Day Only—JANUARY 26th

5.28 Printed handlist for *The
Carnival of Venice* exhibition,
Julien Levy Gallery, New York,
January 26, 1933. Max Ewing
Papers.

Yale, interleaved in his scrapbooks of ephemera illustrating the vagaries of queer history in the United States and Europe from the 1910s until his death in 1964.[26]

Ewing's one-day exhibition at the Julien Levy Gallery on Madison Avenue took place on January 26, 1933. The names of his sitters are noted in a printed handlist (fig. 5.28) with a brief introduction by the prominent critic Gilbert Seldes, the former editor of the *Dial* and a close friend of Muriel Draper's. The event was thrilling for Ewing and his friends, and presented a fine excuse for a grand celebration at the gallery. A raucous "preview party" was held on the night of January 25, and many of the sitters arrived in the costumes they had worn for their portraits or — as many observed — wore very little, despite the cold of the January night. As the critic Henry McBride put it in his review in the *New York Sun*, Ewing was "very subtle in choosing sitters and still more subtle in encouraging them to psychoanalyze themselves while posing … Some of the gentlemen sitters, for instance, were but lightly attired. Looking at these prints, Miss [Lorna] Lindsay [*sic*] … remarked that the exhibition was giving her renewed confidence in the innate modesty of her own sex, for it was only the gentlemen who felt the urge to strip for the camera."[27]

Gilbert Seldes, who appears in the series with his wife Amanda (fig. 5.29), saw the exhibition rather differently. In his short introduction, printed on the checklist above the names of the sitters, he characterizes Ewing's endeavor as a lighthearted "lark" that showcased Ewing's wide and varied social circle. Generously describing Ewing's recently published novel *Going Somewhere* as "the contemporary version of the baroque," Seldes goes on to link Ewing's mannered writing to his photography project, explaining that the photos were all taken in Ewing's "New York studio-apartment" simply to entertain the artist and his friends. "Into this apartment," he continued:

> entered … some representatives of the Faubourg Sainte-Germain, of Piccadilly, of Wall Street, of Broadway, and of Coney Island. The photographer was not serious about his business. The subjects came because he invited them and told them they could be whatever they liked in Venice. I doubt Mr. Ewing was trying to penetrate the subconscious desires of his subjects. I think that he wanted to make a series of entertaining and admirable photographs. In that endeavor, as in all his others, he has succeeded.[28]

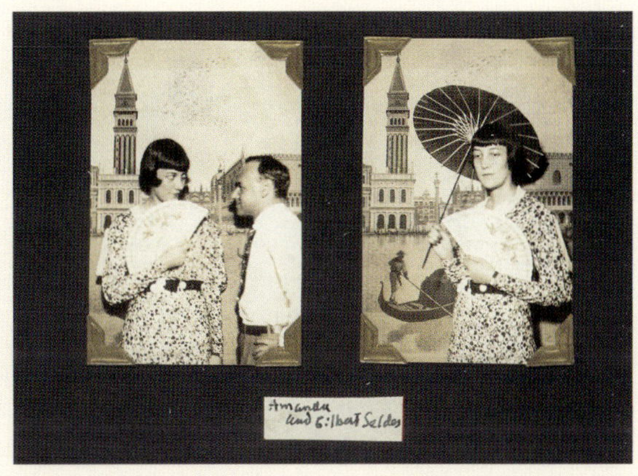

5.29 Max Ewing, *Amanda and Gilbert Seldes*, from *Les Amants de Venise*.

Indeed, Seldes's reading was right on the mark: Ewing went to some effort to reassure his friends of his lighthearted intentions, hoping to make it clear that his photos offered no threat to the serious artistic work they were doing.

As he wrote to Van Vechten a few weeks before the Levy Gallery opening, "You may know already that Julien Levy is going to show my Carnival of Venice briefly late this month between two more reputable shows." He went on:

> on the night of the 25th there is to be a party to which the people photographed are to be invited to come as they were photographed — in the same costumes. As some of them have worn

no costumes at all, it will be hard on them if the night is cold. Others
are expected in fur coats and dressing gowns. It promises to be
alarmingly miscellaneous as to personnel as well. It won't be
complete without you and Fania ... My pictures lay no claim to being
portraits. They are taken from the point of view of being
appropriately lunatic additions to my closet, it now being difficult to
get new additions for it without taking them myself! Perhaps the
most lunatic of all is a recent one of Namara on the canal decked out
in a whole jungle of paradise feathers.[29]

The fact that Ewing's photographs were also exhibited at a *thé dansant* at
the Waldorf Astoria in February 1933, hosted by a committee of prominent
women including Muriel Draper, Mary Garden, Marion Tiffany Saportas, "Princess
Paul Chavchavadze," Kay Francis, and Madame Alma Clayburgh, bears out the
impression that he had "arrived," not only in the art world, but at the pinnacle of
New York society. As the invitation stated, "Mr. Max Ewing, author of 'Going
Somewhere' will be present during the tea hour at an exhibit of his amusing
photographs of International Celebrities, called 'The Carnival of Venice,' with a
great many celebrities also present."[30] Guests were entertained by both "Nat
Brandywynne and his Orchestra" and "Harold Stern and his Orchestra" at a ticket
price of $1.50, a hefty sum. And there were human costs for the event as well,
although Ewing preferred to glide over these without comment when he boasted
about the gala to his mother: "They are going to show all the pictures I showed
at the Levy Gallery except the Negroes," he stated matter-of-factly, "who do not
seem to rank showing at the Waldorf-Astoria!"[31]

GLIMPSES OF THE ART WORLD

Throughout the months that Ewing worked on his photo project, George Lynes
kept a close watch on his progress, helping him with printing (when the drugstore
refused), enlarging, and lighting; more important, in contrast to Van Vechten,
Lynes seemed to take him seriously as an artist.[32] While Ewing wasn't very happy
to have Lynes critique his work, reacting defensively when Lynes
told him that the *Carnival of Venice* samples he sent along
"weren't good enough," he appreciated his friendship, and the
two men maintained an intimate and good-natured relationship,
particularly when it came to queer experiences and adventures
in Harlem and elsewhere, sharing photographs of Sansone, the
Ritter brothers, and themselves. In addition to taking numerous
portraits of Ewing, Lynes sat for his own portrait and persuaded
Ewing to exchange a collection of twenty-six *Carnival of Venice*
images for his own work.[33] Though Lynes was, by this point,
moving in a very different professional direction from Ewing, seeking to make a
name for himself in both fashion and homoerotic photography, the two men
collaborated on projects throughout 1931 and '32, including a portrait of Lynes in
front of one of Ewing's Venice travel posters (fig. 5.30), which is preserved in
Lynes's own scrapbooks at Yale as well as in Ewing's collection.[34]

Ewing's relationship with the photographer Berenice Abbott was far less
intimate, but, as we saw in chapter 3, they were briefly very close during the
period in 1929 when Abbott, newly arrived from Paris, fell head over heels in love

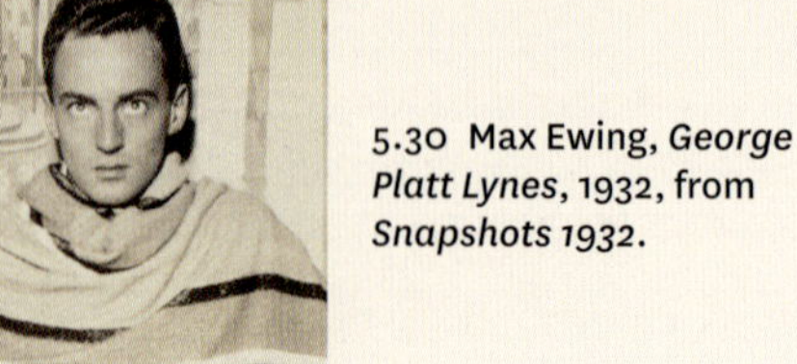

5.30 Max Ewing, *George
Platt Lynes*, 1932, from
Snapshots 1932.

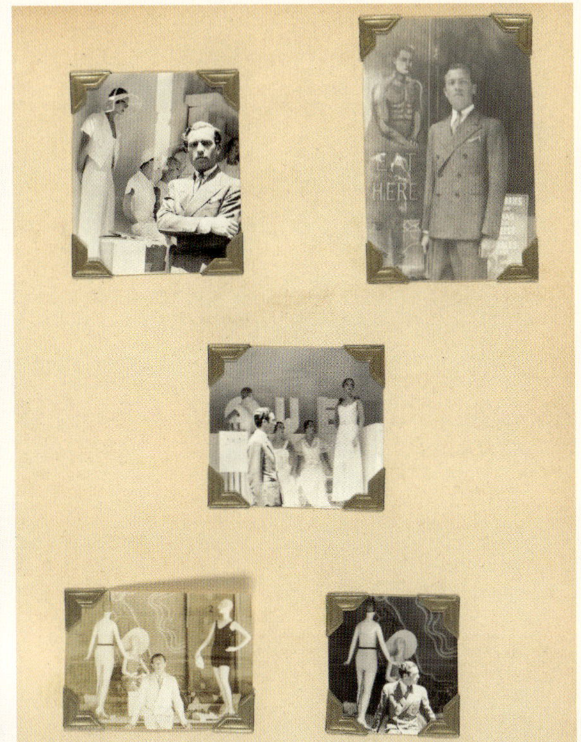

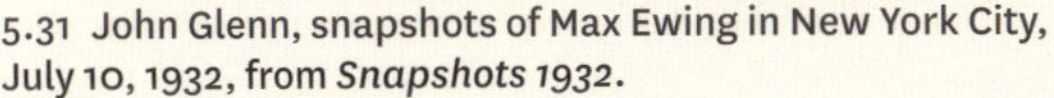

5.31 John Glenn, snapshots of Max Ewing in New York City, July 10, 1932, from *Snapshots 1932*.

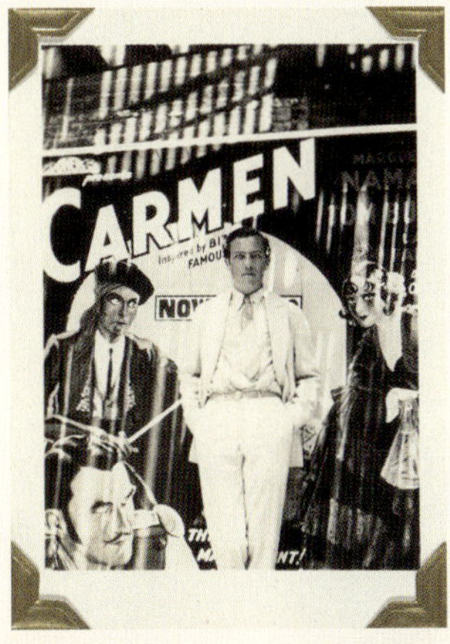

5.32 John Glenn, Max Ewing with poster for *Carmen*, July 10, 1932, from *Snapshots 1932*.

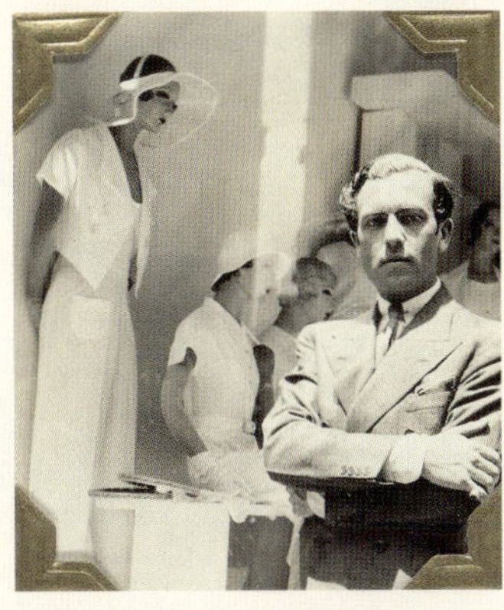

5.33 John Glenn, snapshot of Max Ewing with mannequins in a shop window, July 10, 1932, from *Snapshots 1932* (detail of 5.31).

with the erratic and manipulative Princess Eugénie Murat, whose extraordinary portrait Abbott created in 1930. In July 1929, Ewing and Abbott even collaborated on a sort of "payback" project, a "speak-o-phone" recording entitled "Isn't it Awful: A Lament," with Abbott taking the part of Murat in a mock interview that parodied the hapless princess's snobbish tastes and cluelessness about life in New York.[35] A second recorded dialogue made the same day, in which Ewing's cousin Doris plays the role of Murat, is called "Etes-vous Polygame?" — a title that pokes fun at the queer princess's arch language as well as her tendency to misplace people and things. Ewing and Abbott were friends, and that relationship had some important consequences for his life and career.

We know that Abbott took Ewing's portrait for the jacket of his book *Going Somewhere* (see fig. 3.37) in April 1932, and that both he and Lynes were very much aware of Abbott's effort to preserve the work of Eugène Atget in concert with their friend, the gallerist and collector Julien Levy.[36] Moreover, both men knew Abbott's work at MoMA, where Lynes, Abbott, Robert Locher, and a number of other friends participated in the *Murals by American Painters and Photographers* exhibition in May 1932.[37] Like Walker Evans, another member of the extended Draper circle, Abbott photographed the city around her throughout this period, capturing the glamorous lights, romantic vistas, and transparent shop windows of a changing New York in an entirely new way.[38]

While Ewing never, to our knowledge, turned his camera on the urban landscape, focusing instead on making portraits of his many friends, there appears to be more than a hint of Atget's influence, via Abbott, in a series of self-portraits Ewing created with his friend John Glenn on July 10, 1932 (figs. 5.31–5.33). In these snapshots, Ewing poses on the street against backdrops of shop windows, mannequins, and movie posters, capturing quirky signage and unlikely

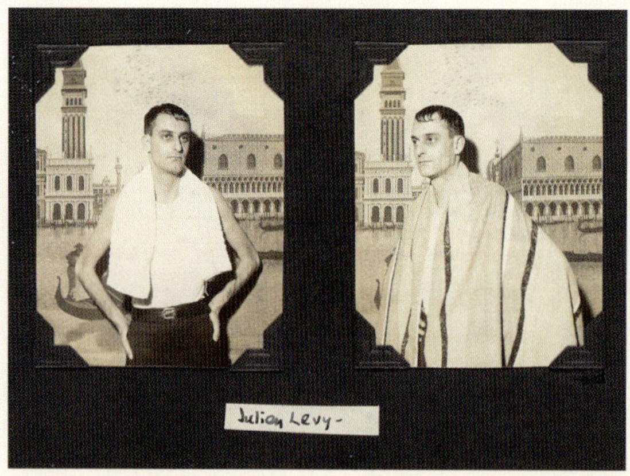

5.34 Max Ewing, *Julien Levy Swimming on the Grand Canal*, from *Les Amants de Venise*.

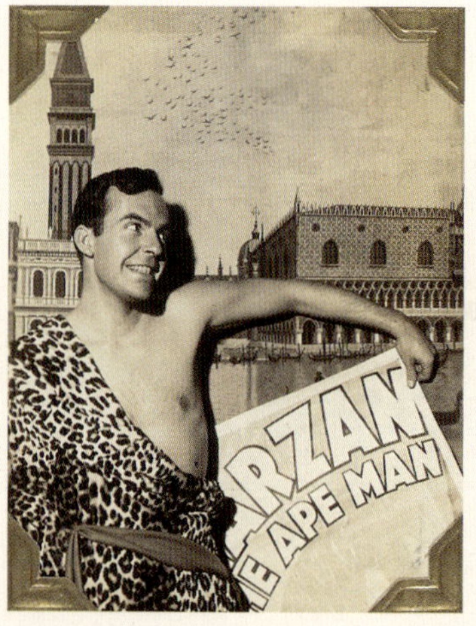

5.35 Max Ewing, *John McAndrew as Tarzan*, from *The Carnival of Venice*.

juxtapositions in closely cropped images. He was particularly proud of a photo in which he stood in front of an advertisement for Marguerite Namara's *Carmen*, writing to his mother to point out that he "looked very Spanish myself" and seemed to be "part of the poster."[39]

Not surprisingly, many portraits in Ewing's *Carnival of Venice* series represent artists and curators associated with the Julien Levy Gallery.[40] In Ewing's photo of the gallerist himself, Levy poses with a towel around his shoulders as if he had just emerged from a swim, though he still wears his dress trousers (fig. 5.34); his wife Joella, the daughter of artist Mina Loy, appears in a companion photo. A portrait of the young art historian John McAndrew, a Harvard classmate of Levy's who had recently been appointed as an assistant professor at Vassar and would go on to a distinguished career at both MoMA and Wellesley College, shows him wearing a leopard-print Tarzan costume and carrying a helpful cue card (fig. 5.35); in another image, McAndrew and Lynes, in brightly patterned tunics, look adoringly at the up-and-coming Hollywood actress Lois Moran, whom Lynes had brought to Ewing's apartment in November (fig. 5.36).[41]

McAndrew organized the *Surréalisme* show at the Levy Gallery, which included two of Ewing's *Muriel* sculptures, and he shared an apartment on the far east side of Manhattan with Lynes and Lloyd Wescott. He was Levy's first secretary and curator at the gallery.[42] McAndrew was thus part of two overlapping circles that proved to be enormously important to Ewing in these years: one, the crowd of young Harvard graduates, including Levy himself, as well as Lincoln Kirstein, Philip Johnson (1906–2005), Henry-Russell Hitchcock (1903–87), and Everett "Chick" Austin, who championed modern art and architecture; the other, the circle of queer young men, including many of the above but also Lynes, Wescott, Wheeler, and other men who socialized and worked together. While never an insider in the former group — he was, after all, a Midwesterner who had attended the University of Michigan without graduating, and thus not fully part of their elite circle — he was nonetheless an important participant in the latter, although here as well he was at something of a disadvantage because of his tendencies toward camp "effeminacy" and breathless enthusiasms, including his obsession with Muriel Draper. These overtly queer characteristics annoyed Kirstein in particular, who aspired to project a more "manly" persona, and like McAndrew, identified as bisexual.

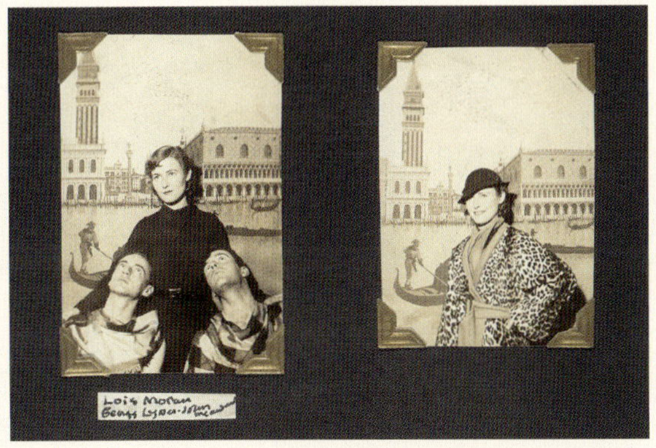

5.36 Max Ewing, *Two Portraits of Lois Moran*: L) *with John McAndrew and George Platt Lynes in Costume*, and R) *Posing in a Leopard Coat*, from *Les Amants de Venise*, 1932.

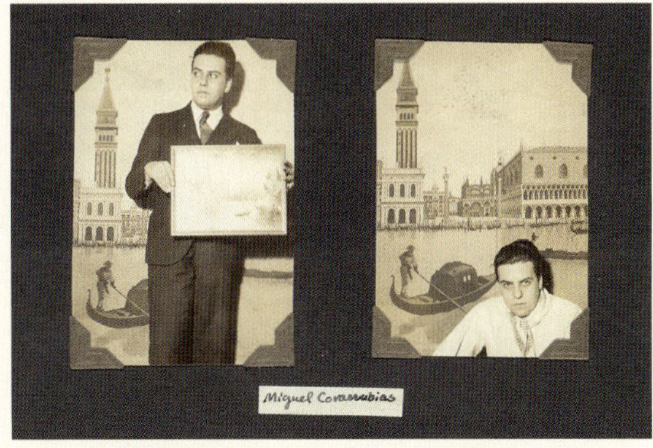

5.37 Max Ewing, *Two Portraits of Miguel Covarrubias*, from *Les Amants de Venise*.

Although most of the people depicted in Ewing's *Carnival*, including many of those who were famous in their own time, are no longer familiar to us in the twenty-first century — people such as Lois Moran, or Marguerite Namara, both beloved by Ewing and, more important, recognizable to his mother as stars — it is surprising to discover how many of the young, up-and-coming artists he depicted became household names during their own lives. These include Miguel Covarrubias (fig. 5.37) whom Ewing had known since 1923, thanks to Van Vechten. Ewing first met him at a party and described him as a "caricaturist" who had "done" Van Vechten (representing him as Black man in the well-known image with the caption "A prediction") and his wife, Fania. Ewing reported to his family that Covarrubias came to his apartment in 1923 and sketched his portrait in March 1927. A frequent participant in the raucous parties and Harlem gatherings that Van Vechten organized in this period, Covarrubias would contribute the illustrations to Taylor Gordon's autobiography *Born to Be* in 1929.[43] In Florine Stettheimer's *Cathedrals of Fifth Avenue*, discussed in the previous chapter, Covarrubias and his wife were depicted standing close to Ewing and Muriel Draper.

Ewing also knew and photographed a very young Isamu Noguchi (see fig. 5.22), whom he had perhaps met in Paris when Noguchi was working as an assistant to Constantin Brâncuși, a friend of Margaret Anderson. Ewing and Anderson had visited Brâncuși's studio (where he served them coffee and "did a Charleston or two") in June 1926.[44] The artist Winold Reiss depicted Noguchi in his portrait series representing figures of the "Harlem Renaissance," and it is likely that Ewing knew him as a member of that circle as well.[45]

Ewing first met the very young choreographer and dancer Agnes de Mille (1905–93) (fig. 5.38) at a party at Natalie Hammond's in May 1930. He later encountered de Mille at Hammond's parties a number of times over the years and finally snapped her portrait, looking regal and confident in a shiny satin gown, at the end of December 1932. Through the same connection, he met Tallulah Bankhead, a member of Hammond's lesbian theater set, which also included Alice DeLamar and her friend, the actress Eva Le Gallienne, as well as Hammond's partner Alice Laughlin, an artist and stage designer. Bankhead appeared in the *Gallery* in a number of views, and Ewing made a few attempts to arrange for the actress to sit for *The Carnival of Venice*, but to no avail.[46] He had also hoped to photograph the

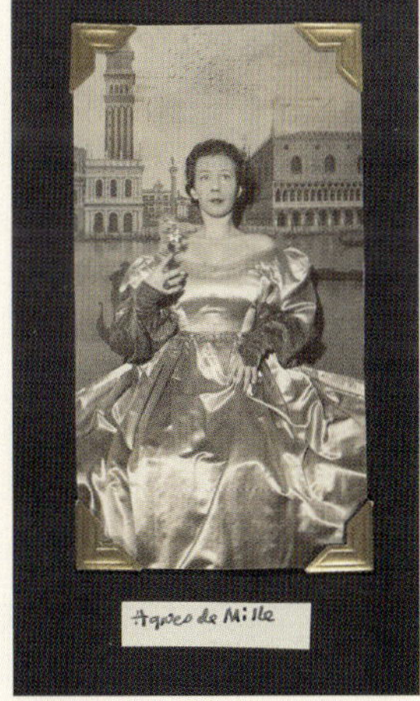

5.38 Max Ewing, *Agnes de Mille*, from *Les Amants de Venise*.

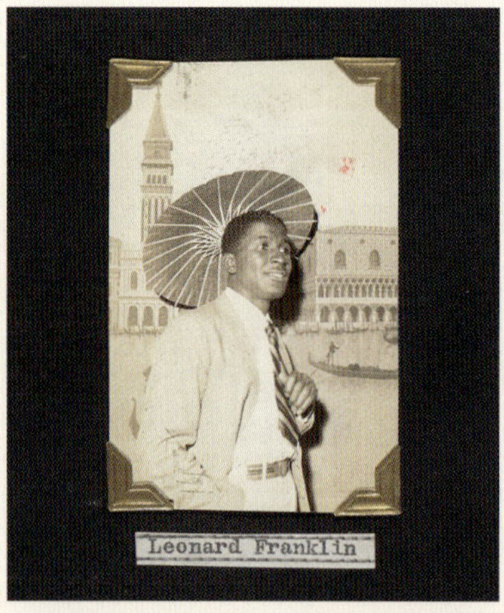

5.39 Max Ewing, *Leonard Franklin with a Parasol*, from *Les Amants de Venise*.

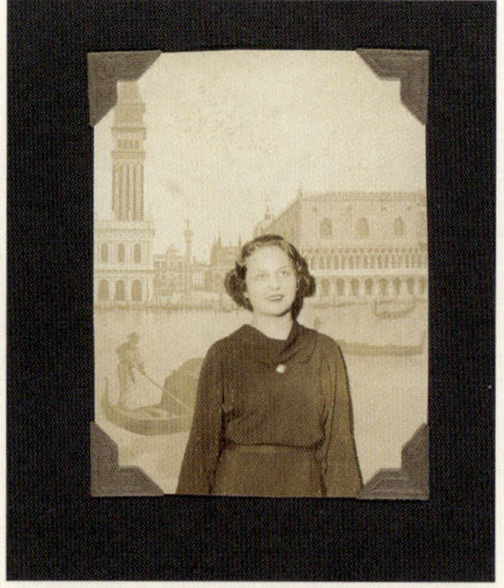

5.40 Max Ewing, *Unidentified Woman, probably a performer in Four Saints in Three Acts*, from *Les Amants de Venise*.

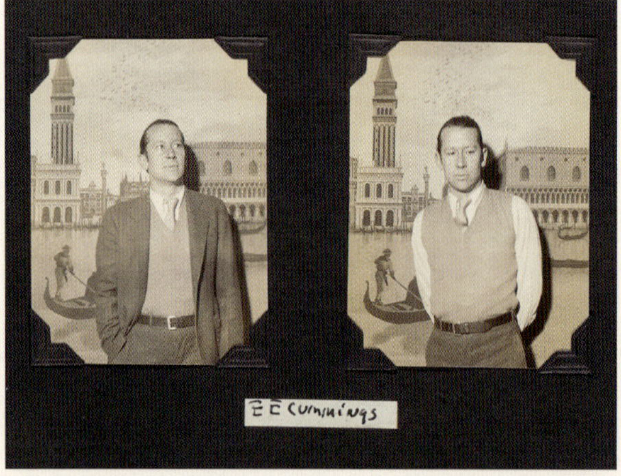

5.41 Max Ewing, *E. E. Cummings*, from *Les Amants de Venise*.

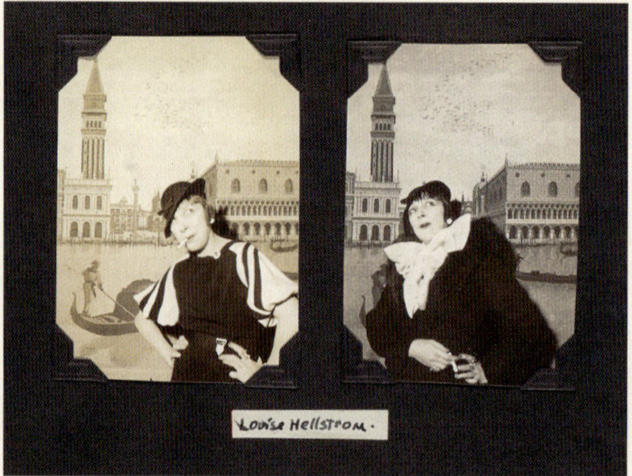

5.42 Max Ewing, *Louise Hellstrom*, from *Les Amants de Venise*.

glamorous Hollywood actress Anna May Wong (who had sat for Carl Van Vechten in April 1932 and attended one of Ewing's parties the previous year) "as a Venetian," but they were never able to arrange a date.[47]

He had better luck with young performers based in New York. These included two performers from *Four Saints in Three Acts*, Leonard Franklin (fig. 5.39) and an unidentified African American woman (fig. 5.40). Although the latter is not identified in Ewing's album — little is known about most of the performers in that production — the presence of these images in the collection serves as an important reminder of how closely he watched the evolution of that project, no doubt attending rehearsals and conferring with his friend Florine Stettheimer about the progress of her set designs. As with Noguchi, however, and a few others, including the well-known writer E. E. Cummings (fig. 5.41) — who was soon to be romantically paired with Ewing's beloved Marion Morehouse — or Balanchine's assistant, Lucia Davidova (a lover of Alice DeLamar), there is little information about their friendship.[48] No doubt he met Davidova through DeLamar, but he also associated her with Lincoln Kirstein, who was then busy promoting Balanchine and getting the American Ballet Theatre off the ground. Similarly, it is likely he met Cummings through Draper; Morehouse had herself only recently met the poet in 1932.[49] This was a small world, as we know, but Ewing's many connections within it, and the positive reception of his efforts with so many people, say a great deal about the intellectual and creative energy of New York in these years. It also says a lot about the collector's zeal Ewing displayed as he sought out his subjects: like the avid celebrity hunter that he was, he succeeded in capturing a likeness of almost everyone he knew for his portrait series.

QUEER NEW YORK

Although Van Vechten was deeply engrossed in his photography work for much of 1932 and thus had virtually stopped giving parties entirely, Ewing could still count on Muriel Draper, Edward Wasserman, and Natalie Hammond for invitations and introductions to a wide array of people, some of whom sat for portraits. It was thanks to Wasserman, for example, that he came to photograph Joe Carstairs (fig. 5.43) and Ruth Baldwin (fig. 5.44), a prominent lesbian couple from England, when he attended a "small gathering" for Carstairs, who "had just arrived for a month in New York" with two of her girlfriends, "before going on a cruise up the Amazon River on their own schooner."[50] Carstairs had leased an apartment next to Natalie Hammond's modern penthouse (where Alice Laughlin lived in an adjacent unit furnished in a "Spanish" style), and Ewing reported to his mother that they all were coming to "have me photograph them in Venice next week."[51] Ewing's letter, written when he first met Carstairs in September 1931, provides a bit of catty commentary about the women's gender-bending appearance: "You may have seen the Carstairs girl in newsreels or papers," Ewing gleefully confided:

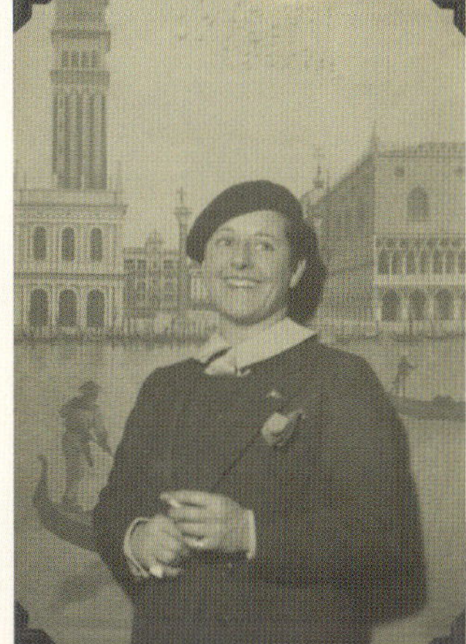

5.43 Max Ewing, *Joe Carstairs*, from *The Carnival of Venice*.

> She is the English girl who goes for boat racing … She looks like a N.Y. truck driver. And a very husky one. She has a haircut that is practically a shave. And she came to the party in an old sweater, surrounded by her harem of girls whom she carries with her wherever she goes at her expense. An amazing creature sounding like a bass drum … Ruth Baldwin used to be a friend of Addison Pelletier who lives with Natalie H. But Addison warns Ruth not to even telephone her now, because Natalie would be apt to knife her in the back if she did. Which sounds a little drastic.[52]

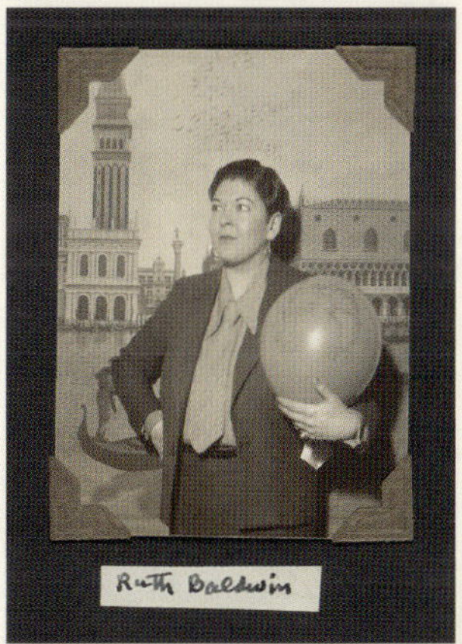

5.44 Max Ewing, *Portrait of Ruth Baldwin*, from *Les Amants de Venise*.

Like "Spivy" (fig. 5.45), the queer nightclub owner who poses with her friend Paul Flato, the society jeweler, and Gladys Bentley, the Harlem entertainer whose cross-dressing performances made her famous, Carstairs and Baldwin are rare examples of queer women who lived independently as an "out" couple. In all of these cases, unusual

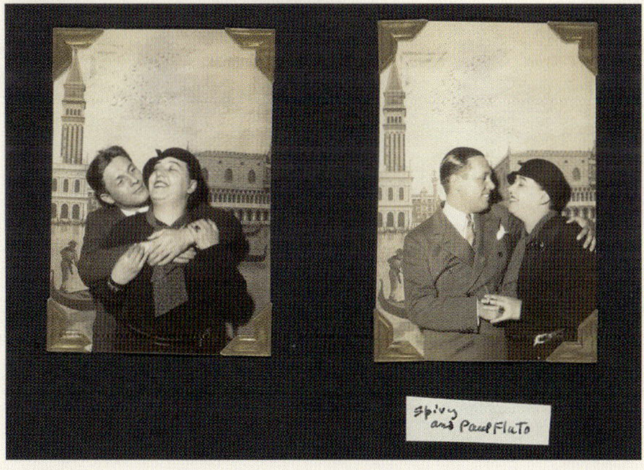

5.45 Max Ewing, *Paul Flato and "Spivy,"* from *Les Amants de Venise*.

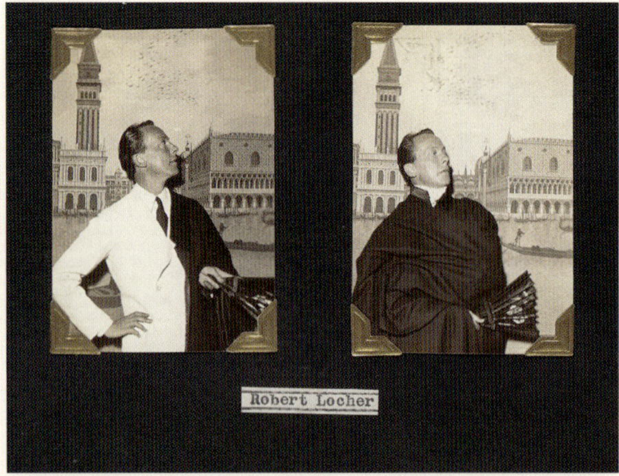

5.46 Max Ewing, *Two Portraits of Robert Locher*, from *Les Amants de Venise*.

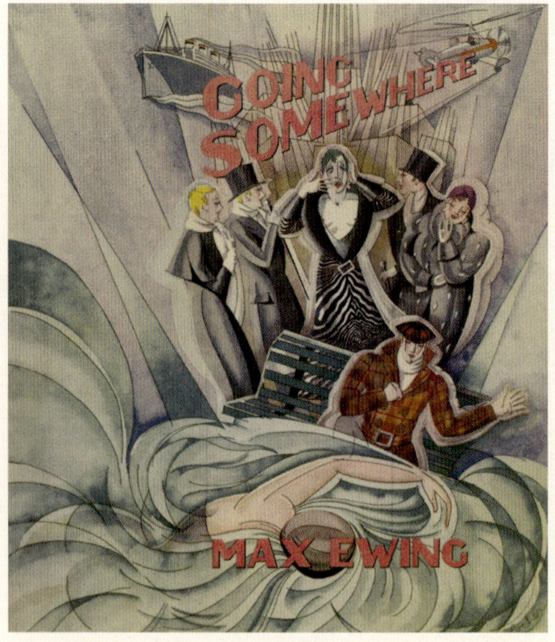

5.47 Robert Locher, cover design for Max Ewing's *Going Somewhere* (1933). Max Ewing Papers.

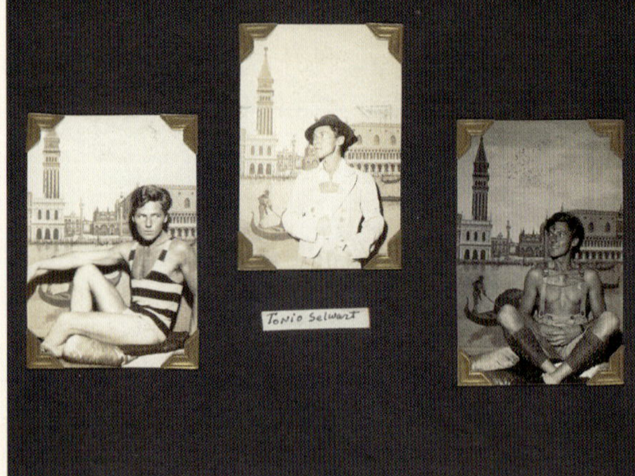

5.48 Max Ewing, *Three Portraits of Tonio Selwart*, from *Les Amants de Venise*.

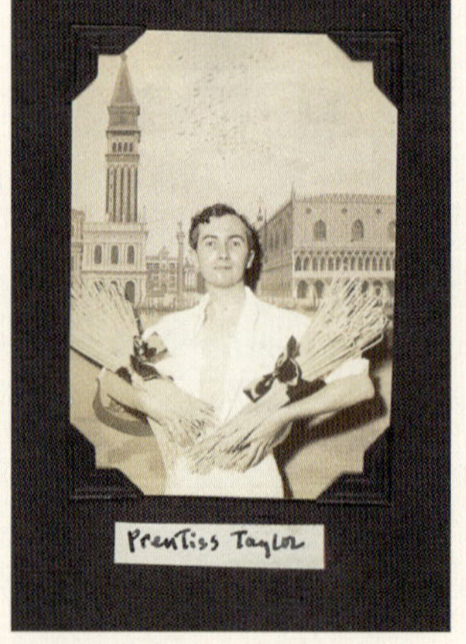

5.49 Max Ewing, *Prentiss Taylor*, from *Les Amants de Venise*.

circumstances — extreme wealth in the case of Carstairs, and the tolerant atmosphere of New York's entertainment world in the case of Bentley and Spivy — made their relative freedom possible, but Ewing's photos nonetheless remain rare evidence of the complex identities they fashioned for themselves (see also fig. 4.20).

Ewing's portrait of the graphic artist and interior designer Robert Locher is another significant image for the history of New York's queer culture and for Ewing's own biography.[53] Locher (fig. 5.46), born in 1889, was a prominent member of the Draper and Stettheimer circles and the life partner of the prominent American artist Charles Demuth, despite the fact that the two men lived apart and Locher remained married until the mid-1930s, when Demuth died and left him a substantial number of artworks and a house in Lancaster, Pennsylvania.[54] By 1932, Ewing had known Locher socially for a number of years, thanks to their shared connection with Muriel Draper — "Bobby is one of the best designers and decorators and architects" in New York, he informed his mother, "He and Beatrice have been great friends of Muriel's for many years" — and to the queer community of design professionals in New York.

Among his accomplishments, Locher had created many distinctive book covers for Knopf, including Van Vechten's novels and Ewing's *Going Somewhere*.

He was an associate editor at *House and Garden* and an illustrator for *Vanity Fair*, as well as an industrial artist and a teacher at Parsons School of Design.[55] Ewing was thrilled when he accepted an invitation from Blanche Knopf (1894–1966) to design Ewing's cover, and he sent the mock-up of the book (fig. 5.47) to his mother, instructing her to test it out on any comparable book in her own library so that she could see how well it fit.

Through Locher, Ewing expanded his connections in the queer design and journalism worlds, visiting Locher's large home in Staten Island over the summer of 1932, particularly while Beatrice Locher (b. 1886) was away on excursions of her own. In August, he began a new friendship with the photographer known as Horst (see fig. I.28), an up-and-coming star newly arrived in the United States to work for *Vogue*. As Ewing wrote to his mother on August 18:

> I have a new friend, a German boy named Horst Bohrmann.
> A photographer whom Vogue has brought over from Germany and
> London to do fashion photographs for the magazine. He has been
> photographing only a year, and is paid $200.00 a sitting! He brought
> letters of introduction to Bobby Locher from Paris, and he and
> I are going out to Bobby's tomorrow to spend the night and go to the
> beach on Saturday. Sunday I am invited to the Stettheimers again
> with Carl Van Vechten, and may go or may not.[56]

For reasons unknown, the large-format print of Locher's portrait in the *Carnival* album (see fig. I.28) is the only one that is touched up to highlight the eyes, as though he were wearing eyeliner and mascara.

Like Van Vechten, Locher was an important role model for Ewing as he navigated his life as a queer, young man in New York, though it is important to stress that both men were also married to women. This sent a clear message — not that Ewing and others needed reminding — about the dangerous isolation that a person might face if the issue of sexual orientation were pushed too far or spoken about too loudly. In Ewing's queer circle, many friends were in heterosexual marriages (Kirstein and McAndrew among them) or, like Esther Murphy, tried it out, with varying degrees of success. For some men, like the actor Tonio Selwart (fig. 5.48) who had appeared in Van Vechten's queer group portraits, heterosexual marriage was a viable option and a helpful cover. For many others — like Ewing, or Donald Angus, or the campy, queer Prentiss Taylor (fig. 5.49) — that route appears to have been neither desirable nor possible. Clearly, the question of evidence in matters of sexual orientation remains complex, and conventional markers are often indecipherable. This is especially true when we consider Ewing's homoerotic nude portraits and the status of models like Paul Meeres and Jack Pollock, both of whom were married to women but nevertheless happily took part in the queer social and visual culture that Ewing, Van Vechten, and Lynes were creating in these years.

NAKED MEN AND NUDES

For some time, Max Ewing had been sailing close to the wind when it came to his nude photographs: he had been using the Ritters as male models for his art projects since 1930, but unlike Lynes, who was always careful about displaying and circulating nude images, he took many risks, perhaps expecting his privileged status in the art world to protect him. We know that he sent nude photos to Van Vechten and others through the mail, and he even asked the local drugstore to print the snapshots he had taken in preparation for his sculpture of male nudes in *Muriel Destroying Young Men*.[57] Moreover, he expected all of his friends to accept his models as his social companions regardless of their own notions of propriety. While this did not extend to Paul Meeres, who seemed to have little interest in socializing with his white admirers beyond occasional visits to their homes, or the Ritter brothers, who didn't venture far from the world of bodybuilding, Harlem nightclubs, and gay parties, Ewing often insisted on bringing his so-called "trainers" — Roy Setliff, whom he referred to as "the Marine," and Jack Pollock, a boxer — with him when he visited his friends, both gay and straight, pushing the boundaries of class and sexuality.

Nevertheless, with his family back in Ohio or even with his cousin Doris, Ewing never deviated from the camp ambiguities and veils that his queer persona allowed. The difference in tone between Ritter's chatty descriptions of the queer haunts in Harlem that he visited in his life as a young man-about-town and Ewing's coy letters to his mother are revealing. For example, in a letter to Ewing written November 27, 1933, Fred Ritter fills his friend in on his recent activities:

> This town is also giving some of them "Gay Nineties" parties, Eddie Wasserman and that crowd gave one which we attended called the Hurdy Gurdy Ball, they hired three floors in the fifties and decorated them in old time barroom style and everyone came dressed as Bowery characters ... George Lynes [is] back from abroad he gave [a] little party, have gone [to] Harlem for some reason and get up there most every Saturday nite, frequent Clinton Moores the Hotcha [*sic*] which by the way is not so gay maybe because Jimmy [*sic*] Daniels [is] not there he [is] in London right now expects [to] be back by first of year ... still getting my share of propositions latest from some Marcoue and a Don Campbell Jr., they offer me the world but all I want is a small island in the South Sea's [*sic*], where I can spend my old age watching tropical sunsets, ahem, so its [*sic*] no dice.[58]

By contrast, Ewing wrote to his mother on June 26, 1930:

> My ex-prize fighting, ex-Marine friend from South America, Nicaragua, California, and points east and west and north and south — Roy Setliff — left for Philadelphia today. He insists that he is going west to build himself a mountain lodge in the Sierra Nevada mountains and as soon as it is habitable I have to come and share it and let him BUILD ME UP to his own middle-weight champion proportions. I might even do it for three months sometime. He is a superb creature and terribly sweet. I was tempted to ask him to stop off at Clear Lake [the Ewing family's vacation cottage in Indiana] for a week, on his way west, but decided not to, because I could not get enough work done with him there. Namara asked him and me out to her house to dine Sunday night, and the Sheldons had us to dinner Monday night. They both sat spellbound before his tales of wild adventure in Central America.[59]

Ewing's photographs reveal a different sort of experience altogether, one that he never wanted or expected his family to see. His awkward photograph of Setliff (fig. 5.50), the self-conscious and clearly uncomfortable "superb creature" whom he referred to in his letter, suggests that, for "the Marine" at least, the parties with Ewing's friends and the nude photography may have strayed into altogether too-explicit queer territory. After all, Setliff was a "steeplejack" and handyman who helped out around his apartment and at Muriel's house: as Ewing wrote to his mother, in September 1932, "My ex-Marine friend Roy showed up — the boy who helped paint Muriel's house two years ago. I got him to paint my bathroom pink. I took a brush and did the pipes and corners myself and had a grand time."[60]

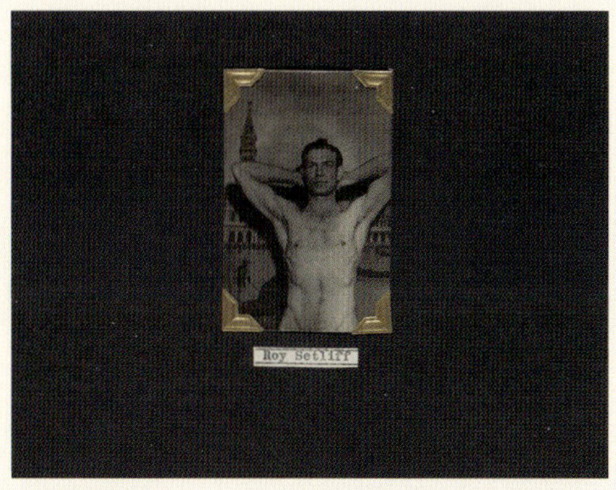

5.50 Max Ewing, *Roy Setliff ("The Marine")*, from *Les Amants de Venise*.

The Ritters were performers, and their modeling ability clearly resulted in a different sort of image and an altogether different "imaginary" in queer visual narrative. Thus, when Fred and his brother Bill posed for Ewing "in Venice," they did so with a clear awareness of being looked at by men and propositioned by men, just as they were in bars and at parties.[61] When Fred stood fully exposed in Ewing's bedroom with his hands above his head, or when Bill did handstands (fig. 5.51) that gave the viewer a peek at his genitals — albeit upside down (the only "uncensored" image of male nudity in the Ewing collection) — they sometimes look directly at the camera, confident in their bodies and in control of their images as reflected in Ewing's appreciative gaze, or display themselves, bronzed and beautiful, like the icons they were.

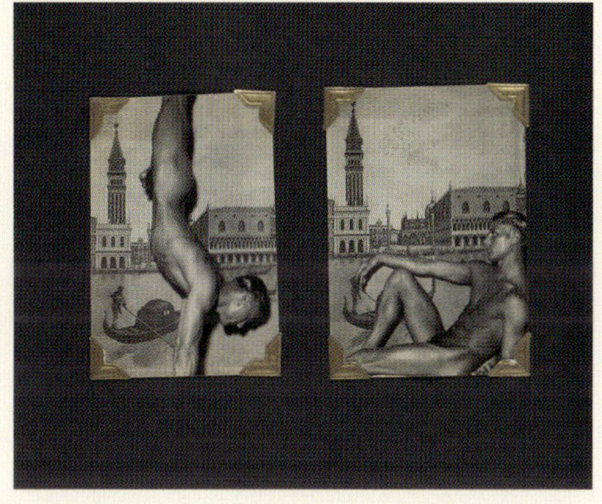

5.51 Max Ewing, *Bill Ritter Doing a Handstand Nude*, and *Bill Ritter Reclining*, from *Les Amants de Venise*.

It is for this reason, perhaps, that the Ritter images from the *Carnival* were so appealing to Carl Van Vechten. They readily lent themselves to the combination of queer visual pleasure and camp humor that Van Vechten appreciated and — if the tropes that often reappear in the scrapbooks over a period of decades are any indication — never tired of. Indeed, the reclining image of Bill Ritter appears twice in Van Vechten's scrapbooks, once with the caption "Blond Beauty and Very Swish" (fig. 5.52) pasted opposite three willowy male figures labeled "A Dutchess [*sic*] is a Dutchess is a Dutchess," and a second time with the collaged captions "Eager For Harness Again," and "Well Worth The Work," (fig. 5.53) juxtaposed with Ewing's handstand photo (captioned "Lovelier

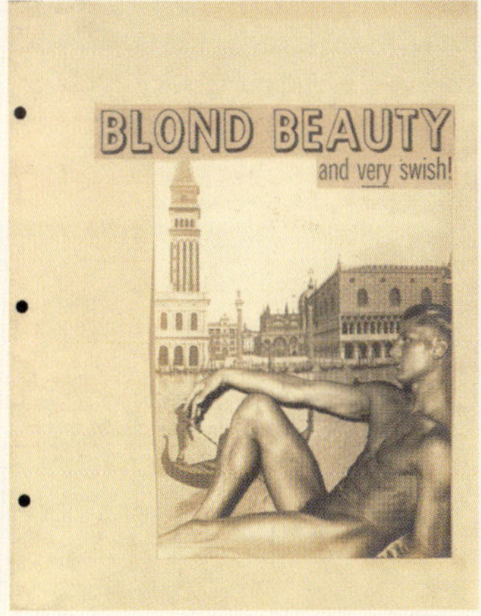

5.52 Carl Van Vechten, "Blonde Beauty … and very swish," collage with Max Ewing's photographs of Bill Ritter and found text, from Carl Van Vechten's scrapbook. Carl Van Vechten Papers.

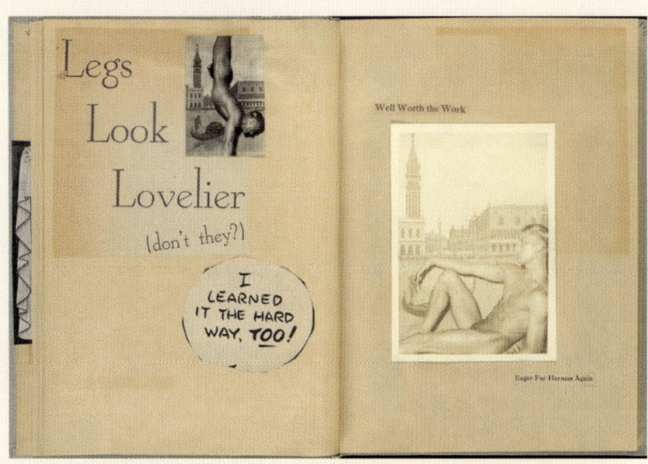

5.53 Carl Van Vechten, "Legs Look Lovelier" and "Well Worth the Work," double page collage with Max Ewing's photographs of Bill Ritter and found text, from Carl Van Vechten's scrapbook.

and lovelier"). While it isn't clear when Van Vechten created these pages — they could have been made any time between the 1930s and the 1960s — they clearly put Ewing's photographs to good use as both homoerotic images and objects of camp irony that go well beyond the photographer's original intentions. The same can be said for another spread in the scrapbook, which adds the caption "Playing on Both Legs" to Ewing's large-format image from the Levy Gallery exhibition, and pairs it with a photo of Ritter as a cigarette-smoking street tough entitled "New 1938 Play Yard" (fig. 5.54).

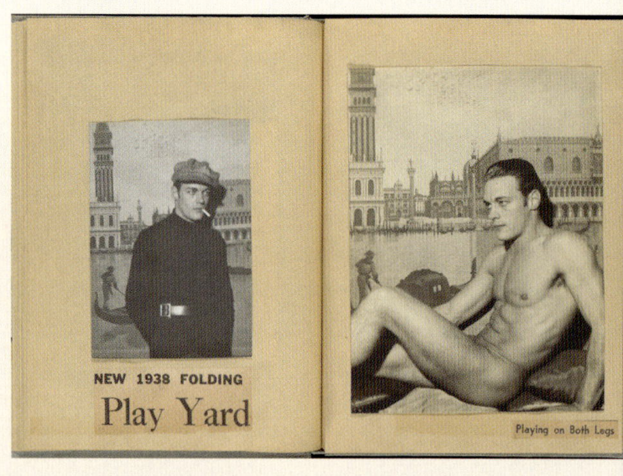

5.54 Carl Van Vechten, "Play Yard" and "Playing on Both Legs," double page collage with Max Ewing's photographs of Fred Ritter and found text, from Carl Van Vechten's scrapbook.

A number of photographs from 1932 fall into the same category. These include two that show the Ritter brothers sitting on the bench in front of the view of Venice, their bodies entwined: one is given the title "Love at First Night," while the other bears the caption "Gay Honeymoon" (fig. 5.55). Again, there is no indication of when the words and images were brought together. Whatever the date, the newly narrativized photos fulfil a number of significant tasks. First, Van Vechten clearly recognized that the literal reading of these images as snapshots of real people rather than works of art like George Platt Lynes's artistically lighted and carefully posed photographs of the Ritters was unavoidable. As such, Ewing's photos are explicitly and emphatically queer. Second, with their new narratives, Van Vechten's images read as both performative camp and as paeans to gay culture. Unlike either Lynes's art photography, which takes the subject out of the real world and places it on the plane of beautiful fantasy, or even Ewing's own strategically cropped nudes, Van Vechten's collages of the Ritters make a statement: in their unedited realism, they offer a clear image of two queer, well-built bodies juxtaposed in a photographer's home. So much for Van Vechten's declaration to Ewing's cousin Doris that the "nudes are gone, destroyed or otherwise disposed of."[62]

The Paul Meeres portraits are equally compelling, yet for different reasons. By showing him both clothed and unclothed (albeit cropped) in the

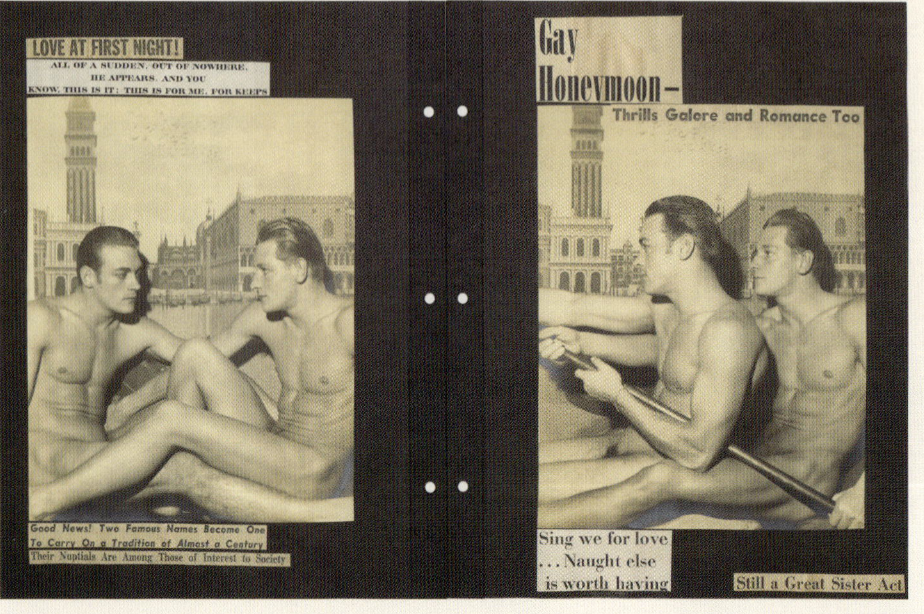

5.55 Carl Van Vechten, "Love at First Night" and "Gay Honeymoon," double page collage with Max Ewing's photographs of the Ritter brothers and found text, from Carl Van Vechten's scrapbook.

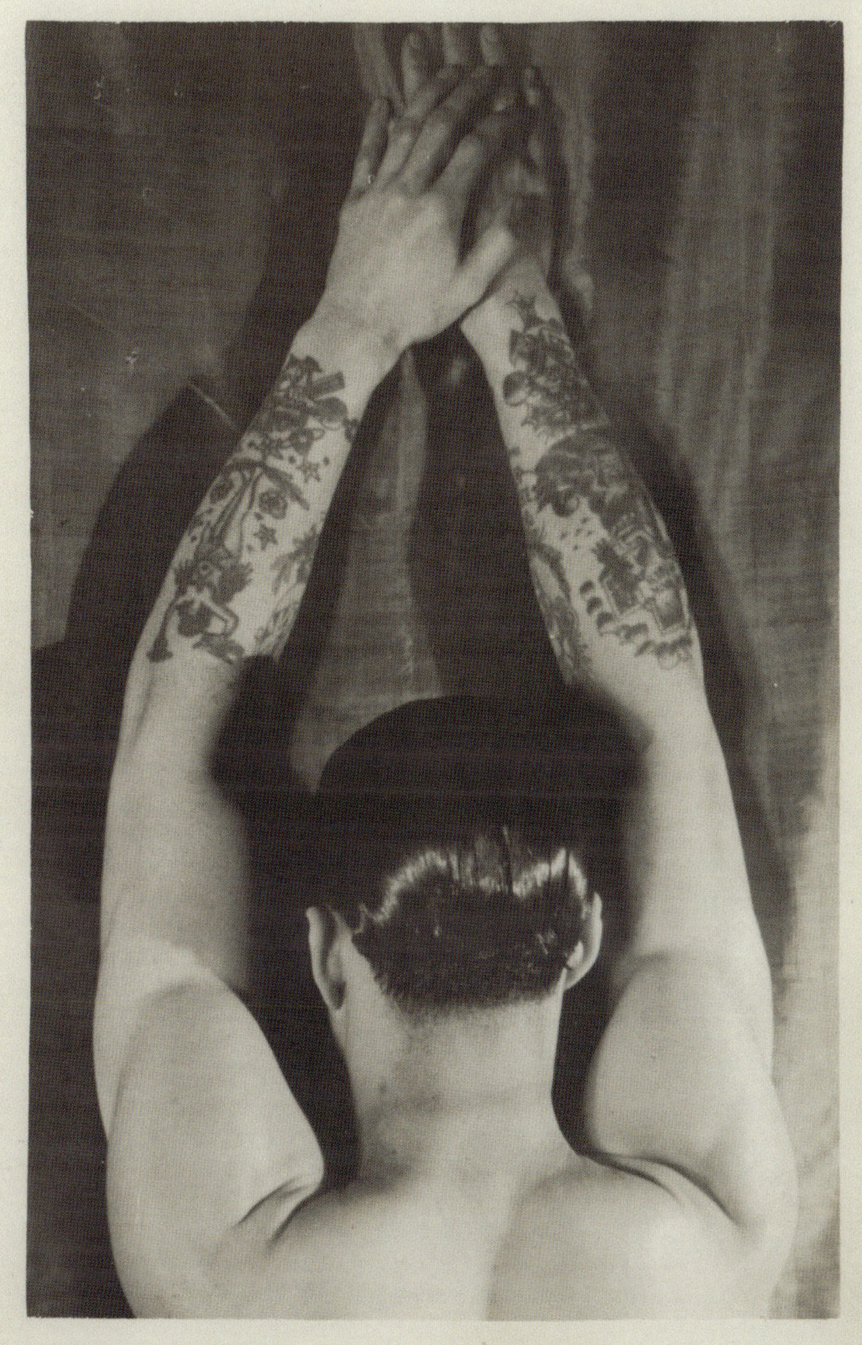

Carnival (see fig. 5.13) Ewing suggested that the possibility of nudity was always there: for the much-admired entertainer and star, that was part of the narrative bargain that the performer struck with his audience. Ewing's photographs never deviate from Meeres's role as a performer and pinup, focusing on clothing and costume (or lack thereof) or on his role as an artist's model, standing in conventional poses. These are different from the way in which Van Vechten had portrayed him in his own photographs in April 1932, presenting Meeres as a beautifully lighted, highly objectified face and body, often looking away from the camera: in one striking image of this type, Meeres turns his back and raises his arms above his head to reveal his tattoos (fig. 5.56), an abstracted and aestheticized form in the manner of Stieglitz or other artists.

It is fascinating to see what Van Vechten made of Ewing's portraits of Meeres when he got his hands on them in the private realm of his own scrapbooking activities. In Van Vechten's uncropped versions of the Ewing photos, Meeres's body is fully revealed to the gaze of the viewer. Thus, the caption "Meat and the Body" (fig. 5.57) is particularly graphic and sexualized camp, as is the full-frontal "A Feast for the Eyes" (fig. 5.58), which presents Meeres's nude body to the gaze of the spectator with the explicitness of the porn magazines and postcards that Van Vechten loved. Van Vechten's captions for the cropped images, including the one of Meeres wearing a sailor's hat, are more ironic and campily suggestive, adding phrases like "Rare Bird," "This is Perhaps the One Coffee You Haven't Tasted Before," and "You Can't Write Too Strong an Ad About It."

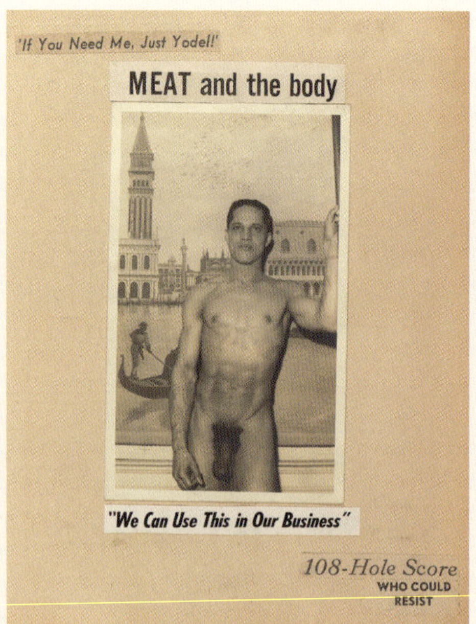

5.57 Carl Van Vechten, "Meat and the Body," collage with Max Ewing's photograph of Paul Meeres and found text, from Carl Van Vechten's scrapbook.

Ewing's portraits and snapshots of the boxer Jack Pollock (figs. 5.59 and 5.60), his friend, "trainer," and perhaps also occasional lover, are altogether different from any of his other nudes. Despite the differences between them, the two men became intimate friends and companions, spending time together not only in New York, but also in California, where Pollock visited Ewing in the fall of 1933, and later in Pioneer in the winter and spring of 1934. Despite his lack of money, Pollock had travelled from Idaho to Ohio to try to help his friend shake off the deep depression he was sinking into following his mother's nervous breakdown and, ultimately, her death in April 1934. Pollock even took up residence with Max in the Ewing family home for a period of time, and it was the boxer who was with Ewing at the time of his suicide the following month.

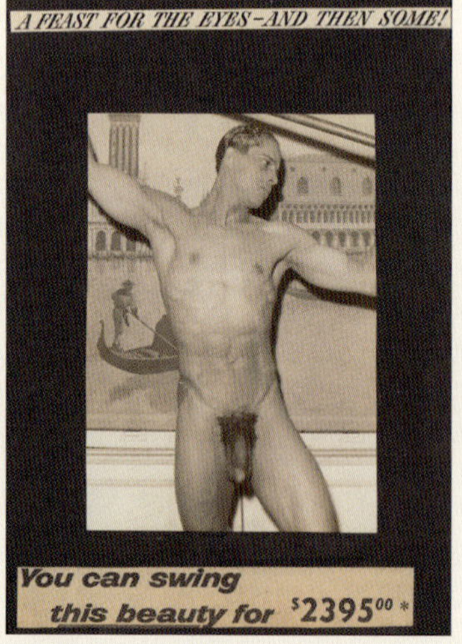

5.58 Carl Van Vechten, "You Can Swing This Beauty," collage with Max Ewing's photograph of Paul Meeres and found text, from Carl Van Vechten's scrapbook.

Regardless of his family's suspicions about Pollock's motives, Ewing himself never wavered in his love, even as he continually failed to defer to, or even acknowledge, the challenges that his devotion to the boxer presented for the "polite society" of Pioneer, Ohio. On the contrary, he was proud to have the companionship of such a handsome and unlikely new friend, and happy to show him off to the members of his circle. As he wrote to Muriel Draper soon after the two met, Pollock was "MUCH MORE ATTRACTIVE" even than Roy Setliff, the ex-marine and sometime boxer who had introduced them, adding archly, "So isn't it awful? Just when marine boxers were quite off our mind? He is several years younger than Roy, effectively battle-scarred, and looks like a composite of Dempsey and Carpentier … He has been photographed, and I will show you the results soon … At any rate he is apt to make quite a stir."[63]

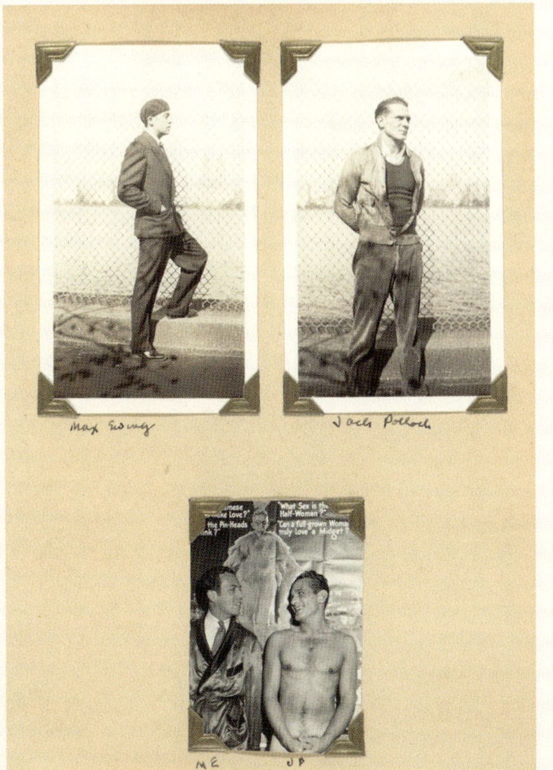

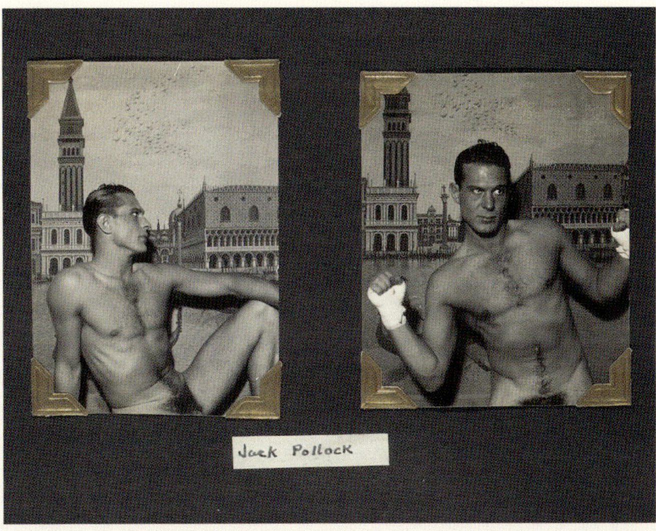

5.59 Snapshots of Max Ewing and Jack Pollock from Ewing's *Snapshots 1932*.

5.60 Max Ewing, *Two Nude Portraits of Jack Pollock*, from *Les Amants de Venise*.

While Ewing was more guarded when he shared the news about Pollock with his mother, he gleefully wrote to tell her how pleased he was by his new friend:

Here I am fresh from a workout in Central Park with my trainer! This is a new development. For two or three years I have been exercising (as you know) in a makeshift and haphazard way … So now I have someone who is training me right, and I am very much excited. A young man named Jack Pollock, a magnificent athlete, who was introduced to me by Roy, my ex-Marine friend. Pollock is in training himself, and has taken me in charge for a small sum per week. I don't train as strenuously as he does and he is starting me in light. He gets me up at seven-thirty and takes me around the reservoir in the Park, a two-mile clip, at an easy pace. … On Wednesday I was invited to the Conrads at Montclair. I asked them if I might bring my "trainer." They were quite intrigued and said of course. So I took him and we had a grand time. We talked so much in the evening we missed the last train back to New York and so we stayed there all night and played tennis yesterday A.M. and came back later in the day … Pollock says in three months he can quite transform me. I am delighted by this new regime and you will be too when you see me.[64]

In October 1932, he shared further news about the friendship, reporting that "My trainer and I went to Fieldston to the Winslows … stayed for dinner … everyone is very much excited over meeting him, as he is like a refreshing breeze off a body of water we have never had a breeze from before, if you follow me."[65] By November, the two men were inseparable, attending parties, luncheons, and formal dinners with all of Ewing's friends.[66]

Ewing's snapshots of Pollock, preserved both in his own scrapbooks (fig. 5.59) and in the *Carnival of Venice* series (see fig. 5.60), reflect the intimacy and informality of their relationship, one clearly dedicated to celebrating the boxer's muscular beauty as he posed in the guise of a classical bodybuilder or as a reclining, Michelangelesque nude. Unlike Ewing's other images of male nudes, the Pollock photos very clearly reveal the photographer's loving gaze and declare his presence, sometimes quite literally, in the frame in snapshots where the two laugh and camp it up at the beach or in front of the treasured *Freaks* poster in Ewing's apartment.

Ewing knew that the Pollock images would make an excellent gift for his friend Carl Van Vechten, and he sent along a few examples, including one reclining nude that he attached to a letter, preserved in Van Vechten's scrapbooks. In his letter, Ewing asks rather coyly whether Van Vechten might be able to help his friend find a job, since "My contacts with the kind of job he might conceivably get are slight." He also noted that Pollock was "quite delightful in many ways, and is full of hair-raising and blood-curdling stories of his prowess in the ring from Boston to Honolulu. I think you would be amused to meet him."[67] The results of Ewing's request are unknown, but Van Vechten liked the image so much that he reproduced it a few times, adding the caption "A Resting Beauty" to one of the photos. (fig. 5.61).

It is unlikely that Van Vechten ever warmed to Pollock, however, especially after the boxer had been summarily dismissed by Draper and rejected by Ewing's friends and family following Ewing's death.[68] Indeed, Van Vechten made his opinion of Pollock quite clear when he added the captions "Party-perfect," "Sensational Trade" (fig. 5.62), and "Eager for Sex" to Ewing's photos of him in his scrapbooks.

LEAVING NEW YORK

Perhaps it was Van Vechten's tepid reaction to his latest photography and writing projects that made Ewing start to feel restless in New York, and perhaps he simply had "a western bug" in his "bonnet," as he told his mother. Either way, it seemed like time to move on. "I have been here [meaning his West 31st Street apartment] about five years," he explained:

> These years covered a definite period of my life, a period of readjustment, a squaring away of some plans, and a taking on of others. With the publication of this book I feel that a new era is beginning. With Dad's death I feel that certain aspects of another era are finished. I'm not sure that it would not be a good thing psychologically to move, and make a new start in new surroundings for 1933.[69]

His dreams of becoming a concert pianist were well and truly over, and he was beginning to think he should try his luck as a screenwriter in Hollywood, as so many of his friends had done. He also began to separate himself from his mother

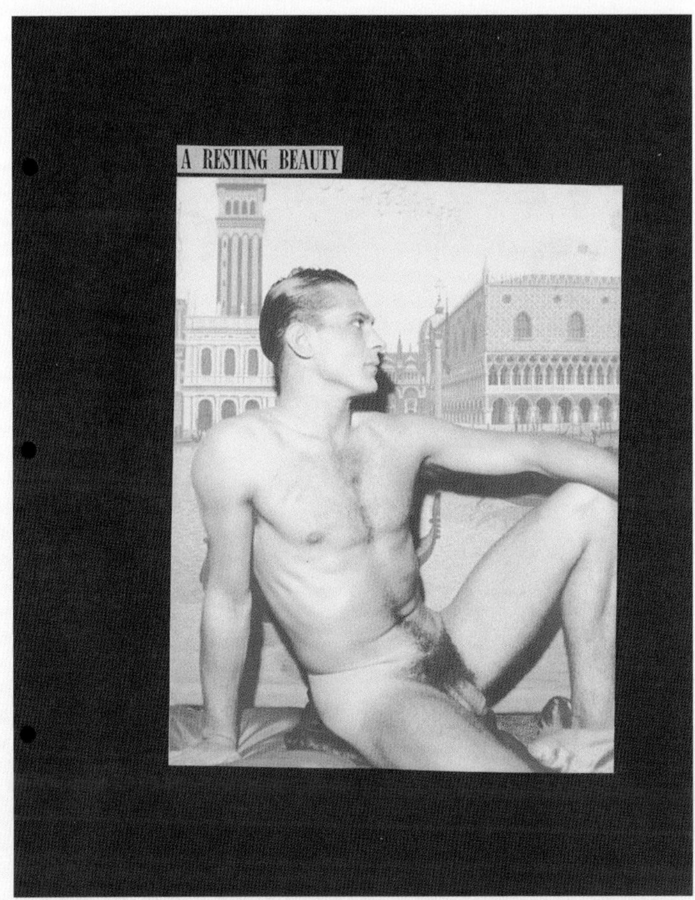

5.61 Carl Van Vechten, "A Resting Beauty," collage with Max Ewing's photograph of Jack Pollock and found text, from Carl Van Vechten's scrapbook.

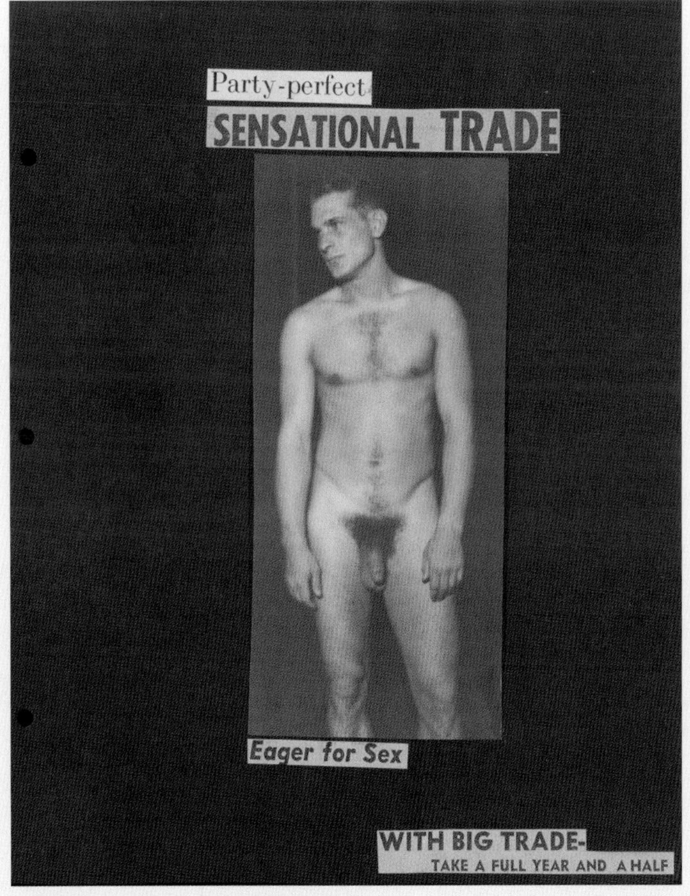

5.62 Carl Van Vechten, "Sensational Trade," collage with Max Ewing's photograph of Jack Pollock and found text, from Carl Van Vechten's scrapbook.

and from Pioneer, setting his sights on the sort of success that the Stettheimers encouraged him to pursue. He was looking forward to seeing his book in print and to the celebration of his *Carnival of Venice* at the Julien Levy Gallery the following month. He had invited his mother to join him for the opening and meet his friends, but he knew she wouldn't come; he was finished with being disappointed about that, and resigned to the fact that they lived in different worlds.

Thus, as Ewing wrote just before Christmas, marking the first holiday he had not been at home in Pioneer, he would always remember the happy years of Christmas celebrations with his "loving family," and be grateful that "for a week or two we completely overlooked the differences in our lives and ways of living the rest of the year." Yet even as he longed to strike out on his own, he never stopped being Clara Ewing's devoted son, adding reassuring words of love as so often before: "Whatever success I may win I want to bring it all to you," he confessed, "for you are responsible for it all, and yours is half the glory!! I send you a hundred kisses, and I wish I could make it clear how dear you are to me."[70]

Ewing still had one more antic project to complete before he left town, one that he hoped would help prepare him for his trip to Hollywood. He founded an organization called "The GaryFlappers" to bring Gary Cooper's most devoted fans together, and he printed up membership cards for everyone who joined, including Van Vechten, Muriel Draper (fig. 5.63), and his cousin Doris. A few of these, bearing the motto, "The GaryFlappers (A New Cooper Union) and listing Ewing's address, survive in the archive and in Van Vechten's scrapbook. He later reported to George Platt Lynes that he

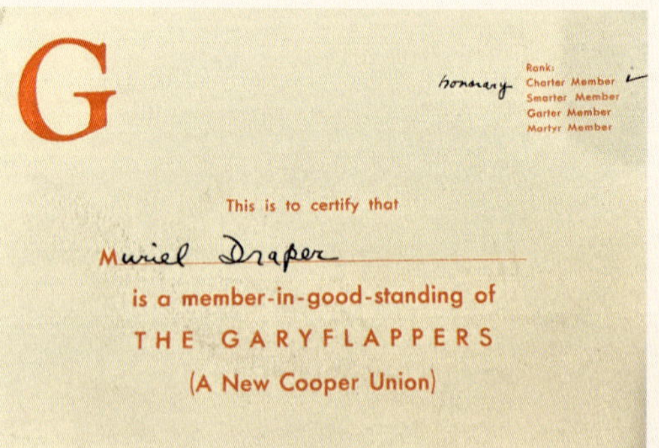

5.63 Muriel Draper's membership card for "THE GARRYFLAPPERS (A New Cooper Union)." Max Ewing Papers.

was "sick with a cold, as a result of too much strenuous Garyflapping at the Central Park Casino Night before last," noting that he hoped Lynes could attend his party at the Waldorf as he had missed him at his "Garyflapper Gala."[71]

Once again, Ewing put his things in storage, writing on Mother's Day, 1933 that he "wouldn't be surprised if I stayed away from New York six or seven months."[72] He carefully filed the clippings and photographs from his *Gallery*, marking the end of an era, and he packed up his collection of programs and books in preparation for his new life. He was excited to be heading to San Francisco to stay with Noël Sullivan (1890–1956), a wealthy patron of artists and writers (including Langston Hughes) whose home had become a center of queer social and cultural life, and he was looking forward to seeing many old friends in Hollywood — the Hoffensteins and the Seldeses among them, as well as the many young actresses and socialites, including Lilyan Tashman, Peggy Fears, and Mercedes de Acosta, whom he had befriended in New York. He celebrated his success in New York with an all-night party that marked the great distance he had come since he had first arrived in the city. As he wrote to his friend Edgar Ailes:

> The night before I left I stayed out all night because my apartment was too torn up to go back to! I more or less covered all the waterfronts with Tallulah Bankhead who was at loose ends, and Irene Barrymore (Mrs. Lionel) and various cronies. We did all the high

spots such as the Mayfair Yacht Club and the Embassy Club, and
ended up next morning in the low spots such as the Ha-ha, and the
Hotcha [*sic*]. And I took a train that afternoon feeling that I had
exhausted all there was for me in New York for the immediate time
being! I have never been west of Chicago, and I must say I am very
eager for the first time to look around Out West.[73]

Little did Ewing realize, as he boarded the train the following morning,
that the coming months would bring more disillusionment than he had ever
known, and that his westward journey would end with his mother's death as well
as his own. For now, Ewing was filled with excitement about his new adventures
and confident that he would soon realize his dreams.

THE QUEER EYE OF THE 1920S AND '30S

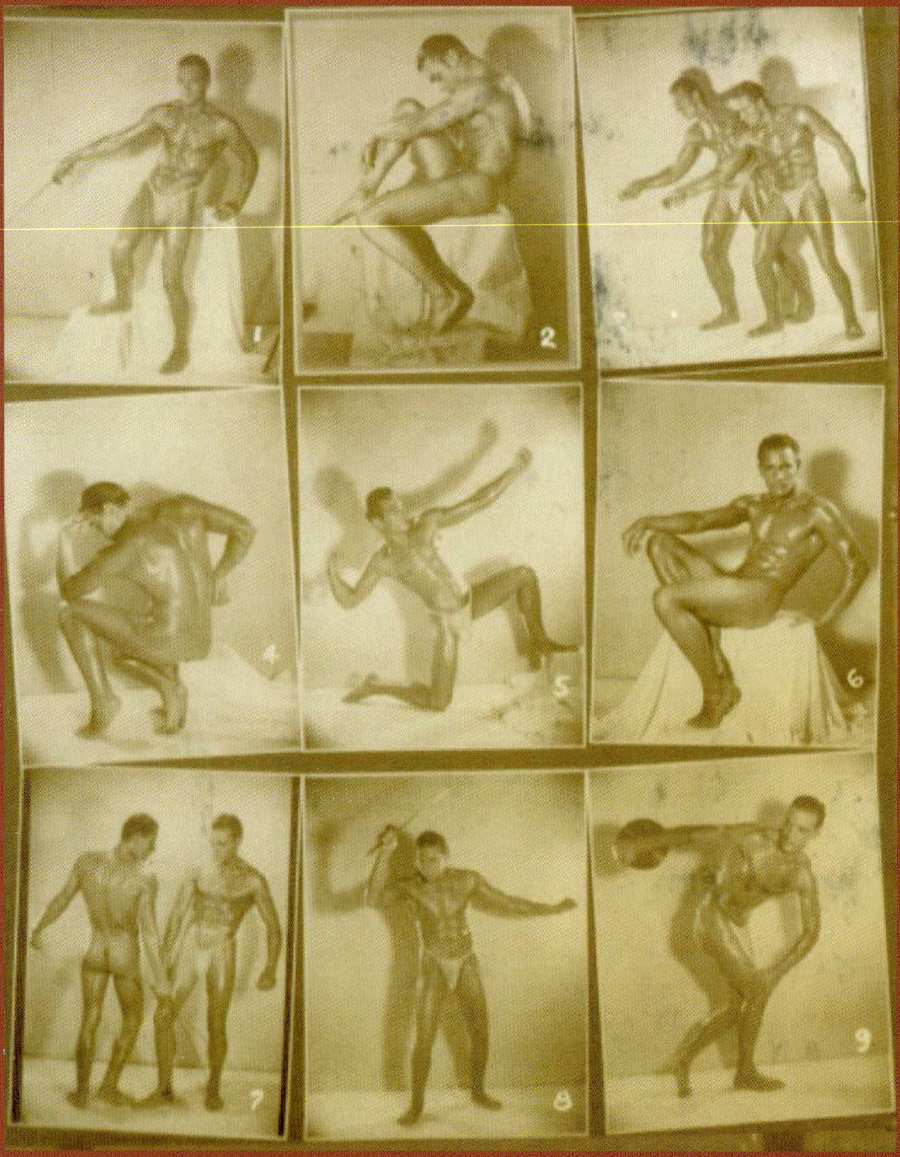

I.1 Publicity photos showing the Ritter brothers in "classical" poses, from George Platt Lynes's scrapbooks, c. 1934. Beinecke Rare Book & Manuscript Library, Yale University.

As the work of a queer photographer, Max Ewing's images represent a rare survival, preserving both the likenesses of his extended community of artists, actors, friends, and acquaintances — the "queer moderns" of my title — and his own distinctive point of view, a view shaped by the "queer eye" behind the lens of an amateur's camera. This can be seen not only in what Ewing chose to look at and photograph, but also in the way he staged, framed, and represented his subjects. Together with a handful of other artists whose work depicted scenarios from queer life, including Carl Van Vechten, George Lynes, Charles Demuth, Robert Locher, and Paul Cadmus, his images contribute enormously to our knowledge of a world that existed alongside and within the better-known artistic, cultural, and social environments occupied by members of New York's avant-garde as a group.

Thus, as we near the end of Ewing's own story, it is worth stepping back to consider the broad question of the "queer eye" and the significance of the images presented here for the history of US culture in the 1920s and early '30s. Ewing's photographs and photo collections were produced and exhibited in his own self-invented queer space: the studio and gallery that he created within his apartment. Here he could entertain his friends, tell stories, play music on the piano, enjoy informal performances of song and dance and — most important — establish an alternative zone of artistic production and queer sociability in his adopted city. He circulated his images widely, sharing them with family, friends, and acquaintances, thus sending his distinctive way of seeing to places well beyond the physical space of his home. As such, he expanded his network in ever-widening circles of influence and established his queer presence far beyond the boundaries of his physical environment: indeed, despite being produced almost one hundred years ago, Ewing's photographs introduce his queer milieu — physical, psychic, and cultural — and his point of view to present-day observers with the same dramatic flair that they did when he first exhibited them. He is thus an invaluable guide to an unfamiliar world.

Like all works of art, Ewing's photographs reflect the visual culture of his time and place as well as his own experience of the world around him and the centuries of art history that preceded him. Paintings, sculptures, sketchbooks, newspapers, billboards, fan magazines, advertising illustrations, snapshots, and the broad spectrum of images with which he was familiar, both consciously or unconsciously, inform his choices, as do the particularities of the queer visual culture that he inhabited. He was an avid museumgoer who studied the history of art and photography in both the United States and Europe: his portraits drew on those resources as well as his own sense of the new possibilities for contemporary photography and portraiture, which were being intensively explored by his artist friends.[1] As we have seen, he was also an energetic collector of queer ephemera, including bodybuilding magazines and photographs, humorous postcards, and erotica.

Despite his sophisticated knowledge of art, Ewing composed his own images in a rather conventional manner, often representing women in the familiar "glamour" poses of movie stars, fashion models, and divas (which, of course, many of them actually were), or snapping informal photos of couples clowning around, as in the case of the Seldeses or Paul Flato and Spivy illustrated in the previous chapter. As we know, he asked his friends to choose costumes and props for their photographic sojourns "in Venice," recreating the familiar tropes of popular snapshots in his made-up scenes. Similarly, when photographing male nudes for the *Carnival of Venice* series, he frequently posed his subjects in the familiar gestures and stances of artists' models, holding spears like classical Roman warriors or reclining on their elbows like Michelangelo's Sistine nudes, thus mediating between the reality of his focused scrutiny of naked male bodies and the fictive realm of conventional artistic imagery. This was also the format favored by the bodybuilder Anthony Sansone and by the Ritter brothers (fig. I.1), whose modeling photos both Ewing and George Platt Lynes collected.[2]

Unlike Lynes, whose images unfailingly express the immediacy of sensual beauty and sexuality, even when his models, both male and female, are staged in narrative scenarios, Ewing consistently maintained a distanced gaze, reflecting his rather old-fashioned notions of propriety, even as he sought and embraced the pleasure of looking. Despite being a passionate connoisseur and a committed modernist, Ewing was limited by both his amateur ambitions and goals: he had spent his life studying and performing music, after all, not in the studio or with a sketchbook in hand. What he most enjoyed was observing the world around him in the company of his illustrious friends, just as Florine Stettheimer had depicted him in her *Cathedrals of Fifth Avenue*.[3] Ultimately, he was a collector, an impresario, and a commentator whose photos were aids to memory and storytelling: he brought people and pictures together, preserving and narrating his experiences through his images and, of course, in his wonderfully vivid letters. The gallery in his walk-in closet, his *Collection of Extraordinary Portraits* (with its catalogue), and his *Carnival of Venice* series were his most significant contributions to the art of his time, capturing the extraordinary appearance of the men and women he knew or admired and preserving the ephemeral existence of a magical circle in which he was accepted and valued.

In his life as in his art, Ewing was deliberate and circumspect, choosing his role models carefully, and fashioning his queer identity and stylish persona out of the bits and pieces of other people's attitudes and habits. He modeled his sophisticated hauteur about art and music on Muriel Draper's charismatic manner and adapted his camp performance and frenzied collecting activities from the example set by Carl Van Vechten. Surrounded by a large group of queer friends of various ages and backgrounds, Ewing learned to deploy layers of camouflage and codes of communication needed to protect himself in his queer world-within-a-world. These were the codes that he mastered as he performed a variety of roles and identities, wending his way through the complex, intersecting networks that he encountered in the city.[4] Most important, these were the codes that informed the images he created.

As a photographer, Ewing lacked the self-discipline and training of the serious artists he knew, but his tastes and aspirations — like so many of his habits and attitudes — reflected theirs: with the full-length male nudes he created for *The Carnival of Venice*, he sought to impress the members of his circle and to bring them, and himself, the pleasure of looking. While that series can be seen both as a reflection of the emerging genre of informal, relational portraiture epitomized by the work of Berenice Abbott and Carl Van Vechten, and as an offshoot — however distant — of the new narrative approach to fashion photography created by George Lynes and others in the 1930s, Ewing's photographs ultimately are most valuable as a record of the look and spirit of the avant-garde in New York City in the '30s and, perhaps more important, as evidence of one of the many ways of seeing practiced among them.

IMAGING QUEER NEW YORK

The social and cultural geography of New York's avant-garde art world has been
extensively documented and analyzed by historians such as Steven Watson
and Edward White, as have various aspects of the Harlem Renaissance and the
many forms of popular entertainment, especially those related to the immigrant
experience in the period from the 1910s to the 1930s.[5] As we have seen,
Ewing and his friends often moved freely from one milieu and neighborhood to
another, crisscrossing the city, from Greenwich Village to the Upper West Side,
and from Times Square to Harlem.[6] Even within these circles, however, queer
sexuality and social life, though tacitly acknowledged, were highly circumscribed
and rarely if ever named: the lingua franca of the time is reflected in the discourse
of fictional characters like Van Vechten's Duke of Middlebottom, "a British,
monocle-sporting bisexual dandy" who spouted phrases like "a thing of beauty is
a boy forever," setting a tone of knowing innuendo characteristic of what
Kirsten MacLeod calls "arched brow modernism."[7] Indeed, as historians like
George Chauncey, Kevin Mumford, and Lisa Barg have shown, though many young
men and women participated in the broad sexual and cultural revolution of
their time, embracing queer and interracial relationships, they often remained
content to let the details of their own or their friends' private lives and
unconventional marriages remain shrouded by veils of irony and humor and
hidden behind closed doors.[8]

Given this secrecy, can we ever know what queer New York looked like or
sounded like, or imagine the spaces that queer men and women inhabited?
Fortunately, a handful of surviving works of art and ephemera offer valuable
clues. Even the most accomplished camp performers occasionally let down their
guard and, as in Max Ewing's case, even the most closely guarded secrets
sometimes slip from behind the curtain. Taken together, fragments of diaries,
letters, and snapshots, along with the rare drawings, watercolors, and
photographs that have survived and come to light, form a legible picture, like
pieces of a jigsaw puzzle, if we look at them as a group.[9] What thus emerges is a
new geography, a sort of "queer archipelago" of spaces and places, both public
and private, dispersed throughout the city and known to a select few: cabarets,
bars, dance halls, and cafeterias of the sort described by Chauncey in *Gay New
York*, bookstores that functioned as gathering places for friends and kindred
spirits, like those run by Sylvia Beach and Adrienne Monnier in Paris in the 1920s,
and, of course, the many private homes and studios like Van Vechten's or Draper's
or Max Ewing's where parties, readings, informal concerts, and private
conversations took place.[10]

The making and circulation of images by the denizens of this archipelago
yield evidence, both visual and textual, which can be read "against the grain"
of homophobic repression. Despite the challenges for historians, we know that
the period of the 1920s and '30s in New York was a time when queer artists
and writers often pushed the boundaries of "propriety," creating images of queer
celebration and resistance across a wide spectrum of forms, from Van Vechten's
collages of erotic and humorous clippings, to Charles Demuth's private sketches
and watercolors showing scenes of gay life, to George Lynes's explicit and joyful
celebration of queer sexuality and desire. By circulating these images, these
artists participated in what Nick Mauss and Angela Miller have called "queer
world-making," documenting and validating their alternative realm.[11] In this same

way, with his *Gallery*, his scrapbooks, and his *Carnival of Venice*, Max Ewing was very much a maker and preserver of queer space.

VAN VECHTEN'S SECRET SCRAPBOOKS

As we have with so many other aspects of Max Ewing's life, it is to Carl Van Vechten, his friend, mentor, and archivist, that we must turn first. As Jonathan Weinberg first pointed out in an essay entitled "Boy Crazy," Van Vechten's quest for queer and unconventional imagery was an outgrowth of his tireless pursuit of celebrity and his experience of queer and mixed-race cabarets and bars throughout his adult life: "His art ... was eclipsed by the pursuit of what might be called the extracurricular activities of modernism," as Weinberg wrote, "knowing the right people, having the right things, above all being seen in the right places at the right time."[12] Illustrating his observation with a watercolor of a "cabaret interior" from 1918 by Charles Demuth (fig. I.2), Van Vechten's friend and fellow denizen of the queer demimonde, Weinberg noted the fascinating mix of people who gathered in such places to talk, drink, and dance. On the far left of the image, we can recognize Van Vechten himself — tall, blonde, white-faced, and clearly relaxed in his element — as he sits on a sofa and carries on an animated conversation with a fashionably dressed woman. In the middle of the group, Demuth placed himself, wearing a brown corduroy suit and soft, black hat, and standing in his characteristic, hipshot posture (the result of a childhood injury), his hand in his back pocket, leaning against a small, white chair that he tips away from himself to support his weight. On the far right, a group of musicians, including one with brown skin, plays a song for the benefit of two sailors who dance in a tight clutch of arms and legs: here, as was his habit, Demuth carefully outlines the muscular legs and buttocks of the sailor who faces away from him.

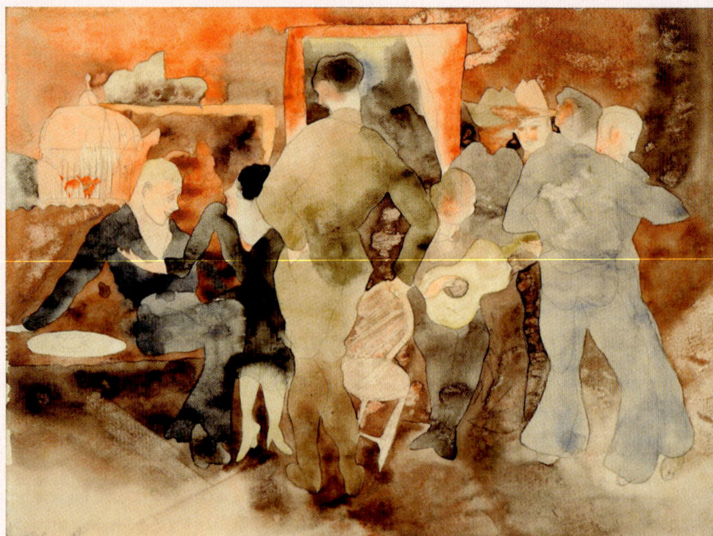

I.2 Charles Demuth, *Cabaret Interior with Carl Van Vechten*, 1917, watercolor, pen, and pencil on paper, 7¾ × 10¾ in. (19.7 × 27.3 cm). Collection of Barbara Millhouse, Reynolda Museum of Art.

Here as elsewhere, Demuth's work opens a window onto this little-known milieu, not only visually describing the lively scene, but placing himself and Van Vechten squarely in the middle of it. This was the world of queer people and experiences that greeted Max Ewing when he first arrived in New York and sat in Van Vechten's "red and yellow silk-lined" living room in the Fairfax Arms in 1923, five years after Demuth's watercolor was painted, and this is the world that Van Vechten documented in his diaries, novels, photographs, and scrapbooks as he set about the work of recording, collecting, and cataloguing the habits, words, faces, and, wherever possible, the intimate experiences of the those around him. Van Vechten never shied away from including himself in this ever-expanding miscellany. Indeed, his autobiography describes the origins of his insatiable quest for images and texts in the loss he experienced as a child when his father decided to burn the bundles of old letters that Carl and his mother had retrieved from the attic: his mother "wept softly" beside him, he recalled, and he himself came to "regret ... and wish [he] had them back, for they were filled with a discussion of old matters that it would be pleasant to read about today, and some of them were love letters, and I should have liked to know how my father made love to my mother."[13]

While Ewing, unlike Van Vechten, wasn't inclined to plumb the depths of his own psyche or interrogate the motives that lay behind his zeal for collecting, both men shared their passion, and, of course, their best "finds," with their mothers; indeed, both took comfort in surrounding themselves with the clippings and photos that brought a jumble of famous people, distant places, and private memories into their living rooms and albums. As Van Vechten's biographer Edward White put it, "The scrapbooks were his attempt to possess beauty in much the same way that a lepidopterist pins butterflies to a board. Held in stasis between the covers of his books, the luminaries of the theater who swept into town never really left: they and the glamour they exuded were with Carl, always."[14] We saw a similar process in Ewing's *Gallery* and in his *Carnival of Venice* series.

A fascination with celebrity clearly dominated the lives of both Van Vechten and Ewing, but both men also harbored other passions, as is clearly shown by their collections of male nudes and queer erotica. For his *Carnival of Venice* series, Ewing took control of those images, stage-managing and producing full-length, nude photographs of a handful of friends. The fact that many of these photographs were removed from Ewing's archive after his death and subsequently repurposed (without attribution) in Van Vechten's scrapbooks highlights their value as evidence of the diversity of queer experiences and artistic ambitions that flourished in the 1920s and '30s.[15]

It is also significant that while Ewing's photographic archive was sanitized by literally cropping out evidence of male nudity as well as any suggestion of erotic intent, Van Vechten's own homoerotic scrapbooks at Yale had a different fate: sealed for twenty-five years after his death, they were only made available to librarians and scholars in 1989, some twenty years after Stonewall. Perhaps he had an inkling of the sea change that the gay liberation movement would produce in the intervening years. Indeed, in many ways, Van Vechten's scrapbooking activities set the stage for these changes: assembled between the 1920s and his death in 1964, they document a wide array of queer images and erotica, popular slang, significant events, and the homophobia that persisted across the span of Van Vechten's life. In many ways they also serve as a collaged and multilayered autobiography that sheds new light on both Van Vechten and his self-imposed task as collector, archivist, and historian of queer — albeit mostly male — life and culture.[16]

Nevertheless, it is only after we are able to get past the campy slogans and the sometimes-startling array of queer erotica, that the significance of Van Vechten's accomplishment fully emerges. Looking at the eighteen scrapbooks as a group, it is easy to be overwhelmed by the sheer profusion of collaged pages or lulled into an overloaded stupor by the obsessively collected and frequently repetitious examples of camp humor. Moreover, for some observers, as the historian James Smalls explains, the eroticism of the nudes and the stark depictions of interracial sexuality can be powerful and distracting in a visceral and emotional sense, making them difficult to scrutinize objectively as historical evidence.[17]

Much is revealed if we persevere: for Van Vechten, the scrapbooks were a repository not only of queer imagery but also of queer experience as he knew it in his lifetime, showcasing the wide array of tastes and types that he encountered.

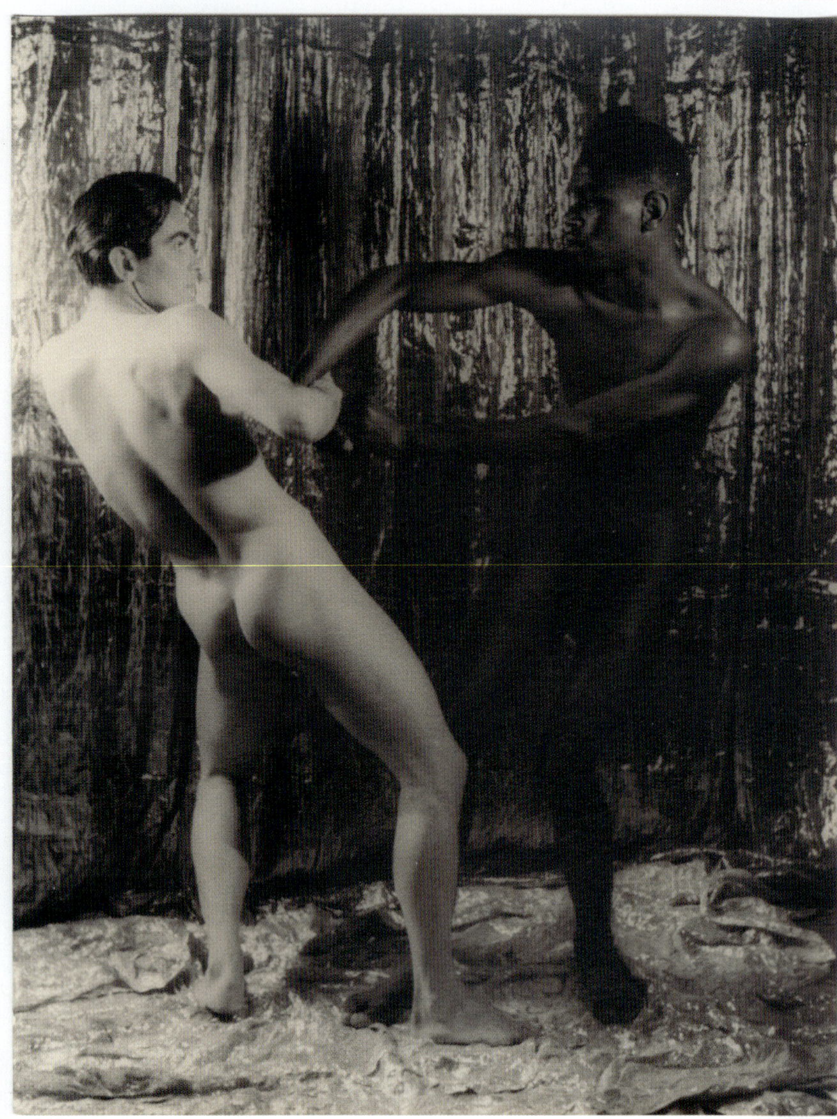

When compared with the many items of explicit erotica that Van Vechten pasted into his scrapbooks — racist photos of naked, dark-skinned boys, or of sailors masturbating, or sketches of men engaged in sex acts of various kinds — Ewing's images appear rather tame and prurient, suggesting an almost childlike curiosity about the nakedness of other people that could only be satisfied by the pleasure of convincing them to remove their clothing in his studio-bedroom. Moreover, when compared with a photographer like George Platt Lynes, who always foregrounds sexuality and erotic beauty in his images, both Ewing and Van Vechten seem more old-fashioned, camp, and "arched brow" than ever. Ewing's nude models almost always look away from the camera, for example, modestly refusing the photographer's gaze: only Paul Meeres, an experienced performer with his extraordinary body fully exposed, confidently looks back and engages with the camera. Even in the rare instances where more than one person occupies the frame, opening up the possibility of narrative and intersubjective engagement — as is the case with his snapshots of the Ritter brothers — the awkward pairings seem more goofy than sexy, especially when viewed side by side with Lynes's artistic images of the Ritters' nude, entwined bodies (discussed in the prologue).

Van Vechten's interests, both historical and sexual, were realized through the images in his private archive, which ranged from explicit erotica to humorous ephemera, like the menu showing the Marx Brothers in drag that Ewing presented to Van Vechten as an addition to his "Collection of Amatory Curiosa," as Ewing called it (see fig. 0.6). Like Ewing, he told stories through pictures, using collaged texts to create new, camp meanings for the images; unlike Lynes, who achieved his artistic effect through the skillful deployment of the subtle "amorous glance," as critic Elspeth Brown put it, the images that Van Vechten preferred left little to the imagination.[18]

In Van Vechten's own explicitly queer photographs — a genre he only began to experiment with in the mid- to late 1930s — he never seems to have moved beyond awkward, staged scenarios: he consistently focused on highly choreographed poses of naked teenagers and young men in interracial pairs, either standing in front of reflective foil backdrops in his studio (fig. I.3), or posing dramatically in pastoral, outdoor settings.[19] Often the interactions between his favorite young models — the African American teenager Allen Juante Meadows and the white ballet dancer Hugh Laing — suggested the possibility of sexual encounters between the two young men through highly stylized, and often cringeworthy poses and implied narratives. When he added examples of these photographs to his scrapbooks, he sometimes also included the sort of collaged joke texts that he added to Ewing's snapshots of the Ritter brothers, Paul Meeres, and others. In some cases, he reused the same photographs multiple times, simply adding different captions to create new meanings, and swapping images in and out of the scrapbooks to suit his whims over a period of decades.

Ewing's photographs are different: he used props and costumes as elements of masquerade that enabled his sitters to assume their chosen roles in his fictive carnival; for him, Venice was both the literal backdrop and the dramatic setting for the characters — gondoliers, Venetian ladies, sailors, and so on — that his sitters assumed. As such, they seem far more like the characters that Ewing and his childhood friends created using the costumes from the dress-up box in the room above his parents' store than objects of desire. Ewing's purpose was primarily to have fun and to collect portraits of the people he knew. If they took off their clothes, so much the better: he liked to look and he loved the shock value of the images when he showed them to his friends.

The alterations that Van Vechten made to Ewing's photos shed light on his own, more far-reaching ambitions. When he added these images to his scrapbooks, he sometimes cropped out the heads and legs (fig. I.4) to better focus on the form of the torso and genitals (although sometimes obscured by later overpainting), just as Arnold Genthe had done with his *Modern Torso* in 1918 or as Alfred Stieglitz did in his portrait series of Georgia O'Keeffe. More often, he left these images intact as documentation, adding to the encyclopedic quality of his project. As James Smalls noted in his study of Van Vechten's homoerotic images, for Van Vechten,

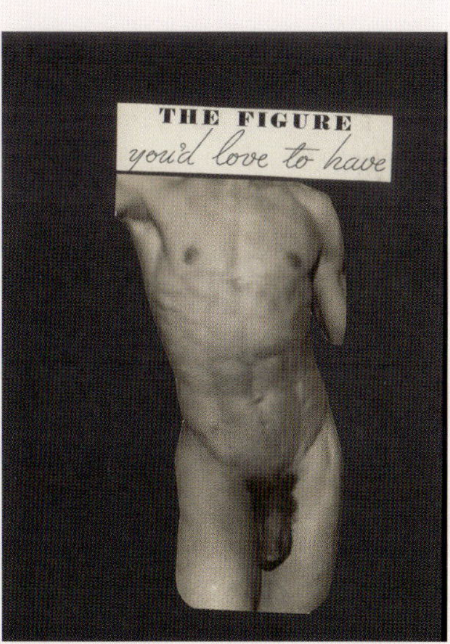

I.4 Carl Van Vechten, "The Figure You'd Love to Have," collage with Max Ewing's photograph of Paul Meeres (cropped) and found text, from Carl Van Vechten's scrapbook.

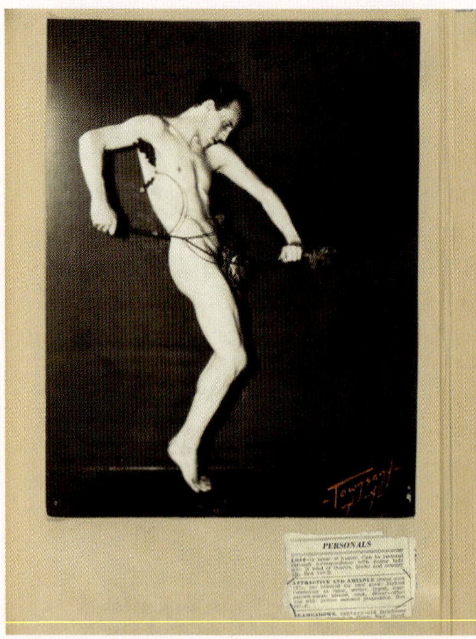

I.5 Carl Van Vechten, "Personals," collage with Edwin F. Townsend's photograph of Robert Gorham (inscribed to Max Ewing) and found text, from Carl Van Vechten's scrapbook.

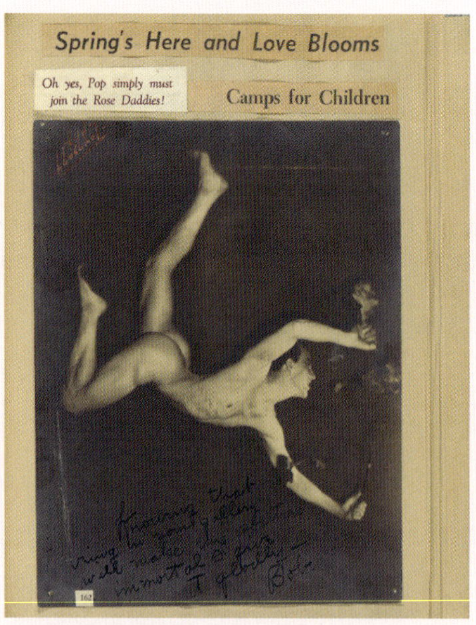

I.6 Carl Van Vechten, "Spring's Here," collage with Edwin F. Townsend's photograph of Robert Gorham (upside down) and found text, from Carl Van Vechten's scrapbook.

the act of photography was critical to [his] psychological and social definition. Not only was it his intention to use it as outlet for both artistic expression and instrument of cultural/racial documentation, he also employed the medium as a means of popular myth-making about himself in relationship to African-Americans and to modern gay culture — a strategy that helped to bolster his success and notoriety during and even after the period of "negromania" … that typified the Harlem Renaissance.[20]

Drawing on his broad knowledge of the history of art and steeped in the codes of queer culture, Van Vechten treated his scrapbooks as a complex and multilayered fabric of differing artistic modes, changing registers, and shifting viewpoints, alternating between portraiture, homoerotic fantasy, camp performance, and historical evidence gathering.[21] Thus, as Jonathan Weinberg remarked in "Boy Crazy," while these scrapbooks may not be unique in the history of queer collecting, the variety and breadth of the images, as well as their "encyclopedic and historical quality," makes them an extraordinary resource.[22]

This is especially true of the many nudes by other photographers that Van Vechten removed from Ewing's collection and repurposed in his own. These images include three striking, high-contrast studies made in the studio of Edwin Townsend — the go-to photographer for body builders like Sansone and the Ritters — showing Ewing's friend Robert Gorham, who was "just about the handsomest spectacle the world," as Ewing put it in 1926.[23] One, inscribed "To Max" (fig. I.5) is clearly visible at the bottom of the wall in the photo of Ewing's *Gallery* as it existed in 1928, while another (fig. I.6), also inscribed, was rotated ninety degrees to make the figure appear to be flying through space. A third photo depicts Gorham as though he were running across a stage carrying large round shields or cymbals in his hands (fig. I.7); here Van Vechten added the words "Clad Only in a Shriek, Was Too Gay for the Romans." Another Townsend nude, inscribed

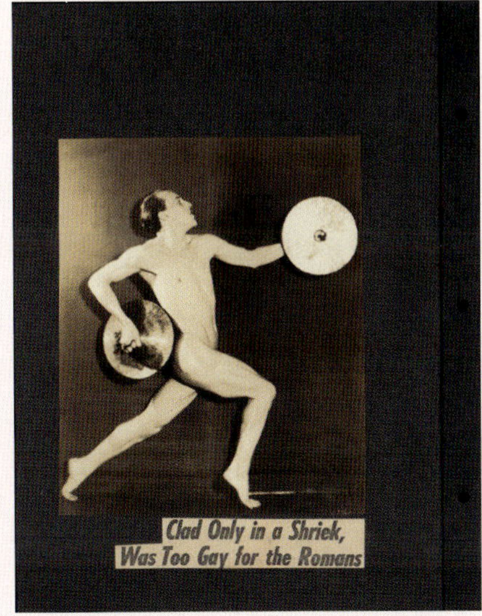

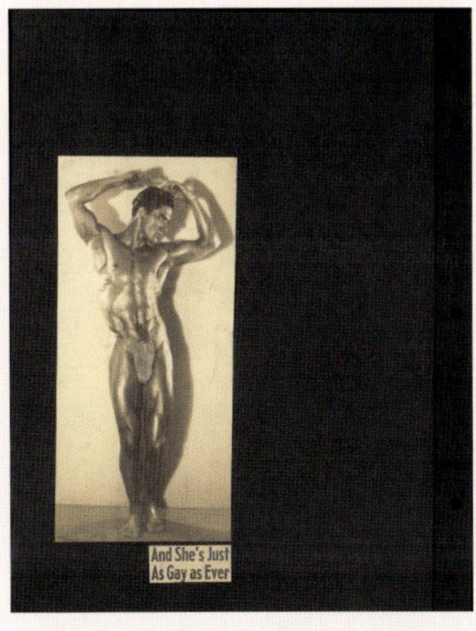

I.7 Carl Van Vechten, "Clad Only in a Shriek," collage with photograph of Robert Gorham and found text, Carl Van Vechten's scrapbook.

I.8 Carl Van Vechten, "As Gay as Ever," collage with photograph of Anthony Sansone and found text, from Carl Van Vechten's scrapbook.

"to Max" by "James Stewart," a friend about whom nothing more is known, also appears in the scrapbooks with the caption "such a vast ass" and "Fag Record." These were clearly the sort of photos that Ewing's family wanted destroyed.

Van Vechten had other ideas. Although these images appealed to his taste for camp and sometimes childish humor, the historical aspect of his work as a collector was also important to him. Both he and Ewing continually strove to stay up to date with the latest developments in music, theater, film, politics, and culture, including the study of homosexuality and the exploration of changing attitudes toward men like themselves: as noted earlier, in December 1930, they attended a three-hour lecture in German (no doubt illustrated with slides) by the queer sexologist Magnus Hirschfeld who was then touring the United States ("we didn't understand all he said by any means," Ewing admitted to his mother).[24] The two men followed the marathon presentation with a meal at a German restaurant where they talked and compared notes on what they had heard. In another example of their shared interest, Van Vechten wrote to Ewing in November 1933 to ask if he had read the recently published *The Young and Evil* (an explicitly queer novel by Charles Henri Ford and Parker Tyler), adding that he'd had a party for another queer writer, the expat American Julien Green, "to which you would probably have been invited had you been here."[25]

Given his wide-ranging interests, it isn't surprising that Van Vechten's scrapbooks also contain examples of virtually every homophobic epithet and stereotype in existence, from swish "boyish" types — like the dancer Paul Swan who was "as light as a matchstick" — to buff bodybuilders like Anthony Sansone (fig. I.8), whose portrait was captioned "And She's Just as Gay as Ever." Another photo of Sansone is juxtaposed with a small newspaper clipping that noted "Of course all artists aren't queer … but some of them are acting that way for commercial reasons," a sentiment that both Ewing and Van Vechten would both have considered hilarious. Although we don't know exactly when these collages were assembled, most of the homophobic terms we find in them were in circulation during Ewing's lifetime, including the familiar "pansy" and "fairy" and "gay" — as we saw in a newspaper clipping that Ewing sent to Muriel Draper

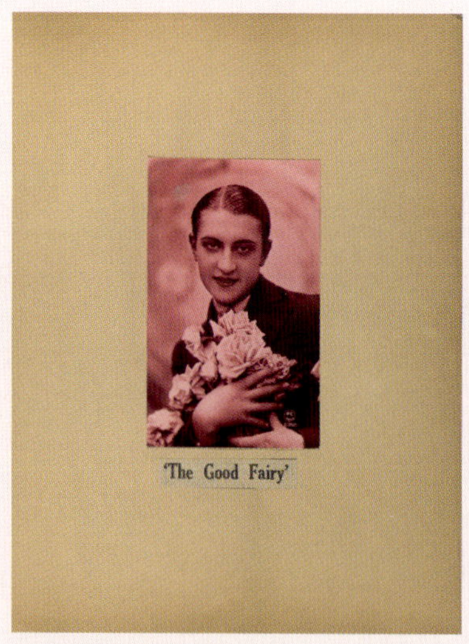

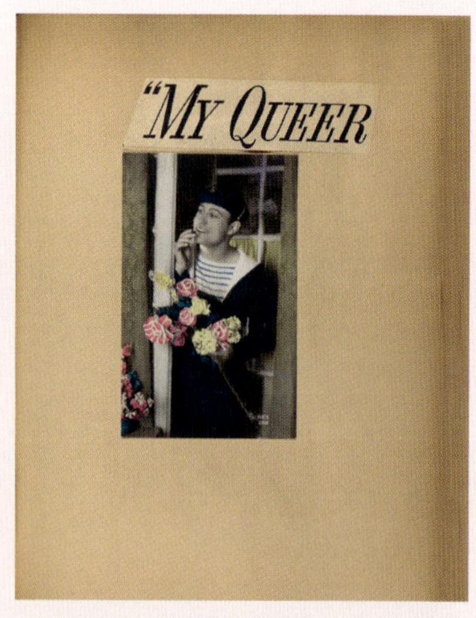

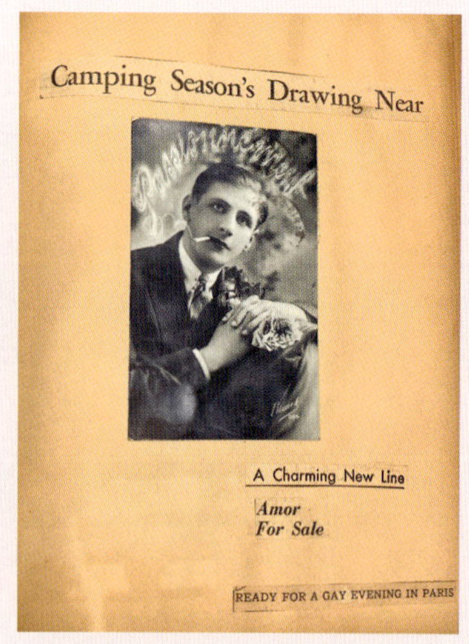

I.9 Carl Van Vechten, "The Good Fairy," collage with hand-colored postcard and found text, from Carl Van Vechten's scrapbook.

I.10 Carl Van Vechten, "My Queer," collage with hand-colored postcard and found text, from Carl Van Vechten's scrapbook.

I.11 Carl Van Vechten, "Camping Season," collage with found photograph and found text, from Carl Van Vechten's scrapbook.

because she "liked gay things" — as well as "queer," "sissy," and "fag."[26] A page in the scrapbooks assembled in the 1930s includes listings for the "Pansy Club," the 1931 "Pansy Ball," and a cabaret revue titled "Pansies on Parade"; there is also a rare "Certificate of Membership" for the "Ancient Order of Pansies of America" that touted "full opportunities to meet each other's friends and sailors." There are numerous examples of "fairies," "sissies," "queens," and "queers," including "The Good Fairy" (fig. I.9), "My Queer" (fig. I.10), and a "Greek Queen" who "Lives Up to Her Advance Billing." These pages are loaded with all sorts of other double-entendres as well, from "Back Room Belle" and "Ready for a Gay Evening in Paris" (fig. I.11), to "There's one in Every Town" and "[If] You Want a Wife: Write Me at Once."

As his friends and acquaintances knew very well, Van Vechten *had* a wife, Fania Marinoff, whom he loved, fought with, and remained close to in a marriage that lasted for fifty years. As a role model who showed his young friends how to manage "the closet," Van Vechten was unequaled: he even had himself photographed standing in his bathrobe beside the open door of the closet in his home, both alone and with his wife by his side (see chapter 2). On one of his scrapbook pages, Van Vechten even pasted two small snippets of text that say it all: "Do I have to be Frustrated?" and "I have been leading a double life and I don't intend to stop." These words appear next to five images of athletic men in bathing trunks and bikinis: on the top right of the page is a photo of a boyish Fred Ritter in Florida, probably removed from Ewing's collection.[27]

Van Vechten had sufficient wealth and privilege to afford an enormous amount of latitude in his daily life, both professional and private, and in his domestic arrangements. He clearly refused to have his identities — as a white man with many Black friends, as a husband with an active gay life, or as a denizen, and a cultural leader, of New York's queer and avant-garde bohemia — limited by external categories or marked by labels imposed by others. He shrugged off the disappointment and anger of his friends among the leaders of the Harlem Renaissance who chastised him for using the N-word in the title of his novel, and he turned a deaf ear to sexologists who labeled him a pervert.[28] While many critics and scholars have been unable to account for these seemingly contradictory values and views, or for his fetishistic pursuit of Black and Asian bodies (so clearly reflected in the erotic fantasies depicted in his photographs of Meadows and Laing, for example), it seems clear that he approached matters of race in much the same way as he navigated the challenges of sexuality: he simply did what he wanted, refusing all efforts to describe and, more important, to categorize, restrain, or stigmatize him. The more we know him, the more he seems like a radical change-maker who embraced the sort of poetic and unfettered risk-taking encouraged by the notion of "fugitivity": "consent not to being a single individual," wrote the critic and philosopher Fred Moten — this could easily have served as Van Vechten's motto as he navigated the many worlds of avant-garde New York.[29] He certainly had the privilege and the insatiable curiosity about his own evolving identity to carry it off.

VAN VECHTEN'S QUEER GAZE

As literary scholar Emily Bernard has suggested, Van Vechten represents a rare instance of someone who could hold more than one idea, or one emotion, in his head at a time, even if these were contradictory or ultimately rejected and cast aside over the course of his long life. As Bernard described him in a talk at Yale's Beinecke Library in 2017:

> He loved black bodies, and he loved the spectacle of blackness, just like any other white pleasure-seekers who made pilgrimages uptown. Like those he spirited uptown, Van Vechten was attracted to the tolerant atmosphere toward homosexuality that colored Harlem nightlife. But while Carl's early interest in blackness may have been inspired by sexual desire and his fascination with primitivism, these features were not what sustained his interest in black people and black culture, and his beliefs changed and expanded over the course of his forty-year love affair with black art.[30]

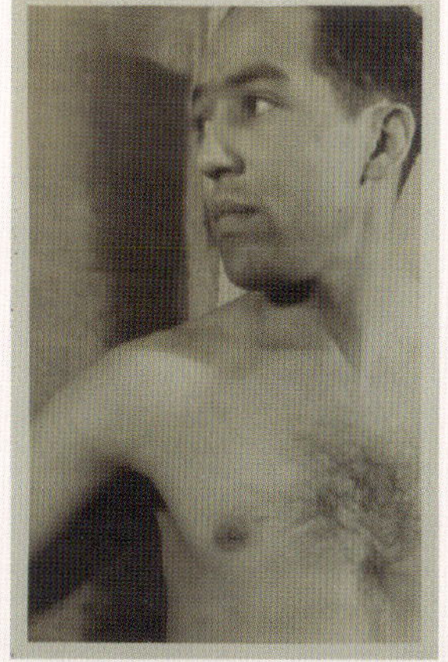

I.12 Carl Van Vechten, *Portrait of Langston Hughes*, March 27, 1932.

Close associates like Langston Hughes (fig. I.12), who was also gay, and Paul Robeson (fig. I.13), who emphatically wasn't, accepted these idiosyncrasies as unique to their friend, and perhaps even recognized that his "love affair with black art," as Bernard put it, extended to them as artists and not simply as Black men. Why else would they have been among the first to subject themselves to his queer gaze, posing in his studio seminude (according to the standards of the time), with their shirts off, as the entertainers Jimmie Daniels and Tonio Selwart (see figs. 4.32–4.34) had done? Van Vechten refused all limits, and he even turned the same inquisitive gaze on himself, going so far as making a series of seminude, shirtless portraits of his own, chubby, white body, seemingly without even a hint of self-consciousness (fig. I.14). His pose suggests camp performance, but his lack of clothing and his imperfect physique make him vulnerable in significant ways.

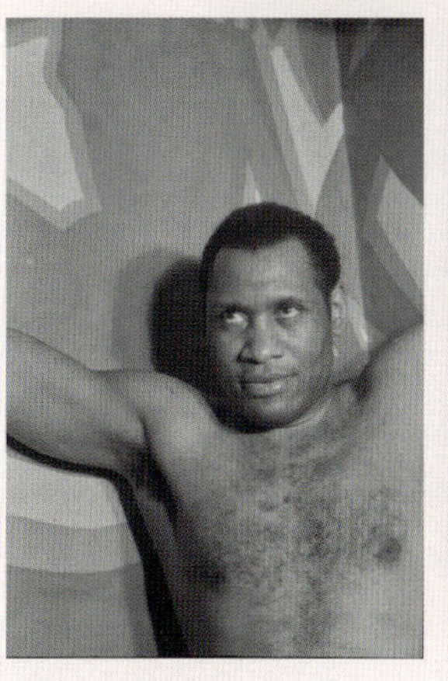

I.13 Carl Van Vechten, *Portrait of Paul Robeson*, March 7, 1932.

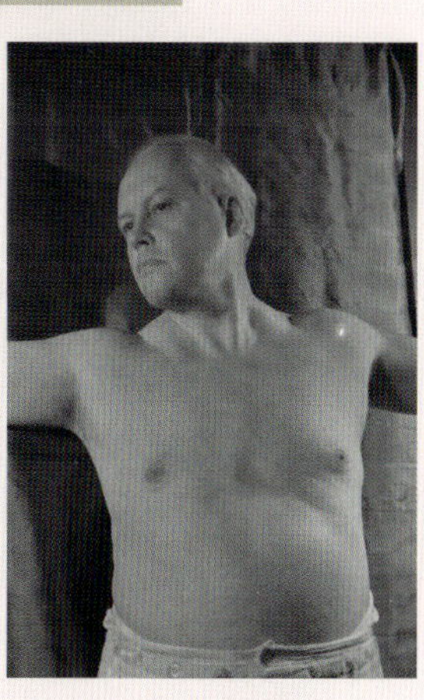

I.14 Carl Van Vechten, *Self-Portrait*, April 16, 1932.

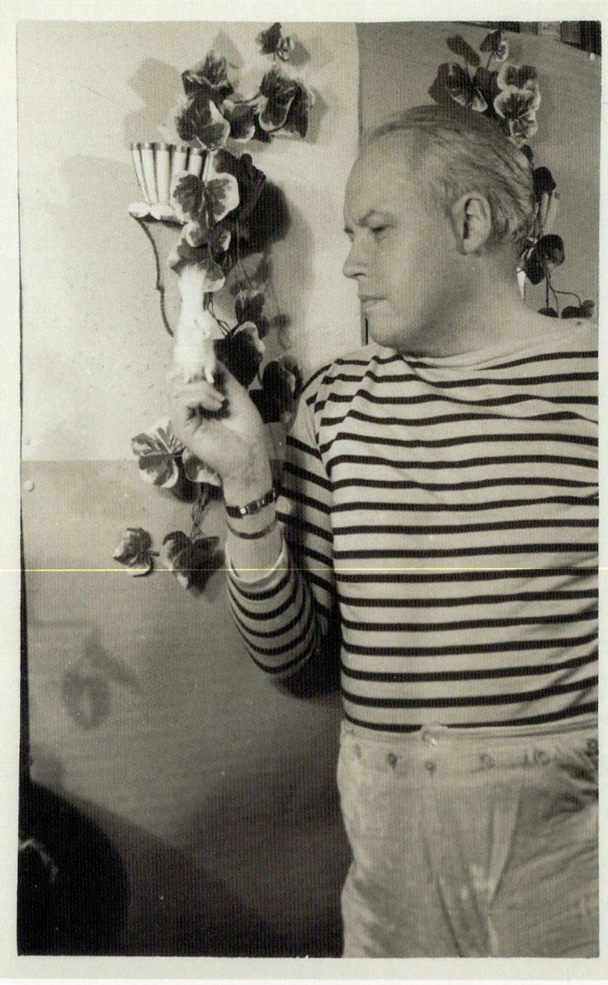

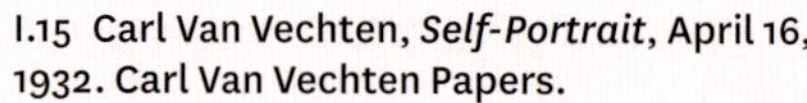

I.15 Carl Van Vechten, *Self-Portrait*, April 16, 1932. Carl Van Vechten Papers.

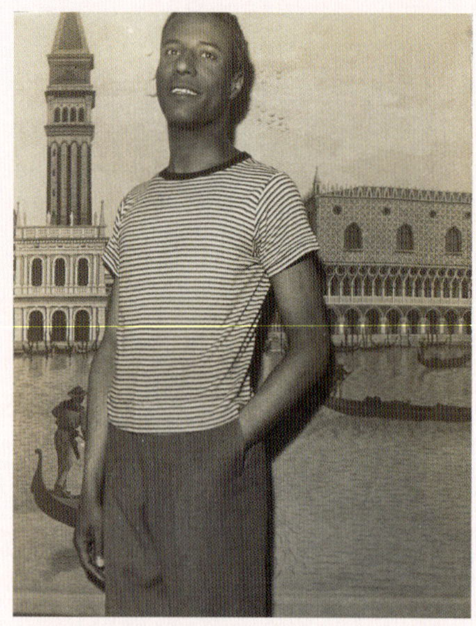

I.16 Max Ewing, *Harold Jackman*, from *The Carnival of Venice*.

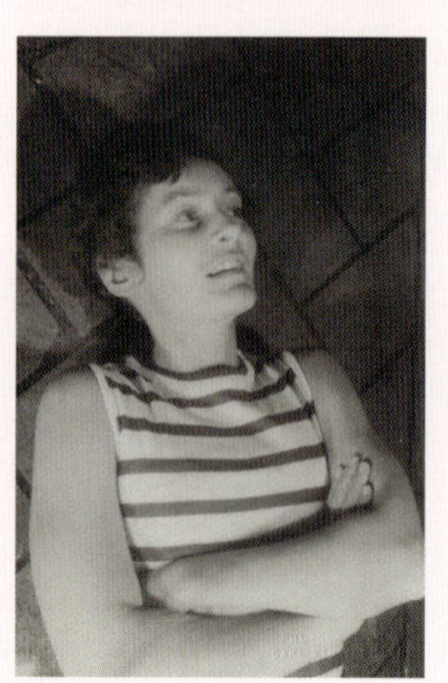

I.17 Carl Van Vechten, *Alice DeLamar*, May 2, 1932. Carl Van Vechten Papers.

Van Vechten loved posing, and he loved dressing up in costumes of all kinds, donning a sailor's striped jersey and white velvet trousers for a campy series of self-portraits in which he holds a stuffed toy of a white cat (fig. I.15). By 1932, when the self-portrait was made, sailors' uniforms had become ubiquitous among the fashionable elite and among expats on the Riviera and could be worn without irony or erotic intent: Ewing's portrait of Harold Jackman in *The Carnival of Venice* (fig. I.16) and Van Vechten's May 1932 portrait of Ewing's friend Alice DeLamar (fig. I.17) are just two of many such examples, as is the relatively early portrait of George Lynes sporting sailor pants and a skimpy jersey in Villefranche in 1928 that Ewing included in his *Gallery*.[31] By the end of the 1920s, the fad included white sailor pants like the ones in Van Vechten's self-portrait, as well as white or blue sailors' blouses, examples of which recur frequently in the pages of the *Carnival*, notably in the portraits of Muriel Draper's sons Paul (1909–96) and Saunders (1913–43) (nicknamed "Smudge") standing next to the Bridge of Sighs (fig. I.18). Like Van Vechten, Ewing sometimes wore a striped jersey, and even posed in a sailor's blouse and beret in 1932 with his cousin Doris (fig. I.19); he posted the image to her with the joking message that if she wasn't "very good" he would send a dozen copies of the postcard to the headmistress of the school where she

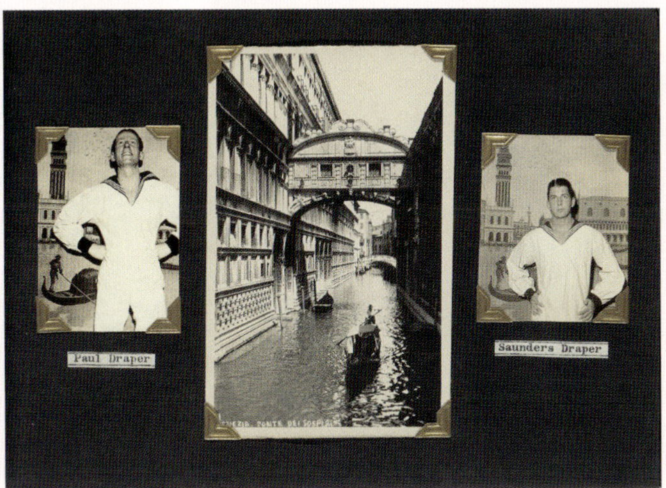

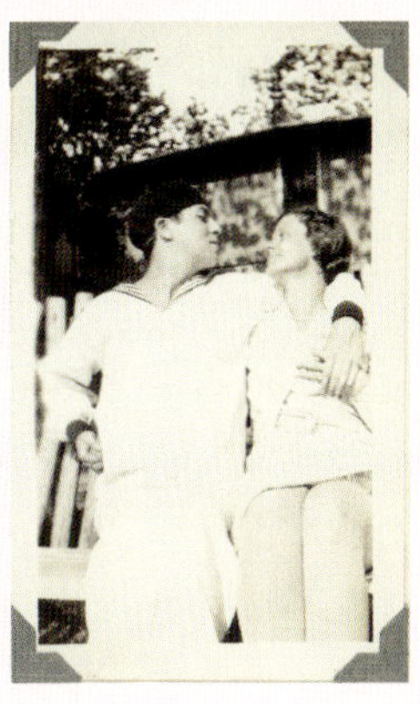

I.18 Max Ewing, *Paul and Saunders ("Smudge") Draper*, from *Les Amants de Venise*.

I.19 Anon., snapshot of Max Ewing in sailor shirt, with his cousin Doris Ewing, c. 1928. Max Ewing Papers.

worked: "Just try to convince her, if you can," he teased, "that I'm not a sailor you found somewhere."[32]

The images of sailors that Van Vechten preferred went well beyond popular enthusiasm for their distinctive, fashionable clothing, of course: in the scrapbooks, they are often depicted as the object of admiration or actor in erotic fantasies, both in humorous collages with repurposed texts ("Let this be the ONE HOT DISH") and in explicit images and stories depicting and describing sexual encounters.[33] The availability of sailors for every sort of risqué entertainment, including paid sex and quick hookups, was both a trope of fiction and a reality in the "slumming" adventures of Ewing and his friends. The evidence for this is everywhere in Ewing's archive, including photos of Ewing and his friends clowning around with a sailor they picked up in Paris in 1927, and numerous descriptions in his letters.[34] A letter from Alice DeLamar, written in May 30, 1934, when Ewing was seeing to his mother's financial and legal affairs in Pioneer, Ohio, offers a rare bit of gossip: she wrote that she wished he were back in New York: "Lots of fun is expected this week," she joked, "with the entire fleet in town — sorry you are not here to go bumming, as I have gotten some very superior information about some very special festivities that are to be staged in various sailors dives."[35] As Van Vechten quipped in his caption for one of Ewing's photos of Paul Meeres, showing him entirely nude except for a sailor's cap jauntily perched on his head and gesturing in a sprightly salute, "THE NAVY CALLS IT … and the Navy Knows."[36]

This was all serious fun but also seriously risky, as everyone knew. Only Van Vechten would have the audacity to push the limits of propriety still further, pasting a pair of condoms onto the page and exhorting his readers to "Play Safe" (fig. I.20). "Take This Precaution," he advised: here as in everything else in the unconventional world that Van Vechten created for himself and his friends, judgments might be suspended in favor of shock-effect and humor.

For Ewing and other young men, Van Vechten's queer collections told the story of queer life as they lived it, spoke it, heard it, and saw it. The scrapbooks allowed these men to see themselves in

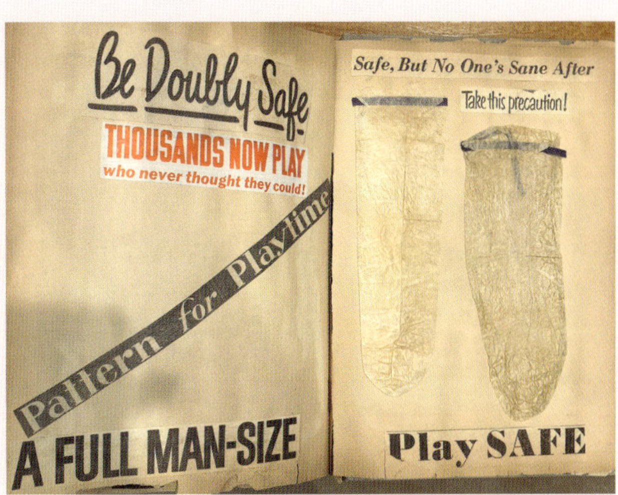

I.20 Carl Van Vechten, "Play Safe," collage with found text and condoms, from Carl Van Vechten's scrapbook.

ways that no other documents did. Van Vechten was their leader and mentor in this as in other areas of their lives, and the bonds that connected them were strong, even when they were physically apart. As he wrote to Ewing in the fall of 1933, some months after the younger man had left New York to try his luck in Hollywood, "I didn't see you very often in New York but it was nice to know you were here."[37] For Ewing and others — including the many poets, writers, models, and entertainers, Black and white, whose careers he supported and whose private lives he shared — the feeling was certainly mutual.

ON "THAT" STREET: QUEER IMAGERY IN THE WORK OF CHARLES DEMUTH
The image of the sexy sailor, like the examples discussed above, is ubiquitous in queer ephemera and fashion, and also, somewhat surprisingly, in some rare, private images painted by the American artist Charles Demuth. Like Carl Van Vechten, his friend and contemporary, Demuth had considerable experience in the queer and bohemian demimonde — as evidenced by the *Cabaret Interior with Carl Van Vechten* discussed above — and the two men shared a preference for erotic images of masculine, sexually available young men. A small but significant part of Demuth's artistic output was dedicated to exploring those fantasies and to recording images of the things he saw or simply imagined in that realm. Although it seems at first impossible that twenty-first-century viewers might be allowed glimpses of that secret, queer world, that is indeed what Demuth allows his viewers to do.

Thanks to the foundational work of art historians like Barbara Haskell, Betsy Fahlman, and Jonathan Weinberg, among others, and to the recent "Demuth Reinterpretation Project" (2022) that enabled the Demuth Museum to commission a handful of new studies interrogating the artist's relationship to LGBTQ culture, we now know a great deal more about the life and work of this brilliant yet elusive artist than we did a few decades ago.[38] Essays by Susan Ferentinos and Jonathan Katz are particularly helpful in situating Demuth in New York, Provincetown, and Paris and exploring the queer visual culture of those places. Other contributions to the museum's collection of new scholarship describe the artist's attraction to vaudeville and his affinity for the art of the sideshow. Because the artist created so many works related to queer life and locales, and because he remained closely associated with Max Ewing's good friends the Stettheimers, Carl Van Vechten, Robert and Beatrice Locher, and Muriel Draper until the time of his death in 1935, he is an indispensable source of visual information relating to the world that he and Ewing inhabited, and to closely guarded secrets rarely if ever shared beyond the queer demimonde.

Demuth's subjects included lovingly delineated views of sailors dancing together and with women (fig. I.21), as well as explicit images of men engaged in sexual encounters, both in the city (such as the 1930 *Two Sailors Urinating*, revisited by Barbara Haskell in a recent essay) and on the isolated beaches of Provincetown, a place that Demuth visited regularly. He patronized the cabarets of Harlem — though with nothing like the zeal or commitment of Van Vechten or Ewing — and the bars of Greenwich Village, and produced a number of extraordinary views of the Turkish bathhouses that catered to gay men, in some versions including himself among a group of naked men who chat among themselves while a variety of sexual encounters unfold around them (fig. I.22). Moreover, he was fearless, though characteristically rather camp and quirky,

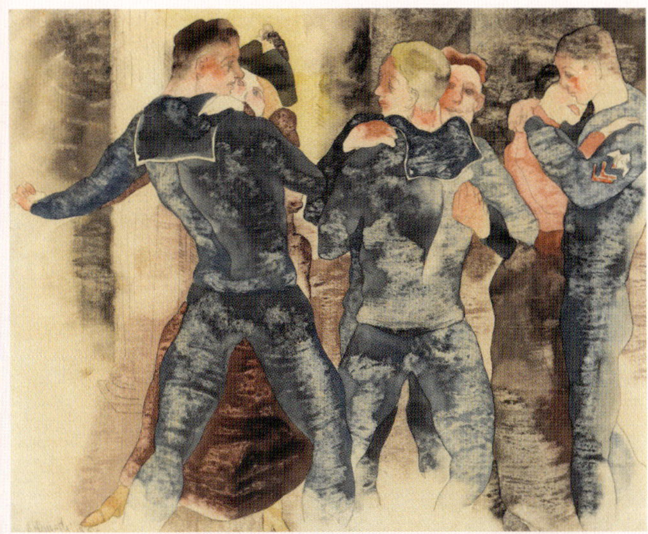

I.21 Charles Demuth, *Dancing Sailors*, 1918, watercolor and pencil on paper, 8 × 10 in. (20.3 × 25.4 cm). Museum of Modern Art, Abby Aldrich Rockefeller Fund, 147.1945.

I.23 Charles Demuth, *On "That" Street*, 1932, watercolor over graphite, on cream laid paper, laid down on ivory board, 11 × 8⁹⁄₁₆ in. (27.8 × 21.7 cm). Art Institute of Chicago, Alfred Stieglitz Collection, 1949.528.

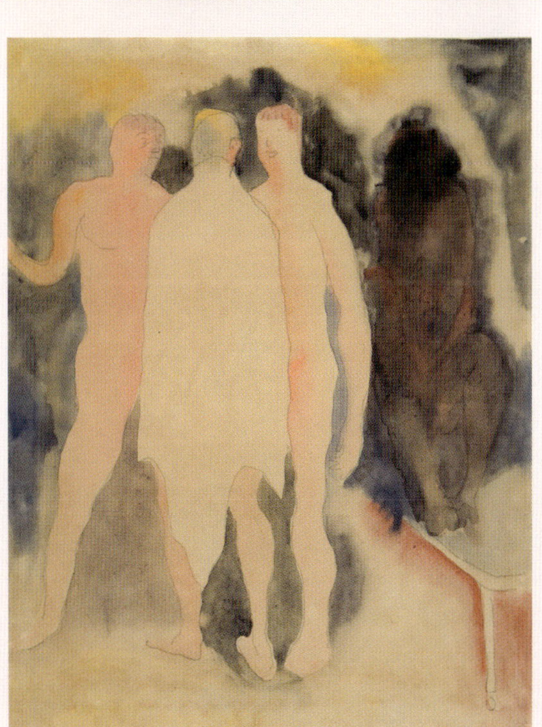

I.22 Charles Demuth, *Turkish Bath*, 1915, watercolor over graphite underdrawing, 8⁷⁄₁₆ × 10⁷⁄₈ in. (21.4 × 27.6 cm). Yale University Art Gallery. Gift of George Hopper Fitch, BA, 1932 1980.83.2.

in his depiction of a darkened street corner where older, middle-class men like himself met and picked up sailors. His 1932 watercolor, entitled *On "That" Street* (fig. I.23), showed a real place, identified by Jonathan Katz as Sands Street, near the Brooklyn Navy Yard, in which Demuth is clearly recognizable, hand on hip in his brown coat and hat, as an active participant, engaged in conversation with two sailors who, according to Katz, represent two poles in the spectrum of effeminate and masculine/butch types that were well-known to gay men.

Demuth was unique in his matter-of-fact representation of the erotic and titillating aspects of everyday life, but he also used his remarkable abilities as an artist to explore even more mundane subjects, such as the shame and sadness that could accompany one-night stands and hookups with the sex workers who catered to gay men. He depicted these in a series of three unprecedented sketches entitled *Eight O'Clock (Evening)*, *Eight O'Clock (Early Morning #1)*, and *Eight O'Clock (Morning #2)*, that were analyzed by Jonathan Weinberg in his study

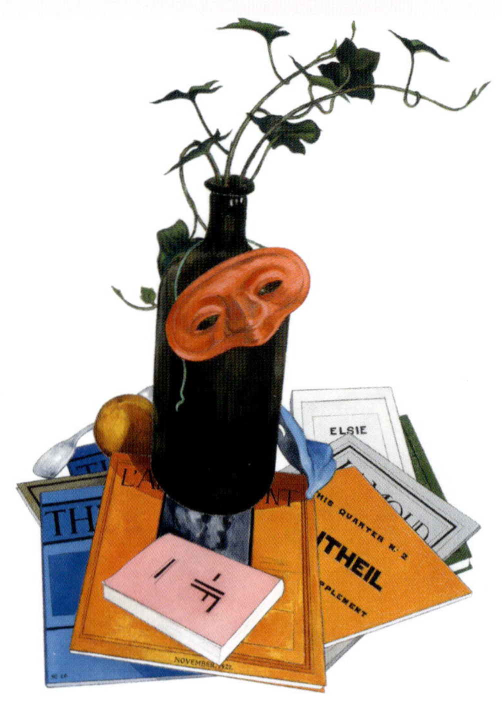

I.24 Charles Demuth, *Longhi on Broadway*, 1928, oil on board, 33⅞ × 27 in. (84.7 × 68.6 cm). Museum of Fine Arts, Boston. Gift of William H. Lane Foundation, 1990.397.

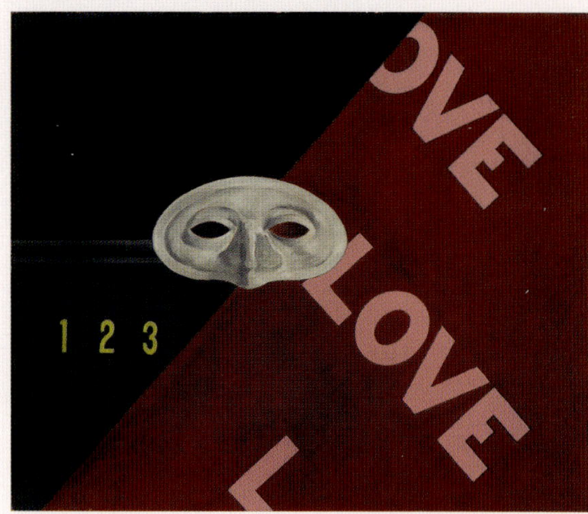

I.25 Charles Demuth, *Love, Love, Love: Homage to Gertrude Stein*, 1928 [1929], oil on panel, 20⅛ in. × 20⅞ in. (51 × 53 cm). Museo Nacional Thyssen-Bornemisza, Madrid.

of Demuth's queer art.[39] Here as elsewhere, his work offers access to private scenarios, emotions, and codes that he and his contemporaries knew so well.[40]

Viewed through the lens of Demuth's private life and in the context of the body of work under discussion here, two other large-scale works in oil, including *Longhi on Broadway* (fig. I.24) and *Love, Love, Love* (fig. I.25) can be read as encoded love letters to Locher, with whom Demuth was in almost daily contact throughout his life.[41] The use of bold text and color in these works recalls Locher's designs for posters and book jackets, including the one he produced for Ewing's *Going Somewhere* (1932) (see fig. 5.47), and the assemblage of secret signs and private details included in both works is strongly suggestive of his deep connection to Locher, rather than to more distant but better-known figures including Eugene O'Neill and Gertrude Stein, who are usually associated with these works. This reading, in turn, makes a stronger case for Demuth's association with Max Ewing and the queer, New York culture that all three men shared in New York in the 1920s and '30s.

As denizens of overlapping social circles, including the Draper and Stettheimer salons, and as close friends of Robert Locher and his wife Beatrice, it is probable that Ewing and Demuth knew each other as acquaintances, despite the lack of specific evidence documenting such a connection. While Demuth's name doesn't show up in Ewing's letters describing the people he met or socialized with, the artist does appear, just below Florine Stettheimer, on an undated list of his "Guests," numbering more than four hundred, preserved among Ewing's papers.[42] Nothing is known about the circumstances that motivated Ewing to compile such a list, but the inclusion of Demuth's name in it is intriguing.

The two men, although separated by a generation (like Ewing and Van Vechten), had many things in common: Demuth was a brilliant conversationalist with a camp, fin de siècle manner (described after his death by Marsden Hartley as a "quaint, incisive sort of wit with an ultra-sophisticated, post eighteen-ninety touch to it"); he was a dandy who loved beautiful clothes and colorful ties, which he might sometimes wrap around his waist "in place of a belt, following the fashion trend among effete young men in New York," as Bruce Kellner described him; and he was a "bachelor" who remained close to his mother and assiduously shielded his private life from public view.[43] Unlike Ewing, however, Demuth left only a handful of letters and documents behind after his death, but each in his own way was a remarkable chronicler of the world around them, and both delighted in the camp humor and lovingly detailed observation of the bodies, clothes, manners, quirks, and foibles of their friends and contemporaries in queer New York.

Moreover, in Florine Stettheimer's *Cathedrals of Fifth Avenue*, Demuth — distinguished by his crooked stance and cane, and by the bright-eyed expression of an observer — stands next to Max Ewing and Muriel Draper on the right side of the composition, between the Stettheimer sisters and a tight clutch of people that includes Miguel Covarrubias and his wife as well as Virgil Thomson. Though he stands alone in a scene filled with couples and families and focused on the marriage of an anonymous bride and groom, it is clear from a great deal of external evidence that Demuth was happily embedded in any number of social and intellectual circles, including the New York art world and the queer communities that flourished under the radar in New York, Provincetown, and even Lancaster, Pennsylvania.[44] As historian Susan Ferentinos and earlier scholars have explained, though primarily based in Lancaster, Demuth made frequent visits to New York and had many friends and professional associates there, including Stieglitz, O'Keeffe, Henry McBride, Muriel Draper, and the Lochers. This is borne out by a series of snapshots taken by Van Vechten in May 1932, which shows Demuth and O'Keeffe smiling and laughing in the sunshine on a New York street (fig. I.26), clearly contradicting the impression, created by some scholars, of the frail and sickly recluse exiled to the "province," as Demuth called it, of western Pennsylvania.[45] Like Ewing, the artist was extremely well connected and beloved by a wide circle of friends.

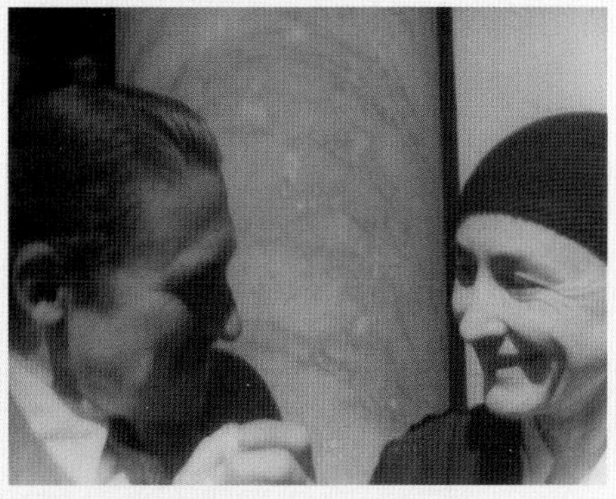

I.26 Carl Van Vechten, *Charles Demuth and Georgia O'Keeffe in front of the Museum of Modern Art*, New York City, May 3, 1932. Carl Van Vechten Papers.

COMPLEXITY AND CONTRADICTION: CHARLES DEMUTH AND ROBERT LOCHER

While Demuth seems to have been content to let his sexuality remain unspecified in the minds of his heterosexual friends, he was clearly not at all shy about sharing the details of his life and sexuality with his queer circle. While he always guarded his privacy, he was scrupulous in recognizing his intimate friends with gifts of art during his lifetime and with bequests following his death. As is well-known, he stipulated in his will that all of his unsold watercolors should go to Robert Locher after his death, together with his home and studio in Lancaster.[46] In the 1920s, Demuth and Locher collaborated in redecorating that prominent eighteenth-century building, now the Demuth Museum, and its interior in the Colonial style with an "exactitude of detail," as Marsden Hartley put it; the home and its contents passed to Locher after Demuth's mother died in 1943.[47] From that point until the mid-1950s, Locher and his then partner, the dancer Richard Weyand, occupied the property, establishing an antiques shop and clothing store in the front rooms. Demuth's estate and remaining works of art eventually passed to Yale after Weyand's death.

As historian Susan Ferentinos explains, "Whether or not they were lovers at one time, Demuth and Locher maintained a strong friendship throughout their lives. Locher did not live in Lancaster during Demuth's final fifteen years there, but he wrote Demuth and his mother regularly and sometimes visited."[48] Despite Locher's marriage to the Boston socialite Beatrice Howard in 1915, the two men lived together in Europe, with and without Beatrice, in the 1920s, and they continued to travel and socialize as a threesome for many years, up until the couple divorced in 1933. As we know, such triangular configurations were common in a time when many gay men were married and many queer people (and many women, whatever their orientation) had to be creative about their domestic arrangements in order to ward off scrutiny or censure of their private lives.[49]

The Lochers and Demuth seem to have found that marriage offered a respectable cover that suited their intimate attachments. Throughout their adult lives, the two men addressed each other in the casual manner of intimate friends and treated each other, in conversation and in public at least, like brothers. We know that in November 1921, for example, the Demuths, mother and son, gave the Lochers a sum of money on Demuth's birthday, "as they are rather hard up, on account of some money still owed him from the theater job of the past summer."[50] The following year, a postcard from Locher, written in January 1922, refers to him as "Charles Darling."[51] Though little more evidence survives, there are hints in Demuth's letters to Henry McBride and Alfred Stieglitz, his friend and dealer: they often refer to "Bobby" with affectionate disdain, and allude to the closeness of the two men in various unconventional ways. A note to McBride from August 25, 1929, for example, is gossipy and casual, remarking that "Robert returned to us for the wedding, and seemed generally insulting, — not to us, however. I am spending the week-end with him on the Island. 'Come for a long weekend,' said the command, 'with Muriel. We'll ruin you all in four days.' You better come along, otherwise you won't be safe."[52] Another note, written to Stieglitz a month later, reveals an even stronger bond: "Bobby took the poster with the white mask" (the painting we know as *Love, Love, Love*), Locher wrote, and "said it was the only painting which touched Broadway, — & New York. I was so touched that I let him have it. It's still 'unfinished,' — and he says that he will not allow me to work on it now that it's his."[53] Although the painting has sometimes been associated with Gertrude Stein, whom Demuth had met in Paris, the artist's words to Stieglitz make it clear that it is Locher rather than Stein, and Broadway's ebullience and unconventionality rather than modernist Paris, that are represented here. Though the Lochers became fans of Stein and Toklas when they lived in Paris, and Gertrude even wrote a word-portrait of Beatrice Locher, neither of the three women are referred to in the painting and that period of their lives seems long in the past.[54] Indeed, with its pink mask and bold, pink letters, the painting makes clear references not just to love but specifically to queer love with its masquerades and codes. It is therefore not surprising at all that Locher wanted to have it and keep it close.

Ewing had met the Lochers through Muriel Draper in the mid-1920s, and he became friends with both of them in the latter part of decade. Ewing reported to his mother on August 20, 1928 that he had been with the Lochers at their estate on Staten Island, but the couple don't make regular appearances in his letters until the early '30s, when he began to spend more time with them: "Bobby is one of the best designers and decorators and architects in N.Y.," he boasted to his mother in September 1931, "He and Beatrice have been great friends of Muriel's for many years … Muriel and I are invited to their place on Staten Island for the weekend … it's a beautiful house and they are divine people. I spent a weekend there two years ago but I did not know the Lochers nearly as well as I do now."[55] Ewing even took a car trip to New England with Beatrice Locher at around this time and recorded the experience in a group of snapshots preserved in his photograph album.[56]

In 1931, Muriel Draper wrote an appreciation of Locher's work for the magazine *Creative Arts*, and he enjoyed enormous success both as a graphic artist and as an interior decorator with an active practice. He was particularly well known as an interpreter of both modern and historical styles.[57] Like many others in their circle, Ewing took note of Locher's quick wit, urbane manner, and expert knowledge of the worlds of theater, fashion, and interior design. These are the elements of Locher's persona that are included by Demuth in the "poster portrait" entitled *Longhi on Broadway*: two masks, one red and one blue, are conjoined by a green glass vase filled with trailing ivy; a Colonial-style spoon (perhaps a reference to their collaboration on the painstaking renovation of the Demuth home) and a ripe peach are placed together on a floating surface, next to a pile of art books and high-end magazines that connected Demuth and Locher to the international scene. These include a volume titled "Antheil" and a book embellished only with the word "Elsie," surely a reference to Elsie de Wolfe, the famous celebrity decorator; both also appear in Ewing's *Gallery*. When these signs are decoded and fully explicated in the context of the art-world experience of New York and Paris that Locher and Demuth shared, the portrait comes into focus as an image by Demuth of his beloved friend.[58]

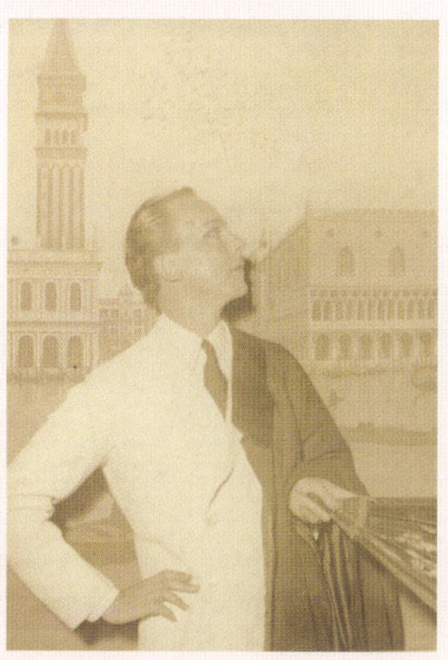

I.27 Max Ewing, *Robert Locher*, large version (retouched) from *The Carnival of Venice*.

Max Ewing was also well versed in such coded references. This was a period when he was frequently out at parties, nightclubs, and concerts with a very diverse group of friends, and an active participant in the queer scene. He even acquired a group of new boyfriends, including the handsome actor Richard Clemmer, "whom I like immensely and who is wonderful looking," as he matter-of-factly informed his mother.[59] Many of these friends appeared in Ewing's *Carnival of Venice*, including Locher, who donned a swirling, black cape and held a paper fan in his hand, and posed dramatically. In the large version of Ewing's portrait (fig. I.27), Locher's face has been made up with mascara, eyebrow pencil, and lipstick, making him appear particularly dramatic, like an actor in a play. Beatrice does not appear in the series, although a group of Ewing's snapshots from a road trip he took with her in September 1931 suggests that the two had their own friendship.[60]

Ewing visited the Lochers on Staten Island in January 1932, reporting to his mother that they were "on their last financial pins":

They think they will have to give up their elegant NY showroom the
end of the month, as it costs several hundred dollars a month rent,
and there is no business. Also they may give up the big Staten island
house. They think everything will go overboard this month. Beatrice
doesn't care much, but Bobby of course does. Beatrice may give me
one of her newly acquired grand pianos to keep for a while, wherever
they go.[61]

In May 1932, Ewing and his friend Frank Bishop motored to Staten Island,
where he joined Locher and "his cousin" for the evening. The term was one that
Locher and Demuth, and others no doubt, deployed as code for their boyfriends
and intimate friends. Perhaps Ewing was referring to Demuth here, though it is
more likely that he would have mentioned such a distinguished guest by name.
It is also possible that by this time Locher had begun his new relationship with
Richard Weyand and thus Demuth wasn't present.[62] In either case, it seems clear
that by this time that the Lochers were separated and Robert was on his own.
"We did not speak of Beatrice," Ewing added rather cryptically, noting that "Bobby
is very bored and depressed over having little money and nothing to do."[63]

In July, Ewing was thrilled to report that Robert Locher had agreed to
design the cover of *Going Somewhere* for Knopf, just as he had done for a number
of Van Vechten's works. Ewing had suggested Locher to his publishers, knowing
that it was unlikely that he would take on the project, given that he had "become
so famous and successful," and fearing that he might be too expensive, but
Locher had agreed to do it for whatever they could pay.[64] He was also excited that
Blanche Knopf had agreed to give him an advance of fifty dollars for the book, and
he lost no opportunity to boast about that to his parents and friends. On July 28,
he wrote, "Tomorrow I'm going to Staten Island to consult with Bobby Locher
about doing my book's jacket. We may go to a Staten island [*sic*] beach for
awhile"; once again, Beatrice was absent, although Ewing didn't explain why,
adding only that she was "in Newport because its [*sic*] cheap!"[65]

The two men worked on the project throughout the summer, and Ewing
was thrilled by Locher's design, sending a mockup of the cover (see fig. 5.47) to his
mother so that she could follow the progress of the book as it moved through the
various stages of the publication process, which he described for her in detail.[66]
Ewing's frequent meetings with Locher on Staten Island also gave him an
opportunity to relax in the company of his charming friend: Locher had many
connections to the worlds of fashion and illustration, many of them gay (including
Porter Woodruff, the *Vogue* artist), which afforded Ewing new social
opportunities. On August 18, for example, he reported that he had a "new friend"
named Horst Bohrmann; soon Ewing and Horst (who, with his partner George
Hoyningen-Huene, would go on to invent a style of fashion photography that
changed the industry) were spending a great deal of time together. As Ewing
reported: "Friday and Saturday I was at Bobby Lochers [*sic*] with Horst, the
German boy. Had a lovely time. Delicious Italian dinners and lay on the beach all
day Saturday with the Korotnovs and the Stewarts, Staten Island friends of
Bobby."[67] A photograph of Horst from 1931 by Hoyningen-Huene (fig. I.28)
provides ample evidence of both the glamorous new approach to photography
and the appeal of his new friend. Once again, Ewing said nothing about the
whereabouts of Beatrice Locher on these occasions, but the scene that Ewing

described speaks volumes about the changes taking place in the Locher household at that time. Beatrice remarried as soon as her divorce from Robert was finalized.[68]

Locher would remain close to his many New York friends, including the Stettheimers and their circle, after Ewing's death in 1934, and he appeared as the "compere," opposite Florine's depiction of herself as the "commère" — roles adapted from *Four Saints in Three Acts* — in her *Cathedrals of Art* (1942).[69] He cuts a dapper, elegant figure in that painting, an image that Ewing would have appreciated and emulated, as he would Locher's unique position in the art world that Stettheimer depicted. By that point, of course, Charles Demuth had died, having finally succumbed in 1935 to diabetes. The world that these men had inhabited as "cousins" and "friends" since before World War I had changed in almost every other respect as well, but Demuth would live on in his friends' memories as a sort of hothouse product of the 1920s and '30s — like the lush exotics and brightly colored flowers he painted — with his elegant, camp, manners and distinctively queer appearance. As the artist George Biddle put it, "He was a homosexual, '*fin de siècle*,'" using a rare bit of slang that referred to the sort of queer forms of speech, flamboyant gestures, and fashionable dress that were associated with Oscar Wilde and his contemporaries at the end of the nineteenth century.[70]

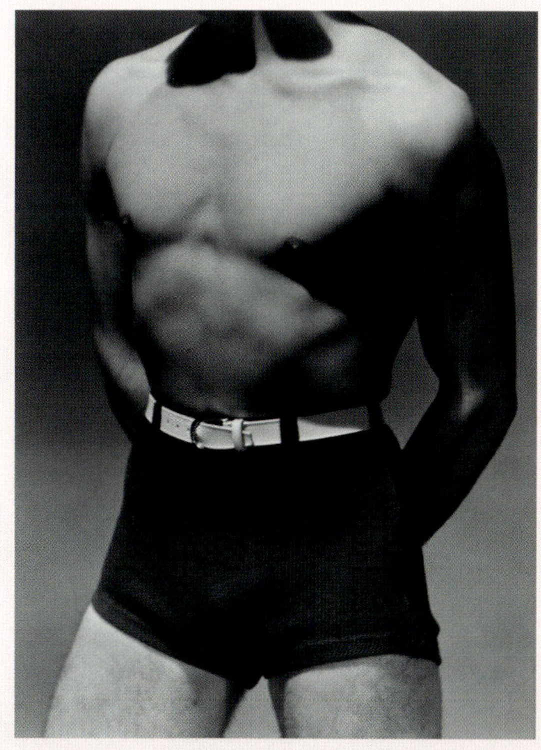

I.28 George Hoyningen-Huene, *Horst Torso with Beachwear*, 1930. George Hoyningen-Huene Estate Archive.

That Ewing was familiar with the term is revealed by his handwritten caption on a scrapbook page that included a photo of him from December 1931, bundled up in a heavy coat and beret and glowering seductively at the camera on a cold winter's day by the shore in Asbury Park, New Jersey. The page is decorated with a circle of custom-made, novelty "stamps" imprinted with a glamorous portrait of his beautiful beau Richard Clemmer (fig. I.29). "Fin de siècle," Ewing simply stated, announcing to anyone who knew the code that he and Clemmer were not only "homosexual," in the same way that Demuth was, but also worthy exemplars of the debonair, dandified look and knowing tone that the artist had perfected.

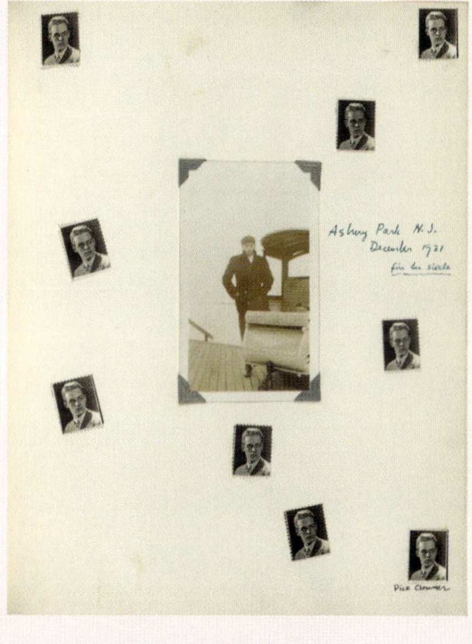

I.29 Max Ewing, "Fin de Siècle," collage with portrait of Max Ewing in Asbury Park, NJ, December 1931, surrounded by novelty postage-stamp portraits of Richard Clemmer. Max Ewing Papers.

GEORGE PLATT LYNES: A NEW WAY OF SEEING

A great deal has already been said here about Max Ewing's friendship with George Lynes, and the differences and similarities between them, both as photographers and as queer men in New York City. When the two met in 1927, Lynes had only recently embarked on the path that would define the course of his private life as a member of a long-term threesome with Glenway Wescott and Monroe Wheeler. His artistic aspirations and the aestheticized style of his work, as well as his distinctive character, both as a person and as an artist, were also fully formed by 1930 or 1931.[71]

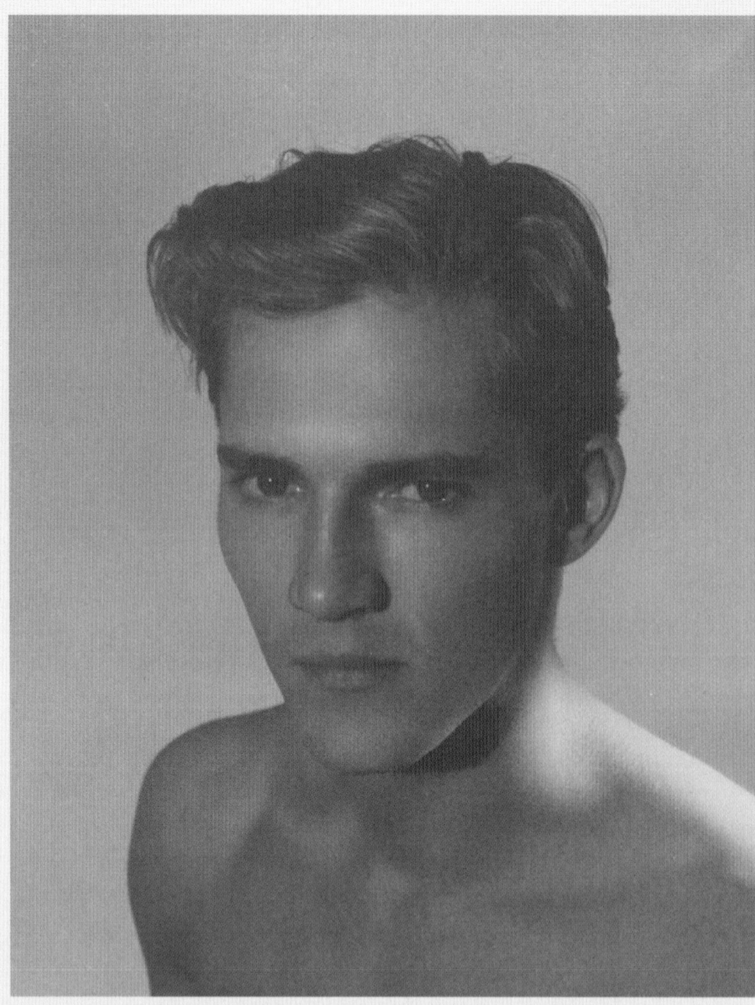

I.30 George Platt Lynes, *Portrait of Lloyd Wescott*, c. 1930. Max Ewing Papers.

Whatever Ewing may have hoped, Lynes had already moved far ahead as a photographer by this point, as a comparison of portraits of Glenway's younger brother Lloyd Wescott by the two men clearly shows. In Ewing's 1932 snapshot of Lloyd "playing basketball on the Grand Canal" (see fig. 5.12), Wescott appears shirtless and wearing only a pair of shorts, yet he is so fully distanced from the viewer by the quality of the lighting and his awkward, upturned gaze that there is little to suggest either erotic intent or interest. By contrast, Lynes's photograph (fig. I.30), which survives in Ewing's own scrapbooks, is a different sort of image altogether, one that captures both the sultry gaze of the handsome young man and the photographer's appreciation for his beauty. While Lynes had only just begun to ramp up his professional technique when the photo was taken, he was clearly already on his way to creating a distinctive and recognizable approach.[72]

Like Van Vechten and Demuth, Lynes and Ewing joked about sailors and idly fantasized about their sexual availability, but it was Lynes, with his openness to real sexual experiences and his ability to dramatize male nudity through composition and lighting, who would invent a new genre both of fashion photography and queer imagery. Compared with Lynes, all three of the others seem like survivors from an earlier era, which, indeed, they were, despite the similar ages of Ewing and Lynes. Yet even Lynes — whose passion for Wheeler is evidenced by his poetic love letters and the lyrical photographs that are preserved in the "travel albums" published by Anatole Pohorilenko — kept a secret portfolio of his most intimate, erotic images.[73] These exceptional, tender

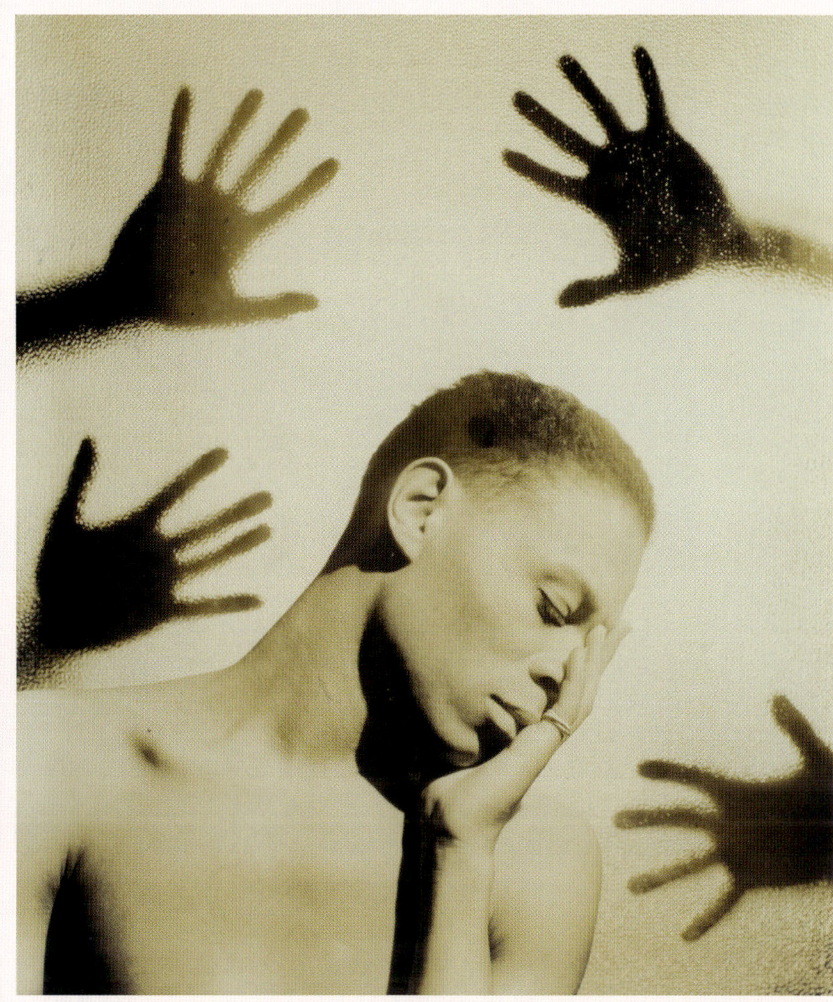

I.31 George Platt Lynes, *Jimmie Daniels, Singer at Le Ruban Bleu*, 1933. Gibbes Museum of Art.

photographs were recently discovered in Monroe Wheeler's private archive in a plain, brown envelope marked simply "GPL/MW Private." Thanks to a series of lucky accidents, they were brought to the attention of curator Jarrett Earnest who exhibited and published them in collaboration with the David Zwirner Gallery in 2019.[74]

Lynes's photos, taken in the early months of his rapturous affair with Wheeler, include close-ups of their angelic, sleeping faces and exquisitely produced platinum prints of their genitals and lovemaking. Like much of Lynes's work, and unlike Ewing's nude snapshots or the scrapbooks compiled by Van Vechten, these images are truly game changers for the history of queer visual culture. Lynes not only shows us things we never expected to see, and hints at private scenarios we weren't meant to witness, but also does so in a completely new way, free of camp irony or shame. This paradigm shift can't be emphasized strongly enough: just as he did when he first encountered Wescott and Wheeler in the winter of 1927 and boldly announced to Monroe that he "would be his," Lynes was unrepentant about viewing the world through his own unique, self-absorbed, queer lens and making himself — his sexuality, his feelings, his body, his artistic vision — both part of the process and part of the image. In this way, he revolutionized not only queer photography, but also fashion photography and the depiction of the male nude.

Two final examples, including Lynes's dance portrait of Jimmie Daniels (fig. I.31) and his camp depiction of the white choreographer Frederick Ashton,

fully clothed and posed with the nude, Black
dancers from *Four Saints in Three Acts* (fig.
I.32), demonstrate the evolution of this new
way of seeing. The former, in which Daniels's
extraordinary face and torso are surrounded
by blurry, silhouetted hands that capture the
motion and vibrancy of dance, reminds us of
the peculiarity of the photographic process
itself, with its lenses and variable depth of
field, with objects moving in and out of focus,
just as the photographer's own eye adjusted
what he saw. Moreover, with the queer gaze of
the photographer foregrounded, the image
jumps out at us as something entirely modern
and new. Similarly, the photo of Ashton and
"his" dancers — one in which his white hands

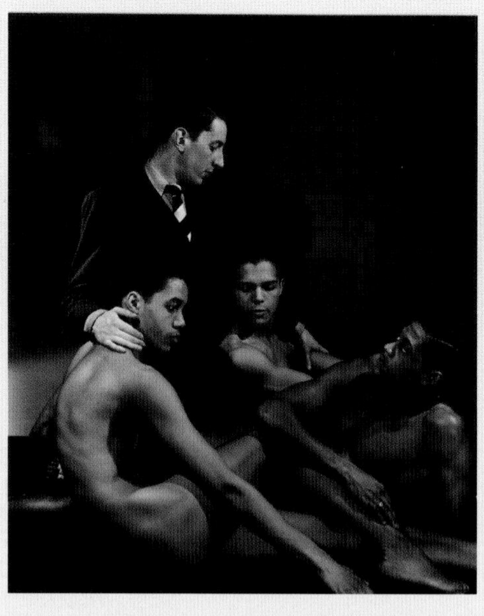

I.32 George Platt
Lynes, *Frederick
Ashton and Dancers*,
1934. Collection of the
Kinsey Institute.

caress the dark skin of one of the men and the bicep of another — encodes queer
erotic content and racial difference in the language of performance, creating an
aura of camp deniability much like that of Van Vechten's "arched brow"
modernism, the ironic tone that enabled writers and artists to simultaneously
declare and retract the queer meanings of their work.

This ambiguity at first makes the photo seem awkwardly performative
and, frankly, racist, like many of the images of Black men in Van Vechten's private
archive. Yet here the element of parody, and the undeniable beauty and agency
of the Black men (one of whom stares back at the white choreographer),
ultimately overtake the cringeworthy racial hierarchies embedded in the image.
They also reveal the ways in which Lynes manipulated the conventions of
traditional pictorial organization (the triangular composition and the recumbent
nudes, for example) to turn expected relationships upside down by showing them
through an unashamedly queer lens. Ultimately, *Four Saints* itself strove to
achieve something of the same effect through a combination of parody, irony, and
celebration of the talents and dignity of its Black performers. It is fitting that
Lynes's image continues in this vein.

Like Romaine Brooks's portrait of Carl Van Vechten from 1936 (discussed
in chapter 2), in which the subject sits on a throne-like chair behind which the
beautiful faces of young, Black men loom in the darkness, Lynes's photograph
can be read in multiple ways simultaneously. Close attention to such images
offers a new vantage point on the intersectional values that shaped modern forms
and meanings among a group of people who strove to challenge racism,
homophobia, and artistic conventions through their art. That the works of George
Platt Lynes or Romaine Brooks can withstand such close scrutiny is a testimony to
their complexity, and to a level of sophistication that Ewing, as an amateur in the
realm of art and photography, neither aspired to nor had the talent to achieve.
In this respect, he knew himself very well: he was a musician first and foremost,
but also a man who put his energy into trying new things and fully experiencing
the modern city. As he had written to his cousin Doris in August 1932, when
"a thing ceases to be a caprice, I lose interest in it and am not so good at it."[75]

Thus, in the spring and summer of 1933, he turned his gaze toward
Hollywood, writing reviews for movie magazines and sketching out treatments

for the screenplays that he would later submit to the big film studios. Ewing was filled with optimism as he packed up his things, taking down the photographs in the *Gallery* and carefully filing them away, yet the process was bittersweet. The injury to his finger, sustained as he performed Antheil's *Ballet Mécanique* at Carnegie Hall in April 1927, was clearly not going away, and he had known for some time that he could never have a career as a serious musician.

Ewing was proud of the glamorous life he had led in New York among the beloved artists and celebrities that he had only dreamt about before he arrived in the city ten years earlier, but by 1933, that time was over. His *Gallery* no longer had the power to induce the queer, multi-sensory fantasy that it did before, and many of his friends were finding it difficult to live in New York during of the Depression. As he confessed to his mother:

> It is a little bit upsetting to end an era like this, and I hate taking
> down each separate picture, because it is like taking part of myself
> down. But in another way I am quite pleased with the prospect
> of a new place when I return here … I have reached the conclusion
> that the disadvantages of this place outweigh the advantages,
> so I'm not exactly shedding tears at leaving.[76]

Thus he prepared to leave New York in search of new adventures and what he hoped would be a steady income as a scriptwriter and author in California. Above all, he wanted to make his mother proud, and to have her stop worrying about money. He was enthusiastic and happy — and clearly unprepared for the disasters that would befall him in the year to come.

Chapter 6

THE END OF THE ROAD, 1933–34

Although the tragic conclusion to Max Ewing's story has been known to readers since the very first pages of this study, the event never fails to come as a shock. No doubt neither Max Ewing nor his mother expected how close the end of their relationship was when they corresponded in their usual bantering way throughout 1933, and — oddly enough — neither do we when we read their letters. For much of his life, Ewing was generally so upbeat and confident that it is hard to imagine the profound despair that led him to take his own life. His mother was his bulwark, unfailingly believing in his brilliance, his beauty, and their collective ability to overcome whatever obstacles, including homophobia, might stand in their way.

Nevertheless, when we listen for the change in tone of their more fractious exchanges and examine their relationship in the context of the disturbing events of 1933–34 — the deepening economic Depression in the United States, the impending war in Europe, and the repeated rejections of Ewing's work by Hollywood agents and studios in particular — we can begin to detect the fissures that eventually broke the foundations of their life apart. Indeed, Clara Ewing's increasingly fragile mental and physical state, her many anxieties and fears, and the profound disconnect between Max Ewing's queer way of life and the social and cultural mores of small-town America are all painfully and poetically on view here. The Ewing family had stood strong for decades, sustained by money, education, and their status in the town of Pioneer, but without the emotional and financial support of his father (who died in April 1932) and his mother (who died in April 1934), Max Ewing and those around him stopped believing in his genius.

Ewing's suicide in Binghamton, New York, where he and the boxer Jack Pollock had stopped for lunch en route to New York, provided the motivation for Carl Van Vechten to swiftly and expeditiously gather Ewing's extraordinary archive together and deposit it at Yale, carefully preserving the hundreds of letters, photographs, and ephemera accumulated in New York and back in Pioneer. As Van Vechten recognized, these documents create an extraordinary portrait of a queer man in urban and rural America in the 1920s and '30s, stitched together by a chorus of diverse American voices that are often reminiscent of the novels of F. Scott Fitzgerald. Read alongside Ewing's plaintive letters to his friends — Alice DeLamar and Muriel Draper in particular — after his mother's death, and the communications that Jack Pollock sent to these women from Pioneer after he joined Ewing there, the story of Max Ewing's tragic rise and fall takes on the epic quality of American tragedies like *The Great Gatsby* or *Tender Is the Night*, both of which were conceived and written, as we know, within Ewing's New York milieu. More than any other novelist, Fitzgerald understood both the bright lights and the loneliness of the city, even as the jazz music, the raucous drinking and dancing, and the frenzied moving from place to place went on uninterrupted like a merry-go-round, whether or not people like Max Ewing stayed on or fell off. Though he clearly didn't have Fitzgerald's talent, Van Vechten tried, through his novels and his photographs (particularly those that portrayed the range and diversity of his Black and white contemporaries) to capture the same spirit, and he recognized that his young friend was both a victim and, strangely enough, a beneficiary of the unusual times in which they lived. Perhaps it is ultimately his resonances with the romance of fiction that make Max Ewing — the talented, queer boy who came to New York in search of glamour and a glittering career — such a vivid and compelling figure.

For most of 1933, Ewing's letters are filled with the usual sunny reports of his social conquests and the sort of breathless stargazing that he never failed to report to his mother: he boasted about his exhibition at the Julien Levy Gallery in January and the party at the Waldorf Astoria that followed, he described the plays and concerts and parties he attended, and a series of gatherings and get-togethers that he hosted, attended by a broad swath of New York's bohemia. He was out at one event or another almost every night. Although his father had died the previous year, and despite the incessant news of bank failures and worthless stocks, things seemed to continue on as usual for the Ewings, both in New York and Pioneer, Ohio.

Positive reviews of Ewing's *Going Somewhere* appeared throughout the spring of 1933, but those notices — which pleased Ewing greatly, and which he shared with his mother — are largely overshadowed by his attention to the *Carnival of Venice* project and his plans to travel to California. In his letters, he readily corrects his mother's misperceptions of the business of book publishing ("There is nothing 'strange' about the circulation of my book. It will circulate to anyone who orders it," he wrote) and regularly chides her for not taking "proper care" of herself by off-loading some of the responsibilities for maintaining her home and store, but it is notable that these communications suggest a new tone of impatience with his mother that begins to appear with greater regularity.[1] In one undated letter from March or April 1933, for example, he highlights the tensions between them on the matter of her health, noting, "Any advice or suggestion I make, you take as adverse criticism, and go right on as before. I have never offered a word of criticism of a thing you ever did, except overwork … I only know that it makes me more unhappy than anything in the world, and I am so upset about it that I can't concentrate on anything or get anything done at all."[2]

On February 16, Ewing and the "GaryFlappers" hosted a midnight party in the (of course, absent) star's honor. Many friends saved the membership cards for his new club that Ewing distributed (see fig. 5.63). Ewing wrote home with all the details of the event, sparing no effort to describe his glamorous life to his mother: "Sorry to write you so often," he commented, "but something tremendous happens almost every hour, and I have to keep you posted!"[3]

Ewing's mother must have responded to the news of these events with uncharacteristic anxiety, suggesting that the lavish party and the printed cards were unnecessary extravagances in a time when the family needed to save money. Max wrote back to her with a sharp rebuke: "Don't get excited and DON'T worry about things like the Garyflappers," he scolded:

> I never start what I cannot finish. I have more than the necessary fifty subscribers already, and still three days to go. The dollars have been pouring in. Everyone wants to attend. Rita Romilly [one of the Gurdjieff crowd] rang up Muriel yesterday very indignant because she had not been asked to be a Garyflapper. She said everyone in N.Y. whom she knew had become a Garyflapper and she was insulted at being left out … so I called her up as if I hadn't heard of all this, and she was all smiles, and said she would send me two dollars right away.[4]

Although Clara and Max had made elaborate plans for her to attend his exhibition opening reception at the Waldorf on February 18, she wrote to him just two days before to say that she did not feel able to come. Ewing's response foreshadows the ongoing health and money concerns that would ultimately incapacitate both of them in the winter and spring of 1934, and demonstrates the extreme psychological interdependence between mother and son:

> It is true what you say about my Pioneer problems being very serious if anything should "happen" to you. But even though serious, they would be solved and settled in some way. They always are. But nothing could be done about you by that time. And what happens to you is the main thing to consider. I couldn't bear to have anything bad happen to you. I feel very close to you, closer now than I think I ever did before. We are not together much in point of time, yet I never think of us as being separate or apart. I keep in constant communication with you, and have you always at the back of my mind, no matter how much I am seemingly absorbed in something else. You must stay with me to give me incentive to do more things and better ones.[5]

Ewing had always made it clear to his parents and anyone else who would listen that he loathed Pioneer, Ohio and hoped never to return there, protesting that he was much too sensitive, intelligent, and psychologically vulnerable to withstand the onslaught of banality that had caused him so much pain in his childhood. A story he told after spending the summer of 1925 in Pioneer hits all of the familiar notes:

> I saw Tom Dewey [his college friend] when I came back here [New York] in September, he remarked that I had suddenly grown extremely mature over the summer. I laughed and said that he should have seen me in August when my mind had apparently reverted to a childishness that approached imbecility: Of course that childishness was real only during the two or three days when I was so very sick. After that I sort of kept it up as a defense mechanism. You really can not imagine what it means to me to sit in that house alone all day and realize acutely every minute that on every side are barbarians, that I am caged in … and not one of them has ever had an esthetic emotion in his or her life, and that if I were to die that minute I could not talk to them because they would not know what I was saying. Fish, babies parties, and front porch gossip sends me into the state you saw me in in early September. The futility of the thing enervates me so I just let go and wait.[6]

Ewing's parents loved him and their neighbors tolerated him, but everyone recognized that Max Ewing was strange. He wasn't like other people from Pioneer, and whether that was because he was simply a brilliant and eccentric specimen — a "hot house plant," as he had described himself — or because he really wasn't a "normal" boy in the ways that the gossips whispered

about behind his back, it was obvious that his parents, with their store and
their social prominence, provided him with a buffer against the realities of life in
small-town America. Without that, he was no match for the tidal wave of
judgment and loneliness that came his way.

All of those troubles were still in the distant future, however. Ewing's
letters to friends and family from the spring and summer of 1933 were filled with
anticipation and hope, despite his bittersweet emotions about the ways in which
his life — and all of their lives — had changed over the course of the past ten
years. He had turned thirty in April, and he was ready to begin something new:

> I expect to be very much refreshed and brightened up by the West,
> and when I return to New York I would like to make a whole fresh
> start of some sort, and not just fall back on my old routine. I feel that
> this year is a turning point of some sort. Dad's death definitely
> terminated something. And the appearance of my book in some way
> terminated something else, or rather started something else. I feel as
> if I were bringing the nineteen-twenties, as well as my own twenties,
> to a close, and that a new period is beginning. I have lived nearly ten
> years in New York, and I have loved every year. I haven't done exactly
> what I planned to do when I came here, but that is the result of many
> new circumstances, and I am just as pleased over what I have done
> as over what I might have done. New York is a different city entirely
> from what it was ten years ago, and the whole world is a different
> place. Everything is caught up in a whirlwind of change these days,
> and we have to change too, or be left behind in the rush.[7]

Ewing acknowledged that he had been "very snobbish" about things like
popular books and movies in the past, adding that he had become more
"tolerant" now and was anxious "to make a stab at them."[8] Moreover, even if he
didn't get any work out West, he said, he wanted to see for himself if the weather
in California, or Colorado, or Arizona, might be better for his health than New York
City's — he had long suffered from hay fever and what he described as "catarrhal
and bronchial discharge," which he regularly medicated with infusions of
cocaine.[9] As he explained to his mother, he was buying a new suit "to wear to the
BEST PLACES" in Hollywood, and he joked about seeing Dietrich and Garbo.
Although he still stayed out all night at raucous parties and filled his letters with
anecdotes about familiar topics like doing "such a good Black Bottom" with Alice
DeLamar at the Club Deauville or how she had organized a "tea date … in her roof
house on top of a Park Avenue skyscraper," he was also clearly aware that dark
forces were massing on the horizon. "Aren't you glad you are not a Jew in
Germany?" he scrawled at the end of a long, chatty letter to his mother; indeed,
while the social whirl of his New York world went on unabated, the old certainties
of the 1920s had begun to resound with a hollow ring.[10]

In June, Ewing went to Pioneer to visit his mother, and in July he finally left
for "the West," stopping only briefly in Chicago to see the *Century of Progress*
exhibition.[11] His California adventure began with a wonderful stay at the luxurious
San Francisco home of his friend Noël Sullivan. When he arrived, he was picked
up at the station by a chauffeur in a limousine and taken to a "palatial" house,
perched "on a high hill over-looking the bay"; his room was filled with flowers and

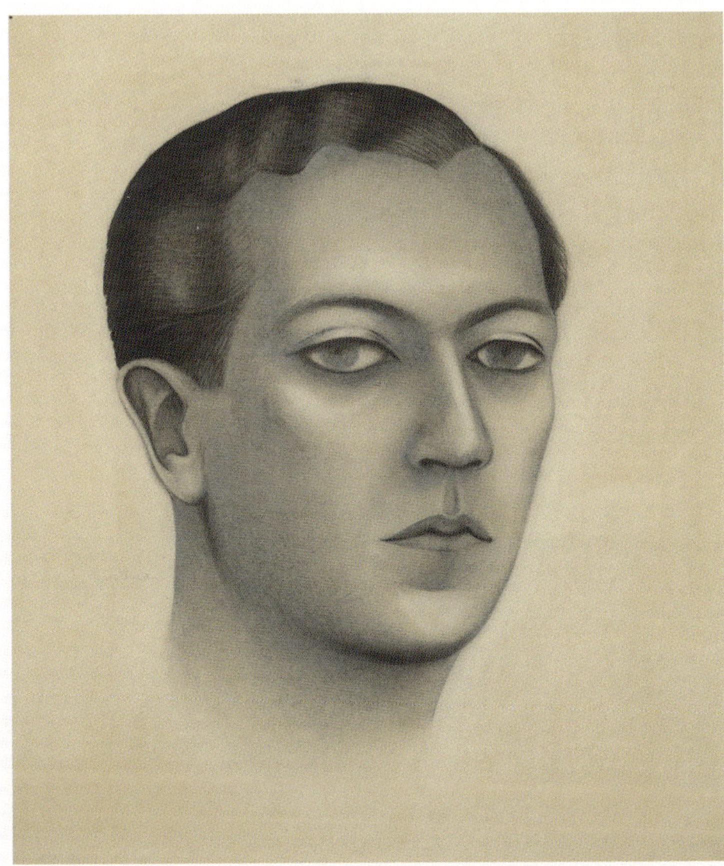

6.1 Billy Justema, *Portrait of Max Ewing*, undated (1933). Max Ewing Papers.

looked out on an "Italian roof garden filled with fountains and ferns and all sorts of lovely things."[12] He was introduced to a tight-knit, queer, and interracial circle of friends, many of whom — not least of all Langston Hughes — were already familiar to him from his experience of Van Vechten's coterie in New York.[13] A letter from Sullivan, written in August 1933, suggests the composition of the group:

> Langston arrived a week ago and the enrichment of life which his presence means is hard for me to describe. His experiences in the past year, culminating with a rather inhospitable reception in Japan, are thrillingly interesting. He was very sorry to miss you and hopes to see you soon. He plans to remain here until the end of the month and then go down to Carmel to write his book of reminiscences of Soviet Asia and perhaps also a novel. ... Ramon Novarro returned to Los Angeles by way of San Francisco ten days ago and I have just written him saying you are at the Roosevelt, so I'm sure you will hear from him soon ... Billy [Justema] is planning to go south this week. He is doing a portrait of Langston now. For quite a few days after his last "spree," he was almost suicidally contrite, and the operation of the law of Karma decreed for him a sharp attack of neuritis which lasted a number of days. From both of these, however, he has recovered.[14]

Billy Justema (1905–87) made a portrait of Max Ewing (fig. 6.1), which survives among Van Vechten's papers, along with a letter from Ewing from December 1933, reporting that Justema was also painting "a lovely sailor friend of mine whom he is drawing in his sailor hat" and another portrait of Ewing himself: "I pose in a derby hat at the typewriter and Billy draws me from the floor. The scene is fanciful."[15] Alas, neither of the latter two works survives.

Ewing spent most of the fall in Hollywood, and life went on pretty much as he had planned: he made a number of new friends, went to parties, met up with people he knew from New York like the writer Gilbert Seldes and his wife Amanda, and spent a great deal of time people-watching at the big studios and around town. He confided to his mother that he had plans to collaborate on a new show with a his friend Peggy Fears, a glamorous former "Ziegfeld girl" and Broadway producer whom he had photographed for *The Carnival of Venice*. Fears had recently married the wealthy developer, A. C. Blumenthal, and, although queer, had figured out how to navigate the complexities of her bicoastal, bisexual world.[16] Ewing was bursting with optimism about the prospect of fame and fortune, as he gushed to his mother: "Peggy Fears is a grand girl and a good person for me to know, for she is producing shows all the time on Blumenthal's money … She would like me to be her new Noel [*sic*] Coward and it begins to look as if it might be!"[17] In late August, he sent a postcard from the "Garden of Allah" hotel and spa, a venue owned by the lesbian actress Alla Nazimova (1879–75) and frequented by a coterie of queer women Ewing knew well, including Peggy Fears and Tallulah Bankhead. He had "cocktails 'chez' Fears and Bankhead" on August 7, 1933, reporting that he had spent the night at the hotel because he stayed too late at the party to get the streetcar back to his apartment.[18]

A few days later, he described a visit to the Metro-Goldwyn studios with his new friend Adrian, a costume designer: to Ewing's great delight, the two men had spent the afternoon with the screen idol Ramon Novarro, whose portrait graced the pages of Van Vechten's scrapbooks (fig. 6.2) and no doubt those of many other fans as well. Dropping Novarro's name as well as Adrian's was a surefire way of establishing his Hollywood bona fides with friends in New York and his mother in Pioneer.

Despite his best efforts, however, none of Ewing's grand designs for professional success were realized: indeed, his big plans always seemed to fizzle out just as quickly as they came into his head. He clearly found it difficult to gain any traction with Hollywood agents or studios, and he hadn't gotten any songs accepted. He refused to sign a long-term contract with one agent and insisted that the term of the agreement be shortened, confessing to his mother that he "was not signing even

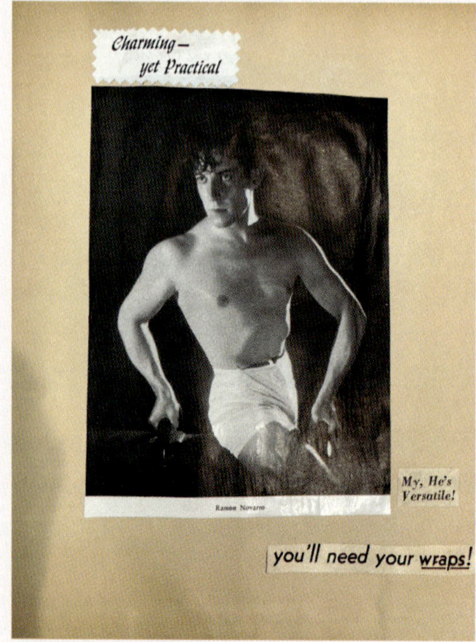

6.2 Carl Van Vechten, "Charming—Yet Practical," collage with photograph of Ramon Novarro and found text, from Carl Van Vechten's scrapbook.

that until they make some appointments for me."[19] He was "going to play songs for an executive at Paramount," he reported, but nothing came of that either, since fewer musicals were being produced as a result of the Depression. It seemed clear that Hollywood was not all he had imagined it to be.

Even Ewing's beloved Gary Cooper proved to be something of a disappointment. In a letter to Cary Ross, his friend from the Museum of Modern

Art and Alfred Stieglitz's American Place Gallery (the two men had spent a "quiet evening" in the company of Walker Evans some months before), he shared "the few bits of Cooperiana" that he had acquired thus far.[20] One brief and banal sighting at the Paramount studio had taken place after many hours spent waiting around — "the custom of the country," as Ewing called it — with his friend, the actress Lilyan Tashman, in her dressing room. Cooper had wandered in with his secretary to share "champagne and sandwiches," saying little before he aimlessly walked out again. Then he went "for a ride around the lot on a bicycle … he went nowhere, just rode around and around in a detached way":

> While he was riding his secretary (who resembles Joseph Stella and makes a grotesque foil for Gary) informed us that what Gary really enjoyed most was to roam around his ranch bare-assed (the phraseology is the secretary's) playing a mouth organ. Also that he loved to fuss with little pieces of leather and make himself belts or other little leather things with his own hands … It all sounded extremely eccentric.[21]

He confessed that he had had only one other glimpse of "Mr. C" since then: "At the Colony Club one night when he was intoxicated, and doing a little solitary roulette playing in a dusty linen suit … He looks distrait and miserable and as if it were all too much to cope with." It was true, Ewing said, that Cooper stood out even in the Paramount dining room, where the tables were filled with the likes of "Cary Grant, Chevalier, Buster Crabbe, Randolph Scott, etc.," because of his extraordinarily beautiful eyes — "as blue as only Geraldine Farrar's" — and his striking, dark tan. "Gary stands out most prominently," Ewing quipped, but "Maybe it is just a matter of height."[22] With characteristic style, he summed up his Cooper sightings for Muriel Draper: "He is at once amiable and anti-social, poised and restless, and more *detached* than anyone alive."[23]

Long hours of work, lots of waiting around, and disappointing movie stars: in real life, Hollywood offered very little to write home about — quite literally. Ewing described the place as "the hardest working factory town I know of in the world," confessing in a letter to his friend Joe Brewer that he

> worked hard [there] because there was so little else to do. Everyone I know worked hard all day and fell into bed exhausted by nine at night. Miss Garbo retires every night before eight, and rises every day before 4 AM. Likewise Miss Crawford and all the rest. They must all be on their sets in full make up, looking too beautiful, at half past eight every morning, so it means they cannot do a thing the night before, except drink some orange juice and nibble a carrot and have a massage and go to sleep.[24]

Worst of all, Ewing had discovered that Los Angeles was more like Pioneer than he ever imagined: it was filled with "farmers" and farmers' wives, he observed, "all looking as though they were on their way to a Kay Francis Barn Dance in their horses and buggies." In his opinion, "Los Angeles probably has more farmers in it than any spot on earth":

> All the retired farmers from Iowa, Kansas, Nebraska and all that
> region, come here as fast as they can. They come by the thousands,
> they come by the hundreds of thousands, and once in Los Angeles,
> they remain just the farmers they were. Other cities too have big
> populations recruited from the farms, but other cities seem to
> assimilate them ... But not so Los Angeles. There were only farmers
> there from the start, and only more and more farmers have been
> added. So that it is primarily a gigantic community of farmhands ...
> For a city of its size it is probably the most illiterate on earth. Only a
> supremely illiterate city could take Aimee McPherson seriously as
> a spiritual leader ... I guess they bring their overalls right along from
> Iowa and that's what they wear even on a night out in Chinatown.[25]

Even more troubling than the banality and ignorance of the place was the fact that
Clara Ewing was becoming uneasy about her son's lack of money and success,
and every letter brought more news of her health problems and rumblings of what
seemed like paranoia about friends and neighbors. When Clara told him in no
uncertain terms that she didn't want to hear anything more about movie stars "or
anything they do," he replied with dismay:

> You always seemed to me to be distinctly interested. But if you are not
> then I won't need to write you about that. I have put considerable
> effort into writing you about them, but if it does not interest you then
> it has been time wasted ... I am sorry too that you feel that nothing I
> do ever 'gets me anywhere.' I do not know of anyone who shares this
> opinion with you.[26]

Suddenly believing her son to be a failure, and herself increasingly
unstable, Clara Ewing began to insist that he return to Pioneer — his worst
nightmare — as soon as possible. The litany of paranoid anxieties that she recited
on November 9 is typical of her declining faculties in November and December of
1933: "I don't know what you could salvage if you came home," she wrote, "and
I don't know how you could stand it here but of course you will have to eventually
... To have you pointed out as a failure would just kill me — and even if you won't
need money for a long time, I don't think I could ever send any ... It would only
increase my misery for you to come home and not be able to do a thing to help."[27]
She wasn't "off [her] head," she insisted, "I am just crazy with stern reality." She
went on and on: she "doubted" that his "cheeriness" was "real," she admitted,
adding a few days later, "If you should be disappointed in your play I don't see how
you can stand it. You have been so brave and sweet thro [sic] it all when I *know*
you are heartbroken — have all your big friends forsaken you?"[28]

Mother and son had always been close to the point of "telepathy," as Clara
Ewing called it, but to his credit, Ewing kept trying to reason with her, and he kept
on moving forward with his writing. As he told his mother on November 18,
"I don't like that you are so convinced that I can NEVER make any money," he wrote:

> After all, you and Dad did not commence to make any money that you
> could really call MONEY until you were past thirty, and I am just that
> now. You both served long apprenticeships before the money began to

roll in. Well, so have I served a long apprenticeship. It has been an
expensive one but it will be profitable in the end. And when I cash in
on it there will be more money than you made, I'm sure. So no more
wailing about how I am going to be miserable all my life in Pioneer.
I'm not going to spend my life in Pioneer. I'm going to get you out of
there instead … It half broke my heart when my book came out and
Dad was not on hand to see it. And it would break my heart
completely if my play should go in New York and you would not be
able to attend the opening. So now you get a move on and get better.[29]

By mid-December, Clara Ewing was in a downward spiral, and the
panicked letters that Max received from family, servants, and neighbors all but
guaranteed that she was taking her son with her. Still he tried to right the ship,
protesting that "The people write me the most terrifying letters, about how you
keep threatening suicide and the most hair-raising things … It has got me into a
state of absolute panic, and if you have the slightest regard for my well-being you
will make super human efforts to curb yourself in these wild threats." He chose
his words carefully in order to reassure her, "I am not saying that it is all
delusional on your part. You are sick and run down, of course. But a lot of this
hysteria is plainly self-induced by this incessant preoccupation with money,
money, money. And you have simply got to stop it."[30]

These protests proved to be futile. Clara Ewing's repeated suicide
attempts — she had to be "pulled from the cistern" three times, Ewing's uncle
reported — and the alarming accounts of her former friends about her now-
shattered grasp on reality forced him to return to Pioneer in January 1934, a place
that he had vowed to leave forever.[31] We know Ewing would himself follow in his
mother's footsteps over the course of the six months that followed, falling
into a world of delusion and paranoia that caused him to doubt both his own
financial security and the validity of the relationships he had formed in New York.
Thus, he realized his mother's worst fears and fulfilled her darkest prophesies,
proving to himself, in a twisted way, that the love they had shared, at least — their
"telepathy" — had been real.

Ewing's own precipitous decline and death in mid-June 1934 came as a shock to
everyone he knew, largely because his letters to his friends throughout the
first six months of the year were lucid, often humorous, with sometimes beautiful
descriptions of his mental state and the problems he faced. As he wrote to Alice
DeLamar on January 9, he had been called back to Pioneer "by the serious illness
of my mother here. I hurried to her and find that she is suffering from a serious
nervous breakdown, brought on partly by heart trouble and partly from
exaggerated worry about financial matters."[32] He then went on to ask his wealthy
friend for a big favor: to help him reassure his mother of his solvency by
pretending to offer him a substantial loan if he ever needed it, confessing to her
that "I am forced to resort to sundry devices, some childish and others eccentric.
This one is definitely eccentric … I am doing *anything* to quiet her apprehensions
that I will end up destitute!" In closing, he joked that the ruse was clearly worthy
of a psychiatrist, adding that, given the state of things, he himself "should really
be at a post in Vienna."[33]

He also shared the news of his return to Pioneer with George Lynes and his college friend Edgar Ailes in February 1934, telling Lynes, "Last month in Hollywood I received an S.O.S. wire, to return here at once because of the critical illness of my mother."[34] He explained that she was now in a hospital in Toledo, confessing that it wasn't clear when or if she would get better. He also let both of them know that he was deeply disappointed to be missing the premiere of *Four Saints in Three Acts*, asking for news of the event. As he wrote to Ailes:

> It is a situation in which I am not at my best, and I don't yet see my way out of it. As long as my mother has been in the hospital, I of course have to be on hand. So here I just am in the lower depths of Ohio, and of spirit too. Tonight more than any night too, because this is the evening when the 4 saints in 3 acts make their N.Y. bow, and it is of course a great occasion from my prejudiced point of view.[35]

By mid-April, even small reminders of life in New York were beginning to fade and, as he told Alice DeLamar, his own health was beginning to be affected:

> Here things get steadily and almost unbearably worse. Mother's heart finally gave out after such a long strain of nervousness + high blood pressure and she has been just barely alive for nearly three weeks. It is so ghastly. We think every day will be the last — but there is always another — until I am almost as much of a wreck as she is. ... I feel utterly alone and so desperately unhappy. I'll hope to see you somewhere later this spring or summer.[36]

Clara Ewing died at the end of April, and her son was inconsolable. Now he was alone in the world, he felt, and unable to cope. Without his mother, he had no idea who he was. He had spent his life trying to live up to her expectations — she was "both the backer and the audience of the show," as he put it — and he was now at a complete loss. As Ewing admitted to DeLamar, his predicament was "not a financial impasse but an emotional and psychological impasse. Bewilderment and loneliness so acute that it is almost unbearable."

> I am sure that you can appreciate this more sympathetically than most people. It is hard to explain to you how dependent I have always been on my Mother, without being with her a great deal in recent years. She has been a real <u>alter ego</u> to me, much more so than I realized. And out of a mistaken generosity, she never allowed me to shoulder a single responsibility of any kind, not the slightest kind ... my life seems torn in two, and all my identity lost. The whole universe is suddenly unfamiliar ground, since my relation to everything in it has suddenly changed. To re-establish some measure of sanity and balance and confidence in myself is my problem now, and I don't know how I can do [that] here, or how I can get away. ... I have been appointed sole executor of both my mother's and my father's estates, and the confusion I am in is beyond recounting. ... But what I need from you most, Alice, is a secure feeling of fellowship and friendship

which I can count on. My friendships, which have been largely
acquaintanceships, have been numerous, profuse and often
indiscriminate. But in a situation like mine at present one does take
stock, and eliminate a great many false values in one's life. I hope
that we may become better friends. I really mean this.[37]

Uncharacteristically, Ewing asked for help, clearly at his wit's end, just
three weeks before his suicide:

What I have to fight most at present is a lack of interest and incentive.
My "work" is hardly worthy of that name. I have always played _at_ my
work, whatever it was, and I have little confidence in its real worth
or in its chances for economic return. A great deal of effort all my life
has gone into playing up to my mother's conception of me. She was
both the backer and the audience of the show. And now I feel like
a lost performer, whose performance isn't very good anyway … It is of
course only an attitude, but something or someone will have to get me
out of it. I hate to resort to Mrs. Eddy! So, please send me anything
you can in the way of bracing me up, or re-instating myself or at least
my illusion of myself. People tell me I am in a condition comparable
to shell shock. I can't see my way through it, and it is comforting
to think of you and of Betsy too on the other side of it somewhere.
I should really love to see you. Until I do, don't forget me![38]

Although a great number of his friends — the Stettheimers, Esther
Murphy, Muriel Draper, Carl Van Vechten, Edward Wasserman, and many
others — wrote letters of support, condolences, and offers of help, Ewing seemed
to be moving steadily toward a point of no return.[39] He was barely holding his
head above water, as he told Ettie Stettheimer:

I do so appreciate letters, or attention of any sort, because I am so
very lonely, doubly lonely, because of the loss of my parents who were
always here when I was here, and because of the loss of all
companionship with my friends, which was always constant and
abundant in New York. Here I have no one, for my interests have
diverged so widely from everyone's interests here that there is almost
no communication at all. Of course people have been very kind and
helpful in many ways, but I feel all alone just the same. And I cannot
get away, because of such a multitude of things to do, and I do not
know how to do any of them. There are odds and ends of real estate in
three states, all difficult or impossible to dispose of, and impossibly
expensive to keep. I have never had any such responsibilities and I
don't know how to assume them. The whole past seems so swept away
and the future so impenetrable, while the present is so solitary and so
confused and stricken. I won't burden you with separate grievances,
but I do want you to know that I need you, all of you, and that I deeply
appreciate all your kindnesses to me in the past, and look forward
to a still firmer friendship with you sometime later.[40]

Though Alice DeLamar wrote on May 22 with an offer of a substantial loan ($1,000 or, "if he preferred," $1,500) that might enable him to "leave Pioneer a little sooner," Ewing was now completely immobilized.[41] As he explained, "I would love to see you and all my other friends, but I am ill myself now and laden down with endless legal and financial responsibilities so I don't see when I can ever get away from this tortured countryside … I am simply stupefied by the turn of events and only trying to avoid a breakdown myself."[42]

Ever loyal, Alice DeLamar wrote again on May 30 with great compassion, encouraging him to do what he needed to do to get out of Pioneer and focus on the future. She encouraged him not to "give yourself up to the situation," but instead to remember that he was ultimately in charge of his own life, adding that "it will doubtless have to mean some form of work taken rather seriously and methodically and not, as formerly, for amusement alone, but for the purpose of buying yourself your freedom to come and go, and live where you choose." She went on:

> You don't need any Mrs Eddys or any "spiritual props" unless I mistake you very much indeed, but you need the encouragement of your friends and the restoration of your self-confidence and above all the urge to get to work at some self-supporting occupation as soon as these estate matters permit your absence. The change of scene, when that time comes, will surely be a god send in itself. … in a few months you will look back on it … so take courage and carry on.

She wrote that, although it may sound banal, "I'm glad you wrote me all about it in more details, as one often feels less haunted by ones [*sic*] depressions after telling about them. Let me hear more any time you feel the urge to write about things, and be sure to let me know, when daylight starts to break through all this, and the impasse begins to dissolve." She signed off, "As ever Alice."[43]

Everyone offered to help, but no one came — and Ewing felt all alone in "that ghost house in Pioneer" with "no diversions … and none of *my people*, just nothing but silence and memories of past pleasures and recent tortures," as he wrote to his friend Joe Brewer.[44] In an undated letter to his uncle from May 1934, Ewing revealed just how far his mental state had fallen: he confessed that he had come to realize that his mother's money worries were "real," and began to blame himself for not taking her more seriously, writing that he was "swamped and bewildered by everything that got mother down." He had no idea how to handle financial affairs — "It is as though I was transplanted to China and alone had to rebuild the great wall," as he put it — and he was beginning to succumb to the despair that he always knew awaited him in Pioneer.

In his own distinctive language, and in the veiled terms that the situation required, he explained to his uncle that he knew himself to be bereft of the companionship that had sustained him in a world of homophobic prejudice:

> I am beside myself with missing the old companionship of Dad and Mother, which is all that ever tied me here, and with missing the abundant companionship of my New York friends, who are all so far away, and while they are sympathetic, and solicitous, they cannot

possibly understand the ramifications of the situation here, and
I cannot share anything with them. If there were only some one some
where for me to really turn to and have around and have things
in common with. But I am as alone as a Pyramid and as confused as
a beetle. My whole past seems swept away in one swoop, the present
seems unbearable, and the future impenetrable.[45]

He ended by saying that he felt like "a trapeze performer with the net taken away,"
and "physically like a wrungout rag." "I don't see how I can get hold of myself here.
I don't see how I can get away. I don't see anything clearly. In short I don't see …
I am really questioning the universe for the first time in my life, and my relation to
any thing in it. I feel as tho I had no identity at all."[46]

Anyone who had been paying attention to Max Ewing for the past ten years
could see that the biggest gaping hole in his life during the spring and early
summer of 1934 was caused by the near complete absence of Muriel Draper.
Throughout 1933, the two had corresponded in chatty letters, and Max had filled
her in with all the news of his adventures in San Francisco and Hollywood, his
progress on his screenplay, and his sightings of mutual friends and movie stars.[47]
Now Muriel's letters were even less frequent, but when she did write, her letters
give a vivid impression of the charisma and enthusiasms that made so many men
and women — Max Ewing included — yearn to be around her; from the sound of
her rapid-fire reminiscences of people and places, she was just as lively and
irresistible now as she had been in London twenty years earlier or in New York.[48]
In September, she described a visit to her old friend Mabel Dodge and her new
husband Tony Luhan in Taos (Mabel had sent the money for the ticket), capturing
details of their eccentric home and peculiar attire in her own distinctive voice and
breathless sentences: "How can I tell you of arriving in plain, bright, high, empty
Raton," she wrote:

> driving through a harsh, beautiful canyon of silver cottonwood and
> pinon trees, crossing hot brooks and cool valleys, arriving before a
> high, phallic adobe wall, going through a gate with a singing bell in it,
> meeting Mabel amidst the burning bush and hollyhocks and green
> sword blades of leaves growing from a pink paved court … Mabel in a
> child's white embroidered short dress and pink shawl? How can I?
> Or of Tony in pink braided hair and blue shirt and turquoise and
> silver jewels and a purple tie and English boots and breeches? … and
> servants in high wide and handsome boots of white deerskin
> and dresses of violet and scarlet cotton? And of Indians dancing in
> the dining-room to Tony and friends' singing and drum beating —
> for hours, lifting their weight up from the ground with it, in
> Dionysian frenzies.[49]

In October, Draper and Dodge briefly visited Ewing in Los Angeles, and
the three of them went to the movies and had dinner together, leaving Ewing little
time to catch up with his friend.[50] Once back in New York, her letters became
even more sporadic: given the huge number of friends and acquaintances who
demanded her attention, Draper could hardly be expected to keep up with the

sheer volume of correspondence she received, but Ewing felt he was in a different category. He had often complained about her long silences when he was traveling in Europe, but he seems to have been completely unprepared for her muted response to his plight as things got worse for him throughout the spring.

Draper thrived on the thrill of discovering fresh talents and new friendships among the ever-changing parade of characters who trailed through her at-home gatherings, and she clearly had little tolerance for failure. She had seen enough of it in the case of her husband, Paul, who died of alcoholism and depression, and she had had high hopes for Max Ewing as a concert pianist and seemed ready to support him in each of the artistic endeavors — popular music, sculpture, photography, playwriting — to which he turned his hand. Nevertheless, while she genuinely loved her young friend and enjoyed his sophisticated company when they went to concerts or the theater, when he left New York City, her interest began to stray toward other people and problems, notably the young and energetic Lincoln Kirstein, the School of American Ballet, and their shared enthusiasm for both Balanchine and Soviet Russia.[51] Kirstein's diaries for April and May of 1934 are filled with descriptions of parties and gatherings with friends for cocktails and gossip, notes recording the arrival of Gurdjieff in New York in late April and their almost daily meetings with him, and his recollections, often verbatim, of the anecdotes Muriel told and what she wore, just as Ewing's letters had been.[52] Muriel Draper had clearly moved on. She wasn't cruel or callous, just impatient with weakness and easily bored.

When she did communicate, her advice was to encourage Ewing to return home to New York as quickly as he could; she even offered to put him up at her spare room for as long as he needed to regain his footing. She seemed to have no clue about the morass of legal and family entanglements that preyed on him, nor of the increasingly serious depression he was falling into. On March 26, Ewing tried to put on a brave face and explain the situation to her. "Prepare your chamber à louer," he wrote,

> but I don't know when I can ever get there to occupy it. Anyway, have it padded for a padded cell is what I'll be needing when I do get there. Mother is at home again and not much better after her two months in sanitariums. She hovers between living and not living, and between reason and unreason. Two nights ago we thought surely she was dying, but she rallied … I am literally at my wits end and don't know what to do next. My grandmother gets older, deafer, more exasperating, and *stronger* every day … Whatever am I going to do about these two women? They are entirely alone without relative or friend to assume any slightest responsibility for them. And at the same time they are both utterly unrelated to my life and I cannot establish any contact with them. I cannot exist indefinitely in this backwater town … I am just this side of a breakdown myself.[53]

After his mother died at the end of April, Ewing wrote to Draper to say that he needed her, hinting that "if only someone in NY were at loose ends this spring and could come out and help me by just being with me." He clearly had no idea that she had not the slightest intention of joining him in Pioneer, and he continued to harp on his loneliness:

At present I am unable to do anything … all alone in that ghost house
in Pioneer — trying to decide what to do with their dear belongings
and clothes, and all the accumulation of thirty years of living, in a
house full of memories. I really cannot endure it … I really am in fear
of a complete emotional and physical collapse. I know it must
surprise you for me to give way in this way, just as it surprised me and
seemed incredible that my mother gave way. But we are very much
alike and so identified with each other — my mother and I — that
once I am left in her predicament I almost automatically follow her
process which was just collapse. … I am sick, and utterly alone, and
funds are tied up by mountainous litigation. I have no incentive to go
on at all, except what you and a few other cherished friends can
provide me with … Can't you send me some strength, some part of
yourself, <u>something</u>?[54]

Most of her friends understood that it was a mistake to rely on the
mercurial Muriel Draper for emotional support, yet that was precisely what Max
Ewing was doing, repeatedly asking for more letters and more attention — with
the predictable result. She was unfailingly interested in people and always fun
and amusing; she had two beloved sons of her own, and she did not want to be
confused with anyone else's mother. On the contrary, she flirted, and goaded,
and basked in the admiration and passionate attachment (often sexual) of "her"
young men. Like Carl Van Vechten, she was a gadfly who had created a life of
perpetual motion and innovation for herself in which very few people — Esther
Murphy perhaps, or Alice DeLamar — held her attention for very long. The more
eloquently Ewing described the details of his misery and loneliness, the more
distant she became.

Draper's responses to Ewing's letters — when she bothered to write back
at all — were entirely consistent with the way she lived her own life. She was
fearless in the face of adversity, cobbling together fashionable outfits from dime-
store remnants and hand-me-downs, and ever-hopeful of new conquests and
new opportunities among the men and women who shared her vision for the
burgeoning American cultural revival of the 1920s and '30s. In 1934, she was busy
thinking about the political world and its problems, and she was unmoved by the
harsh realities of Ewing's personal situation. As she wrote to him in an undated
letter from early June 1934:

Dearest Max: Your letters are becoming more and more discouraging,
and I am really puzzled as to how to proceed! You seem so aware
of your dilemma that I cannot believe that you are unable to cope
with it. This is the one time in your life when you CAN realize reality
and if you slide away from it this time, you will find yourself twice as
unable to deal with it the next time — and life doesn't become easier
as it continues, particularly the life that is ahead of all of us during the
next twenty-five years. If you would just DO SOMETHING — wash
the dishes or cook a dinner (I myself taught you how to cook sausages!)
you would find a certain energy coming back to you which you could
direct to other tax-paying and affidavit-signing channels.[55]

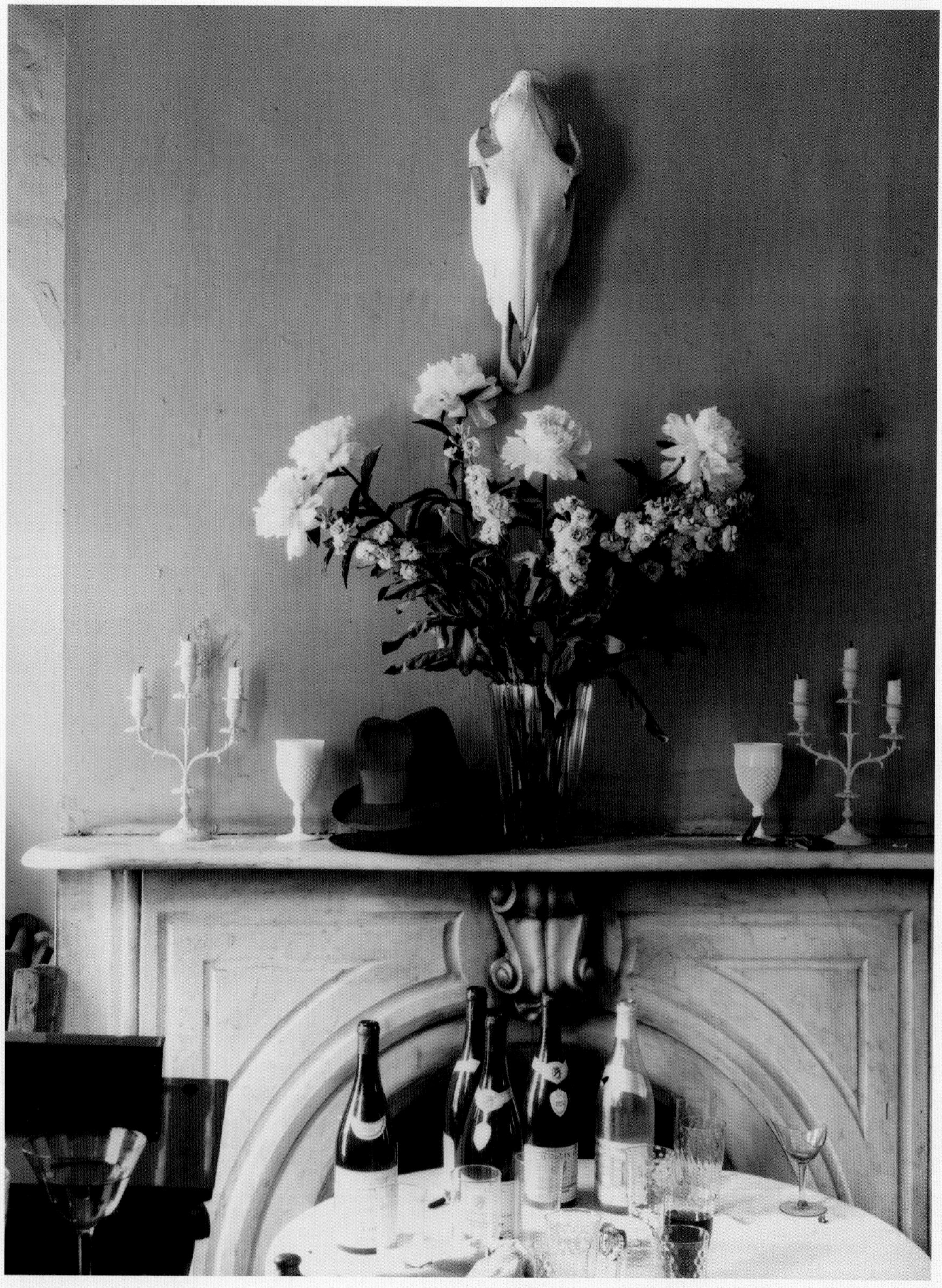

6.3 Walker Evans, *Drawing Room in Muriel Draper's Apartment, New York City*, May 29, 1934, film negative, 6½ × 8½ in. (16.51 × 21.59 cm). Walker Evans Archive, Metropolitan Museum of Art, New York.

Her advice captures the spirit of resilience and curiosity that had always characterized her life in Europe and the United States, a spirit that was clearly entirely missing as Ewing despaired at losing his mother, his New York life, and, eventually, Draper herself. She adamantly refused to accept that he was finally out of "brilliant" ideas, and she encouraged him to treat the situation as an intellectual challenge rather than an emotional disaster. Her suggestions are preposterous, but well-intentioned. "I should think," she wrote:

> that there would be a kind of fascination in delving through all of those dear and memory-laden objects in that very American house, and transforming the cage you speak of trapping your mother and father, into a place to which all your friends would like to come.
> Is there nothing you could do there while getting through all these details which would establish a basis of some sort for a future and diverting life? You are so ingenious and brilliantly resourceful that some fantasy of yours could turn Pioneer into a Central City Salzburg Mecca which would be included in the itinerary of every civilized American in the future which hovers so thrillingly before us, and in which the Pioneers and Green Bays and Grand Rapids will be of much more importance that the Lidos and Monte Carlos and Dolomites of the past.[56]

Her letter continues in the same well-intentioned but tone-deaf fashion: "I do not have to tell you how irksome and unwelcome I know responsibility to be," she noted in closing, "but I can assure you that no burden is as heavy once it is lifted as it is on the ground."

In the last months of Ewing's life, Draper was focused on her own family, her friends, and her life in New York, and she was busy planning the celebration of her son Smudge's wedding and the bachelor party she was hosting for him at her home. The aftermath of that event was captured in all its glorious disarray in a series of extraordinary photographs taken by Walker Evans on May 30, 1934 (figs. 1.18, 6.3). These show not only the profusion of empty wine bottles and half-filled glasses from the night before, but also the extravagant flowers, the cow's skull hung on the wall (reminiscent of the paintings of her friend Georgia O'Keeffe from the early 1930s), and the candelabras on either side of her living room mantle. Here too are Draper's thrift-shop treasures (including the little round table that appears in Ewing's photo of Draper from two years earlier), the billowing silk drapes, and the enormous gilt throne that was her trademark. Lincoln Kirstein noted in his diary for May 30 that he had stopped by Muriel's house at 312 East 53rd Street the afternoon following the party and found Evans photographing the "incredible detritus of the parlor after last night's usher's dinner, a more lushly disastrous scene I never witnessed."[57] As had been the case for the premiere of *Four Saints in Three Acts* earlier in the winter, Max Ewing had missed out on one of the most glamorous events of the season.

Preoccupied with her own affairs, Draper tried to deflect Ewing's attention onto Jack Pollock, the boxer and ex-marine whom she and Ewing had taken up two years earlier and with whom Ewing had remained close. Referring to him as his "trainer," Ewing had, for a period of time in 1932, made Pollock his constant companion in New York, and he had photographed him many times for the

Carnival of Venice series and in informal settings. As discussed earlier, Van Vechten's scrapbooks made frequent use of these images, using captions like "Party Perfect," "Sensational Trade," and "Eager for Sex" to spoof Pollock's beautiful athletic physique and his unlikely role in the lives of both Draper, with whom he had a brief affair, and Ewing, who saw Pollock regularly during his stay in Hollywood and in Pioneer. Like Ewing's family and many of his neighbors in Pioneer, Van Vechten was suspicious of Pollock's motives: his reuse of the photo showing Pollock in his boxer's stance (fig. 6.4) included the captions "Men who like boxers … Love 'em with A Tasty Meat," and "He Knows

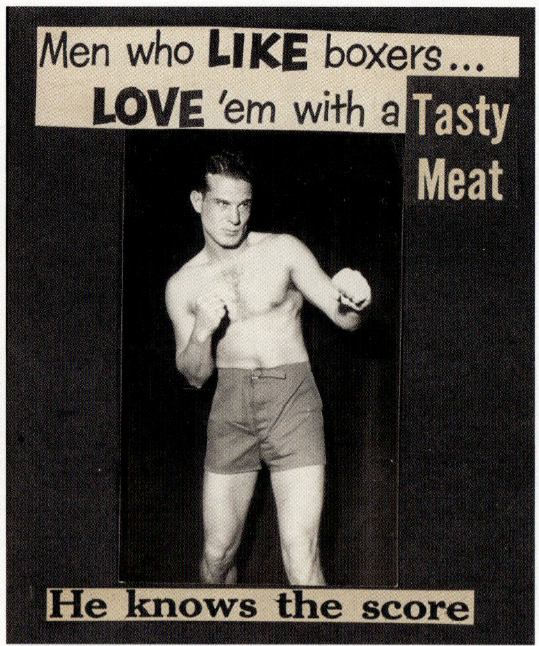

6.4 Carl Van Vechten, "Men Who Like Boxers," collage with photograph of Jack Pollock by Max Ewing and found text, from Carl Van Vechten's scrapbook.

the Score." As with other Pollock photos that he collaged with text in his scrapbook, his humor was hardly subtle: he may have enjoyed looking at Pollock's muscular body, but he got his negative judgment across.

Jack Pollock made regular visits to Ohio starting in January 1934, sometimes staying with Ewing in his parents' home or with nearby neighbors; when Ewing's mother died in April and his mental condition worsened, Pollock came for longer periods and took responsibility for his care, cooking him meals, helping him write letters, and keeping him company. Knowing that Jack was in Pioneer, and anxious to get on her with life, Draper encouraged their friendship: "Jack is the loyal and helpful angel we knew him to be," she advised, "and if you let him down by not responding to his help, I will never forgive you," adding that Ewing should "Thank him for his letter [to her] and for being there when you need him so much."[58] In the same letter, she dropped a bombshell: in July she was going to London and Russia — "yes, RUSSIA I said" — leaving Ewing behind … in Pioneer. Her words were intended to put paid to the feelings of guilt that kept tugging at her heartstrings, and her letter thus has all of the hallmarks of a well-planned breakup speech: "You are very dear and necessary to me," she wrote:

> but are becoming almost a stranger to me in your new state. Nothing is unbearable and you MUST stop nursing yourself, and begin to live again, or you will make yourself into a permanent neurotic for no good reason at all. One's father and mother DO die, but it is ungrateful to them and their memory to refuse life because of it.[59]

Ewing responded as bravely as he could: his last letter is beautifully written, confessional, and abject — and, of course, had exactly the opposite effect from the one he hoped for. "I have basked in your light for so long," Ewing confessed, "and I have been deluded into thinking I was part of that light." He went on:

> I know now that I never was. But I still cling so to the illusion. And more than anything I would like to go with you to Russia.

How magnificent that you can go. You have thought for me and felt
for me so long, I haven't needed to think or feel, and have done
neither, ever … Jack is here, ready to do anything and everything for
me … I do not wonder I seem a stranger to you. I am a stranger to
myself … Dear Muriel, how I need you. I need you.[60]

Jack was handsome and loyal and completely unlike anyone Ewing or
Draper knew in New York or anywhere else — he moved from town to town across
the United States, hitchhiking, hopping freight cars, and picking up odd jobs
when he wasn't able to find work as a boxer. Pollock and Ewing both knew that
nothing could substitute for Draper's presence, and so did she, in her heart of
hearts. Certainly, the relationship between the two men was unusual and
complicated, pushing the boundaries of acceptable behavior, yet it may well have
been exactly what it appears to be: an unusual friendship in which each man got
something from the other — love, praise, intimacy, excitement — that neither had
ever known. As Ewing wrote from Hollywood in September 1933:

This weekend has been pleasant because Jack Pollock, my "trainer"
arrived to spend three days with me. He came down from Reno where
he has been recently. He covers more ground that anyone I know.
Since he left New York last fall for Florida he has been in practically
every state in the Union. And I always knew where he was because he
wrote me every week, and sometimes oftener than that. I have never
known such devotion. He really idolizes me and there is nothing
he would not do for me. And he is the first person I would call on in
an emergency to do anything I could not handle myself. We are so
absolutely unlike each other, and that is undoubtedly part of the bond
between us. He is such an athlete and husky, and able to get about
the country on no funds at all if necessary.[61]

The possibility of a sexual relationship between the two men was always
present, but the evidence is, as usual, inconclusive. Indeed, this may have
been precisely what sustained their connection. The sexual tension was never
completely absent from their communications, and that, of course, added a
consistent element of excitement. Pollock frequently signed his letters "Love,
Jack," or even "Love Always." In August 1933, he wrote at some length to clarify
his meaning, using language that suggests just how awkward and unresolved
his feelings actually were: "I don't know why I'm writing this way pal," he wrote,
"But you did so much for me that Ill [sic] never forget it," adding that "from the
looks" of his letters, "one would think I was married to you & here we are a couple
of regular Boy's. Well I'm positive that no one will see this that's why Im writing
in this way."[62] Another letter from Pollock, written the same month from
San Francisco, chides Ewing for signing his postcards "Love, Max":

It seems as tho you are having a delightfully time in Dear old
Hollywood … you don't ever get to Be to Big a shot but what this lad
will Ball you out when necessary … Max I appreciate the Signature of
Love and the end of your card & feel delighted that you feel that way
about this old horse in the ring. But please Don't address cards that

way for some one might misconstrue the meaning of the word if they didn't know what friends we are & then you know Id [*sic*] politely have to punch the Hell out of some one. In the future just address them Friend or pal "O.K. Max Old boy!"[63]

Jack Pollock had been married before he met Ewing and Draper in New York, and he often wrote about how badly his wife had treated him; he was grateful to his new friends for picking him up when he had sunk so low. In his letters — some of which are no doubt missing from the archive — he wrote to Ewing about his boxing matches, his financial woes (regularly asking for small loans), and his feelings, not just about his prospects in the ring, but also about how he felt about Ewing and others. In October 1933, for example, he sent a long, rambling letter from Burley, Idaho after seeing Ewing in Hollywood:

> Max you know me & you also know that I have taken plenty in my time especially from the girl that was my wife. You called me a gentle men [*sic*] while I was their. You were right Max only lots of other people don't think so Because I never tell them a dam thing. Im just not interested that's all. Why I Became so attached to you is more than I can explain But without a doubt you are the Best person I have ever known in my life or shall ever meet ...[64]

He went on to say that Ewing didn't have to apologize for not showing him a more exciting time or introducing him to more of his friends, "Max I came to see you & Pal Im [*sic*] glad I did for you are you & all I wanted to see so knock off the apologies it isn't necessary & if I live to be a thousand I could never spend a happier week end."

Between the nude photographs that Ewing took for *The Carnival of Venice* in 1932, the boxer's regular visits to see his friend in New York, Hollywood, and Pioneer in 1933 and 1934, and the fact Pollock often wrote to Ewing about how much he cared for him, the evidence certainly suggests intimacy that went beyond friendship. As Jack suggested more than once, anyone reading their letters would certainly have found them queer, yet only the two men themselves knew for certain what went on between them. Ewing loved looking at his beautiful friend, especially when he took his clothes off, and he enjoyed having a devoted friend like Pollock to pal around with: that may have been enough, given his scruples and his closeness with his mother. Pollock seemed to confirm this when he wrote to Alice DeLamar after Ewing's death that while Max Ewing "did have emotions at times," and "would always be the one lovely boy in my life," Max "didn't have the nerve to make an approach and follow them through."[65] Though very few of Ewing's friends or family members believed a word Jack Pollock said in this or any other regard, this may have been the truth.

Up until the end of April 1934, Pollock seems to have remained, for the most part, in Idaho and Washington state, filling his letters with chatty news. He often wrote about how busy he was, adding in one note that he was trying to exercise more and hoped to "get Back down to [his] old form when [he] was Exquisite and Decorative and such and such," flirtatiously quoting words that had obviously been used by Ewing. In another letter from about the same time, he thanked Ewing for sending his photo, writing "Your picture is swell.

Gee punk why the hell did they make you so good looking & with so Many
Brains & cheat me out of Both."[66] In March, he again visited Pioneer and stayed
long enough to lend a hand with some of the driving and housework, but he soon
left, saying that he planned to travel to Alaska, and that he was hoping to
go to China.[67]

Pollock's letters from May take a very different tone, making it clear that
his reaction to Ewing's dark communications after his mother's death was similar
to that of other friends: he encouraged Ewing to be brave and to get on with the
business that needed to be done — but he kept his distance. "My poor old heart
goes out to you Max," he wrote, saying that "sooner or later all must go But its
terrible hard when they are so close to you."[68] Yet, even Pollock was shocked by
the change in his friend in the weeks that followed, writing that Ewing's letters
"frightened" him, and adding that he knew Max had a "hard assignment" but
needed to "pull [himself] together & finish your job." He also told Ewing that, in his
estimation, he was "as Brave as any fighter that ever crawled through the ropes or
any cop that ever shot it out as man to man with a thug as any Body."[69] Hoping to
cheer him up, he reminded him that the experience they "went through" in
Pioneer would "Bring us lots closer & I can safely say that I shall always want you
for my own favorite friend."

Despite his good intentions, and Draper's encouragement, Pollock's decision to
return to Pioneer in late May threw the little town into a state of confusion and
opened up the flood gates of suspicion among family members and neighbors.[70]
What was the itinerant, plain-spoken "prize-fighter" doing in town again if not
trying to manipulate their friend and take his money? He had certainly arranged
for a number of loans from the Ewings' neighbors, and then left them to be settled
by Max's estate.[71] What was going on between them anyway? Pollock's ideas
about how to cheer up his friend mostly extended to holding nightly parties in the
Ewing home, drinking wine, and playing records; years later, Doris Ewing reported
to Carl Van Vechten that it was "hard for the Pioneeronians to pass the house
and see shades drawn in daylight and lights on all night, all with MUCH REVELRY
and WHOOPLA before the sun rose!"[72] Jack cozied up to the ladies and held hands
with the married telephone operator who lived next door, but Ewing refused to
leave the house and wouldn't buy food, claiming, as his mother had, that there
was no money.[73]

Ewing's elderly grandmother — nicknamed "Doddy" — lived across town
and, almost from the first, took against Jack and made her feelings clear in her
own, plainspoken way. Ewing had written to her from New York from time to time,
but her bad temper, always buffered by her daughter, Clara, during her lifetime,
made Ewing agitated and morose. Even the usual banter and humor from
Jack — so much a part of their earlier life — didn't help. As Pollock wrote to
Draper in an undated letter, written in the middle of June:

> here is a boy you may think you know But Im [*sic*] pretty sure you
> don't know. Max Ewing has never had an affair with Man Woman or
> Child. A Boy 31 Years old that has with out a doubt Been everything
> I am not. I was Ill in 1932 if you will refresh your memory & Max
> Ewing and I must say your self helped to pull me out of it. Now there

has come a time in my life where I'm doing the Best I know how to
pull Max back to Par & its such a difficult job that I don't think I can
stick much longer.[74]

In June, Pollock realized that he was out of his depth and
concluded — along with Ewing's family in Grand Rapids — that the only person
who could help his friend was Muriel Draper herself. A half-finished letter
to her from Ewing, written the week before his death, trails off mid-page, ending
with a hastily scrawled note from Jack:

Max feels he can't go on and write you any more. But that is part
of his case. He calls himself unworthy of just every thing which is
untrue for that Boy is a great unusual kid as we both know.
And Muriel he is coming on out of this and will see you next week
if possible. I do hope nothing interferes with his coming.[75]

Pollock wrote to Draper later to sum up the situation:

We both knew Max when. But the Max of today is so different and
very difficult for I'm no Brother or anything altho I treat him like
a two year old Bro. or have but now it is so different & he has changed
so. I shall do all I can to try and get him there with you awhile but it
does seem quite hopeless at times for he make [*sic*] it so difficult.
He does seem quite normal some times and then again so far from me
or anyone at times. Love Jack.[76]

It was all becoming just too much to bear, and eventually Draper broke her
long silence, writing to Ewing that she loved him too much to let him die:

Dearest Max, I am where you need me, close to you always and
forever. I haven't written because words seem so inadequate, and I
have been trying so hard to go out to you and be beside you in the
flesh, and give you the strength you justly need but I haven't been able
to arrange it ... This is just to tell you that what does not kill you
makes you stronger and that you cannot die yet — I love you too much
and need you too much for such a thing to be possible, even if you
wanted it, which you do *not*, even for a second ... More tomorrow.
Proceed, proceed and all other things will fall away. Love, Muriel.[77]

She added a breezy postscript: "Very busy with weddings, and sailings, and
review of fleets, and publishers and sheriffs."

As we know, her words arrived too late to make a difference. On June 16,
1934, Ewing's uncle A. E. Ewing wrote to Draper to warn her that his nephew and
Jack Pollock were on their way:

I have just received long distance advice from Pioneer, Ohio, that
Max and his friend Pollock left Pioneer yesterday by auto for New
York ... Max is in Poor health, and in my judgment, should not have
attempted the New York trip ... in addition I am informed that

Max did not wish to make the trip, and that Mr. P. virtually dragged
him into it … He told me a month ago that the one person who would
be a comfort to him was you.[78]

What he didn't know was that the two men had only made it as far as Binghamton,
New York, where they stopped for lunch and to fill up the car. Left unattended in a
small café, Ewing walked to the steep bank of the nearby Susquehanna River,
removed his clothes, folded them neatly on the ground, and plunged into the
water. A. E. Ewing wrote to Draper to give her the news: "Max Ewing was drowned
in the river this PM … I have been advised by the undertaker at Pioneer that 'Jack'
Pollock will return to Pioneer with the body. Presume the burial will take place
Wednesday-Thursday at latest."[79]

Ewing's suicide was traumatic for everyone but the most callous of his
acquaintances, and Draper took the news particularly hard. Nevertheless,
still unwilling to concede an inch to his former rival, Lincoln Kirstein casually
noted the event in his diary, adding that Muriel Draper was struggling to come to
terms with her guilt and anger, but that he was unmoved.[80] "Mools is silent and
remote," Kirstein wrote a few days later, "taking most of the responsibility
of Max Ewing's suicide. She naturally can find little comfort in me, since when she
prophesied it a month ago I said 'and a good thing for him.'"[81]

Jack Pollock was, understandably, completely undone by the
tragedy — exhausted, guilty, and alone. Having returned briefly to Pioneer, his
only thought was to get back to Muriel in New York City, where he found her
surrounded by the usual assortment of friends and hangers-on. No one was in
mourning for Max Ewing. In the short period that he had been absent from the
New York scene, the parade had moved on and other people had taken his place:
Kirstein and his friends were ascendant, and Draper was — as she had herself
written — busy with her own affairs and planning her trip to Russia. Pollock had
never been a true insider in that world in any case: he never really was more than
a good-looking curiosity whom Draper and Ewing had picked up along the way.
Worse still, as Kirstein noted, he kept bursting into tears, talking about Max
Ewing, and making pronouncements of the sort that filled his letters. Nobody
really found Pollock amusing any more.

It wasn't long before Draper was searching for ways to get rid of him.
First, she tried to pass him off to Edward Wasserman, but he soon wore out his
welcome in the queer, luxurious milieu of Wasserman's Long Island summer
retreat, refusing to join in the festivities. Meeting a few days later for cocktails
with Kirstein and other friends, Draper ridiculed his cowboy drawl, his Stetson
hat, and the way he seemed always to be playing a role: Kirstein reported that
"Mools says it is difficult to over-estimate the effect of the films on the idea he has
of himself as Clark Gable, hopping freights etc."[82] She couldn't bear the
melodrama or the despair. When Pollock confessed it was taking all of his "self-
control" not to throw himself off of the fourth floor of her house, she flew into a
rage and called him a "coward."[83] He was a "crashing bore and a drunk," she told
her friends, and she sent him away.[84]

Soon Draper's friends circled the wagons, ready to assure her that
Ewing's death wasn't her fault. One of the clearest statements came from Carl
Van Vechten: "Thinking everything over dearest Madraper" — the name
he gave her to complement his own "Carlopa" — he assured her that he was

almost convinced that Max's act was the result of a realization on his
part that he was (at least partially) insane, a fear that you would
recognize this and an inability to face the (probable) consequences.
If he were insane, and Jack Pollock's report of his reaction to burned
carrots is pretty good evidence, he is thrice blessed for doing what
he did. Think all that he and we have avoided! Whether or no [*sic*] he
was insane, I think it must have been <u>fear</u> of insanity that drove him
to this walk into the river.

He concluded that he, too, was "haunted by the whole story, more even today
than I was last night, but I don't think you have any reason to reproach yourself.
Had you acted differently you might have precipitated something worse."[85]

Van Vechten channeled his grief (and curiosity, no doubt) into doing what
he did best: he turned Max Ewing's life into a story — a glamorous, beautiful,
American tale of a queer, young man's rise and fall — from which he, and others,
could learn. Ever the collector, Van Vechten was quick to realize that Ewing's
papers would be a gold mine for the sort of queer history that interested him
most, writing to Ewing's uncle to suggest that perhaps there would be a way to
preserve his books and papers in an archive:

> I was in Europe when Max died and only returned recently, or you
> should have heard from me. Inexpressibly shocked by the tragedy
> which, however — and the more I hear about it the more I am
> convinced of this — seems unavoidable. Before I had your letter I had
> talked at length with Muriel Draper and Jack [*sic*] Brewer: so I had a
> pretty good idea of what happened ... Max had a pretty interesting
> collection of books, photographs and manuscripts (I believe that even
> during his sojourn in Hollywood he wrote two plays). Couldn't
> something be done to preserve this collection (or a part of it) intact as
> a slight memorial to his charming soul. I think it would be a pity for
> his more personal effects to be scattered and I would like to think they
> could be gathered together somewhere where persons like myself,
> personally interested, could examine them at leisure some day.[86]

With the family's blessing, Van Vechten began putting together an archive,
relying heavily on Max's cousin Doris, a teacher only a few years older than he,
with whom Ewing had shared many years of family visits, childhood dress-up
performances, and any number of New York adventures, dancing in Harlem and
admiring his collections. Doris Ewing thus became Van Vechten's staunchest
ally in the creation of the Max Ewing Archive at Yale. For nearly ten years,
she dug into nooks and crannies and opened drawers to look for letters, returning
a number of times to Pioneer, contacting Ewing's friends, and enduring Van
Vechten's frequent hectoring and reminders that she needed to try harder.

Doris Ewing had been worried that people would see the nude photos and
judge her cousin — in one letter of 1943, she termed these images his "naked
SEX assortments" — and she wanted to protect him from posthumous
humiliation. She was not just worried about her cousin's homosexuality, but also
about his peculiar tastes and habits. In fact, she wasn't far wrong, yet she

realized, eventually and with Van Vechten's help, that this was precisely why it was important to tell Max Ewing's story: soon after he died, people began to whisper that it was his homosexuality that had made him susceptible to the sort of insanity that would cause him to take his own life. One such comment came in a letter to Jack Pollock from a neighbor, Frances Bollinger, who had worked for the Ewings: seeking to comfort him, she wrote that "people like Max that are not normal as you and I all do it; his uncles and their wives told me that was at the bottom of the whole thing."[87]

Van Vechten confronted these anxieties head on: as he wrote to Doris Ewing, "You quoted a doctor in one of your letters as saying … being what he was and having what he had, Max wouldn't last long, or words to that effect. Do you know this doctor? Would he write you a letter or could you ask him what he meant by all this?"[88] As he had reassured her many times, Ewing wasn't well-known or famous, and he wasn't even able to sell his plays and novels while he was alive. Ewing's collection had no monetary value, yet Van Vechten (and he hoped Doris as well) wanted him to be remembered and useful to later historians — "persons like myself," as he had written to Doris's father, "personally interested."

Writing to Doris Ewing in 1942 as their project drew to a close, Van Vechten was kind and unusually relaxed and happy: "Let us, indeed, congratulate ourselves in everything being in order," he declared, "Max is on his own now BUT NOT OUT IN THE RAIN. We will see what posterity makes of all this!"[89] In January 1943, he celebrated again: "The Good News," he told her, "is that the letters and the scrapbooks and the photographs and the whatnots are practically ready to go to Yale." Noting that his friend (and lover) Mark Lutz had done a "superb job" cataloguing the letters and making notes — "Practically a life's work and he had done it in about three months, spending every minute of his time on this job" — he declared himself satisfied. Van Vechten then symbolically threw open the doors of the archive, offering up exactly the sort of energetic, optimistic challenge to his audience that he made so often, in word and deed, across the span of his long career: "We have all done Max PROUD," he declared, "and he is laid out for future generations to make what they can of. I prophesy that it will be a lot."[90] Van Vechten was entirely correct, as we know: by placing his faith and energy in preserving the story of Max Ewing's unusual life and times, he ensured that his archive at Yale would become a treasure trove of extraordinary documents and pictures, rich with the promise of new discoveries.

THE POLITICS AND POETICS OF THE ARCHIVE

By committing the better part of a decade to Max Ewing and his archive, Carl Van Vechten was not only able to create a loving memorial to his young friend, but also managed to conjure an unusually joyful and uninhibited queer space where he, and others "like him," as he put it, could study Ewing's life and see themselves in his words and images. Indeed, while Ewing's story ended tragically, for all but the last six months of his life — a period of despair spent in Pioneer, Ohio, exiled from his beloved New York bohemia — he celebrated his distinctive and quirky tastes, his snobbish opinions, and even, more surprisingly, his queer identity, describing his parties for his mother and other correspondents, and detailing his visits to the lesbian-run bookstores of Paris and the queer hotels and cafés of Venice and Villefranche. Toward the end of his life he also wrote about his feelings, drawing back the curtain on emotions that most archives suppress or ignore. His late letters, like the ones written by Jack Pollock in 1933 and 1934, are extraordinarily candid, passionate, and decidedly queer, rare survivals preserved by women — Clara Ewing, Alice DeLamar, Muriel Draper, and Doris Ewing — and sent along to Van Vechten when he asked for them. The chain of events that delivered these papers to Yale, and from there to us, was certainly fragile and extremely unlikely.

The queer space of the Max Ewing archive is also notable because during the last, painful months of his life in Pioneer, Ewing was entirely cut off from the emotional and physical realities of his queer bohemia, and starved for the sort of queer space that he and his friends shared, a space — or rather a "queer archipelago" of safe spaces in the city — that Ewing, quite literally, could not live without. Gone were the pleasures of the little playhouse in the room above his parents' store where he cross-dressed and acted out scenes from opera with his cousin and other girls: now he was no longer seen as a brilliant eccentric boy, protected by his powerful parents; he was an isolated, unhappy queer man stranded in the American Midwest in the middle of the Depression. His mother and his happy family life were gone, and he had nothing with which to replace them.

The radical nature of both Max Ewing's archive and of Carl Van Vechten's commitment to its preservation cannot be overstated: Ewing's voice is unique in queer history, to be sure, but equally, the mere survival of such first-person narratives and vivid images of people and places, is virtually unknown. Moreover, Ewing's photographic projects, from the gallery and catalogue of his *Collection of Extraordinary Portraits* to *The Carnival of Venice*, record a world of queer faces and emotions that would have disappeared entirely were it not for their chance survival here. Foundational scholars from George Chauncey, author of *Gay New York*, to Cassandra Langer, the biographer of Romaine Brooks, to Jonathan Weinberg, the art historian who brought the queer art of Charles Demuth and Marsden Hartley to the attention of a broad public, wove their stories together from diverse fragments: like prospectors sifting for nuggets of gold, they have had to separate the treasures of authentic, queer texts and images from the silt of homophobic legal judgments and critiques.

By contrast, Max Ewing's archive is filled with riches, personal and poetic, that often appear to have been created in a soundproof chamber: he frequently seems oblivious to the world beyond his own private reality. This is a man who sent a roll of film filled with photographs of nude men to his local drugstore to be developed, only to have it returned as "unprintable." Did he really not know, or care, about the consequences? Either way, we are the beneficiaries of his foolhardiness, his privilege, and his unpredictable lack of shame: his archive enables us to see his city and his friends — queer and straight — through his own eyes.

Like Van Vechten's queer scrapbooks and Charles Demuth's watercolors, Max Ewing's letters and photographs open up a world shaped by the language of camp performance and the necessity of evasion that nonetheless rings true with remarkable clarity. This is an archive largely free of the ignorant prejudices of the 1920s and '30s: the performative veils and camp language that Ewing constructed may distract us, but they barely conceal his delighted embrace of who he was and what he became in New York City. The door of his closet, both literal and figurative, was frequently open to his parents, his family, his friends, and his neighbors. He was handsome and charming and more than a little bit reckless in his passion for self-disclosure, secure in his finances and in the knowledge that his family and friends adored him. Perhaps this is why he was so beloved in his own time, and why he emerges as such a compelling and charismatic narrator today. It is also, of course, why his story is so very sad.

In recent years, a number of writers, notably the historian Saidiya Hartman and the poet-philosophers Stefano Harney and Fred Moten, have highlighted the ways in which official descriptions of the lives of people of color, and of women in particular, are robbed of nuance and feeling by the failure of those narratives to record and honor the emotions and experiences of the disempowered.[1] These authors encourage us to shift our attention to the spaces *between* or on the margins of official events and environments: they ask us to look for the incidental, the unplanned, and the unpredicted in the evidence we examine, like the plant on the windowsill in a photograph purporting to record the poverty of a living space, or the words in an oral history describing ordinary day-to-day conversations. In different but similar ways, Hartman, Harney, and Moten thus highlight the politics and the poetics of silences and fragments, and while the experiences of trauma and racism they focus on are fundamentally different from the experiences of the primarily white, middle-class subjects we encounter in many queer archives, our challenge is in many ways very similar: it is through the words of the outliers, and in the fragmented stories of "wayward lives" (Hartman's phrase) and "fugitive" acts (Moten's) that we find new evidence to repair the damage to the historical record.

Perhaps unsurprisingly, the most captivating fragments in Hartman's alternative archive — at least for our purposes here — are those relating to subjects who are both Black and queer, and to lives frequently shared by Black and white friends and lovers, such as the oral history compiled by the lesbian entertainer and activist Mabel Hampton about her adventures as a young woman in the 1920s. These extraordinary recollections are preserved in the Lesbian Herstory Archive, where Hampton describes — among many other things — her visit, together with her white girlfriend, to an all-day and all-night party in the home of A'lelia Walker in Harlem.[2] What she saw and heard expands in startling detail the picture that we already have of such interracial gatherings and their sexual permissiveness from the letters of Max Ewing and the recollections of others in his circle; taken together, these sources open up a world of interracial experience and queer feeling — from love to excitement and joy — that is largely hidden from history, and in so doing, cast new light on the tentative experiment that Ewing, Van Vechten, and their friends pursued.

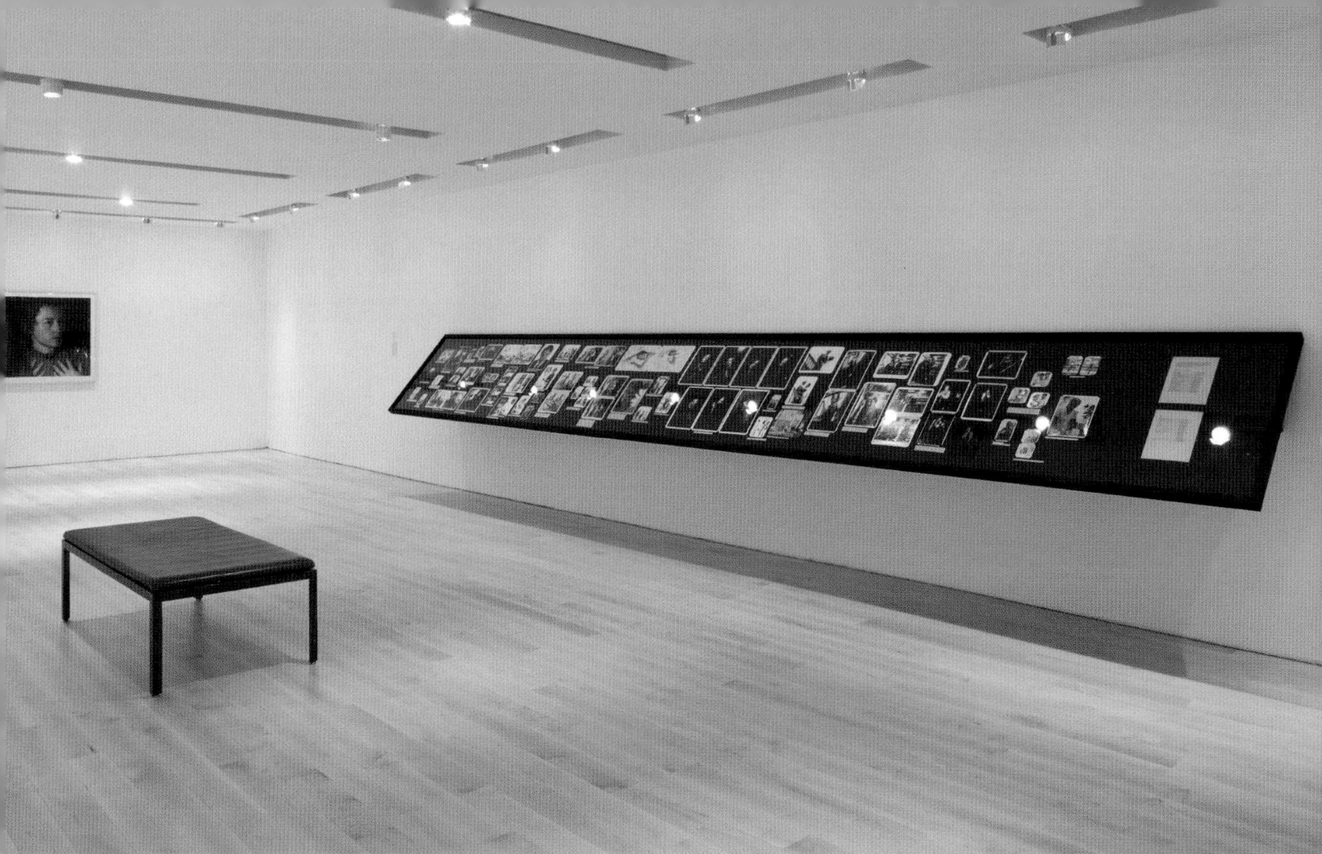

Moreover, Hartman's notion of "critical fabulation" — the imaginative reconstruction of the blank spaces and silences in Black History to create stories rich in emotion and nuance — is an extraordinary tool for historians, one that deftly underscores the fact that the work of writing about the public and private lives of people in the past is both an art and a science, driven by both imagination and data. This notion, while fully described in Hartman's writings, was also explored in the *Fae Richards Photo Archive*, a collaborative installation created between 1993 and 1996 by the photographer Zoe Leonard and the filmmaker Cheryl Dunye that purports to document, through a collection of snapshots and studio portraits, the life of a fictional Black lesbian actress and blues singer in the 1930s. As described by the curator Okwui Enwezor in the catalogue to his 2008 exhibition *Archive Fever: Uses of the Document in Contemporary Art*, "Leonard's *The Fae Richards Photo Archive* (1993–96) draws from … a combination of object, story, and parodic invocation of the archive as the space of lost or forgotten stories," imagining "the existence of such an archive of lost stories moldering in trunk boxes in damp basements."[3]

Here the images (fig. E.1) are entirely convincing as evidence from an individual's life story, and they are especially vivid when they are brought together as a chronological, group display of photos of various shapes and sizes, with all of the irregularities of "real" documents, haphazardly preserved. Following philosopher Michel Foucault, Enwezor describes "the archive" as "an active, regulatory discursive system," rather than "a dim, musty place full of drawers, filing cabinets, and shelves laden with old documents, an inert repository of historical artifacts"; this is the view of artists like Leonard and Dunye, and a foundational concept in Hartman's work. In short, if official histories did not recognize archives of queer, or Black, or female experiences, these artists decided to create and celebrate them.

E.1 Zoe Leonard, *The Fae Richards Photo Archive*, 1993–96, gelatin silver prints and chromogenic prints, partial installation view, 1997 Biennial Exhibition at the Whitney. Whitney Museum of American Art, New York. Purchased with funds from the Contemporary Painting and Sculpture Committee and the Photography Committee 97.51addddd. Artwork © Zoe Leonard; digital image, © Whitney Museum of American Art.

For the literary critic Ann Cvetkovich, like Hartman, the notion of an "archive of [queer] feelings," is radical precisely because, as she explains, "emotional experiences and intimacies are frequently ephemeral and hence not always assumed accessible via the print records and other documents conventionally found in institutionally based archives."[4] While her foundational efforts focused on texts, in her more recent work, Cvetkovich explores the photography of both Tammy Rae Carland and Zoe Leonard as evidence of the ways in which images can document the ordinary experiences of queer lives, enlarging the emotional range of the archive by their very presence. This is certainly true in the case of Ewing's *Collection of Extraordinary Portraits*, in which he creates a record not only of his fictive family of friends — Black and white, queer and straight — but also of his emotional enthusiasms, up to and including, in some cases, his feelings of love, albeit implied and not expressed. While Ewing clearly resisted displays of emotion in real life — as we know, for example, from his tortured response to his unconsummated affair with the composer Constant Lambert — it is nevertheless through his photographs, including the nudes of Paul Meeres and Jack Pollock, that one ultimately gets a sense of how he felt about the men he loved — or, more accurately, lovingly admired. By contrast, in Ewing's letters and those of Pollock, what stands out most clearly is their *resistance* to expressions of love, and the barriers that both men erected to moderate and deflect their emotions. At the other end of the spectrum are the letters filled with Ewing's expressions of emotional despair, fully articulated and framed, in response to his abandonment by Muriel Draper. All of these passionate, loving relationships were queer in every sense of the word and as rich as they were diverse, and it is the chance survival of the letters that enables us to know and understand them.

The efforts by scholars to find meaning in archival texts and images, both real and fictive, and the ongoing search for traces of experience and emotion in collections that so often resist such intimacies, underscore just how remarkable the survival of Max Ewing's archive truly is. As noted throughout this book, his words and adventures often read like the "unreal" fictions of creative writing, while the names of prominent artists and famous people that casually crop up in his stories suggest that Ewing might well be a real-life Zelig who appears everywhere across time and space.

Yet Max Ewing's papers and photos are neither works of fiction nor the poetic fragments from a queer heterotopia fashioned by a romantic imagination. On the contrary, Ewing's archive, like Van Vechten's, documents the real-life struggles of an interracial group of queer outsiders and unconventional intellectuals who tried to bridge the gaps of race, class, and sexuality that separated them. Despite all of their shortcomings and poor decisions — like the "regrettable choice" (as historian Emily Bernard put it) made by Van Vechten when he included the N-word in the title of his novel, or Ewing's cowardly decision to go along with the policy of the Waldorf Astoria and exclude the portraits of his Black friends in his *Carnival of Venice* exhibition there — the members of this circle challenged the status quo of racism and homophobia in their daily lives and went to considerable effort to document their efforts in doing so.[5]

Ewing's letters and photographs thus tell us things we would never have otherwise known, and for that, Van Vechten — the controversial, arrogant writer and photographer of many thousands of portraits documenting his relationships with prominent friends and acquaintances, many of them Black — is to be celebrated. Were it not for him, so much that we are moved by in the lives of these people would be lost, and while his friendship and support — intermittent, preoccupied, and haphazard during the last year of Ewing's life — weren't enough to save his friend from isolation and despair as he moldered away in Pioneer, Ohio in the spring of 1934, his Herculean efforts to gather and preserve his archive did in the end succeed in carving out precisely the sort of fragile, messy, and yet entirely believable queer space — a space of contradictions, alive with politics, poetry, and feelings — that we must fully embrace as we try to reimagine Ewing's queer life and the experiences of other men and women throughout history.

Max Ewing's Jazz Age New York
A Brief Guide to People and Places
With Dates of Max Ewing's Participation and His Key Contacts in Each Circle

NEW YORK, 1923–33

Circle of Carl Van Vechten
(1880–1964) writer, photographer, collector, and host
and Fania Marinoff
(b. Odessa, 1890–1971) actress
151 E. 19TH STREET
AND 150 W. 55TH STREET (FROM 1924)

Gertrude Stein (1874–1946) .... *writer and saloniste*
Alice B. Toklas (1877–1967) .... *editor, critic, and partner of Stein*
Mabel Dodge Luhan (1879–1962) .... *activist and arts patron*
Muriel Draper (1886–1952) .... *writer and saloniste*
Alfred A. Knopf (1892–1984) .... *publisher*
Blanche Knopf (1894–1966) .... *editor and publisher*
F. Scott Fitzgerald (1896–1940) .... *writer*
James Weldon Johnson (1871–1938) .... *writer, diplomat, and activist*
Walter White (1893–1955) .... *activist and leader of the NAACP*
Paul Robeson (1898–1976) .... *actor, performer, writer, and activist*
Nora Holt (1885–1974) .... *musicologist and singer*
Langston Hughes (1901–67) .... *poet, writer, and activist*
Nella Larsen (1891–1964) ....*writer,*
.... *m. to scientist Elmer Imes from 1919 to 1933*
Harold Jackman (1901–61) .... *teacher and librarian*
Edward Wasserman, later "Waterman" (c. 1890–c. 1955) .... *financier, host*
Taylor Gordon (1893–1971) .... *singing partner of Rosamond Johnson*
....*and author of* Born to Be, *1929*
Donald Angus (1899–1990) .. *writer and lover/intimate friend of Van Vechten*
Miguel Covarrubias (1904–57) .... *artist and illustrator*
Jimmie Daniels (1907–84) .... *singer and cabaret performer*
.... *at Harlem's Hot-Cha club*
Prentiss Taylor (1907–91) .... *artist and activist*
Paul Meeres (1902–62) ....*Bahamian dancer and*
.... *nightclub entertainer at Small's Paradise and Connie's Inn in Harlem*
Tonio Selwart (1896–2002, b. Germany) .... *Broadway and film actor*

Circle of Robert Winthrop Chanler
(1872–1930) muralist, painter, and host
147–149 E. 19TH STREET ("THE HOUSE OF FANTASY")

Shared many friends with Van Vechten
and created diverse social networks in Greenwich Village
and Woodstock, New York

Salon of Louise Hellstrom
(b. 1891, active 1910s–30s) partner of R. W. Chanler,
lived in NYC and Woodstock, NY

Edgard Varèse (1883–1965) ....*French composer*
Jane Heap (1883–1964) .... *curator, editor of the* Little Review,
....*and former partner of Margaret Anderson)*
Joseph Stella (1877–1946, b. Italy) ....*painter*

Salon of Kirk Askew
(1903–74) art gallery director and host
and Constance Askew (1895–1984)
166 E. 61ST STREET
HELD ON SUNDAYS

Julien Levy (1906–81) .... *art dealer and gallerist*
Lincoln Kirstein (1907–96) ...., *curator and arts patron;*
....*founder of American Ballet Theater*
Philip Johnson (1906–2005) ....*curator and architect*
Henry-Russell Hitchcock (1903–87) ....*curator and art historian*
Allen Porter (1902–87) .... *curator*
John McAndrew (1904–78) ....*art historian and curator*

The Grand Street Follies actors and their friends

Albert Carroll (1895–1956) ....*actor and drag artist, active 1920s*
Aline MacMahon (1899–1991) .... *Broadway and film actress*
Marion Morehouse (1906–69) ....*fashion model and partner of E. E. Cummings*

Circle of Muriel Draper

(c. 1886–1952) writer, lecturer, interior designer, and activist

240 E. 40TH STREET AND, FROM 1929, 312 E. 53RD STREET
HELD ON FRIDAYS

Included many of the Van Vechtens,' the Askews,' and Hellstrom's friends

Paul Draper (1909–96)..*dancer and choreographer*

Raimund "Smudge" Draper (1913–43) ....*RAF pilot*

Esther Murphy (1897–1962).......................................*writer and intellectual, sister of Gerald and Sarah Murphy*

Glenway Wescott (1901–87) ....*writer and partner of Wheeler and Lynes*

Monroe Wheeler (1899–1988) ....*curator and partner of Wescott and Lynes*

Lloyd Morris (1893–1954) ....*author, critic, and Glenway Wescott's agent*

George Platt Lynes (1907–55) ....*photographer; from 1927 to mid-1940s, partner of Wescott and Wheeler*

E. E. Cummings (1894–1962) ....*poet and writer*

Robert Locher (1888–1956) ....*designer and graphic artist*
and Beatrice Locher (b. 1886, divorced 1933) ....*m. Thomas Farrar; later in Fire Island, NY*

Walker Evans (1903–75) ....*photographer*

Circle of Alice DeLamar

(1895–1983) arts patron and lesbian saloniste

Eva Le Gallienne (1899–1991) ....*actress and director*

Cecil Beaton (1904–80) ....*British photographer*

Lucia Davidova (b. Russia) ....*active 1930s, dancer, associate of Balanchine, and partner of Alice DeLamar*

Natalie Hammond (1904–85) ....*artist, designer, and arts patron*

Agnes de Mille (1905–93) ....*dancer and choreographer*

Tallulah Bankhead (1902–68) ....*actress*

Salon of
Gertrude Stein

(1874–1946) writer, collector, and lesbian saloniste

and *Alice B. Toklas*

(1877–1967) writer and hostess

27 RUE DE FLEURUS

Leading French and American intellectuals,
artists, and rising stars

Long-time friends of Carl Van Vechten and Muriel Draper

Paul Tchelitchew (1898–1957, b. Russia) .... *artist*
René Crevel (1900–35) .... *French writer*
Noël Haskins Murphy (1895–1982)...*(singer; m. Frederic Murphy [d. 1924],*
...........*sister-in-law of Esther, Gerald, and Sara Murphy, partner of Janet Flanner*
Sylvia Beach (1887–1962) .... *bookseller, publisher, and partner of Monnier*
Adrienne Monnier (1892–1955) .... *French bookseller and partner of Beach*
Constant Lambert (1905–51) .... *British composer*

Salon of
Natalie Barney

(1876–1972) writer and lesbian saloniste

20–22 RUE JACOB
HELD ON FRIDAYS

Gathering place for queer expats and their friends,
especially visiting Americans

Romaine Brooks (1874–1970) ....*artist and life partner of Barney*

"At Miss Barney's one met lesbians;
Paris ones and those only passing through town"

— SYLVIA BEACH

("Max Ewing" listed in the diagram of visitors
to her Temple de l'Amitié
published in *Adventures de l'Esprit*, Paris, 1929.)

Circle of Margaret Anderson

(1886–1973) writer and editor of the *Little Review* and partner of Jane Heap

Georgette Leblanc (1869–1941) ....*French actress and partner of Margaret Anderson*
George Antheil (1900–59)..*composer*
Constantin Brâncuși (1876–1957, b. Romania) ....*Romanian sculptor and painter*

Salon of Florine (1871–1944), Ettie (1875–1955), and Carrie Stettheimer (1869–1944)

ALWYN COURT, WEST 69TH STREET;
STUDIO IN THE BEAUX-ARTS BUILDING (BRYANT PARK)

Leading salon for American and European avant-garde artists,
writers, and musicians, including
many of Van Vechten's and Draper's friends

Charles Demuth (1883–1935) ....*painter*
Georgia O'Keeffe (1887–1986) ....*painter*
Alfred Stieglitz (1864–1946) ....*photographer and gallerist*
Marcel Duchamp (1887–1968) ....*French painter and sculptor*
Virgil Thomson (1896–1989) ....*composer and critic*

Salon of A'lelia Walker

(1885–1931) Arts patron and founder of "The Dark Tower"

108–110 WEST 136TH STREET;
80 EDGECOMBE AVENUE

Center for avant-garde arts in Harlem,
included Van Vechten, Draper, and their friends,
leaders of the Harlem Renaissance,
young writers and entertainers, visitors from Europe

Max Ewing's "Mondays"

19 WEST 31ST STREET

Included Van Vechten, Draper and many of their friends. Hosted visiting artists, writers, and
musicians from Europe; Harlem entertainers and friends; bodybuilders and athletes

Roy Setliff (active 1930s) ...."*The Marine*"
Jack Pollock (active 1930s) ....*boxer*
Anthony Sansone (1905–87) ....*body builder and model*
Fred and Bill Ritter (active 1930s) ....*body builders and models*
Derek Patmore (1908–72) ....*British writer, designer, and protégé of Lloyd Morris*
George Dangerfield (1904–86) *and* Mary Dangerfield..................................*British writer and historian*

Circle of Noël Sullivan

(1890–1956) singer and arts patron; friend of Langston Hughes

Billy Justema (1905–87).. *artist*

Actors, Producers, and Friends from New York

Alla Nazimova (1879–1945)..*actress and producer*
Mercedes de Acosta (1892–1968)....................................*writer and lover*
....*of Dietrich and Garbo, among others*

Peggy Fears (1903–94) .... *Broadway and Hollywood actress and producer*
Gilbert (1893–1970) *and* Amanda Seldes (c. 1903) .... *editor and critic;*
....*friends of Carl Van Vechten from New York*

Samuel Hoffenstein (1890–1947, b. Odessa)....................*journalist and*
....*screenwriter from New York*

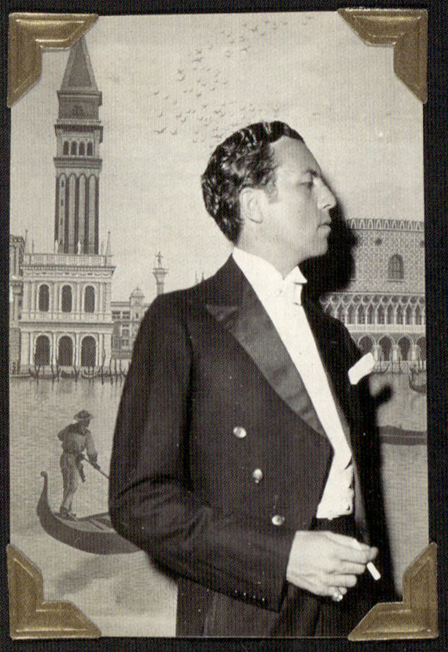 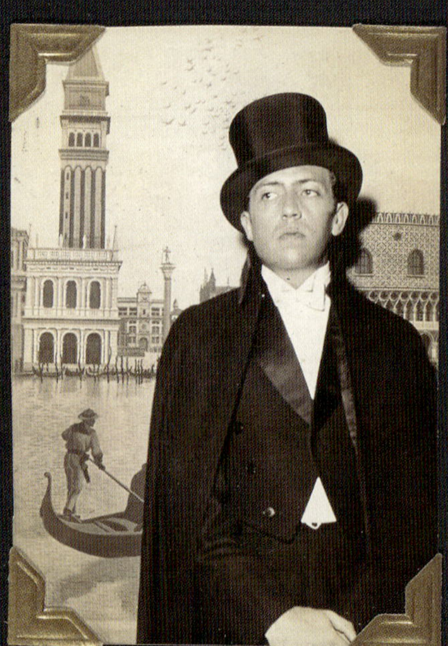

Max Ewing

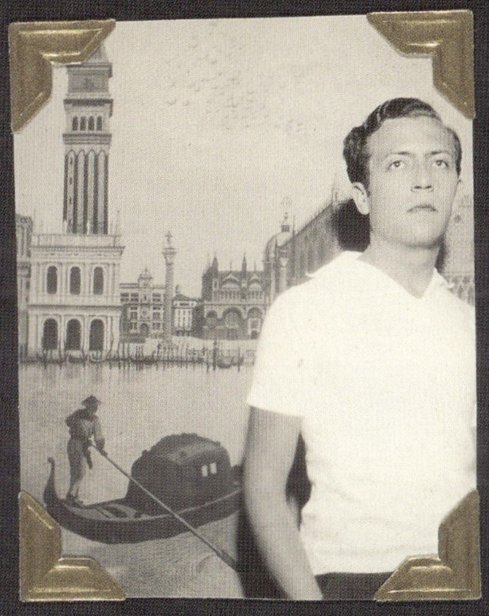

The Venetian Glass Nephew
Max Ewing.

Acknowledgments

I encountered Max Ewing by chance in the winter of 2018 while I was a research fellow at the Beinecke Rare Book & Manuscript Library at Yale University. At the time I was studying the lives and living spaces of queer American ex-pats in France in the 1920s and '30s, and I soon discovered that Max Ewing's long, gossipy letters had a great deal more to say about these people and their choices than those of any other writer I knew. Like so many of his friends and acquaintances, I was captivated by his humor and charm, and intrigued by the sheer number and variety of the "queer moderns" he photographed. Ewing's obsessive and infectious enthusiasm for his projects, and his talents as a composer, photographer, and socialite, immediately inspired me to drop everything and devote myself to telling his story.

It is thus fitting that I begin by acknowledging the rich collections and dedicated staff of the Beinecke Library for all their help. I am especially grateful to Moira Fitzgerald, Genevieve Coyle, Mary Ellen Budney, John Monahan, Paul Civitelli, Rebecca McGuire, Adrienne Leigh Sharp, and Matt Nelson for tirelessly making files and images available to me, and for producing scans for use in my research, especially during the period between March 2020 and May 2022 when I was unable to visit the library in person because of the COVID-19 pandemic. Particular thanks are due to Max Ewing's cousin Wallace Ewing, not only for publishing *Genius Denied: The Life and Death of Max Ewing* (2012), which includes transcriptions of many of his letters, but also for his collegiality and advice over the years. The materials from the Max Ewing Collection at the Beinecke Library that are included in this book are published with his permission.

Wellesley College supported my scholarship and publications with research grants and travel funds throughout my long career as a faculty member. As Grace Slack McNeil Professor of the History of American Art at Wellesley, I was fortunate to have the resources to organize seminars and conferences related to this project and many others, and to invite colleagues to campus for lectures and presentations. These included an event in fall 2022 that featured significant contributions on queer studies and design history by John Potvin, Timothy Rowan, and Kevin Murphy. Thanks to Christy Anderson, the editor of *The Art Bulletin*, their essays were published in that journal in March 2024. Many Wellesley librarians, colleagues, and staff generously supported my work on this and other projects over the years, including Jeanne Hablanian (tireless and always good-humored provider of books and articles), Brooke Henderson, Meghan Murray, and Samara Pearlstein. I am also very grateful to Provost Andrew Shennan for his support and encouragement.

My initial research on New York's "High Bohemia" was conducted in spring 2019 while I was the Rea S. Hederman Visiting Critic at the American Academy in Rome. I am grateful to John Ochsendorf, the former director, for inviting me to become part of that inspirational community. It is also a pleasure to thank Yale University for the research fellowships that enabled me to conduct my work at the Beinecke Library over many months and for the opportunity to present some of my conclusions at Yale, most recently in the spring of 2022 at a conference organized by the Program in Lesbian, Gay, Bisexual, and Transgender Studies.

Kevin Murphy read the complete manuscript more than once and generously wrote up his comments, as did Daniel Abramson. Martin Brody offered invaluable advice and a specialist's knowledge of the history of modern music, as he has done so often in the past as a friend, colleague, and teaching partner. The section of this book about avant-garde music in New York and Paris, and about George Antheil in particular, owes a great deal to him. Pat Berman kindly read and commented on the *Carnival of Venice* chapter. Jacki Musacchio, Margaret Carroll, Judith Black, Salem Mekuria, Martha McNamara, Jennifer Jasmin, and Quaker Case also generously gave their time to discussing aspects of this project with me. I am grateful to all of them. Jules Spector, my former student in the Architecture Program at Wellesley College, has been a dedicated and resourceful research assistant, particularly in the matter of recording and tracking the detailed information for the captions and credits. Jules and other former students at Wellesley and Harvard contributed enormously through their comments and critiques in my advanced seminars.

Many specialists in art history and queer studies have communicated via email or spoken with me on Zoom, and I am indebted to all for their advice and counsel. These include Steven Watson, whose books laid the foundations for the study of the American avant-garde and the Harlem Renaissance; Allan Ellenzweig, biographer and scholar of the work of George Platt Lynes; and Nick Mauss, author of a new study (with Angela Miller) of Lynes, Paul Cadmus, and PaJaMa. I also want to thank Betsy Fahlman for her advice about Charles Demuth and Robert Winthrop Chanler, and Barbara Bloemink for commenting on my readings of Florine Stettheimer's paintings. Lisa Cohen's three-part biography of Esther Murphy, Mercedes de Acosta, and Madge Garland is a model of scholarship that opened my eyes to many aspects of Max Ewing's network of women friends. Nona Footz, biographer of Alice DeLamar, contributed valuable information from her archive. Michael K. Johnson offered advice about Taylor Gordon, the subject of his recent book. Donald Albrecht, curator and historian of design, was the first to include an image of Ewing's *Gallery* in his 2016 exhibition *Gay Gotham: Art and Underground Culture in New York* at the Museum of the City of New York, and I am also grateful to him for meeting with me and discussing a possible collaboration. Emily Bernard's foundational scholarship on Carl Van Vechten helped shape my understanding of the man who was uniquely responsible for much of Max Ewing's queer collecting and exploration of the queer visual arts and literature. I am enormously grateful to her for speaking with me about "Carlo" and the choices he made, especially those related to issues of racial politics and identity. Finally, it is a pleasure to acknowledge the contributions made by Ken Silver and Jarrett Earnest in the area of queer studies and visual culture, particularly those related to the latter's exhibition (at David Zwirner Gallery, New York, in 2019) and catalogue *The Young and Evil: Queer Modernism in New York* (2020). Their recent work has been enormously helpful to me as I endeavored to frame answers to my questions.

My earliest efforts to write about the *Gallery of Extraordinary Portraits* in Max Ewing's clothes closet appeared in fall 2019 in a two-part essay, published online in *Platform*. I am grateful to Matt Lasner, Swati Chattopadhyay, and Marta Guttman, the editors of that journal, for making that work possible and for helping me adapt my scholarship to shortform writing. I am also indebted to John Potvin for including my chapter about Max Ewing in his book on *The Senses in Interior Design* (Manchester University Press, 2023).

Michelle Komie, my editor at Princeton University Press, was an early supporter of this book and has worked closely with me on many previous projects. I want to thank her for her commitment and patience over the past years. The editorial team at Princeton — Annie Miller, Terri O'Prey, and Steven Sears — helped move this book through the publishing process and gave their sharp-eyed attention to the text and illustrations. Their skill and professionalism have been invaluable. Thanks also to Jenny Chan for her thoughtful and beautiful design.

At the outset, my friend Valerie Fraser challenged me to think about how my interest in Max Ewing related to the history of architecture, a question that helped shape my subsequent explorations of queer spaces and domesticities. Many other friends, family members, and colleagues have also supported and engaged with this project over the years. These include Tim Butler, Jeffrey and Cheryl Katz, Virginia Carabine (who helped me find Max Ewing's apartment and roof garden at the Life Hotel in New York), Lee Ann Custer (who found the plan), Jared Friedman, Stephanie Tracy, John Friedman, Polly Heavenrich, and Aliah Werth, who visited the Museo Hendrik Christian Andersen in Rome (another distinctively queer space) with me. For unfailing friendship and thoughtful comments during innumerable dinner-table conversations, I am grateful to Elizabeth Gildersleeve. Most of all, I want to acknowledge the support of my partner Cameran Mason and thank her for her patience and good humor over the many years that we have been cohabiting with Max Ewing. For better or worse, we have all come to think of him as a member of our family.

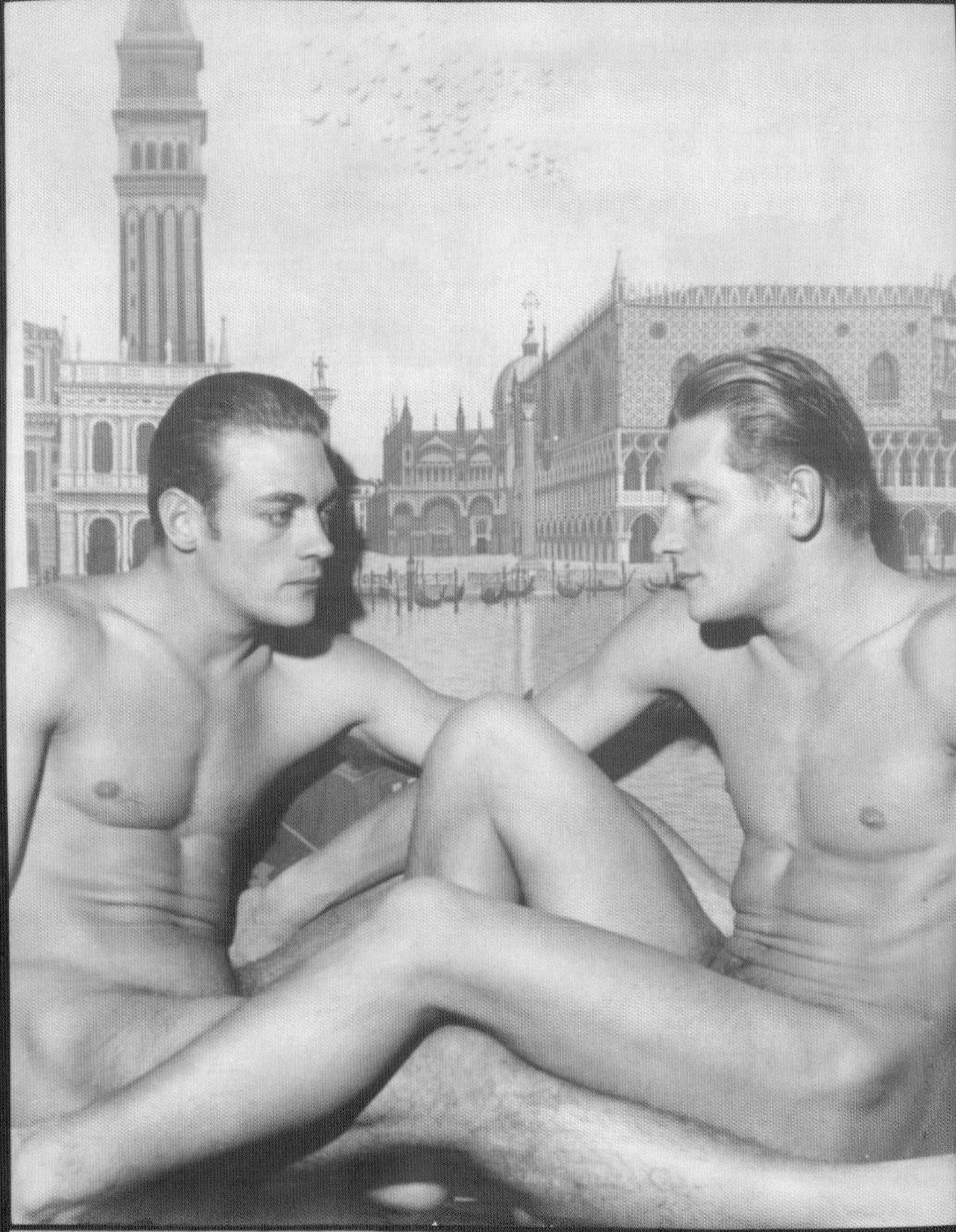

LOVE AT FIRST NIGHT!
ALL OF A SUDDEN, OUT OF NOWHERE,
HE APPEARS. AND YOU
KNOW, THIS IS IT; THIS IS FOR ME, FOR KEEPS
Good News! Two Famous Names Become One
To Carry On a Tradition of Almost a Century
Their Nuptials Are Among Those of Interest to Society

Gay
Honeymoon –
Thrills Galore and Romance Too 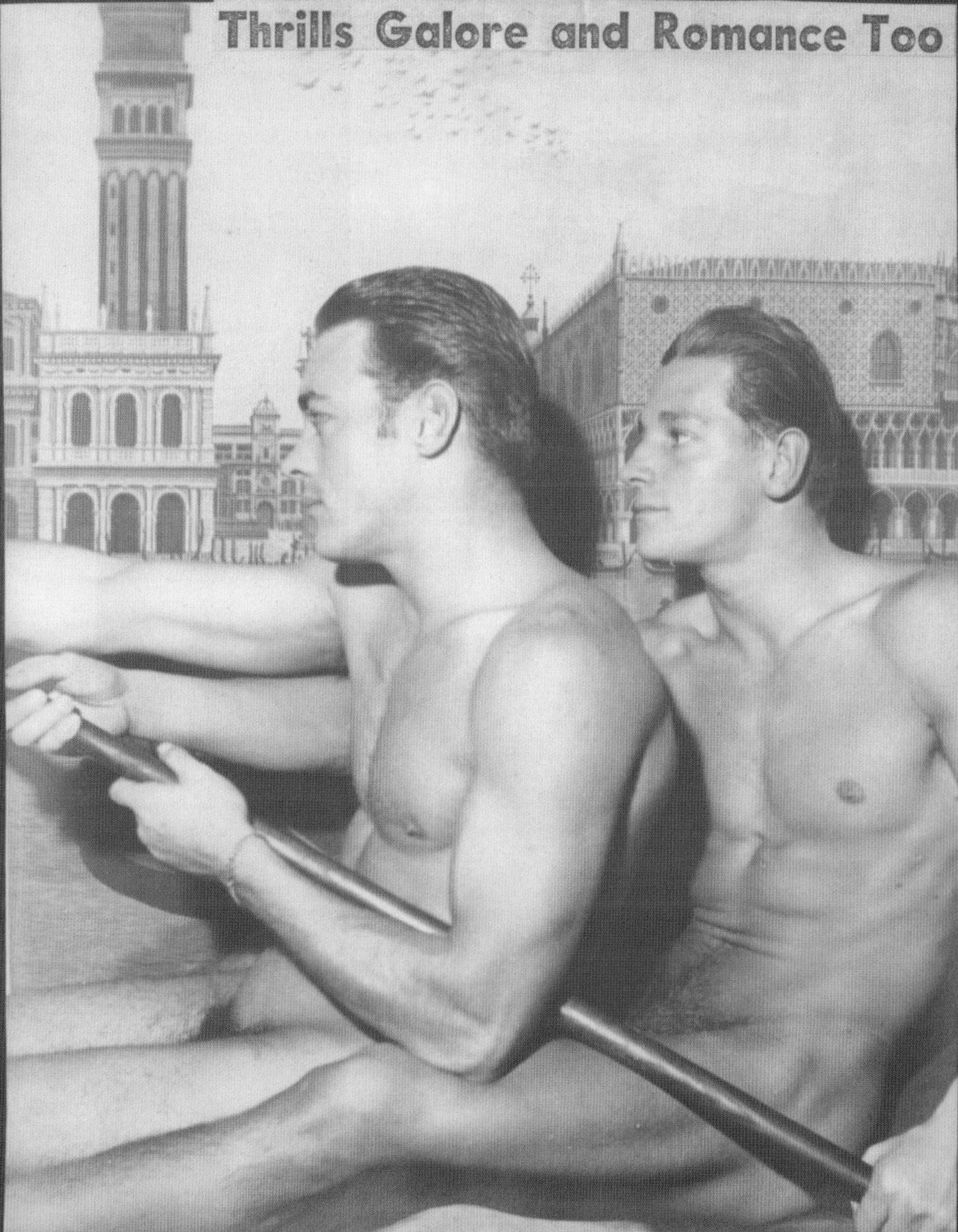
Sing we for love
... Naught else
is worth having
Still a Great Sister Act

Notes

Prologue
Rediscovering Queer New York

1   Though Max Ewing's letters are known to scholars of the period for the rich detail they offer, he has not been studied as a musician, collector, and photographer. Many of his letters, particularly from the last year of his life, were published by his cousin Wallace K. Ewing in *Genius Denied: The Life and Death of Max Ewing* (CreateSpace Independent Publishing, 2012). I am very grateful for Wallace Ewing's permission to publish materials from the Max Ewing Collection at the Beinecke Library and for his generosity to me throughout this book project. *The Gallery of Extraordinary Portraits* was first discussed as a queer space by Donald Albrecht, ed., *Gay Gotham: Art and Underground Culture in New York* (New York: Rizzoli, 2016), 84–89. Ewing generally referred to the installation simply as "my gallery," but Carl Van Vechten and later archivists, including the Beinecke Library at Yale, catalogued his collection and photographs of the installation as the *Max Ewing Closet Gallery of Extraordinary Portraits*. This the label, usually shortened to *Gallery of Extraordinary Portraits*, is used here.

2   Bill Ritter to Max Ewing [hereafter ME], n.d. [winter 1934], Max Ewing Papers, Yale Collection of American Literature, Beinecke Rare Book & Manuscript Library, YCAL MSS 656, box 9, folder 68. Unless otherwise noted, all documents cited in this book are from this collection. Here, as elsewhere, I have retained original spelling and punctuation where possible. I use the term "queer" in this book in conformity with current practice in academic, activist, and queer communities: in most contexts, this term improves upon the narrow designations "lesbian" and "gay" by suggesting a broader range of nonconforming behaviors, sexualities, and experiences. So too do the terms "sapphist" or "sapphic," with their broad implication of affective and not simply erotic attachment; the term had been used since the eighteenth century and was current in the 1920s. For current terminologies, see Sherron E. Knopp, "If I Saw You Would You Kiss Me": Sapphism and the Subversiveness of Virginia Woolf's *Orlando*," *PMLA* 103, no. 1 (January 1988): 24–34; and Simonetta Fraquelli and Cindy Kang, *Marie Laurencin: Sapphic Paris* (New Haven, CT: Yale University Press,

2023). When appropriate, I use more familiar words — in phrases like "gay man" or "lesbian friends" — to reflect usage that Ewing and his contemporaries would have understood to designate sexual orientation and social affinities: for the most recent discussion of these issues, see Marko Jobst and Naomi Stead, "Introduction," and Olivier Vallerand, "On the Uses of Queer Space Thinking," in Marko Jobst and Naomi Stead, eds., *Queering Architecture: Methods, Practices, Spaces, Pedagogies* (London: Bloomsbury Visual, 2024), 10–24 and 26–43, respectively. Ewing didn't explicitly label either himself or his friends, although there is evidence that he knew and sometimes used the terms "gay" and "queer" to characterize places (such as bars) and people in ways we can recognize and understand. For Clinton Moore's Harlem club, and the entertainments offered there, see Chad Heap, *Slumming: Sexual and Racial Encounters in American Nightlife, 1885–1940* (Chicago: University of Chicago Press, 2010), 258–59. For gay Harlem, see Thomas H. Wirth, ed., *Gay Rebel of the Harlem Renaissance: Selections from the Work of Richard Bruce Nugent* (Durham, NC: Duke University Press, 2002); and Eric Garber, "A Spectacle in Color: The Lesbian and Gay Subculture of Jazz Age Harlem," in *Hidden From History: Reclaiming the Gay and Lesbian Past*, ed. Martin Duberman, Martha Vicinus, and George Chauncey (New York: New American Library, 1989), 318–31.

3   The donation of the archive is fully documented in the Carl Van Vechten Papers, New York Public Library, box 11.

4   See Okwui Enwezor, "Archive Fever: Photography between History and the Monument," in *Archive Fever: Uses of the Document in Contemporary Art*, ed. Okwui Enwezor (New York: International Center of Photography, Steidl Publishers, 2008), 11–51. Enwezor included Zoe Leonard and Cheryl Dunye's *Fae Richards Photo Archive* in his exhibition as an example of queer ephemera. The work of Saidiya Hartman, including *Wayward Lives, Beautiful Experiments: Intimate Histories of Social Upheaval* (New York: W. W. Norton, 2019), while focused primarily on notions of "race" and the experiences of formerly enslaved people, further expands discussion of the politics, poetics, and limits of archives as institutional and historical repositories.

5   The three hundred portraits exhibited in Ewing's gallery were listed by number in a self-published

catalogue entitled *Max Ewing Collection of Extraordinary Portraits* and its supplement, *Max Ewing Collection of Incredible Portraits*, box 14, folder 139. The installation changed frequently, and the list does not include every portrait from Ewing's collection preserved in his archive at Yale. For self-portraiture, See Amelia Jones, "The 'Eternal Return': Self-Portrait Photography as a Technology of Embodiment," *Signs* 27, no. 4 (summer 2002): 947–78. Though Ewing was an amateur, unlike Alfred Stieglitz, Cindy Sherman, Lyle Ashton Harris, and other artists that Jones discusses, his efforts, like theirs, were intended to create both a relational connection with his viewers and the promise of immortality, the latter being particularly notable in light of his suicide in June 1934.

6   George Chauncey, *Gay New York: Gender, Urban Culture, and the Making of the Gay Male World, 1890–1940* (New York: Basic Books, 1994).

7   Chauncey, *Gay New York*, 227–67.

8   Recent scholarship extends this inquiry into a wide range of previously uncharted private spaces and networks, notably those inhabited by middle-class, Black lesbians in the 1920s: see Cookie Woolner, *The Famous Lady Lovers: Black Women and Queer Desire before Stonewall* (Chapel Hill: University of North Carolina Press, 2023), esp. chapter 4.

9   Iris Origo, *The Merchant of Prato* (New York: Knopf, 1960).

10   For a comprehensive introduction to the Harlem Renaissance, see Steven Watson, *The Harlem Renaissance: Hub of African-American Culture, 1920–1930* (New York: Pantheon Books, 1995).

11   Henry McBride, "Max Ewing as a Camera Man: Strange Qualities are Revealed in Novelist's Photography," *New York Sun*, January 27, 1933, 4.

12   Bill Ritter to ME, n.d. [July 1933?], and February 12, 1934, box 9, folder 68.

13   For Lynes's homoerotic imagery and the visual conventions of gay male erotica, see Jarrett Earnest, ed., *The Young and Evil: Queer Modernism in New York, 1930–1955* (New York: David Zwirner Books, 2020), and Thomas Waugh, *Hard to Imagine: Gay Male Eroticism in Photography and Film from Their Beginnings to Stonewall* (New York: Columbia University Press, 1993), 102–32. For Lynes and fashion, see Elspeth Brown, *Work!* (Durham, NC: Duke University Press, 2017), chapter 3; and Nick Mauss and Angela Miller, *Body*

Language: The Queer Staged Photographs of George Platt Lynes and PaJaMa (Oakland: University of California Press, 2023). Watson, *The Harlem Renaissance*, 98–163, sketches out the broad cultural context.

14   For Abbott, see Julia Van Haaften, *Berenice Abbott: A Life in Photography* (New York: Norton, 2018).

15   For the early history of their arrangement, see Anatole Pohorilenko and James Crump, *When We Were Three: The Travel Albums of George Platt Lynes, Monroe Wheeler and Glenway Wescott, 1925–1935* (New York: Arena Editions, 1998).

16   Woolner, *The Famous Lady Lovers*, 106. For their Harlem residence and additional information, see "Edna Thomas, Lloyd Thomas & Olivia Wyndham Residence," NYC LGBT Historic Sites Project, accessed December 8, 2023, https://www.nyclgbtsites.org/site /edna-thomas-lloyd-thomas-olivia -wyndham-residence/.

17   See Michel Foucault, "Friendship as a Way of Life," in *Ethics*, ed. Paul Rabinow (New York: The New Press, 1994), 135–40; and Sharon Marcus, *Between Women: Friendship, Desire, and Marriage in Victorian England* (Princeton, NJ: Princeton University Press, 2007). The three artists who worked together as PaJaMa in the later 1930s and '40s — Paul Cadmus, Jared French, and Margaret French — were a queer couple (Cadmus and French) and a married couple (Jared and Margaret): for their work in photography, see Mauss and Miller, *Body Language*.

18   This argument is elaborated on in John Potvin, "The Materials of Shame: Decoration, Masculinity, and the Birth of Modern Interior Design," *The Art Bulletin* 106, no. 1 (March 2024): 7–19. The article began as a paper presented at the McNeil Seminar at Wellesley College in November 2022.

19   Ewing mentions seeing the Fitzgeralds at parties and makes a note of their move to Delaware in 1928; in one gossipy letter, he also mentions Dos Passos. In the latter text, however, he was more concerned with describing his 3 a.m. meeting with Mae West — a queer icon — after a performance of *Diamond Lil* that he attended with Muriel Draper, and by the spot-on imitation of West by Dorothy Sands in the *Grand Street Follies*. See ME to John and Clara Ewing [hereafter ME to parents], n.d. [1928], box 9, folder 67.

20   Lisa Cohen, *All We Know: Three Lives* (New York: Farrar,

Straus and Giroux, 2012), 24, 54, and part I ("A Perfect Failure").

21   On the subject of Gerald's sexuality and discomfort with Hemingway's homophobic hyper-masculinity, see Linda Patterson Miller, ed., *Letters from the Lost Generation: Gerald and Sara Murphy and Friends* (New Brunswick, NJ: Rutgers University Press, 1991), 4–7; and Kenneth E. Silver, "The Murphy Closet and the Murphy Bed," in *Making it New: The Art and Style of Sara and Gerald Murphy*, ed. Deborah Rothschild (Williamstown, MA: The Williams College Museum of Art, 2007), 107–18.

22   Kirsten MacLeod, "The 'Librarian's Dream Prince': Carl Van Vechten and America's Modernist Cultural Archives Industry," *Librar-ies & the Cultural Record* 46, no. 4 (2011): 360–87.

23   Carl Van Vechten [hereafter CVV] to A. E. Ewing, July 16, 1934, box 9, folder 70.

24   James Weldon Johnson Memorial Collection, Beinecke Rare Book & Manuscript Library, Yale University, https://beinecke.library .yale.edu/collections/curatorial -areas/james-weldon-johnson -memorial-collection.

25   *Duck Soup to Nutty Nuts*, program from the Egyptian Theater, Hollywood, n.d. [December 1933], Carl Van Vechten Papers, YCAL MSS 1050, box 213, vol. 8.

Chapter 1
All That Glamour and Loneliness:
New York in the 1920s

1   For Ewing's biography, see Ewing, *Genius Denied*; and Alice T. Friedman, "Max Ewing's Closet and Queer Architectural History," *Plat-form*, October 8 and 21 [parts 1 and 2, respectively], 2019, https://www .platformspace.net/home/max -ewings-closet-and-queer -architectural-history-part-1-1 and https://www.platformspace.net /home/max-ewings-closet-and -queer-architectural-history\part-2.

2   ME to parents, n.d. [August 1928], box 4, folder 21. Walter Pater's *Studies in the History of the Renaissance* (1873) was one of the foundational texts of art history and criticism.

3   ME, "Diary," 1917, box 30, folder 225. See also ME to parents, June 16, 1923, box 1, folder 6; and ME to parents, October 15, 1923, box 1, folder 5. For the growing pop-ularity of movies, vaudeville, and fan magazines that catered to the population of urban workers, see David Nasaw, *Going Out: The Rise and Fall of Public Amusements*

(Cambridge, MA: Harvard University Press, 1993).

4   A. E. Ewing, "John Caleb Ewing," c. 1934, box 12, folder 126. This document also includes a detailed chronology and description of the last days of Max Ewing's life, including his suicide in Binghamton, NY on June 16, 1934.

5   See the online Amortization Table, https://www.amortization table.org/inflation-calculator /125000/1932.

6   ME to parents, n.d., box 1, folder 5.

7   ME to parents, June 16, 1923, box 1, folder 6.

8   Max Ewing, "About Carl Van Vechten: One of the Rarest Figures in the Whole Galaxy of Contempo-rary American Writers," *Detroit Free Press*, February 4, 1923, 4–5.

9   ME to CVV, n.d. [February 1923], YCAL MSS 1050, box 43, folder 588.

10   CVV to ME, January 26 and February 6, 1923, box 8, folder 59.

11   ME to parents, May 17, 1923, box 1, folder 6.

12   In June 1926, as he mulled over his future needs and finances in New York, Ewing chided his parents for working so hard and encouraged them to spend "a load of money" on themselves, adding that "there is no reason why I should spend any more money any year for the next 20 years than I've spent this year, around $3000." He also noted that he intended to start making money of his own the following year, adding "You must know that I have no ten-dency toward weddings, or houses or lots or automobiles or things like that." ME to parents, June 21, 1926, box 3, folder 15.

13   For Van Vechten, see Emily Bernard, ed., *Remember Me to Harlem: The Letters of Langston Hughes and Carl Van Vechten, 1925–1964* (New York: Knopf, 2001); Emily Bernard, *Carl Van Vechten and the Harlem Renaissance: A Portrait in Black and White* (New Haven, CT: Yale University Press, 2012); Edward White, *The Taste-maker: Carl Van Vechten and the Birth of Modern America* (New York: Farrar, Straus and Giroux, 2014); and Kirsten MacLeod, "Introduction: The Blind Bow-Boy; 'A Great Forgotten American Novel of the 1920s,'" in Carl Van Vechten, *The Blind Bow-Boy* (Cambridge, UK: Modern Humanities Research Association, 2018), vii–xxii. These historians discuss Van Vechten's complex relationships with African American writers and artists, his casual racism, and his undeniable impact on the Harlem Renaissance.

14   ME to parents, October 9, 1923, box 1, folder 6.

15   ME to parents, October 10, 1923, box 1, folder 6.

16   Charles Barber, *Lost in the Stars: The Forgotten Music of Alexander Siloti* (Lanham, MD: Scarecrow Press, 2002).

17   ME to parents, December 5, 1923, box 2, folder 8.

18   ME to parents, October 15, 1923, box 1, folder 6.

19   ME to parents, October 15, 1923, box 1, folder 6.

20   ME to parents, October 30, 1923, box 1, folder 6.

21   ME to parents, October 30, 1923, box 1, folder 6.

22   ME to parents, May 9, 1924, box 1, folder 6.

23   The work was performed by William Rainey, the founder of the Cherry Lane Playhouse, on November 22, 1925: Ewing saved the program, box 2, folder 12, for his parents. See also Edward Burns, ed., *The Letters of Gertrude Stein and Carl Van Vechten, 1913–1946* (New York: Columbia University Press, 2013), 129n2; and "William Rainey, Theater Man, Dies," *New York Times*, September 14, 1964, 37.

24   ME to parents, May 15, 1924, box 2, folder 9.

25   ME to parents, October 27, 1924, box 2, folder 10.

26   ME to parents, November 10, 1924, box 2, folder 10.

27   For Draper, see Betsy Fahlman, "The Great Draper Woman: Muriel Draper and the Art of the Salon," *Woman's Art Journal* 26, no. 2 (autumn 2005–winter 2006): 33–37; Steven Watson, *Strange Bedfellows: The First American Avant-Garde* (New York: Abbeville Press, 1991), 91–94, 206; and Steven Watson, *Prepare for Saints: Gertrude Stein, Virgil Thomson and the Mainstreaming of American Modernism* (New York: Random House, 1999), 174–86.

28   For the *Follies* and the Neighborhood Playhouse, see Margaret M. Knapp, "Theatrical Parody in the Twentieth-Century American Theatre: The Grand Street Follies," in "Popular Theatre," special issue, *Educational Theatre Journal* 27, no. 3 (October 1975): 356–63.

29   ME to parents, n.d. [May 1924], box 2, folder 8.

30   For the tight-knit "family" group created at the Playhouse, see John Strangeland, *Aline MacMahon: Hollywood, the Blacklist, and the Birth of Method Acting* (Lexington, KY: University Press of Kentucky, 2022), chapter 2, esp. 44–46. Carroll's gender-bending roles in the *Follies* were featured in a photo essay in *Vanity Fair*, November 1, 1924, 44, suggesting a level of respectability that distinguished his comic performances from more ris-qué acts presented in Harlem clubs and in the "interzones" in other cities: see Chad Heap, *Slumming*, 240ff; and Kevin Mumford, *Inter-zones: Black/White Districts in Chicago and New York in the Early Twentieth Century* (New York: Columbia University Press, 1997). For "female impersonators" as family entertainment and the ambiguous relationship between gender parody and homosexuality, see the Prologue to Daniel Hurewitz, *Bohemian Los Angeles and the Making of Modern Politics* (Oakland: University of California Press, 2007), esp. 26–39.

31 ME to [his aunt] Alice Manning, June 5, 1924, box 2, folder 8.

32 Stangeland, *Aline MacMahon*, 44. Cummings was listed in the catalogue of the Max Ewing *Collection of Extraordinary Portraits* (no. 65) in 1928.

33 ME to parents, n.d. [April 1925], box 2, folder 11. Ewing's "Silver Cord Song," written for the 1927 *Follies*, was later published as "Silver Apron Strings" by the Edward B. Marx Music Corporation.

34 ME to parents, October 5, 1924, box 2, folder 11.

35 ME to parents, May 29, 1924, box 2, folder 11.

36 As his uncle A. E. Ewing put it, Ewing "never recovered from his taste of New York City life" or his acquaintance "with others of 'artistic' bent." A. E. Ewing, "John Caleb Ewing," n.d. [June or July 1934], box 12, folder 126.

37 Gina Wouters and Andrea Gollin, eds., *Robert Winthrop Chanler: Discovering the Fantastic* (NY: Monacelli, 2016), and especially Betsy Fahlman, "Reclaiming an American Modernist," in Wouters and Gollin, eds., *Robert Winthrop Chanler*, 21–49.

38 ME to parents, February 2, 1925, box 2, folder 10.

39 ME to parents, March 12, 1925, box 2, folder 10.

40 See the Smithsonian American Art Museum's Photograph Study Collection online: https://sirismm .si.edu/siris/julquickstart.htm. Over a hundred works by Chanler, including murals and painted screens, are included among the Juley photographs.

41 Smithsonian American Art Museum, negative J0050335. For the costume, see ME to Muriel Draper [hereafter MD], June 20, 1926, box 6, folder 1; for his portrait "dressed for the Marchesa Casati's ball," see ME to parents, February 25, 1929, box 4, folder 23.

42 Wouters and Gollin, eds., *Robert Winthrop Chanler*, 47–48.

43 See Michael K. Johnson, *Can't Stand Still: Taylor Gordon and the Harlem Renaissance* (Jackson, MI: University Press of Mississippi, 2019), and Gordon's autobiography, *Born to Be* (New York: Knopf, 1929).

44 Walker's salon, the Dark Tower, is discussed at length in chapter 3.

45 See Bruce Kellner, ed., *The Splendid Drunken Twenties: Selections from the Day Books 1922–30* (Urbana: University of Illinois Press, 2003), 153–58; White, *Tastemaker*, 169–78.

46 For the range of Harlem venues and offerings, see Heap, *Slumming*; Mumford, *Interzones*; and Eric Garber, "A Spectacle in Color," 318–33. See also Steven Watson, *Harlem Renaissance*, 124–44. For a detailed "night-club map" of Harlem drawn by E. Simms Campbell in 1932, see the Library of Congress, https://www.loc.gov/ resource/g3804n.ct007809/?r= 0.089,0.031,0.805,0.354,0. For Jimmie Daniels, see the Amistad Collection, Tulane University, https://www.amistad researchcenter.org/single-post /2016/06/06/50-years50-collections -jimmie-daniels-the-king-of -nightlife-in-new-york.

47 For The Sugar Cane, see Kellner, ed., *Splendid Drunken Twenties*, 154n48 ("Few whites and fewer educated blacks went slumming at this raunchy speakeasy on the fringe of Harlem's actual slums. It was patronized largely by black pimps, prostitutes, and petty gamblers").

48 Henry Louis Gates, Jr., "The Black Man's Burden," in Michael Warner, ed., *Fear of a Queer Planet: Queer Politics and Social Theory* (Minneapolis: University of Minnesota Press, 1993), 230–38. See also Eric H. Newman, "Ephemeral Utopias: Queer Cruising, Literary Form, and Diasporic Imagination in Claude McKay's 'Home to Harlem' and 'Banjo,'" *Callaloo* 38, no. 1 (winter 2015): 167–85. For an introduction to the overlapping cultures in Harlem in this period, see Bruce Nugent, *Gay Rebel of the Harlem Renaissance: Selections from the Work of Richard Bruce Nugent*, ed. Thomas H. Wirth (Durham, NC: Duke University Press, 2002); and Mumford, *Interzones*, chapter 6.

49 Kellner, ed., *Splendid Drunken Twenties*, 153.

50 Though little is known about Edward Wasserman (later Waterman), a pair of letters sent to him by Nella Larsen in 1928 shows that he was both a supporter of her work and an intimate member of the interracial circle; he appears often in Ewing's correspondence as a party-giver and queer bon vivant. See Nella Larsen Letters, Sc MG 407, Schomburg Center for Research in Black Culture, Manuscripts, Archives and Rare Books Division, New York Public Library. Kellner, ed., *Splendid Drunken Twenties*, 108, writes that "on occasion his apartment became privately notorious as a white version of a black buffet flat where impromptu homosexual shows sometimes were staged, featuring mixed casts."

51 Carl Van Vechten, *Parties* (New York: Knopf, 1930), 172.

52 Cary D. Wintz and Paul Finkelman, eds., *Encyclopedia of the Harlem Renaissance: K–Y* (New York: Taylor and Francis, 2004), 916.

53 Bernard, ed., *Remember Me to Harlem*, xix.

54 Bernard, ed., *Remember Me to Harlem*, xviii–xix.

55 Bernard, ed., *Remember Me to Harlem*, xxii.

56 White, *Tastemaker*, 190–91.

57 Kellner, ed., *Splendid Drunken Twenties*, 101.

58 Chris Albertson, *Bessie* (New Haven, CT: Yale University Press, 2003), 172–74.

59 ME to parents, March 19, 1926, box 3, folder 14.

60 White, *Tastemaker*, 150–51.

61 MacLeod, "Blind Bow-Boy," xiii.

62 MacLeod, "Blind Bow-Boy," xv.

63 ME to MD, Muriel Draper Papers, n.d., YCAL MSS 49, box 3, folder 108.

64 Albertson, *Bessie*, 169.

65 ME to Edgar Ailes, November 27, 1925, box 6, folder 37.

66 ME to [his grandmother] Josephine Barto ["Doddy"], June 3, 1925, box 2, folder 11.

67 For Draper's ideas about gender, love, and sexuality, see the draft manuscript of her *America Deserta* (1932), especially the chapter "Men Will Be Boys," which describes the philosophy that motivated her frequent sexual relationships with young men, YCAL MSS 49, series II, box 12, folder 415.

68 Both Watson, *Strange Bedfellows*, and Fahlman, "Great Draper Woman," provide details of her pre–New York life.

69 Muriel Draper, *Music at Midnight* (New York: Harper & Brothers, 1929).

70 Draper's role as a "muse" to her many artistic admirers is the subject of Olivia Armandroff, "Drawing for an Audience of One: Art in Muriel Draper's Archives" (MA thesis, University of Delaware, 2020); for Tobey, see 88–93. YCAL MSS 49, series I. Draper donated these papers to Yale in 1951 and 1952.

71 "Interviews," Steven Watson, February 12, 2003, https://steven -watson.com/interviews/.

72 See, for example, ME to MD, letters from Europe, May–June 1926; ME [from Pioneer, Ohio] to MD, YCAL MSS 49, n.d. [1933–34], box 3, 106.

73 For Kirstein's complicated, decades-long relationship with Draper, see Martin Duberman, *The Worlds of Lincoln Kirstein* (Evanston IL: Northwestern University Press, 2008), 86–88, 149–54, 254–55.

74 ME to MD, June 9, 1926, box 6, folder 42.

75 ME to parents, n.d. [June 1925], box 2, folder 11.

76 Fahlman, "Great Draper Woman," 33–37.

77 Duberman, *Lincoln Kirstein*, 86.

78 ME to Edgar Ailes, October 6, 1925, box 6, folder 36.

79 ME to parents, December 17, 1925 and January 26, 1926, box 2, folder 13.

80 Her designs for a number of interior projects are preserved in her archive, YCAL MSS 49, series III, Personal Papers 1881–1977, "Interior Decoration."

81 "Interviews," Steven Watson, February 12, 2003.

82 ME to parents, November 29, 1925, box 2, folder 13.

83 ME to parents, December 2, 1925, box 2, folder 12.

84 ME to parents, June 16, 1923, box 1, folder 5.

85 ME to parents, February 1926, box 2, folder 13.

86 ME to parents, February 8, 1926, box 2, folder 13.

87 ME to parents, February 1 and 3, 1926, box 2, folder 13.

88 April 1926, box 3, folder 14.

89 ME to parents, April 1, 8, 11, 1926, box 3, folder 14.

90 ME to parents, April 8, 11, 14, box 6, folder 42.

Chapter 2
Paris, the Riviera, and Venice, 1926–27

1 Max Ewing, "About Carl Van Vechten," 6.

2 ME to parents, May 4, 1926, box 3, folder 14.

3 ME to MD, May 1, 1926, box 6, folder 42.

4 ME to parents, May 16, 1926, box 3, folder 14.

5 ME to parents, May 6 and May 9, 1926, box 3, folder 14.

6 ME to Clara Ewing [hereafter CE], June 25, 1926, box 3, folder 15.

7 ME to MD, May 15, 1926, box 6, folder 1.

8 ME to CE, May 6, 1926, box 3, folder 14.

9 See Alice T. Friedman, "Queer Old Things: Glamour,

Memory, and Spatial Imagination," *Places Journal* (February 2015): https://placesjournal.org/article /queer-old-things/.

10   The phenomenon is discussed in a number of recent studies, including Richard Meyer, "Threesomes: Lincoln Kirstein's Queer Arithmetic," in *Lincoln Kirstein's Modern*, ed. Samantha Friedman and Jodi Hauptman (New York: Museum of Modern Art, 2019), 98–105. See also Nick Mauss, *Transmissions* (New York: Whitney Museum, 2017); and Mauss and Miller, *Body Language*.

11   ME to parents, May 3, 1926, box 3, folder 14.

12   These details are included in a typewritten biography of "John Caleb Ewing" completed by his brother after Max Ewing's death in 1934, box 12, folder 126.

13   See John Potvin, *Deco Dandy: Designing masculinity in 1920s Paris* (Manchester: Manchester University Press, 2020).

14   ME to parents, May 20, 1926, box 3, folder 14.

15   For tailoring as a signifier of queer identity, see George Chauncey, *Gay New York*, 4, 50–56, 187–88.

16   ME to parents, May 16, 1926, box 3, folder 14.

17   ME to parents, May 30, 1926, box 3, folder 14.

18   ME to parents, June 17, 1926, box 3, folder 15.

19   ME to parents, June 8, 1926, box 3, folder 15. Cassandra Langer's invaluable study *Romaine Brooks: A Life* (Madison: University of Wisconsin Press, 2015) and the Smithsonian exhibition *The Art of Romaine Brooks* (2016), based on new research, revised much of the chronology and thinking about Brooks's life and works. See also "Artist: Romaine Brooks," Smithsonian American Art Museum, https://americanart.si.edu/artist /romaine-brooks-599. For Diaghilev, see Lynn Garafola and Nancy Van Norman Baer, eds., *The Ballets Russes and Its World* (New Haven, CT: Yale University Press, 1999). For the Ballets Russes and fashion, see Mary E. Davis, *Ballets Russes Style: Diaghilev's Dancers and Paris Fashion* (Chicago: University of Chicago Press, 2010).

20   ME to parents, May 6, 1926, box 3, folder 14.

21   ME to MD, May 7, 1926, box 6, folder 42. He had dismissed the first Antheil piece he had heard in Paris the previous week, writing to Draper that it was "as uneventful and unarriving as any quartet at the Composer's Guild," but he soon changed his mind.

22   ME to MD, May 7, 1926, box 6, folder 42. He deemed the Ballet Suédois "too new even for New York." ME to parents, December 5, 1923, box 2, folder 8. This was also his first time seeing the dancer Jean Börlin, for whom he composed a sonnet included in his *Twenty-Six Sonnets from the Paronomasian and Other Languages Commencing with 'P'*—a self-published volume that appeared in 1924. Börlin's photo in Ewing's *Gallery of Extraordinary Portraits* was inscribed "A Monsieur Max Ewing Merci Pour le Beau Sonnet." For Börlin and the queerness of the Ballets Suédois, see Potvin, *Deco Dandy*, chapters 1 and 2; and Ramsay Burt, "Interpreting Jean Borlin's *Dervishes*: Masculine Subjectivity and the Queer Male Dancing Body," *Dance Chronicle* 22, no. 2 (1999): 223–38.

23   ME to parents, May 13, 1926, box 3, folder 14.

24   For Antheil and his modernist contemporaries, see Carol J. Oja, *Making Music Modern: New York in the 1920s* (Oxford: Oxford University Press, 2000), chapter 5.

25   Antheil to Muriel Draper, n.d., [1920?] and December 21– May 1922, YCAL MSS 49, series I, folders 6–7.

26   ME to parents, June 8, 1926, box 3, folder 15.

27   ME to parents, September 19, 1926, box 3, folder 16.

28   Ewing saved the program from the concert on April 20, 1927 and circled the phrase "distinguished pianists," adding (ironically) that this was "a new name for them," box 32, folder 244. For his descriptions of the rehearsals and performance, see ME to parents, box 3, folder 17 (esp. March 25–30).

29   ME to parents, March 30, 1927, box 3, folder 17.

30   The story is told in Oja, *Making Music Modern*, chapter 5.

31   See ME to parents, March 5, 1926, box 2, folder 13: "Sunday afternoon Aaron Copland is coming to play his new piano pieces for me. He has written some grand things and his new Theater Music was played by the Boston Symphony this season. He is a good friend of Leo and Donald and I have long meant to ask him here but just got around to it. He sails to Paris March 27." Ewing joined him for dinner in Paris soon after he arrived (ME to parents, May 3, 1926, box 3, folder 14).

32   ME to parents, May 6, 1926, box 3, folder 14: "I'm going to hear Arthur Rubinstein and Heifitz this next week. The season—musical and social—is at its height now, and its even worse than in New York to keep up with it. Leo Linder [violinist] and Henry Cowell [composer] will be here May 21."

33   ME to parents, May 28, 1926, box 3, folder 14.

34   The best introduction to this extended community remains Shari Benstock, *Women of the Left Bank, Paris 1900–1940* (Austin: University of Texas Press, 1987). See also Simonetta Fraquelli and Cindy Kang, *Marie Laurencin*.

35   For Anderson, see Mathilda Hills, ed., *Forbidden Fires* (Tallahassee, FL: Naiad Press, 1996); and Margaret Anderson, *My Thirty Years' War: An Autobiography* (New York: Friede, 1930).

36   Oja, *Making Music Modern*, 74.

37   Genêt, "A Life on a Cloud," *The New Yorker*, June 3, 1974, 44–67.

38   ME to parents, May 9, 1926, box 3, folder 14.

39   ME to MD, May 26, 1926, box 6, folder 42.

40   ME to MD, June 2, 1926, box 6, folder 42.

41   ME to parents, June 11, 1926, box 3, folder 15.

42   ME to MD, May 21, 1926, box 6, folder 42. Ewing had a photograph of Baker in his *Gallery*, listed in the catalogue (no. 141) as "Josephine Baker (Nude With Necklace and Bracelets)."

43   Cohen, *All We Know*, 54–58.

44   Ewing kept a copy of Barney's printed diagram among his souvenirs, box 32, folder 248.

45   For an introduction to Barney, see her bio on the Library of Congress online: https://guides .loc.gov/feminism-french-women -history/famous/natalie-clifford -barney. See also Melanie Hawthorne, "Clans and Chronologies: The Salon of Natalie Barney," in *A Belle Epoque? Women and Feminism in French Society and Culture*, eds. Diana Holmes and Carrie Tarr (New York: Berghahn Books, 2007), 65–78; and Melanie Hawthorne, *Women, Citizenship and Sexuality: The Transnational Lives of Renée Vivien, Romaine Brooks, and Natalie Barney* (Liverpool: Liverpool University Press, 2022), esp. chapter 3 (on Brooks).

46   Quoted by Brenda Wineapple, *Genêt: A Biography of Janet Flanner* (New York: Ticknor and Fields, 1989), 85–86.

47   See Friedman, "Queer Old Things."

48   ME to MD, June 26, 1926, box 6, folder 1.

49   ME to MD, n.d. [June 1926], box 6, folder 42.

50   ME to parents, July 23, 1926, box 3, folder 15.

51   For the relationship between Brooks and Barney, including the details of their unconventional marriage with Lily de Gramont, see Langer, *Romaine Brooks*, 87–102.

52   ME to parents, June 25, 1926, box 3, folder 15.

53   ME to MD, June 22, 1926, box 6, folder 1.

54   ME to parents, March 25, 1927, box 3, folder 17.

55   ME to parents, March 4 and 7, and 27, box 3, folder 17.

56   ME to parents, July 4, 1926, box 3, folder 15.

57   ME to parents, July 4, 1926, box 3, folder 15.

58   ME to parents, October 3, 1926, box 3, folder 16.

59   ME to MD, n.d. [August 2, 1926], box 6, folder 43.

60   ME to parents, August 5, 1926, box 3, folder 15.

61   ME to parents, August 2, 1926, box 3, folder 15.

62   Maria Sophia Quine, "Daisy, Countess di Robilant," *Encyclopedia*, https://www .encyclopedia.com/women /encyclopedias-almanacs -transcripts-and-maps/di-robilant -daisy-countess-fl-1922-1933.

63   Langer, *Romaine Brooks*, 10–11.

64   ME to parents, August 5, 1926, box 3, folder 15.

65   ME to parents, August 31, 1926, box 3, folder 16.

66   ME to parents, September 1, 1926, box 3, folder 15.

67   Cliff Eisen, ed., *The Letters of Cole Porter* (New Haven, CT: Yale University Press, 2019), 53–71.

68   ME to parents, September 1, 1926, box 3, folder 16.

69   ME to parents, September 1, 1926, box 3, folder 16. For the guestbook, see "Visitor's Book," *Villa Foscari: La Malcontenta*, https:// www.lamalcontenta.com/index .php/en/life-in-villa/life-in-villa -1924-1965/libro-degli-ospiti.

70   ME to parents, August 12, 1926, box 3, folder 15.

71   ME to parents, September 27, October 3 and 14, 1926, box 3, folder 16.

72   ME to parents, September 27, October 3 and 14, 1926, box 3, folder 16.

73   ME to parents, October 14, 1926, box 3, folder 16.

74   Mark I. Lurie, *Galantière: The Lost Generation's Forgotten Man* (New York: Overlook Press, 2017). Galantière's wife, Dorothy, a dancer and close confidant of Ewing's (she appears in *The Carnival of Venice*), would soon leave him for the sculptor Roy Sheldon.

75   ME to parents, October 31, 1926, box 3, folder 16.

76   ME to parents, November 19 and December 2, 1926, box 3, folder 16.

77 ME to parents, December 10, 1926, box 3, folder 16.

78 ME to parents, n.d. [December 1926], box 3, folder 16.

79 For the early history of the relationship, see Allen Ellenzweig, *George Platt Lynes: The Daring Eye* (Oxford: Oxford University Press, 2021), chapter 6.

80 ME to parents, March 7, 1927, box 3, folder 17.

81 ME to parents, March 7, 1927, box 3, folder 17.

82 ME to parents, March 28, 1927, box 3, folder 17.

83 Oja, *Making Music Modern*, 72. Ewing kept the handbill for the concert, box 3, folder 16. ME to parents, April 15, 1927, box 3, folder 17. Carl Van Vechten attended the performance: Kellner, ed., *Splendid Drunken Twenties*, 160, as well as the after-party at the Club Deauville, which was attended by A'lelia Walker, Nora Holt, the Robesons, and Muriel Draper as well as Antheil. The group went on to another party, and he returned home at 5 a.m.

84 Oja, *Making Music Modern*, 71.

85 Letter from Boni and Liveright to ME, April 18, 1927, box 3, folder 17.

86 ME to parents, April 18, 1927, box 3, folder 17.

87 ME to parents, May 9, 1927, box 3, folder 17.

88 ME to parents, May 9, 1927, box 3, folder 17.

89 ME to parents, May 9, May 13, and n.d. [May] 1927, box 3, folder 17; ME to parents, May 31 and June 12, 1927, box 3, folder 18.

90 For Alice DeLamar, see the extensive information collected by Nona Footz over the past ten years and summarized on *Alice DeLamar* (blog), accessed March 20, 2018, https://alicedelamar.wordpress.com/. See also the information about DeLamar on "Queer Places," *Elisa Rolle* (blog), accessed August 12, 2023, http://www.elisarolle.com/queerplaces/a-b-ce/Alice%20Delamar.html.

91 Derek Patmore, *I Decorate My Home* (New York: Harper & Brothers, 1936); and Derek Patmore, *Decoration for the Small Home* (London: Putnam, 1938). Patmore also published *Private History: An Autobiography* (London: Jonathan Cape, 1960), with a lengthy description of his life in these years (chapters 5–7).

92 ME to parents, July 30, 1927, box 3, folder 18.

93 ME to parents, July 25, 1927, box 3, folder 18.

94 ME to parents, August 5, 1927, box 3, folder 18.]

95 ME to parents, August 12, 1927, box 3, folder 18.]

96 ME to parents, August 17, 1927, box 3, folder 18. In the catalogue of the *Max Ewing Collection of Extraordinary Portraits*, one of these images (unspecified) is listed as number 26: "Esther Murphy and Natalie Barney in a Renaissance Courtyard (Photography by Max Ewing, Verona, 1927)."

97 ME to parents, August 17, 1927, box 3, folder 18.

98 ME to parents, August 17, 1927, box 3, folder 18.

99 For Van Vechten's adventures in Berlin, see White, 253–54.

100 ME to parents, June 17, 1926, box 3, folder 15.

101 ME to parents, June 21, 1926, box 3, folder 15.

102 Meyer, "Threesomes."

103 For the offerings, artistic and otherwise, made by Ewing, Tobey, Kirstein, and others among Draper's coterie of young men, see Olivia Armandroff, "Drawing for an Audience of One."

104 ME to parents, June 17, 1926, box 3, folder 15.

105 Duberman, *The Worlds of Lincoln Kirstein*, 86–88, 90, 149–54, 254–55, describes Kirstein's sexual relationship with Draper, which is also detailed in sections of Kirstein's diaries from this period: New York Public Library Digital Collections, Jerome Robbins Dance Division, [S]* MGZMD 123. Duberman notes that Walker Evans described Draper in a 1971 interview as "completely artificial and phony to the fingertips" adding that Evans had also called her "a remarkable woman … who was very useful in the education of young men like me at that time."

106 No. 209, *The Max Ewing Collection of Incredible Portraits*, described by Ewing below the title as a "Supplement to Catalogue of Extraordinary Portraits, Both Collections on Permanent Exhibition in Apartment Quatre Vingt-Quatre, 19 West 31st Street, New York City, Telephone Lackawanna 6400," box 14, folder 139.

107 ME to MD, n.d. [June 1926], and July 16, 1926, box 6, folders 42–43.

108 ME to MD, June 9, 1926, box 6, folder 42.

109 Ewing's obsession with celebrity was shaped by Oscar Wilde and Sarah Bernhardt, who carefully curated public perceptions of their personalities and courted the attention of fans through their manipulations of the media. See Sharon Marcus, "Salomé!! Sarah Bernhardt, Oscar Wilde, and the Drama of Celebrity," in "Celebrity, Fame, Notoriety," special issue, *PMLA* 126, no. 4 (October 2011): 999–1021.

110 The details are provided in Ellenzweig, *George Platt Lynes*, chapter 6.

111 ME to Parents, April 1, 1926, box 3, folder 14.

112 ME to Parents, July 29, 1926, box 3, folder 15.

113 ME to Parents, July 29, 1926, box 3, folder 15.

114 Ellenzweig, *George Platt Lynes*, 67–68.

115 Ellenzweig, *George Platt Lynes*, 67.

116 In addition to Ellenzweig's *George Platt Lynes*, see Anatole Pohorilenko and James Crump, *When We Were Three*, 17.

117 For photos of the couple with and without Lynes in the mid-1920s, see George Platt Lynes, *Travel Album*, 1927, gelatin silver prints, Philadelphia Museum of Art.

118 See Glenway Wescott, *Continual Lessons: The Journals of Glenway Wescott, 1937–1955* (New York: Farrar, Straus and Giroux, 1991), 8–10. Wescott titled his next novel *The Pilgrim Hawk: A Love Story* (New York: Harper & Brothers, 1940).

119 ME to parents, February 28, 1927, box 7, folder 50, "Restricted." He wrote on February 28 to say that "Saturday evening was spent with George Lynes, and Friday at Esther Murphy's party in Park Avenue."

120 ME to parents, April 19, 1927, box 3, folder 17.

121 ME to parents, May 30, 1926, box 3, folder 14.

122 ME to MD, June 2, 1926, box 6, folder 42.

123 ME to parents, June 8, 1926, box 3, folder 15.

124 ME to parents, June 11, 1926, box 3, folder 15.

125 ME to MD, postscript written June 11, 1926, box 6, folder 42.

126 ME to parents, June 11, 1926, box 3, folder 15.

127 ME to Constant Lambert, n.d. [June 15, 1926?], box 9, folder 67. In the list of papers that Carl Van Vechten sent to Yale in 1943, he speculated that the note had never been sent; there is no record of Lambert sending it back to either Ewing or to Van Vechten for the Yale collection (Carl Van Vechten Papers, New York Public Library, box 11, folder 11).

128 Ewing kept the programs for *Façade* and for Pound's performance of the poetry of Francois Villon, box 6, folder 43.

129 Andrew Motion, *The Lamberts: George, Constant and Kit* (New York: Farrar, Straus and Giroux, 1986), 160.

130 ME to MD, June 9, 1926, box 6, folder 42.

131 ME to MD, July 1, 1926, box 6, folder 43.

132 "George Dangerfield, Historian," *New York Times*, January 6, 1987, 84.

133 ME to parents, October 28, 1927, box 7, folder 50.

134 ME to parents, October 31, 1927, box 3, folder 18.

135 In fact, Ewing did see Dangerfield again in New York, and rather often as it turned out: in 1930, he and his wife Mary emigrated to the United States and became part of Ewing's — and Draper's — circle; Ewing included portraits of both of them in his photo albums and they also appeared in *The Carnival of Venice*.

136 This argument draws on Amelia Jones, "The 'Eternal Return'," 947–78.

137 Edward Burns, ed., *The Letters of Gertrude Stein and Carl Van Vechten*, 321.

138 Patmore, *Private History*, 111–112. In the same passage he writes about other members of the Draper circle, including Esther Murphy and Lorna Lindsley (Ewing's friend from Paris who had purchased the Orgeval house with Noël Murphy), noting about the latter that "she had numerous amorous adventures with sailors in different parts of the world," and "would think nothing of inviting a dozen brash young American sailors from Brooklyn to join the more socialite guests" (112).

139 Burns, ed., *Letters of Gertrude Stein and Carl Van Vechten*, 472, 475, 485, 488, 490, 493. The portrait, which Van Vechten was pleased with, was given to Yale; in a note from January 23, 1941, Van Vechten explained that Brooks had given the painting to him and then, "subsequently, by a ruse, took it away and never returned it." Langer, *Romaine Brooks*, 149–55, discusses these works without explaining the artist's choice of sitters; as Langer notes, she completed only four portraits after 1934.

140 Fahlman, "Great Draper Woman," 36.

141 Patmore, *Private History*, 110.

142 Langer, *Romaine Brooks*, 148–55.

143 Romaine Brooks's "Memoir," in the Beinecke Library at Yale (YCAL MSS 461, box 1), reveals nothing on the subject, and Draper doesn't mention it. A letter from Natalie Barney to the critic Gilbert Seldes (whose portrait appears in *The Carnival of Venice*), dated December 12, 1958 notes that Romaine Brooks had "enjoyed Muriel's settings [sic]," adding "it seems to me that this tell-tale portrait conveys the rest," University of Delaware

Library, MSS 0099, F0519. Langer, *Romaine Brooks*, 155.

Chapter 3
The Gallery of Extraordinary Portraits, 1928–33

1   ME to parents, January 17, February 20 and 28, April 28, 1928, box 4, folder 21.

2   The use of new apartment-hotels by gay "bachelors" was first identified by George Chauncey in *Gay New York*. For gay Harlem, see Bruce Nugent, *Gay Rebel of the Harlem Renaissance*; and Mumford, *Interzones*, chapter 6. For bachelor flats, see Elizabeth Collins Cromley, *Alone Together: A History of New York's Early Apartments* (Ithaca, NY: Cornell University Press, 1990), 187–90; and Chauncey, *Gay New York*, chapter 6.

3   ME to Edgar Ailes, December 27, 1927, box 6, folder 37. I am indebted to Lee Ann Custer, postdoctoral fellow at Vanderbilt University, for locating the 1932 plan online in the "I-card" file of the New York City Department of Housing Preservation (https://hpdonline .nyc.gov/hpdonline/building/32176 /overview). See Lee Ann Custer, "The Clean Open Air of John Sloane's Tenement Paintings," *American Art* 37, no. 2 (summer 2023): 28–52.

4   ME to parents, November 27, 1927, box 3, folder 20.

5   ME to parents, November 28, 1927, box 3, folder 20.

6   ME to parents, August 1926, box 3, folder 15.

7   Christopher Breward, "The Closet," in *Queering the Interior*, ed. Matt Cook and Andrew Gorman-Murray (London: Bloomsbury Publishing, 2017), 187–97.

8   ME to parents, April 7, 1929, box 4, folder 23.

9   See Marcus, "Salomé!! Sarah Bernhardt, Oscar Wilde," 99–1021; for opera fandom, see Wayne Koestenbaum, *The Queen's Throat: Opera, Homosexuality and the Mystery of Desire* (New York: Poseidon Press, 1993).

10   Catalogue of the *Max Ewing Collection of Extraordinary Portraits* and its supplement, the *Max Ewing Collection of Incredible Portraits*, box 14, folder 149.

11   Whitney Davis, "Queer Family Romance in Collecting Visual Culture," *GLQ: A Journal of Lesbian and Gay Studies* 17, nos. 2–3 (2011): 309–29.

12   ME to Alice DeLamar, May 24, 1934, box 6, folder 62.

13   Henry Urbach's reading of the "ante-closet" immediately in front of the closet door as a space of simultaneous disclosure and nondisclosure seems particularly apt for our understanding of camp performance in this case. See Henry Urbach, "Closets, Clothes, dis-Closure," *Assemblage* 30 (August 1996): 62–73. See also Christopher Breward, "The Closet," 187–96.

14   Eve Kosofsky Sedgwick, "Shame, Theatricality, and Queer Performativity: Henry James's *The Art of the Novel*," in *Touching Feeling: Affect, Pedagogy and Performativity* (Chapel Hill, NC: Duke University Press, 2003), 35–66.; the issue is taken up by John Potvin in chapter 2 of *Deco Dandy*.

15   The range of topics shared with Ewing and an intimate circle of queer friends is suggested by their letters, notably CVV to ME, November 13, 1933, box 8, folder 60: responding to an anecdote that ME had told him about Mae West, Van Vechten suggests that "if you haven't told it to Langston, please do." Later in the same document he notes that "I gave a party for [Paris-based writer] Julian Green last night to which you would probably have been invited had you been here, although the others were mostly colored … Tonio [Selwart] and [Donald] Angus [CVV's close friend and former lover] were there." He closes with another bit of queer in-group gossip, "Eddie Wassermann [*sic*] has a Man now instead of Hannah and I'm told there is a sporting house for sailors on Park Avenue." The postscript, "Have you read the *Young and Evil* by Charles Ford and Parker Tyler?," further suggests the close watch both men kept on new developments in queer culture.

16   ME to parents, n.d. [December 1930], box 5, folder 28.

17   ME to parents, "Friday," n.d. [March 1927], box 3, folder 17.

18   ME to parents, February 3, 1930, box 4, folder 25.

19   The X-ray is listed as no. 64 in the *Catalogue*.

20   See Steven Watson, *Strange Bedfellows*. For Florine Stettheimer's paintings, see Elizabeth Sussman and Barbara Bloemink, eds., *Florine Stettheimer, Manhattan Fantastica* (New York: Whitney Museum of Art, 1995); and Barbara Bloemink, *Florine Stettheimer: A Biography* (New Haven, CT: Yale University Press, 2022). See also Linda Nochlin's foundational study, "Florine Stettheimer — Rococo Subversive," *Art News*, 1980, https://www.artnews.com /art-in-america/features/from-the -archives-florine-stettheimer -rococo-subversive-63262. For the queer and "ultra-feminine" character of the Stettheimers' salon, see Cécile Whiting, "Decorating with Stettheimer and the Boys," *American Art* 14, no. 1 (spring 2000): 24–49; and Christopher Breward, "Styling *Four Saints in Three Acts:* Scene, Costume, Fashion and the Queer Modern Movement," in *4 Saints in 3 Acts: A Snapshot of the American Avant-Garde in the 1930s*, eds. Patricia Allmer and John Sears (Manchester: Manchester University Press, 2017), 82–102. For Ewing's game-changing encounter with the Stettheimers, see ME to parents, January 28, 1929, box 7, folder 50.

21   ME to parents, November 18, January 29, 1930, and n.d. [November 1929], box 5, folder 28, mention attending the Stettheimers' parties; in the undated letter, Ewing notes that Florine and Charles Demuth visited to his apartment. In July 1932, Ewing accompanied Florine Stettheimer to the top of the Empire State Building: ME to CE, n.d. [July 1932], box 5, folder 32. The Stettheimer sisters showed Ewing the photos that Van Vechten had taken of them, noting that he "was the only person alive they would show them to, they were so bad": ME to CE, December 3, 1932, box 5, folder 33.

22   Whiting, "Decorating with Stettheimer and the Boys," 36.

23   A series of postcards showing the interior of Van Vechten's apartment includes a view of his study with the portrait prominently displayed on the wall, box 8, folder 60.

24   *Catalogue of the Max Ewing Collection of Extraordinary Portraits*, no. 86.

25   Taylor Gordon, *Born to Be*, introduction by Muriel Draper, foreword by Carl Van Vechten, and illustrations by Covarrubias (New York: Covici-Freide, 1929). See Michael K. Johnson, *Can't Stand Still*.

26   For Cunard and her influence, see Carla Kaplan, *Miss Anne in Harlem: The White Women of the Black Renaissance* (New York: Harper, 2013).

27   Max reported to his mother about a July 25, 1928 party at Van Vechten's: "After dinner Friday night we went to Harlem to see Paul Meeres, the brown Valentino who dances at Small's Paradise," box 4, folder 21.

28   Allen Ellenzweig, *George Platt Lynes*. In the same letter, he reported that he had photographed "Max, Zena, Demetrious Vilan (a dancer), and Paul Meeres (also a dancer)"; quoted in Anatole Pohorilenko and James Crump, *When We Were Three*, 67.

29   Van Vechten took the photos on April 1, 1932: Carl Van Vechten Papers Relating to African American Arts and Letters, Beinecke Rare Book & Manuscript Library, Yale University, New Haven, Connecticut.

30   ME to parents, October 14, 1928, box 4, folder 22: "Paul Meeres, the brown Valentino, is an enchanting person. I had him downtown once again, and he is as refreshing as a breeze from the Bahamas where he came from." On October 28, Ewing reported that Paul Meeres came to see him: "Everyone gives him their phone number and asks him to come over but he never does." Ewing noted gleefully that Meeres had never visited Van Vechten: ME to parents, October 28, box 4, folder 22. See also ME to parents, December 9, 1931, box 5, folder 30: "Mary Garden says she wants to have herself photographed in Paul Meeres Indian costume … this may be arranged with George Lynes next week."

31   ME to parents, November 19, 1930, box 5, folder 28. A different image of the Rocky twins, from 1928, appears in the 1929 photo of the *Gallery*.

32   ME to parents, March 11, 1930, box 4, folder 25: "My Mondays are becoming quite a regular and established event."

33   ME to CVV, October 28, 1928, YCAL MSS 1050, box 43, folder 589.

34   ME to parents, November 29, 1928, box 4, folder 22.

35   ME to parents, November 29, 1928, box 4, folder 22.

36   ME to parents, September 27, 1926, box 3, folder 15.

37   ME to parents, December 14, 1928, box 7, folder 50.

38   ME to parents, March 20 and 28, 1924, box 2, folder 8. The camera was either a Kodak 1a or 2a Autographic, both of which took the Kodak 116 film that Ewing advised his father to use when he sent the camera back to him on September 30, 1930, box 4, folder 27. This is probably the same popular model that George Platt Lynes borrowed from Monroe Wheeler when he photographed his friends in the south of France in 1928: in Ewing's *Carnival of Venice* portrait series, Lynes is shown as a tourist in Venice, holding a similar camera.

39   ME to parents, March 11, 1930, box 4, folder 26: Ewing notes that Marguerite d'Alvarez visited the closet for the first time.

40   Catalogue entries for Ewing's portraits of Glenway Wescott: 43 left profile; 128 "Glenway Wescott with sheers"; 171 "Glenway Wescott"; 186 "GW drawing by Cocteau"; 197 "GW seated at a table"; 201 "GW"; 202 "GW riding on a horse in New Mexico."

41   Earnest, *The Young and Evil*, especially Anne Reynolds, "No Strangers," 25–35, on the notion of

"erotic spectatorship." For Cadmus and Lynes, see Mauss and Miller, *Body Language*.

42 ME to parents, April 7, 1929, box 4, folder 23. He also mentioned that he was invited to lunch by their English friend Zena Naylor; she is also mentioned a number of times in Van Vechten's diaries, and he notes that he attended a going-away party for Naylor at Max Ewing's on April 30, 1929: Kellner, ed., *Splendid Drunken Twenties*.

43 Ellenzweig, *George Platt Lynes*, 98–99.

44 Ellenzweig, *George Platt Lynes*, 107–11.

45 ME to George Platt Lynes [hereafter GPL], n.d. [spring 1932], box 7, folder 54.

46 ME to parents, n.d. [December 1929], box 9, folder 67. In a letter of December 6, 1929, from GPL to Monroe Wheeler, he reported that he had photographed "Max, Zena, Demetrious Vilan, Paul Meeres." In the same letter, Lynes notes that the photos of Meeres and Vilan were "nudes and near nudes," and that Meeres was "the most beautiful man I have ever seen." Ellenzweig, *George Platt Lynes*, 112–13. He added that he had made a set of these images for Wheeler. Lynes's portrait of Naylor wearing Ewing's sailor hat from Villefranche is also in the Ewing collection.

47 ME to parents, February 3, 1930, box 4, folder 25.

48 ME to parents, December 11, 1930, box 5, folder 28.

49 See Ellenzweig, *George Platt Lynes*, chapter 8, 532n54.

50 Ellenzweig, *George Platt Lynes*, 117–18.

51 All entries are from the catalogue of the *Max Ewing Collection of Extraordinary Portraits*, [December 1928], box 14, folder 139.

52 Potvin, *Deco Dandy*, chapter 3; and David Bathrick, "Max Schmeling on the Canvas: Boxing as an Icon of Weimar Culture," *New German Critique*, no. 51 (autumn 1990): 113–36.

53 ME to parents, August 1928, box 4, folder 21.

54 For Robeson, see Jeffrey Stewart, ed., *Paul Robeson: Artist and Citizen* (New Brunswick, NJ: Rutgers University Press, 1998).

55 *Catalogue of the Max Ewing Collection of Extraordinary Portraits*, no. 106.

56 For Beaton's early career, the Sitwells, and Constant Lambert, see Robin Muir, *Cecil Beaton's Bright Young Things* (London: National Portrait Gallery, 2020), 10–39, 54–59, 142–45.

57 Catalogue no. 76, *Beatrice Lillie and Sir Robert Peel at Home*. I am grateful to Ella Mints, a student

in my advanced seminar at Wellesley College (spring 2022) for pointing this out.

58 See Van Haaften, *Berenice Abbott*.

59 ME to parents, April 7, 1932, box 5, folder 31.

60 ME to parents, October 3, 1926, box 3, folder 16. He couldn't make up his mind about whether to sail with Heap or with his handsome friend Robert Gorham, joking in an earlier letter that "on the principle that handsome boy is always handsomer than a handsome woman, I would rather sail with him than with Jane": ME to parents, September 27, 1926, box 3, folder 16.

61 *Catalogue of the Max Ewing Collection of Extraordinary Portraits*, no. 117.

62 *Catalogue of the Max Ewing Collection of Incredible Portraits*, no. 215 and no. 141.

63 A plaster version of the bust by Sheldon survives in the Beinecke at Yale.

64 For the notion of "self-fashioning" through clothes and portraitures, see Stephen Greenblatt, *Renaissance Self-Fashioning from More to Shakespeare* (Chicago: University of Chicago Press, 1980).

65 See Van Haaften, *Berenice Abbott*, 144–47, 152–57.

66 Max Ewing, "Êtes-vous Polygame," an "interview," and Max Ewing, "Isn't It Awful," a "lament" by Princess Eugénie Murat (played by Berenice Abbott), were recorded on "aluminum instantaneous phono disc," July 27, 1929, box 35, folder 250. Two other skits, entitled "Reminiscences and Hysterics" and "An Intelligence Test" were recorded by Ewing with his cousin Doris Ewing, August 3, 1929, box 35, folder 251.

67 ME to parents, February 26, 1929, box 3, folder 23. On June 27, 1929, he noted that "Dorothy Caruso has opened a recording studio in 62nd street where you can have records made of yourself very cheap," adding that he was going to make a recording, box 4, folder 24.

68 ME to parents, March 7, 1929, box 4, folder 23.

69 ME to parents, n.d. [May 1929], box 4, folder 23. Dudley Murphy was a film director who directed the *Ballet Mécanique* in 1924.

70 ME to parents, February 26, 1929, box 4, folder 23. For de Acosta, see Cohen, *All We Know*, part 2. In the early 1920s, de Acosta was romantically involved with Eva Le Gallienne, who later turned her attentions to Gladys Calthorp; Calthorp and Le Gallienne lived and worked together in New York, but had already separated by the time of Ewing's party in 1929. For the

complex personal and professional relationships among these women, see Helen Sheehy, *Eva Le Gallienne: A Biography* (New York: Alfred A. Knopf, 1996), part 3.

71 ME to parents, n.d. ["Sunday" 1929], box 4, folder 23.

72 ME to parents, February 11, 1929, box 4, folder 23.

73 The first mention of Beaton in Van Vechten's New York daybooks occurs on December 31, 1928: see Kellner, ed., *Splendid Drunken Twenties*, 230. For Beaton's use of camp artifice and irony, see John Potvin, *Bachelors of a Different Sort: Queer Aesthetics, Material Culture and the Modern Interior in Britain* (Manchester: Manchester University Press, 2015), chapter 7. Potvin notes that "While artifice, affect and creativity were the sources of Beaton's fame and fortune, these would also provide innumerable ambivalent experiences of shame," an observation that might equally be made of Ewing: Potvin, *Bachelors*, 248.

74 *Max Ewing Collection of Incredible Portraits*, no. 218. Muir, *Cecil Beaton's Bright Young Things*, 56–57, 138–41. Ewing kept the program in his collection.

75 According to Van Vechten, who was also there, along with most of the usual suspects, including Esther Murphy, Alice DeLamar, Beatrice and Robert Locher, Lewis Galantière, and even Mabel Luhan: Kellner, ed., *Splendid Drunken Twenties*, 230.

76 Potvin, *Bachelors*, 276–77.

77 Muir, *Cecil Beaton's Bright Young Things*, 10–18.

78 Quoted in Potvin, *Bachelors*, 260ff. Flanner wrote to her lover Natalia Danesi Murray about her feelings of shame in letters collected by Murray in *Darlinghissima: Letters to a Friend, Janet Flanner* (New York: Random House, 1985).

79 A'lelia Bundles, *On Her Own Ground: The Life and Times of Madam C. J. Walker* (New York: Scribner, 2002). Bundles's biography of A'lelia Walker, her great-grandmother, is in progress; most of the Walker papers and photographs remain in the family's hands with limited access for outside researchers.

80 ME to parents, May 4, 1927, box 3, folder 17.

81 A'lelia Walker to ME, April 18, 1928, box 9, folder 65. On October 15, 1927, Van Vechten recorded in his daybook that "The Dark Tower, A'lelia's new tearoom [speakeasy] opens tonight." Kellner, ed., *Splendid Drunken Twenties*, 179.

82 "A'lelia Robinson Pied-a-terre," September 4, 1940, JWJ MSS 1050, box 225.

83 See "Villa Lewaro," accessed July 21, 2024, https://en.wikipedia.org/wiki/Villa_Lewaro. The hybrid nature of both residences is discussed in Alice T. Friedman, "Shifting the Paradigm: Houses Built for Women," in *Design and Feminism: Re-Visioning Spaces, Places, and Everyday Things*, ed. Joan Rothschild (New Brunswick, NJ: Rutgers University Press, 1999), 85–97.

84 Tara Dudley, "Seeking the Ideal African-American Interior: The Walker Residences and Salon in New York," *Studies in the Decorative Arts* 14, no. 1 (fall–winter 2006–7): 80–112.

85 ME to parents, April 29, 1929, box 4, folder 21. Walker also visited with "two friends" in July (n.d. [July], box 4, folder 24).

86 ME to parents, April 28, 1929, box 4, folder 21.

87 ME to parents, June 1929, box 4, folder 24, describes a party at the Dark Tower in honor of Nella Larsen and Walter White.

88 Ewing first met Mills at a party given by Edgard Varèse on "Memorial Day, 1925," box 2, folder 11. In January 1926, Ewing attended a concert by Florence Mills before going to a party at Carl Van Vechten's where Taylor Gordon sang "Negro songs": ME to parents, n.d. [November 1925], box 2, folder 12. The event is also recorded in Van Vechten's diary: see Kellner, ed., *Splendid Drunken Twenties*, 108. On May 1, 1929, Ewing and Van Vechten were in Harlem buying Gladys Bentley's recordings: ME to parents, May 7, 1929, box 4, folder 26.

89 Langston Hughes, *The Big Sea* (New York: Hill and Wang, 1940), 224, https://gutenberg.ca/ebooks/hughesl-bigsea/hughesl-bigsea-00-h-dir/hughesl-bigsea-00-h.html#chapter0117.

90 Hughes, *The Big Sea*, 227.

91 Hughes, *The Big Sea*, 228.

92 Mabel Hampton, interviewed by Joan Nestle, January 13, 1983, Lesbian Herstory Archives, accessed March 2020, http://herstories.prattinfoschool.nyc/omeka/collections/show/29. Hampton's life and career are explored at length by Hartman in *Wayward Lives, Beautiful Experiments*.

93 ME to parents, n.d. [late November 1929], box 4, folder 25.

94 Hughes, *The Big Sea*, 225.

95 ME to parents, October 2, 1931, box 5, folder 30.

96 Hughes, *The Big Sea*, 247.

97 ME to parents, October 2, 1931, box 5, folder 30.

98 The event is described in ME to parents, April 8, 1928, box 5, folder 21. Ewing was proud of his

photos of the socialite and considered her a friend, see catalogue no. 41: photos of Emily Vanderbilt and Max Ewing signed "Emily Davies Vanderbilt May 20, 1928."

99 See the Introduction to Chauncey, *Gay New York*.

Chapter 4
The Making of an Artist

1 Ewing continued to invite his friends to the performances of the *Grand Street Follies*: on May 1, 1929, for example, Van Vechten attended the opening and went to an after-party with Eddie Wasserman, where he met Ruth Draper and saw "Philip Moeller, Mina Curtiss, Muriel Draper, Albert Carroll … Max Ewing, etc." See Kellner, ed., *Splendid Drunken Twenties*, 244.

2 Despite a year of "x-rays and electrical treatments" following Antheil's *Ballet Mécanique*, Ewing's finger was no better: ME to parents, October 10, 1928, box 4, folder 22. For the *Surréalisme* exhibition and other foundational shows in the winter of 1932, see the Julien Levy Gallery Records, Philadelphia Museum of Art, Series V Scrapbooks, 1925–41; and Julien Levy, *Memoir of an Art Gallery* (New York: G. P. Putnam's Sons, 1977), esp. 100–106.

3 De Acosta is one of the three extraordinary women (with Esther Murphy and *Vogue* editor Madge Garland) who are of the subjects of Lisa Cohen's *All We Know*.

4 White, *Tastemaker*, 248–54.

5 Levy, *Memoir*, 101.

6 The full story, based on interviews with Thomson and others, is told in Watson, *Prepare for Saints*.

7 ME to parents, January 28, 1929, box 7, folder 50.

8 ME to MD, May 7, 1926, box 6, folder 43; ME to parents, February 26, 1929, box 4, folder 23; ME to parents, December 19, 1932, box 5, folder 34.

9 ME to parents, October 28, 1928 and October 27, 1929, box 7, folder 50.

10 As Henry McBride wrote in his essay in the catalogue of the MoMA exhibition, *Florine Stettheimer* (New York: Simon and Schuster, 1946), 10, "The artists who came to these parties came there because of her, most of them in the avant garde, such as Gaston Lachaise, Charles Demuth, Pavel Tchelitchew, et al., but all the others in attendance, the writers, singers, dancers, and sometimes even scientists, were definitely interested and amused by Florine's paintings." For an overview of Florine's oeuvre and the Stettheimers' salon, see Barbara Bloemink,

Florine Stettheimer; and Matthias Muhling, Karin Althaus, and Susanne Boller, eds., *Florine Stettheimer* (Munich: Hirmer, 2015).

11 Kirsten MacLeod, "Introduction: The Blind Bow-Boy," vii–xxii.

12 ME to parents, January 29, 1930, box 4, folder 25.

13 Cecily Swanson, "Conversation Pieces: Circulating Muriel Draper's Salon," *Journal of Modern Literature* 36, no. 4 (summer 2013): 23–43.

14 ME to parents, April 14, 1926, box 3, folder 14: "Everything went into storage. I'm taking the Chanler portrait to Muriel's and the statues. Sascha is taking lamps and dishes. Hotel [Warrington] is keeping the chest of drawers. You have been marvelously sweet about this going of mine, and I can't tell you how much I appreciate it."

15 The photographer Ralph Steiner had been a friend of Ewing's at least since the spring of 1926, when he invited Ewing to an exhibition of his work at J. B. Neumann's Print Room and asked if he could bring Carl Van Vechten along with him. Invitation to Steiner exhibition with ME to CVV, February 16–March 1, 1926, YCAL MSS 1050, box 44, folder 589. See also "Ralph Steiner: American, 1899–1986," MoMA, accessed June 22, 2023, https://www.moma.org/artists/5631, for biographical information and a selection of images.

16 Carl Van Vechten, "Ma Draper," *Yale University Library Gazette* 37, no. 4 (April 1963): 127, 128. He also described their lasting friendship and connection with Max Ewing: "Muriel and I were always more or less acquainted; we had to be because we associated with so many of the same people. It probably was not before the early thirties that we became friends and she began to ask me to her parties, but I saw a good deal of her even before that, and I was constantly aware of her presence, her golden throne, and her potential celebrity. Our mutual friends Max Ewing, Gilbert Seldes, and Robert Chanler inevitably asked us both to the same gatherings." Van Vechten, "Ma Draper," 12.

17 ME to parents, February 3, 1930, box 4, folder 23.

18 ME to parents, February 21, 1930, box 4, folder 25. The photos are from box 15, folder 145.

19 ME to parents, January 29, 1930, box 4, folder 25.

20 Kellner, ed., *Splendid Drunken Twenties*, 278; ME to parents, February 3, 1930, box 4, folder 25.

21 For Max Ewing's and others' images of Muriel Draper, see

Armandroff, "Drawing for an Audience of One," esp. 61–74.

22 *Inlander* 10, no. 4, (June 1930): 39–40, box 11, folder 102. The photographer's visit in May 1930 is recorded in ME to parents, May 14, 1930, box 4, folder 26.

23 ME to parents, February 21, 1930, box 4, folder 25.

24 ME to parents, February 25, 1930, box 4, folder 25.]

25 ME to parents, May 20, 1930, box 4, folder 25: new statue of Glenway Wescott, "my masterpiece."

26 ME to parents, n.d. [October 1929], box 4, folder 27.

27 ME to parents, October 27, 1930, box 4, folder 27, and n.d. [March 1931], box 5, folder 28.

28 See box 31, folder 237.

29 Doris Ewing suggested in a number of letters that the nudes weren't worth saving, and Van Vechten delayed, finally writing back (untruthfully) to say that "The nudes are gone, destroyed or otherwise disposed of." CVV to Doris Ewing, August 1, 1942, YCAL MSS 1050, box 43, folder 587.

30 For an overview of the contradictions presented by Van Vechten's scrapbooks, see James Smalls, "Van Vechten's Secret," *Gay and Lesbian Review Worldwide* 13, no. 3 (May–June 2006): 25–29, and James Smalls, *The Homoerotic Photography of Carl Van Vechten: Public Face, Private Thoughts* (Philadelphia: Temple University Press, 2015). For the scrapbooks, see Jonathan Weinberg, "Boy Crazy: Carl Van Vechten's Queer Collecting," *Yale Journal of Criticism* 7, no. 2 (January 1994): 25–49.

31 ME to GPL, n.d. [April 1930], box 7, folder 54.

32 ME to GPL, n.d. ["Friday"], box 7, folder 54.

33 ME to GPL, n.d. ["Friday"], box 7, folder 54.

34 ME to GPL, n.d. ["Wednesday"], box 7, folder 54. See also Ellenzweig, *George Platt Lynes*, 112–13. A postcard from Ewing to Lynes postmarked January 5, 1930 refers to prints of those photographs and to portraits of Ewing with his piano. ME to GPL, January 5, 1930, box 7, folder 54.

35 ME to parents, February 1 and 3, 1926, box 2, folder 13.

36 For example, when he told her about his plan to visit Nino Ronchi, the Milanese painter, during his visit to Europe in the summer of 1926, he joked that "it looks as if there will be a girl, *or a boy*, in every port." ME to parents, February 1, 1926, box 2, folder 13.

37 See Thomas Waugh, *Hard to Imagine*; and David Leddick, *Naked Men Too: Liberating the Male Nude, 1950–2000* (New York: Uni-

verse Publishing, 2000). For "the amorous regard" of Lynes's male nudes, and Lynes's career in fashion photography, see Elspeth H. Brown, "Queering Glamour in Interwar Fashion Photography," *GLQ: A Journal of Lesbian and Gay Studies* 23, no. 1 (July 2017): 289–326.

38 Doris Ewing to CVV, July 8 and 21, 1942, YCAL MSS 1050, box 43, folder 586.

39 Chauncey, *Gay New York*, 18ff.

40 Duberman, *The Worlds of Lincoln Kirstein*, 93–94.

41 "I at last got Paul Meeres, the Brown Valentino, down here last Saturday night. He is that marvelous looking boy who dances at Small's Paradise in Harlem, and is the greatest sheik of them all. He does look exactly like Rudolph Valentino, save that he is brown. I think he must be only half negro … He said that everyone who came to Smalls gave him their telephone number and begged him to come and see them, but that it was very few he went to see. He said he had never even gone to see Mr. Van Vechten, though all Harlem worshiped Carl. But he came to see me, and made it emphatic that this was a great distinction." ME to parents, October 10, 1928, box 4, folder 22.

42 GPL to Monroe Wheeler, December 4, 1931, quoted in Ellenzweig, *George Platt Lynes*, 169n46.

43 ME to parents, February 21, 1930, box 4, folder 25; quoted in Wallace Ewing, *Genius Denied*, 33.

44 MD to CVV, September 2, 1930, YCAL MSS 1050, box 41, folder 540.

45 Quoted by Betsy Fahlman, "The Great Draper Woman," 33–37.

46 CVV to Muriel Draper, June 8, 1946, in Bruce Kellner, ed., *Letters of Carl Van Vechten* (New Haven, CT: Yale University Press, 1987), 221.

47 *Surréalisme*, January 9–29, 1932, Philadelphia Art Museum, Julien Levy Gallery Records, series III, "Exhibition Announcements and Other Ephemera," box 36, folder 3, https://findingaids.library.upenn.edu/records/PMA_PMA.005.

48 ME to parents, January 15, 1932, box 5, folder 31.

49 Margaret Anderson and Mathilda M. Hills, *Forbidden Fires* (Kansas City, MO: Naiad Press, 1996). I am grateful to Professor Hills for sharing her work on Anderson, Solita Solano, and Flanner, and for talking about her relationship with her life partner, Elizabeth Jenks Clark, who had known the group since the 1930s and lived with Solano from the 1940s until Solano's death in 1975. Clark left the Anderson archive to Hills at her death;

these papers and photographs were later transferred to the Beinecke as the Elizabeth Jenks Clark Collection of Margaret Anderson.

50 Muriel Draper Invitation List, n.d. [late 1920s], YCAL MSS 49, box 15, folder 510.

51 Florine Stettheimer, manuscript of *Crystal Flowers*, Florine and Ettie Stettheimer Papers, YCAL MSS 20, box 8, folder 133, n.p., from the section entitled "Moods." The poems were edited by Ettie Stettheimer and privately printed in *Crystal Flowers*, 1949. See Muhling, Althaus, and Boller, eds., *Florine Stettheimer*, 174–81; and Irene Gammel and Suzanne Zelazo, eds., *Florine Stettheimer: New Directions in Multimodal Modernism* (Toronto: Book Hug Press, 2019).

52 ME to parents, November 18, 1929, box 4, folder 25.

53 For Stettheimer's views on the gallery system and the art market, see Heather Hole, "Florine Stettheimer, the Department Store, and the Spaces of Display, New York, 1916–26," *Panorama: The Journal of the Association of Historians of American Art* 3, no. 2 (fall 2017), https://journalpanorama .org/article/florine-stettheimer/.

54 Henry McBride, *Florine Stettheimer*, 24.

55 Christopher Reed, *Bloomsbury Rooms: Modernism, Subculture, Domesticity* (New Haven, CT: Yale University Press, 2004), 236–37; and Christopher Reed, "A *Vogue* That Dare Not Speak Its Name: Sexual Subculture during the Editorship of Dorothy Todd, 1922–1926," *Fashion Theory* 10, nos. 1–2 (2006): 39–72, esp. 42–43. See also Jane Stevenson, *Baroque Between the Wars: Alternative Style in the Arts, 1918–1939* (New York: Oxford University Press, 2018).

56 ME to parents, November 7 and December 11, 1930, box 5, folder 28.

57 ME to parents, February 5, 1931, box 5, folder 28.

58 ME to parents, April 6, 1931, box 5, folder 29.

59 ME to parents, June 18 and July 3, 1931, box 5, folder 29; July 9, 1931, box 5, folder 30.

60 *Crystal Flowers*, Beinecke Library, YCAL MSS 20, box 8, folder 133, https://collections .library.yale.edu/catalog/17054802 (image 336).

61 ME to CE, June 4, 1932, box 5, folder 32.

62 Bloemink, *Florine Stettheimer*, 290–94; and Linda Nochlin, "Florine Stettheimer — Rococo Subversive," *Art in America*, September 1980, 64–83. I am grateful to Barbara Bloemink for corresponding with me via email about

this new reading of the painting (correspondence with the author, April 9 and 10, 2023).

63 McBride, *Florine Stettheimer*, 7.

64 McBride, *Florine Stettheimer*, 31–32.

65 Bloemink, *Florine Stettheimer*, 290.

66 For Wanamaker's Belmaison Gallery (curated by the Stettheimers' friend Louis Bouché from 1921), see Hole, "Florine Stettheimer, the Department Store, and the Spaces of Display," n44.

67 Peter A. Juley Collection, Photography Study Collection, Smithsonian American Art Museum, J0050373. For Dudensing's Valentine Gallery records, see Archives of American Art, accessed March 20, 2023, https://www.aaa.si.edu /collections/valentine-gallery -records-7103.

68 H. T., "Lucie Bigelow Rosen Heard," *New York Times*, February 1, 1938, 18.

69 See Anne M. Lampe, *Robert E. Locher, A Modern Classic* (Lancaster, PA: The Demuth Museum, 2017). A photo of Beatrice Locher and Max Ewing in Newport in September 1931 is in one of Ewing's photo albums, box 24, image 115.

70 In the opinion of Barbara Bloemink, the differing eye color of the two male figures makes the identification of the groom with Robert Locher unlikely. Barbara Bloemink, email communication to author, April 10, 2023.

71 ME to CE, July 1932, box 5, folder 33.

72 ME to CE, August 22 and n.d. [August 1932], box 5, folder 33.

73 White, *Tastemaker*, 151–52. He writes that the term was coined by Jacques-Emil Blanche to describe Luhan's coterie of young men.

74 Postcards from CVV to ME, *Famous Beauties of the XX Century*: "Prentiss Taylor, December 22, 1931"; "Donald Angus Circa 1919" (sent December 15, 1931); "Edward Wasserman circa 1919" (sent December 14, 1931); "Max Ewing" (labeled "[— ?] 1928"). Box 8, folder 60. Ewing listed the dates of each of the portraits in a note of February 17, 1932, together with captions for views of Van Vechten's apartment and other places he had lived throughout his life. Prentiss Taylor's papers are in the Archives of American Art, https://www.aaa .si.edu/collections/prentiss -taylor-papers-9232.

75 The handwritten list includes the notation "Complete, ME." ME to CVV, MSS 1050, box 43, folder 591.

76 Smalls, *Homoerotic Photography of Carl Van Vechten*, 23; and White, *Tastemaker*, 259, which references Van Vechten's interest in Covarrubias's new Leica. A similar message was written on an undated postcard showing the "Early home of Carl Van Vechten Cedar Rapids Iowa," n.d. [January 1932], box 8, folder 60: "I am getting a camera and am going to become an Artist Photographer — with subjects that the others have missed."

77 Postcard, n.d. [January 1932], box 8, folder 60.

78 CVV to ME, February 4, 1932, (real-photo postcard) showing "The View from Carl Van Vechten's Window," box 8, folder 60. On May 3, 1932, Van Vechten photographed O'Keeffe in front of MoMA; some of the images from this session show her with their old friend, the artist Charles Demuth: YCAL MSS 1050, box 343, folder 4466. (See fig. 6.25.)

79 Preserved in Prentiss Taylor Papers, Archives of American Art, https://www.aaa.si.edu/collections /prentiss-taylor-papers-9232.

80 Carl Van Vechten, contact sheets, February 27, 1932, YCAL MSS 1050, box 84, folder 1404.

81 CVV to ME, February 18, 1932, in Kellner, ed., *Letters of Carl Van Vechten*, 125.

82 For Van Vechten as a portrait photographer, see "Carl Van Vechten's Portraits," Beinecke Rare Book & Manuscript Library, https:// beinecke.library.yale.edu /collections/highlights/carl-van -vechtens-portraits; and the Carl Van Vechten Collection, Prints and Photographs Division, Library of Congress, https://www.loc.gov /collections/van-vechten /about-this-collection/.

83 Fania Marinoff and Edith Ramsay, photographed March 9, 1932, roll number XII, box 566, folder 10474.

84 In this regard, the work of the artist J. C. Leyendecker, the subject of a recent exhibition entitled *Under Cover: J. C. Leyendecker and American Masculinity*, May 5–August 13, 2023, curated by Donald Albrecht at the New York Historical Society, is relevant for its veiled but unmistakable homoerotic content.

85 ME to CE, December 3, 1932, box 5, folder 33.

Chapter 5
The Carnival of Venice, 1932

1 ME to CE, April 21, 1932, box 5, folder 32.

2 ME to CE, April 21, 1932, box 5, folder 32.

3 Nancy Martha West, "Operated by Any School Boy or Girl: The Marketing of the Brownie Camera,"

in *Kodak and the Lens of Nostalgia* (Charlottesville: University Press of Virginia, 2000), chapter 3.

4 For Warhol's polaroid snapshots, see Robert B. Woodard, *Andy Warhol Polaroids 1958–1987* (New York: Taschen, 2017). A selection of these images is online at the RISD Museum, https://risdmuseum .org/exhibitions-events/exhibitions /andy-warhols-photographs.

5 ME to CVV, April 22, 1932, YCAL MSS 1050, box 43, folder 591.

6 ME to CVV, April 22, 1932, YCAL MSS 1050, box 43, folder 591.

7 CVV to ME, n.d. [April 1932], photo postcard of Gertrude Stein, box 8, folder 60.

8 ME to CVV, June 23, 1932, YCAL MSS 1050, box 43, folder 591.

9 For Chanler's paintings on screens, see Betsy Fahlman, "Robert Winthrop Chanler: Reclaiming an American Modernist," in *Robert Winthrop Chanler: Discovering the Fantastic*, eds. Gina Wouters and Andrea Gollin (New York: Monacelli, 2016), 20–49. A similar screen showing Chanler's *Fighting Zebras* (1926), in the collection of Carol Taylor Gray, Woodstock, New York, is illustrated on page 84.

10 CVV to ME, June 25, 1932, box 8, folder 60.

11 As the project moved forward, Van Vechten expressed his feelings more candidly in private, writing to Donald Angus on October 1, 1932: "Max went to Eddies' yesterday, set up a tripod and lights and took pictures. Now, really!!" Kellner, ed., *Letters of Carl Van Vechten*, 125.

12 ME to CVV, n.d. "Monday," YCAL MSS 1050, box 43, folder 586.

13 ME to Edward Wasserman, January 19, 1933, box 8, folder 61: "Be sure to leave Wednesday night Jan 25th and come to the Venetian soiree at Julien Levy's 9 to 12 pm. Wear your blue Bavarian jacket, and if practicable, bring En Cas. He is listed in the catalogue."

14 For Robeson's biography and political activism, see Martin Duberman, *Paul Robeson* (New York: New Press, 1989). Van Vechten kept copies of Ewing's Robeson portraits in his own collection and donated them to Yale in 1941, along with other photographs, manuscripts, books, and papers, when he established the James Weldon Johnson Memorial Collection.

15 ME to CE, July 8, 1932, box 5, folder 32.

16 CVV to ME, July 25, 1932, box 8, folder 60. The name was drawn from the title of a novel by their friend Elinor Wylie, published in 1925.

17 ME to GPL, July 25, 1932, box 7, folder 54.

18 For a discussion of Kirstein's Harvard circle, see Douglas Shand-Tucci, *The Crimson Letter: Harvard, Homosexuality, and the Shaping of American Culture* (New York: St. Martin's Press, 2004).

19 For Neel, see Alice Neel, *Alice Neel: People Come First* (New York: Metropolitan Museum of Art, 2021); and Eleanor Nairne, et al., *Alice Neel: Hot Off the Griddle* (London: Barbican, 2023).

20 ME to CVV, July 22, 1932, YCAL MSS 1050, box 43, folder 591.

21 The Lynes portrait was made in October, as suggested by a letter, ME to GPL, October 11, 1932, box 7, folder 54: "Stop for me at six and be prepared to let me snap you in the piazza." In an undated note to Lynes, Ewing mentions another portrait of him, "pensive in a towel," which is now missing (ME to GPL, n.d., box 7, folder 54).

22 ME to CE, June 19, 1932, box 5, folder 32. I am grateful to Pat Berman for sharing her analysis of the camp imagery and conventions of portraiture in Ewing's *Carnival*.

23 ME to CE, December 3, 1932, box 5, folder 33: "Namara was so excited by my exhibition of photos of Venice that she came in to have hers taken."

24 ME to Doris Ewing, August 10, 1932, box 7 folder 50. Ewing saved the clipping from *Town and Country*, February 1, 1933, 15, which included his portrait along with those of Lois Moran, "Princess Chavchavadze," and Mrs. Tiffany Saportas: box 31, folder 239.

25 All but the Van Vechten scrapbooks have been digitized: *The Carnival of Venice*, box 20, (large format prints) presentation photographs of forty-eight individuals; *Les Amants de Venise*, vols. 1–4, box 21, Green vol. 1 (thirty-three sitters), Brown "The International Festival of Venice" (thirty-one sitters), Blue (thirty-four sitters), Brown no. 2 (ten sitters, including puppets). "Handlist" from the *Carnival of Venice* exhibition at the Julien Levy Gallery, January 26, 1933, box 7, folder 54: list of seventy-six sitters with an introductory note by Gilbert Seldes, https://collections .library.yale.edu/catalog/11692111.

26 Unlike the photos in the Ewing archive, the homoerotic material in the Van Vechten scrapbooks has not been digitized or made available online.

27 "Handlist" from the *Carnival of Venice* exhibition at the Julien Levy Gallery, January 26, 1933, box 7, folder 54.

28 Gilbert Seldes, "The Carnival of Venice: Photographs by Max Ewing," January 26, 1933, box 7, folder 54. The exhibition was also reviewed by Henry McBride, "Max Ewing as a Camera Man: Strange Qualities Are Revealed in Novelist's Photography," *New York Sun*, January 27, 1933, 7, Henry McBride Papers, YCAL MSS 31, series II, box 15, folder 433.

29 ME to CVV, January 9, 1933, box 44, folder 592.

30 Advertisement from the Waldorf Astoria, box 31, folder 232.

31 Ewing, *Genius Denied*, 85.

32 ME to CE, November 27, 1932, box 5, folder 33, wrote that he was "Going out to George Platt Lynes's house in Englewood New Jersey to make enlargements of his prints." He also had help from Eddie Moeller, "who lives with John Glenn, [who] says he will teach me and let me use his apparatus until I can afford to buy some. I am going to learn about enlarging on Monday night." ME to CE, August 8, 1932, box 5, folder 32.

33 ME to GPL, various dates, box 7, folder 54.

34 See George Platt Lynes, scrapbooks, YCAL MSS 139, box 6, folder 163: "Twenty six shots of men and women posed individually and together in front of Max Ewing's Carnival of Venice backdrop."

35 Max Ewing, "Êtes-vous Polygame," an "interview," and Max Ewing, "Isn't It Awful," a "lament" by Princess Eugénie Murat (played by Berenice Abbott), were recorded on "aluminum instantaneous phono disc," July 27, 1929, box 35, folder 250.

36 Van Haaften, *Berenice Abbott*, 141–42, 152–55.

37 See "Murals by American Painters and Photographers," MoMA, accessed June 19, 2019, https://www.moma.org/calendar /exhibitions/2045.

38 For Berenice Abbott's 1928 notebook in the Metropolitan Museum of Art, see https://www .metmuseum.org/exhibitions /berenice-abbott. ME to CE, April 26, 1933, notes that he spent a "Quiet evening with Cary Ross and Walker Evans," quoted in Ewing, *Genius Denied*, 129.

39 ME to CE, July 21, 1932, box 5, folder 32.

40 Katharine Ware, *Photography at the Julien Levy Gallery* (New Haven, CT: Yale University Press, 2006).

41 ME to CE, November 23, 1932, box 5 folder 32: "George Lynes is coming in tonight bringing a movie star Lois Moran." For McAndrew, see Mardges Bacon, *John McAndrew's Modernist Vision: From The Vassar College Art Library to the Museum of Modern Art in New York* (New York: Princeton Architectural Press, 2019).

42 Bacon, *John McAndrew's Modernist Vision*, 41–57.

43 See Miguel Covarrubias, *Carl Van Vechten*, c. 1925, ink and watercolor over graphite, National Portrait Gallery, Smithsonian, https://npg.si.edu/object/npg _NPG.2000.36; and Beverly J. Cox, *Miguel Covarrubias Caricatures* (Washington, DC: Published for the National Portrait Gallery by the Smithsonian Institution Press, 1985). See also ME to CE, October 30, 1923, box 1 folder 5; and ME to CE, March 7, 1926, box 2, folder 13.

44 ME to MD, n.d. [1926], box 6, folder 42.

45 See Marilyn Satin Kushner, *The Art of Winold Reiss: An Immigrant Modernist* (New York: New York Historical Society, 2021).

46 ME to CE, December 28, 1932, box 5, folder 33.

47 ME to CE, June 4, 1932, box 5, folder 32. Samuel Hoffenstein went on to win an academy award for the screenplay of *Laura* (1944), a story that hinges on the murderous tendencies of the gay protagonist, Waldo Lydecker, played by Clifton Webb, a queer, New York actor. For homophobic stereotypes in films of that period, see Alice. T. Friedman, "'I Noticed His Attention Was Fixed upon My Clock': Masculinity and the Queer Film Interior," *Interiors* 10, nos. 1–2 (2019): 85–102. For Ewing's connections to Natalie Hammond and her friends, including Alice Laughlin and Addison Pelletier, see ME to parents, n.d. [1927], box 7, folder 40; ME to parents, May 4, 1930, box 4, folder 25; ME to parents, October 27 1930, January 7, 1931, and February 16, 1931, box 5, folder 28.

48 Jennifer Homans, *Mr. B: George Balanchine's Twentieth Century* (New York: Random House, 2023), 188–89.

49 See Richard S. Kennedy, "The Elusive Marion Morehouse," in "Marion Morehouse Memorial Issue," special issue, *Spring*, n.s., no. 5 (October 1996): 8–17.

50 "Max Ewing's Diary" for January 4, 1933, box 30, folder 227. For Carstairs, see Brock Switzer, "Not Your Average Joe," Mariners Museum and Park, September 3, 2020, https://www.mariners museum.org/2020/09/not -your-average-joe/.

51 ME to CE, November 26, 1932, box 5, folder 33.

52 ME to parents, September 21, 1931, box 7, folder 50.

53 See also nitrate negative, box 34. For Locher's work, see Lampe, *Robert E. Locher*.

54 New work on Demuth's identity as a queer artist was produced as part of the Demuth Museum's Reinterpretation Project in 2022, including Susan Ferentinos, "The Queer Life of Charles Demuth," Demuth Museum Reinterpretation Project, accessed April 1, 2023, https://www.demuth.org/charles -demuth, and contributions by Barbara Haskell, Jonathan Frederick Katz, M. Alison Kibler, Erin Pauwels, Jonathan Frederick Walz, and Keri Watson. Some of these materials are archived online at https://static1 .squarespace.com/static /5f3d65a8b0e9ed3a96b44be6 /t/64271079e4a9000494854e1f /1680281721802/DemuthLGBTQ .Report.pdf; and https://static1 .squarespace.comstatic /5f3d65a8b0e9ed3a96b44be6 /t/642713564e6cbc5da36efa82 /1680282457905/Scholar +Essays.pdf.

55 "Interior Decorator Is Dead," *New York Times*, June 21, 1956, 29, https://timesmachine.nytimes.com /timesmachine/1956/06/21/94295571 .html?pageNumber=29.

56 ME to CE, August 18, 1932, box 5, folder 32.

57 ME to GPL, n.d. [April 1930?], box 7, folder 54.

58 Fred Ritter to ME, November 27, 1933, box 9, folder 68.

59 ME to parents, June 26, 1930, box 4, folder 26.

60 ME to CE, September 15, 1932, box 5, folder 33.

61 See Bill Ritter to ME, n.d. [spring 1933–February 1934], box 9, folder 68.

62 CVV to Doris Ewing, August 1, 1942, YCAL MSS 1050, box 43, folder 587.

63 ME to MD, n.d. [September 1932], YCAL 49, box 3, folder 106.

64 ME to CE, September 30, 1932, box 5, folder 33.

65 ME to CE, October 10, 1932, box 5, folder 33.

66 ME to CE, November 19 and November 28, 1932, box 5, folder 33.

67 ME to CVV, YCAL MSS 1050, box 223, vol. 18.

68 Lincoln Kirstein, "Diary" (1934), and partial transcription, "January 25–December 4, incomplete," Lincoln Kirstein Papers, Jerome Robbins Dance Division, New York Public Library for the Performing Arts, (S)*MGZMD 123, box 4 (transcription), and box 5 ("Diary"). Ewing and Pollock are mentioned in the "Diary," 125–34.

69 ME to CE, November 15, 1932, box 5, folder 33.

70 ME to CE, December 22, 1932, box 5, folder 34.

71 ME to GPL, n.d. [January 1933], box 7, folder 54.

72 ME to CE, "Mother's Day," 1933, box 6, folder 34.

73 ME to Edgar Ailes, n.d. [June 1933?], box 6, folder 37.

Intermezzo
The Queer Eye of the 1920s and '30s

1 Watson, *Prepare for Saints*; and Steven Watson, *The Harlem Renaissance*. For race and racism in Thomson's opera and the Harlem Renaissance, see Lisa Barg, "Black Voices/White Sounds: Race and Representation in Virgil Thomson's Four Saints in Three Acts," *American Music* 18, no. 2 (summer 2000): 121–61. For Draper, see Betsy Fahlman, "Great Draper," 33–37; and Armandroff, "Drawing for an Audience of One."

2 In addition to the photos that Sansone circulated, he published a compilation of images, titled *Modern Classics*, in 1932. See John Massey, *American Adonis: Tony Sansone: The First Male Physique Icon* (New York: Universe, 2004).

3 Breward, "Styling *Four Saints in Three Acts*," 82–102.

4 For an extensive bibliography related to queer history in the fin de siècle period and in the early twentieth century, see Susan Ferentinos, "The Queer Life of Charles Demuth," made available online March 2023, https://static1 .squarespace.com/static /5f3d65a8b0e9ed3a96b44be6/t /64271079e4a9000494854e1f /1680281721802/DemuthLGBTQ .Report.pdf. Among the many foundational histories, see Jonathan Katz, *The Invention of Homosexuality* (New York: Dutton, 1995); Christine Stansell, *American Moderns: Bohemian New York and the Creation of a New Century* (New York: Metropolitan Books, 2000); Jay Hatheway, *The Gilded Age Construction of Modern American Homophobia* (New York: Palgrave Macmillan, 2003); and Siobhan B. Somerville, *Queering the Color Line: Race and the Invention of Homosexuality in American Culture* (Durham, NC: Duke University Press, 2000).

5 See Watson, *Strange Bedfellows*; White, *Tastemaker*; and David Nasaw, *Going Out*.

6 George Chauncey, *Gay New York*, 227–67; and Eric Garber, "A Spectacle in Color," 318–33.

7 Kristen MacLeod, "Introduction: The Blind Bow-Boy," vii–xxii.

8 Mumford, *Interzones*; Lisa Barg, "Black Voices/White Sounds," 121–61; and Chad Heap, *Slumming*.

9 For the latest discussion of this queer subculture, see Mauss and Miller, *Body Language*.

10 For the idea of the "lesbian archipelago," see Friedman, "Queer Old Things." This idea is explored in Mumford, *Interzones*, 73–92.

11 The publication of the essays in Earnest, ed., *The Young and Evil*, and the exhibition that the volume documented, marked a milestone in this area, bringing many previously unknown images to light. The multimedia, performance, and dance exhibition *Transmissions*, curated by Nick Mauss at the Whitney Museum of Art in 2018, also changed the way in which these artists and their work, particularly Lynes's dance and fashion photography, are seen.

12 Weinberg, "Boy Crazy," 25–49.

13 Quoted by Weinberg, "Boy Crazy," 27–28, from Van Vechten, "The Tin Trunk," in *Sacred and Profane Memories* (New York: Alfred A. Knopf, 1932), 12.

14 White, *The Tastemaker*, 28. A similar experience of sharing movie magazines and scrapbooking with his mother was described by Andy Warhol. See Blake Gopnik, *Andy Warhol: A Life as Art* (New York, Ecco Press, 2020); and Kathryn M. Duda, "At Home in Pittsburgh: Andy Warhol's Youth," *Carnegie Magazine*, https:// carnegiemuseums.org/magazine -archive/1996/julaug/feat2.htm.

15 Carl Van Vechten's "Homoerotic Scrapbooks," YCAL MSS 1050, series III, boxes 206–23. All references to Van Vechten's scrapbooks derive from this source unless otherwise noted.

16 See Ellen Gruber Garvey, *Writing with Scissors: American Scrapbooks from the Civil War to the Harlem Renaissance* (New York: Oxford University Press, 2012).

17 James Smalls, *The Homoerotic Photography of Carl Van Vechten*, 18–19. See also James Smalls, "Public Face, Private Thoughts: Fetish, Interracialism, and the Homoerotic in Carl Van Vechten's Photographs," in *The Passionate Camera: Photography and Bodies of Desire*, ed. Deborah Bright (London: Routledge, 1998), 78–102.

18 Elspeth H. Brown, "Queering Glamour in Interwar Fashion Photography," 289–326.

19 Thomas Waugh, *Hard to Imagine*. For "primitivism" in these images, see Smalls, *Homoerotic Photography of Van Vechten*, 39.

20 Smalls, *Homoerotic Photography of Van Vechten*, 3.

21 The conventions of the genre are described by Allen Ellenzweig, *The Homoerotic Photograph: Male Images from Durieu/Delacroix to Mapplethorpe* (New York: Columbia University Press, 1992).

22 Weinberg, "Boy Crazy," 47.

23 ME to parents, September 27, 1926, box 3, folder 16.

24 ME to parents, n.d. [December 1930], box 5, folder 28.

25 CVV to ME, November 13, 1933, box 8, folder 60. Noël Sullivan wrote to Ewing on August 21, 1933, box 5, folder 34, that "Langston arrived a week ago" and "the enrichment of life which his presence means is hard for me to describe … he was very sorry to miss you and hopes to see you soon. He plans to remain here until the end of the month and then go down to Carmel," noting that Billy Justema was doing a portrait of Langston.

26 ME to MD, n.d. [June 1926], box 3, folder 108, Muriel Draper Papers. Van Vechten also included a glossary in his much-maligned *Ni***er Heaven*.

27 YCAL 1050, box 223, vol. 18.

28 The homophobic codes used in these criticisms are discussed by Scott Herring, "'Slightly Known Territory': Renaissance Admixture and the So-Called Van Vechten School," in *Queering the Underworld: Slumming, Literature, and the Undoing of Gay and Lesbian History* (Chicago: University of Chicago Press, 2007).

29 Fred Moten, *Stolen Life* (Durham, NC: Duke University Press, 2018).

30 "Emily Bernard on Carl Van Vechten," Beinecke Rare Book & Manuscript Library, January 23, 2017, https://beinecke.library.yale .edu/article/emily-bernard-carl -van-vechten.

31 Andrew Stephenson, "'Our Jolly Marin Wear': The Queer Fashionability of the Sailor Uniform in Interwar France and Britain," *Fashion, Style, Popular Culture*, 3, no. 2 (March 2016): 157ff.

32 ME to Doris Ewing, n.d. [1930?], box 9, folder 67.

33 YCAL 1050, series III, box 208, vol. 3, and box 209, vol. 4. In this context, Jarrett Earnest's recent essay on "Tom of Finland," entitled "Tom's Men," *New York Review of Books*, May 4, 2024, is particularly helpful.

34 See box 24, photo album, "Of Friends."

35 Alice DeLamar to ME, May 30, 1934, box 6, folder 62.

36 YCAL 1050, series III, box 212, vol. 7.

37 CVV to ME, November 13, 1933, box 8, folder 60.

38 Essays commissioned by the Demuth Museum's Reinterpretation Project in 2022, accessed April 1, 2023, https://www.demuth.org /charles-demuth. See also Barbara Haskell, *Charles Demuth* (New York: Whitney Museum of American Art, 1987); Jonathan Weinberg, *Speaking for Vice: Homosexuality in the Art of Charles Demuth, Marsden Hartley and the First American Avant-Garde* (New Haven, CT: Yale University Press, 1995); and Betsy Fahlman, *Pennsylvania Modern: Charles Demuth of Lancaster* (Philadelphia: University of Pennsylvania Press, 1983). An earlier study by Emily Farnham, *Charles Demuth: Behind a Laughing Mask* (Norman: University of Oklahoma Press, 1971), is filled with interviews and recollections of the artist.

39 Weinberg, *Speaking for Vice*, 24–29.

40 See Sally R. Munt, *Queer Attachments: The Cultural Politics of Shame* (London: Taylor & Francis, 2007).

41 For Locher, see Lampe, *Robert E. Locher*. Kellner, ed., *Letters of Carl Van Vechten*, 15n4, notes that "There is no evidence that they were ever lovers," but their constant communication, collaboration, and intimate manner with one another contradict that assertion; as with Ewing and most other queer people in this period, anything more revealing than a passing comment would be courting danger in a period of severe repression of homosexuality. For the "poster-portraits," see Robin Jaffee Frank, *Charles Demuth Poster-Portraits, 1923–1929* (New Haven, CT: Yale University Art Gallery, 1994). Although sometimes associated with Gertrude Stein, the painting seems to have little connection to her; Kellner, ed., *Letters of Carl Van Vechten*, 126n2, also disputes that association, noting that "even a shallow familiarity with Stein's life and work contradict" the assertion, since "she had no connections with Broadway and only a casual acquaintance with Demuth." See also Alice T. Friedman, "Interior Decorator is Dead," *The Art Bulletin* 106, no. 1 (March 2024): 34–39.

42 ME, "Guests," n.d., box 12, folder 126.

43 Bruce Kellner, ed., *The Letters of Charles Demuth, American Artist, 1883–1935* (Philadelphia: Temple University Press, 2000), xvii. Marsden Hartley, "Farewell Charles," *The New Caravan*, 1936, reprinted in Kellner, ed., *Letters of Charles Demuth*, 171–77 (quote on 171–72).

44 The painting may, in fact, represent the wedding of Otto Kahn's younger daughter, imaginatively removed from their home, where it took place, to St. Patrick's Cathedral. Barbara Bloemink, email communications to author, March 2023.

45 Kellner, ed., *Letters of Charles Demuth*, xvi.

46 Haskell, *Charles Demuth*, 24–26. This history is described in Charlie Schroeder, "Uncle Bob," in Lampe, *Robert E. Locher*, 3–6. Quoting Bruce Kellner, Schroeder writes that Locher's marriage was "widely considered to be a marriage of convenience." The couple were divorced in 1933 and Beatrice married four days later, building Pride House on Fire Island.

47 Marsden Hartley, "Farewell Charles," in Kellner, ed., *Letters of Charles Demuth*, 171–77.

48 Susan Ferentinos, "The Queer Life of Charles Demuth," 18.

49 Useful studies include Brenda Helt and Madelyn Detloff, eds., *Queer Bloomsbury* (Edinburgh: University of Edinburgh Press, 2016); and Mauss and Miller, *Body Language*.

50 Kellner, ed., *Letters of Charles Demuth*, 36.

51 Robert Locher, "Postcard to Charles (Demuth)" (January 12, 1922), Locher to Demuth folder, Demuth Foundation, Lancaster, PA. Cited by Ferentinos, "The Queer Life of Charles Demuth," 24. Portraits of Locher by Man Ray and Baron de Meyer from this period suggest a distinctively camp element in his manner.

52 Kellner, ed., *Letters of Charles Demuth*, 123.

53 Kellner, ed., *Letters of Charles Demuth*, 125–26.

54 Gertrude Stein, *Portraits and Prayers* (New York: Random House, 1934), 144–45.

55 ME to parents, February 5, 1931, box 4, folder 21; and ME to parents, September 21, 1931, box 5, folder 28.

56 ME, photo album "Of Friends," box 24.

57 Muriel Draper, "Robert Locher," *Creative Arts* 9, no. 1 (July 1931): 53.

58 A very different reading for both *Longhi* and *Love, Love, Love* is suggested by Frank, *Charles Demuth Poster-Portraits*, 90–106.

59 ME to parents, n.d. [November 1931], box 5, folder 30.

60 Photo album, "Of Friends (red)," box 24. For Beatrice (Locher) Farrar's marriage to Thomas Farrar following her divorce from Locher, and her importance to the queer community in Fire Island, see Esther Newton, *Cherry Grove, Fire Island: Sixty Years in America's First Gay and Lesbian Town* (Durham, NC: Duke University Press, 2014), 23–28, 74–75.

61 ME to parents, January 15, 1932, box 5, folder 31.

62 ME to CE, n.d. ["Mothers Day"], box 5, folder 32. See Kellner, ed., *Letters of Charles Demuth*, 67–68, 102. For Demuth's use of the term, see Ferentinos, "The Queer Life of Charles Demuth," 25–26. In a June 25, 1925 letter to McBride, Demuth camps it up: "This, my dear Mr. McBride, is all, it seems, that there is to it. I trust that you will be successful in your venture. If all this is unclear let me know and if you wish I will have my cousin (as you invented) [drive] me down. … My cousin thinks that you are grand. I am sorry we caused you that hour or was it only an half hour? Some time you must come up and see my real cousin, here, — there is one." Kellner, ed., *Letters of Charles Demuth*, 68, esp. n1. In the 1920s, the term "cousin" was in wide circulation as gay code.

63 ME to CE, n.d. ["Mothers Day"], box 5, folder 32.

64 ME to CE, July 21, 1932, box 5, folder 42.

65 ME to CE, July 28, 1932, box 5, folder 42.

66 ME to CE, August 2 and 16, 1932, box 5, folder 42.

67 ME to CE, August 1932, box 5, folder 42.

68 Schroeder, "Uncle Bob," 3–6.

69 For the identification of these figures, and a discussion of the camp and subversive messages in Stettheimer's painting, see Linda Nochlin, Florine Stettheimer — "Rococo Subversive," *Art in America*, 1980, available online through *Art in America*: https://www.artnews.com/art-in-america/features/from-the-archives-florine-stettheimer-rococo-subversive-63262/.

70 Emily Farnham, "Charles Demuth: His Life, Psychology and Works" (PhD diss., Ohio State University, 1959), 88.

71 In addition to Allen Ellenzweig's definitive biography, *George Platt Lynes: The Daring Eye*, see his earlier study, *The Homoerotic Photograph: Male Images from Durieu/Delacroix to Mapplethorpe*.

72 For the evolution of his approach, see Elspeth H. Brown, *Work!: A Queer History of Modeling* (Durham, NC: Duke University Press, 2019), esp. chapter 3, on Lynes. See also James Crump, "Photography as Agency: George Platt Lynes and the Avant-Garde," in James Crump, *George Platt Lynes: Photographs from the Kinsey Institute* (Boston: Bullfinch Press, 1993), 137–48.

73 Crump, *When We Were Three*.

74 Earnest, ed., *The Young and Evil*.

75 ME to Doris Ewing, August 10, 1932, box 7, folder 50.

76 Ewing, *Genius Denied*, 150–51.

Chapter 6
The End of the Road, 1933–34

1 Many letters from 1933 and 1934, including letters from Jack Pollock that remained in the Ewing family archives, were published by Wallace Ewing, the nephew of Max's first cousin Doris, in *Genius Denied*. His transcriptions are quoted without comment. Some of these letters were given to the Beinecke in March 2024 and catalogued as YCAL 656, series VII, box 37.

2 ME to CE, n.d. ["Wednesday"], box 5, folder 34. Max Ewing's collection of clippings related to *Going Somewhere* is in box 29, folder 233.

3 Ewing, *Genius Denied*, 78–79.

4 Ewing, *Genius Denied*, 86.

5 Ewing, *Genius Denied*, 88.

6 ME to parents, n.d. [1925], box 2, folder 12.

7 Ewing, *Genius Denied*, 141 (n.d. [December 1932], box 5, folder 35).

8 Ewing, *Genius Denied*, 141 (n.d. [December 1932], box 5, folder 35).

9 See ME to his uncle, December 13, 1933, published in Ewing, *Genius Denied*, 22. I am grateful to Steven Watson for sharing an anecdote about Ewing's cocaine use, told to him by Joella Levy (Zoom conversation with author, May 27, 2020).

10 Ewing, *Genius Denied*, 143; Nazi Germany mentioned on 116.

11 ME to MD, July 1, 1933 and n.d. [July 1933], box 6, folder 45.

12 ME to CE, n.d. ["Friday AM"], box 5, folder 34.

13 For Langston Hughes's loyalty to Van Vechten and his queer, interracial "underworld," see Herring, *Queering the Underworld*, 104–8. Langston Hughes, Richard Bruce Nugent, Wallace Thurman, Noël Sullivan, and Billy Justema were all members of the bicoastal confraternity as well.

14 Noël Sullivan to ME, August 21, 1933, box 5, folder 35.

15 ME to CVV, December 31, 1933, YCAL MSS 1050, box 44, folder 44. The portrait, which was kept by Van Vechten, is preserved in YCAL 1050, series 4, "Art."

16 Ewing, *Genius Denied*, 78–79. For Fears, de Acosta, and Bankhead in Hollywood, see ME to CE, August 8, 11, and 13, 1933, box 5, folder 35.

17 Ewing, *Genius Denied*, 79.

18 ME to CE, "Garden of Allah," n.d. [August 1933], box 5, folder 35. See also Ewing's "Diary" for 1933, box 30, folder 227.

19 ME to CE, n.d. [1933], box 5, folder 35.

20 ME to Cary Ross, n.d, ("Hollywood, Monday") [fall 1933], box 8, folder 60. Ross was a Harvard-educated poet and lover of Philip Johnson who worked at the Museum of Modern Art from 1930 to 1932 and became secretary to Alfred Stieglitz; see "Queer Places," Elisa Rolle (blog), accessed March 12, 2023, http://www.elisarolle.com/queerplaces/a-b-ce/Cary%20Ross.html.

21 ME to MD, n.d. [fall 1933], box 6, folder 44.

22 ME to Cary Ross, n.d. [fall 1933], box 8, folder 60.

23 Ewing, *Genius Denied*, 162.

24 ME to Joseph Brewer, n.d. [January 1933], box 8, folder 60.

25 Ewing, *Genius Denied*, 174.

26 Ewing, *Genius Denied*, 180.

27 CE to ME, November 9, 1933, box 7, folder 47.

28 CE to ME, November 9, 13 and December 11, box 7, folder 47.

29 Ewing, *Genius Denied*, 220–21.

30 Ewing, *Genius Denied*, 228–29.

31 A. E. Ewing to ME, paraphrased in Ewing, *Genius Denied*, 247.

32 ME to Alice DeLamar, January 9, 1934, box 6, folder 31.

33 ME to Alice DeLamar, January 9, 1934, box 6, folder 31.

34 ME to GPL, February 14, 1934, box 6, folder 41.

35 ME to Edgar Ailes, February 20, 1934, box 6, folder 37.

36 ME to Alice DeLamar, April 13, 1934, box 6, folder 41.

37 ME to Alice DeLamar, May 24, 1934, box 6, folder 41.

38 ME to Alice DeLamar, May 24, 1934, box 6, folder 41.

39 Ettie Stettheimer to ME, letter dated the "penultimate day of April 1934," box 8, folder 62. She wrote that she had heard the unhappy news of his mother's passing: "One has to steel oneself and be as hard as possible if one is to live at all and one must try to live as fully as possible for many reasons and one is to justify the sacrifice one's mother has brought to the cause of life by giving birth … This is only to let you know of my warm sympathy, in which Carrie and Florine join me and express the hope that life will soon compensate you for what you have been through."

40 ME to Ettie Stettheimer, May 9, 1934, box 8, folder 58. See also Florine Stettheimer to ME, and Ettie Stettheimer to Edward Wasserman, June 18, 1934, box 8, folder 58. Ewing was in frequent touch with the Stettheimers throughout the spring of 1934, and wrote to Florine to say how sorry he was to miss *Four Saints*: see Ewing, *Genius Denied*, 252.

41 Alice DeLamar to ME, May 22, 1934, box 8, folder 62.

42 ME to Alice DeLamar, "Toledo," n.d. [June 1934], box 6, folder 31.

43 ME to Alice DeLamar, May 30, 1934, box 8, folder 62.

44 ME to Joseph Brewer, n.d. [April 1934], box 9, folder 67.

45 ME to A. E. Ewing, n.d. [June 1934: with note "Copy of most of Max's last letter to us"], box 7, folder 46.

46 ME to A. E. Ewing, n.d. [June 1934: with note "Copy of most of Max's last letter to us"], box 7, folder 46.

47 ME to MD, "Saturday," n.d. [fall 1933], box 6, folder 43; and MD to ME, n.d. [fall 1933], box 6, folder 44.

48 Muriel Draper had published a memoir entitled *Music at Midnight* (New York: Harper and Brothers, 1929); in it, she described the musical evenings held at her prewar salon and the luminaries — from Arthur Rubinstein to Henry James — she had entertained in her London home before the death of her husband and her move to New York. See Cecily Swanson, "Conversation Pieces: Circulating Muriel Draper's Salon," 23–43; Betsy Fahlman, "Great Draper Woman," 33–37; and Carl Van Vechten, "Ma Draper," 129.

49 MD to ME, "September 1933 Taos," n.d., box 6, folder 44.

50 Max Ewing, "Diary," October 21–22, 1933, box 30, folder 227.

51 Curiosity and enthusiasm about the economic system of Soviet Russia was far more widespread in the early 1930s than it would later become. I am grateful to James Oles for pointing out Diego Rivera's cover for the March 1932 issue of *Fortune* magazine, showing a parade in Moscow's Red Square, as well as the illustrations by Rivera in an appreciative article on Joseph Stalin in *Cosmopolitan* from September 1932. See James Oles, *Diego Rivera's America* (San Francisco: University of California Press, 2022).

52 Lincoln Kirstein, "Diary," 1934, and partial transcription, "January 25–December 4, incomplete," Lincoln Kirstein Papers, Jerome Robbins Dance Division, The New York Public Library for the Performing Arts, (S)*MGZMD 123, box 4 (transcription), and box 5 ("Diary").

The Gurdjieff material is in Kirstein, "Diary," 125–34.

53 ME to MD, March 26, 1934, box 6, folder 45.

54 ME to MD, n.d. ["Toledo, Friday"], box 6, folder 45.

55 MD to ME, n.d. [June 1934], box 6, folder 44.

56 MD to ME, n.d. [June 1934], box 6, folder 44.

57 Kirstein, "Diary," May 30, 124–25 (transcription).

58 MD to ME, n.d. [June 1934], box 6, folder 44.

59 MD to ME, n.d. [June 1934], box 6, folder 44.

60 MD to ME, n.d. [June 1934], box 6, folder 44.

61 ME to CE, September 11, 1933, box 5, folder 35.

62 Ewing, *Genius Denied*, 281.

63 Ewing, *Genius Denied*, 282.

64 Ewing, *Genius Denied*, 286.

65 Jack Pollock to Alice DeLamar, n.d. [June 1934], box 9, folder 70.

66 Ewing, *Genius Denied*, 292.

67 Ewing, *Genius Denied*, 300–301. Ewing recorded his departure in his "Diary," March 6, 1934, box 30, folder 227.

68 Ewing, *Genius Denied*, 303–4.

69 Ewing, *Genius Denied*, 306.

70 Ewing's "Diary" records his arrival on May 26, 1934, box 30, folder 227.

71 Ewing, *Genius Denied*, 327.

72 Ewing, *Genius Denied*, 327.

73 For Jack's correspondence with Bessie Durbin Herrell, see box 9, folder 70. Bessie wrote to Alice DeLamar to ask for money on Jack's behalf; she sent him $75 ($1,700 in today's dollars). Jack had also written to Alice to tell her his side of the story of Ewing's death.

74 Ewing, *Genius Denied*, 311–12.

75 ME and Jack Pollock to MD, n.d. [June 1934], box 8, folder 70.

76 Jack Pollock to MD, n.d. [June 1934], box 6, folder 45.

77 MD to ME, n.d. [June 1934], box 6, folder 44.

78 A. E. Ewing to MD, June 16, 1934, box 9, folder 70.

79 A. E. Ewing to MD, June 17, 1934, box 9, folder 70.

80 "Max Ewing killed himself on his way to see Muriel with her ex boxer Pollock. She will of course blame herself … I should have, myself, no remorse. But then I got no letters from him." Kirstein, "Diary," June 18, 1934, 125.

81 Kirstein, "Diary," June 19, 1934, 126.

82 Kirstein, "Diary," June 24, 1934, 133.

83 Kirstein, "Diary," 130; Jack Pollock to MD, n.d. [June 1934], box 9, folder 70.

84 Kirstein, "Diary," June 24, 1934, 133.

85 CVV to MD, n.d., "Thursday" [July? 1934], box 9, folder 70.

86 CVV to A. E. Ewing, July 16, 1934, box 43, folder 587.

87 Frances Bollinger to Jack Pollock, n.d. [July 1934], box 9, folder 70.

88 CVV to Doris Ewing, August 1, 1944, YCAL 1050, box 43, folder 587.

89 CVV to Doris Ewing, n.d. [1942], YCAL 1050, box 43, folder 587.

90 CVV to Doris Ewing, January 16, 1943, YCAL 1050, box 43, folder 587.

Epilogue
The Politics and Poetics of the Archive

1 Hartman, *Wayward Lives, Beautiful Experiments*; Fred Moten and Stefano Harney, "The University and the Undercommons," in *The Undercommons: Fugitive Planning and Black Study* (New York: Autonomedia, 2013), 25–43, available online at https://www.minorcompositions.info/wp-content/uploads/2013/04/undercommons-web.pdf.

2 Mabel Hampton Oral History Collection, 1976–1989, Lesbian Herstory Archives, http://herstories.prattinfoschool.nyc/omeka/collections/show/29.

3 Okwui Enwezor, "Archive Fever," 44–45.

4 Ann Cvetkovich, "Photographing Objects as Queer Archival Practice," in *Feeling Photography*, ed. Elspeth H. Brown and Thy Phu (Durham, NC: Duke University Press, 2014), 273–96.

5 Emily Bernard, *Black Is the Body: Stories from My Grandmother's Time, My Mother's Time, and Mine* (New York: Vintage Books, 2019), 94–95.

Index

Image Credits

Please note that unless otherwise specified all images are courtesy of the Beinecke Rare Book & Manuscript Library, Yale University.

© Art Institute of Chicago (4.13, I.23)

© Man Ray Trust (2.13)

© Cecil Beaton Archive, Condé Nast (1.8, 3.34, 3.44, 3.45)

© Center for Creative Photography, Arizona Board of Regents (1.16)

© Condé Nast (1.7)

© The Estate of Alice Neel, courtesy The Estate of Alice Neel and David Zwirner (5.17)

© Estate of Berenice Abbott, Getty Images (1.6, 3.36, 3.40)

© Used with permission of The George Platt Lynes Estate (0.4, 2.24, 3.24, 3.25, 3.26, 4.1, 4.13, I.30, I.31, I.32)

© George Hoyningen-Huene Estate Archive (I.28)

© Gibbes Museum of Art / Carolina Art Association (I.31)

Photo by Jerry L. Thompson (2.2)

© The Metropolitan Museum of Art (1.18, 4.14, 6.3)

© Museo Nacional Thyssen-Bornemisza, Madrid (I.25)

© Museum of Fine Arts, Boston (2.25, I.24)

Digital Image © The Museum of Modern Art/Licensed by SCALA / Art Resource, NY (0.4)

© Reynolda Museum of American Art (I.2)

© Scala / Art Resource (0.4, 2.9, 2.13, 2.15, 3.24, 4.14, I.21, 6.3, E.1)

© Smithsonian American Art Museum (1.9, 1.10, 1.11, 1.12, 1.13, 2.9, 2.15)

© The Trustees of Indiana University on behalf of the Kinsey Institute, 2024 (I.32)

© Walker Evans Archive (1.18, 6.3)

© Whitney Museum of American Art (E.1)

Yale University Art Gallery (3.8, I.22)

© Zoe Leonard (E.1)

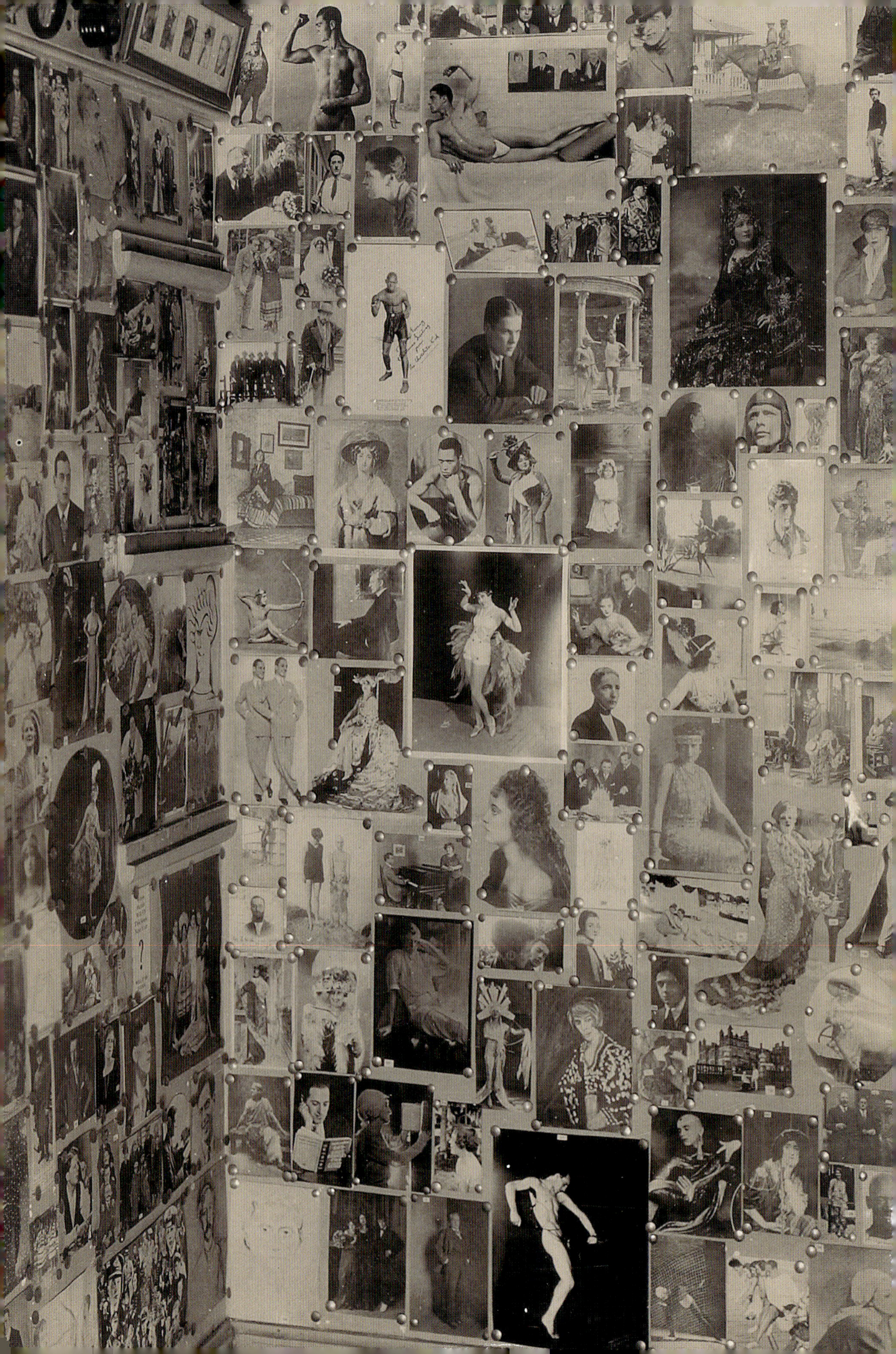